New Perspectives on

Microsoft® Access 7 for Windows® 95

INTRODUCTORY

The New Perspectives Series

The New Perspectives Series consists of texts and technology that teach computer concepts and the programs listed below. Both Windows 3.1 and Windows 95 versions of these programs are available. You can order these New Perspectives texts in many different lengths, software releases, bound combinations, and CourseKits™. Contact your CTI sales representative or customer service representative for the most up-to-date details.

The New Perspectives Series

Computer Concepts

dBASE

Internet Using Netscape Navigator

Lotus 1-2-3

Microsoft Access

Microsoft Excel

Microsoft Office Professional

Microsoft PowerPoint

Microsoft Windows 3.1

Microsoft Windows 95

Microsoft Word

Microsoft Works

Novell Perfect Office

Paradox

Presentations

Quattro Pro

WordPerfect

New Perspectives on

Microsoft® Access 7 for Windows® 95

INTRODUCTORY

Joseph J. Adamski
Grand Valley State University

A DIVISION OF COURSE TECHNOLOGY
ONE MAIN STREET, CAMBRIDGE MA 02142

an International Thomson Publishing company I(T)P

Albany • Bonn • Boston • Cincinnati • London • Madrid • Melbourne • Mexico City
New York • Paris • San Francisco • Singapore • Tokyo • Toronto • Washington

New Perspectives on Microsoft Access 7 for Windows 95 — Introductory is published by CTI.

Managing Editor	Mac Mendelsohn
Series Consulting Editor	Susan Solomon
Senior Product Manager	Barbara Clemens
Product Manager	Rachel Bunin
Developmental Editor	Terry Ann Kremer
Production Editor	Roxanne Alexander
Text and Cover Designer	Ella Hanna
Cover Illustrator	Nancy Nash

For more information contact:

Course Technology
One Main Street
Cambridge, MA 02142

International Thomson Publishing Europe
Berkshire House 168-173
High Holborn
London WCIV 7AA
England

Thomas Nelson Australia
102 Dodds Street
South Melbourne, 3205
Victoria, Australia

Nelson Canada
1120 Birchmount Road
Scarborough, Ontario
Canada M1K 5G4

International Thomson Editores
Campos Eliseos 385, Piso 7
Col. Polanco
11560 Mexico D.F. Mexico

International Thomson Publishing GmbH
Königswinterer Strasse 418
53227 Bonn
Germany

International Thomson Publishing Asia
211 Henderson Road
#05-10 Henderson Building
Singapore 0315

International Thomson Publishing Japan
Hirakawacho Kyowa Building, 3F
2-2-1 Hirakawacho
Chiyoda-ku, Tokyo 102
Japan

ISBN 0-7600-3542-3

Printed in the United States of America

10 9 8 7 6 5 4 3

From the New Perspectives Series Team

At Course Technology, we have one foot in education and the other in technology. We believe that technology is transforming the way people teach and learn, and we are excited about providing instructors and students with materials that use technology to teach about technology.

Our development process is unparalleled in the higher education publishing industry. Every product we create goes through an exacting process of design, development, review, and testing.

Reviewers give us direction and insight that shape our manuscripts and bring them up to the latest standards. Every manuscript is quality tested. Students whose backgrounds match the intended audience work through every keystroke, carefully checking for clarity and pointing out errors in logic and sequence. Together with our own technical reviewers, these testers help us ensure that everything that carries our name is error-free and easy to use.

We show both *how* and *why* technology is critical to solving problems in college and in whatever field you choose to teach or pursue. Our time-tested, step-by-step instructions provide unparalleled clarity. Examples and applications are chosen and crafted to motivate students.

As the New Perspectives Series team at Course Technology, our goal is to produce the most timely, accurate, creative, and technologically sound product in the entire college publishing industry. We strive for consistent high quality. This takes a lot of communication, coordination, and hard work. But we love what we do. We are determined to be the best. Write us and let us know what you think. You can also e-mail us at info@course.com.

The New Perspectives Series Team

Joseph J. Adamski
Judy Adamski
Roy Ageloff
David Auer
Rachel Bunin
Joan Carey
Patrick Carey
Barbara Clemens
Kim Crowley
Kristen Duerr
Jessica Evans
Kathy Finnegan
Robin Geller
Chris Greacen
Roger Hayen
Charles Hommel
Chris Kelly
Terry Ann Kremer
Melissa Lima
Mac Mendelsohn
Dan Oja
June Parsons
Sandra Poindexter
Mark Reimold
Ann Shaffer
Susan Solomon
Christine Spillett
Susanne Walker
John Zeanchock
Beverly Zimmerman
Scott Zimmerman

Preface The New Perspectives Series

What is the New Perspectives Series?

Course Technology's **New Perspectives Series** combines text and technology products that teach computer concepts and microcomputer applications. Users consistently praise this series for innovative pedagogy, creativity, supportive and engaging style, accuracy, and use of interactive technology. The first New Perspectives text was published in January of 1993. Since then, the series has grown to more than 30 titles and has become the best-selling series on computer concepts and microcomputer applications. Others have imitated the New Perspectives features, design, and technologies, but none have replicated its quality and its ability to consistently anticipate and meet the needs of instructors and students.

How is the New Perspectives Series different from other microcomputer applications series?

The **New Perspectives Series** distinguishes itself from other series in at least four substantial ways: sound instructional design, consistent quality, innovative technology, and proven pedagogy. The texts in this series consist of two or more tutorials, which are based on sound instructional design. Each tutorial is motivated by a realistic case that is meaningful to students. Rather than learn a laundry list of features, students learn the features in the context of solving a problem. This process motivates all concepts and skills by demonstrating to students why they would want to know them.

Instructors and students have come to rely on the the high quality of the **New Perspectives Series** and to consistently praise its accuracy. This accuracy is a result of Course Technology's unique multi-step quality assurance process that incorporates student testing at three stages of development, using hardware and software configurations appropriate to the product. All solutions, test questions, and other CourseTools (see below) are tested using similar procedures. Instructors who adopt this series report that students can work through the tutorials independently, with a minimum of intervention or "damage control" by instructors or staff. This consistent quality has meant that if instructors are pleased with one product from the series, they can rely on the same quality with any other New Perspectives product.

The **New Perspectives Series** also distinguishes itself by its innovative technology. This series innovated Course Labs, truly *interactive* learning applications. These have set the standard for interactive learning.

How do I know that the New Perspectives Series will work?

Some instructors who use this series report a significant difference between how much their students learn and retain with this series as compared to other series. With other series, instructors often find that students can work through the book and do well on homework and tests, but still not demonstrate competency when asked to perform particular tasks outside the context of the text's sample case or project. With the **New Perspectives Series**, however, instructors report that students have a complete, integrative learning experience that stays with them. They credit this high retention and competency to the fact that this series incorporates critical thinking and problem solving with computer skills mastery.

How does the book I'm holding fit into the New Perspectives Series?

New Perspectives microcomputer applications books are available in the following categories:

Brief books are about 100 pages long and are intended to teach only the essentials of the particular microcomputer application.

Introductory books are about 300 pages long and consist of 6 or 7 tutorials. An Introductory book is designed for a short course on a particular application or for a one-term course to be used in combination with other introductory books. The book you are holding is an introductory book.

Four-in-One books and **Five-in-One** books combine a Brief book on Windows with 3 or 4 Introductory books. An Essential Computer Concepts section is also included.

Comprehensive books consist of all of the tutorials in the Introductory book, plus 3 or 4 more tutorials on more advanced topics. They also include the Brief Windows tutorials, 3 or 4 Additional Cases, and a Reference Section.

Intermediate books take the 3 or 4 tutorials at the end of three or four Comprehensive books and combine them. Reference Sections and Additional Cases are also included.

Advanced books begin by covering topics similar to those in the Comprehensive books, but cover them in more depth. Advanced books then go on to present the most high-level coverage in the series.

Finally, as the name suggests, **Concepts and Applications** books combine the *New Perspectives on Computer Concepts* book with various Brief and Introductory microcomputer applications books.

Custom Books Course Technology offers you two ways to customize a text to fit your course exactly: *CourseKits*, 2 or more texts packaged together in a box, and *Custom Editions*, your choice of New Perspectives books bound together. Both options offer significant price discounts.

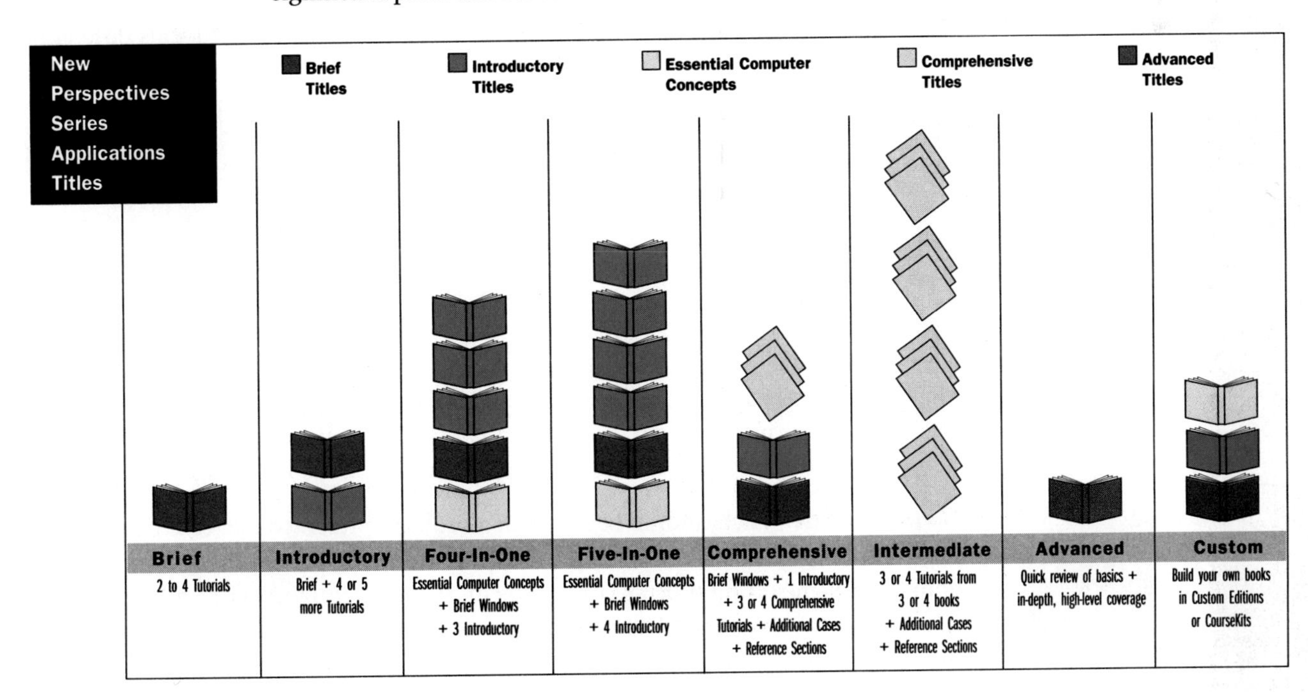

In what kind of course could I use this book?

This book can be used in any course in which you want students to learn the most important topics of Microsoft Access 7 for Windows 95, including planning, creating, and maintaining Access databases. Students learn how to retrieve information using queries and develop professional-looking reports, as well as create customized forms to access and enter data in a database. This book assumes that students have learned basic Windows 95 navigation and file management skills from Course Technology's *New Perspectives on Microsoft Windows 95 Brief* or an *equivalent* book.

How do the Windows 95 editions differ from the Windows 3.1 editions?

Larger Page Size If you've used a *New Perspectives* text before, you'll immediately notice that the book you're holding is larger than the Windows 3.1 series books. We've responded to user requests for a larger page, which allows for larger screen shots and associated callouts. Look on page AC 12 for an example of how we've made the screen shots easier to read.

Sessions We've divided the tutorials into sessions. Each session is designed to be completed in about 45 minutes to an hour (depending, of course, upon student needs and the speed of your lab equipment). With sessions, learning is broken up into more easily-assimilated chunks. You can more accurately allocate time in your syllabus. Students can better manage the available lab time. Each session begins with a "session box," which quickly describes which skills the student will learn in the session. Furthermore, each session is numbered, which makes it easier for you and your students to navigate and communicate about the tutorial. Look on page AC 5 for the session box that opens Session 1.1.

Quick Checks Each session concludes with meaningful, conceptual questions—called Quick Checks—that test students' understanding of what they learned in the session. The answers to all of the Quick Check questions are at the back of the book preceding the Index. You can find examples of Quick Checks on pages AC 30, AC 48, and AC 69.

New Design We have retained the best of the old design to help students differentiate between what they are to *do* and what they are to *read*. The steps are clearly identified by their shaded background and numbered steps. Furthermore, this new design presents steps and screen shots in a larger, easier-to-read format. Some good examples of our new design are on pages AC 18 and AC 19, and AC 46 and AC 47.

What features are retained in the Windows 95 editions of the New Perspectives Series?

"Read This Before You Begin" Page This page is consistent with Course Technology's unequaled commitment to helping instructors introduce technology into the classroom. Technical considerations and assumptions about hardware and software are listed in one place to help instructors save time and eliminate unnecessary aggravation. The "Read This Before You Begin" page for this book is on page AC 2.

Tutorial Case Each tutorial begins with a problem presented in a case that is meaningful to students. The problem turns the task of learning how to use an application into a problem-solving process. The problems increase in complexity with each tutorial. These cases touch on multicultural, international, and ethical issues—so important to today's business curriculum.

1.
2.
3.

Step-by-Step Methodology This unique Course Technology methodology keeps students on track. They enter data, click buttons, or click or press keys always within the context of solving the problem posed in the tutorial case. The text constantly guides students, letting them know where they are in the course of solving the problem. In addition, the numerous screen shots include callouts that direct students' attention to what they should look at on the screen. On almost every page in this book, you can find an example of how steps, screen shots, and callouts work together.

TROUBLE?

TROUBLE? Paragraphs These paragraphs anticipate the mistakes or problems that students are likely to have and help them recover and continue with the tutorial. By putting these paragraphs in the book, rather than in the Instructor's Manual, we facilitate independent learning and free the instructor to focus on substantive conceptual issues rather than on common procedural errors. Two representative examples of Trouble?s are on pages AC 9 and AC 12.

Reference windows Reference Windows appear throughout the text. They are short, succinct summaries of the most important tasks covered in the tutorials. Reference Windows are specially designed and written so students can use them for their reference value when doing the Tutorial Assignments and Case Problems, and after completing the course. Page AC 10 contains the Reference Window for Exiting Access.

Task Reference The Task Reference is a summary of how to perform common tasks using the most efficient method, as well as helpful shortcuts. It appears as a table at the end of the book. In this book the Task Reference is on pages AC 277–AC 280.

Tutorial Assignments, Case Problems, and Lab Assignments Each tutorial concludes with a Tutorial Assignment, which provides students with additional hands-on practice of the skills they learned in the tutorial. The Tutorial Assignment is followed by four Case Problems that have approximately the same scope as the tutorial case. In the Windows 95 applications texts, there is always one Case Problem in the Instructor's Manual that requires students to solve the problem independently, with minimum guidance. Finally, if a Lab (see below) accompanies the tutorial, a Lab Assignment is included. Look on page AC 30 for the Tutorial Assignment for Tutorial 1. See pages AC 70 through AC 74 for examples of Case Problems. The Lab Assignment for this book is on page AC 31.

Exploration Exercises The Windows environment allows students to learn by exploring and discovering what they can do. Exploration Exercises can be Tutorial Assignments or Case Problems that might challenge students, encourage them to explore the capabilities of the program they are using, and extend their knowledge using the Windows Help facility and other reference materials. Pages AC 157–AC 160 contain Exploration Exercises for Tutorial 4.

The New Perspectives Series is known for using technology to help instructors teach and administer, and to help students learn. The technology-based teaching and learning materials available with the New Perspectives Series are known as CourseTools. What CourseTools are available with this textbook?

Course Labs Computer skills and concepts come to life with the New Perspectives Course Labs—highly interactive tutorials that guide students step-by-step, present them with Quick Check questions, allow them to explore on their own, and test their comprehension. Lab Assignments are also included in the book at the end of each relevant tutorial. The lab available with this book and the tutorial in which it appears is:

Databases
Tutorial 1

Course Test Manager Course Test Manager is a cutting-edge Windows-based testing software that helps instructors design and administer pretests, practice tests, and actual examinations. The full-featured program generates random practice tests, provides immediate online feedback, and generates detailed study guides. Online pretests help instructors assess student skills and plan instruction. If students take tests at the computer, tests can be automatically graded and statistical information generated for the instructor on individual and group performance. Instructors can also use Course Test Manager to produce printed tests.

Online Companions When you use a New Perspectives product, you can access Course Technology's faculty and student sites on the World Wide Web. You may browse the password-protected Faculty Online Companion to obtain all the materials you need to prepare for class. Please see your Instructor's Manual or call your Course Technology customer service representative for more information. Students may access their Online Companion in the Student Center using the URL http://www.vmedia.com/cti/.

Instructor's Manual Instructor's Manuals are written by the authors and are quality-assurance tested. They are available in printed form and through the Course Technology Faculty Online Companion on the World Wide Web. Call your customer service representative for the URL and your password. Each Instructor's Manual contains the following items:

- Instructor's Notes for each tutorial prepared by the authors and based on their teaching experience. Instructor's Notes contain a tutorial overview, tutorial outline, troubleshooting tips, and lecture notes.
- Printed solutions to all of the Tutorial Assignments and Case Problems.
- An Additional Case Problem for each tutorial to augment teaching options.
- Solutions disk(s) containing every file students are asked to create or modify in the Tutorials, Tutorial Assignments, and Case Problems.

Student Files Disks Student Files Disks contain all of the data files that students will use for the Tutorials, Tutorial Assignments, and Case Problems. A README file includes technical tips for lab management. These files are also available online. See the inside covers of this book and the "Read This Before You Begin" page before Tutorial 1 for more information on student files.

Instructor's Resource Kit

You will receive the following Course Tools in the Instructor's Resource Kit:

- Course Labs Setup Disks
- Course Test Manager Test Bank Disks
- Course Presenter CD-ROM
- Instructor's Manual and Solutions Disks
- Student Files Disks

Acknowledgments

I want to thank Charles Hommel, University of Puget Sound, for his perceptive ideas, good humor, and tireless work in revising this book to meet Windows 95 standards. Thanks also to Anna Hommel for her help.

I also thank the dedicated and enthusiastic Course Technology staff, including Mac Mendelsohn, Managing Editor; Susan Solomon, Series Consulting Editor; Barbara Clemens, Senior Product Manager, for their support; special thanks to the Course Technology Production staff, including Roxanne Alexander, Production Editor, and GEX; and thanks to Jim Valente, Manuscript QA Coordinator, and student testers Patrick Reilly and Tia McCarthy.

Special thanks to Rachel Bunin for her excellent managerial skills, and Terry Ann Kremer for her literary contributions and her thoroughness.

Joseph J. Adamski

Brief Contents

Table of Contents

TUTORIAL 6

Creating Reports

New Perspectives on

Microsoft® Access 7 for Windows® 95

INTRODUCTORY

TUTORIALS

Read This **Before You Begin**

TO THE STUDENT

STUDENT DISKS

To complete the tutorials, Tutorial Assignments, and Case Problems in this book, you need three Student Disks. Your instructor will either provide you with Student Disks or ask you to make your own.

If you are supposed to make your own Student Disks, you will need three blank, formatted high-density disks. You will need to copy a set of folders from a file server or standalone computer onto your disks. Your instructor will tell you which computer, drive letter, and folders contain the folders you need. The following table shows you which folders go on each of your disks, so that you will have enough disk space to complete all the tutorials, Tutorial Assignments, and Case Problems:

Student Disk	Write this on the disk label	Put these folders on the disk
1	Tutorials 1-6, Tutorials and Tutorial Assignments	Tutorial from Disk 1 folder
2	Case Problems 1 and 2	Cases from Disk 2 folder
3	Case Problems 3 and 4	Cases from Disk 3 folder

When you begin each tutorial, be sure you are using the correct Student Disk. See the inside front or inside back cover of this book for more information on Student Disk files, or ask your instructor or technical support person for assistance.

COURSE LABS

Database

This book features an interactive Course Lab to help you understand database concepts. There is a Lab Assignment at the end of Tutorial 1 that relates to this Lab. To start the Lab, click the Start button on the Windows 95 taskbar, point to Programs, point to Course Labs, point to New Perspectives Applications, then click Databases.

USING YOUR OWN COMPUTER

If you are going to work through this book using your own computer, you need:

- **Computer System** Microsoft Windows 95 and Microsoft Access 7 for Windows 95 must be installed on your computer. This book assumes a full installation of Access.
- **Student Disks** Ask your instructor or lab manager for details on how to get the Student Disks. You will not be able to complete the tutorials or exercises in this book using your own computer until you have Student Disks. The student files may also be obtained electronically over the Internet. See the inside front or inside back cover of this book for more details.
- **Course Lab** See your instructor or technical support person to obtain the Course Lab for use on your own computer.

VISIT OUR WORLD WIDE WEB SITE

Additional materials designed especially for you are available on the World Wide Web. Go to **http://www.vmedia.com/cti/**.

TO THE INSTRUCTOR

To complete the tutorials in this book, your students must use a set of Student Files. These files are stored on the Student Files Disk(s) included in the Instructor's Resource Kit. Follow the instructions on the disk label(s) and the Readme.doc file to copy them to your server or standalone computer. You can view the Readme.doc file using WordPad.

Once the files are copied, you can make Student Disks for the students yourself, or tell students where to find the files so they can make their own Student Disks. Make sure the files get correctly copied onto the Students Disks by following the instructions in the Student Disks section above, which will ensure that students have enough disk space to complete all the tutorials, Tutorial Assignments, and Case Problems.

COURSE LAB SOFTWARE

Tutorial 1 features an online, interactive Course Lab that introduces basic database concepts. This software is distributed on the Course Labs Setup Disk(s), included in the Instructor's Resource Kit. To install the Lab software, follow the setup instructions on the disk label(s) and in the Readme.doc file. Once you have installed the Course Lab software, your students can start the Lab from the Windows 95 desktop by clicking Start, pointing to Programs/Course Labs/New Perspectives Applications, and clicking Databases.

CTI SOFTWARE AND STUDENT FILES

You are granted a license to copy the Student Files and Course Lab to any computer or computer network used by students who have purchased this book. The Student Files are included in the Instructor's Resource Kit and may also be obtained electronically over the Internet. See the inside front or inside back cover of this book for more details.

TUTORIAL 1

Introduction to Database Concepts and Access 7 for Windows 95

Planning a Special Magazine Issue

OBJECTIVES

In this tutorial you will:

- Learn terms used with databases
- Start and exit Access
- Identify the components of Access windows
- Open and close an Access database
- Open and close Access objects
- Print an Access table
- View an Access table using a datasheet and a form
- Use the Access Help system and shortcut menus

CASE

Vision Publishers

Brian Murphy is the president of Vision Publishers, which produces five specialized monthly magazines from its Chicago headquarters. Brian founded the company in March 1973 when he began publishing *Business Perspective*, a magazine featuring articles, editorials, interviews, and investigative reports that are widely respected in the financial and business communities. Using the concept, format, style, and strong writing of *Business Perspective* as a model, Brian began *Total Sports* in 1975, *Media Scene* in 1978, *Science Outlook* in 1984, and *Travel Vista* in 1987. All five magazines are leaders in their fields and have experienced consistent annual increases in circulation and advertising revenue.

Brian decides to do something special to commemorate the upcoming 25th anniversary of *Business Perspective* and schedules a meeting with three key employees of the magazine. At the meeting are Judith Rossi, managing editor; Harold Larson, marketing director; and Elena Sanchez, special projects editor. After reviewing alternatives, they agree that they will create a special 25th-anniversary issue of *Business Perspective*. The issue will include several articles reviewing the past 25 years of the magazine as well as the business and financial worlds during those years. Most of the special issue, however, will consist of articles from previous issues, a top article from each year of the magazine's existence. The *Business Perspective* team expects to sign up many advertisers for the issue and to use it as an incentive bonus gift for new and renewing subscribers.

Brian instructs Judith to select past articles and Elena to plan for the special issue. Brian will decide on the concept for the new articles and will communicate assignments to the writers.

Judith begins her assignment by using the Vision Publishers database that contains all articles published in the five magazines. From this Microsoft Access 7 for Windows 95 database, Judith will review the articles from *Business Perspective* and select the top articles.

Elena will also use Access for her assignment. Once Judith and Brian determine which articles will be in the special issue, Elena will use Access to store information about the selected business articles and their writers.

In this tutorial, you will work with Judith to complete her task. You will also learn about databases and how to use the features of Access to view and print your data.

Using the Tutorials Effectively

These tutorials will help you learn about Microsoft Access 7 for Windows 95. The tutorials are designed to be used at a computer. Each tutorial is divided into sessions, such as Session 1.1 and Session 1.2. The headings identify the tutorial and session number; for example, Tutorial 2 will have Session 2.1 and 2.2. Each session is designed to be completed in about 45 minutes, but you can take as much time as you need. It's also a good idea to take a break between sessions.

Before you begin, read the following questions and answers. They are designed to help you use the tutorials effectively.

Where do I start?

Each tutorial begins with a case, which sets the scene for the tutorial and gives you background information to help you understand what you will be doing in the tutorial. Ideally, you should read the case before you go to the lab.

How do I know what to do on the computer?

Each session contains steps that you will perform on the computer to learn how to use Access. Read the text that introduces each series of steps. The steps you need to do at a computer are numbered and are set against a colored background. Read each step carefully and completely before you try it.

How do I know if I did the step correctly?

As you work, compare your computer screen with the corresponding figure in the tutorial. Don't worry if your screen display is somewhat different from the corresponding figures. The important parts of the screen display are labeled in each figure. Check to make sure these parts are on your screen.

What if I make a mistake?

Don't worry about making mistakes—they are part of the learning process. Paragraphs labeled "TROUBLE?" identify common problems and explain how to get back on track. Follow the steps in a TROUBLE? paragraph *only* if you are having the problem described. If you run into other problems:

- Carefully consider the current state of your system, the position of the pointer, and any messages on the screen.
- Complete the sentence, "Now I want to...." Be specific, because you are identifying your goal.
- Develop a plan for accomplishing your goal, and put your plan into action.

How do I use the Reference Windows?

Reference Windows summarize the procedures you learn in the tutorial steps. Do not complete the actions in the Reference Windows when you are working through the tutorial. Instead, refer to the Reference Windows while you are working on the assignments at the end of the tutorial.

How can I test my understanding of the material I learned in the tutorial?

At the end of each session, you can answer the Quick Check questions. The answers for the Quick Checks are at the end of the tutorials.

After you have completed the entire tutorial, you should complete the Tutorial Assignments. The Tutorial Assignments are carefully structured so you will review what you have learned and then apply your knowledge to new situations.

What if I can't remember how to do something?

You should refer to the Task Reference at the end of the tutorials; it summarizes how to accomplish commonly performed tasks.

To follow the tutorials, you need to know how to use menus, dialog boxes, the Help facility, and My Computer in Microsoft Windows 95. Course Technology, Inc. publishes two excellent texts for learning Windows 95: *New Perspectives on Microsoft Windows 95—Brief* and *New Perspectives on Microsoft Windows 95—Introductory.*

Now that you've read how to use the tutorials effectively, you are ready to begin.

SESSION 1.1

In this session, you will learn how to start and exit Access. You will also learn how to open a database, view and print a table, and close an object window. With these skills, you will be able to open, view, and print tables in Access databases.

Introduction to Database Concepts

Before you work along with Judith on her Vision Publishers assignment, you need to understand a few key terms and concepts associated with databases.

Organizing Data

Data is a valuable resource to companies. At Vision Publishers, for example, writers' names, payments, past magazine article titles, and publication dates are data of great value. Organizing, creating, maintaining, retrieving, and sorting such data are important activities that lead to the display and printing of information useful to a company.

When you plan to create and store new types of data, either manually or on a computer, you follow a general three-step procedure:

1. Identify the individual fields.
2. Group fields for each entity in a table.
3. Store the field values for each record.

You first identify the individual fields. A **field** is a single characteristic of an entity and is also called a data element, data item, or attribute. An **entity** is a person, place, object, event, or idea. For example, Vision Publishers uses one entity, magazine articles (which includes several fields, such as Article Title and Article Length) to store data about its published articles. It uses another entity, writers (which includes the fields Writer Name and Writer Phone) to maintain information about the writers who have contributed to its magazines. Descriptive **field names**, such as Article Title and Writer Name, are used to label the fields.

Next, you group together all fields for a specific entity into a **table**. Corresponding to the entities discussed above, Vision Publishers has a MAGAZINE ARTICLES table and a WRITERS table, as shown in Figure 1-1. The MAGAZINE ARTICLES table has fields named Article Title, Magazine Issue, Magazine Name, and Article Length (number of words). The WRITERS table includes fields named Writer ID, Writer Name, and Writer Phone. By identifying the fields for each entity and then organizing them into tables, you have created the physical structure for your data.

Figure 1-1 Fields organized in two tables

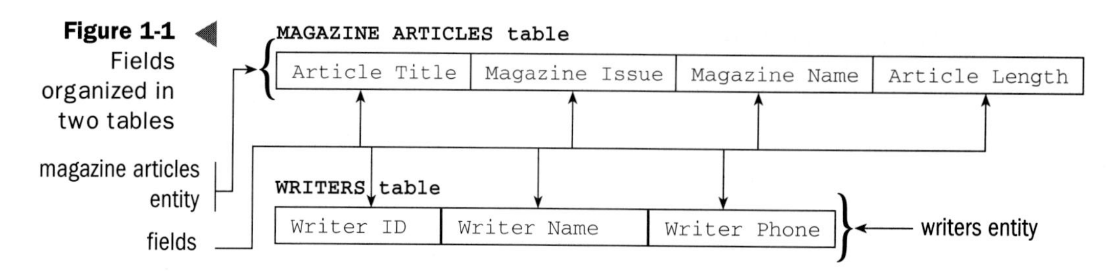

Your final step is to store specific values for the fields of each table. The specific value, or content, of a field is called the **field value**. In the MAGAZINE ARTICLES table shown in Figure 1-2, for example, the first set of field values for Article Title, Magazine Issue, Magazine Name, and Article Length are, respectively, Trans-Alaskan Oil Pipeline Opening, 1977 JUL, Business Perspective, and 803. This set of field values is called a **record**. Each magazine article that appears in the MAGAZINE ARTICLES table is a separate record. In Figure 1-2, nine records are shown, corresponding to the nine rows of field values.

Figure 1-2 Data organization for a table of magazine articles

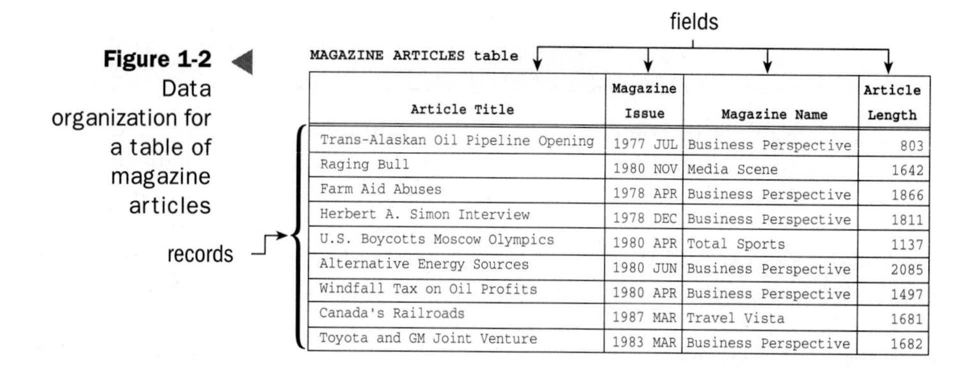

MAGAZINE ARTICLES table (fields; records)

Article Title	Magazine Issue	Magazine Name	Article Length
Trans-Alaskan Oil Pipeline Opening	1977 JUL	Business Perspective	803
Raging Bull	1980 NOV	Media Scene	1642
Farm Aid Abuses	1978 APR	Business Perspective	1866
Herbert A. Simon Interview	1978 DEC	Business Perspective	1811
U.S. Boycotts Moscow Olympics	1980 APR	Total Sports	1137
Alternative Energy Sources	1980 JUN	Business Perspective	2085
Windfall Tax on Oil Profits	1980 APR	Business Perspective	1497
Canada's Railroads	1987 MAR	Travel Vista	1681
Toyota and GM Joint Venture	1983 MAR	Business Perspective	1682

Databases and Relationships

Organizing information in tables helps database users obtain information easily. However, what if you need information that is stored in more than one table? For example, suppose Judith wants information about a specific writer, Leroy W. Johnson, and the articles he wrote. To be able to access this information, the WRITERS table would have to be related to the MAGAZINE ARTICLES table. A collection of related tables is called a **database**, or a **relational database**.

To have a relational database, records must be connected from the separate tables through a **common field** that appears in all tables. For the WRITERS table and the MAGAZINE ARTICLES table, that common field is named Writer ID (Figure 1-3). For example, Leroy W. Johnson is the third writer in the WRITERS table and has a Writer ID field value of J525. This same Writer ID field value, J525, appears in the first and third records of the MAGAZINE ARTICLES table. Using these related tables, Judith can now find out specific information about Leroy W. Johnson and the articles he wrote.

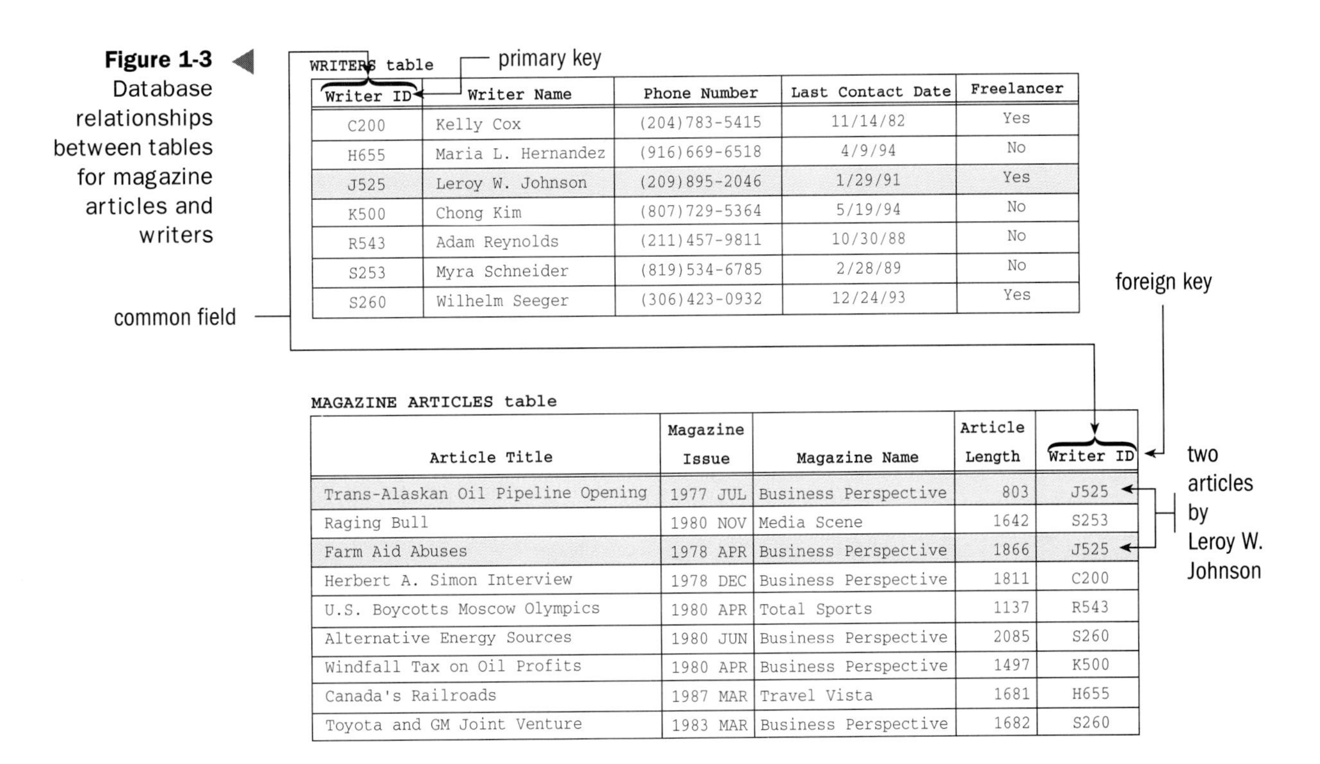

WRITERS table

Writer ID	Writer Name	Phone Number	Last Contact Date	Freelancer
C200	Kelly Cox	(204)783-5415	11/14/82	Yes
H655	Maria L. Hernandez	(916)669-6518	4/9/94	No
J525	Leroy W. Johnson	(209)895-2046	1/29/91	Yes
K500	Chong Kim	(807)729-5364	5/19/94	No
R543	Adam Reynolds	(211)457-9811	10/30/88	No
S253	Myra Schneider	(819)534-6785	2/28/89	No
S260	Wilhelm Seeger	(306)423-0932	12/24/93	Yes

MAGAZINE ARTICLES table

Article Title	Magazine Issue	Magazine Name	Article Length	Writer ID
Trans-Alaskan Oil Pipeline Opening	1977 JUL	Business Perspective	803	J525
Raging Bull	1980 NOV	Media Scene	1642	S253
Farm Aid Abuses	1978 APR	Business Perspective	1866	J525
Herbert A. Simon Interview	1978 DEC	Business Perspective	1811	C200
U.S. Boycotts Moscow Olympics	1980 APR	Total Sports	1137	R543
Alternative Energy Sources	1980 JUN	Business Perspective	2085	S260
Windfall Tax on Oil Profits	1980 APR	Business Perspective	1497	K500
Canada's Railroads	1987 MAR	Travel Vista	1681	H655
Toyota and GM Joint Venture	1983 MAR	Business Perspective	1682	S260

Figure 1-3 Database relationships between tables for magazine articles and writers

Notice that each Writer ID value in the WRITERS table is unique, so that we can distinguish one writer from another and identify the writer of specific articles in the MAGAZINE ARTICLES table. We call the Writer ID field the **primary key** of the WRITERS table. A primary key is a field or a collection of fields, whose values uniquely identify each record in a table.

When we include a primary key from one table in a second table to form a relationship between the two tables, we call it a **foreign key** in the second table. For example, Writer ID is the primary key in the WRITERS table and is a foreign key in the MAGAZINE ARTICLES table. Although the primary key Writer ID has unique values in the WRITERS table, the same field as a foreign key in the MAGAZINE ARTICLES table does not. The Writer ID values J525 and S260, for example, each appear twice in the MAGAZINE ARTICLES table. Each foreign key value, however, must match one of the field values for the primary key in the other table. Each Writer ID value in the MAGAZINE ARTICLES table, for instance, appears as a Writer ID value in the WRITERS table.

Relational Database Management Systems

As you might imagine, a company relies on numerous databases to store its data. To manage its databases, a company uses **database management system (DBMS)** software to let its employees create databases and then manipulate data in the databases. Most of today's database management systems, including Access, are called relational database management systems. In a **relational database management system**, data is organized as a collection of tables. These tables are formally called relations, which is how the term relational databases originated.

A relationship between two tables in a relational DBMS is formed through the common field. A relational DBMS (Figure 1-4) controls the physical databases on disk storage by carrying out data creation and manipulation requests. Specifically, a relational DBMS allows you to:

- create database structures containing fields, tables, and table relationships
- add new records, change field values in existing records, and delete records
- obtain immediate answers to the questions you ask about your data through its built-in query language
- produce professional-looking, formatted, hardcopy reports from your data through its built-in report generator
- protect databases through its security, control, and recovery facilities

Figure 1-4 A relational database management system

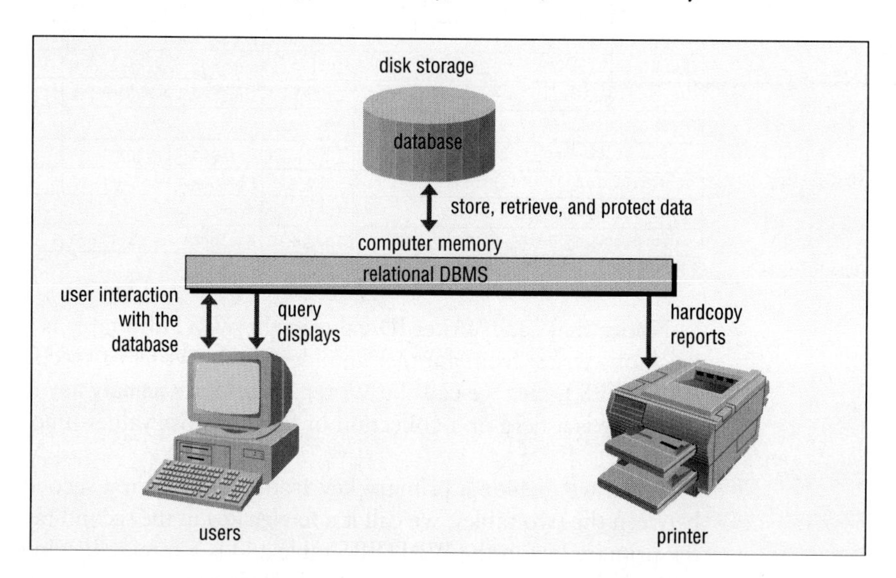

A company like Vision Publishers additionally benefits from a relational DBMS because it allows several people working in different departments to share the same data. More than one person can enter data into a database, and more than one person can retrieve and analyze data that was entered by others. For example, Vision Publishers keeps only one copy of the WRITERS table, and all employees use it to meet their specific needs for writer information.

A DBMS can handle massive amounts of data and can easily form relationships among multiple tables. Each Access database, for example, can be up to 1 gigabyte in size and can contain up to 32,768 tables.

Starting and Exiting Access

Access is rapidly becoming one of the most popular relational DBMSs in the Windows 95 environment. For the rest of this tutorial, you will learn to use Access as you work with Judith and Elena on their project.

You first need to learn how to start Access, so let's do that now.

To start Access:

1. Make sure you have created your copy of the Access Student Disk and that you have started Windows 95.

   TROUBLE? If you don't have a Student Disk, then you need to get one before you can proceed. Your instructor will either give you one or ask you to make your own. See your instructor for information.

2. Click the **Start** button.

3. Point to **Programs** to display the programs list.

4. Point to **Microsoft Office**. See Figure 1-5.

Figure 1-5 Starting Microsoft Access

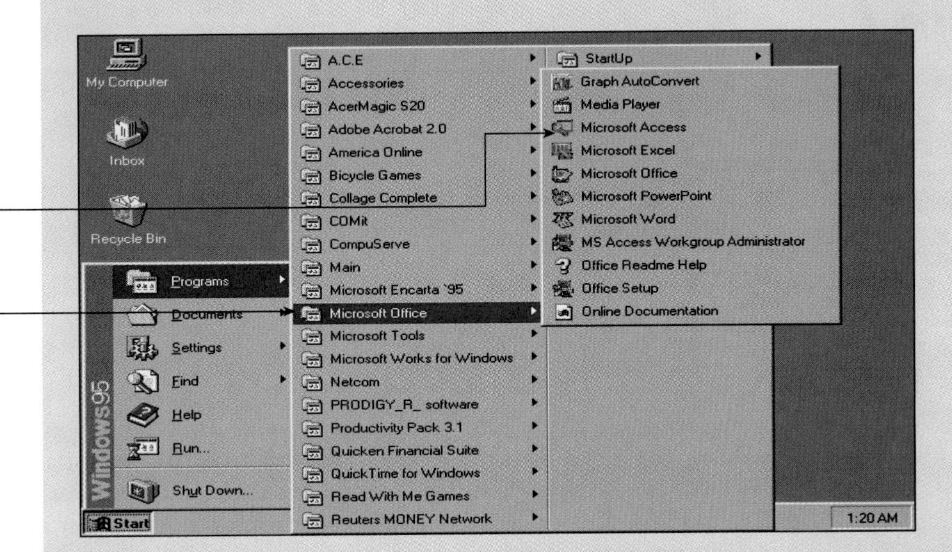

   TROUBLE? If you don't see a Microsoft Office in the program list, then look for a program labeled Microsoft Access and use it instead. If you do not have either of these, ask your technical support person or instructor for help finding Microsoft Access. Perhaps Access has not been installed on the computer you are using. If you are using your own computer, make sure you have installed the Access software.

5. Click **Microsoft Access** to start Access. After a short pause, the Access copyright information appears in a message box and remains on the screen until Access displays the Microsoft Access window. See Figure 1-6.

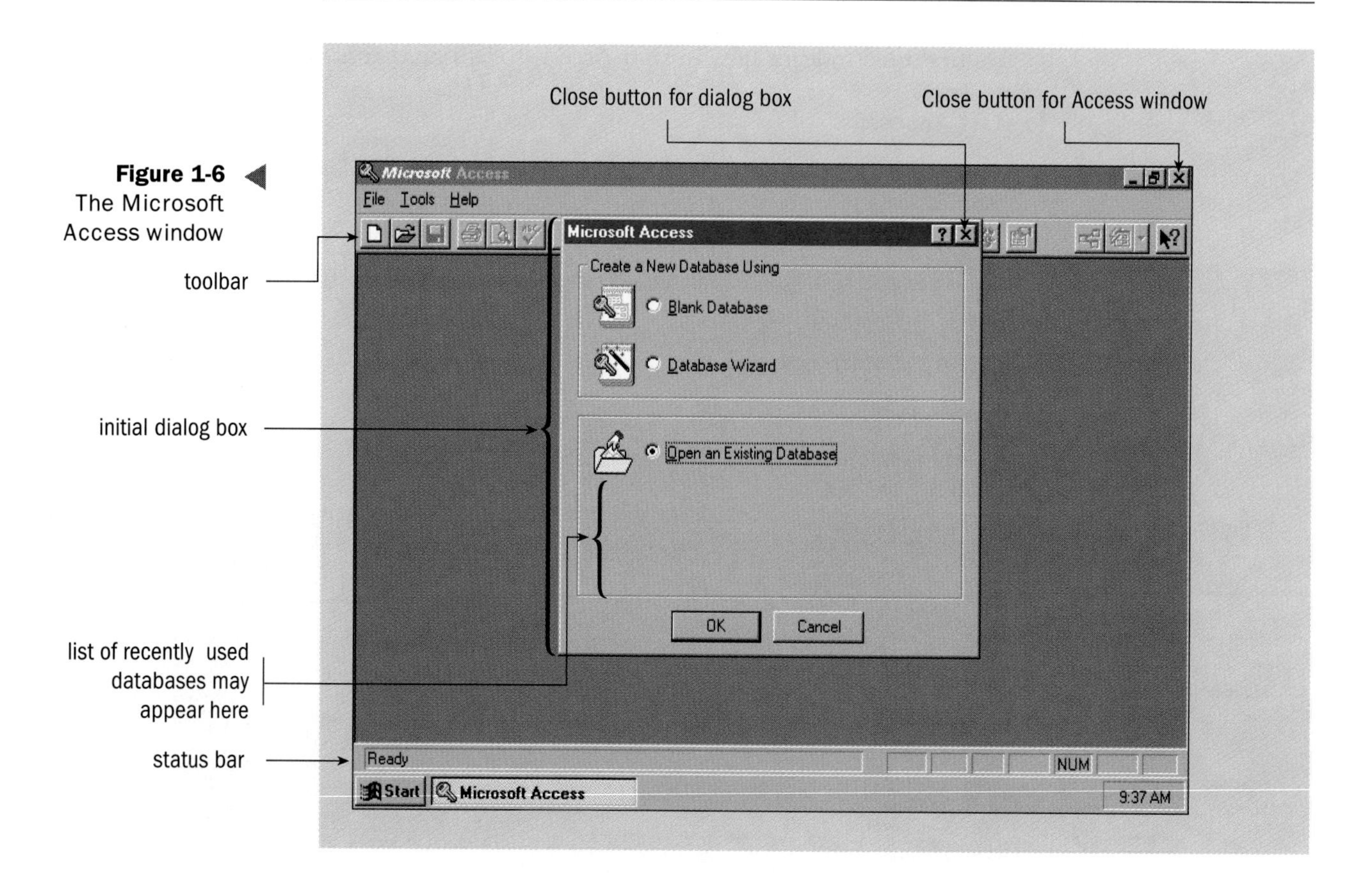

Figure 1-6 The Microsoft Access window

Access is now loaded into your computer's memory. When you start Access, the Access window contains a dialog box that allows you to create a new database or open an existing database. Although Judith wants to work with an existing database, it's always a good idea to know how to exit a software application when you first start working with it.

The Reference Window called "Exiting Access" lists the general steps for exiting Access. Don't try the steps in the Reference Window now. Instead, just read the information in the Reference Window to get a general idea of what you are going to do. Specific instructions that you will follow are provided in the next section of numbered steps.

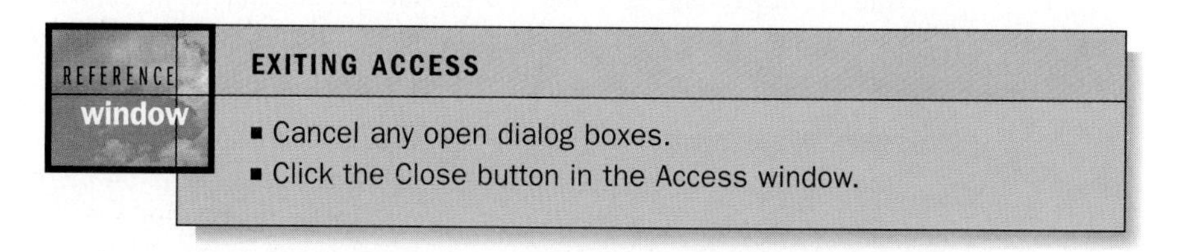

REFERENCE window

EXITING ACCESS

- Cancel any open dialog boxes.
- Click the Close button in the Access window.

By completing the following set of steps, you can exit Access at almost any time, no matter what you are doing. If you ever try to exit Access and find you cannot, your active window is likely to be an open dialog box. An open dialog box will prevent you from immediately exiting Access. Simply cancel the dialog box, and you will then be able to exit Access.

To exit Access:

1. Click the **Close** button ☒ to close the dialog box.
2. Click the **Close** button ☒ in the upper-right corner of the Access window.

You have now exited Access. In the next section of the tutorial, as the first step in helping Judith complete her assignment, you'll learn how to open a database.

Opening a Database

To select the articles for the 25th anniversary issue, Judith will work with an existing database, so her first step is to open that database. When you want to use a database that was previously created, you must first open it. When you open a database, a copy of the database file is transferred into the random access memory (often referred to as RAM) of your computer and becomes available for your use. You can then view, print, modify, or save it on your disk.

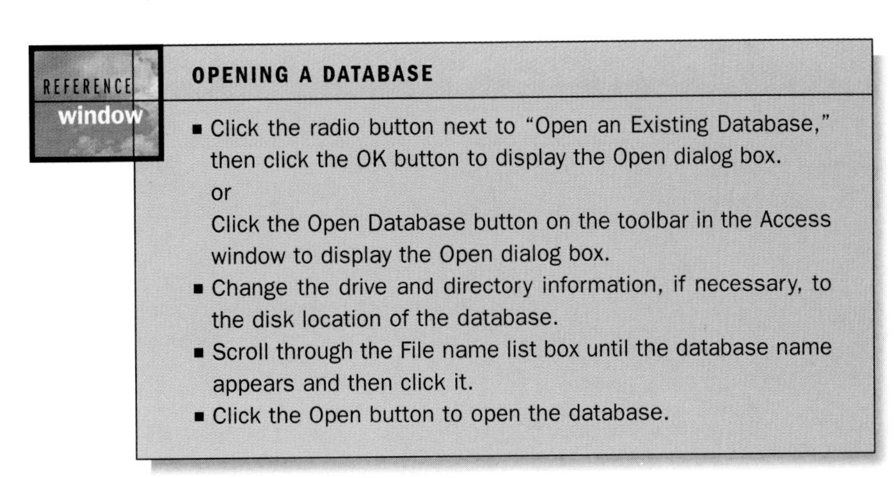

REFERENCE window

OPENING A DATABASE

- Click the radio button next to "Open an Existing Database," then click the OK button to display the Open dialog box.
  or
  Click the Open Database button on the toolbar in the Access window to display the Open dialog box.
- Change the drive and directory information, if necessary, to the disk location of the database.
- Scroll through the File name list box until the database name appears and then click it.
- Click the Open button to open the database.

Judith opens the database for Vision Publishers now.

To open an existing database:

1. Start Access by following the steps described earlier. The Access window appears with the initial dialog box.
2. Make sure your Access Student Disk is in the appropriate drive—either drive A or drive B.

   You may see a list of databases in a list box below the Open an Existing Database radio button. This is a list of databases recently used on your machine. The first entry in the list, More Files, gives you access to databases not shown in the list. If this list box is visible, make sure that More Files is highlighted.
3. Make sure the radio button next to "Open an Existing Database" is selected. Click the **OK** button to display the Open dialog box. See Figure 1-7.

Figure 1-7 Open dialog box

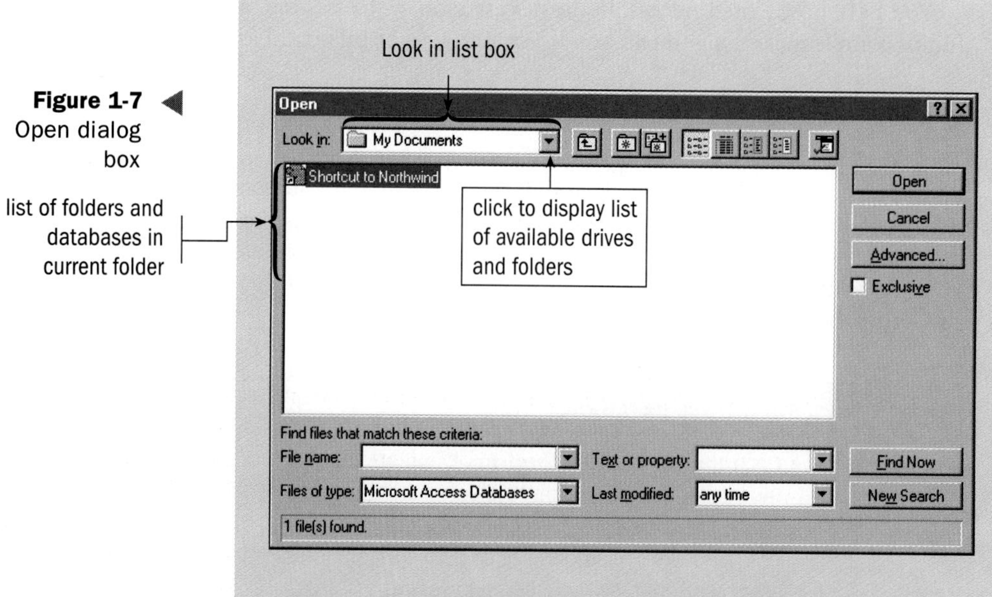

4. Click the **Look in** list arrow. A list of available drives drops down. Click the icon of the drive in which you put your Student Disk. The panel below the Look in list box now displays a list of folders and databases on your disk.

5. Click **Tutorial** in the folders list to select it, then click the **Open** button.

6. Click **Vision** in the database list to select it. See Figure 1-8.

Figure 1-8 Completed Open dialog box

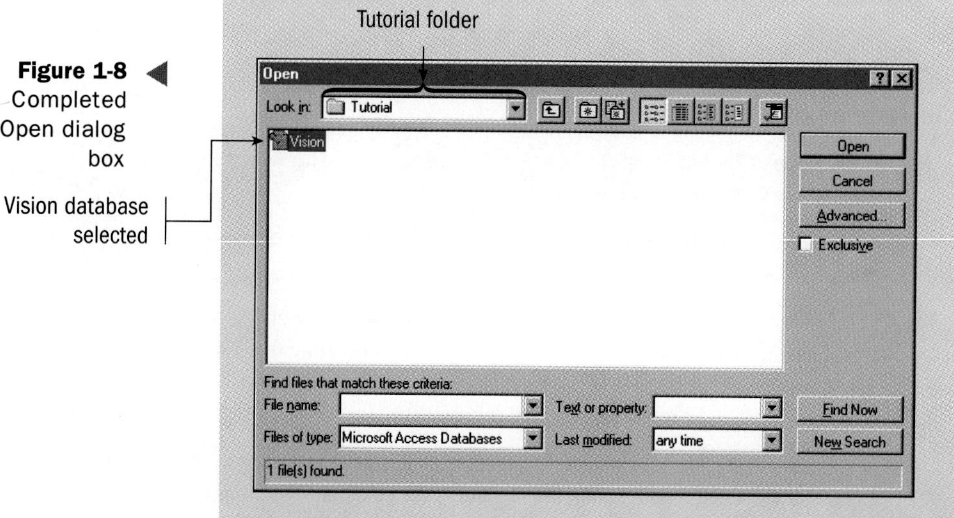

TROUBLE? Depending on your computer configuration, your screen may show the database name with the extension name. In that case, click Vision.mdb to select the database.

TROUBLE? If you can't find a file named Vision, check that the Look in list box indicates the Tutorial folder of your Student Disk. If the Look in list box shows the correct folder, perhaps you are using the wrong disk in the drive. Check your disk to be sure it's your Student Disk. If it is the correct disk, check with your technical support person or instructor. If it is not the correct disk, place the correct Student Disk in the drive and resume your work from Step 4.

7. Click the **Open** button to let Access know you have completed the Open Database dialog box. Access opens the Vision database and displays the Database window in the Access window.

Before beginning her assignment for Brian, Judith checks the window on the screen to familiarize herself with her options. You should also.

Access Windows

Access windows, like other Windows software such as Word and Excel, contain toolbars and menu bars that vary depending on the window you are viewing. As in other Windows programs, the toolbar buttons represent common operations you perform with the software you are using—in this case, databases.

When you first view the toolbar, you might be unsure of the function associated with each toolbar button. Fortunately, when you stop the mouse pointer on a toolbar button, Access displays a ToolTip under the button and a description of the button in the status bar at the bottom of the screen. A **ToolTip** is a boxed caption showing the name of the indicated toolbar button.

Judith displays the ToolTip for the Print button.

To display a ToolTip:

1. Move the mouse pointer to the toolbar and stop the pointer on [Print button]. It is the fourth button from the left. After a short pause, Access displays a ToolTip under the button and the button's description in the status bar. See Figure 1-9.

Figure 1-9 The Print ToolTip in the Access window

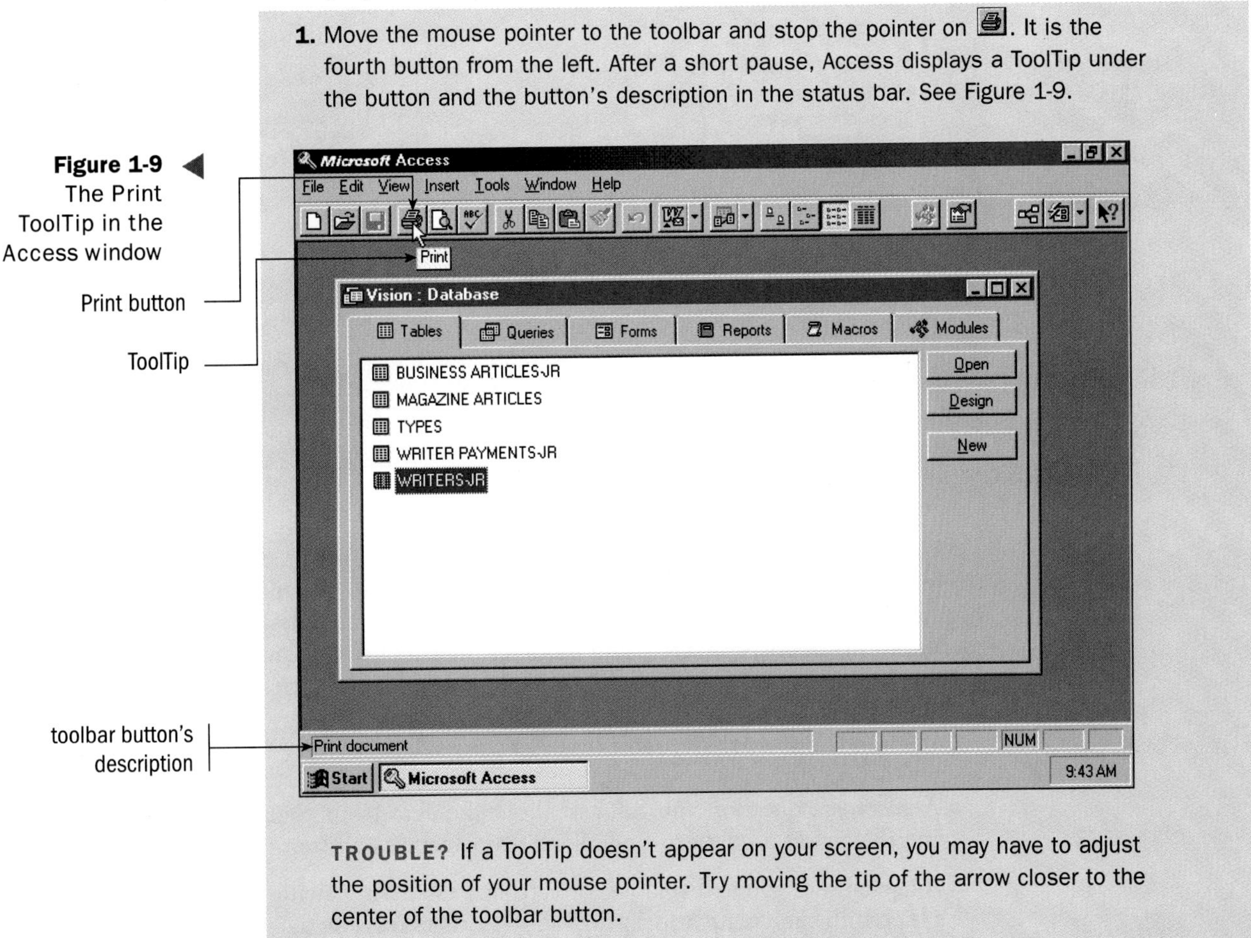

TROUBLE? If a ToolTip doesn't appear on your screen, you may have to adjust the position of your mouse pointer. Try moving the tip of the arrow closer to the center of the toolbar button.

Some toolbar buttons, such as the Format Painter button, appear dimmed because they are not active now. They will become active later, after you have opened a database or taken some other action. Spend a few moments now stopping at active toolbar buttons to view their ToolTip and status bar descriptions.

The Database Window

After a database is opened, Access displays the Database window, shown in Figure 1-10. Because you already have experience with the Windows 95 graphical user interface (GUI), you will recognize the following components of the Database window: the Access window title bar, the Access window sizing buttons, the menu bar, the toolbar, the toolbar buttons, the Database window sizing buttons, and the status bar.

Figure 1-10 The Database window

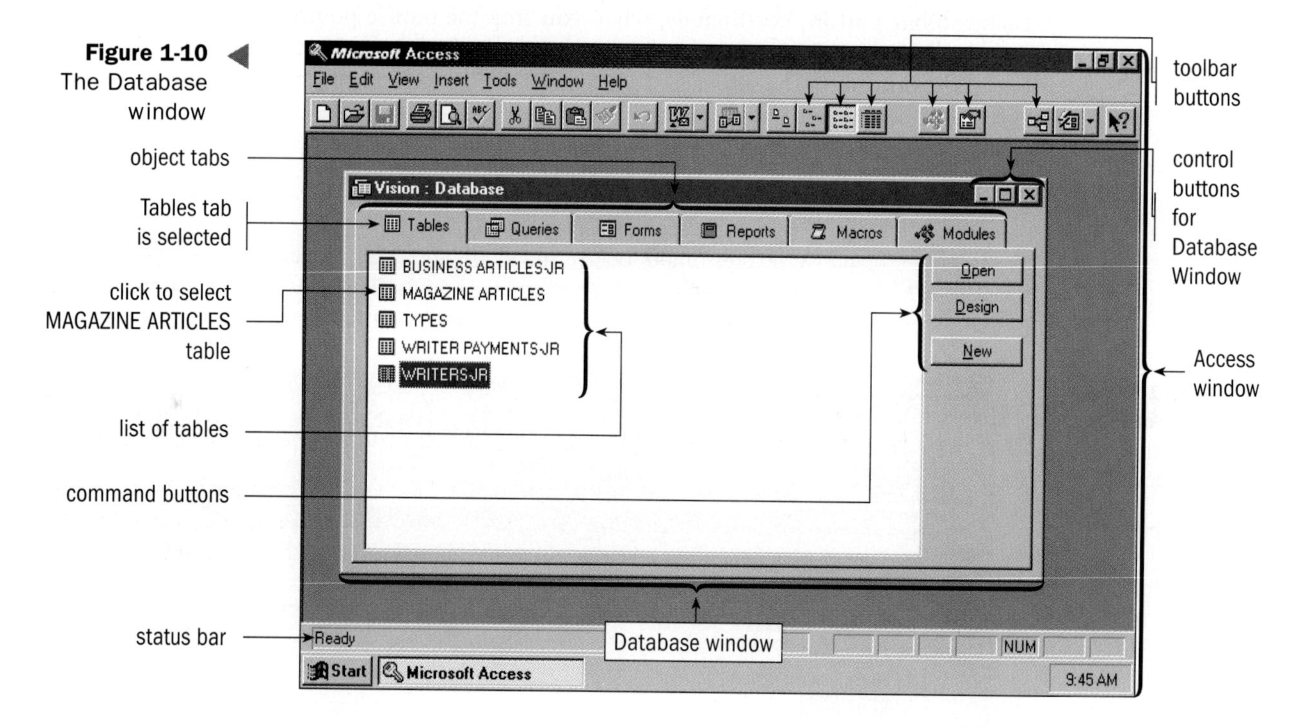

You might not be familiar with the six object tabs and the three command buttons. The object tabs represent the six types of objects you can create for an Access database. Unlike most other DBMSs, Access stores each database, which includes all of its defined tables, queries, forms, reports, macros, and modules, in a single file. Each object is handled separately so that if Vision Publishers has three tables, five queries, and four reports in a database, Access treats them as 12 separate objects.

You already know what a table is, so let's consider the other five objects:

- A **query** is a question you can ask about the data from your tables. For example, Judith can use a query to find all magazine articles written by a particular writer.
- A **form** allows you to display records from a table for viewing or editing. For example, Judith can create a form that allows others to view data one record at a time from the WRITERS table.

- A **report** is a customized format for printing the data from tables. If Brian needs to review all writer information, a report can be generated to display this data in a readable format.
- A **macro** is a saved list of operations to be performed on data. Judith can use a macro, for example, to open a special form automatically whenever someone opens the company database.
- A **module** is a set of one or more Visual Basic procedures (Visual Basic is Access's built-in programming language). At Vision Publishers, for example, a module is used to calculate payments to writers.

The three command buttons in the Database window represent the major operations performed on tables. You can create a new table by clicking the New button. For an existing table, click the Open button to view table records or click the Design button to change the table structure.

The Tables tab is automatically selected when you first open a database, and a list of available tables for the database appears. When you click one of the other object tabs to select it, a list of available objects of that type appears.

Viewing and Printing a Table

Now that you have opened a database and familiarized yourself with the components of the Database window, you are ready to view and print an existing Access table. If you want to look up information contained in just a few records in a table, you usually view the table on the screen. If you need information from a large number of records or need to present the information to other people, however, you usually print a hardcopy of the table.

Datasheet View

The Vision Publishers table named MAGAZINE ARTICLES contains data about all the magazine articles published by the company. Judith opens this table to start her selection of top past articles from *Business Perspective* magazine for use in the special issue.

OPENING THE DATASHEET VIEW WINDOW FOR A TABLE

- Scroll through the Tables list until the table name appears and then click it.
- Click the Open button.

Judith opens the MAGAZINE ARTICLES table for Vision Publishers.

To open the Datasheet View window for the MAGAZINE ARTICLES table:

1. If necessary, click **MAGAZINE ARTICLES** to select it, then click the **Open** button. The Datasheet View window for the MAGAZINE ARTICLES table appears on top of the previous windows. See Figure 1-11.

Figure 1-11 The Datasheet View window

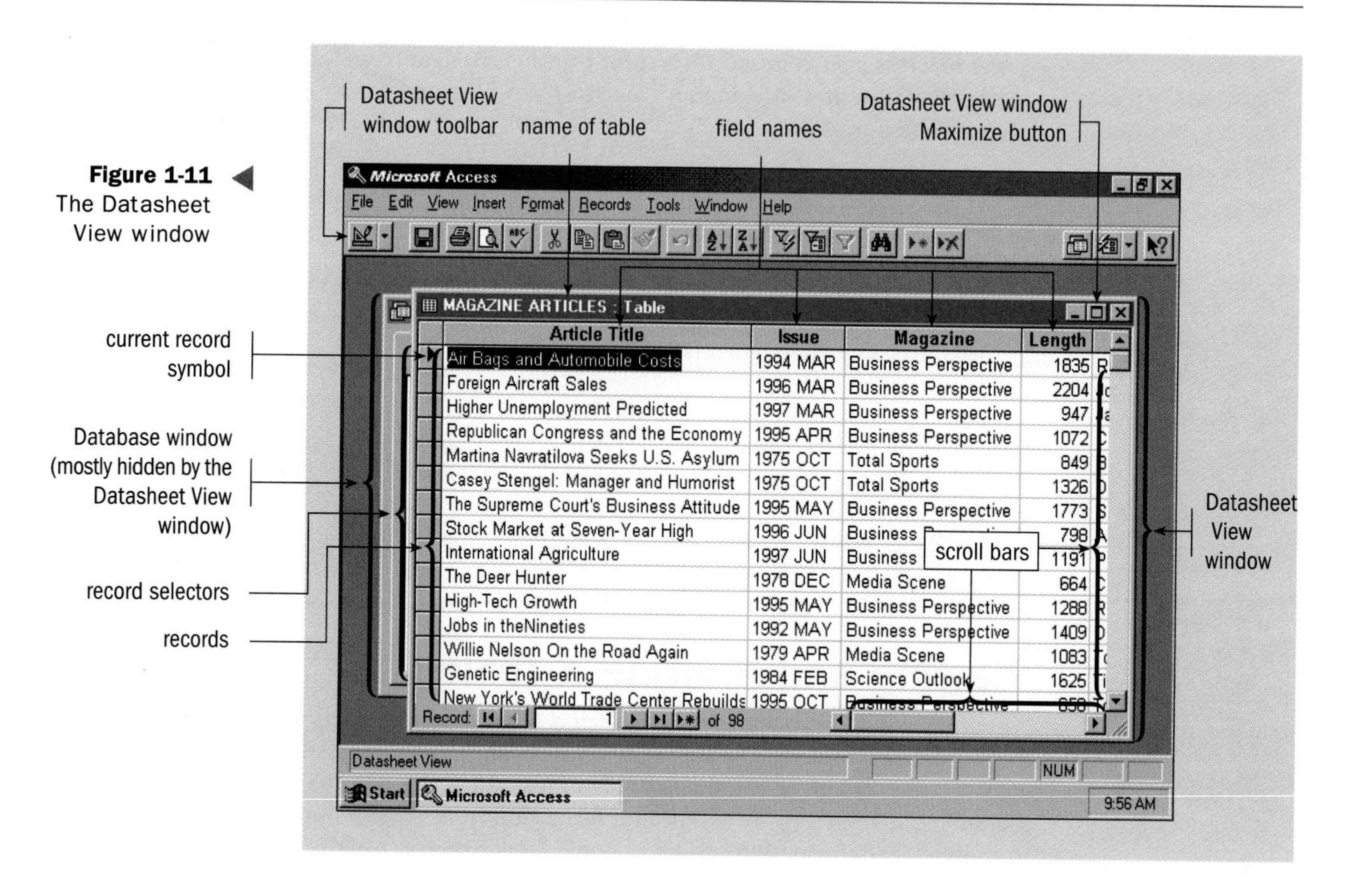

The **Datasheet View** window shows a table's contents in rows and columns, the way a spreadsheet does. Each row is a separate record in the table, and each column contains the field values for one field from the table. When you first open a datasheet, Access automatically selects the first field value in the first record for processing. This field is highlighted and a darkened triangle symbol, called the **current record symbol**, appears in the record selector to the left of the first record. If you move your mouse pointer over any field value, the pointer shape changes to I. If you then click the I on a field value in another row, that field value becomes the currently selected field and the current record symbol moves to that row. Although the entire field value is not highlighted, the insertion point stays where you clicked, and the new record becomes the current record. Practice clicking the I on different fields and records and notice the changes that occur in the datasheet.

Even though the MAGAZINE ARTICLES table has only five fields, depending on your computer system the Datasheet View window may not be large enough to display all the fields across the screen. You may only see only the first group of records from the table. To see more of the table on the screen, you can maximize the Datasheet View window in the Access window.

To maximize the Datasheet View window:

1. Click the **Maximize** button for the Datasheet View window. Notice that a Restore button replaces the Maximize button and that the table title appears in the Access title bar.

   TROUBLE? If your datasheet is not maximized, you probably clicked the Datasheet View window Minimize button or one of the Microsoft Access window sizing buttons instead. Use the appropriate sizing button to restore your screen to its previous condition, and then refer to Figure 1-11 for the location of the Datasheet View window Maximize button.

Even though the Datasheet View window is maximized, depending on your computer system, the fields in the MAGAZINE ARTICLES table may still be too wide to fit on the screen and there might be too many records to see them all on the screen at one time. One way to see different parts of a table is to use the vertical and horizontal scroll bars and arrows on the right and bottom of the datasheet. Practice clicking these scroll bars and arrows to become comfortable with their use. Use the vertical scroll bar (also called the elevator) to move vertically through the table to display different records. Use the horizontal scroll bar to scroll right and left to display different fields.

Using the lower-left navigation buttons, shown in Figure 1-12, is another way to move vertically through the records. From left to right, respectively, the four **navigation buttons** select the first record, the previous record, the next record, and the last record in the table. The last button ▶* creates a blank (new) record. The current record number appears between the two sets of navigation buttons. The total number of records in the table appears to the right of the navigation buttons. Practice clicking the four navigation buttons (but not the blank record button) and notice the changes that occur in the datasheet, in the current record number, and in the placement of the current record symbol.

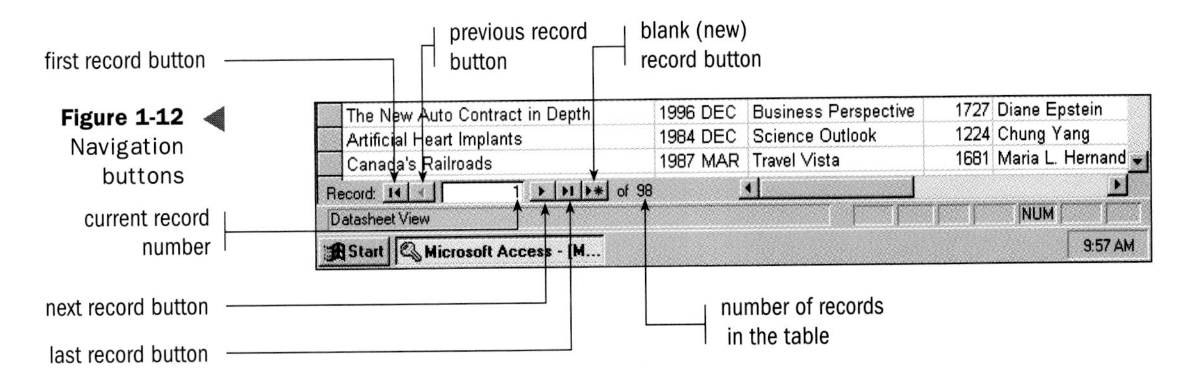

Figure 1-12 Navigation buttons

The Datasheet View window displays the table records on the screen. To obtain a hardcopy of the records, you can print them on your printer. Because the table contains several datasheet pages, Judith decides to print only the records from the first datasheet page to study their contents more closely. Remember, a datasheet page allows you to view the actual records.

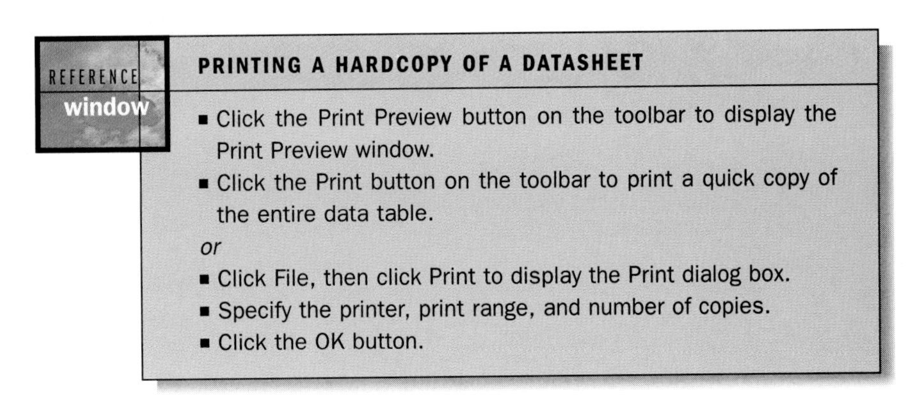

REFERENCE window

PRINTING A HARDCOPY OF A DATASHEET

- Click the Print Preview button on the toolbar to display the Print Preview window.
- Click the Print button on the toolbar to print a quick copy of the entire data table.

or

- Click File, then click Print to display the Print dialog box.
- Specify the printer, print range, and number of copies.
- Click the OK button.

Before you actually print the records, it is sometimes useful to preview them on the Print Preview screen. The Print Preview screen displays the records as they will appear on the hardcopy.

Judith previews the datasheet and then print its first page.

To preview and print a datasheet:

1. Click the **Print Preview** button on the toolbar. The Print Preview window opens. See Figure 1-13.

Figure 1-13 The Print Preview window

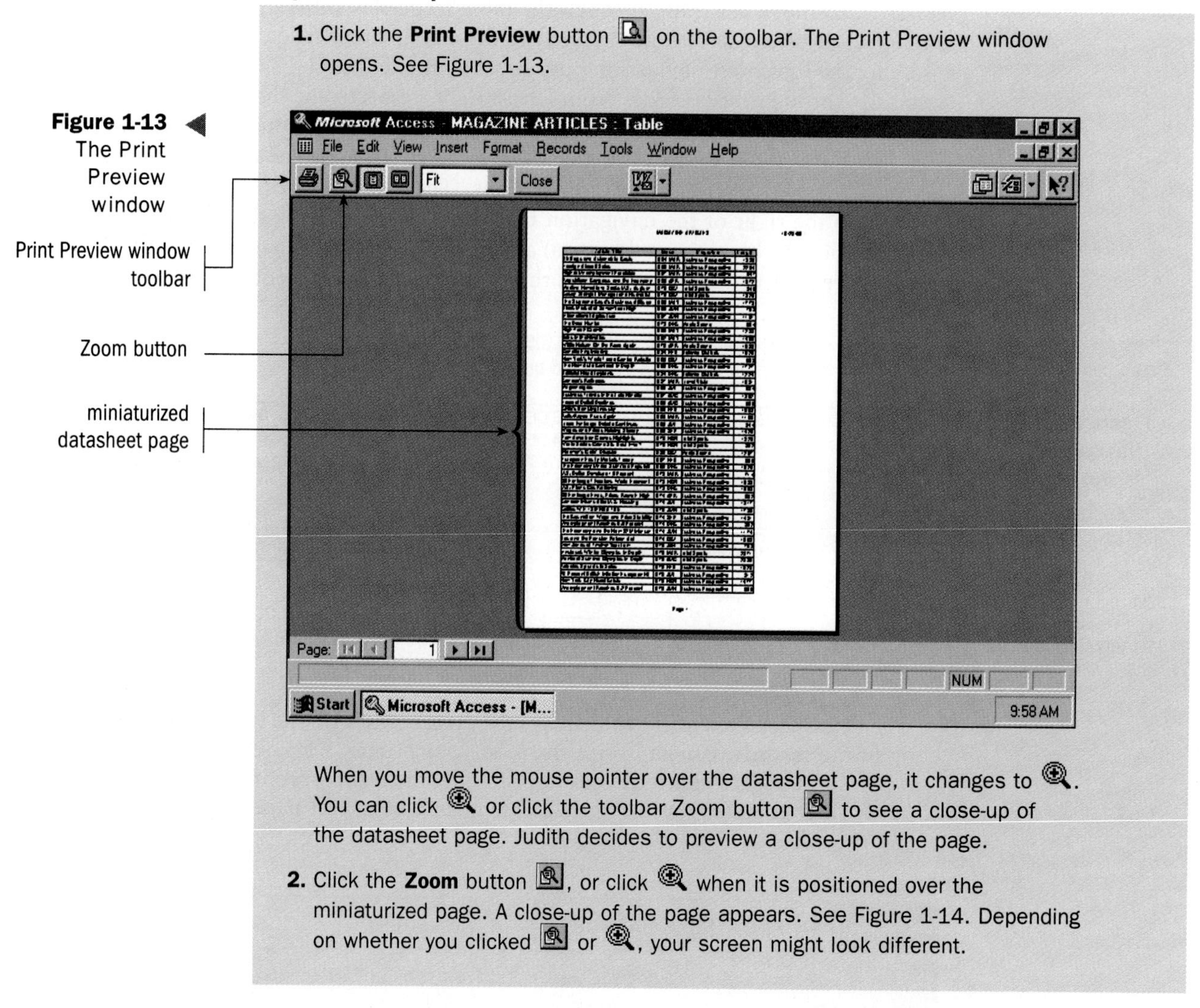

When you move the mouse pointer over the datasheet page, it changes to . You can click or click the toolbar Zoom button to see a close-up of the datasheet page. Judith decides to preview a close-up of the page.

2. Click the **Zoom** button , or click when it is positioned over the miniaturized page. A close-up of the page appears. See Figure 1-14. Depending on whether you clicked or , your screen might look different.

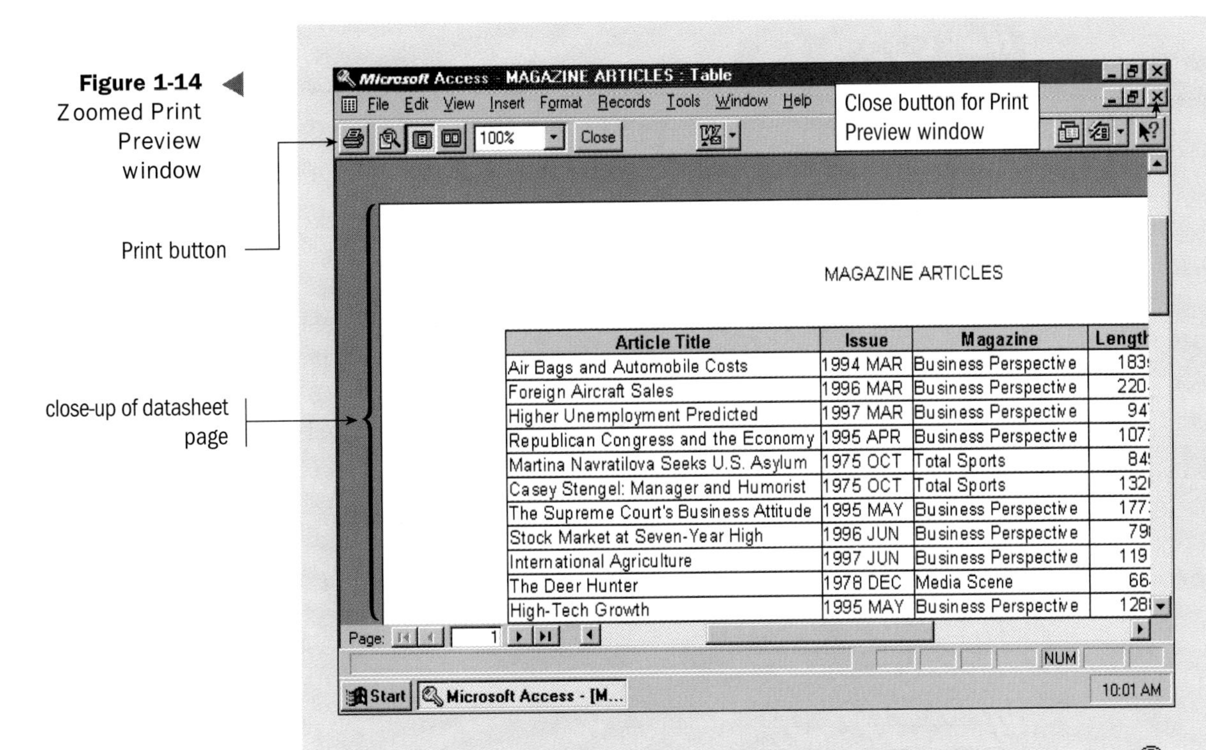

Figure 1-14 Zoomed Print Preview window

When you move the mouse pointer over the datasheet page, it changes to . If you click or , the page returns to its original miniaturized view. Practice clicking , , , and the navigation buttons. When you are done practicing, you are ready to print the datasheet page.

Microsoft Access offers two ways to print a datasheet. If you click the Print button on the toolbar, Access will immediately print the entire datasheet. If you want to print only selected pages or selected records, you can specify this in the Print dialog box that appears when you choose the Print option from the File menu.

3. Make sure your printer is on-line and ready to print. Because you want to print just the first datasheet page, click **File**, then click **Print**. The Print dialog box opens. Check the Printer section of the dialog box to make sure your printer is selected.

   TROUBLE? If the correct printer is not selected, click the list arrow in the Name text box and select the correct printer from the printer list.

4. Click the radio button next to "**Pages**" in the Print Range panel, then type **1**, press the **Tab** key, type **1** to print just the first page of the datasheet, then click the **OK** button. A dialog box informs you that your datasheet page is being sent to the printer.

5. After the dialog box closes, click the Print Preview window **Close** button to return to the Database window.

   TROUBLE? If Access displays a message box asking if you want to save changes, click the No button. You accidentally changed the datasheet and do not want to save the modified version in your table.

   TROUBLE? If your document hasn't printed yet, check the print status in the print queue for your printer. Remove your document from the print queue before returning to your datasheet and then print the first datasheet page again. If it still doesn't print, see your technical support person or instructor.

Quick Check

1. What three steps should you generally follow to create and store a new type of data?
2. What are fields and entities, and how are they related?
3. What are the differences between a primary key and a foreign key?
4. Describe what a DBMS is designed to do.
5. Describe the six different objects you can create for an Access database.
6. What do the columns and rows of a datasheet represent?

Use the data in Figure 1-15 to answer Question 7.

Figure 1-15

CHECKING ACCOUNTS table

Account Number	Name	Balance
2173	Theodore Lamont	842.27
4519	Beatrice Whalley	2071.92
8005	t Zambrano	1132.00

CHECKS table

Account Number	Check Number	Date	Amount
4519	1371	10/22/98	45.00
4519	1372	10/23/98	115.00
2173	1370	10/24/98	50.00
4519	1377	10/27/98	60.00
2173	1371	10/29/98	20.00

7. Name the fields in the CHECKS table. How many records are in the CHECKS table? What is the primary key of the CHECKING ACCOUNTS table?

Now that you've completed Session 1.1, you can exit the program or continue on to the next session. If you want to take a break and resume the tutorial at a later time, you can exit Access by clicking the Access window Close button in the upper-right corner of the screen. When you resume the tutorial, place your Student Disk in the appropriate drive and start Access. Open the database Vision, maximize the Database window, and then continue working on the next session of the tutorial.

SESSION 1.2

In this session, you will learn to view table records in a form, close a database, and use Access Help and shortcut menus.

Form View

Judith now opens an existing form to view the records from the MAGAZINE ARTICLES table. As we discussed earlier, a form gives you a customized view of data from a database. You use a form, for example, to view one record at a time from a table, to view data in a more readable format, or to view related data from two or more tables. The way you open a form is similar to the way you opened a datasheet.

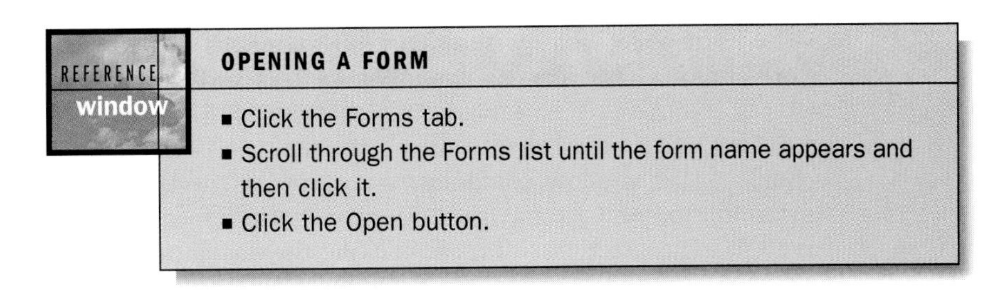
REFERENCE window

OPENING A FORM

- Click the Forms tab.
- Scroll through the Forms list until the form name appears and then click it.
- Click the Open button.

Judith now opens the form named Magazine Articles.

To open a form:

1. Make sure that the Database window is open and maximized, then click the **Forms** tab. A list of available forms appears in the Forms list. See Figure 1-16.

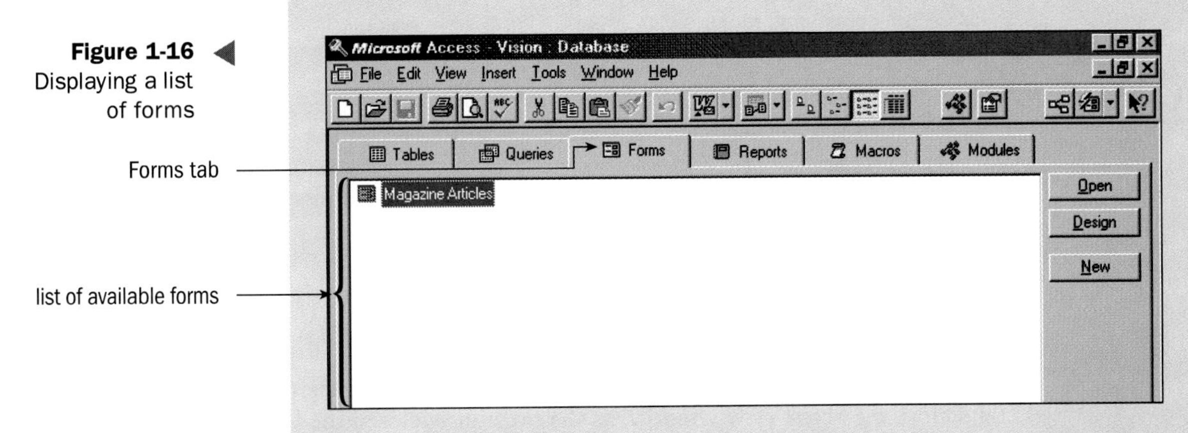

Figure 1-16 Displaying a list of forms

2. Only one form is listed, so it is already highlighted, or selected. Click the **Open** button. The Form View window opens. The Form View window is maximized because the Database window was maximized. See Figure 1-17.

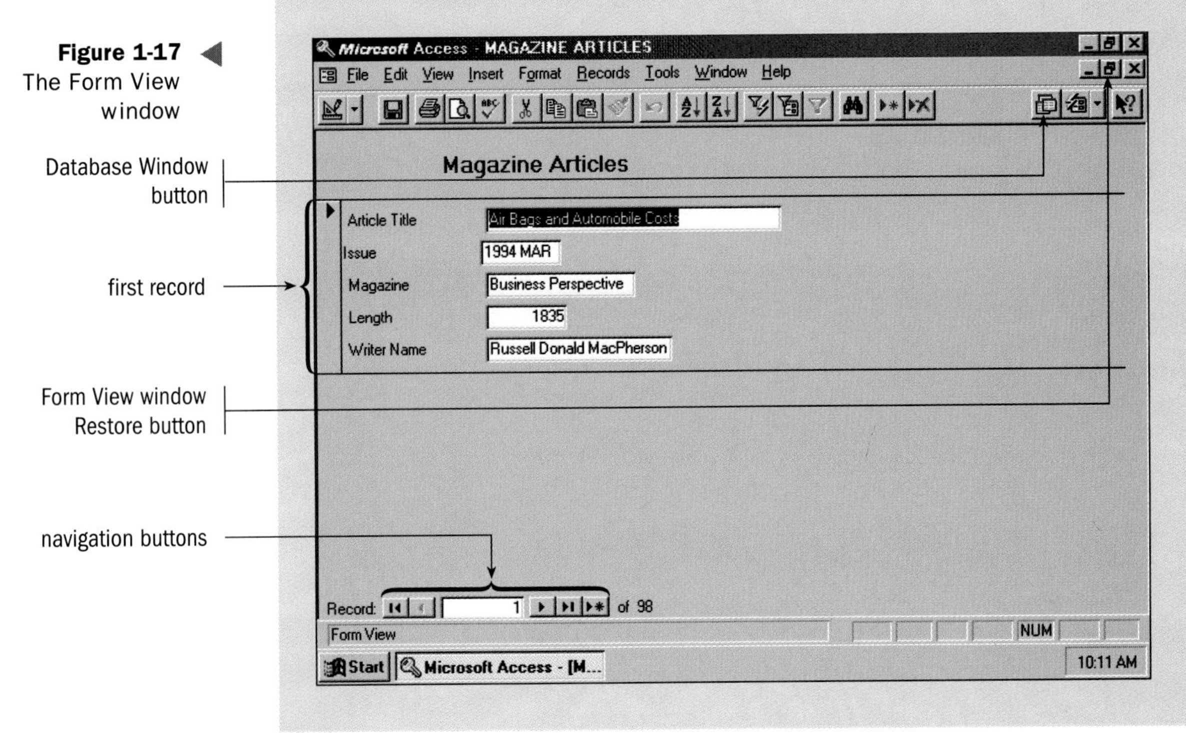

Figure 1-17 The Form View window

The Form View window shows a table's contents in a customized format, usually one record at a time. The form shown in Figure 1-17 vertically displays all five fields from the MAGAZINE ARTICLES table for a single record. Each field has a label (the field name) on the left and a boxed field value on the right.

Some of the window components you saw in the Datasheet View window (e.g., the Restore button and the navigation buttons) also appear in the Form View window and have the same functions. Practice clicking the navigation buttons and clicking different field values. Notice the changes that occur in the form.

Judith decides to print the first page of records from Form View. Access prints as many form records as can fit on a printed page. Judith decides not to use the Print Preview option. The steps you follow to print from Form View are similar to those used to print in Datasheet View.

To print a form page:

1. Before continuing, make sure you are in Form View with the first record displayed in a maximized window. Click **File**, then click **Print**. The Print dialog box opens.
2. Make sure your printer is on-line and ready to print. Check the Printer panel of the dialog box to make sure the correct printer is selected. Click the radio button next to "**Pages**" in the Print Range panel, type **1**, press the **Tab** key, type **1**, and then click the **OK** button. A dialog box informs you that your form page is being sent to the printer. After the dialog box closes, Access returns you to Form View.

Closing a Database

Judith is done viewing both the form and the database, so she closes the database. She could close the Form View window, as she previously closed the Datasheet View window, and then close the database. However, whenever you close a database without closing the Form View window or any other open object window, Access automatically closes all open windows before closing the database.

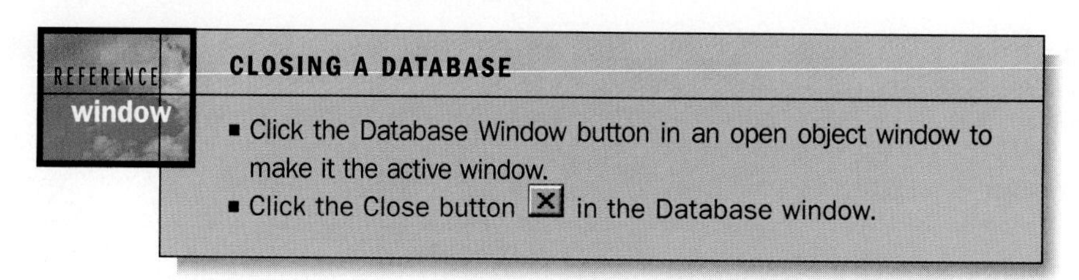

Judith closes the Vision Publishers database.

To close the Vision database:

1. Click the **Database Window** button on the toolbar to activate the Database window. See Figure 1-18.

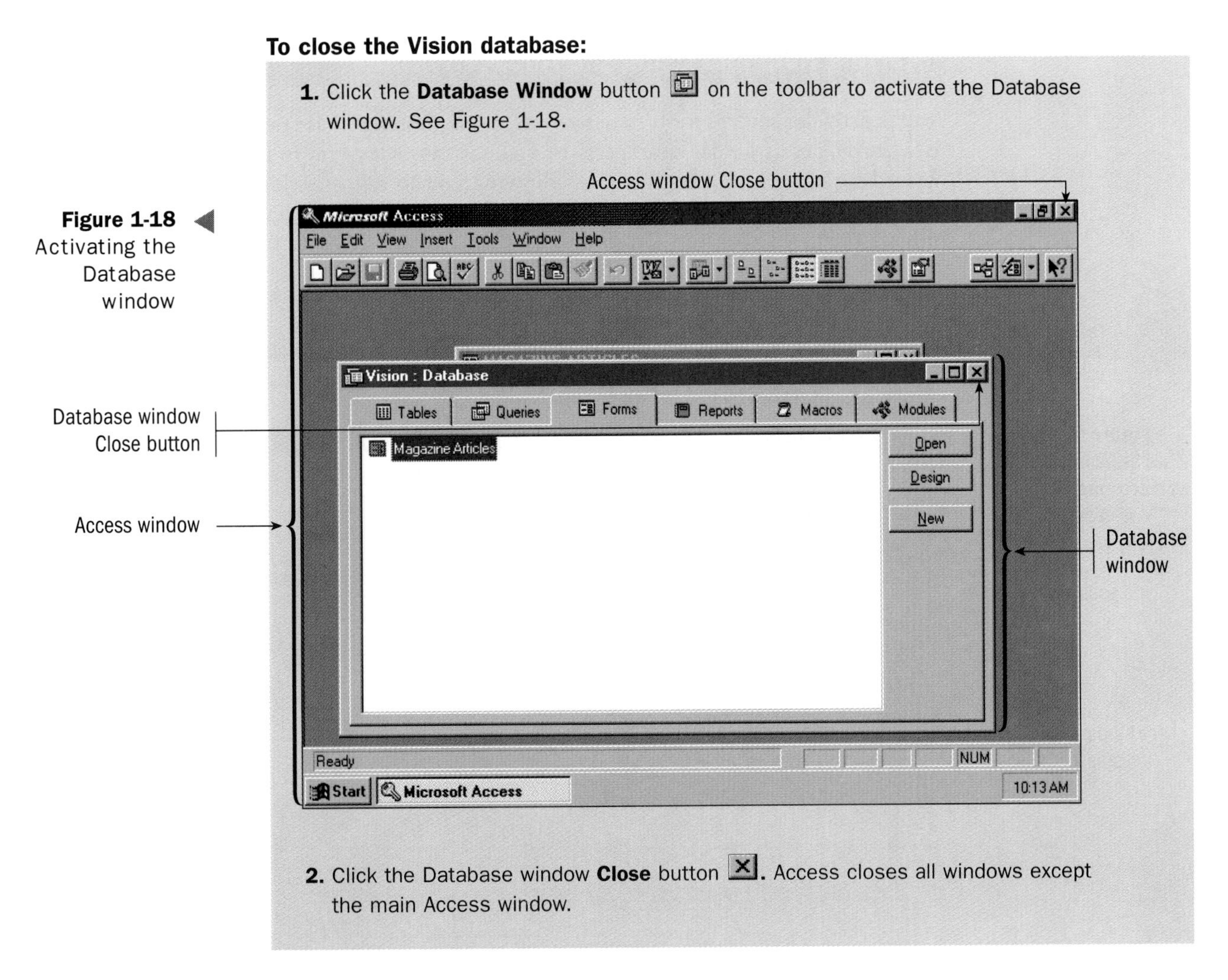

Figure 1-18 Activating the Database window

2. Click the Database window **Close** button. Access closes all windows except the main Access window.

Getting Help

While you are using Access on your computer, there might be times when you are puzzled about how to complete a task—or, you might need to clarify a definition or Access feature or investigate more advanced Access capabilities. You can use Access's Help system to give you on-line information about your specific questions. Access offers you five ways to get on-line help as you work: the Answer Wizard, the Help Contents, the Help Index, the Find feature, and the context-sensitive Help system. Let's practice using Answer Wizard, the Help Index, and the context-sensitive Help system, the three methods you will find most useful as you work through the tutorials.

Starting Help and Using the Answer Wizard

Access provides several tools to assist you in common database tasks. These tools, known as wizards, act as guides or experts to make it easier for you to use Access. The Answer Wizard assists you in using Help by allowing you to ask questions in ordinary language and finding a list of useful help topics for you to read. Judith has some questions about moving the toolbar on the screen and uses the Answer Wizard to find the answer.

To use the Answer Wizard to get help on moving the toolbar:

1. Click **Help** and then click **Answer Wizard**. The Access Help window opens and the Answer Wizard page is visible. See Figure 1-19.

Figure 1-19 The Answer Wizard page of the Access Help window

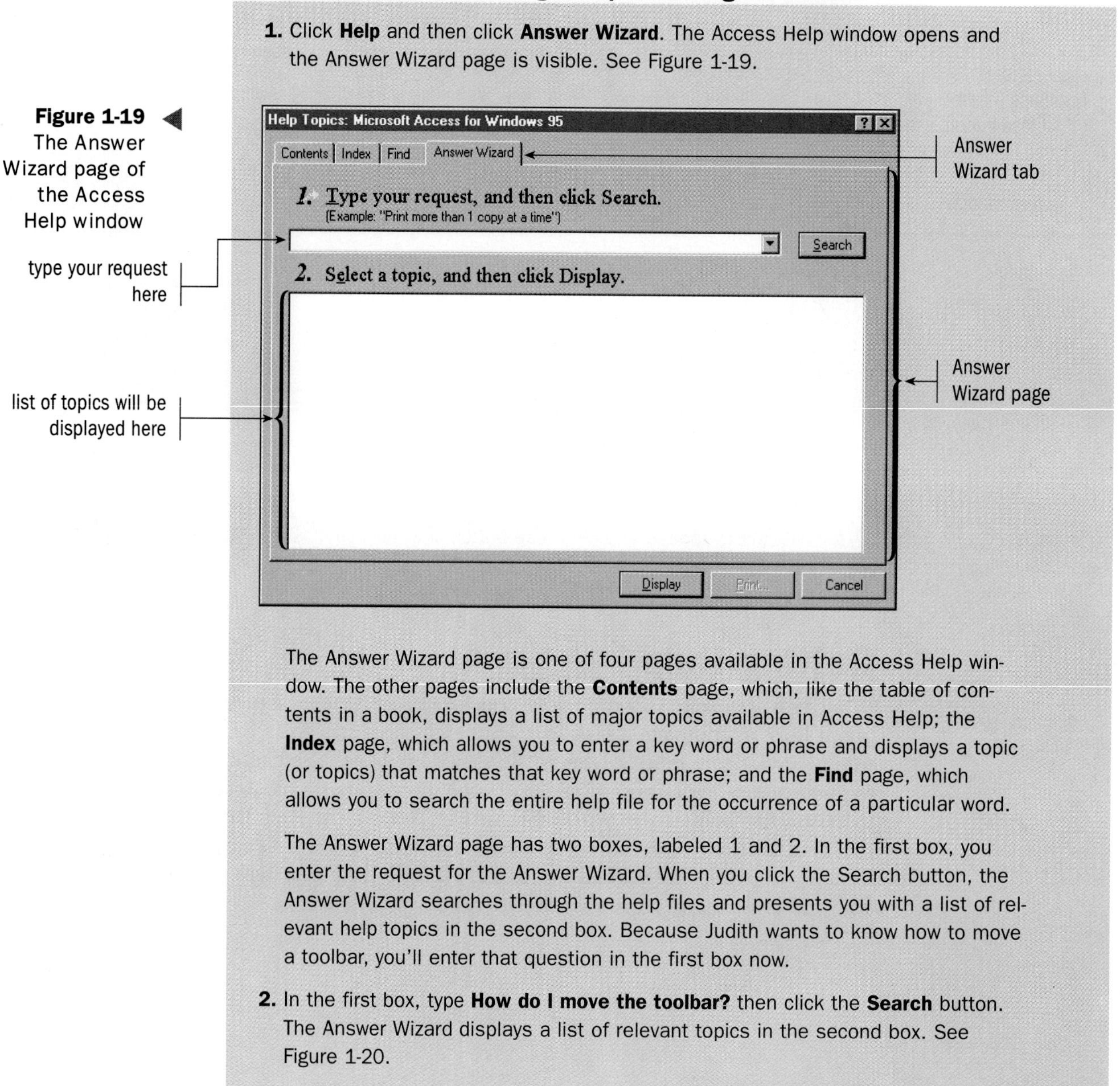

The Answer Wizard page is one of four pages available in the Access Help window. The other pages include the **Contents** page, which, like the table of contents in a book, displays a list of major topics available in Access Help; the **Index** page, which allows you to enter a key word or phrase and displays a topic (or topics) that matches that key word or phrase; and the **Find** page, which allows you to search the entire help file for the occurrence of a particular word.

The Answer Wizard page has two boxes, labeled 1 and 2. In the first box, you enter the request for the Answer Wizard. When you click the Search button, the Answer Wizard searches through the help files and presents you with a list of relevant help topics in the second box. Because Judith wants to know how to move a toolbar, you'll enter that question in the first box now.

2. In the first box, type **How do I move the toolbar?** then click the **Search** button. The Answer Wizard displays a list of relevant topics in the second box. See Figure 1-20.

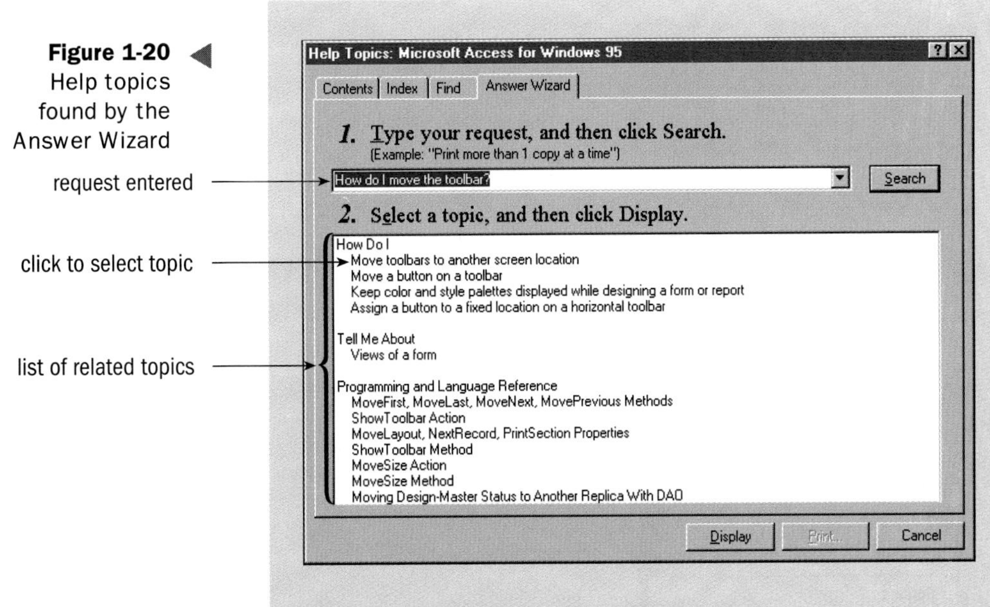

Figure 1-20 Help topics found by the Answer Wizard

The list box displays several different topics. The second line in the box lists a topic that should provide Judith with the answer to her question. Let's look at that Help topic.

3. Click **Move toolbars to another screen location** to select that topic.

4. Click the **Display** button. The Answer Wizard finds the help text for you and displays it in the Help window. See Figure 1-21.

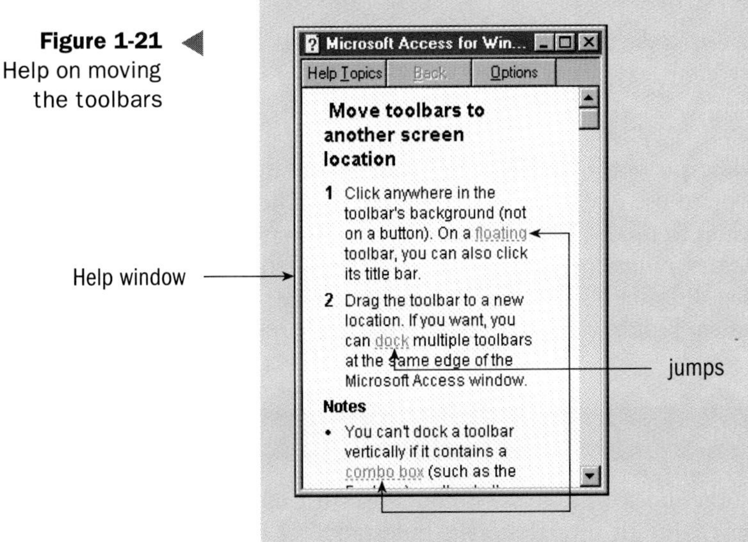

Figure 1-21 Help on moving the toolbars

TROUBLE? If you see the message "Help topic does not exist," you might not have the complete Access Help system installed on your system. Ask your technical support person or instructor for assistance.

The Help window displays the answer to Judith's question. Notice that some words in the Help window are in color and underlined and that the mouse pointer changes to [pointer] when you move it over these words. These underlined words or topics in the Help window are called **jumps**. A jump provides a link to other Help topics or to more information or a definition of the current word or topic. Judith wants to view the definition of a floating toolbar.

5. Move the pointer over the word **floating** and click the left mouse button when the pointer changes to [pointer]. Access Help displays a definition of the term. See Figure 1-22.

Figure 1-22 Definition of "floating"

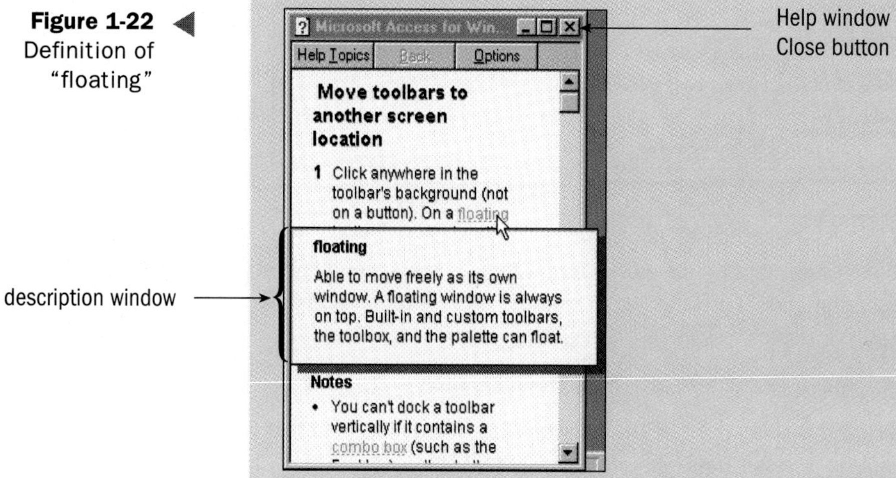

Microsoft Access for Win...
Help Topics | Back | Options
Move toolbars to another screen location
1 Click anywhere in the toolbar's background (not on a button). On a floating
floating
Able to move freely as its own window. A floating window is always on top. Built-in and custom toolbars, the toolbox, and the palette can float.
Notes
• You can't dock a toolbar vertically if it contains a combo box (such as the

Help window Close button

description window

6. Click in the help text to close the definition window. Click the Help window **Close** button [X] to close the Help window.

The Answer Wizard assists you by interpreting your question and suggesting possible help topics. Another way to use Access Help is to search for a key word or phrase in the Help Index. Judith decides to use the Help Index to find information about some printing options. By default, Access prints the datasheet across the narrow dimension of a page, called **portrait orientation**. Printing "sideways," across the longer dimension of a page, is called **landscape orientation**. Judith wants to find out how to change the default orientation for a page.

Using the Help Index

The Help Index is like the index of a book. It contains a list of key words and phrases that describe Help topics. Judith uses the Help Index to find information about page orientation.

To use the Help Index in Access Help:

1. Click **Help**, then click **Microsoft Access Help Topics**. The Access Help window is displayed. Notice that the Answer Wizard page is visible, since that was the last page you used in Help.

2. Click the **Index** tab to display the Index page. See Figure 1-23.

Figure 1-23 Index page in the Help window

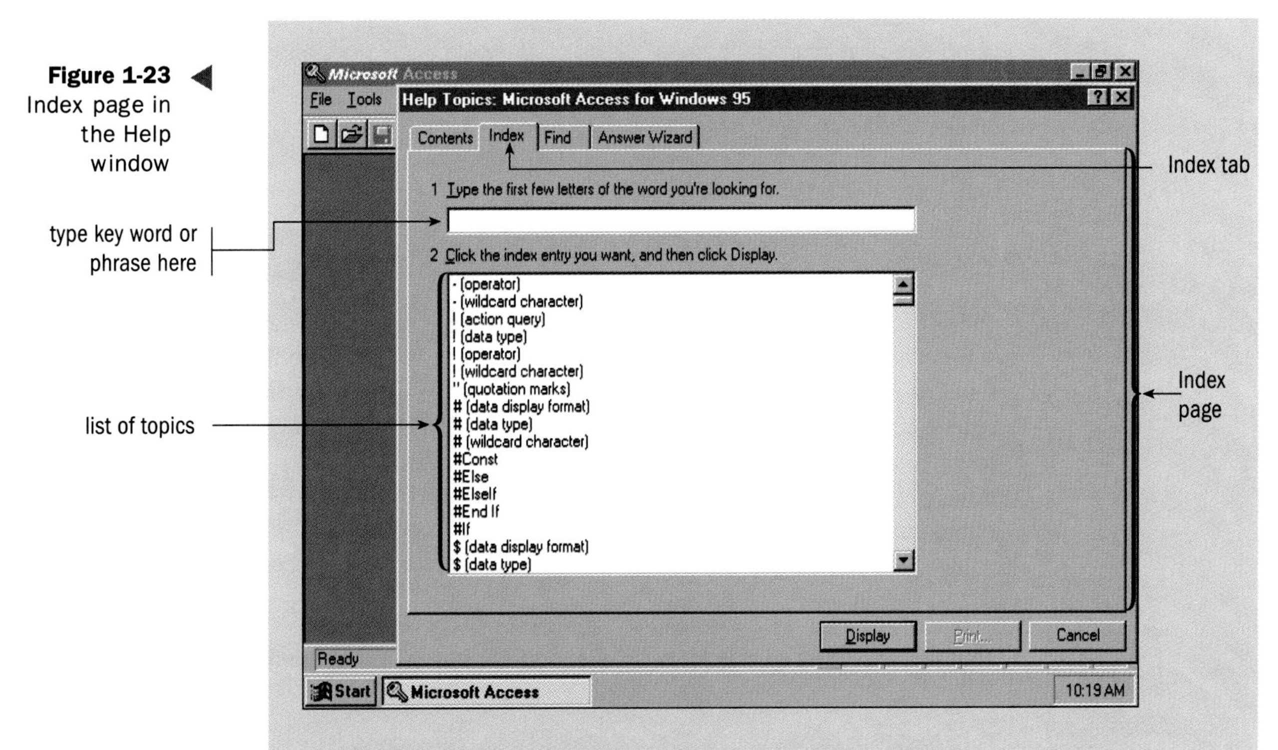

Like the Answer Wizard page, the Index page has two boxes. You enter the key word or phrase for which you want help in the upper box. As you type, the lower box displays the list of topics that match what you have typed.

3. Type **o** in the upper text box. The list of topics shown changes to those topics starting with "o."

4. Type **ri** after the "o" in the text box. The list of topics shown changes to those starting with the letters "ori" and the topic "orientation, page" is highlighted.

5. Click the **Display** button. Access Help displays a description of the steps needed to set up the page orientation and other characteristics of a printed page. See Figure 1-24.

Figure 1-24 Help on setting up the characteristics of a printed page

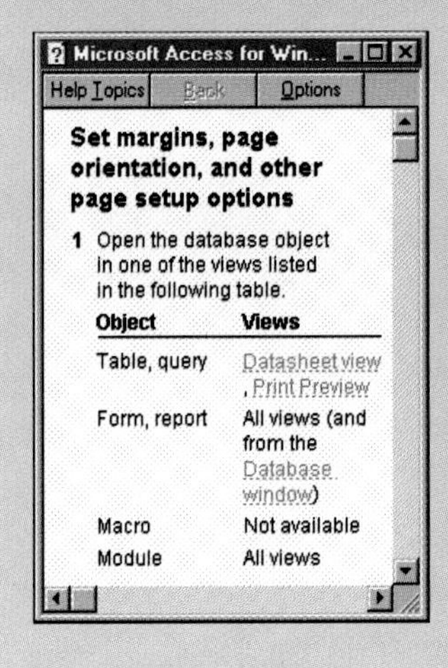

7. Read the information about setting up the page orientation, using the scroll bar to view the entire topic.
8. Click the **Close** button on the help topic window. The Help window closes.

Using Context-Sensitive Help

In addition to the Help menu, Access provides a Help button on the toolbar. This Help button is context-sensitive, which means that it displays information that is relevant to the window or operation that is currently active. If you want Help information about a particular component of an Access window, click the Help button on the toolbar. The mouse pointer changes to ?, which is the Help pointer. You then click the ? on the window component about which you want information, and Help opens a window specific to that component.

Judith is interested in learning more about the purpose of the on the Access toolbar by clicking the Help button.

To use context-sensitive Help on a specific window component:

1. Click the **Help** button on the toolbar. The mouse pointer changes to ?. See Figure 1-25.

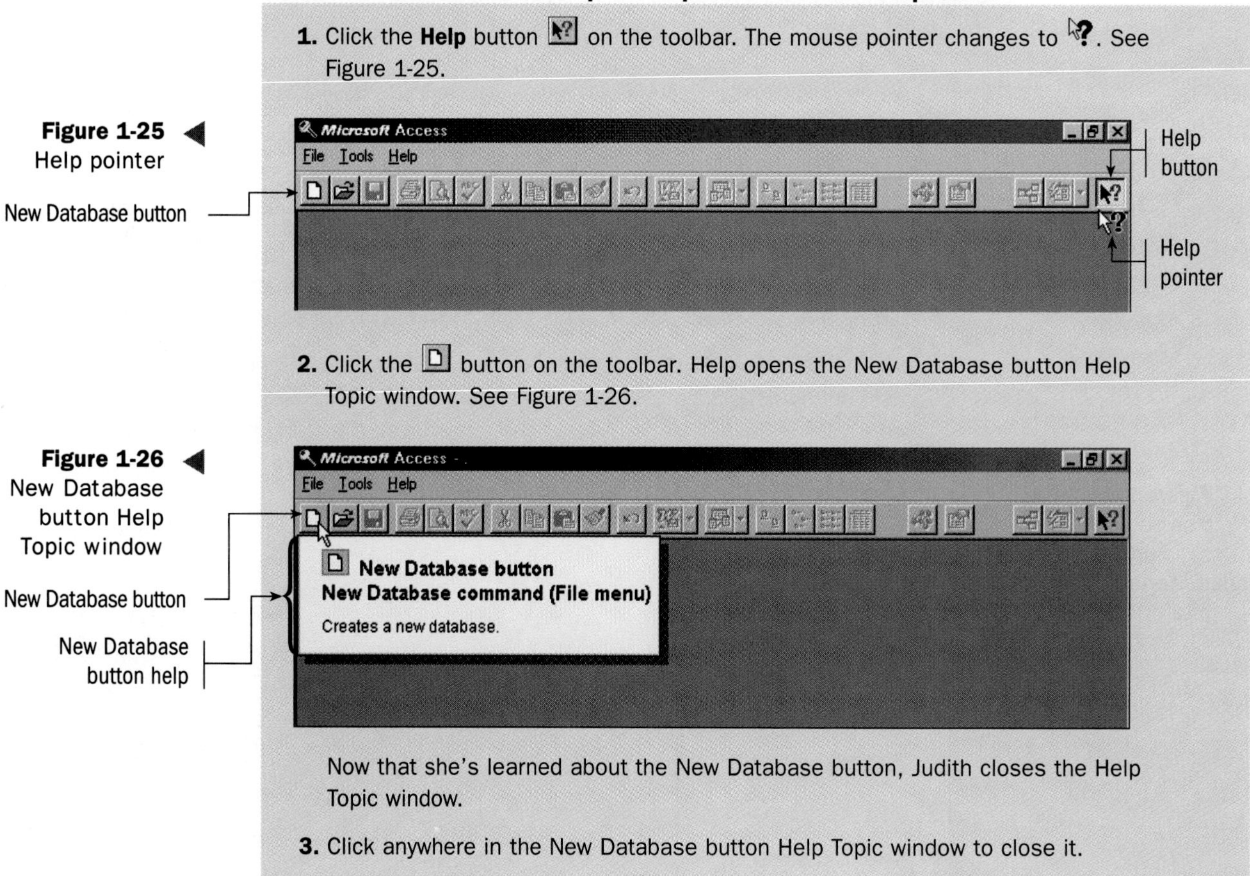

Figure 1-25 Help pointer

2. Click the button on the toolbar. Help opens the New Database button Help Topic window. See Figure 1-26.

Figure 1-26 New Database button Help Topic window

Now that she's learned about the New Database button, Judith closes the Help Topic window.

3. Click anywhere in the New Database button Help Topic window to close it.

Judith now feels comfortable about using Access's Help system when she needs it. But before she does any more work on her assignment, she decides that learning about shortcuts will save her valuable time.

Shortcut Menus

As you work with Access objects, you may find it helpful to use a shortcut menu. A shortcut menu contains a list of commands that relate to the object you click. To display a shortcut menu, you position the mouse pointer on a specific object or area and click the right mouse button. Using a shortcut menu is often faster than using a menu option or toolbar button.

Judith opens the Vision database, and then displays a shortcut menu.

To open a database:

1. From the main Access window, click the **Open Database** button to display the Open dialog box.
2. Click **Vision** to select it, then click the **Open** button.

Judith now opens the shortcut menu for the table objects.

To display a shortcut menu:

1. Click the **Tables** tab to display the list of tables.
2. Move the mouse pointer into the Database window and position it on the last table listed.
3. Click the right mouse button. Access displays the shortcut menu. See Figure 1-27.

Figure 1-27 The shortcut menu

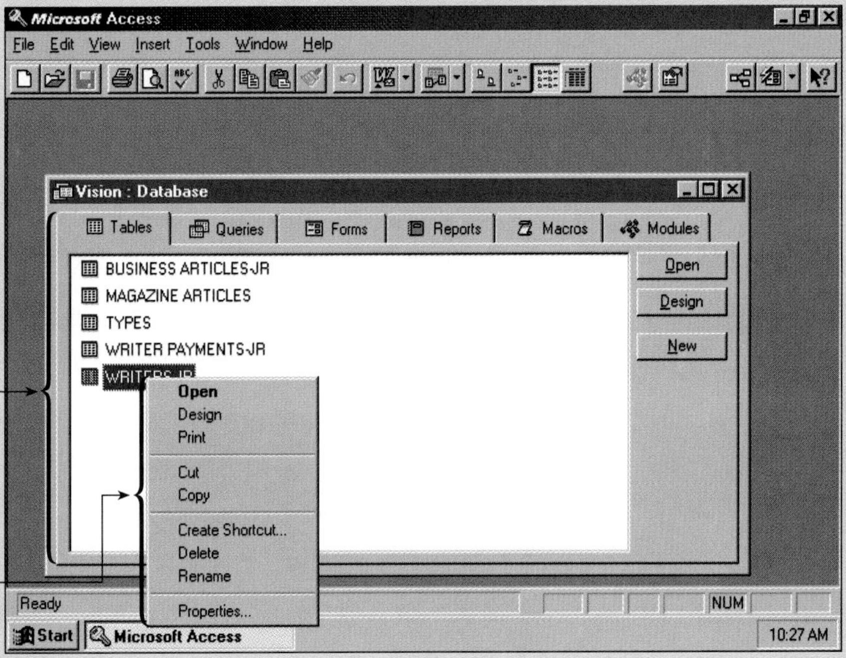

Tables page

shortcut menu

If you select a shortcut menu command, it applies to the highlighted table. Judith does not want to select a command, so she closes the shortcut menu.

To close a shortcut menu:

1. Move the pointer off the shortcut menu and click the left mouse button to close the shortcut menu.

Judith feels confident that she can use Access effectively to complete her assignment and exits Access.

To exit Access:

1. Click the **Close** button [X] to close the main Access window and return to the Windows 95 desktop.

Now Judith knows how to use the Vision database to select articles for the special issue. In the next tutorial you will assist Elena, who will create a specific database for the 25th anniversary issue.

Quick Check

1. What does the Form View window show?
2. Name the five ways you can use Access's Help system to get on-line information.
3. How does the Help Index differ from the Answer Wizard?
4. How would you find out the meaning of the [Spelling] button?
5. What is the purpose of a shortcut menu, and why would you use it?
6. How do you open and close a shortcut menu?

Tutorial Assignments

Start Access, open the Vision database in the Tutorial folder on your Student Disk, and do the following:

1. Open the MAGAZINE ARTICLES table in Datasheet View.
2. Preview the datasheet for printing.
3. Print the first page of the datasheet.
4. Close the Print Preview window and then the Datasheet View window.
5. Open the Magazine Articles form.
6. Preview the form for printing. What is the page number of the last page?
7. Print the last two pages of the form.

8. Look at the toolbars that are available in the following active windows: the Database window, the Datasheet View window, and the Print Preview window. Describe the differences you see from toolbar to toolbar. Use the context-sensitive Help button to learn about the different toolbar buttons available.

Lab Assignment

This Lab Assignment is designed to accompany the interactive Course Lab called Database. To start the Database Lab, click the Start button on the Windows 95 taskbar, point to Programs, point to Course Labs, point to New Perspectives Applications, and click Database. If you do not see Course Labs on your Programs menu, see your instructor or lab manager.

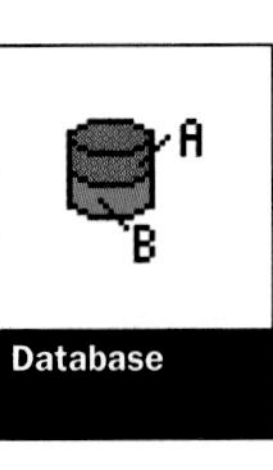

Database This Database Lab demonstrates the essential concepts of file and database management systems. You will use the Lab to search, sort, and report the data contained in a file of classic books.

1. Click the Steps button to review basic database terminology and to learn how to manipulate the classic books database. As you proceed through the Steps, answer the Quick Check questions that appear. After you complete the Steps, you will see a Quick Check Report. Follow the instructions on the screen to print this report.

2. Click the Explore button. Make sure you can apply basic database terminology to describe the classic books database by answering the following questions:
   a. How many records does the file contain?
   b. How many fields does each record contain?
   c. What is the contents of the Catalog # field for the book written by Margaret Mitchell?
   d. What is the contents of the Title field for the record with Thoreau in the Author field?
   e. Which field has been used to sort the records?

3. Manipulate the database as necessary to answer the following questions:
   a. When the books are sorted by title, what is the first record in the file?
   b. Use the Search button to search for all the books in the West location. How many do you find?
   c. Use the Search button to search for all the books in the Main location that are checked in. What do you find?

4. Use the Report button to print out a report that groups the books by Status and sorted by title. On you report, circle the four field names. Put a box around the summary statistics showing which books are currently checked in and which books are currently checked out.

TUTORIAL 2

Creating Access Tables

Creating the WRITERS Table at Vision Publishers

OBJECTIVES

In this tutorial you will:

- Design a database
- Create a database
- Create tables using the Design View window and the Table Wizard
- Define the fields for a table
- Change field properties
- Modify a table's structure
- Create and delete an index

Vision Publishers

Vision Publishers' Brian Murphy, Judith Rossi, and Elena Sanchez meet to exchange ideas about the cover design and article layout for the 25th-anniversary issue of *Business Perspective*. Now that Judith has selected the articles to be included in the special issue, Elena needs to create a database to store information about the articles and writers so that she can coordinate production of the issue. Her first task will be to contact the writers of these past articles.

Elena will also record information about reprint payments that Vision Publishers will make to the writers. Elena realizes, therefore, that the database she will create for the special issue will contain several tables: a table each for writers, past articles, and reprint payments. She decides to concentrate first on creating a table of all the writers. After that she will create a table in which to record the reprint payments. Elena knows from her previous work with databases that—before she can create any of her database tables on the computer—she must first design the database.

Designing a Database

A database management system can be a useful tool, but only if you first carefully design your database to represent your data requirements accurately. In database design, you determine the fields, tables, and relationships needed to satisfy your data and processing requirements. Some database designs can be complicated because the underlying data requirements are complex. Most data requirements and their resulting database designs are much simpler, however, and these are the ones we will consider in the tutorials.

When you design a database, you should follow these guidelines:

- *Identify all fields needed to produce the required information.* Because, for example, Vision Publishers has a policy that only freelancers will be paid for reprints of their articles, Elena needs to know if a writer is a freelancer and, if so, what the reprint payment amount is. After looking over the list of past articles chosen for the special issue, Elena notes that the 25 articles were written by only 13 writers and Chong Kim wrote four of them. Brian points out that the writer of "Cola Advertising Wars" is a different Chong Kim, so Elena realizes that a writer name is not unique. She will need to identify the writer of each article with a unique Writer ID. Only after carefully considering her requirements is Elena able to determine the fields that will produce the information she needs (Figure 2-1).

Figure 2-1 Elena's data requirements

article title	writer phone number
issue of Business Perspective	is the writer a freelancer?
length of article	freelancer reprint payment amount
writer name	writer ID
writer age	check number
reprint check amount	check date

- *Determine the entities involved in the data requirements.* Recall that an entity is a person, place, object, event, or idea for which you want to store and process data. Elena's data requirements, for example, involve entities for articles, writers, and payments. The type of entity in a table usually suggests the name for the table in a database.

- *Group the identified fields by entity to form tables.* Elena groups the fields in her list under each entity name, as shown in Figure 2-2. So far, Elena's database design has three tables: BUSINESS ARTICLES, WRITERS, and WRITER PAYMENTS. Elena's design and using more than one table eliminates unnecessarily redundant information in the database. When Elena enters the data for a new payment in the WRITER PAYMENTS table, for example, she needs to enter only the Writer ID to identify the writer to whom the payment is made. It is not necessary for her to enter the writer's name, phone number, etc., since that information is kept in the WRITERS table. Information about each writer is stored as a single record in the WRITERS table, and each payment can be linked to the writer through the Writer ID field.

Figure 2-2 Elena's fields describing each entity

Business Articles	Writers	Writer Payments
article title	writer ID	check number
issue of Business Perspective	writer name	check amount
length of article	writer phone number	check date
	is the writer a freelancer?	
	freelancer reprint payment amount	
	writer age	

- *Designate each table's primary key.* A primary key uniquely identifies each record in a table. Although not mandatory, it's usually a good idea to have a primary key for each table to help you select records accurately. For example, Elena has decided to include a Writer ID field in the WRITERS table to identify each writer uniquely because she needs to distinguish between the two writers named Chong Kim. The primary key for the WRITER PAYMENTS table will be Check Number. At this point, however, Elena does not have a primary key for the BUSINESS ARTICLES table because no field in this table is guaranteed to have unique field values. Elena delays a final decision on a primary key for this table until later in the database design process.
- *Include a common field in related tables.* You use a common field to link two tables. In the BUSINESS ARTICLES and WRITER PAYMENTS tables, Elena includes the Writer ID field, the primary key for the WRITERS table, to serve as a foreign key. Doing so will allow Elena quick access to information in the WRITERS and BUSINESS ARTICLES tables, telling her who wrote which article.
- *Avoid data redundancy.* **Data redundancy**, which occurs when you store the same data in more than one place, can cause inconsistencies. For example, Figure 2-3 shows an example of what might happen if Elena designs her database incorrectly. Here, the BUSINESS ARTICLES table has a redundant field (Writer Name), which results in inconsistent spellings of the same name (Leroy Johnson vs. Leroy W. Johnson vs. Leroy W. Jonson; Kellie Kox vs. Kelly Cox). In contrast, Figure 2-4 shows a correct database design for the BUSINESS ARTICLES and WRITERS tables, where the only data redundancy is the Writer ID field, which serves as the common field to link the two tables.

Figure 2-3 Incorrect database design with redundancy

BUSINESS ARTICLES table

Article Title	Issue of Business Perspective	Length of Article	Writer ID	Writer Name
Trans-Alaskan Oil Pipeline Opening	1977 JUL	803	J525	Leroy Johnson
Farm Aid Abuses	1978 APR	1866	J525	Leroy W. Jonson
Herbert A. Simon Interview	1978 DEC	1811	C200	Kellie Kox
Alternative Energy Sources	1980 JUN	2085	S260	Wilhelm Seeger
Windfall Tax on Oil Profits	1980 APR	1497	K500	Chong Kim
Toyota and GM Join Venture	1983 MAR	1682	S260	Wilhelm Seeger

inconsistent data

WRITERS table

Writer ID	Writer Name	Writer Phone Number	Freelancer	Freelancer Reprint Payment Amount
C200	Kelly Cox	(204)783-5415	Yes	$100
J525	Leroy W. Johnson	(209)895-2046	Yes	$125
K500	Chong Kim	(807)729-5364	No	$0
S260	Wilhelm Seeger	(306)423-0932	Yes	$250

Writer Name redundant in BUSINESS ARTICLES table

Figure 2-4 Correct database design without redundancy

BUSINESS ARTICLES table

Article Title	Issue of Business Perspective	Length of Article	Writer ID
Trans-Alaskan Oil Pipeline Opening	1977 JUL	803	J525
Farm Aid Abuses	1978 APR	1866	J525
Herbert A. Simon Interview	1978 DEC	1811	C200
Alternative Energy Sources	1980 JUN	2085	S260
Windfall Tax on Oil Profits	1980 APR	1497	K500
Toyota and GM Joint Venture	1983 MAR	1682	S260

WRITERS table

Writer ID	Writer Name	Writer Phone Number	Freelancer	Freelancer Reprint Payment Amount
C200	Kelly Cox	(204)783-5415	Yes	$100
J525	Leroy W. Johnson	(209)895-2046	Yes	$125
K500	Chong Kim	(807)729-5364	No	$0
S260	Wilhelm Seeger	(306)423-0932	Yes	$250

- *Determine the properties of each field.* The **properties**, or characteristics, of each field determine how the DBMS will store, display, and process the field. These properties include the field name, the field's maximum number of characters or digits, the field's description or explanation, and other field characteristics. Because this is Elena's first time designing and creating a database, she will plan her field properties later.

With these guidelines in mind, Elena completes her initial database design (shown in Figure 2-5) and begins to create her database. Notice that the WRITERS table contains a field for Freelancer Reprint Payment Amount — the amount the writer is paid for each reprint. The WRITER PAYMENTS table contains a field for the Check Amount, which is the amount actually paid to a writer. Because a writer might be paid for more than one reprint, these fields are not redundant.

Figure 2-5 Elena's initial database design

<u>BUSINESS ARTICLES table</u>
Article Title
Issue of Business Perspective
Length of Article
Writer ID — foreign key

<u>WRITERS table</u>
Writer ID — primary key
Writer Name
Writer Phone
Freelancer
Freelancer Reprint Payment Amount
Writer Age

<u>WRITER PAYMENTS table</u>
Check Number — primary key
Writer ID — foreign key
Check Amount
Check Date

SESSION 2.1

In this session, you will learn how to create an Access database, create an Access table, save a table, and switch between Design View and Datasheet View.

Creating a Database

You must first name each database you create. Choose a descriptive name that will remind you of the database's purpose or contents. Elena chooses for her new database the name Issue25, as it will contain all the information necessary to produce the 25th-anniversary issue of *Business Perspective*. Windows 95 and Access allow you to name your database anything you want. When you create a database, Access saves all of the database's tables, forms, queries, and other information in a single disk file identified with the database name.

CREATING A DATABASE

- Click the New Database button on the toolbar (or select the Database Wizard radio button in the initial dialog box and click the OK button). The New Database dialog box opens.
- Click the Blank Database radio button to select it and click the OK button. The File New Database dialog box opens.
- With the File name text box highlighted, type the name of the database you want to create. Do not press the Enter key.
- Change the drive and directory information, if necessary.
- Click the Create button to accept the changes in the New Database dialog box.

Elena creates the Issue25 database.

To create a database:

1. Start Access. The Access window appears with the initial dialog box. See Figure 2-6.

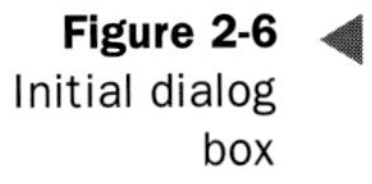

Figure 2-6 Initial dialog box

The initial dialog box provides two ways to create a new database. The Blank Database option creates a new database having no defined tables or other objects. The Database Wizard option allows you to create a blank database or to use one of several predefined databases as models for creating your own. Here Elena will define the database herself. (You will explore using a predefined database model in the Tutorial Assignments for this tutorial.)

TROUBLE? If Access is already running, return to the main Access window, click File, click New Database, select Blank Database, then click the OK button. Then continue with Step 3.

2. Click the **Blank Database** radio button to select it, then click the **OK** button. Access displays the File New Database dialog box. See Figure 2-7. The File name text box contains the highlighted default name, db1.

Figure 2-7 The File New Database dialog box

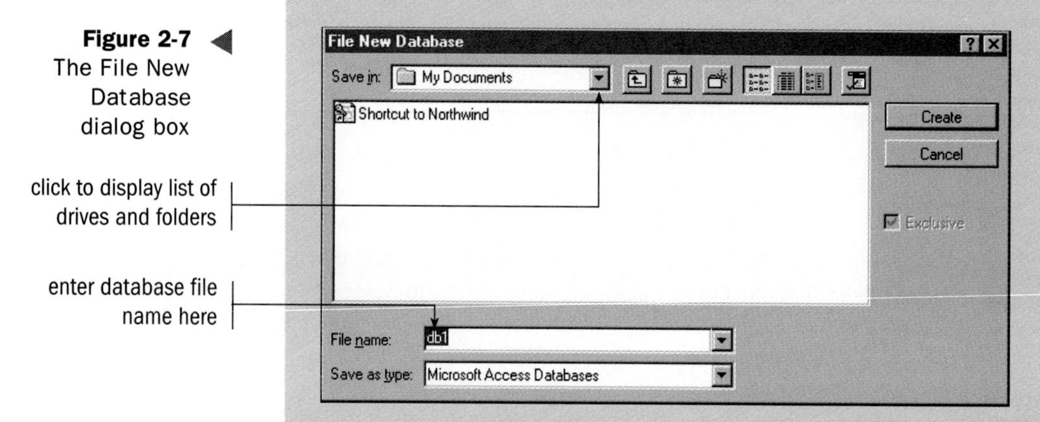

TROUBLE? Depending on your computer's configuration, your screen may show filenames with the .mdb extension.

3. Type **Issue25** in the File name text box.

TROUBLE? If the contents of the File name text box do not show Issue25, the text box might not have been highlighted when you began typing. If this is the case, highlight the contents of the text box and retype Issue25.

4. Click the **Save in** list arrow, then click the drive in which you put your Student Disk. Double-click the **Tutorial** folder to open it. See Figure 2-8.

Figure 2-8 Completed File New Database dialog box

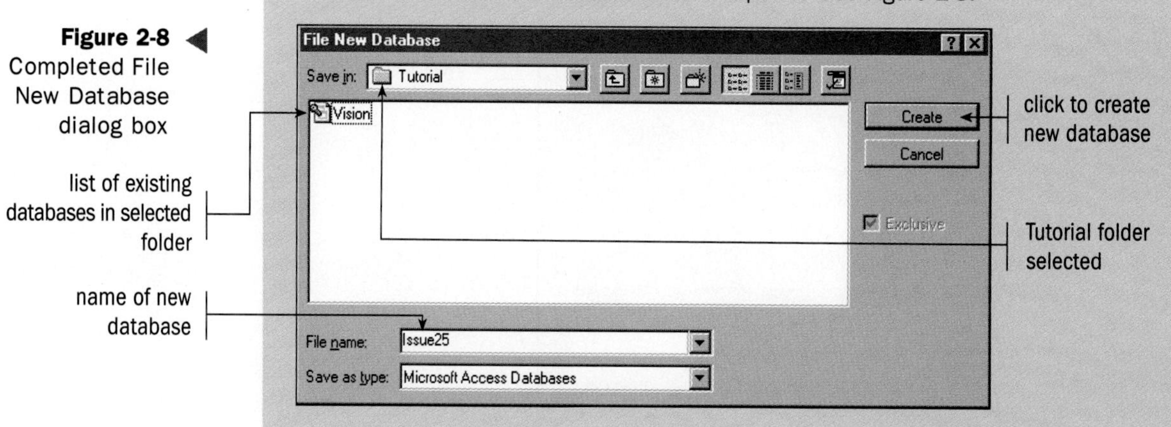

5. Click the **Create** button to let Access know you have completed the New Database dialog box. Access creates the Issue25 database and opens the Database window.

Now that she has created her new database, Elena's next step is to create the WRITERS table structure.

Creating a Table

Creating a table entails defining the table's fields. To create the structure of the WRITERS table, Elena looks at her plan again and notes that the fields that should be included are Writer ID, Writer Name, Writer Phone, Freelancer, Freelancer Reprint Payment Amount, and Writer Age. In Access, you can define a table from the keyboard or use the Table Wizard to automate the table creation process. A **wizard** is an Access tool that asks you questions and creates an object according to your answers. When you use the Table Wizard, for example, you will be asked questions about your table. Access then automatically creates the table based on your answers. Since Elena has already given careful thought to her WRITERS table, she realizes it will be much quicker and easier to define it from the keyboard.

You use the Design View window to define or modify a table structure or the properties for the fields in a table. If you create a table without using the Table Wizard, you enter the fields and their properties for your table directly in this window.

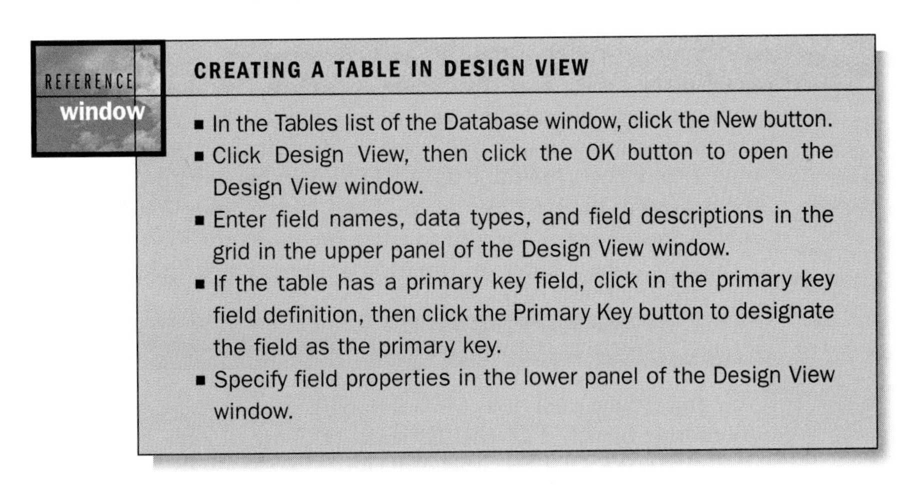
REFERENCE window

CREATING A TABLE IN DESIGN VIEW

- In the Tables list of the Database window, click the New button.
- Click Design View, then click the OK button to open the Design View window.
- Enter field names, data types, and field descriptions in the grid in the upper panel of the Design View window.
- If the table has a primary key field, click in the primary key field definition, then click the Primary Key button to designate the field as the primary key.
- Specify field properties in the lower panel of the Design View window.

To define a table using Design View:

1. If necessary, click the **Tables** tab to display the Tables list, then click the **New** button. Access displays the New Table dialog box. See Figure 2-9.

Figure 2-9 The New Table dialog box

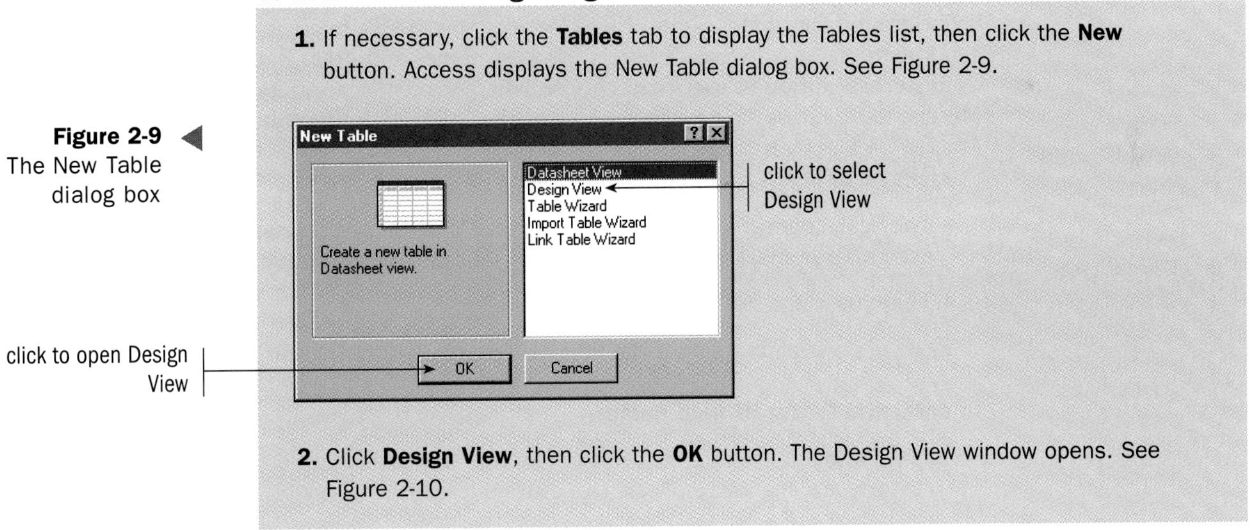

2. Click **Design View**, then click the **OK** button. The Design View window opens. See Figure 2-10.

Figure 2-10 The Design View window

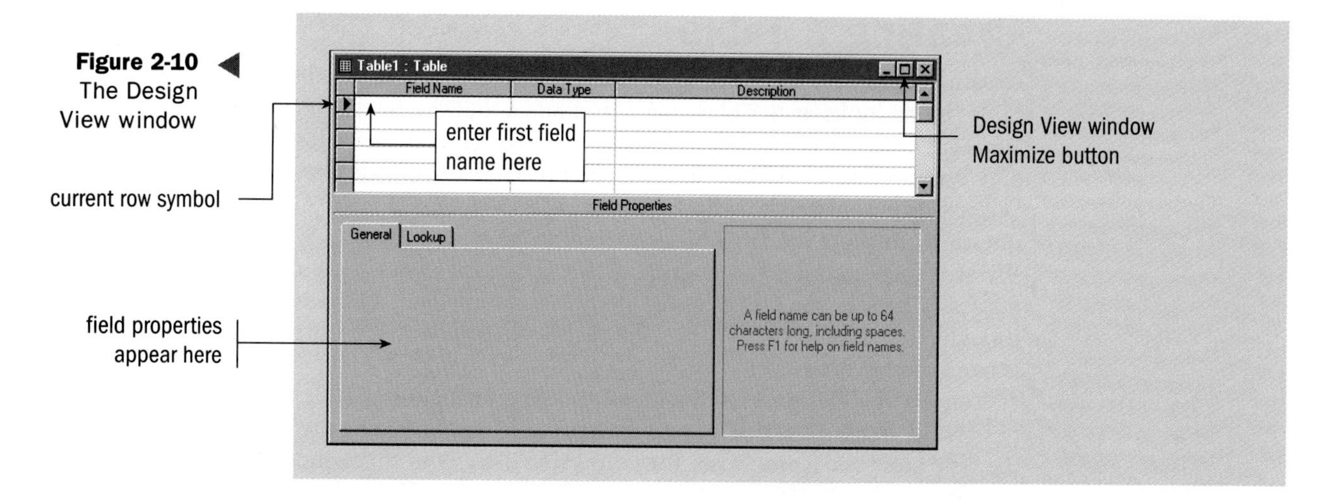

The upper panel of the Design View window contains a grid in which you define each field in the table. The lower-left panel of the window displays the properties associated with the currently selected field. The panel in the lower right displays a short Help message to assist you in defining fields. Note that the title bar will identify the table as Table1 until Elena saves the table as WRITERS (which she'll do later in this tutorial). The cursor is now in the first row of the Field Name column and the row selector is in the first row. Access is ready for you to enter the name for the first field.

Elena can now enter information about the first field in the WRITERS table.

Naming Fields and Objects

You must name each object in a database so that Access can save and retrieve information about the object. For the Issue25 database, Elena will name her tables WRITERS, BUSINESS ARTICLES, and WRITER PAYMENTS, because these names suggest the contents of the tables. For the same reason, she chooses Writer ID, Writer Name, Writer Phone, and Writer Age as some of the field names in the WRITERS table. To differentiate between table and field names, Elena decides to use all uppercase letters for table names, and uppercase and lowercase letters for field names and other database objects.

In Access, although users can choose whether or not to capitalize names of fields and objects, there are some basic conventions that all users must follow regarding names:

- They can be up to 64 characters long.
- They can contain letters, numbers, spaces, and special characters except period (.), exclamation mark (!), square brackets ([]), and accent grave (`).
- They must not start with a space.

Elena is now ready to enter the first field name, Writer ID, into the WRITERS table.

To enter the Writer ID field name:

1. Type **Writer ID**, then press the **Tab** key to move the cursor to the Data Type column of the first row. The Field Properties list displays the default properties for the new field.

Looking at the screen, Elena notes that her next step is to enter a data type for the Writer ID field.

Assigning Field Data Types

You must assign a **data type** for each field. The data type determines what field values you can enter for that field and what other properties the field will have. In Access, you assign one of the following nine data types to each field:

- **Text** allows field values containing letters, digits, spaces, and special characters. Text fields can be up to 255 characters long. You should assign the text data type to fields in which you will store names, addresses, and descriptions, and to fields containing digits that are not used in calculations. Elena assigns the Text data type to the Writer ID field, the Writer Name field, the Writer Age field, and the Writer Phone field. Note that three of these fields contain digits not used in calculations.

- **Memo**, like the Text data type, allows field values containing letters, digits, spaces, and special characters. Memo fields, however, can be up to 64,000 characters long and are used for long comments or explanations. Elena does not have any fields like this, so she does not assign the Memo data type to any of her fields.

- **Number** limits field values to digits. It allows an optional leading sign to indicate a positive or negative value (i.e., + or -) and an optional decimal point. Use the Number data type for fields that you will use in calculations—except those involving money for which there is a special data type. Elena will assign this type to the Writer Age fields.

- **Date/Time** allows field values containing valid dates and times only. Usually you enter dates in mm/dd/yy format, for example, 12/02/98 (December 2, 1998). This data type also permits other date formats and a variety of time formats. With the Date/Time data type, you can perform calculations on dates and times and you can sort them. The number of days between two dates, for example, can be determined. Elena does not have any dates in the table and does not assign the Date/Time data type to any of the WRITERS table fields.

- **Currency** allows field values similar to those for the Number data type. Unlike calculations with Number data type decimal values, however, calculations performed using the Currency data type will not be subject to round-off error. Elena assigns the Currency data type to the Freelancer Reprint Payment Amount field in the WRITERS table.

- **AutoNumber** consists of integers with values that are automatically inserted in the field as each new record is created. You can specify sequential numbering or random numbering. This guarantees a unique field value, so that such a field can serve as a table's primary key. Because the Writer ID field already contains unique field values, Elena does not assign the AutoNumber data type to any of the WRITERS table fields.

- **Yes/No** limits field values to yes and no entries. Use this data type for fields that indicate the presence or absence of a condition, such as whether an order has been filled, or if an employee is eligible for the company dental plan. Elena assigns the Yes/No data type to the Freelancer field in the WRITERS table.

- **OLE Object** allows field values that are created in other software applications as objects, such as photographs, video images, graphics, drawings, sound recordings, voice-mail messages, spreadsheets, and word processing documents. OLE is an acronym for object linking and embedding. You can either import or link to the object, but you cannot modify it in Access. Elena does not assign the OLE Object data type to any of the WRITERS table fields.

- **Lookup Wizard** creates a field that lets you select a value from another table or from a predefined list of values. You'll have a chance to use the Lookup Wizard in Tutorial 3.

Now that Elena is familiar with the data types, she can enter the appropriate type for the Writer ID field. By default, Access assigns the Text data type to each field that is defined. Since Elena wants the Writer ID field to have the Text data type, she does not need to change the default type. She could easily select a different type, however, by clicking on the Data Type text box and then clicking the list arrow that appears. She could then select a different data type. Elena accepts the default Text data type and moves the cursor to the Description column.

To accept the default Text data type and move the cursor to the Description column:

1. Press the **Tab** key. The cursor moves to the Description column.

Assigning Field Descriptions

When you define a field, you can assign an optional description for the field (up to 255 characters long). Later, when you view the field values in the table records, the description will appear on the status bar to explain the purpose or usage of the field. Even if you choose a descriptive field name, you may want to enter a description. For example, Elena decides it will be helpful to enter the description "primary key" for the Writer ID field.

To enter a description for the Writer ID field:

1. Type **primary key**.

Elena has included the description of the Writer ID field, but she still needs to designate the Writer ID field as the primary key.

Selecting the Primary Key

Although Access does not require that tables have a primary key, choosing a primary key has several advantages.

- Based on its definition, a primary key serves to identify uniquely each record in a table. Elena uses Writer ID, for example, to distinguish one writer from another when both have the same name.
- Access does not allow duplicate values in the primary key field. If Elena has a record with N425 as the field value for Writer ID, she will not be allowed to add another record with this same field value in the Writer ID field. Preventing duplicate values ensures the uniqueness of the primary key field.
- Access enforces entity integrity on the primary key field. **Entity integrity** means that every record's primary key field must have a value. If you do not enter a value for a field, you have actually given the field what is known as a **null value**. You cannot give a null value to the primary key field; Access will not store the record for you unless you've entered a field value in the primary key field.
- Access displays records in primary key sequence when you view a table in the Datasheet View window or the Form View window. Even if you enter records in no specific order, you are ensured that you will later be able to work with them in a more meaningful, primary key sequence.
- Access responds faster to your requests for specific records based on the primary key.

To designate the primary key:

1. If necessary, click in the row for the **Writer ID** field, and then click the **Primary Key** button on the toolbar. An icon now appears to the left of the Writer ID field name. See Figure 2-11.

Figure 2-11 ◀ Designating a primary key

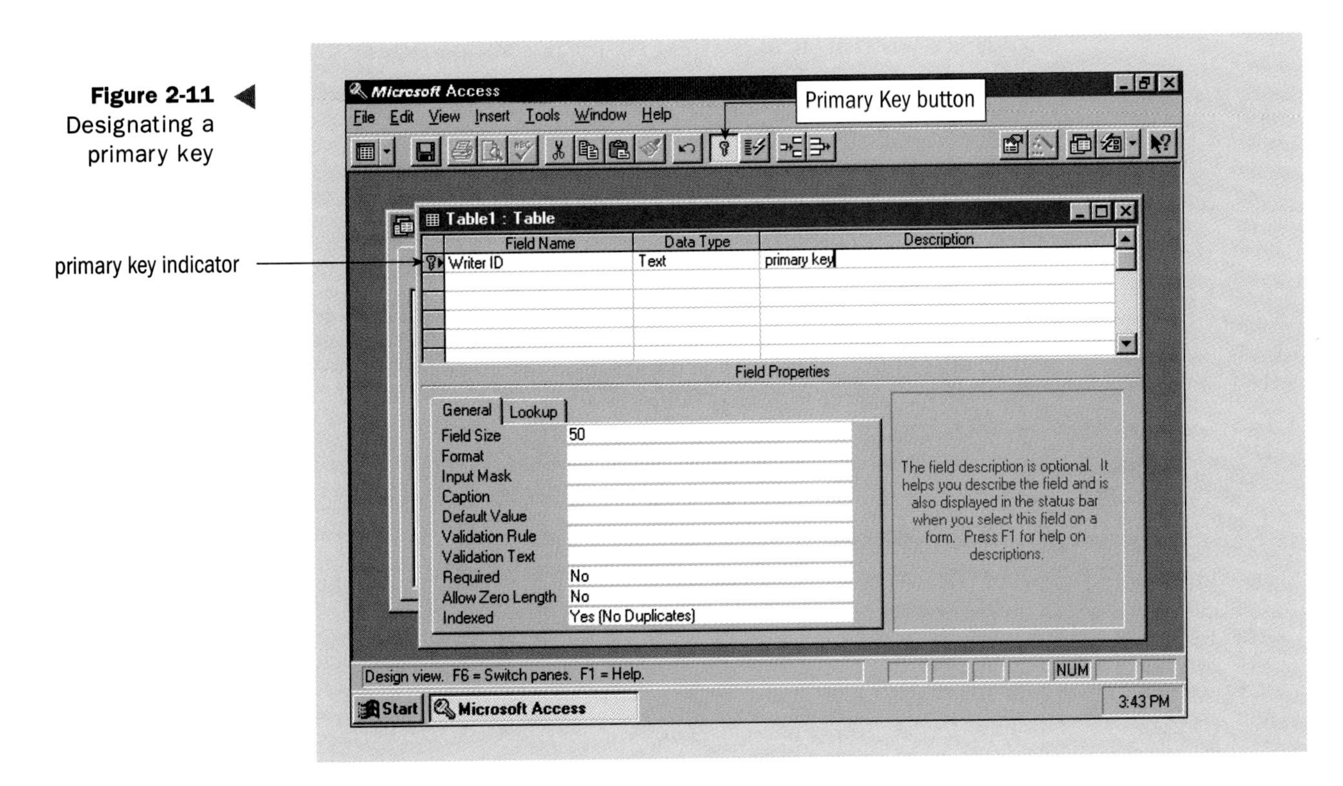

After designating the primary key, Elena moves to the first field property, Field Size.

Assigning Field Sizes

The Field Size property determines a field value's maximum storage size for Text and Number fields. The other data types have no field size property, either because their storage size is a predetermined fixed size (e.g., 8 bytes for a Date/Time field) or because the size is dependent on the actual value stored (e.g., a Memo field). You should document every Text field's maximum size so that you allow enough room for it on entry screens and on reports and other outputs, without wasting space.

A Text field, like Writer ID, has a default field size of 50 characters. You can change its field size by entering a number in the range of 1 to 255 in the text box for the Field Size property in the Field Properties panel. For a Number field, you select the field size from five choices: byte, integer, long integer, double, and single, as shown in Figure 2-12. Double is the default field size for a Number field.

Figure 2-12 ◀ Number data type field size options

Field Size	Storage Size (Bytes)	Number Type	Field Values Allowed
Byte	1	Integer	0 to 255
Integer	2	Integer	–32,768 to 32,767
Long Integer	4	Integer	–2,147,483,648 to 2,147,483,647
Double	8	Decimal	15 significant digits
Single	4	Decimal	7 significant digits

Elena's Writer ID field is a Text field that is always exactly four characters long, so she enters 4 as its field size.

To change a field size:

1. Double-click in the **Field Size** property text box to highlight the current value.
2. Type **4**.

Now that Elena has entered all the information for the first field in the WRITERS table, she returns to her original database design and determines the field data types, sizes, and descriptions for the other fields, as shown in Figure 2-13.

Figure 2-13 Elena's database design for the WRITERS, BUSINESS ARTICLES, and WRITER PAYMENTS tables

	Data Type	Field Size	Description
WRITERS table			
Writer ID	Text	4	primary key
Writer Name	Text	25	
Writer Phone	Text	14	(999) 999-9999 format
Freelancer	Yes/No		
Freelancer Reprint Payment Amount	Currency		$250 maximum
Writer Age	Number	4	byte field size
BUSINESS ARTICLES table			
Article Title	Text	44	
Issue of Business Perspective	Text	8	
Length of Article	Number	4	integer field size
Writer ID	Text	4	foreign key
WRITER PAYMENTS table			
Check Number	Number	16	primary key, double field size
Writer ID	Text	4	foreign key
Check Amount	Currency		
Check Date	Date/Time		

Elena is now ready to define the rest of the fields in the WRITERS table.

To define the remaining fields in the WRITERS table:

1. Click in the **Field Name** column for the second row. Type **Writer Name**, then press the **Tab** key to move to the Data Type column. Press the **Tab** key again to accept the default Text data type. Double-click in the **Field Size** property text box to highlight the current value, then type **25**.
2. Click in the **Field Name** column for the third row. Type **Writer Phone**, then press the **Tab** key to move to the Data Type column. Press the **Tab** key to accept the default Text data type and move to the Description column. Type **(999) 999-9999**.

3. Double-click in the **Field Size** property text box to highlight the current value, then type **14.**

4. Click in the **Field Name** column for the fourth row. Type **Freelancer** and then press the **Tab** key to move to the Data Type column. The Freelancer field is a Yes/No field. You can use the drop-down Data Type list box to select the correct data type.

5. Click the **Data Type** list arrow to display the list of available data types. See Figure 2-14. Click **Yes/No**.

Figure 2-14 Selecting the data type

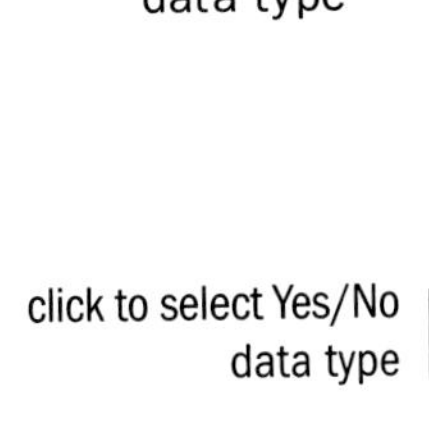

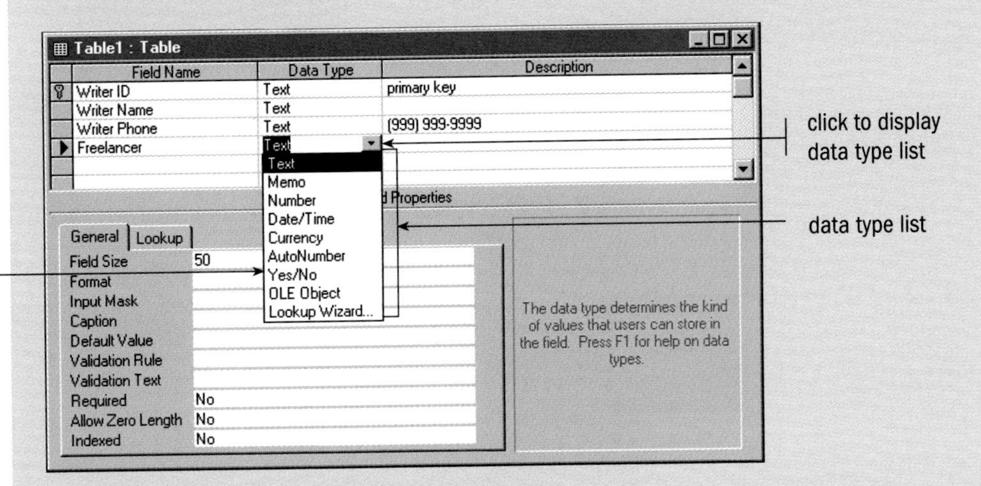

Note that instead of selecting a field's data type by clicking one of the choices in the Data Type list box, you can type the entire data type name in the field's Data Type text box. Alternatively, type just the first character of the data type name to select that data type. You will use this technique in the next step.

6. Click in the **Field Name** column for the fifth row. Type **Freelancer Reprint Payment Amount**, then press the **Tab** key to move to the Data Type column. Since this field is a currency field, type **C**. Access automatically changes the data type to Currency.

7. Click in the **Field Name** column for the sixth row. Type **Writer Age**, then press the **Tab** key to move to the Data Type column. Notice that the field list scrolls so that you can see the Writer Age row.

8. Type **N** to select the Number data type, then press the **Tab** key.

   The Writer Age field will contain the ages of writers. Since these will be integers, probably less than 100, the byte field size is appropriate. The byte field size can store integers from 0 to 256. Using the byte field size rather than the default double field size will save space in the database.

9. Click in the **Field Size** text box, then click the **Field Size** list arrow, then click **Byte**. The list closes and the Field Size property value is changed to Byte.

Elena has now finished defining the fields for the WRITERS table. The final screen is shown in Figure 2-15. Elena wants to save the table structure before proceeding.

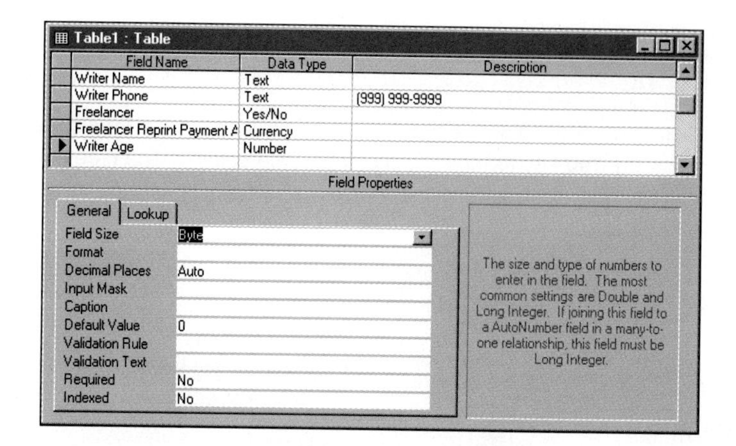

Figure 2-15 Field definitions for the WRITERS table

Saving a Table Structure

When you first create a table, you must save the table with its field definitions to add the table structure permanently to your database.

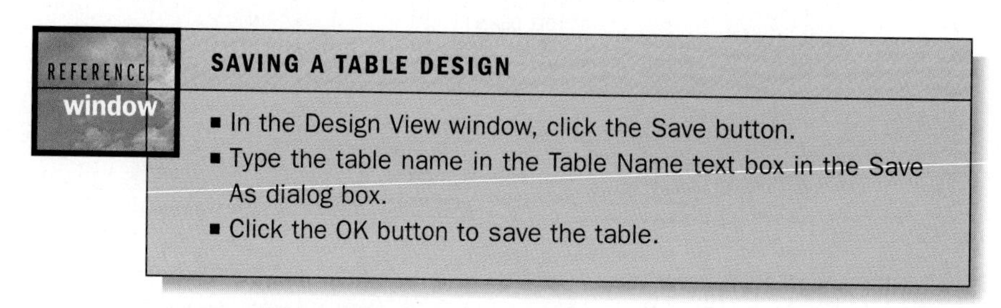

SAVING A TABLE DESIGN

- In the Design View window, click the Save button.
- Type the table name in the Table Name text box in the Save As dialog box.
- Click the OK button to save the table.

To save the WRITERS table:

1. Click the **Save** button on the toolbar. Access displays the Save As dialog box. See Figure 2-16.

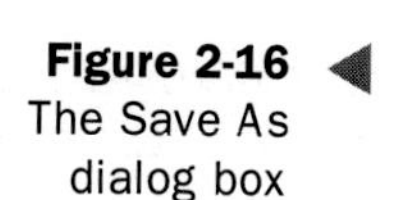

Figure 2-16 The Save As dialog box

2. Type **WRITERS** in the Table Name text box, then click the **OK** button. The dialog box closes and Access saves the WRITERS table on your Student Disk.

Switching to the Datasheet View Window

Once you have defined a table, you can view the table in either Design View or Datasheet View. You use Design View to view or change a table's field definitions and properties, and Datasheet View to view or change the field values and records stored in a table. Even though she has not yet entered any of the field values and records in the WRITERS table, Elena displays the WRITERS table in Datasheet View. She can study the datasheet to determine if she needs to make any changes to the table fields.

To switch to a different view of a table, you use Table View button, which is the left-most button on the toolbar. The appearance of the this button changes, depending on which view is current. The button is currently the icon for Datasheet View and looks like . Clicking the button switches you to Datasheet View, and the button changes to . Clicking again switches you to Design View. If you have more than two views open (such as Datasheet View, Design View, and Form View), clicking the list arrow will display a list of views from which you can choose.

To switch from Design View to Datasheet View:

1. Click the **Table View** button on the toolbar. Access displays the Datasheet View window for the WRITERS table.
2. Click the **Maximize** button for the Datasheet View window to maximize the window. See Figure 2-17.

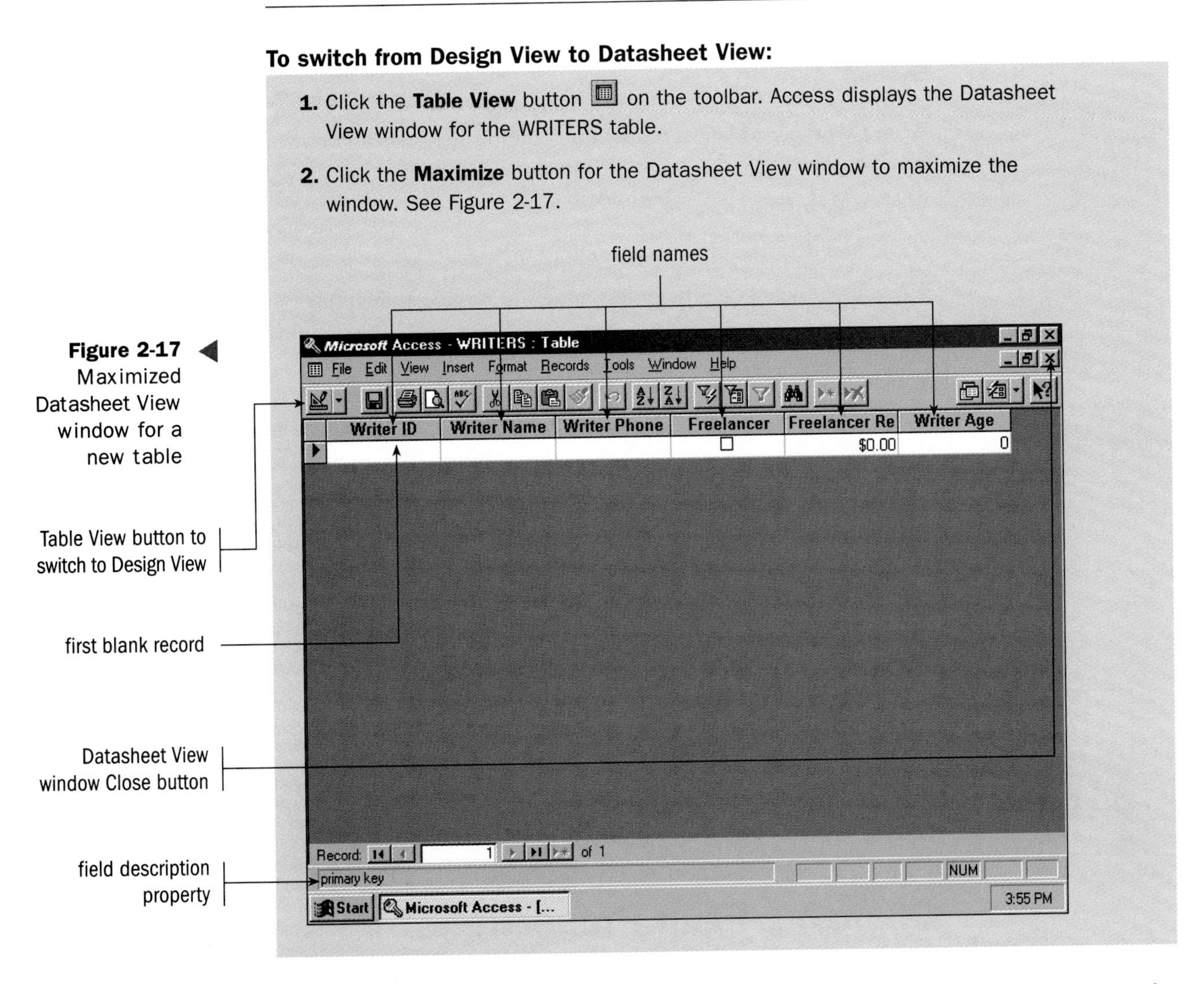

Figure 2-17 Maximized Datasheet View window for a new table

At first glance, Elena is pleased with her table. She notices that all the information for the Writer ID field appears accurate and that its description appears in the status bar. Looking closer, however, Elena sees several problems that she wants to correct. First, some field names, such as Freelancer Reprint Payment Amount, are only partially displayed, and their field value boxes are wider than they need to be to accommodate the field values that will be entered. Second, the Writer Name field value box is too narrow to display the entire field value. Before making these changes, though, Elena prints the datasheet for the WRITERS table so that she can refer to it as she corrects the problems she discovered.

Printing a Datasheet

To print the datasheet:

1. Click the **Print** button on the toolbar. After the message box closes, Access returns you to the Datasheet View window.

Elena switches back to Design View to make her field property changes.

To switch from Datasheet View to Design View:

1. Click the **Table View** button on the toolbar. Access displays the Design View window for the WRITERS table.

Elena is now ready to make her changes, which she'll do in the next session.

Quick Check

1. What two types of keys represent a common field when you form a relationship between tables?
2. What is data redundancy?
3. Name and describe three Access data types.
4. Why might including a field description in a table be helpful?
5. What is one advantage of designating a primary key?
6. Which data types need to have field sizes determined?
7. Describe two different ways to select a field's data type.
8. How do you switch from one view window to another?

If you want to take a break and resume the tutorial at a later time, exit Access. When you resume the tutorial, place your Student Disk in the appropriate drive and start Access. Open the Issue25 database, click the Design button to open the Design View window for the WRITERS table, and maximize the Design View window.

SESSION 2.2

In this session, you will learn to change field properties and change the appearance of the columns in the Datasheet View Window. You will also modify the structure of an Access table, create another table by using the Table Wizard, and create and delete indexes.

Changing Field Properties

Elena has noted several changes she would like to make in the design of her table. She wants to add a caption to the Freelancer Reprint Payment Amount field since that field name is too wide to be displayed. To make data entry easier, she wants to define the default value Yes for the Freelancer field. Elena has heard about the benefit of using input masks. **Input masks** restrict data entry to the appropriate type and format required for the field. She wants to create an input mask for the Writer Phone field that will automatically add the parentheses and hyphen to the phone number. Since the Freelancer Reprint Payment Amount will always be in whole dollars, she wants the values to appear without the two zeros after the decimal. These changes to the field properties can be done i48n the Design View window. Elena also wants to adjust the column widths in the Datasheet View to improve the readability of the table datasheet.

Elena is now ready to change the Caption property for the Freelancer Reprint Payment Amount field.

Entering a Caption

Even though the field name Freelancer Reprint Payment Amount is too wide to fit in the datasheet column heading box, Elena does not want to change it because it is descriptive. Instead, Elena will use the Caption field property. It will replace the field name in the datasheet column heading box and in the label on a form, without changing the actual field name. You can use the Caption property to display a shorter version of a long, more descriptive table field name.

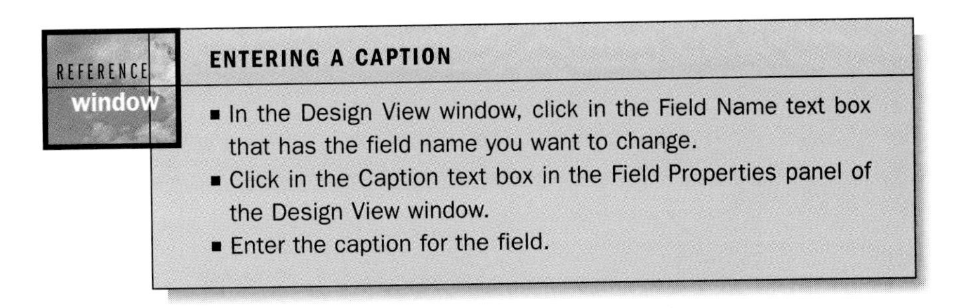

ENTERING A CAPTION

- In the Design View window, click in the Field Name text box that has the field name you want to change.
- Click in the Caption text box in the Field Properties panel of the Design View window.
- Enter the caption for the field.

To enter a caption for the Freelancer Reprint Payment Amount field:

1. Click anywhere in the **Field Name** text box containing Freelancer Reprint Payment Amount. The current row symbol moves to the Freelancer Reprint Payment Amount row and the Field Properties options for this field appear below. Click the **Caption** text box and then type **Amount**. See Figure 2-18.

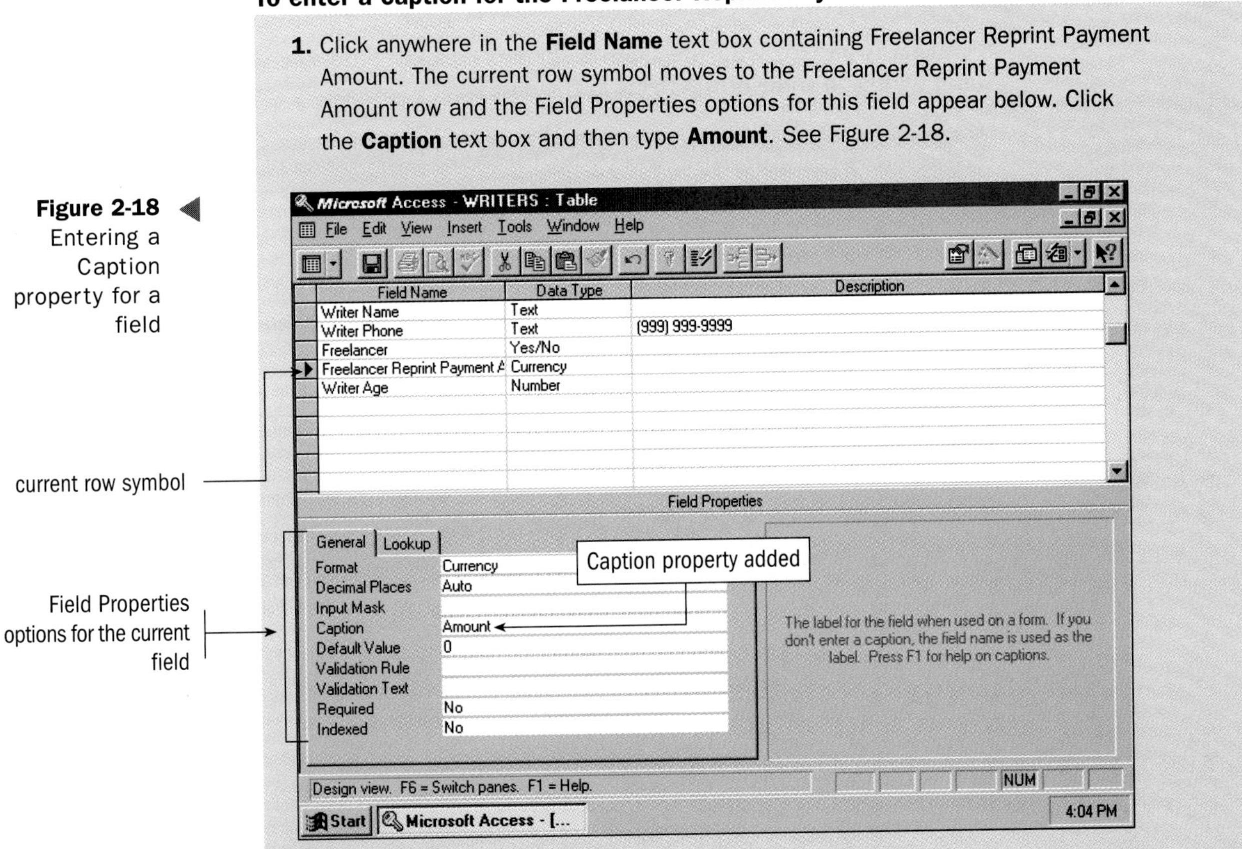

Figure 2-18 Entering a Caption property for a field

Elena switches to Datasheet View to review her change.

To switch to Datasheet View:

1. Click the **Table View** button on the toolbar. Access displays the Save now? dialog box.

   Access makes your table structure changes permanent only when you take action to save the changes or when you close the Design View window. Switching to Datasheet View first involves closing the Design View window, so Access displays the dialog box to ask you about saving your table changes.

2. Click the **Yes** button. (Note that if you wanted to keep the Design View window open and continue making table structure changes, you would click the No button instead.) Access saves your table structure changes, closes the Design View window, and opens the Datasheet View window. See Figure 2-19.

Figure 2-19 Reviewing a change in the Datasheet View window

Elena is pleased with the caption she has created. Now she wants to change the column widths in some of the fields in the datasheet.

Resizing Columns in a Datasheet

As with all software programs, there are often several ways to accomplish a task in Access. In these tutorials, we will show you the simplest and fastest method to accomplish tasks. Because you may not have resized datasheet columns before, however, we'll practice three of the different techniques available: using the Format menu, using the mouse pointer, and the best-fit column width method.

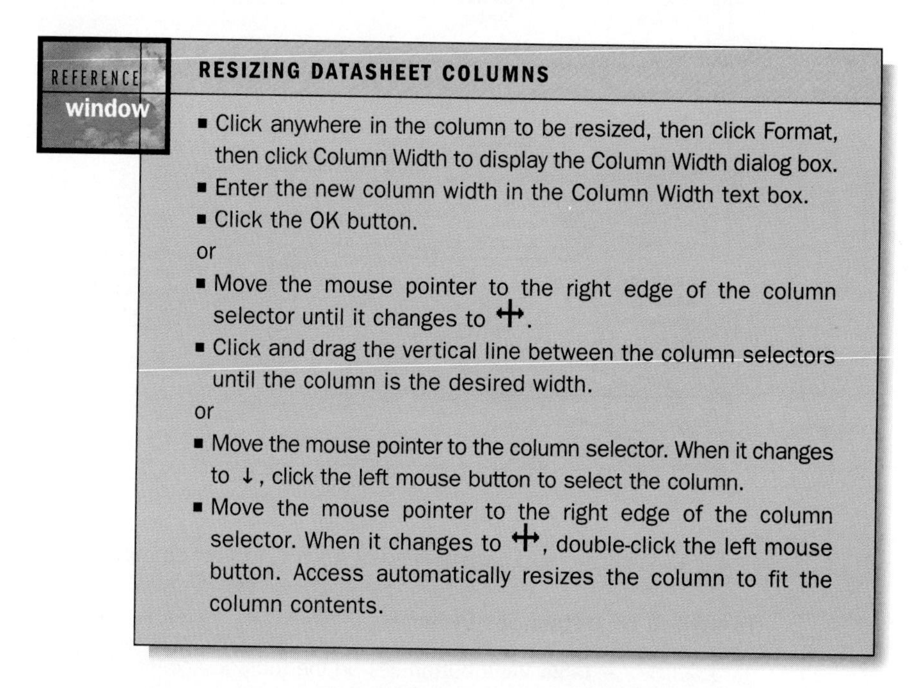

REFERENCE window

RESIZING DATASHEET COLUMNS

- Click anywhere in the column to be resized, then click Format, then click Column Width to display the Column Width dialog box.
- Enter the new column width in the Column Width text box.
- Click the OK button.

or

- Move the mouse pointer to the right edge of the column selector until it changes to ✛.
- Click and drag the vertical line between the column selectors until the column is the desired width.

or

- Move the mouse pointer to the column selector. When it changes to ↓, click the left mouse button to select the column.
- Move the mouse pointer to the right edge of the column selector. When it changes to ✛, double-click the left mouse button. Access automatically resizes the column to fit the column contents.

First, Elena will resize a datasheet column using the Format menu.

To resize a datasheet column using the Format menu:

1. Click anywhere in the **Writer ID** column, click **Format**, and then click **Column Width**. Access opens the Column Width dialog box. See Figure 2-20. Access has automatically selected the default, standard column width of 15.6667 positions and has checked the Standard Width check box.

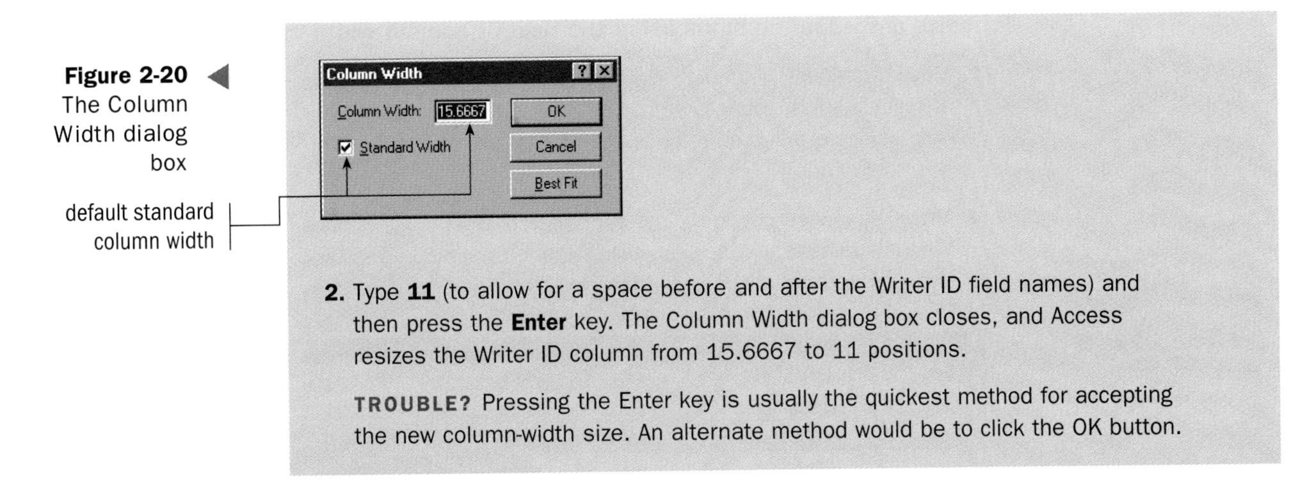

Figure 2-20 The Column Width dialog box

2. Type **11** (to allow for a space before and after the Writer ID field names) and then press the **Enter** key. The Column Width dialog box closes, and Access resizes the Writer ID column from 15.6667 to 11 positions.

   TROUBLE? Pressing the Enter key is usually the quickest method for accepting the new column-width size. An alternate method would be to click the OK button.

Elena resizes the Writer Name field using the second method—dragging the column's right edge with the mouse pointer. To resize this way, you must first position the mouse pointer in the field's **column selector,** which is the gray box that contains the field name at the top of the column. A column selector is also called a **field selector.**

To resize a datasheet column using the mouse pointer to drag the column's right edge:

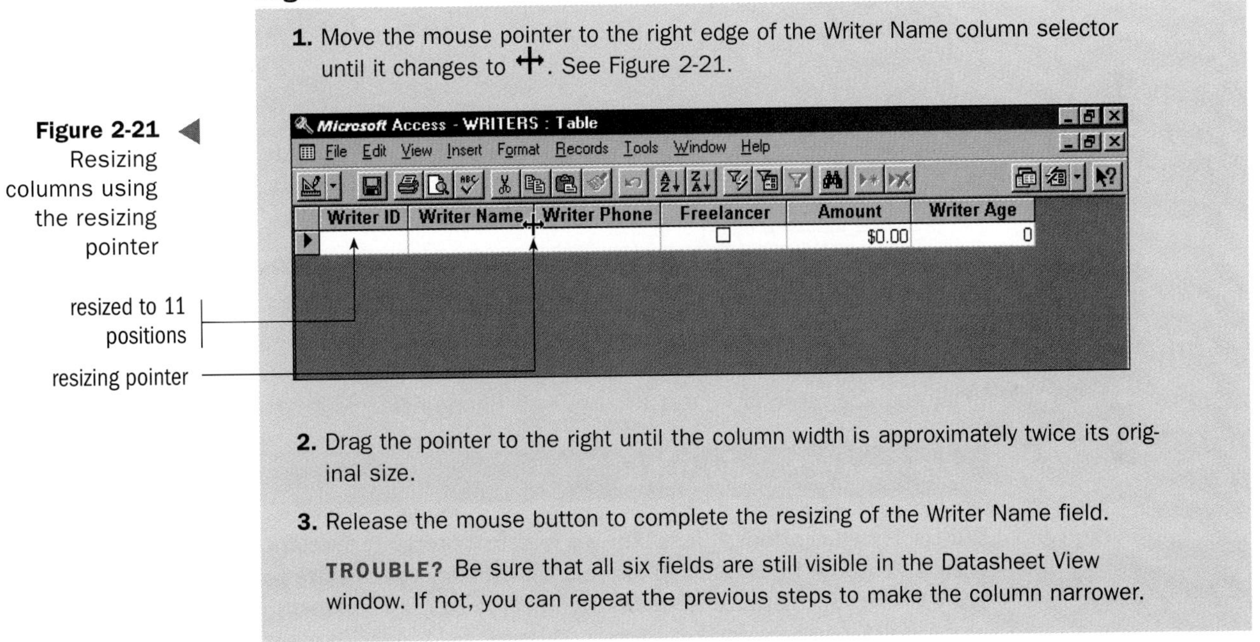

Figure 2-21 Resizing columns using the resizing pointer

1. Move the mouse pointer to the right edge of the Writer Name column selector until it changes to ✛. See Figure 2-21.
2. Drag the pointer to the right until the column width is approximately twice its original size.
3. Release the mouse button to complete the resizing of the Writer Name field.

   TROUBLE? Be sure that all six fields are still visible in the Datasheet View window. If not, you can repeat the previous steps to make the column narrower.

Elena tries a third technique, the best-fit column width method, to resize the Freelancer, Amount, and Writer Age columns. When you use the best-fit column width method, Access automatically resizes the column to accommodate its largest value, including the field name at the top of the column. To use this method, you position the mouse pointer at the right edge of the column selector for the field and, when the mouse pointer changes to ✛, double-click the left mouse button. Access then automatically resizes the column.

For the best-fit method, you can resize two or more adjacent columns at the same time. Simply move the mouse pointer to the column selector of the leftmost of the fields. When the pointer changes to ↓, drag it to the column selector of the rightmost field and then release the mouse button. You then double-click the ✛ at the right edge of the column selector for any field in the group.

To resize datasheet columns using the best-fit column width method:

1. Move the mouse pointer to the Freelancer column selector. When it changes to ↓, click the left mouse button, drag the pointer to the right to the Writer Age column selector, and then release the mouse button. The last three columns are now highlighted.
2. Move the mouse pointer to the right edge of the Freelancer column selector. When it changes to ↔, double-click the left mouse button. Access automatically resizes the three columns to their best fits. See Figure 2-22.

Figure 2-22 Five columns resized

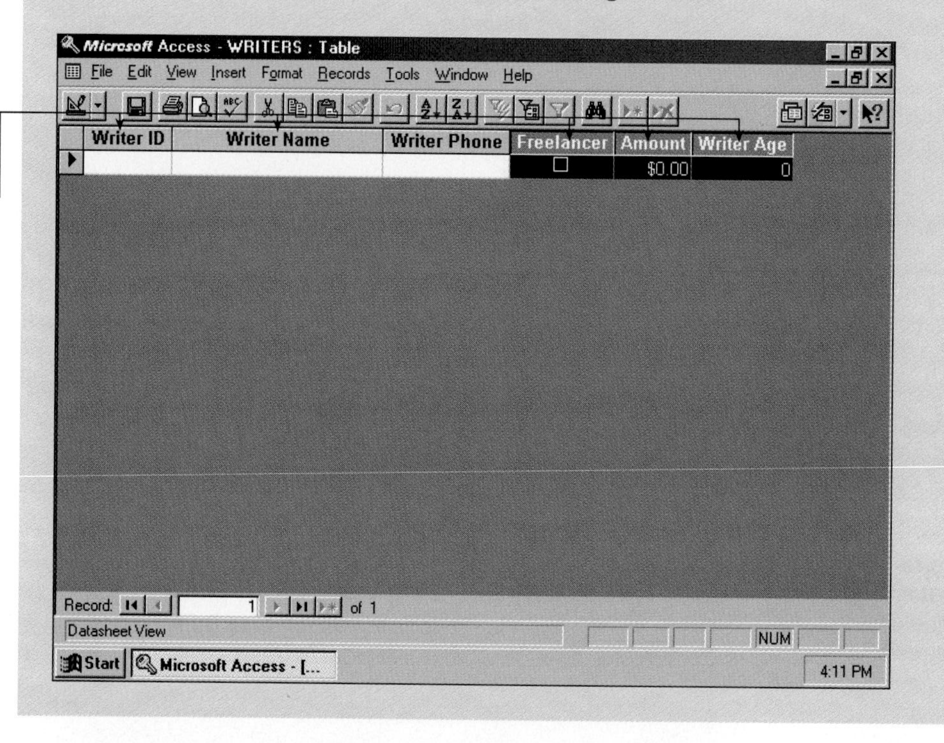

resized columns

For her final set of field property changes, Elena will assign a default value to the Freelancer field, eliminate the decimal places in the Freelancer Reprint Payment Amount field, and add an input mask to the Writer Phone field.

Assigning a Default Value

With a few exceptions, Elena knows which writers are freelancers and which are staff writers. To be safe, Elena will assume that the exceptions are freelancers until she finds out for sure. She assigns the default value Yes to the Freelancer field, which means each writer will have the value Yes in the Freelancer field unless it is specifically changed to No. A default value must be assigned in the Design View window, so Elena first switches from the Datasheet View window.

To assign a default value:

1. Click the **Table View** button on the toolbar to switch to the Design View window.
2. Click anywhere in the **Freelancer** field row to make it the current field, click the **Default Value** property text box, and then type **Yes**. See Figure 2-23.

Figure 2-23 Assigning a default value to a field

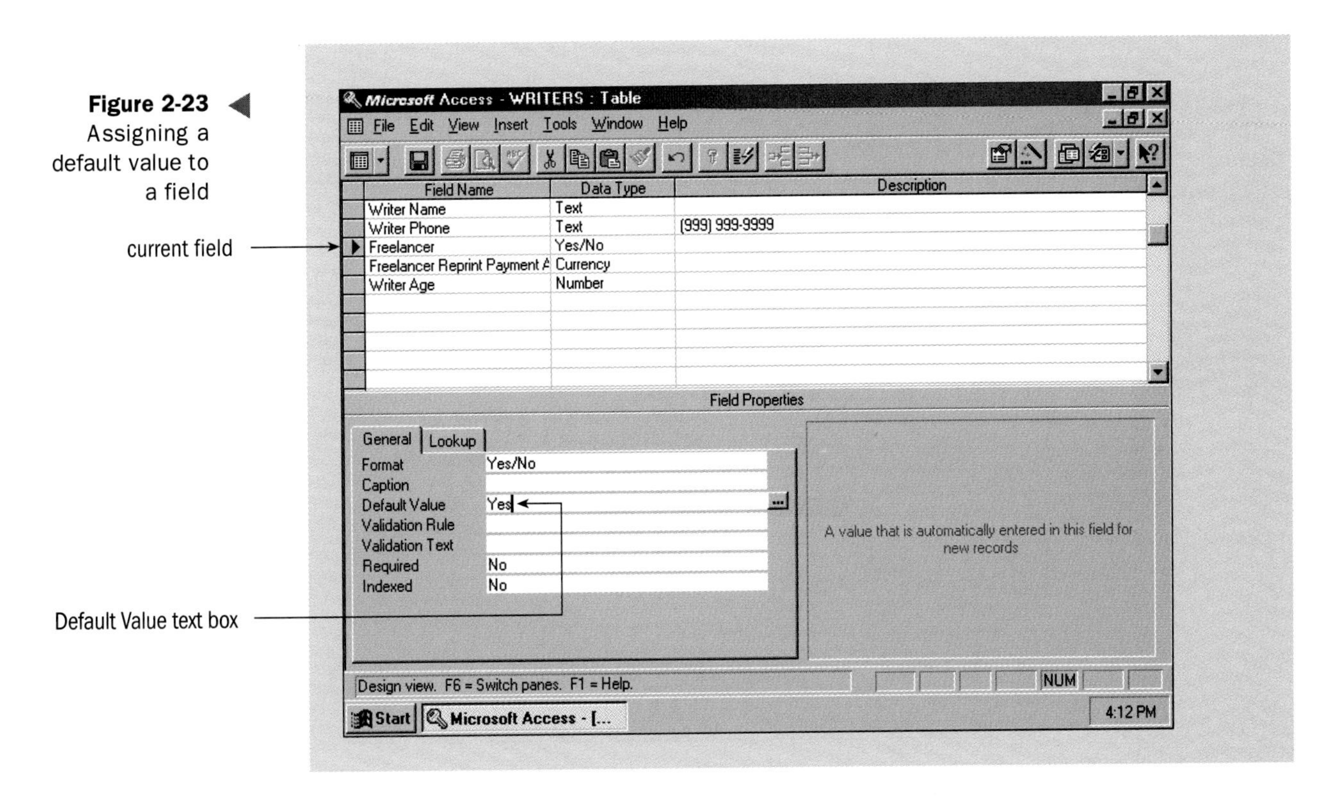

Elena's next change is to eliminate the decimal places in the Freelancer Reprint Payment Amount field.

Changing Decimal Places

Elena knows that the amount that Vision Publishers pays its freelancers is always a whole dollar figure. She therefore changes the Freelancer Reprint Payment Amount field to show only whole dollar amounts. To do this, she modifies the Decimal Places property for the field.

To change the number of decimal places displayed:

1. Click anywhere in the Freelancer Reprint Payment Amount field row to make it the current field and to display its Field Properties options.
2. Click in the **Decimal Places** text box, then click **list arrow** that appears. Access displays the Decimal Places list box. See Figure 2-24.

Figure 2-24
Changing the Decimal Places field property

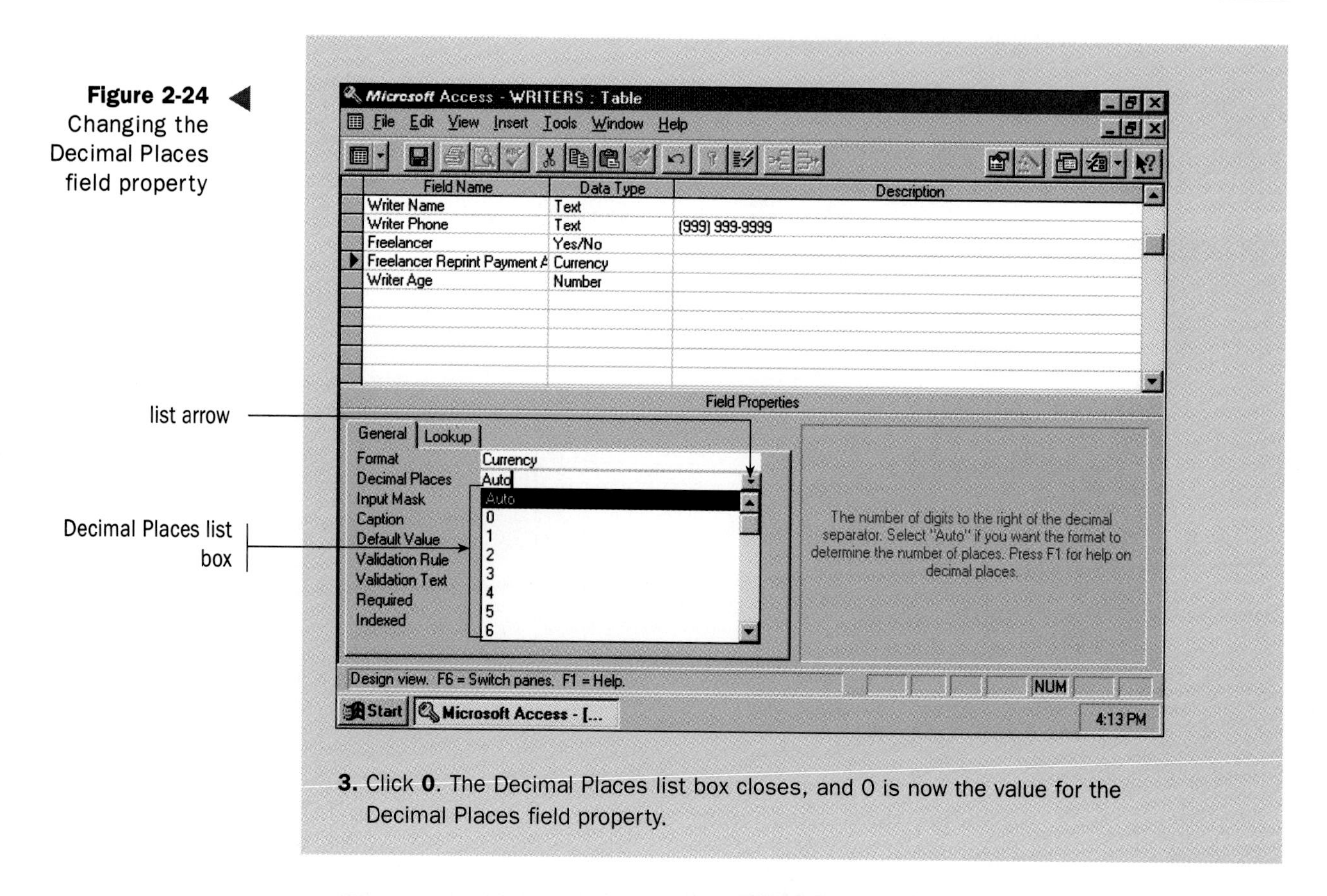

3. Click **0**. The Decimal Places list box closes, and 0 is now the value for the Decimal Places field property.

Elena is now ready to make her final change. She will use the Input Mask Wizard to create an input mask for the Writer Phone field.

Input Masks

One standard way to format a telephone number is with parentheses, a space, and a hyphen as in (917) 555-5364. If you want these special formatting characters to appear whenever Writer Phone field values are entered, you need to create an input mask. Remember that an input mask dictates the format for data entered in a particular field. With an input mask described above for the Writer Phone field, users simply enter the numbers; the parentheses, space, and hyphen are added by Access. An input mask helps to make the data more readable, more consistent, and reduces the chance of error when data is entered.

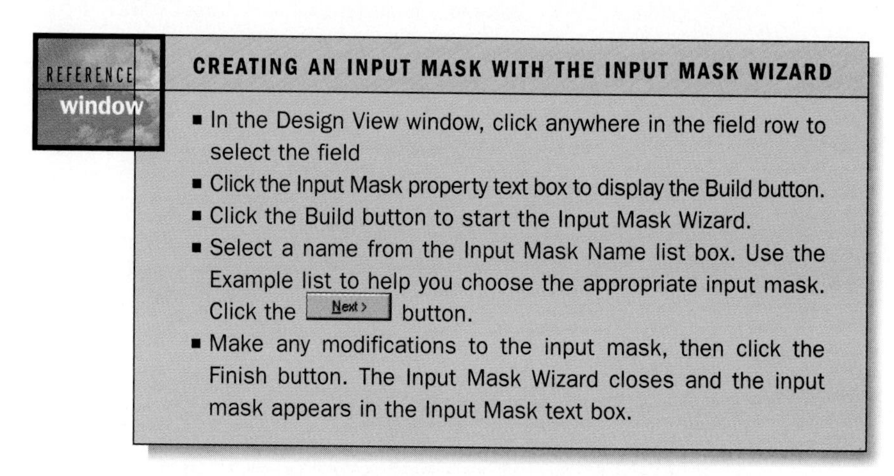

REFERENCE window

CREATING AN INPUT MASK WITH THE INPUT MASK WIZARD

- In the Design View window, click anywhere in the field row to select the field
- Click the Input Mask property text box to display the Build button.
- Click the Build button to start the Input Mask Wizard.
- Select a name from the Input Mask Name list box. Use the Example list to help you choose the appropriate input mask. Click the Next > button.
- Make any modifications to the input mask, then click the Finish button. The Input Mask Wizard closes and the input mask appears in the Input Mask text box.

Elena creates an input mask for the Writer Phone field.

To create an input mask:

1. Click anywhere in the **Writer Phone** field row to make it the current field and to display its Field Properties options.
2. Click in the Input Mask text box to display the Build button. See Figure 2-25.

Figure 2-25 Defining an Input Mask property

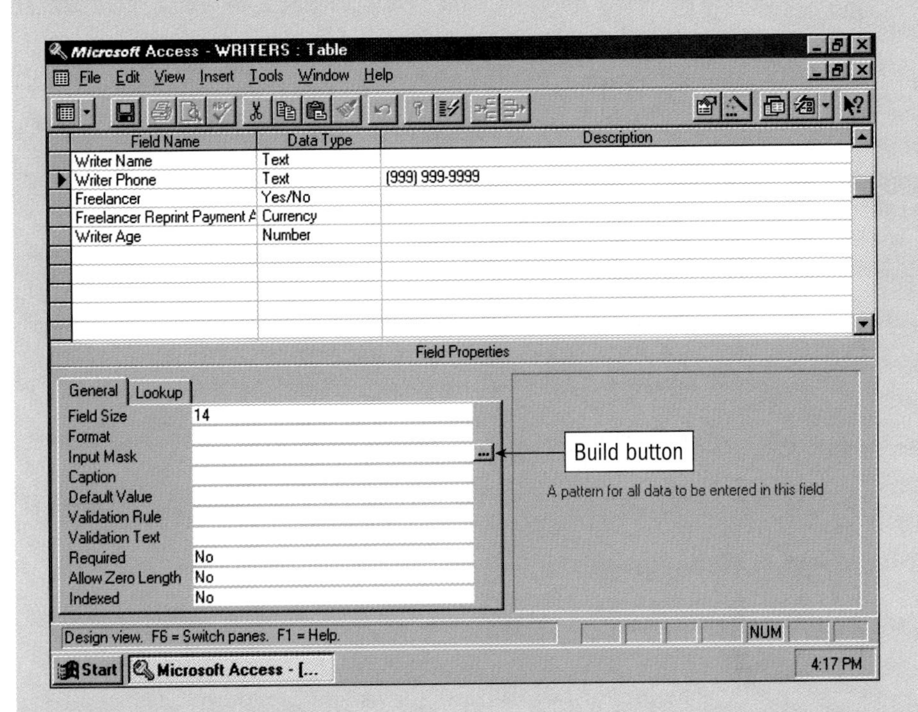

For most common formats it is not necessary to create input masks from scratch. When you click in the Input Mask property text box, Access displays the Build button at the right of the text box. When you click the Build button, Access starts the Input Mask Wizard to assist you in creating an input mask.

3. Click the **Build** button to start the Input Mask Wizard. The Input Mask Wizard lets you select from a list of common input masks, such as masks for social security numbers, zip codes, etc. Before starting the Input Mask Wizard, Access displays the Save now? dialog box. This allows you to save any changes you have made up to this point.
4. Click the **Yes** button to save the changes and close the dialog box. Access saves the WRITERS table and displays the first Input Mask Wizard dialog box. See Figure 2-26.

Figure 2-26 The first Input Mask Wizard dialog box

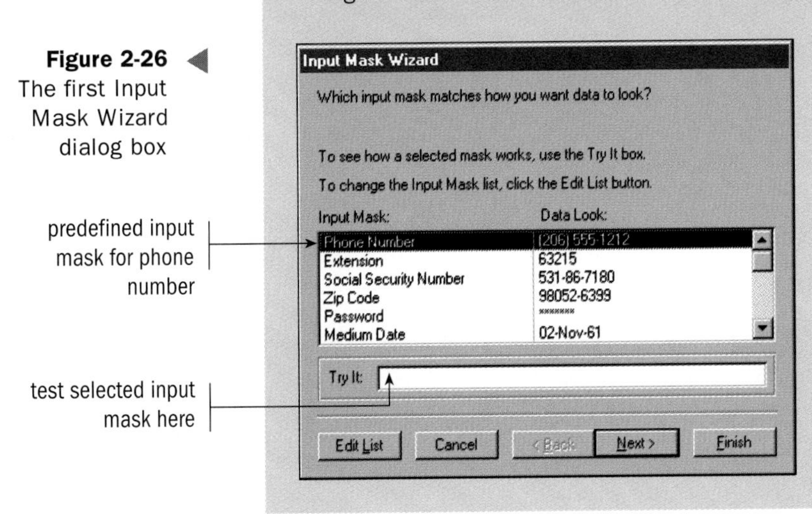

5. If necessary, click **Phone Number** in the Input Mask list box to highlight it.
6. Click in the **Try it** text box. Access displays (___) ___-____ in the text box. The underscores are placeholder characters that are replaced with numbers as you type.
7. Click to the right of the first parenthesis, then type **9876543210** to enter a sample phone number.
8. Click the Next > button. Access displays the next Input Mask Wizard dialog box. See Figure 2-27.

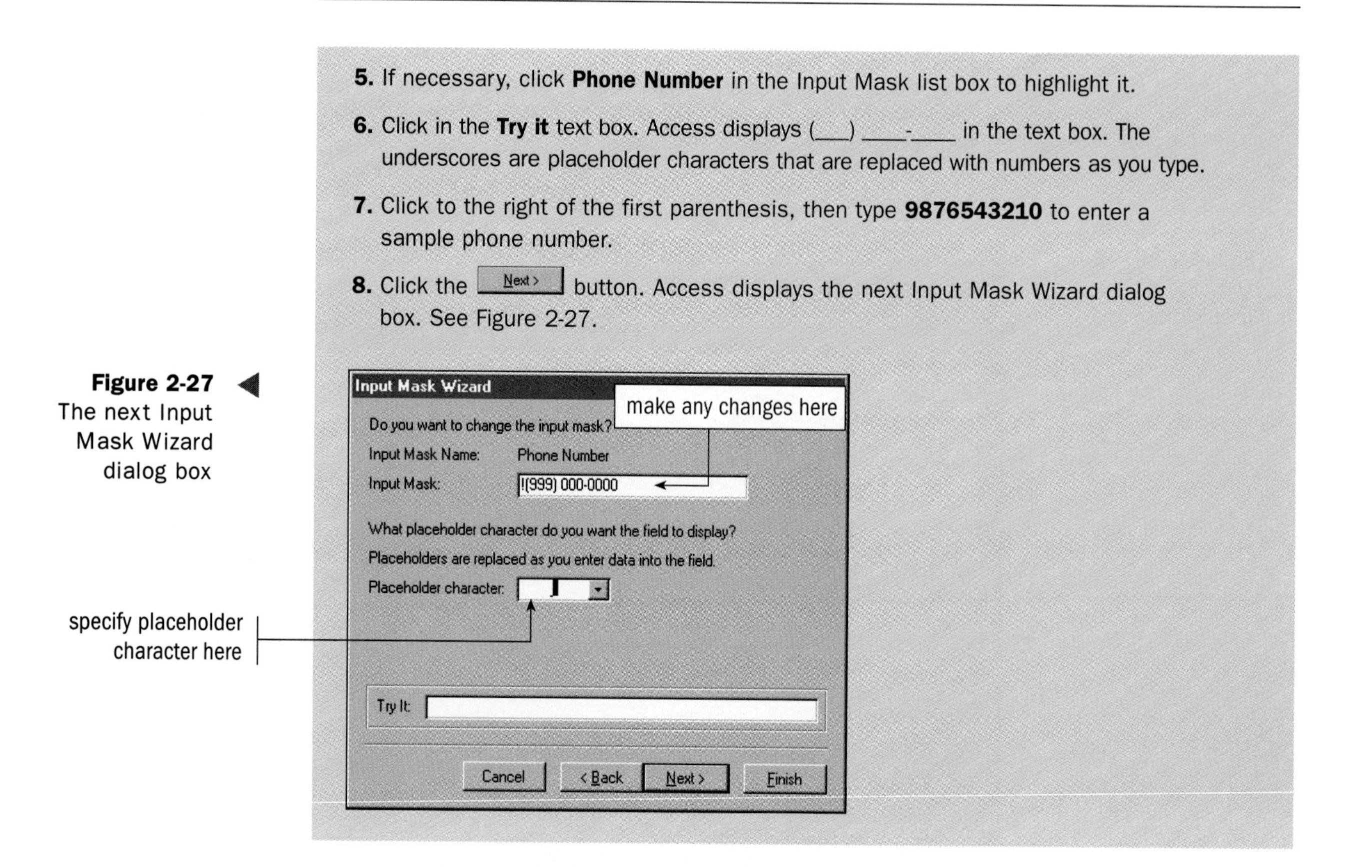

Figure 2-27 The next Input Mask Wizard dialog box

The Input Mask Wizard allows you to modify, or customize, the input mask. You can change the default underscore placeholder character, for example, to a space or one of the following special characters: # @ ! $ % or *. For now, Elena accepts the predefined input mask and continues through the remaining Input Mask Wizard dialog boxes.

To finish an input mask:

1. Click the Next > button. Access displays the next Input Mask Wizard dialog box.
2. Click the top radio button so that you store the data "With the symbols in the mask, like this: (206) 555-1212." Then click the Next > button. Access displays the next Input Mask Wizard dialog box.
3. Click the **Finish** button. Access closes Input Mask Wizard and displays the newly created input mask for the Writer Phone field. See Figure 2-28.

Figure 2-28 The newly created input mask

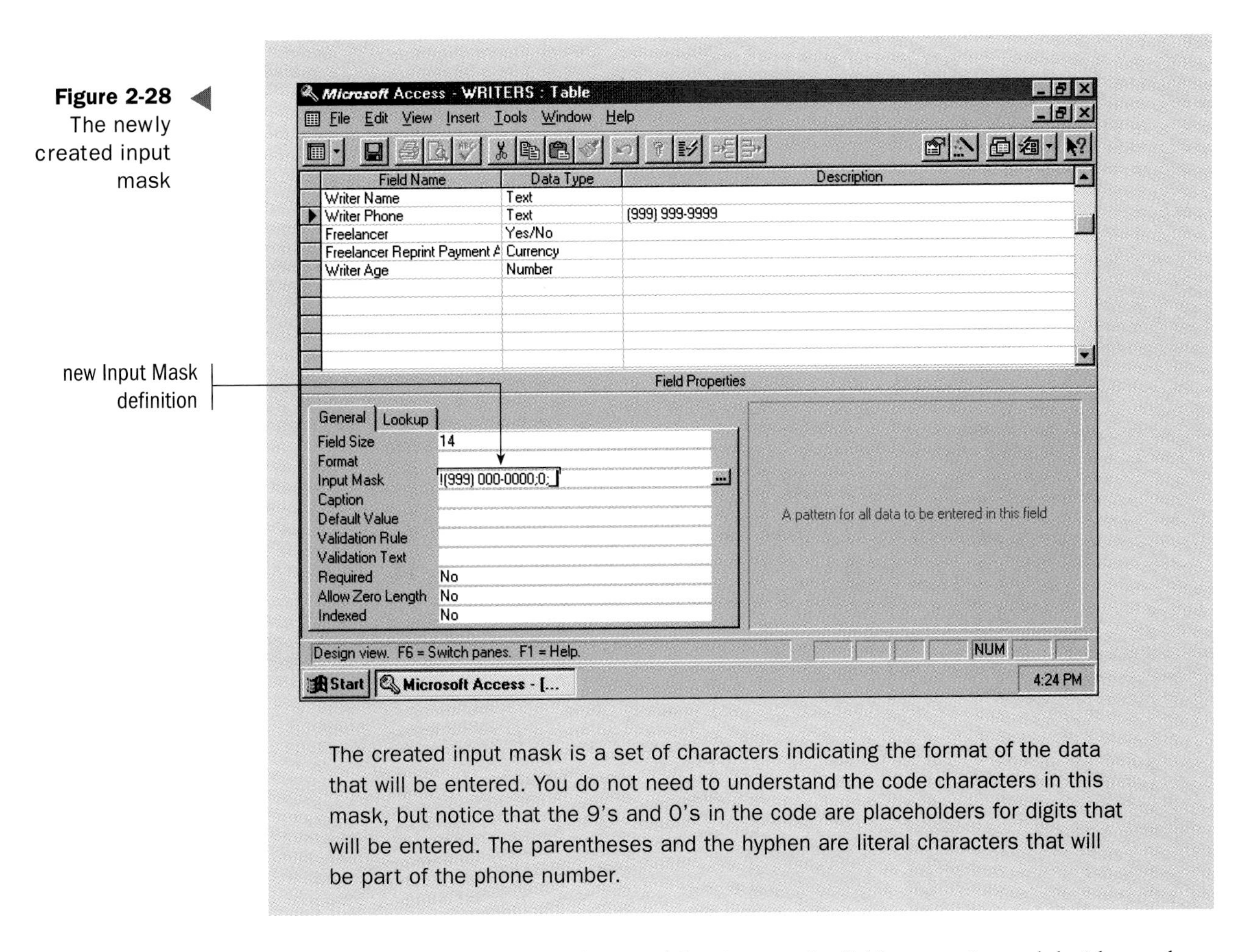

The created input mask is a set of characters indicating the format of the data that will be entered. You do not need to understand the code characters in this mask, but notice that the 9's and 0's in the code are placeholders for digits that will be entered. The parentheses and the hyphen are literal characters that will be part of the phone number.

Elena has finished making her modifications to the field properties and decides to show her table design to Brian for his comments.

Modifying the Structure of an Access Table

When Elena shows Brian her modified WRITERS table, he tells her she has made a good start and then suggests the following structural changes that will improve the table.

- The Writer Age field is unnecessary and could even lead to potential legal problems for Vision Publishers in the future. Brian suggests that Elena delete that information from the table.
- For magazine indexing purposes, Brian needs a list of all the WRITERS table information arranged alphabetically by writer last name. Elena had been planning to enter names in the Writer Name field in the regular order of first, middle, and last name, and now realizes that she needs to change the WRITERS table structure by renaming the Writer Name field Last Name, and then adding a field for First Name, which will include the middle initial, to allow for Brian's list.
- Because Vision Publishers has not contacted some writers for years, Elena needs to add a field named Last Contact Date. That way, she can contact those writers who have a reasonably current contact date first.

While the changes Elena made previously involved changes to individual fields, the changes that Brian wants Elena to make will modify the actual structure of the table.

Deleting a Field

Elena's first priority is to delete the Writer Age field.

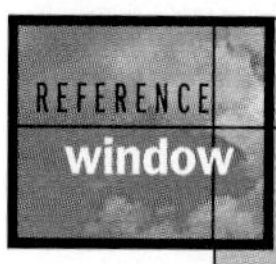

DELETING A FIELD FROM A TABLE STRUCTURE

- In the Design View window, click the right mouse button anywhere in the row for the field you want to delete. Access displays the shortcut menu.
- Click Delete Field in the shortcut menu. Access closes the shortcut menu and deletes the field from the table structure.

To delete a field:

1. Make sure you are in Design View, then move the mouse pointer to the row for the Writer Age field and click the right mouse button. Access displays the shortcut menu. See Figure 2-29.

Figure 2-29 The shortcut menu for Writer Age

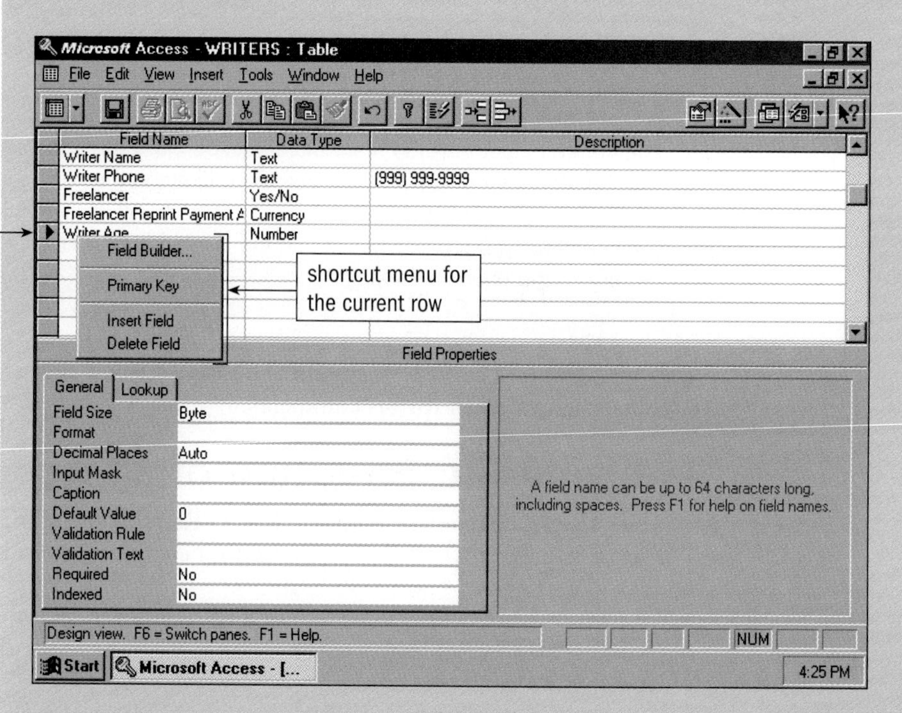

2. Click **Delete Field** in the shortcut menu. Access deletes the Writer Age field from the WRITERS table structure. The row where Writer Age had been positioned is also deleted.

   TROUBLE? If you deleted the wrong field, immediately click the Undo button. The field you deleted is inserted again. (Note that not all changes can be undone, in which case the Undo button will be dimmed). Repeat the deletion steps for the correct field starting with Step 1.

Adding a Field

The order in which the fields are listed in the Design View window determines the order of the fields in the Datasheet View window. Elena wants the new field, First Name, to be positioned right after the Writer Name row, which she will rename Last Name. Then she will position the other new field, Last Contact Date, between the Writer Phone and Freelancer rows.

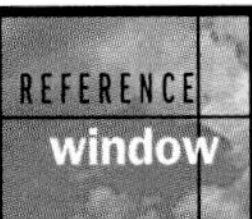

ADDING A FIELD TO A TABLE STRUCTURE

- In the Design View window, open the shortcut menu by clicking the right mouse button anywhere in the row that will fall below the field you are adding.
- Click Insert Field in the shortcut menu. Access inserts a blank row.
- Define the new field by entering a field name, data type, and optional description in the new row.

or

- If the new field is to be added to the end of the table, click the Field Name column for the first blank row. Then enter the field name, data type, and optional description.

Before Elena adds any fields, she wants to change the Writer Name field to Last Name.

To change a field name:

1. Click in the **Field Name** text box for the Writer Name field, then press the **F2** key to highlight the field name.
2. Type **Last Name** to make it the new field name.

Elena is now ready to add two new fields to the WRITERS table.

To add a field to a table structure:

1. Click the right mouse button anywhere in the Writer Phone row. You want to insert the new First Name field above it. Access displays the shortcut menu.
2. Click **Insert Field** in the shortcut menu. Access adds a blank row between the Last Name and Writer Phone rows and closes the shortcut menu. The insertion point is in the Field Name box of the new row. See Figure 2-30.

Figure 2-30 ◀ Preparing to add a new field

row for new field

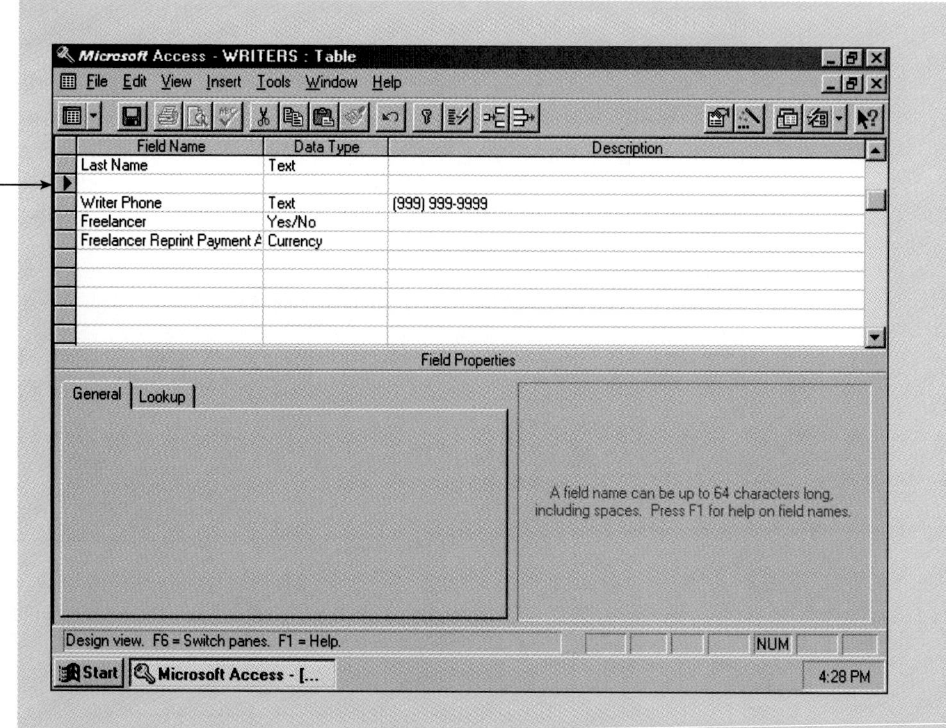

3. Type **First Name** to type in the new field name, then press the **Tab** key.

   Elena estimates that first names and initials should require a field size of 15, and therefore needs to change the field size accordingly.

4. Double-click the **50** in the Field Size box, then type **15**.

   After adding the First Name field, Elena adds the Last Contact Date field to the WRITERS table.

5. Click the right mouse button anywhere in the Freelancer row and then click **Insert Field** in the shortcut menu to insert a row between the Writer Phone and Freelancer rows.

6. Type **Last Contact Date**, press the **Tab** key, type **D** (because it is a Date/Time field), and then press the **Tab** key. See Figure 2-31.

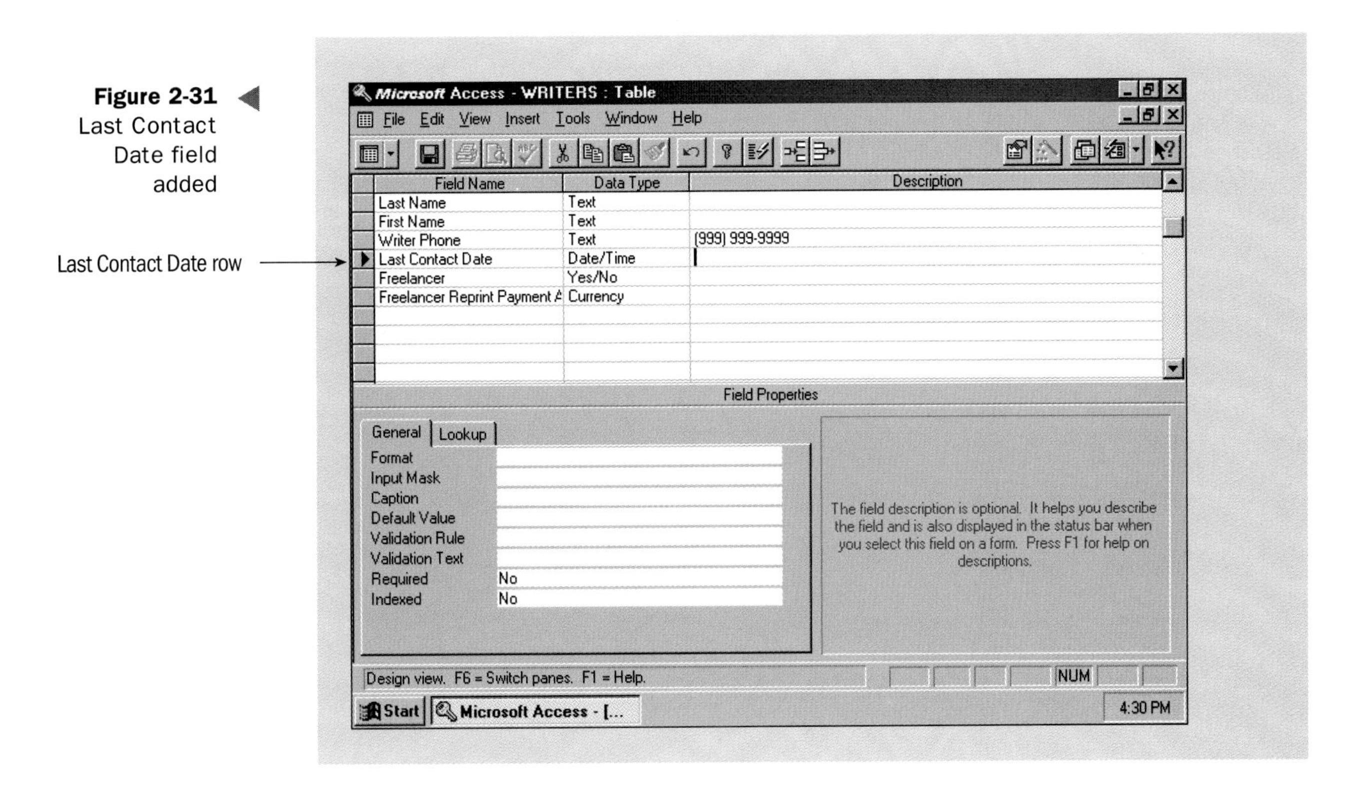

Figure 2-31 Last Contact Date field added

Elena has now modified the WRITERS table structure. Once again, however, she wants to review the appearance of the WRITERS table to see if further modifications are needed.

To review and modify a datasheet:

1. Click the **Table View** button. The Save now? dialog box opens.
2. Click the **Yes** button. Access displays the Datasheet View window. The Last Name and First Name fields appear to the right of the Writer ID field, and Last Contact Date is to the right of the Writer Phone field. The one change that needs to be made is to widen the column for Last Contact Date so the whole field name will be visible.
3. Using the procedure discussed earlier, resize the column for Last Contact Date for best fit so that the entire record is visible. See Figure 2-32.

Figure 2-32 The final Datasheet View window for the WRITERS table

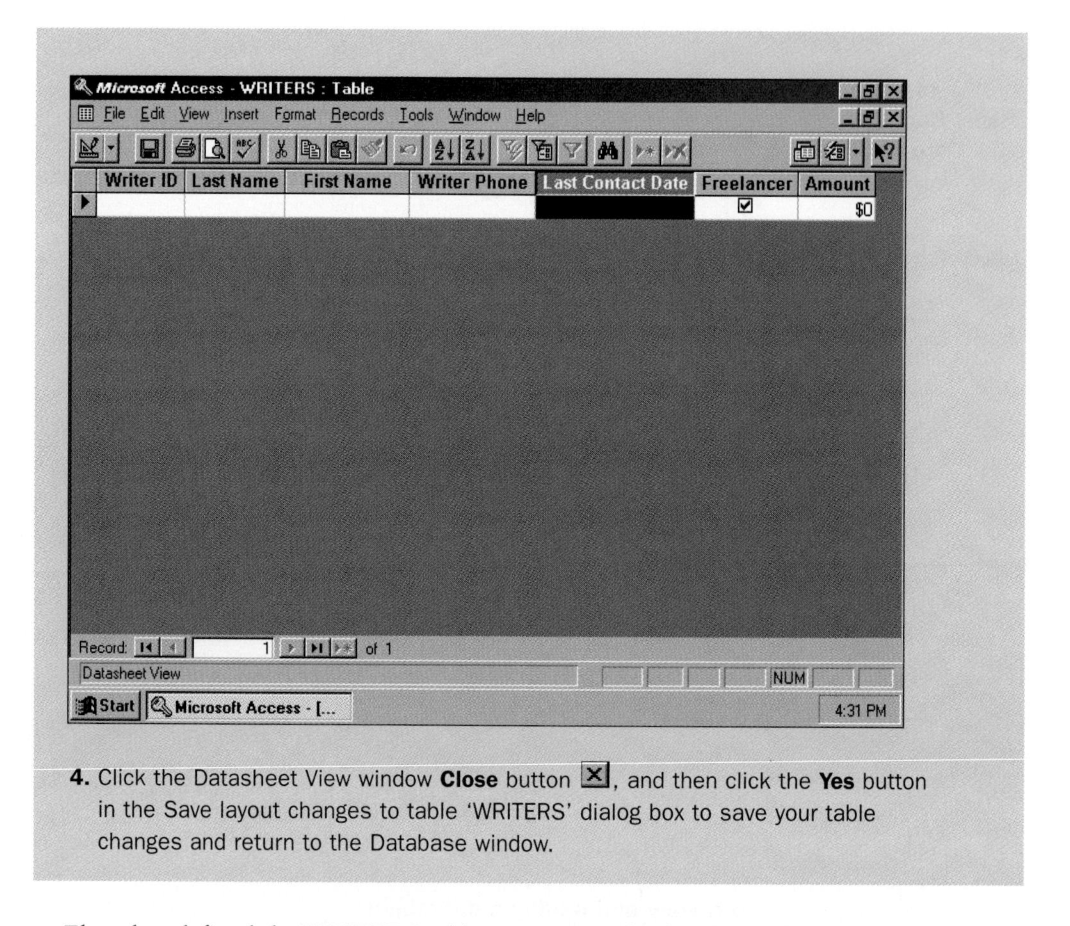

4. Click the Datasheet View window **Close** button, and then click the **Yes** button in the Save layout changes to table 'WRITERS' dialog box to save your table changes and return to the Database window.

Elena has defined the WRITERS table structure and refined the table's datasheet. In the next tutorial Elena will add data to the WRITERS table, but for now she turns her attention to creating a new table for her Issue25 database that will allow her to record reprint payments to writers easily.

Creating a Table with the Table Wizard

As discussed previously, in Access you can define a table from the Design View window—as Elena did with the WRITERS table—or you can use the Table Wizard to automate the table creation process. (In a third method, creating tables from entered data, Access creates a table structure by analyzing data as you enter it in a blank Datasheet View window. In general, it is a good idea to plan and define your table structures carefully before you enter any data.) Because her new table will contain standard fields, Elena will use the Table Wizard to create this table more quickly and efficiently than she could using the keyboard.

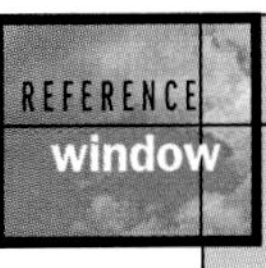

CREATING A TABLE WITH THE TABLE WIZARD

- In the Database window, click the New button. The New Table dialog box opens.
- Click Table Wizard, then click the OK button.
- Click the Business radio button or the Personal radio button to select the types of examples you want to view.
- Select a sample table from the tables list.
- In the sample table, select the fields you want for the new table, then click the Next > button.
- Enter the new table name in the text box and select the primary key option, then click the Next > button.
- If necessary, select the primary key field and specify the data type for the field, then click the Next > button.
- Select the Modify the table design radio button, then click the Finish button.
- After the Table Wizard creates the table, make any necessary modifications to the table structure in the Design View window.

Elena uses the Table Wizard now.

To use the Table Wizard:

1. Make sure you are in the Database window, then click the **New** button. The New Table dialog box opens.
2. Click **Table Wizard**, then click the **OK** button. The first Table Wizard dialog box opens. See Figure 2-33.

Figure 2-33 The first Table Wizard dialog box

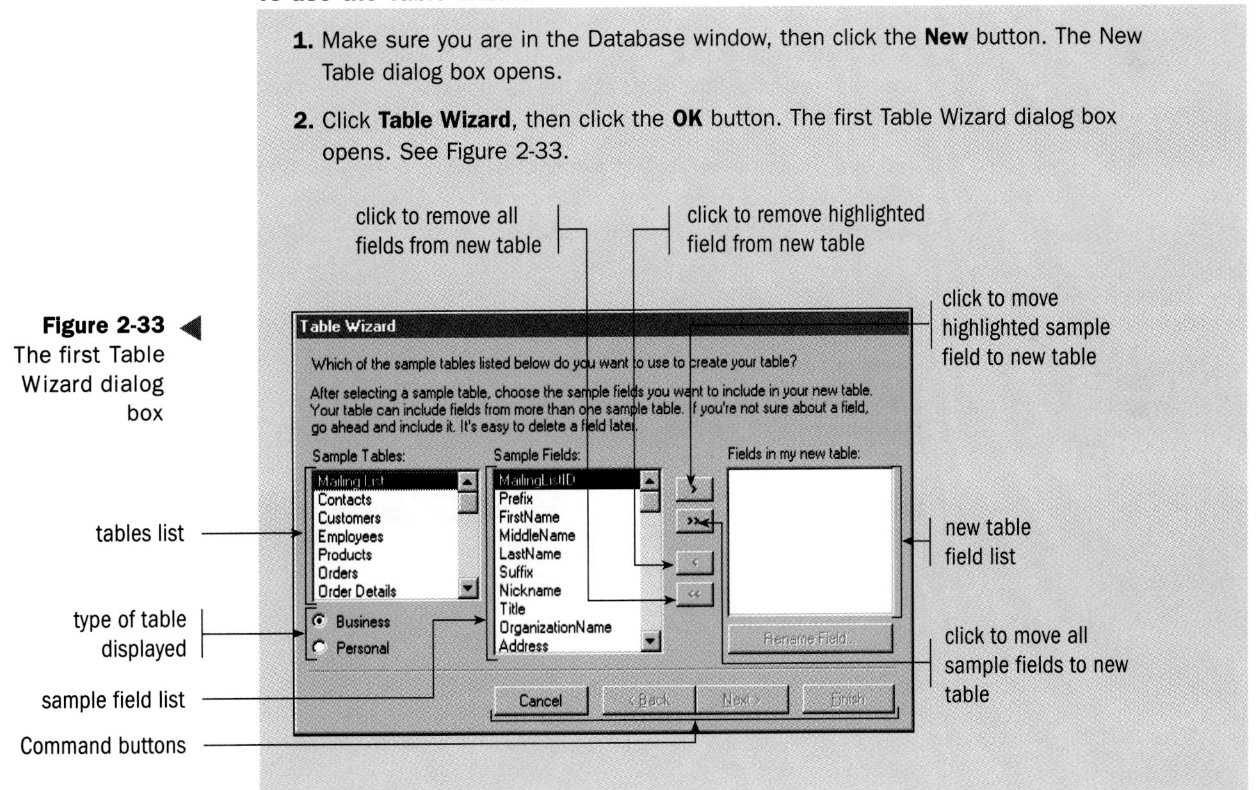

In the first Table Wizard dialog box, you select the fields for your table from sample fields in dozens of sample tables. Two types of sample tables are available: Business and Personal. Simply click the Business or Personal radio button to display the corresponding list of sample tables. Scroll through the Sample Tables list until you find an appropriate table and then select fields to add to your table from the Sample Fields list. If necessary, you can select fields from more than one table. Do not be concerned about selecting field names that exactly match the ones you need—you can change the names later. Instead, select fields that seem like they have the general properties you need for your fields. If a field's properties do not exactly match, you can change the properties later.

You select fields in the order you want them to appear in your table. If you want to select fields one at a time, highlight a field by clicking it, and then click the > button. If you want to select all the fields, click the >> button. The fields appear in the list box on the right as you select them. If you make a mistake, click the < button to remove all the fields from the list box on the right or highlight a field and click the << button to remove one field at a time.

At the bottom of each Table Wizard dialog box is a set of buttons. These buttons allow you to move quickly to other Table Wizard dialog boxes or to cancel the table creation process.

Elena scrolls through the Business sample tables and decides that the Payments sample table contains fields that she will need. She selects fields from the Payments sample table to create the WRITER PAYMENTS table.

To select fields for a new table:

1. Make sure that the Business radio button is selected, and then scroll through the Sample Tables list to find the Payments table.
2. Click **Payments** to select it. Access displays a list of fields available for the Payments table.
3. Scroll through the Sample Fields list box until it displays the CheckNumber field. Click **CheckNumber** in the Sample Fields list box and then click the **>** button. Access places CheckNumber into the list box on the right as the first field in the new table.
4. In order, select **CustomerID**, **PaymentAmount,** and **PaymentDate** for the WRITER PAYMENTS table by clicking the field name in the Sample Fields list box, scrolling as needed, and then clicking the > button. See Figure 2-34.

Figure 2-34 Fields selected for the WRITER PAYMENTS table

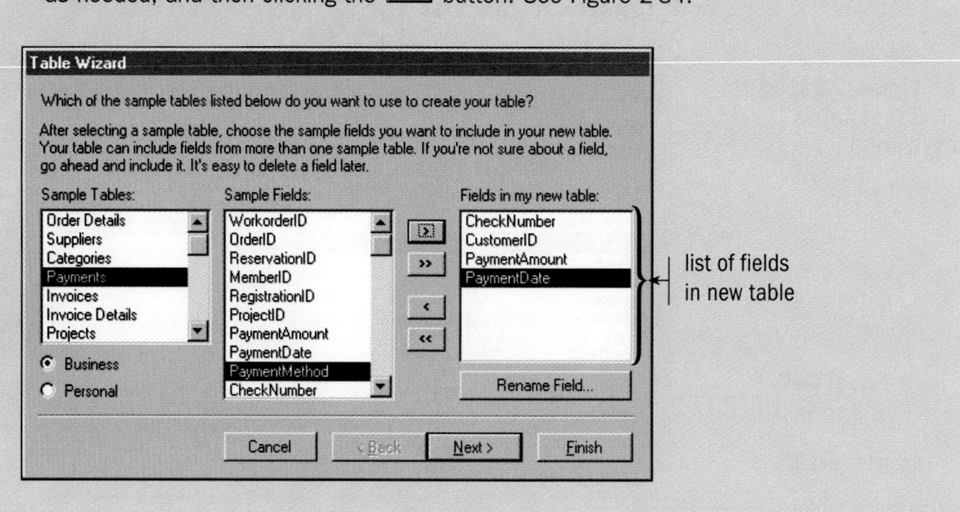

Elena has selected all the fields she needs for her table, so she continues through the remaining Table Wizard dialog boxes to finish creating the WRITER PAYMENTS table.

To finish creating a table using Table Wizard:

1. Click the Next > button. Access displays the next Table Wizard dialog box.
2. Type **WRITER PAYMENTS** in the text box and then click the radio button beside 'No, I'll set the primary key.' See Figure 2-35.

Figure 2-35 Choosing a table name and primary key option

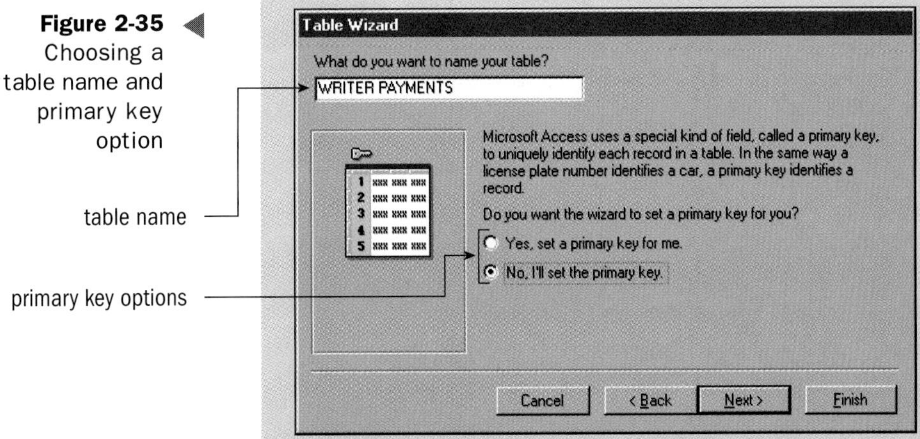

table name

primary key options

Table Wizard

What do you want to name your table?

WRITER PAYMENTS

Microsoft Access uses a special kind of field, called a primary key, to uniquely identify each record in a table. In the same way a license plate number identifies a car, a primary key identifies a record.

Do you want the wizard to set a primary key for you?

Yes, set a primary key for me.

No, I'll set the primary key.

Cancel | < Back | Next > | Finish

3. Click the Next > button. Access displays the next Table Wizard dialog box.
4. Click the **list arrow** in the text box to display the list of fields, then click **CheckNumber**. If necessary, click the middle radio button for the option that reads "Numbers I enter when I add new records." You have now selected the CheckNumber field as the primary key for the table. See Figure 2-36.

Figure 2-36 Choosing the primary key

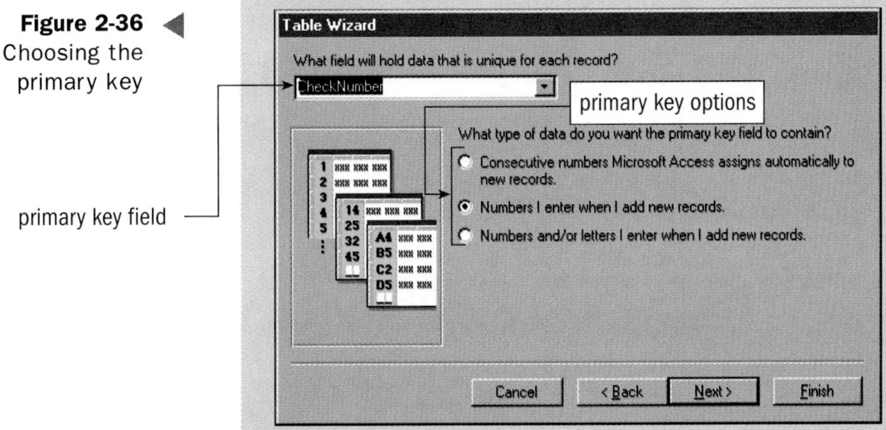

primary key field

primary key options

Table Wizard

What field will hold data that is unique for each record?

CheckNumber

What type of data do you want the primary key field to contain?

Consecutive numbers Microsoft Access assigns automatically to new records.

Numbers I enter when I add new records.

Numbers and/or letters I enter when I add new records.

Cancel | < Back | Next > | Finish

5. Click the Next > button to display the next Table Wizard dialog box.

   Since there is another table in the database (the WRITERS table), Access asks if the WRITER PAYMENTS table is related to it. Defining a relation between two tables is an important tool in building a powerful and useful database. You will investigate defining relations in a later tutorial.
6. Click the Next > button. Access displays the next Table Wizard dialog box.

   Elena needs to change the field names and field properties for the sample fields inserted into the WRITER PAYMENTS table by the Table Wizard so that they agree with her table design. To make these changes she must modify the table design. First, she closes the Table Wizard.
7. If necessary, click the first radio button to select "Modify the table design." Make sure that the box next to Display Help on working with the table at the bottom is unchecked. See Figure 2-37.

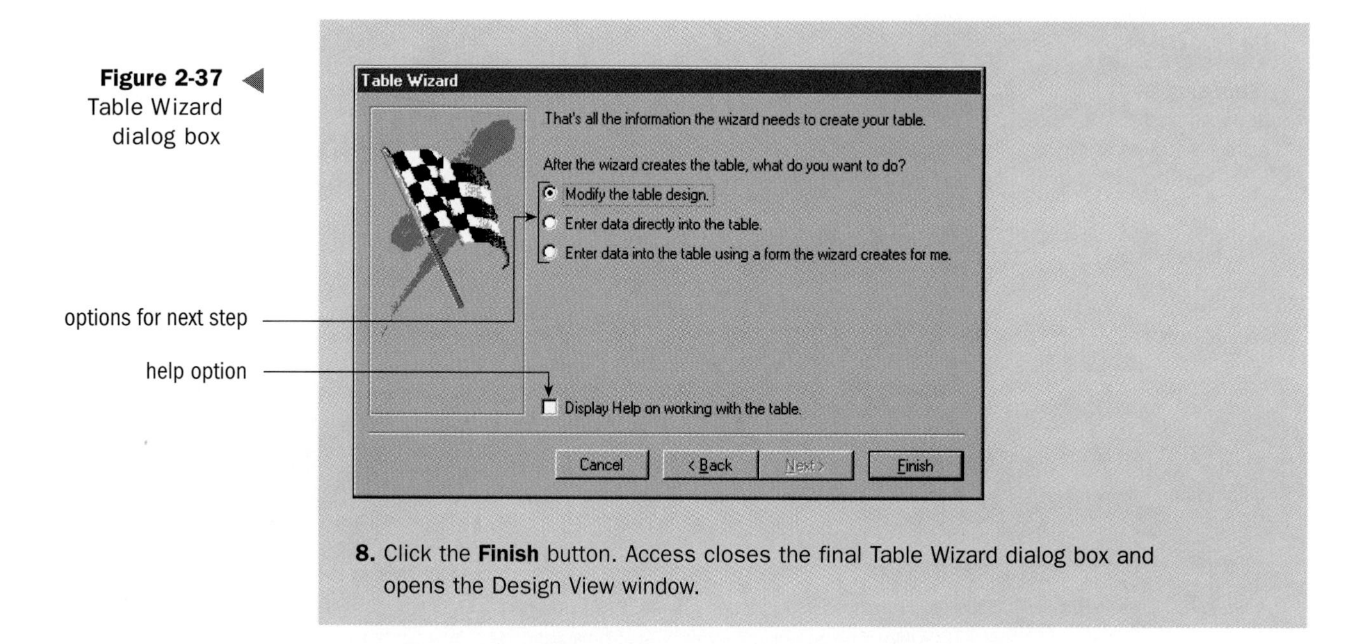

Figure 2-37 Table Wizard dialog box

8. Click the **Finish** button. Access closes the final Table Wizard dialog box and opens the Design View window.

Now that she has created a table using the Table Wizard, Elena realizes that she should view all the fields to make sure the sample field properties are accurate.

Changing the Sample Field Properties

For the first field, CheckNumber, Elena decides to change the field name to Check Number to make it more consistent with the other field names (i.e., by adding a space between the words). She also wants to add "primary key" as a description, and to set the Required property to Yes.

To change the first field's properties:

1. Double-click in the **Field Name** text box for the CheckNumber field to select the name, then type **Check Number**.
2. Click in the Description text box for the Check Number field and type **primary key**.

Elena wants to set the Required property for this field to Yes. Setting the Required property to Yes for a field means you must enter a value in the field for every record in the table. Every primary key field should have the Required property set to Yes, so that each record has a value entered for the primary key field. Fields other than a primary key should have the Required property set to Yes if it is important that a value be entered for each record. Elena decides that the Writer ID, PaymentDate, and PaymentAmount fields also must have data entered for each payment record, so she sets the Required property to Yes for each field.

For the second field, she changes the field name to Writer ID, the data type to Text, the Field Size property to 4, the Required property to Yes. She changes the names of the other fields to check Amount and check Date and sets the Required property to Yes for each of them.

To change the remaining fields' properties:

1. Click in the **Required** property text box, then click the **list arrow** that appears. Click **Yes** to choose that as the property value.
2. Double-click **CustomerID** to highlight it, then type **Writer ID** and press the **Tab** key to move to the Data Type column.

3. Type **T** to select the Text data type, then press the **Tab** key.
4. Double-click the **Field Size** property text box and type **4.**
5. Click in the **Required** property text box and then click the **list arrow** that appears. Click **Yes** to choose that as the property value.
6. Click the **Caption** property text box, press the **F2** key, then press the **Delete** key to delete the caption.
7. Double-click in the **Field Name** text box for the PaymentAmount field to select it, then type **Amount**.
8. Click in the **Required** property text box and then click the **check list arrow** that appears. Click **Yes** to choose that as the property value.
9. Double-click in the **Field Name** text box for the PaymentDate field to select it, then type **Date**.
10. Click in the **Required** property text box and then click the **check list arrow** that appears. Click **Yes** to choose that as the property value.

Elena realizes that she's almost finished creating the WRITER PAYMENTS table; she's defined all the fields, established each field's properties, and designated a primary key. Along with designating a primary key, however, Elena needs to create an index for her table. She does that next.

Creating Indexes

Access automatically creates and maintains an index for the primary key field. An **index** for a field is a list of the field values (in this case, primary key values) and their corresponding record numbers. Indexes serve several functions. First, an index allows Access to sort a table quickly in order by the indexed field. Access uses the primary key index to display the records in primary key order at all times. When you add a new record in the Datasheet View window, Access automatically inserts the new record in its correct place. Second, an index makes searching for a particular field value much more efficient. In large tables, this efficiency greatly increases the speed with which Access can locate the records you want to find. Indexes are also important when you define a relationship between two tables. Access uses the index to match records in the two related tables.

Although it may seem like a good idea to index every field in a table, indexes add to the database disk storage requirements, and they require extra time for Access to maintain them as you add, delete, and modify records. You should, therefore, create indexes only for fields that you will be using frequently for searching and sorting, or for a field you will use as a linking field when you define a relation between two tables.

Elena views the indexes that currently exist for the WRITER PAYMENTS table by using the Indexes button on the toolbar.

To display the indexes for a table:

1. Click the **Indexes** button on the toolbar. Access displays the Indexes window. See Figure 2-38.

Figure 2-38 The Indexes window

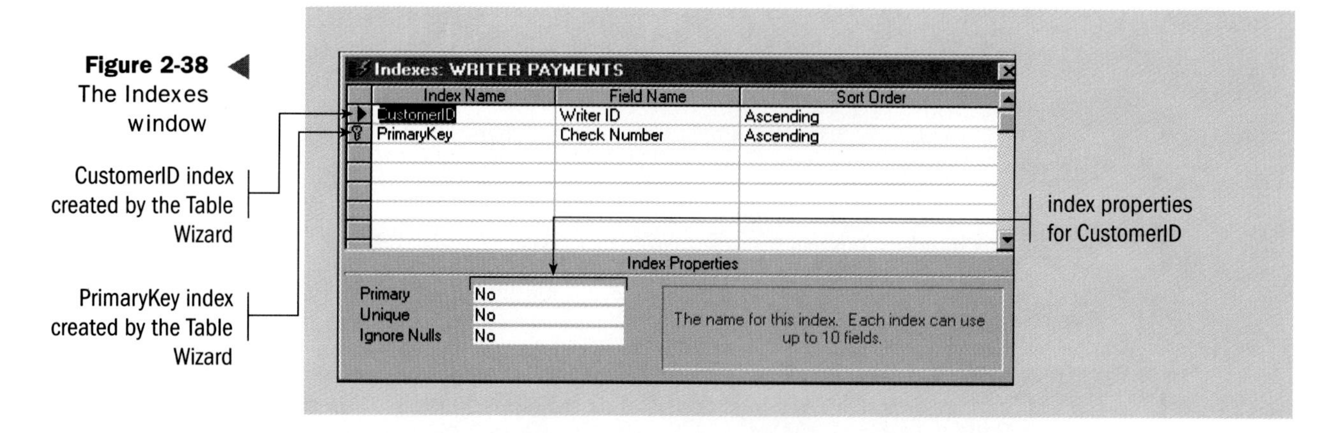

Two indexes appear in the Indexes window: one for the primary key field, Check Number, and a second for the Writer ID field. How was the Writer ID index created? Recall that you used the Table Wizard to create the WRITER PAYMENTS table. When you select Table Wizard fields, you also select all their predefined properties. The original sample table had an index associated with the CustomerID field. When you changed CustomerID to Writer ID, the index for the CustomerID field was retained.

Elena notices that the Writer ID index is still named CustomerID, and that the Check Number index is called PrimaryKey, so she decides to rename them. She does not want to create indexes for the other two fields, but if she ever needs an index for another field in the future, she can create it by using the Indexes window or the Indexed property for the field.

Elena renames the index then saves the changes and exits Access.

To rename an index:

1. If necessary, position the mouse pointer in the first row of the Indexes window under Index Name. Double-click **CustomerID** to highlight it.
2. Type **Writer ID** to rename the index.
3. Position the mouse pointer in the second row of the Indexes window under Index Name. Double-click **PrimaryKey** to highlight it.
4. Type **Check Number** to rename the index.
5. Click the Indexes window **Close** button [X] to close the Indexes window.
6. Click the Design View window **Close** button [X]. Access displays the Save changes dialog box. Click the **Yes** button to save the changes to the table design.
7. Click the Access window **Close** button [X] to exit Access.

Elena has now created two of the three tables for her Issue25 database: WRITERS and WRITER PAYMENTS. The tables will allow her to store information about the writers and record reprint payments made to them. In the next tutorial, she will add data to the WRITERS table.

Quick Check

1. What is a caption?
2. Describe three different ways to resize a datasheet column.
3. Why would you assign a default value to a field?
4. What are the steps for changing decimal places?
5. What is an input mask?
6. Describe two recommended ways to create an Access table.
7. What is an index and why is it useful?

Tutorial Assignments

Elena creates the BUSINESS ARTICLES table structure, as shown in Figure 2-39.

Figure 2-39

BUSINESS ARTICLES table	Data Type	Input/Display Field Size	Description
Article Title	Text	44	
Issue of Business Perspective	Text	8	yyyy mmm format
Length of Article	Number	4	Integer field size
Writer Name	Text	25	

Start Access, open the Issue25 database in the Tutorial folder on your Student Disk, and do the following:

1. Create a new table without using the Table Wizard. Define the fields directly in the Design View window. Use Figure 2-39 to define properties, as appropriate, for each of the four fields in the table. For the Number data type field, use the Description column in Figure 2-39 to set its Field Size property.
2. Save the table and the name it BUSINESS ARTICLES. Do not select a primary key.
3. Switch to the Datasheet View window and resize columns so that the entire field name can be read in the column heading for every field.
4. Print the datasheet for the table.
5. In the Design View window, change the field name Length of Article to Article Length. For the field Issue of Business Perspective, add the Caption property Issue. Resize the columns, if necessary, for these two fields in the Datasheet View window.
6. Print the datasheet for the table.
7. Delete the field Writer Name from the table structure.
8. Add a four-character Text field named Writer ID to the end of the table. For a description, enter "foreign key."
9. Change the data type of the field Issue of Business Perspective to Date/Time.
10. Add a three-character Text field named Type between the Article Length and Writer ID fields. For this new field, enter the description "article type" and the Default Value BUS, which represents a business article.
11. Resize columns, as necessary, in the Datasheet View window.
12. Print the datasheet for the table.

13. Switch the order of the Article Length and Type columns in the datasheet. (Use the Help Index to find help on moving columns.) Do not switch their order in the table structure. Print the datasheet for the table.

EXPLORE

14. Using Access Help for guidance, move the field named Type in the Design View window so that it follows the field named Article Title. Save and print the datasheet for the table and then close the Issue25 database.

15. (This exercise requires approximately 600KB of free disk space. You might want to use a blank formatted disk.) Use the Database Wizard to create a new database called MyMusic. Use the Music Collection model database as a template. Use the default choices in setting up the database.
    a. What tables are in the MyMusic database?
    b. What other database objects were created (forms, queries, etc.)?
    c. Describe the structure of each database table (field names, types, sizes, etc.).
    d. Open the ALBUMS table. What is the primary key field?
    e. What input mask is used for the DatePurchased field?
    f. What indexes are used in the ALBUMS table?

Case Problems

1. Walkton Daily Press Carriers Grant Sherman, circulation manager of the *Walkton Daily Press*, wants a better way to supervise the carriers who deliver the newspaper. Grant meets with Robin Witkop, one of the newspaper's computer experts, to discuss what can be done to improve his current tracking system.

After reviewing Grant's information needs, Robin offers to design a database to keep track of carriers and their outstanding balances. Grant agrees, and Robin designs a database that has two tables: CARRIERS and BILLINGS. Robin first creates the CARRIERS table structure, as shown in Figure 2-40.

Figure 2-40

CARRIERS table

Field Name	Data Type	Input/Display Field Size	Description
Carrier ID	AutoNumber		primary key; unique carrier identification number
Carrier First Name	Text	14	
Carrier Last Name	Text	15	
Carrier Phone	Text	8	
Carrier Birthdate	Date/time		

Do the following:

1. Start Access and create a new database in the Cases folder on your Student Disk. Name the database Press.
2. Create a new table using the Design View window. Use Figure 2-40 to define properties, as appropriate, for each of the five fields in the table.
3. Select Carrier ID as the table's primary key.
4. Save the table with the name CARRIERS.
5. Switch to Datasheet View and resize columns so that the entire field name can be read in the column heading for every field.
6. In Design View, change the field name Carrier Birthdate to Birthdate. Add the Caption property First Name for the field Carrier First Name. Add the Caption property Last Name for the field Carrier Last Name. Resize the columns, if necessary, for the fields in the Datasheet View window.

7. Using Access Help for guidance, move the field named Carrier Last Name in the Design View window so that it follows the field named Carrier ID. Print the datasheet for the table.
8. Save your changes and then close the datasheet.

2. Lopez Lexus Dealerships Maria and Hector Lopez own a chain of Lexus dealerships throughout Texas. They have used a computer in their business for several years to handle payroll and normal accounting functions. Their phenomenal expansion, both in the number of car locations and the number of cars handled, forces them to develop a database to track their car inventory. They design a database that has two tables: CARS and LOCATIONS. They first create the CARS table structure, as shown in Figure 2-41.

Figure 2-41

CARS table

Field Name	Data Type	Input/Display Field Size	Description
Vehicle ID	Text	5	primary key
Manufacturer	Text	13	
Model	Text	15	
Class Type	Text	2	code for type of vehicle; foreign key
Transmission Type	Text	3	code for type of transmission; foreign key
Year	Number	4	Integer field size
Cost	Currency		
Selling Price	Currency		
Location Code	Text	2	lot location within the state; foreign key

Do the following:

1. Create a new database in the Cases folder on your Student Disk. Name the database Lexus.
2. Create a new table using Design View. Using Figure 2-41 as a guide, change the sample field names and properties appropriately.
3. Select Vehicle ID as the table's primary key.
4. Switch to Datasheet View and resize columns using the Column Width dialog box. You want to see all column headings on the screen at one time.

5. Switch to Design View, then move the Location Code field so that it follows the Year field.
6. Save your changes and print the datasheet for the table.

Hector and Maria next create the LOCATIONS table structure, as shown in Figure 2-42.

Figure 2-42

LOCATIONS table

Field Name	Data Type	Input/Display Field Size	Description
Location Code	Text	2	primary key
Location Name	Text	15	
Manager Name	Text	25	

Make sure you are in Database View and do the following:

7. Create a new table without using the Table Wizard. Using Figure 2-42 as a guide, define properties as appropriate.
8. Select Location Code as the primary key and then save the table with the name LOCATIONS.

9. Switch to Datasheet View and resize columns so that the entire field name can be read in the column heading for every field.
10. Save your changes and then print the datasheet for the table.

3. Tophill University Student Employment Olivia Tyler is an administrative assistant in the financial aid department at Tophill University. She is responsible for tracking the companies that have announced part-time jobs for students. She keeps track of each available job and the person to contact at each company. Olivia had previously relied on student workers to do the paperwork, but reductions in the university budget have forced her department to reduce the number of part-time student workers. As a result, Olivia's backlog of work is increasing. After discussing the problem with her supervisor, Olivia meets with Lee Chang, a database analyst on the staff of the university computer center.

Lee questions Olivia in detail about her requirements and then develops a database to reduce her workload. Lee designs a database that has two tables: JOBS and EMPLOYERS. Lee first creates the JOBS table structure, as shown in Figure 2-43.

Figure 2-43

JOBS table

Field Name	Data Type	Input/Display Field Size	Description
Job Order	AutoNumber		primary key; unique number assigned to the job position
Employer ID	Text	4	foreign key
Job Title	Text	30	
Wage	Currency		rate per hour
Hours	Number	2	Integer field size; hours per week

Do the following:

1. Create a new database in the Cases folder on your Student Disk. Name the database Parttime.
2. Create a new table using the Table Wizard. (*Hint:* Select the Time Billed sample table listed in the Business sample tables list.) Using Figure 2-43 as a guide, change the sample field names and properties as appropriate.
3. Select Job Order as the table's primary key.
4. Save the table with the name JOBS.
5. Switch to Datasheet View and resize columns so that the entire field name can be read in the column heading for every field.
6. In the Design View window, remove the caption for the all fields, change the field name Hours to Hours/Week. Add the Caption property Job# for the field Job Order and the Caption property Wages for the field Wage. In the Datasheet View window, resize the columns, if necessary.
7. Move the field named Hours/Week in the Design View window so that it follows the field named Job Order.
8. Save your changes, print the datasheet for the table, and then close the Datasheet View window.

Lee next creates the EMPLOYERS table structure, as shown in Figure 2-44.

Figure 2-44

EMPLOYERS table

Field Name	Data Type	Input/Display Field Size	Description
Employer ID	Text	4	primary key
Employer Name	Text	40	
Contact Name	Text	25	
Contact Phone	Text	14	(999) 999-9999 format

Make sure you are in Database Window and do the following:

9. Open the database named Parttime in the Cases folder on your Student Disk.
10. Create a new table without using the Table Wizard. Using Figure 2-44 as a guide, define properties, as appropriate, for each of the four fields in the table.
11. Select Employer ID as the primary key and then save the table with the name EMPLOYERS.
12. Switch to Datasheet View and resize columns so that the entire field name can be read in the column heading for every field.
13. Save your changes and then print the datasheet for the table.

4. Rexville Business Licenses Chester Pearce works as a clerk in the town hall in Rexville, North Dakota. He has just been assigned responsibility for maintaining the licenses issued to businesses in the town. He learns that the town issues over 30 different types of licenses to over 1,500 businesses, and that most licenses must be annually renewed by March 1.

The clerk formerly responsible for the processing gave Chester the license information in two full boxes of file folders. Chester has been using a computer to help him with his other work, so he designs a database to keep track of the town's business licenses. When he completes his database design, he has two tables to create: LICENSES, which will contain data about the different types of business licenses the town issues, and BUSINESSES, which will store data about all the businesses in town. Chester first creates the LICENSES table structure, as shown in Figure 2-45.

Figure 2-45

LICENSES table

Field Name	Data Type	Input/Display Field Size	Description
License Type	Text	2	primary key
License Name	Text	60	license description
Basic Cost	Currency		cost of the license

Do the following:

1. Create a new database in the Cases folder on your Student Disk. Name the database Buslic.
2. Create a new table without using the Table Wizard. Using Figure 2-45 as a guide, define properties, as appropriate, for each of the three fields in the table.
3. Select License Type as the table's primary key.
4. Save the table with the name LICENSES.
5. Switch to Datasheet View and resize columns so that the entire field name can be read in the column heading for every field.
6. In Design View, change the field name License Name to License Description. Add the Caption property License Code for the field License Type. Change the Decimal Places property of the field Basic Cost to 0. In the Datasheet View window, resize the columns, if necessary.

7. Save your changes, print the datasheet for the table, and then close the Datasheet View window.

Chester next creates the BUSINESSES table structure, as shown in Figure 2-46.

Figure 2-46

BUSINESSES table

Field Name	Data Type	Input/Display Field Size	Description
Business ID	AutoNumber		primary key; unique number assigned to a business
Business Name	Text	35	official business name
Street Number	Number		business street number; Integer field size
Street Name	Text	25	
Proprietor	Text	25	business owner name
Phone Number	Text	8	999-9999 format

Make sure you are in Database View and do the following:

8. Create a new table without using the Table Wizard. Using Figure 2-46 as a guide, define properties, as appropriate, for each of the six fields in the table.
9. Select Business ID as the primary key and then save the table with the name BUSINESSES.
10. Switch to Datasheet View and resize columns so that the entire field name can be read in the column heading for every field.
11. In Design View, add the Caption property Street# for the field Street Number. In the Datasheet View window, resize the columns, if necessary.

12. Move the field named Phone Number in the Design View window so that it follows the field named Street Name.
13. Save your changes and then print the datasheet for the table.

TUTORIAL 3

Maintaining Database Tables

Maintaining the WRITERS Table at Vision Publishers

OBJECTIVES

In this tutorial you will:

- Add data to a table using Datasheet View
- Change table field values
- Delete records from a table
- Import a table to a database and use the Table Analyzer Wizard
- Delete and rename tables in a database
- Change datasheet properties
- Find and replace field values in a table
- Sort records in a datasheet
- Use Access's Spelling feature and Lookup Wizard
- Back up and compact a database

Vision Publishers

Vision Publishers' special projects editor Elena Sanchez meets with the production staff to set the schedule for the special 25th-anniversary issue of *Business Perspective*. After the meeting, she plans the work she needs to do with the WRITERS table. Because Elena has already created the WRITERS table structure, she is now ready to enter data.

Elena decides to begin by entering only three records into the WRITERS table. Then she will review the table structure and the datasheet and make any necessary changes. Elena will then confirm her WRITERS table with president Brian Murphy and managing editor Judith Rossi before entering the remaining records. Finally, Elena will examine the WRITERS table records and correct any errors she finds. Elena takes her written plan, as shown in Figure 3-1, to her computer and begins work.

Figure 3-1 Elena's task list for the WRITERS table

WRITERS table task list:
- Enter complete information for three writers
- Change the table structure and datasheet, if necessary
- Confirm the WRITERS table data
- Enter complete information for remaining writers
- Correct errors

SESSION 3.1

In this session, you will learn to update an Access table by adding records, changing field values, and deleting records. You will also learn to navigate through a table using the mouse, import a table, delete and rename a table, and change datasheet properties.

Adding Records

Elena created the WRITERS table by defining the table's fields and the fields' properties. Before the Issue25 database can provide useful information, however, Elena must **update**, or **maintain**, the database. That is, she must add, change, and delete records in the database tables to keep them current and accurate. When you initially create a database, adding records to the tables is the first step in updating a database. You also add records to an existing database whenever you encounter new occurrences of the entities represented by the tables. For example, an editorial assistant adds a record to the MAGAZINE ARTICLES table in the Vision database for each new article that is published.

Using the Datasheet to Enter Data

In Tutorial 1 you used Datasheet View to look at a table's records. You can also use Datasheet View to update a table. As her first step in updating the Issue25 database, Elena adds the three records to the WRITERS table shown in Figure 3-2. She uses the WRITERS table datasheet to enter these records.

	Writer ID	Last Name	First Name	Writer Phone	Last Contact Date	Freelancer	Amount
Record 1:	N425	Nilsson	Tonya	(909) 702-4082	7/9/97	No	$0
Record 2:	S260	Seeger	Wilhelm	(706) 423-0932	12/24/93	Yes	$350
Record 3:	S365	Sterns	Steven B.	(710) 669-6518	12/13/84	No	$0

Figure 3-2 The first three WRITERS table records

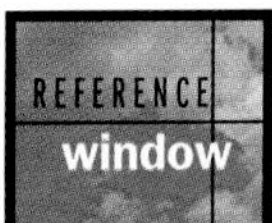

ADDING A RECORD TO A TABLE

- Open the table in Datasheet View.
- If necessary, click the New Record button to position the insertion point in the first field of a new record.
- Type the value for the first field, then press the Tab key. The insertion point moves to the next field.
- Enter the values for the remaining fields in the same way.
- When you press the Tab key after entering the value in the last field, Access saves the record.

To add records to a table's datasheet:

1. If necessary, place your Student Disk in the appropriate drive, start Access, double-click **Issue25** to open the database, maximize the Database window, click **WRITERS**, and then click the **Open** button. The Datasheet View window opens, and the insertion point is at the beginning of the Writer ID field for the first record.

2. Type **N425**, which is the first record's Writer ID field value, and press the **Tab** key. Each time you press the Tab key, the insertion point moves to the right, to the next field in the record.

   Notice that two new symbols appear in the record selectors for rows one and two. The pencil symbol in the first row indicates that you have made changes to the current record and have not yet saved the changes. The asterisk symbol in the second row shows you the next available row for entering a new record.

3. Continue to enter the field values for all three records shown in Figure 3-2. For the Writer Phone field values, type the numbers only. Access automatically supplies the parentheses, spaces, and hyphens from the field's input mask. Notice that the Freelancer field contains a check box. The box contains a check indicating a Yes value—the default value for the Freelancer field. If the value for the Freelancer field is Yes, simply press the Tab key to accept the displayed value and move to the next field. If the value for the Freelancer field is No, place the mouse pointer on the check box and click the left mouse button to remove the check mark. Note that, because the Amount field is defined as a currency field, a dollar sign ($) already appears in the field; you simply enter the numbers. When you've entered the value for the Amount field, press the Tab key to move to the start of the next record. Do not, however, press the Tab key after typing the Amount field for the third record. After entering the three records, your screen should look like Figure 3-3.

Figure 3-3 The WRITERS table datasheet with the first three records entered

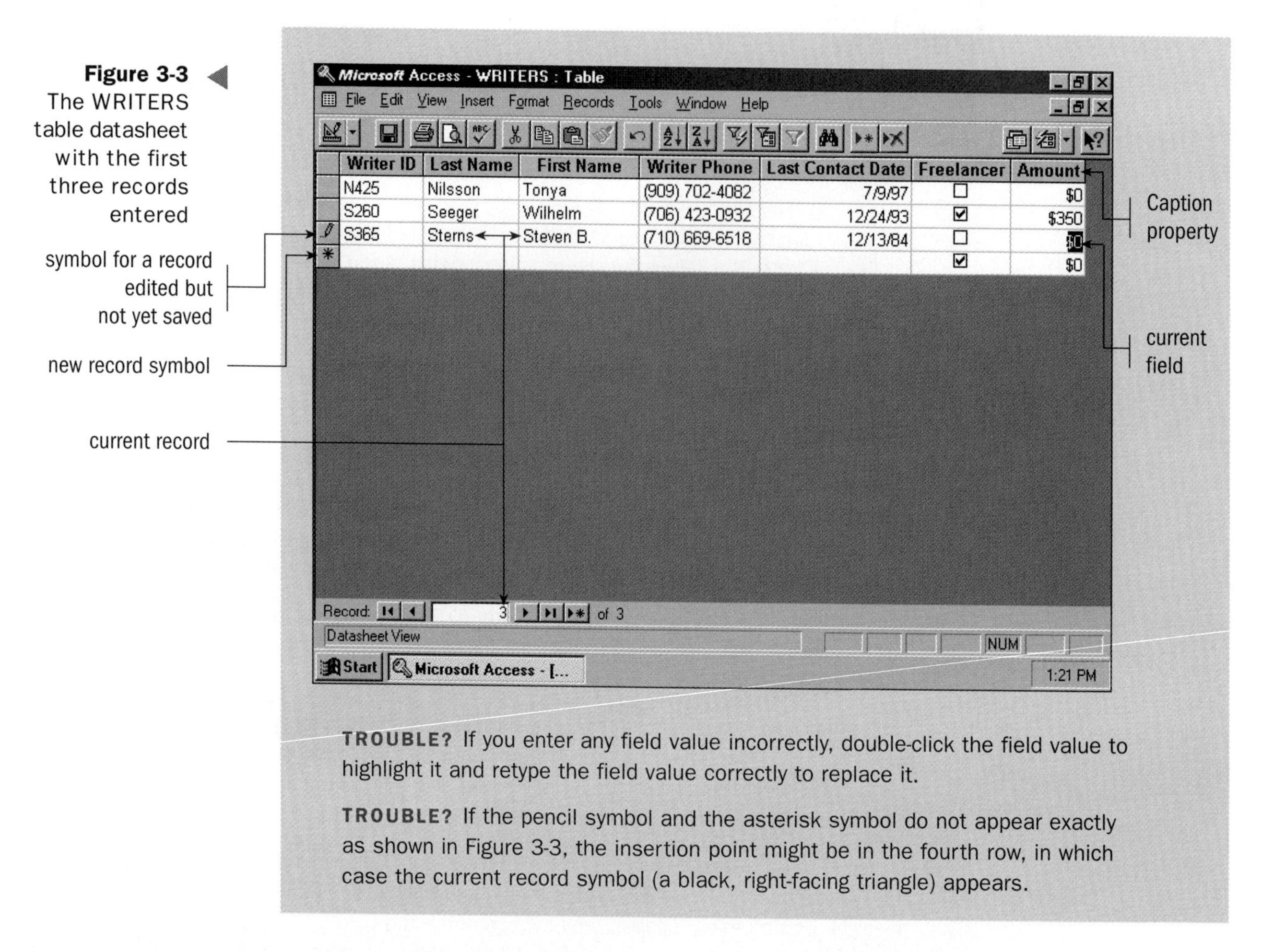

TROUBLE? If you enter any field value incorrectly, double-click the field value to highlight it and retype the field value correctly to replace it.

TROUBLE? If the pencil symbol and the asterisk symbol do not appear exactly as shown in Figure 3-3, the insertion point might be in the fourth row, in which case the current record symbol (a black, right-facing triangle) appears.

Elena has completed her first task, so she continues with the next task on her list: reviewing the table structure and datasheet for any problems.

Changing Records

As Elena looks over the first three records, she realizes that the information she entered is from the preliminary list of writers for the special issue. Upon comparing the preliminary list with the final list that she received at her last meeting with Brian and Judith, Elena notices some differences. First, Tonya Nilsson, who is one of the three writers she just added to the WRITERS table, is a freelancer and will be paid $450 for each of her two reprinted articles. Elena entered Nilsson as a staff writer, so she needs to change both the Freelancer and Amount fields for Nilsson. Also, because Steven B. Sterns does not appear in the final list of writers, Elena needs to delete his record from her WRITERS table.

Before Elena makes any of these changes, however, she decides that she first needs to learn how to select and change a specific record quickly. She investigates different techniques for using the mouse to move through a datasheet.

Using the Mouse to Navigate in a Table

You are probably already familiar with how to use the mouse to move through fields and records in a datasheet or to make changes to field values. The specific mouse techniques you use for movement, selection, and placement are listed in Figure 3-4.

Figure 3-4 ◀ Using the Mouse to navigate in a table

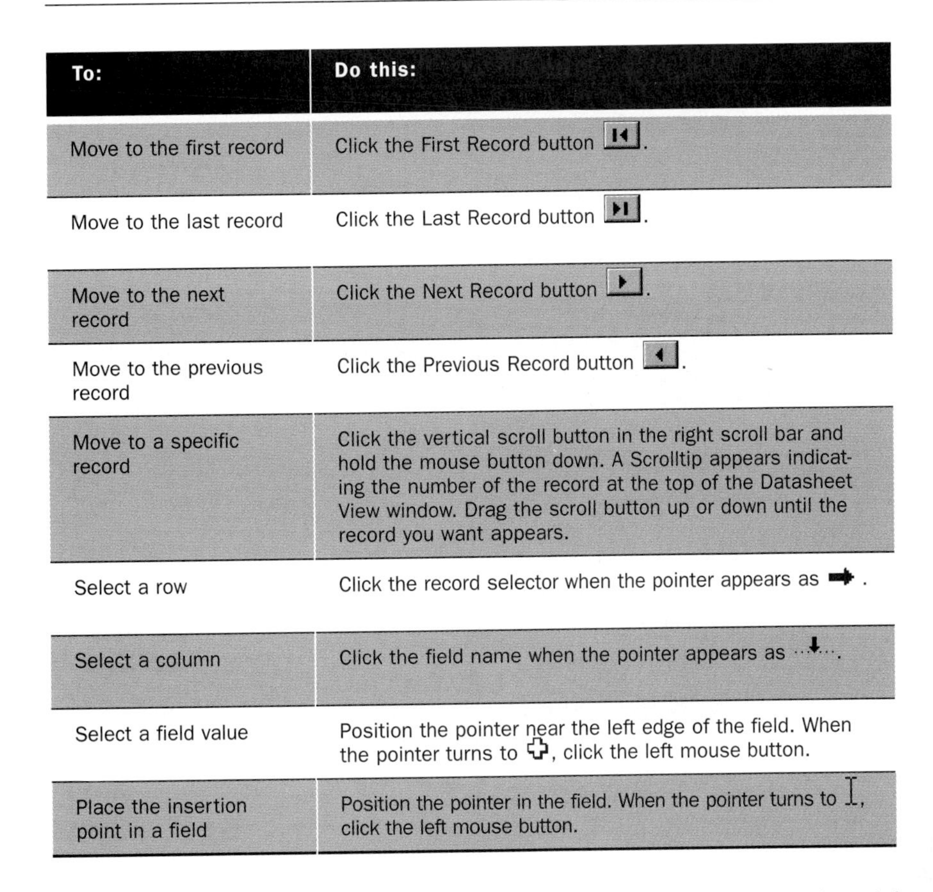

To:	Do this:
Move to the first record	Click the First Record button.
Move to the last record	Click the Last Record button.
Move to the next record	Click the Next Record button.
Move to the previous record	Click the Previous Record button.
Move to a specific record	Click the vertical scroll button in the right scroll bar and hold the mouse button down. A Scrolltip appears indicating the number of the record at the top of the Datasheet View window. Drag the scroll button up or down until the record you want appears.
Select a row	Click the record selector when the pointer appears as ➡.
Select a column	Click the field name when the pointer appears as ⬇.
Select a field value	Position the pointer near the left edge of the field. When the pointer turns to ✚, click the left mouse button.
Place the insertion point in a field	Position the pointer in the field. When the pointer turns to I, click the left mouse button.

Now that Elena is familiar with using the mouse for moving to and modifying records, she is ready to change the field values for Tonya Nilsson in the WRITERS table.

Changing Field Values

Elena's task is to change the field values for Freelancer and for Amount to Yes and $450, respectively.

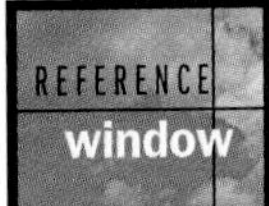

CHANGING A FIELD VALUE IN A RECORD

- Open the table that contains the record to be changed in Datasheet View.
- For a Yes/No field displayed as a check box, click the check box to change the value.
- For any other field, double-click the field value and enter the new value.
- Press the Tab key to move to the next field. Access saves the new value.

To change field values in a datasheet:

1. Click the **check box** in the Freelancer column for the first record, press the **Tab** key, and then type **450**. Both field values in the first record are now correctly changed. See Figure 3-5.

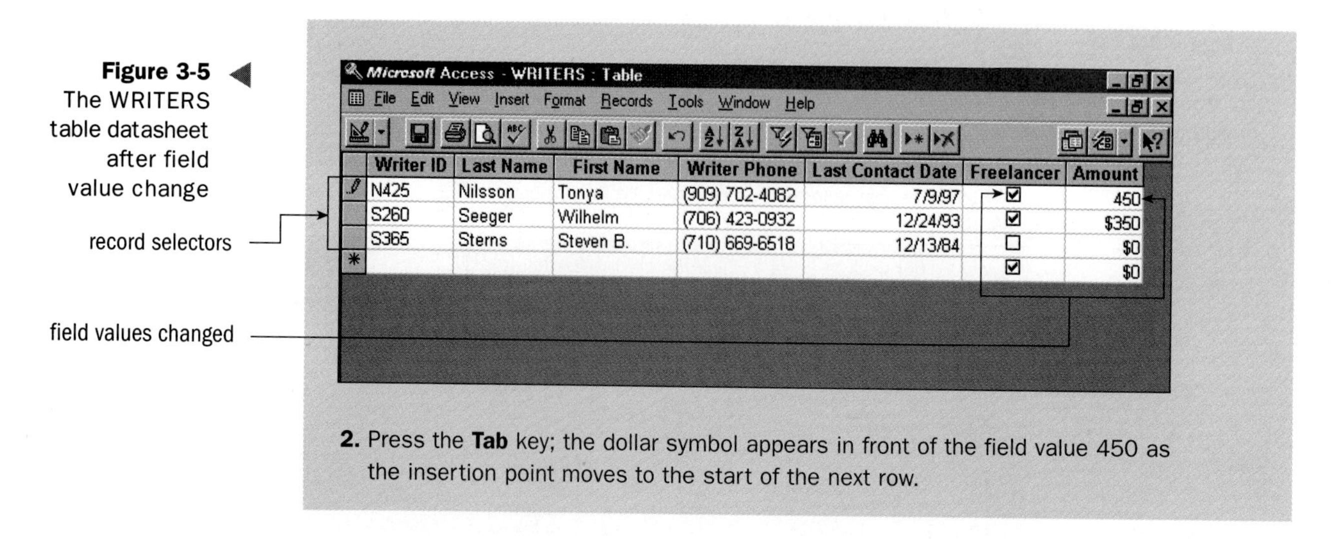

Figure 3-5 The WRITERS table datasheet after field value change

2. Press the **Tab** key; the dollar symbol appears in front of the field value 450 as the insertion point moves to the start of the next row.

Access saves the changes you make to the current record whenever you move to a different record. Your data is kept current as you make changes, and you do not need to worry about losing your changes if a hardware or software problem occurs.

Deleting Records

Elena is now ready to delete Steven B. Sterns from her WRITERS table. After she makes this last change to her initial table, she will print her work and have Brian and Judith confirm the table's structure.

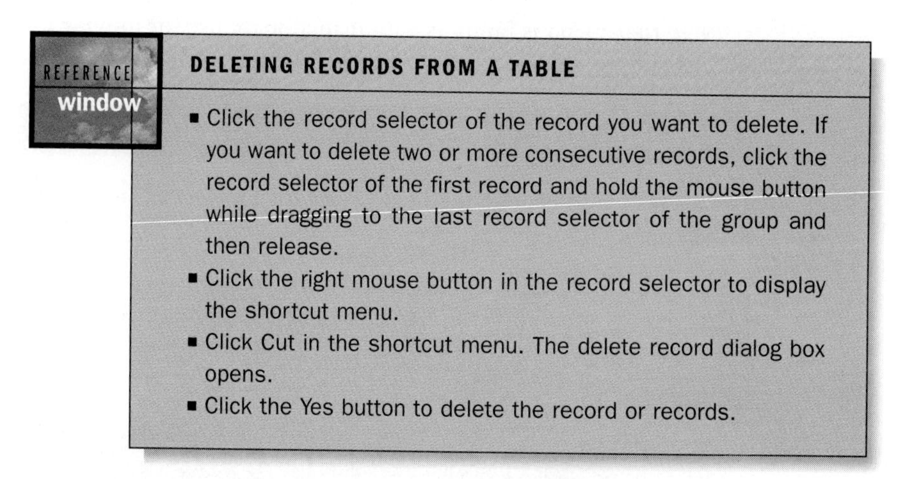
REFERENCE window

DELETING RECORDS FROM A TABLE

- Click the record selector of the record you want to delete. If you want to delete two or more consecutive records, click the record selector of the first record and hold the mouse button while dragging to the last record selector of the group and then release.
- Click the right mouse button in the record selector to display the shortcut menu.
- Click Cut in the shortcut menu. The delete record dialog box opens.
- Click the Yes button to delete the record or records.

Elena deletes the third record from the WRITERS datasheet.

To delete a datasheet record:

1. Click the record selector for the third record. Access highlights the entire third row.
2. Click the right mouse button in the record selector for the third record. Access displays the shortcut menu.
3. Click **Cut** in the shortcut menu. Access displays the delete record dialog box. See Figure 3-6. The current record indicator is positioned in the third row's record selector, and all field values (except default values) in the third record are deleted.

   TROUBLE? If you selected the wrong record for deletion, click the No button. Access ends the deletion process and redisplays the deleted record. Repeat Steps 1–3 to delete the third record.

Figure 3-6 The delete record dialog box

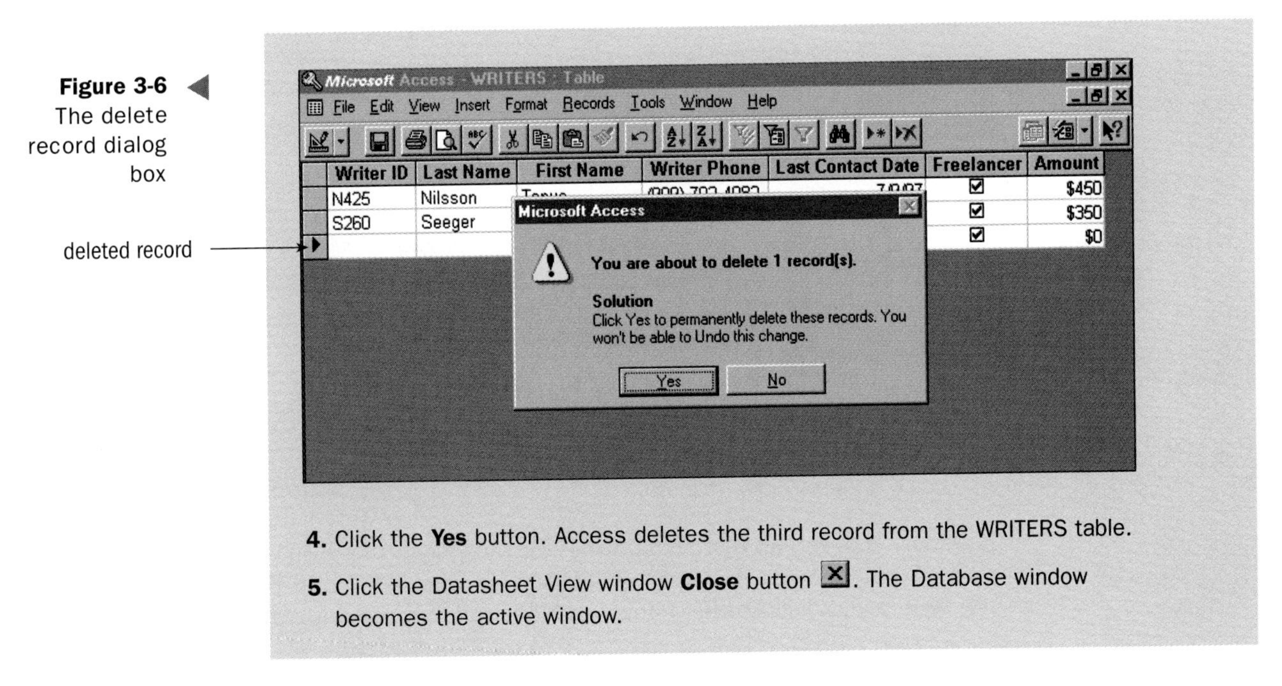

4. Click the **Yes** button. Access deletes the third record from the WRITERS table.
5. Click the Datasheet View window **Close** button. The Database window becomes the active window.

Elena prints the datasheet so that Judith and Brian can confirm the structure of her WRITERS table.

Importing Data

When Elena meets with Brian and Judith, she learns that Judith is also maintaining a table in the company's main database (the Vision database), containing information about the writers selected for the 25th-anniversary issue. Judith and Elena realize that Elena does not need to enter all that information in her Issue25 database. She can simply import the data from Judith's database to Elena's database. This will not only save time but will also reduce the possibility of introducing typing errors.

Importing data involves copying data from a text file, spreadsheet, or database table into a new Access table. You can import objects from an existing Access database, as well as data from Access tables. You can also import from spreadsheets, such as Excel and Lotus 1-2-3; from other database management systems, such as Paradox, dBASE, and FoxPro; and from certain text files. Importing existing data, as shown in Figure 3-7, saves you time and eliminates potential data-entry errors.

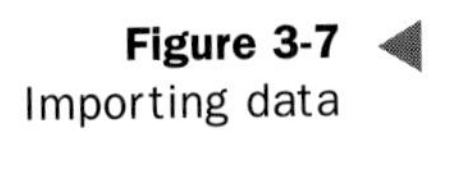
Figure 3-7 Importing data

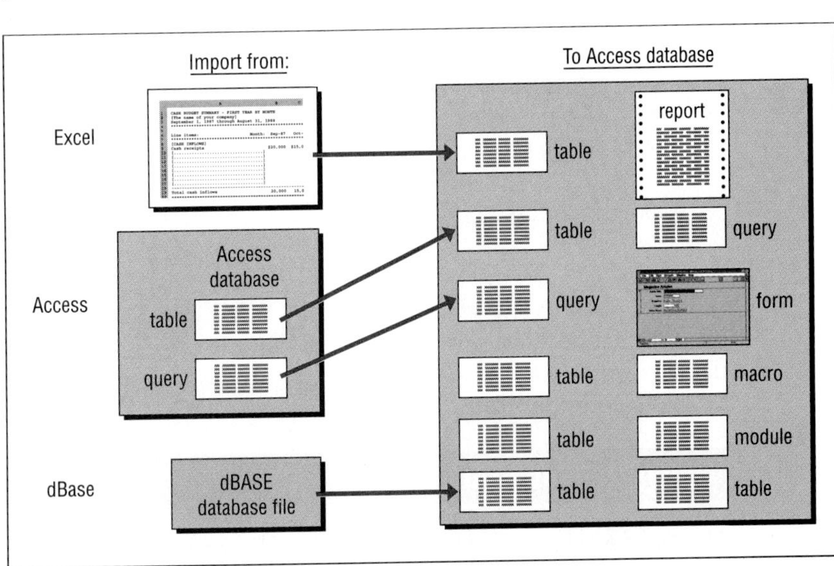

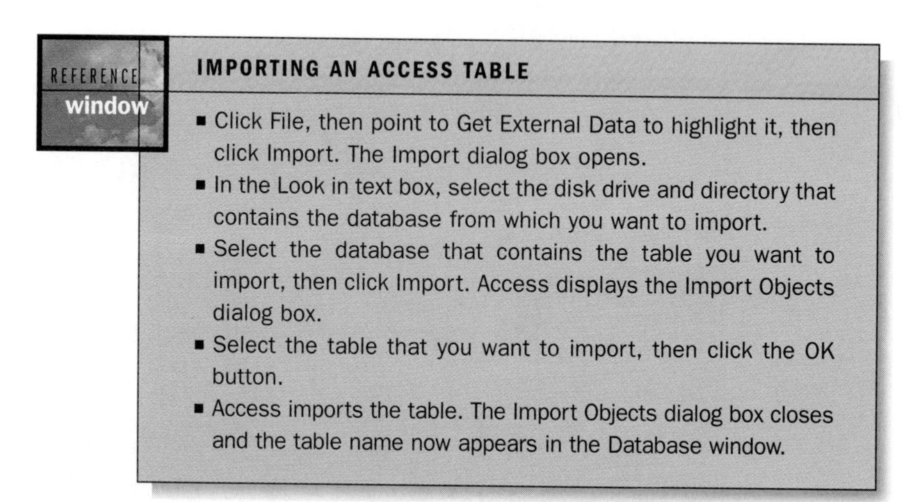
REFERENCE window

IMPORTING AN ACCESS TABLE

- Click File, then point to Get External Data to highlight it, then click Import. The Import dialog box opens.
- In the Look in text box, select the disk drive and directory that contains the database from which you want to import.
- Select the database that contains the table you want to import, then click Import. Access displays the Import Objects dialog box.
- Select the table that you want to import, then click the OK button.
- Access imports the table. The Import Objects dialog box closes and the table name now appears in the Database window.

After Judith verifies that her table has the same fields that Elena needs for her WRITERS table, Elena is ready to import Judith's table (the WRITERS-JR table) to the Issue25 database. Judith includes her initials on all her table names for easy identification.

To import an Access table:

1. Make sure that the Issue25 database is open and the active Database window is maximized, then click **File,** point to **Get External Data** to highlight it, then click **Import**. Access displays the Import dialog box.
2. If necessary, use the Look in text box to select the Tutorial folder on the drive that contains your Student Disk. Click **Vision** in the file list. Click **Import** to display the Import Objects dialog box. See Figure 3-8.

Figure 3-8 The Import Objects dialog box

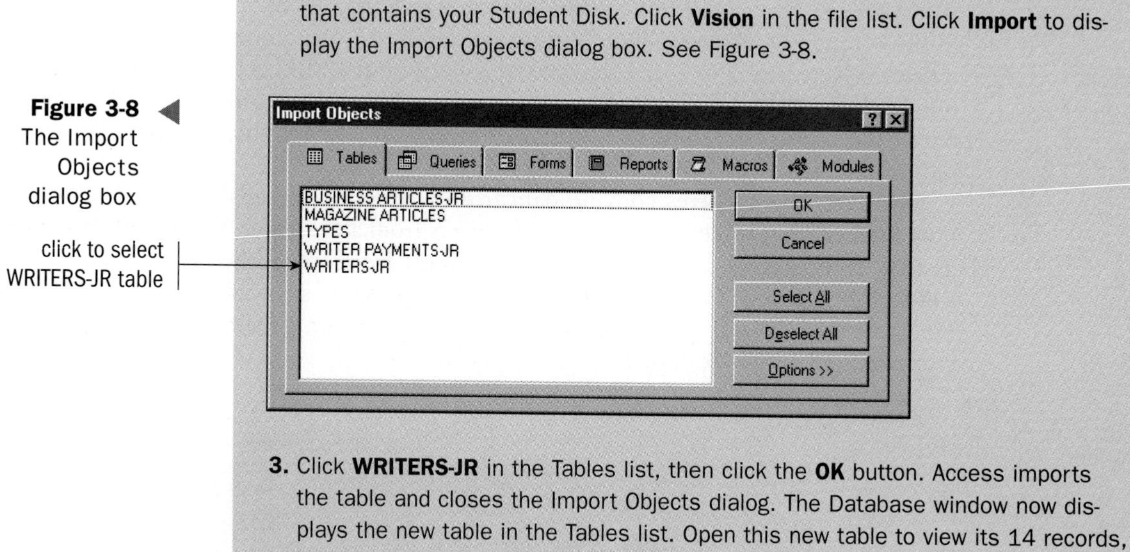

3. Click **WRITERS-JR** in the Tables list, then click the **OK** button. Access imports the table and closes the Import Objects dialog. The Database window now displays the new table in the Tables list. Open this new table to view its 14 records, but do not update any of them. When you are done viewing the records, close the table by clicking the Datasheet View window **Close** button.

Elena quickly views the records of the WRITERS-JR table to confirm that they contain the information she needs. She believes that the table is correctly designed, since it is identical in design to her WRITERS table, but to be sure, she uses the Table Analyzer Wizard to help identify problems.

Using the Table Analyzer Wizard

The **Table Analyzer Wizard** analyzes the table for repeated data and, if necessary, suggests ways to split a table into two or more tables to eliminate data redundancy.

USING THE TABLE ANALYZER WIZARD

- In the Database window, click the Analyze button.
- Click the Next > button twice to move past the first two informational windows.
- Click to select the table to be analyzed, then click the Next > button.
- Click the Yes button to ask the wizard to make suggestions for splitting the table, then click the Next > button. The Table Analyzer Wizard analyzes the table and makes any necessary suggestions for splitting the table.

If the Table Analyzer Wizard suggests splitting the table, do the following:

- Review the suggested changes. Click the Cancel button to ignore the changes or move fields to different tables if desired, name the newly created tables, and then click the Next > button.
- If you desire, specify primary key fields for the tables, then click the Next > button.
- If you want Access to create a query that has the same structure as the original table, select that option, then click the Finish button. Access creates any new tables and the new query. The original table is renamed with its original name followed by the word OLD. Access then opens the new query in Datasheet View. Click the OK button in the dialog box to view the tables or query.

If the Table Analyzer Wizard recommends not splitting the table, click the Cancel button in the dialog box. Access returns to the Database window.

Elena uses the Table Analyzer Wizard to check the design of the WRITERS-JR table.

To use the Table Analyzer Wizard to analyze a table:

1. If necessary, click the **Tables** tab to view the Tables list in the Database window.
2. Click the **Analyze** button on the toolbar. Access starts the Table Analyzer Wizard and displays the first Table Analyzer Wizard dialog box. This dialog box contains examples of the kinds of problems the Table Analyzer Wizard can identify and correct.
3. Click the Next > button to display the next Table Analyzer Wizard dialog box. This dialog box describes how the Table Analyzer Wizard will correct any problems it identifies.
4. Click the Next > button to display the next Table Analyzer Wizard dialog box. In this dialog box, you select the table you want to analyze. See Figure 3-9.

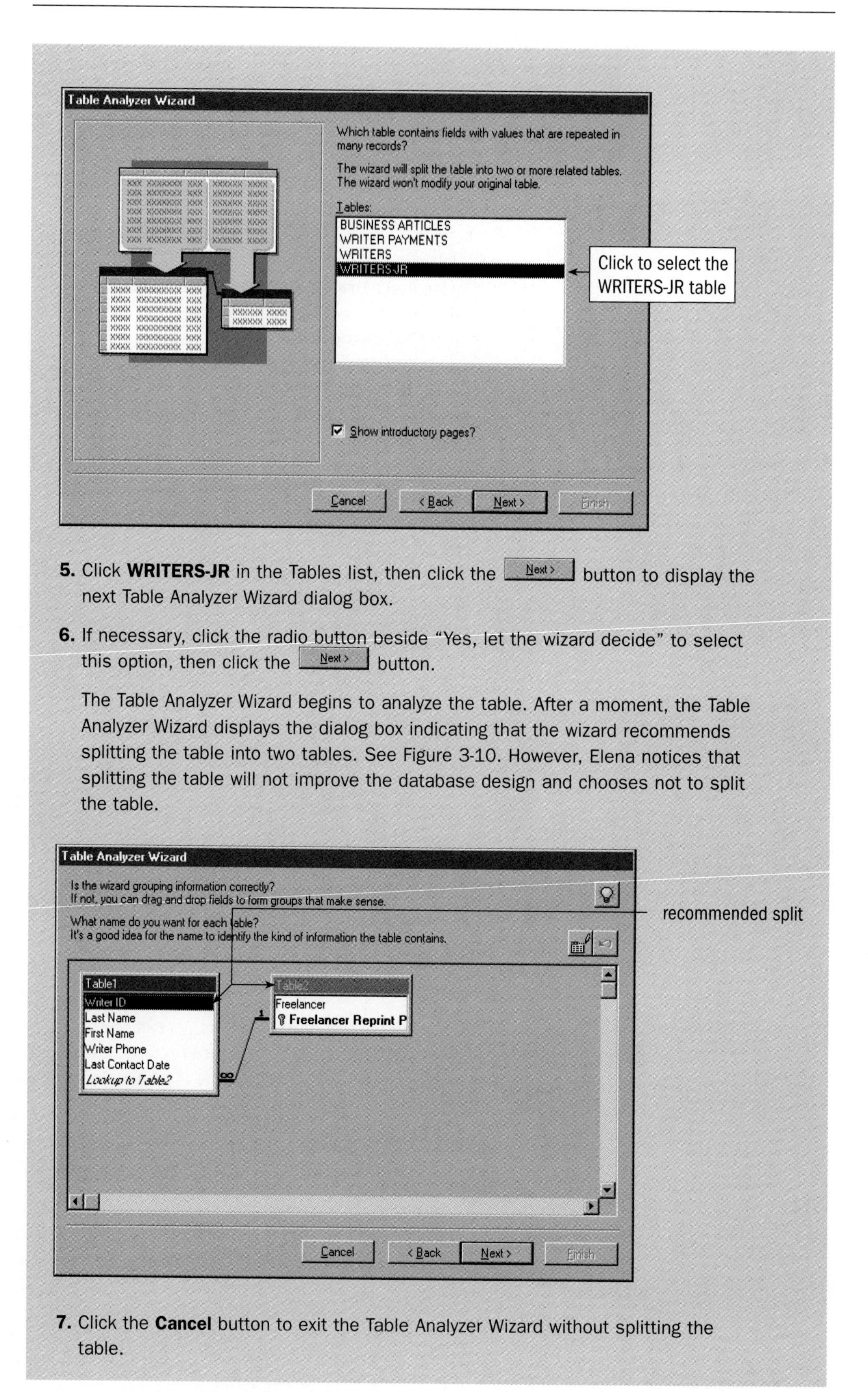

Figure 3-9 Choosing the table to analyze

5. Click **WRITERS-JR** in the Tables list, then click the Next > button to display the next Table Analyzer Wizard dialog box.
6. If necessary, click the radio button beside "Yes, let the wizard decide" to select this option, then click the Next > button.

   The Table Analyzer Wizard begins to analyze the table. After a moment, the Table Analyzer Wizard displays the dialog box indicating that the wizard recommends splitting the table into two tables. See Figure 3-10. However, Elena notices that splitting the table will not improve the database design and chooses not to split the table.

Figure 3-10 The Table Analyzer Wizard recommends splitting the table

7. Click the **Cancel** button to exit the Table Analyzer Wizard without splitting the table.

Deleting a Table

Because the WRITERS-JR table contains the information she needs, and because it appears to be designed correctly, Elena no longer needs the WRITERS table that she initially created. Elena deletes this table from her database to avoid any future confusion.

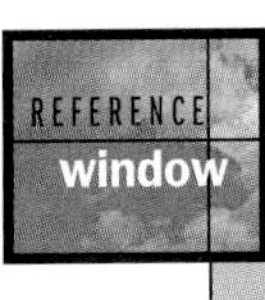

DELETING A TABLE

- In the Database window, click the table you want to delete.
- Click the right mouse button to open the shortcut menu.
- Click Delete. The Delete Table dialog box opens.
- Click the Yes button. The Delete Table dialog box closes, and Access deletes the table. When the active Database window appears, it does not list the table you just deleted.

To delete the WRITERS table:

1. In the Tables list of the Database window, click the **WRITERS** table to select it.
2. Click the right mouse button to display the shortcut menu. Click **Delete**. Access displays a dialog box that asks, "Do you want to delete the table WRITERS?".
3. Click the **Yes** button. The dialog box closes, and the WRITERS table no longer appears in the Tables list.

Renaming a Table

Elena decides that the name for the current writers table, WRITERS-JR, is no longer appropriate. This table will no longer be used only by Judith, but by others at Vision Publishers as well. Because she's already deleted her initial table, Elena is free to rename the WRITERS-JR table WRITERS.

To rename a table:

1. Move the pointer to the WRITERS-JR table in the Tables list and click **WRITERS-JR** with the right mouse button. Access displays the shortcut menu. See Figure 3-11.

Figure 3-11 The shortcut menu for a table

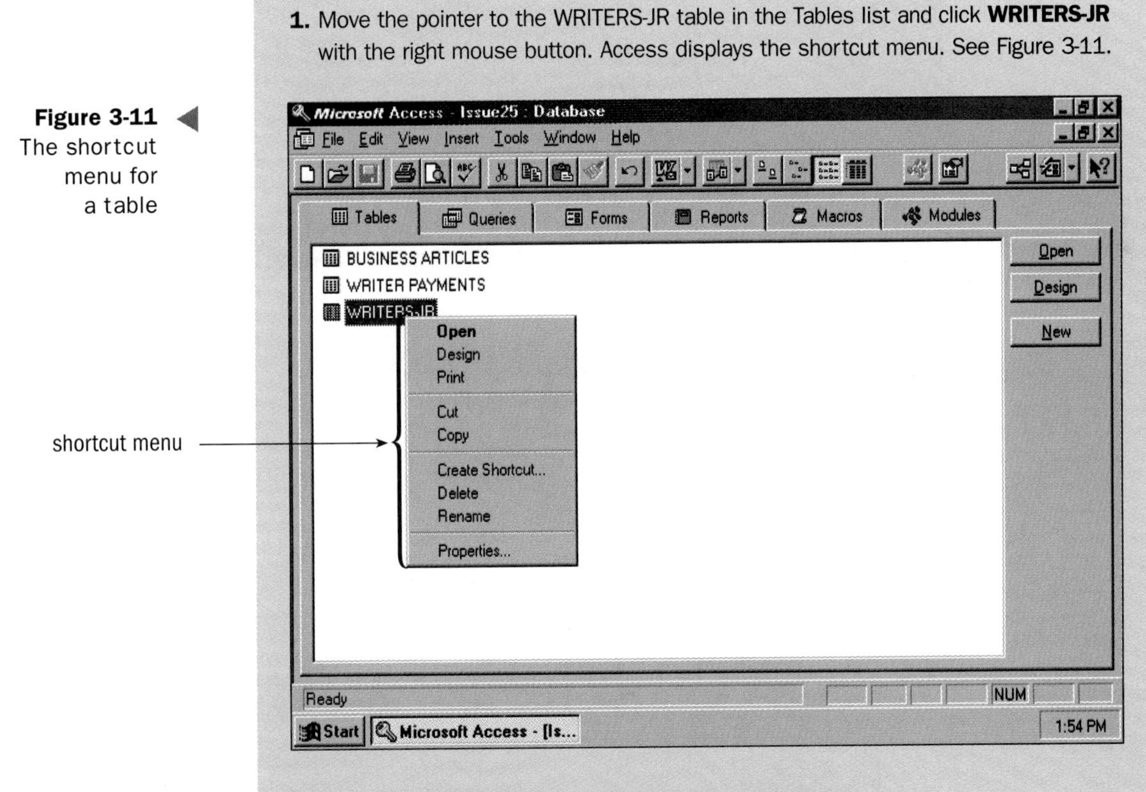

2. Click **Rename**. The name WRITERS-JR is highlighted.
3. Type **WRITERS** in the text box, then press the **Enter** key. The new name, WRITERS, is now displayed in the Tables list.

Although Elena already looked briefly at the imported table records, she now needs to review them more closely for any possible errors. She begins by opening the datasheet. You already know how to open a table's datasheet from the Database window by clicking the table name and then clicking the Open button. You can also open a datasheet by double-clicking the table name. Because this second method is faster, we'll use it from now on.

To open the WRITERS table datasheet:

1. Double-click **WRITERS** in the Tables list. The Datasheet window opens, and the records appear arranged in order by Writer ID, which is the primary key. See Figure 3-12.

Figure 3-12 The WRITERS datasheet with newly imported records

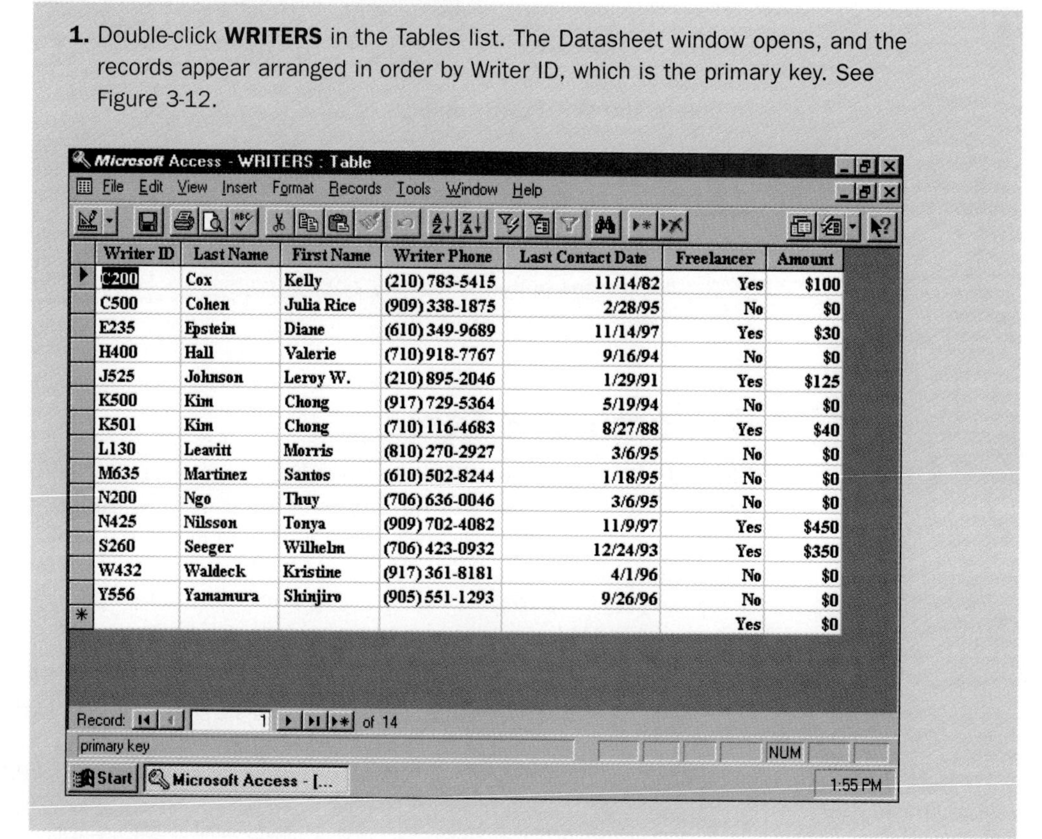

Writer ID	Last Name	First Name	Writer Phone	Last Contact Date	Freelancer	Amount
C200	Cox	Kelly	(210) 783-5415	11/14/82	Yes	$100
C500	Cohen	Julia Rice	(909) 338-1875	2/28/95	No	$0
E235	Epstein	Diane	(610) 349-9689	11/14/97	Yes	$30
H400	Hall	Valerie	(710) 918-7767	9/16/94	No	$0
J525	Johnson	Leroy W.	(210) 895-2046	1/29/91	Yes	$125
K500	Kim	Chong	(917) 729-5364	5/19/94	No	$0
K501	Kim	Chong	(710) 116-4683	8/27/88	Yes	$40
L130	Leavitt	Morris	(810) 270-2927	3/6/95	No	$0
M635	Martinez	Santos	(610) 502-8244	1/18/95	No	$0
N200	Ngo	Thuy	(706) 636-0046	3/6/95	No	$0
N425	Nilsson	Tonya	(909) 702-4082	11/9/97	Yes	$450
S260	Seeger	Wilhelm	(706) 423-0932	12/24/93	Yes	$350
W432	Waldeck	Kristine	(917) 361-8181	4/1/96	No	$0
Y556	Yamamura	Shinjiro	(905) 551-1293	9/26/96	No	$0
*					Yes	$0

With the WRITERS datasheet open, Elena is ready to make any necessary changes to the table. First, she decides to change the font of the table records to make the information easier to read.

Changing Datasheet Properties

When Judith created her version of the WRITERS table, she changed the font to Times New Roman and the font style to bold. Elena believes that Access's default setting (Arial, font size 10) with the normal font style is easier to read. She decides to change the font to improve readability.

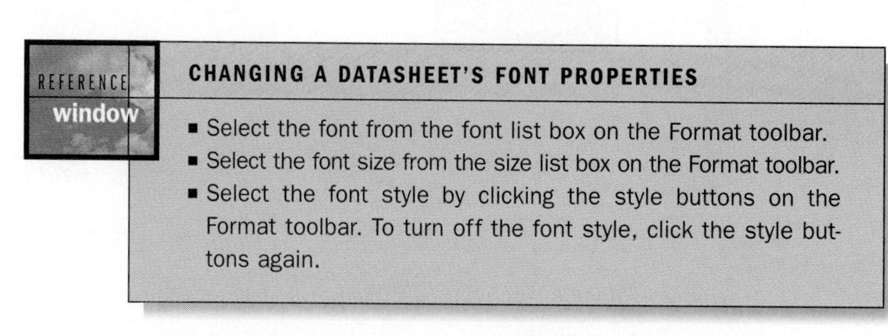

CHANGING A DATASHEET'S FONT PROPERTIES

- Select the font from the font list box on the Format toolbar.
- Select the font size from the size list box on the Format toolbar.
- Select the font style by clicking the style buttons on the Format toolbar. To turn off the font style, click the style buttons again.

To change the datasheet font:

1. If necessary, click **View**, click **Toolbars**, then click **Formatting (Datasheet)** to display the Format toolbar on the screen. Then click the **font name** list arrow. The list of available fonts appears in alphabetical order. See Figure 3-13.

Figure 3-13 The font name list

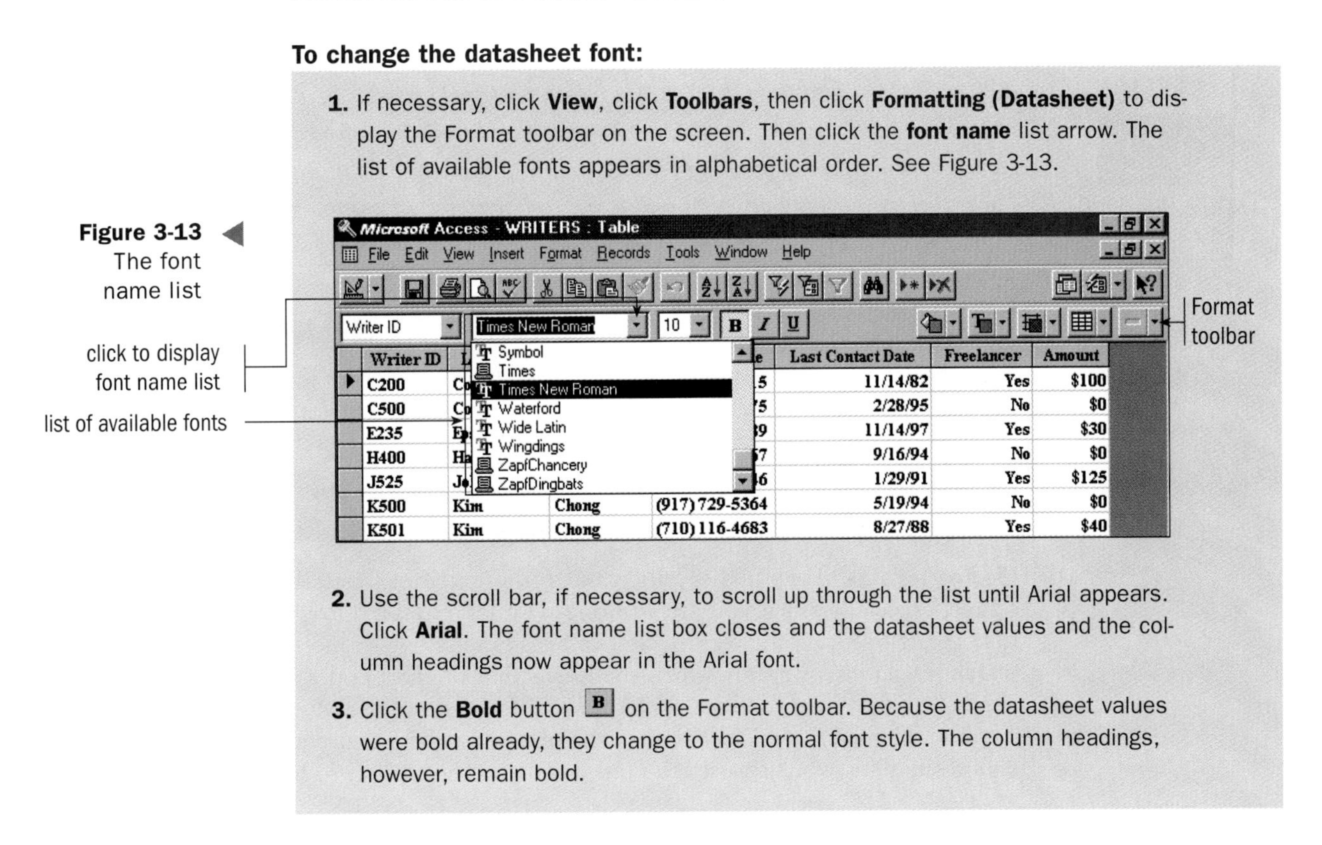

2. Use the scroll bar, if necessary, to scroll up through the list until Arial appears. Click **Arial**. The font name list box closes and the datasheet values and the column headings now appear in the Arial font.

3. Click the **Bold** button **B** on the Format toolbar. Because the datasheet values were bold already, they change to the normal font style. The column headings, however, remain bold.

When you change datasheet fonts, you may need to change the column widths to make some fields fully visible. Access automatically adjusts row heights to accommodate font changes. In this case, Elena realizes that changing the column widths won't be necessary.

The WRITERS table now contains the data Elena needs, in the format she wants. Her next task is to look at the table more closely for any possible errors.

If you want to take a break and resume the tutorial at a later time, exit Access. When you resume the tutorial, place your Student Disk in the appropriate drive, start Access, open the Issue25 database on your Student Disk, maximize the Database window, and open the WRITERS table in Datasheet View.

Quick Check

1. What operations are performed when you update a database?
2. What does a pencil symbol signify in a record selector? An asterisk symbol?
3. Which button do you use to move to the last record in the table?
4. If you change field values in a table, what do you have to do to save your changes?
5. If you delete a record from a table, do all field values disappear? Which field values, if any, remain?
6. What are some advantages of importing data?
7. When would you use the Table Analyzer Wizard?
8. How do you change a datasheet's font?

SESSION 3.2

In this session you will learn how to find data and replace data in a datasheet and how to sort records using a single sort key field and multiple sort key fields. You will also learn to use Access's Spelling feature and link tables by defining a Lookup Wizard field as a foreign key. Finally, you will learn to back up and compact a database.

Finding and Replacing Data in a Datasheet

Even though records are physically stored on disk in the order in which you add them to a table, Access displays them in primary key sequence in the datasheet. Finding a record in the WRITERS table based on a specific Writer ID value, therefore, is a simple process.

Finding Data

Finding records based on a specific value for a field other than the primary key is not so simple, especially when you are working with larger tables. You can spend considerable time trying to locate the records and can easily miss one or more of them in your visual search. Elena discovers this when she learns that the area codes for some writers' phone numbers have changed from 909 to 910. If she quickly reviews the WRITERS table records, she might overlook some of the phone numbers that need to be changed. In situations like this, you can use the Find button on the toolbar to help your search.

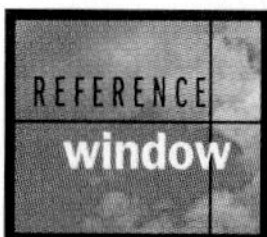

FINDING DATA IN A TABLE

- Click anywhere in the field column you want to search.
- Click the Find button on the toolbar. This opens the Find in field dialog box.
- In the Find What box, type the field value you want to find.
- To find field values that entirely match a value, select Whole Field in the Match box.
- To find a match between a value and any part of a field's value, select Any Part of Field in the Match box; to find a match between a value and the start of a field's value, select Start of Field in the Match box.
- To find all fields that contain the search value, remove the check mark from the Search Only Current Field check box.
- To find matches with a specific pattern of lowercase and uppercase letters, click the Match Case check box.
- To search all records, select All in the Search box.
- To search from the current record to earlier records, select Up in the Search box; to later records, select Down in the Search box.
- Click the Find First button to have Access begin the search at the top of the table, or click the Find Next button to begin the search at the current record as well as to continue the search for the next match. If a match is found, Access scrolls the table and highlights the field value.
- Click the Close button to stop the search operation.

Elena searches the WRITERS table for phone numbers that have a 909 area code.

To find data in a table:

1. Click anywhere in the **Writer Phone** text box for the first record.
2. Click the **Find** button on the toolbar. Access displays the Find in field dialog box. See Figure 3-14.

Figure 3-14
The Find in field dialog box

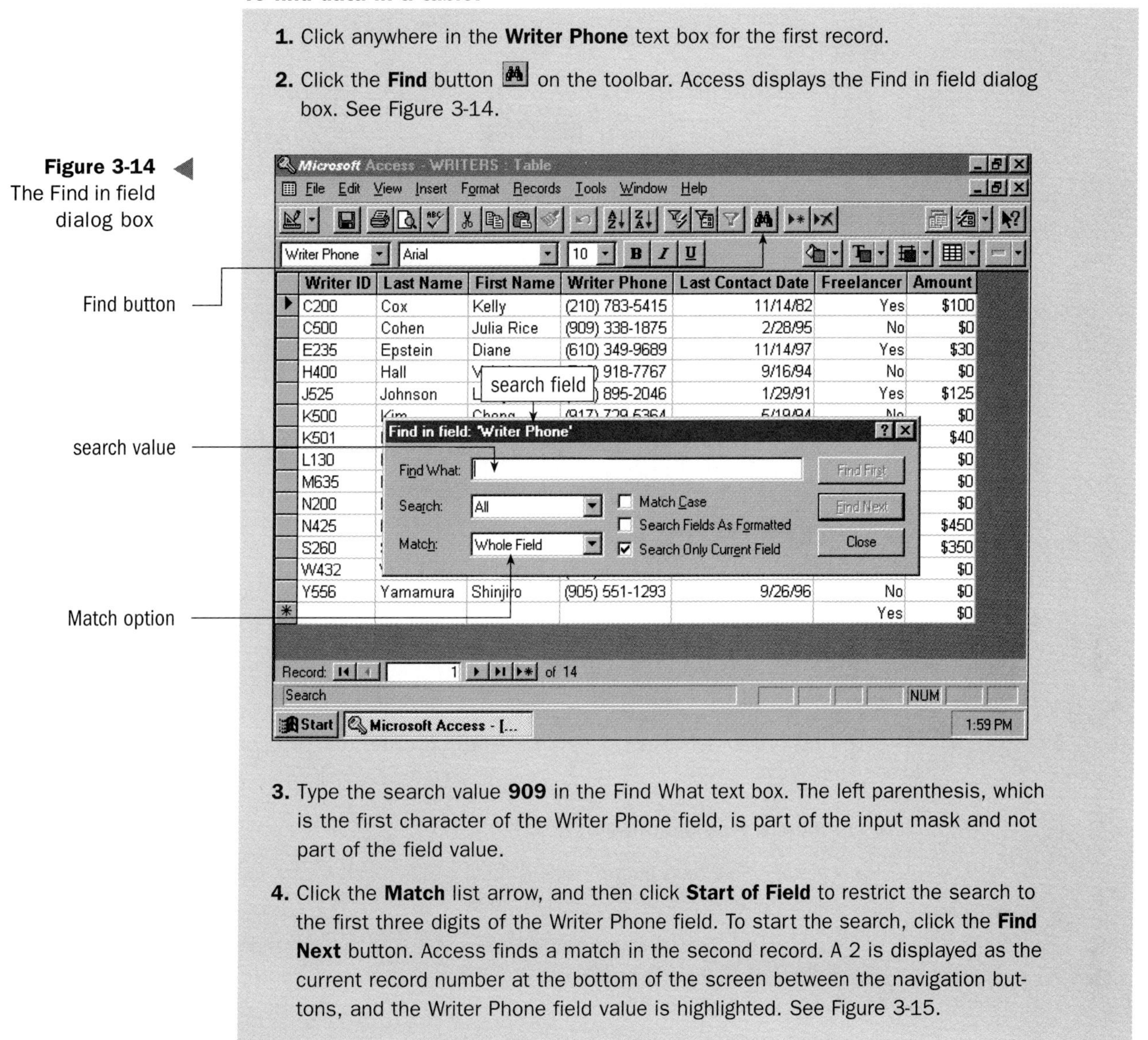

3. Type the search value **909** in the Find What text box. The left parenthesis, which is the first character of the Writer Phone field, is part of the input mask and not part of the field value.
4. Click the **Match** list arrow, and then click **Start of Field** to restrict the search to the first three digits of the Writer Phone field. To start the search, click the **Find Next** button. Access finds a match in the second record. A 2 is displayed as the current record number at the bottom of the screen between the navigation buttons, and the Writer Phone field value is highlighted. See Figure 3-15.

Figure 3-15 Completed Find in field dialog box

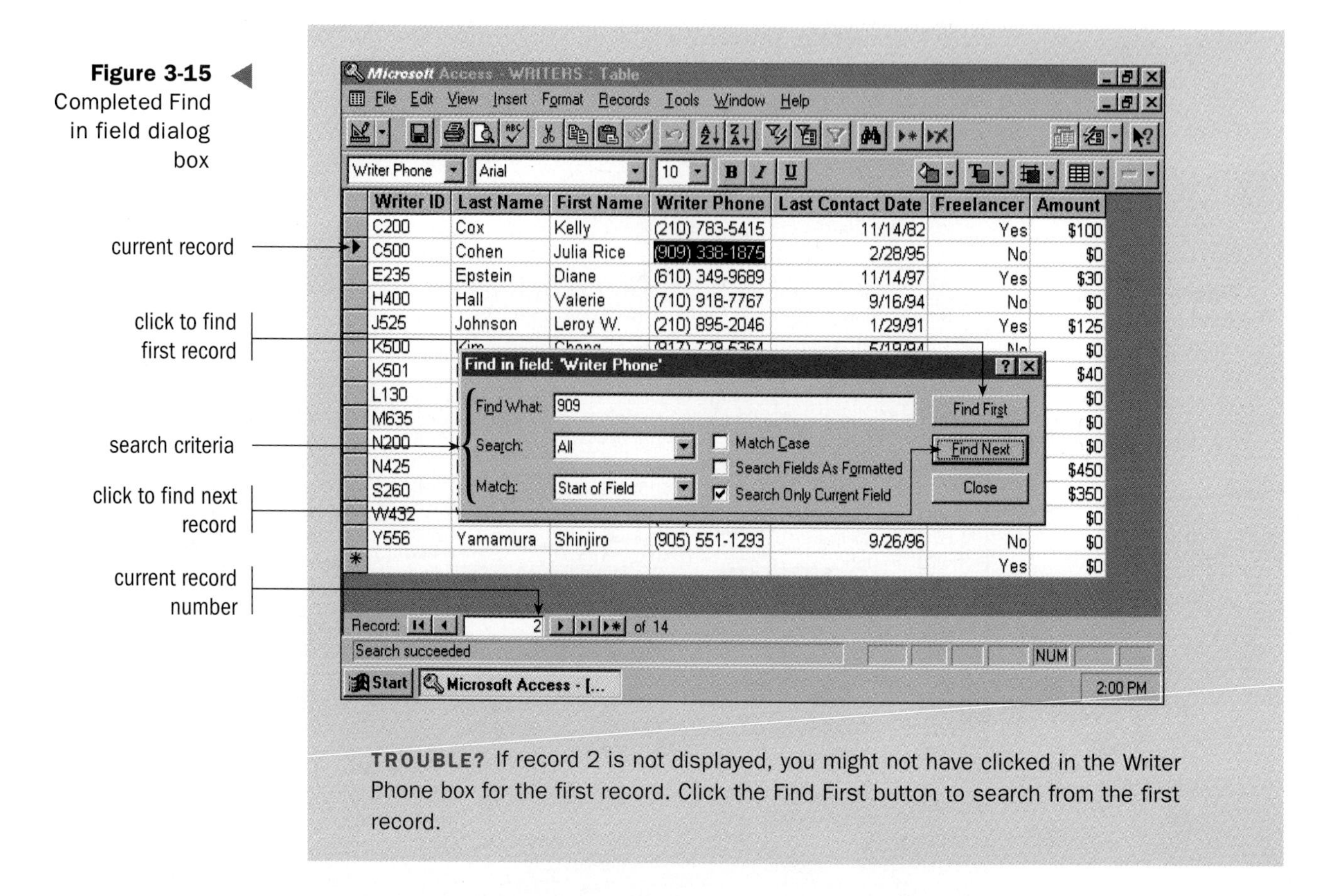

TROUBLE? If record 2 is not displayed, you might not have clicked in the Writer Phone box for the first record. Click the Find First button to search from the first record.

To find other records that match the search criterion, you continue by again clicking the Find Next button.

To continue a Find operation:

1. Click the **Find Next** button. Access finds a match in the 11th record and highlights the entire Writer Phone field value.

   TROUBLE? If the Find in field dialog box obscures the datasheet, drag the dialog box to the lower-right corner of the screen so that it covers less critical parts of the datasheet.

2. Click the **Close** button in the Find in field dialog box. The Find in field dialog box closes.

If you are unsure of the exact text or value you are trying to locate, you can use "wildcard" characters in the Find What text box. Use an asterisk (*) to represent any sequence of characters, a question mark (?) to represent any single character, and the number symbol (#) to represent any single digit. If Elena did not know whether she was looking for 909 or 919 area codes, for example, she would search for "9#9" in her WRITERS table.

You can use the wildcard characters in Find operations, but not for replacing data. Elena will replace data in the WRITERS table next.

Replacing Data

Elena does not want simply to find those area code phone numbers that need to be changed; she wants to replace the value with the new area code, 910. Elena corrects these values by using the Replace option on the Edit menu. You use the Replace option to find a specific value in your records and replace that value with another value.

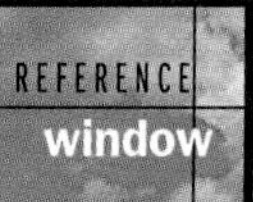

REPLACING DATA IN A TABLE

- Click anywhere in the field column in which you want to replace data.
- Click Edit and then click Replace. This opens the Replace in field dialog box.
- In the Find What box, type the field value you want to find.
- Type the replacement value in the Replace With box.
- To search all fields for the search value, remove the check mark from the Search Only Current Field check box.
- To find and change field values that entirely match a value, click the Match Whole Field check box.
- To find and change matches with a specific pattern of lowercase and uppercase letters, click the Match Case check box.
- Click the Find Next button to begin the search at the current record. If a match is found, Access scrolls the table and highlights the field value.
- Click the Replace button to substitute the replacement value for the search value, or click the Find Next button to leave the highlighted value unchanged and to continue the search for the next match.
- Click the Replace All button to perform the find and replace operations without stopping for confirmation of each replacement.
- Click the Close button to stop the replacement operation.

Elena searches the WRITERS table to replace the 909 phone number area codes with 910.

To replace data in a table:

1. Click in the **Writer Phone** text box for the first record.
2. Click **Edit**, and then click **Replace** to open the Replace in field dialog box. See Figure 3-16. Note that if you previously repositioned the Find in field dialog box, the Replace in field dialog box is similarly positioned. Your previous search value, 909, appears in the new Find What box.

Figure 3-16 The Replace in field dialog box

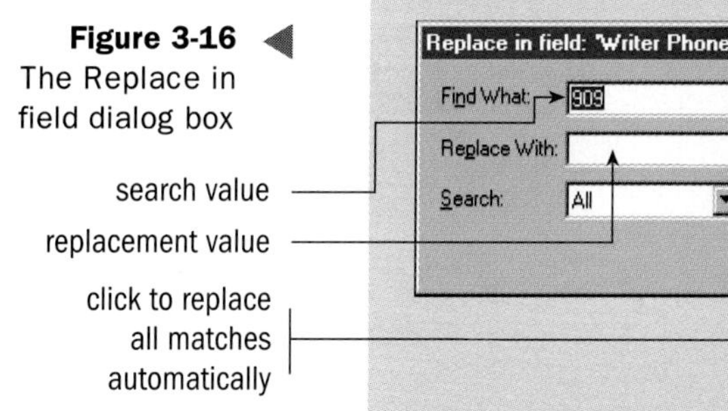

3. Press the **Tab** key and type **910** in the Replace With text box.
4. If necessary, click the **Match Whole Field** check box to remove the check mark.
5. To start the replacement process, click the **Replace All** button.
6. Access displays a dialog box that states, "You won't be able to undo this Replace operation. Do you want to continue?". Access displays this message when more than one replacement occurs, because it cannot undo all the replacements it makes. When this message box appears, click the **Yes** button to complete the replacement operation. Access finds all 909 area codes in the table (in records 2 and 11) and replaces them with 910 area codes.

7. Click the **Close** button [X] in the Replace in field dialog box.

8. Preview and print a copy of the datasheet, using the Print Preview button as you have done before.

   TROUBLE? If a field in the printed datasheet, such as Writer Phone, does not display the whole field value, return to Datasheet View and resize the column. Also, if the printed datasheet takes up two pages, return to Datasheet View and resize the columns to make them narrower without hiding any of the field and names or field values.

Now that Elena has changed the 909 area codes so that all the phone numbers are accurate, she can use the WRITERS table to contact the writers. She feels she will be most successful reaching those writers having a recent contact date. To view the datasheet records arranged by the Last Contact Date field, Elena sorts the records.

Sorting Records in a Datasheet

Sorting is the process of temporarily arranging records in a specified order or sequence. Most companies sort their data before they display or print it because staff use the information differently according to their needs. Brian might want to review writer information arranged by the Amount field, for example, because he is interested in knowing which freelancers will be paid the most for each reprinted article. On the other hand, Elena wants her information arranged by date of last contact because she will be calling the writers. She feels she'll have a better chance of reaching those writers who were contacted most recently.

To sort a table's records, you select the **sort key**—the field used to determine the order of the records in the datasheet. Elena wants to sort the WRITERS data by last contact date, so the Last Contact Date field will be the sort key.

The data type of sort keys can be Text, Number, Date/Time, Currency, AutoNumber, or Yes/No fields, but not Memo or OLE Object. Sort options by data type are shown in Figure 3-17. You sort records in either ascending (increasing) or descending (decreasing) order. Sorting the WRITERS data in descending order by the Last Contact Date field means that the record with the most recent date will be the first record in the datasheet. The record with the earliest date will be the last record in the datasheet.

Figure 3-17 Sorting options for the different data types

Data Type	Ascending order	Descending order
Number, Currency, AutoNumber	numerical, lowest to highest	numerical, highest to lowest
Text	alphabetical, A-Z	alphabetical, Z-A
Yes/No	yes precedes no	no precedes yes
Date	chronological, earliest dates first	chronological, latest dates first

Sort keys can be unique or nonunique. Sort keys are **unique** if the value of the sort key field for each record is different. The Writer ID field in the WRITERS table is an example of a unique sort key, because each writer has a different value in the Writer ID field. Sort keys are **nonunique** if more than one record can have the same value for the sort key field. The Freelancer field in the WRITERS table is a nonunique sort key because more than one record has the same value (either yes or no).

When the sort key is nonunique, records with the same sort key value are grouped together, but they are not arranged in a specific order within the group. If Elena wanted to contact staff writers before freelancers, for example, she could sort by the Freelancer field, which would result in the arrangement shown in Figure 3-18. Notice that the last contact dates are not arranged in a useful order.

Figure 3-18 Sorting by Freelancer field

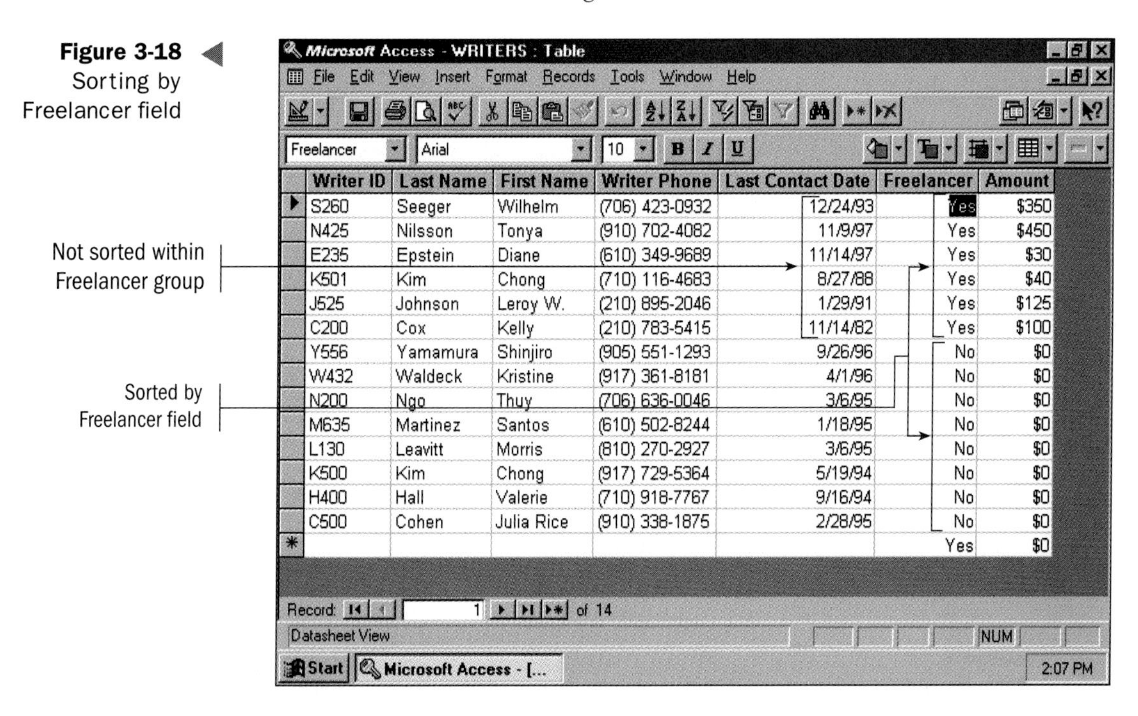

Writer ID	Last Name	First Name	Writer Phone	Last Contact Date	Freelancer	Amount
S260	Seeger	Wilhelm	(706) 423-0932	12/24/93	Yes	$350
N425	Nilsson	Tonya	(910) 702-4082	11/9/97	Yes	$450
E235	Epstein	Diane	(610) 349-9689	11/14/97	Yes	$30
K501	Kim	Chong	(710) 116-4683	8/27/88	Yes	$40
J525	Johnson	Leroy W.	(210) 895-2046	1/29/91	Yes	$125
C200	Cox	Kelly	(210) 783-5415	11/14/82	Yes	$100
Y556	Yamamura	Shinjiro	(905) 551-1293	9/26/96	No	$0
W432	Waldeck	Kristine	(917) 361-8181	4/1/96	No	$0
N200	Ngo	Thuy	(706) 636-0046	3/6/95	No	$0
M635	Martinez	Santos	(610) 502-8244	1/18/95	No	$0
L130	Leavitt	Morris	(810) 270-2927	3/6/95	No	$0
K500	Kim	Chong	(917) 729-5364	5/19/94	No	$0
H400	Hall	Valerie	(710) 918-7767	9/16/94	No	$0
C500	Cohen	Julia Rice	(910) 338-1875	2/28/95	No	$0
*					Yes	$0

To arrange these grouped records in a useful order, you can specify a **secondary sort key**, which is a second sort key field. The first sort key field is called the **primary sort key**. In the example in Figure 3-18, the primary sort key is the Freelancer field, and the secondary sort key can be the Last Contact Date field. Records would then be sorted by last contact date within each group, freelancers and staff writers. Note that the primary sort key is not the same as the table's primary key field. For sorting a table's records, any field in a table can serve as a primary sort key.

Sorting a Single Field Quickly

The **Sort Ascending** and the **Sort Descending** buttons on the toolbar are called quick-sort buttons. **Quick-sort buttons** allow you to sort records immediately, based on the selected field. You first select the column on which you want to base the sort and then click the appropriate quick-sort button on the toolbar to rearrange the records in either ascending or descending order.

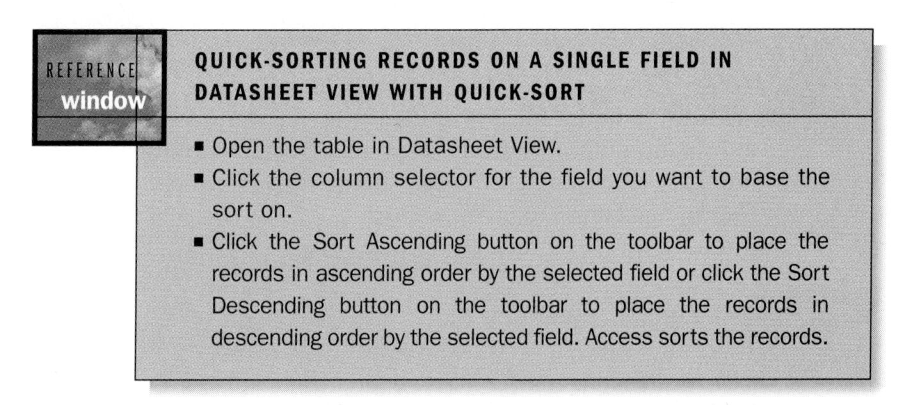

REFERENCE window

QUICK-SORTING RECORDS ON A SINGLE FIELD IN DATASHEET VIEW WITH QUICK-SORT

- Open the table in Datasheet View.
- Click the column selector for the field you want to base the sort on.
- Click the Sort Ascending button on the toolbar to place the records in ascending order by the selected field or click the Sort Descending button on the toolbar to place the records in descending order by the selected field. Access sorts the records.

Elena uses the Sort Descending button to rearrange the records in descending order by the Last Contact Date field.

To sort records in a datasheet with quick-sort buttons:

1. Click anywhere in the **Last Contact Date** column to establish that field as the current field.
2. Click the **Sort Descending** button on the toolbar. Access rearranges the records in descending order by last contact date. See Figure 3-19.

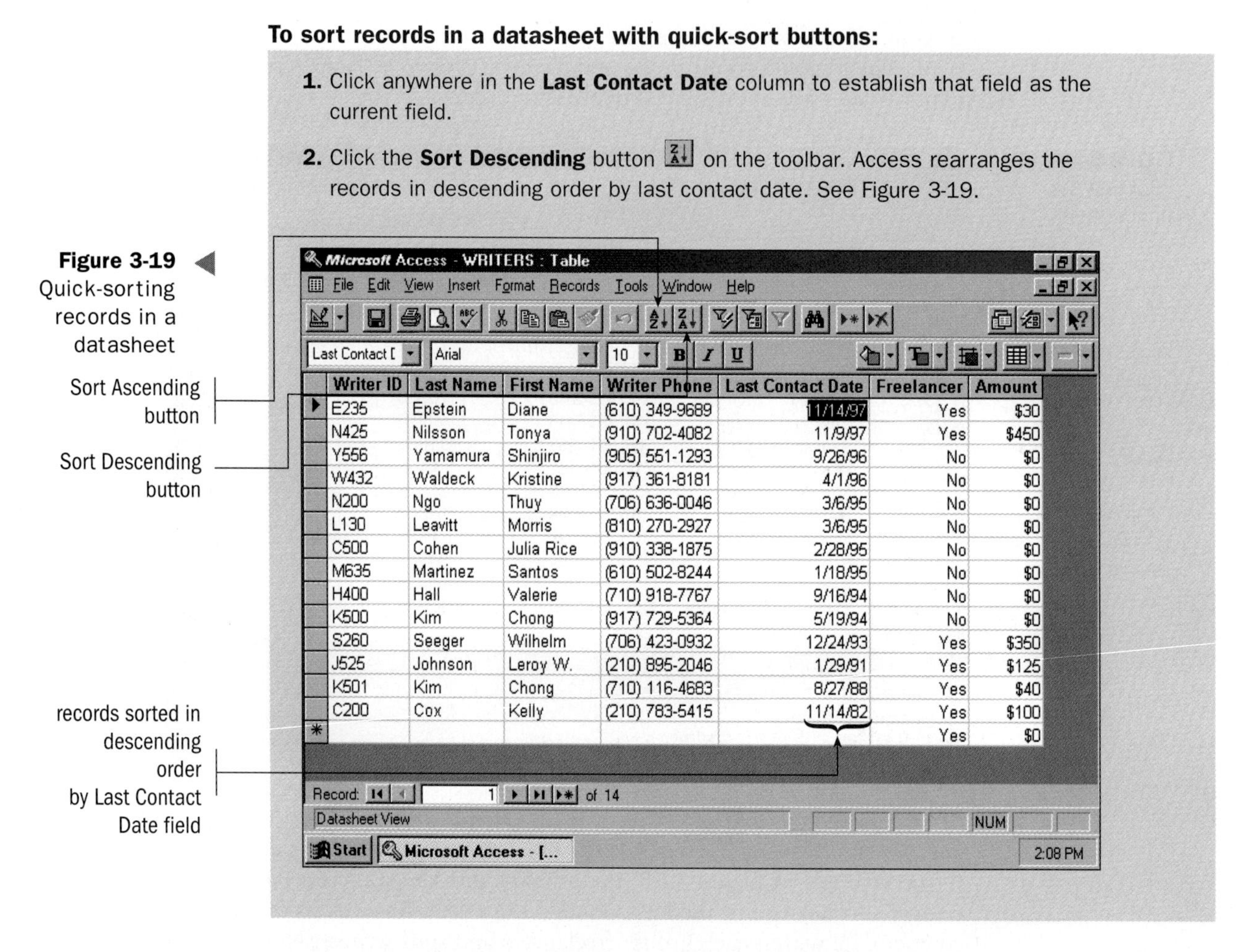

Writer ID	Last Name	First Name	Writer Phone	Last Contact Date	Freelancer	Amount
E235	Epstein	Diane	(610) 349-9689	11/14/97	Yes	$30
N425	Nilsson	Tonya	(910) 702-4082	11/9/97	Yes	$450
Y556	Yamamura	Shinjiro	(905) 551-1293	9/26/96	No	$0
W432	Waldeck	Kristine	(917) 361-8181	4/1/96	No	$0
N200	Ngo	Thuy	(706) 636-0046	3/6/95	No	$0
L130	Leavitt	Morris	(810) 270-2927	3/6/95	No	$0
C500	Cohen	Julia Rice	(910) 338-1875	2/28/95	No	$0
M635	Martinez	Santos	(610) 502-8244	1/18/95	No	$0
H400	Hall	Valerie	(710) 918-7767	9/16/94	No	$0
K500	Kim	Chong	(917) 729-5364	5/19/94	No	$0
S260	Seeger	Wilhelm	(706) 423-0932	12/24/93	Yes	$350
J525	Johnson	Leroy W.	(210) 895-2046	1/29/91	Yes	$125
K501	Kim	Chong	(710) 116-4683	8/27/88	Yes	$40
C200	Cox	Kelly	(210) 783-5415	11/14/82	Yes	$100
*					Yes	$0

Figure 3-19 Quick-sorting records in a datasheet

You can use this same method to restore the records quickly to their original order by clicking in the Writer ID column and then clicking the Sort Ascending button.

To restore records to their original order:

1. Click anywhere in the **Writer ID** column.
2. Click the **Sort Ascending** button on the toolbar. Access rearranges the records in ascending order by Writer ID (the primary key).

Quick-Sorting Multiple Fields

Access allows you to sort a datasheet quickly using two or more sort keys. The sort key fields must be in adjacent columns in the datasheet. You highlight the columns, and Access sorts first by the first highlighted column and then by any other highlighted column, in order from left to right. Because you click either the Sort Ascending or the Sort Descending button to perform a quick-sort, all of the highlighted fields are sorted in either ascending or descending sort order.

REFERENCE window

SORTING RECORDS ON MULTIPLE FIELDS IN DATASHEET VIEW WITH QUICK-SORT

- Open the table in Datasheet View.
- If necessary, rearrange the fields in the datasheet so that the primary sort key field and secondary sort key fields are next to each other, with the primary sort key field on the left.
- Click the column selectors for the fields you want to base the sort on.
- Click the Sort Ascending button on the toolbar to place the records in ascending order by the selected fields or click the Sort Descending button on the toolbar to place the records in descending order by the selected fields. Access sorts the records.

Elena selects the adjacent fields Freelancer and Amount and performs an ascending-order quick-sort.

To use multiple sort keys to sort records in a datasheet using quick-sort:

1. Click the **Freelancer** field selector. (The field selector, remember, is the gray box containing the field name at the top of the column.) While holding down the mouse button, drag the ↓ to the right until both the Freelancer and Amount columns are highlighted. Then release the mouse button.
2. Click the **Sort Ascending** button on the toolbar. Access rearranges the records, placing them in ascending order by Freelancer and—when the Freelancer field values are the same—in ascending order by Amount. See Figure 3-20.

Figure 3-20 Datasheet sorted on two adjacent fields with quick–sort

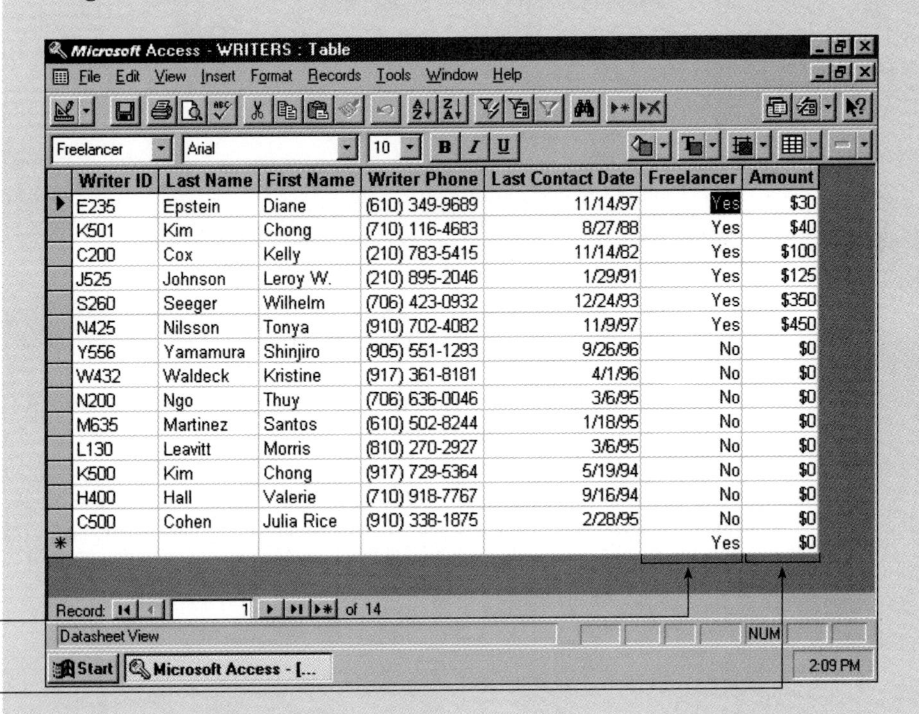

Microsoft Access - WRITERS : Table

Writer ID	Last Name	First Name	Writer Phone	Last Contact Date	Freelancer	Amount
E235	Epstein	Diane	(610) 349-9689	11/14/97	Yes	$30
K501	Kim	Chong	(710) 116-4683	8/27/88	Yes	$40
C200	Cox	Kelly	(210) 783-5415	11/14/82	Yes	$100
J525	Johnson	Leroy W.	(210) 895-2046	1/29/91	Yes	$125
S260	Seeger	Wilhelm	(706) 423-0932	12/24/93	Yes	$350
N425	Nilsson	Tonya	(910) 702-4082	11/9/97	Yes	$450
Y556	Yamamura	Shinjiro	(905) 551-1293	9/26/96	No	$0
W432	Waldeck	Kristine	(917) 361-8181	4/1/96	No	$0
N200	Ngo	Thuy	(706) 636-0046	3/6/95	No	$0
M635	Martinez	Santos	(610) 502-8244	1/18/95	No	$0
L130	Leavitt	Morris	(810) 270-2927	3/6/95	No	$0
K500	Kim	Chong	(917) 729-5364	5/19/94	No	$0
H400	Hall	Valerie	(710) 918-7767	9/16/94	No	$0
C500	Cohen	Julia Rice	(910) 338-1875	2/28/95	No	$0
*					Yes	$0

Record: 1 of 14

Elena prints the results of her sort to use in contacting the writers, then does a final review of the data in the WRITERS table and determines that she is finished with her updates. She closes the WRITERS table Datasheet View window.

To close the Datasheet View window:

1. Click the **Close** button [X] in the Datasheet View window. Access displays the Save changes? dialog box.
2. Click the **Yes** button to save the changes to the WRITERS table and return to the Database window.

Access closes the Datasheet View window and saves the formatting changes made earlier to the table. Access also saves the sort order. Access will display the records in the last sorted order when you open the table again.

Elena next uses Access to work on the other table in her Issue25 database, BUSINESS ARTICLES.

Using Access's Spelling Feature

Judith not only created a WRITERS table, she also maintains a table in the Vision database containing information about the selected business articles for the 25th-anniversary issue. Instead of entering all that information herself, Elena decides to import Judith's database table (BUSINESS ARTICLES-JR) into her Issue25 database. After she confirms that Judith's table contains all the correct information, Elena can delete the BUSINESS ARTICLES table that she initially created.

To import the BUSINESS ARTICLES-JR table:

1. Click **File,** then point to **Get External Data,** then click **Import**. Access displays the Import dialog box.
2. If necessary, use the Look in text box to select the Tutorial folder on the drive that contains your Student Disk. Click **Vision** in the file list. Click the **Import** button to close the Import dialog box
3. Click **BUSINESS ARTICLES-JR** in the Tables list, then click the **OK** button. Access imports the table and closes the Import Objects dialog box. The Database window now displays the BUSINESS ARTICLES-JR table in the Tables list.

   After viewing the table and confirming its contents, Elena decides to use Judith's table instead of her own.
4. Using the procedure for deleting a table described earlier in the tutorial, delete the current BUSINESS ARTICLES table and rename the BUSINESS ARTICLES-JR table BUSINESS ARTICLES.

Elena wants to make sure that the data in the BUSINESS ARTICLES table is accurate. She uses Access's Spelling feature to help her with this. Access's Spelling feature will check the contents of any text field. Each word is checked against Access's internal dictionary. If a word is not found, Access displays a dialog box with a suggested replacement for the word. You can then accept the suggested replacement, select from a list of alternate spellings, or choose to make no changes.

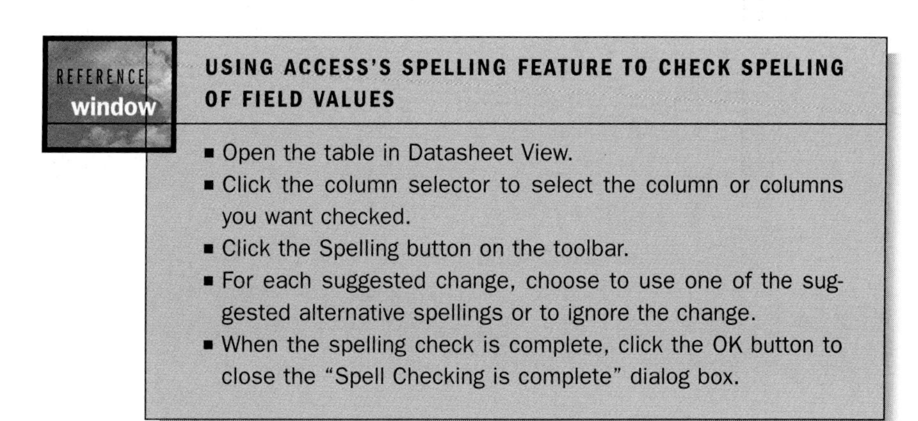

REFERENCE window

USING ACCESS'S SPELLING FEATURE TO CHECK SPELLING OF FIELD VALUES

- Open the table in Datasheet View.
- Click the column selector to select the column or columns you want checked.
- Click the Spelling button on the toolbar.
- For each suggested change, choose to use one of the suggested alternative spellings or to ignore the change.
- When the spelling check is complete, click the OK button to close the "Spell Checking is complete" dialog box.

Elena decides to check the article titles in the BUSINESS ARTICLES table to make sure that they are spelled correctly. She does not check the Type or Writer ID fields because the correct values will not appear in Access's internal dictionary. The Issue field values are dates and are checked for validity by Access when the values are entered. The Article Length field contains numeric values and cannot be checked for spelling.

To check the spelling in the article titles:

1. Double-click **BUSINESS ARTICLES** in the Tables list. Access opens the Datasheet View window of the BUSINESS ARTICLES table.

2. Click the **Article Title** column selector to select the column, then click the **Spelling** button on the toolbar. Access begins checking the spelling of each word in the Article Title column. Access finds a word not in the dictionary and displays the Spelling dialog box. See Figure 3-21.

Figure 3-21 The Spelling dialog box

Access does not find the word "Friedman" in the dictionary and suggests changing it to "Freedman." Elena doesn't want to make this change since this is a correctly spelled name.

3. Click the **Ignore All** button to bypass this suggested change and continue with the spelling check. Clicking the Ignore All button tells Access to ignore any other occurrences of this word in the table. Access next displays the Spelling dialog box for the word "Reagan's."

4. Click the **Ignore All** button to ignore this suggested change and continue with the spelling check. Access next displays the Spelling dialog box for the word "Trans-Alaskan." Although this does not match any entry in the dictionary, Access does not have any suggested alternatives.

5. Click the **Ignore All** button to continue the spelling check. Access next displays the Spelling dialog box for "Pipline" and suggests changing it to "Pipeline." Elena wants to change this to its correct spelling.
6. Click the **Change** button to change "Pipline" to "Pipeline." Access continues the spelling check.
7. Click the **Ignore All** button when Access displays the Spelling dialog box for "Chrysler" and for "Bingham." Access finishes checking the rest of the article titles and displays the "Spell checking is complete" dialog box.
8. Click the **OK** button to close the dialog box.

Access's Spelling feature is useful, but it will not find all misspellings. It only finds words that are not in its dictionary. For example, the word "beast" (as a misspelling of "best") will not be identified as incorrect because "beast" is a correctly spelled word that is found in the dictionary.

Defining a Lookup Wizard Field

In the BUSINESS ARTICLES table, each record has a field for Writer ID, which identifies the writer of the article. If she needs to enter a new article into the table, Elena enters the Writer ID that corresponds to the record for the writer in the WRITERS table. So that she can locate that information more quickly, Elena redefines the Writer ID field in the BUSINESS ARTICLES table to make it a Lookup Wizard field. Then, whenever she enters a new record in the table, Access will display the list of writers from the WRITERS table. Elena can select from the list, and Access will automatically enter the correct Writer ID value. This makes it much easier to enter Writer ID field values for the BUSINESS ARTICLES table and reduces the chance of making an error.

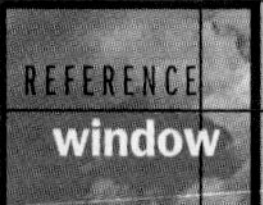

DEFINING A LOOKUP WIZARD FIELD

- Open the table in Design View.
- Click in the Data Type text box of the field for which you want to give the Lookup Wizard data type.
- Click the Data Type text list arrow to display the list of available data types.
- Click Lookup Wizard to start the Lookup Wizard and display the first dialog box.
- Make sure that the radio button for "I want the lookup column to look up values in a table or query" is checked, then click the Next > button. The next Lookup Wizard dialog box opens.
- Click to select the table for the lookup, then click the Next > button to display the next Lookup Wizard dialog box.
- Select the fields you want to appear in the lookup list, then click the Next > button.
- Adjust the width of the columns that will appear in the lookup list, then click the Next > button.
- Select the field that will provide the value for the Lookup Wizard field, then click the Next > button.
- Enter the name you want for the field in the original table. Then click the Finish button to close the Lookup Wizard and return to the Design View window.

To change the Writer ID field to a Lookup Wizard field:

1. Click the **Table View** button on the toolbar to open the Design View window, then click in the **Data Type** text box for the Writer ID row.
2. Click the **Writer ID** list arrow to display a list of available data types, then click **Lookup Wizard**. The first Lookup Wizard dialog box opens. See Figure 3-22.

Figure 3-22 The first Lookup Wizard dialog box

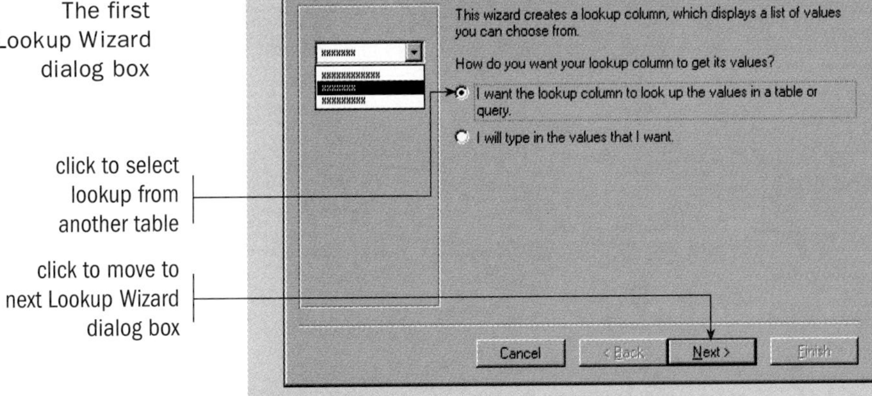

3. Make sure that the radio button next to "I want the lookup column to look up values in a table or query" is checked, then click the Next > button. The next Lookup Wizard dialog box opens.
4. Click **WRITERS** to select it as the table for the lookup, then click the Next > button to display the next Lookup Wizard dialog box. See Figure 3-23.

Figure 3-23 The next Lookup Wizard dialog box

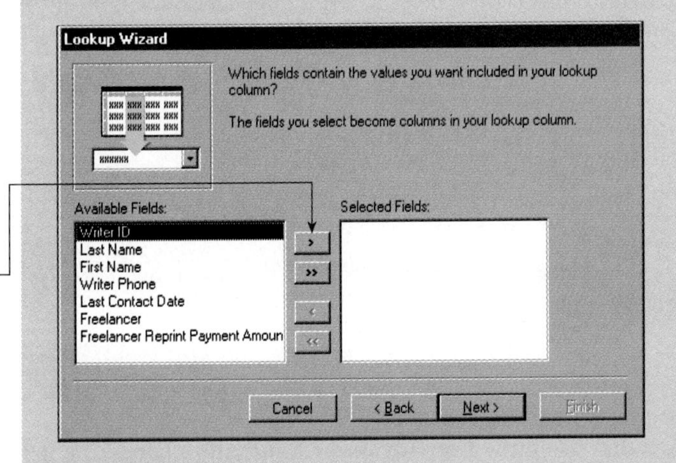

This dialog box allows you to select the fields from the WRITERS table that will appear in the lookup list when you enter a Writer ID value in the BUSINESS ARTICLES table. Select as many fields as you want in order to make it easy to identify the correct Writer ID. Elena decides to have the Writer ID, the Last Name, and the First Name fields displayed.

5. Click **Writer ID** in the Available Fields list then click the Next > button to move it to the Selected Fields list. Click **Last Name**, then click the Next > button. Click **First Name**, then click the Next > button. Then click the Next > button to display the next Lookup Wizard dialog box. See Figure 3-24.

Figure 3-24 The next Lookup Wizard dialog box

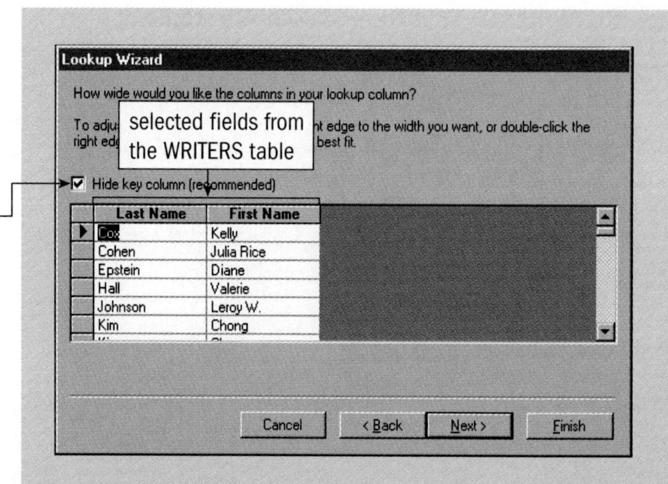

This dialog box allows you to adjust the width of the columns that will appear in the lookup list.

6. Click the **Hide key column** check box to remove the check mark. This makes the Writer ID field visible.

7. Place the pointer on the dividing bar between the column names for the Writer ID and the Last Name fields. When the pointer changes to ✛, click and hold the left mouse button. Move the pointer left to make the Writer ID column narrower. Use the same procedure to make the Last Name and First Name columns narrower as well. Then click the Next > button to display the next Lookup Wizard dialog box.

   This dialog box allows you to select the field from the WRITERS table that will be entered in the Writer ID field in the record for the BUSINESS ARTICLES table.

8. If necessary, click **Writer ID** to select it, then click the Next > button.

   Finally, the Lookup Wizard asks you to enter the name you want for the field in the BUSINESS ARTICLES table. The field's current name, Writer ID, appears in the text box. Since you don't want to change it, you are finished with the Lookup Wizard.

9. Click the **Finish** button to close the Lookup Wizard and return to the Design View window.

10. Click the **Yes** button when Access asks if you want to save the table.

Notice that using the Lookup Wizard does not change the definition of the Writer ID field. The data type of the Writer ID field is still Text, but it is now also defined as a foreign key, linked to the primary key in the WRITERS table. To see how this works when a new record is entered, Elena adds the record shown in Figure 3-25 to the BUSINESS ARTICLES table.

Figure 3-25 New record for the BUSINESS ARTICLES table

Article Title	Type	Issue	Article Length	Writer
Toyota and GM Joint Venture	INT	1983 Mar	1682	Seeger, Wilhelm

To add a new record to the table with a defined Lookup Wizard field:

1. Click the **Table View** button on the toolbar.
2. Click the **New Record** button to move the current record pointer to a new record at the end of the table, then type **Toyota and GM Joint Venture**, and then press the **Tab** key to move to the Type field.
3. Type **INT** to replace the default value BUS for Type, then press the **Tab** key to move to the Issue column.

   Here, the type INT refers to an article about international business. Other types listed in the BUSINESS ARTICLES table include BUS (general business), ITV (interview), LAW (legal article), and POL (politics).
4. Type **1983 Mar**, then press the **Tab** key to move to the Article Length column. Remember that article length refers to the number of words.
5. Type **1682**, then press the **Tab** key to move to the Writer ID column.

   Because the Writer ID field is a Lookup Wizard field, Access displays a list arrow at the right side of the Writer ID field. When you click the arrow, Access displays a list of Writer ID, Last Name, and First Name values from the WRITERS table. To select a writer from the WRITERS table, simply scroll as needed and click on a value from the list. Access automatically inserts the corresponding Writer ID in the data entry field.
6. Click the **Writer ID** list arrow. Access displays a list of Writer ID, Last Name, and First Name values from the WRITERS table. See Figure 3-26.

Figure 3-26 List of Writer ID, Last Name, and First Name values from the WRITERS table

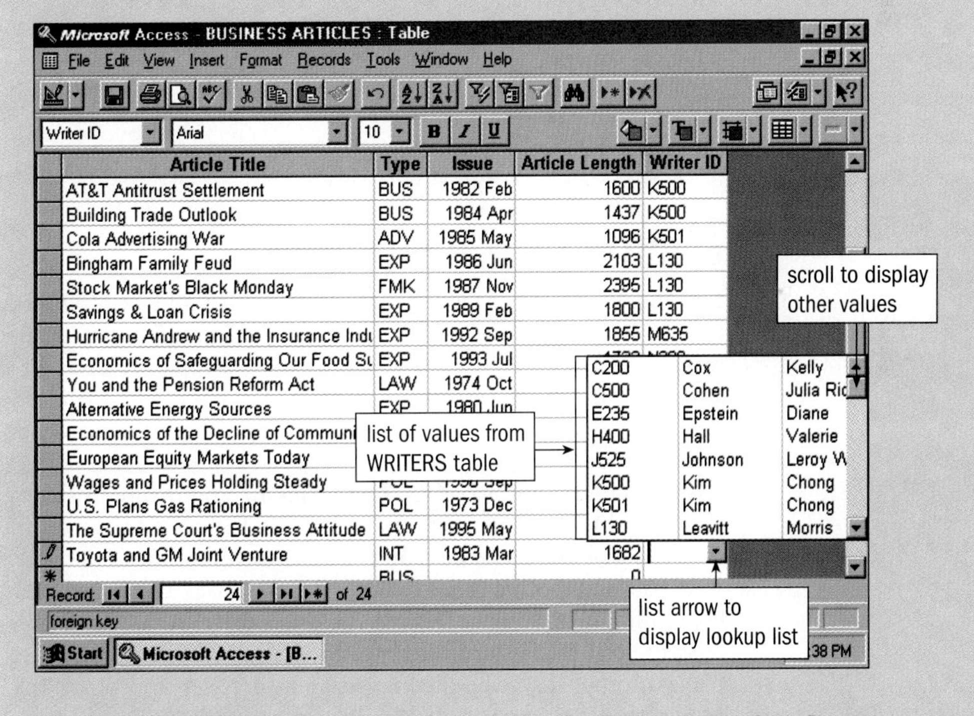

7. Scroll down the list until the name Seeger (Writer ID S260) appears. Click **Seeger**. Access places S260 in the data entry field for the Writer ID. See Figure 3-27.

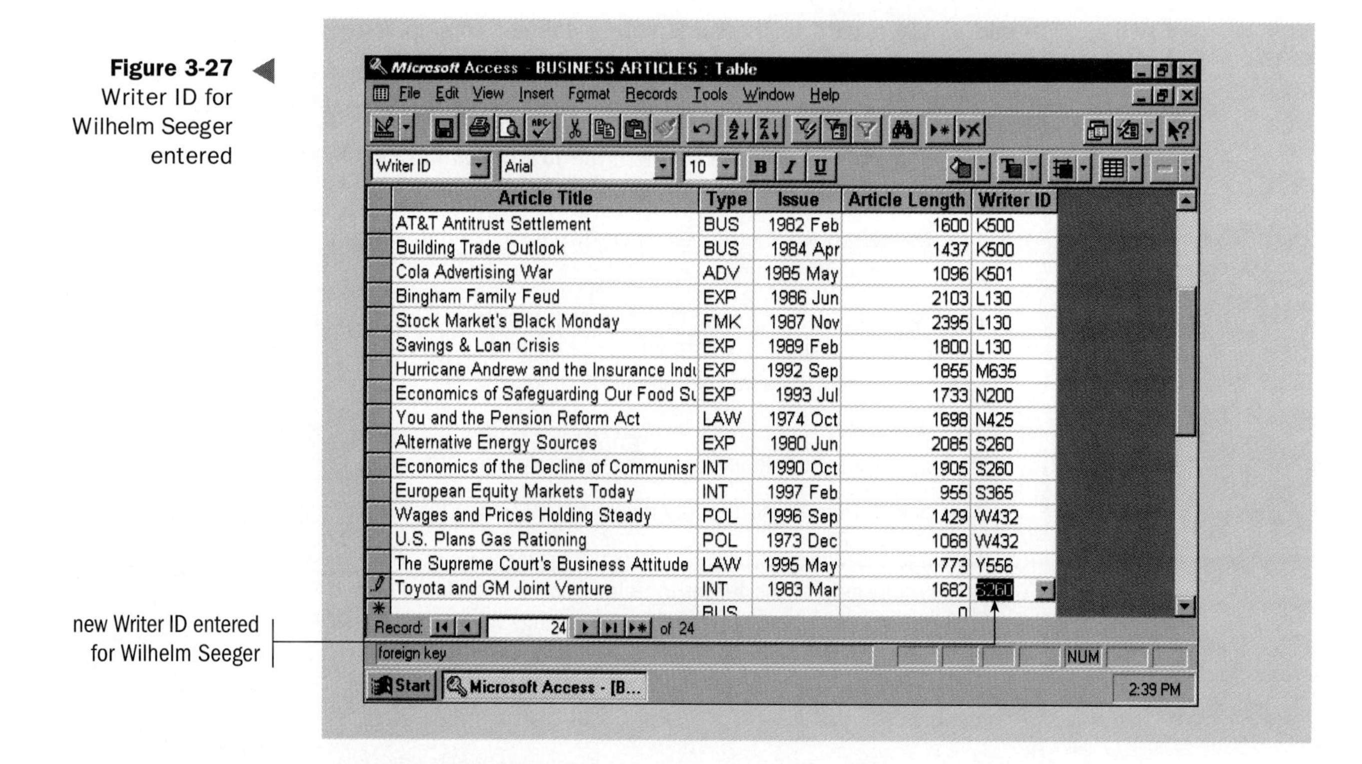

Article Title	Type	Issue	Article Length	Writer ID
AT&T Antitrust Settlement	BUS	1982 Feb	1600	K500
Building Trade Outlook	BUS	1984 Apr	1437	K500
Cola Advertising War	ADV	1985 May	1096	K501
Bingham Family Feud	EXP	1986 Jun	2103	L130
Stock Market's Black Monday	FMK	1987 Nov	2395	L130
Savings & Loan Crisis	EXP	1989 Feb	1800	L130
Hurricane Andrew and the Insurance Indu	EXP	1992 Sep	1655	M635
Economics of Safeguarding Our Food Su	EXP	1993 Jul	1733	N200
You and the Pension Reform Act	LAW	1974 Oct	1698	N425
Alternative Energy Sources	EXP	1980 Jun	2085	S260
Economics of the Decline of Communisr	INT	1990 Oct	1905	S260
European Equity Markets Today	INT	1997 Feb	955	S365
Wages and Prices Holding Steady	POL	1996 Sep	1429	W432
U.S. Plans Gas Rationing	POL	1973 Dec	1068	W432
The Supreme Court's Business Attitude	LAW	1995 May	1773	Y556
Toyota and GM Joint Venture	INT	1983 Mar	1682	S260
	BUS		0	

Figure 3-27 Writer ID for Wilhelm Seeger entered

Elena has now finished entering the new record into the BUSINESS ARTICLES table. She closes the table.

To close the table:

1. Click the **Close** button for the Datasheet View window. Access returns you to the Database window.

Backing Up a Database

Elena is done with her work on the WRITERS and BUSINESS ARTICLES tables. Before exiting Access, however, Elena backs up the Issue25 database. **Backing up** is the process of making a duplicate copy of a database on a separate disk. In Access, remember that a database and all its objects are contained a single file. Elena does this to protect against loss of, or damage to, the original database. If problems occur, she can simply use the backup database.

Access does not have its own backup command. Instead you use Windows' My Computer. (Before backing up a database file, therefore, you must close the database in Access.) The database file icon contains the gray image of a datasheet.

If you have both a drive A and a drive B, copy the Issue25 database file from the drive containing your Student Disk to the other drive. If you have only a drive A, however, you need to copy the Issue25 database file from your Student Disk to the hard disk. Then you place another disk, the backup disk, in drive A and move the database to it from the hard disk.

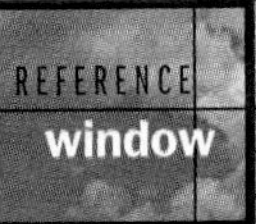

BACKING UP AN ACCESS DATABASE

- Minimize the Access window by clicking the Minimize button in the Access window.
- Open My Computer and copy a database file from one disk to a backup disk, using the procedure appropriate for the disk and hardware configuration.
- Close the My Computer window.
- Be sure that the original disk is in the same drive you've been using for your Access work.
- Switch back to Access. The Access window is the active window.

To back up a database:

1. Click the Database window **Close** button to close the Issue25 database.
2. Minimize the Access window by clicking the **Minimize** button in the Access window.
3. Open My Computer and copy the Issue25 file from your Student Disk to a backup disk, using the procedure appropriate for your disk and hardware configuration.
4. Close the My Computer window.
5. Be sure that your Student Disk is in the same drive you've been using for your Access work.
6. Switch back to Access. The Access window is the active window.

Compacting a Database

Elena deleted a record from the WRITERS table while updating the Issue25 database. She knows that when records are deleted in Access, the space occupied by the deleted records does not automatically become available for other records. The same is true if an object, such as a form or report, is deleted. To make the space available, you must compact the database. When you compact a database, Access removes deleted records and objects and creates a smaller version of the database. Unlike backing up a database, which you do to protect your database against loss or damage, you compact a database to make it smaller, thereby making more space available on your disk. Before compacting a database, you must close it.

REFERENCE window

COMPACTING A DATABASE

- Close any database you are using, so that the Access window is active.
- Click Tools, point to Database Utilities, and then click Compact Database to open the Database to Compact From dialog box.
- In the Look in box, select the drive and directory that contain the database you want to compact.
- In the File name list box, select the database you want to compact.
- Click the Compact button. Access closes the Database to Compact From dialog box and opens the Compact Database Into dialog box.
- In the Save in box, select the drive and directory for the location of the compacted form of the database.
- In the File name text box, type the name you want to assign to the compacted form of the database.
- Click the Save button. The Compact Database Into dialog box closes, and Access starts compacting the database.
- If you use the same name for both the original and compacted database, Access displays the message "Replace existing file?" Click the Yes button to continue compacting the database.
- After the database compacting is complete, Access returns you to the Access window.

Elena compacts her Issue25 database before exiting Access. Because she has just made a backup copy, she uses Issue25 as the compacted database name. You can use the same name, or a different name, for your original and compacted databases. If you use the same name, you should back up the original database first in case a hardware or software malfunction occurs in the middle of the compacting process.

To compact a database and exit Access:

1. Click **Tools**, point to **Database Utilities**, and then click **Compact Database**. Access displays the Database to Compact From dialog box. See Figure 3-28.

Figure 3-28 The Database to Compact From dialog box

database names

2. If necessary, use the Look in list box to select the drive and directory that contain the database to compact.

3. Click **Issue25** in the File name list box.

4. Click the **Compact** button. The Database to Compact From dialog box closes and Access displays the Compact Database Into dialog box. See Figure 3-29.

Figure 3-29 The Compact Into dialog box

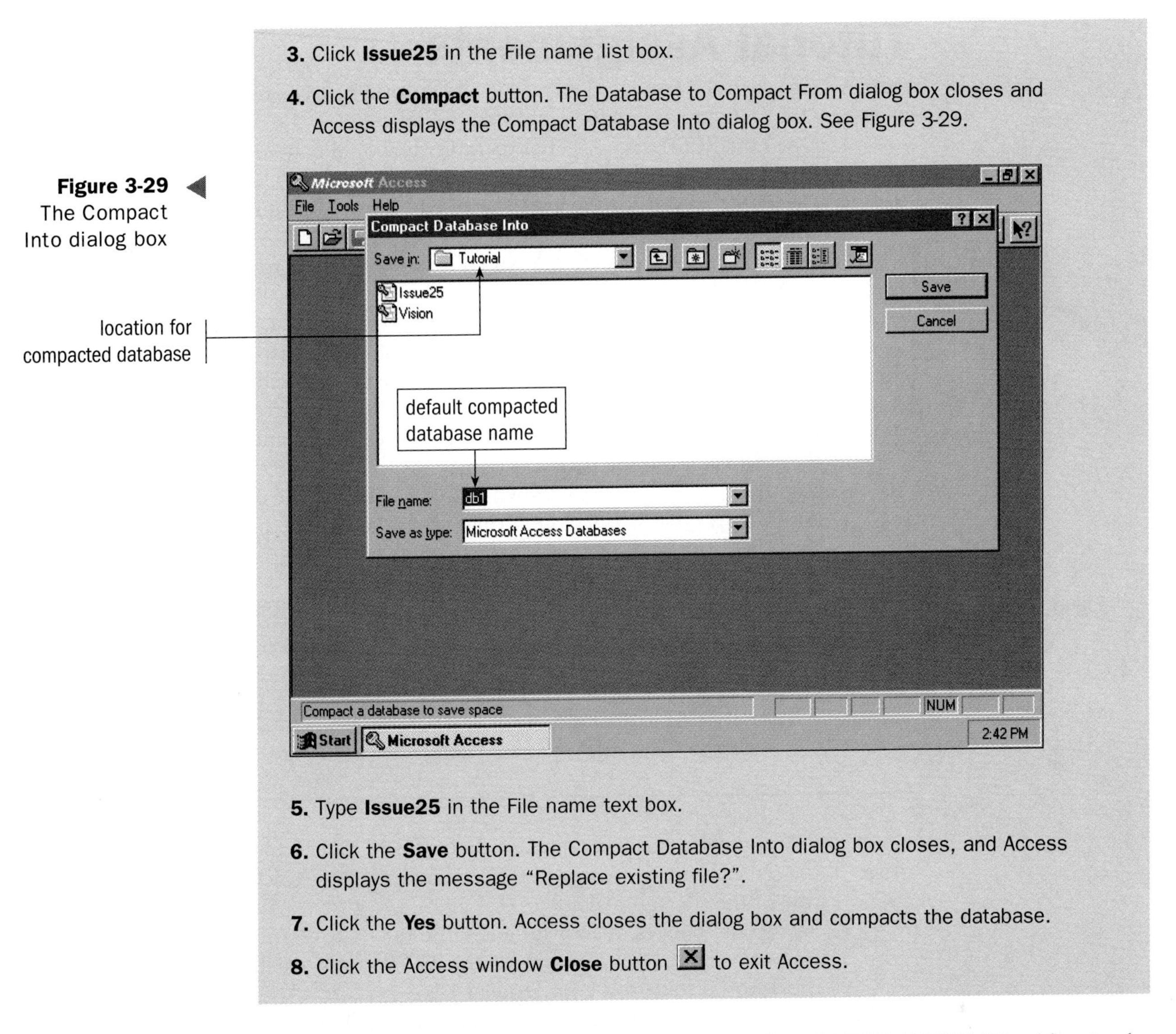

5. Type **Issue25** in the File name text box.

6. Click the **Save** button. The Compact Database Into dialog box closes, and Access displays the message "Replace existing file?".

7. Click the **Yes** button. Access closes the dialog box and compacts the database.

8. Click the Access window **Close** button to exit Access.

Elena has finished updating the WRITERS and BUSINESS ARTICLES tables. In the next tutorial, she will use the Access query feature to answer questions and obtain information from the data in the WRITERS and BUSINESS ARTICLES tables.

Quick Check

1. How can you find a specific field value in a table?
2. Why do you need to be cautious about using the Replace All option when replacing table field values?
3. What are the advantages of sorting a datasheet's records?
4. When might you consider using a secondary sort key?
5. What are some advantages of using Access's Spelling feature?
6. What is the purpose of the Lookup Wizard?
7. How many different files do you copy when you back up one Access database that includes three tables?
8. What is the purpose of compacting a database?

Tutorial Assignments

Start Access, open the Issue25 database in the Tutorial folder on your Student Disk, maximize the Database window, and do the following:

1. Open the BUSINESS ARTICLES table. It should contain 24 records.
2. Print the BUSINESS ARTICLES datasheet.
3. Delete the record for the article entitled "European Equity Markets Today," which is an article that appeared in a 1997 issue.
4. In the Type field, change the type of the 1988 article from LAW to POL.

5. Switch to Design View. Make the row for the Issue of Business Perspectives field the current field, click in its Format property box, and start the Access Help system. Click Index, type date/time, click the Display button, click the jump for Date/Time display formats, and read the discussion of Custom Formats. Explain the meaning of the date/time format yyyy mmm. Exit the Access Help system, switch back to Datasheet View, and observe the format of the field values in the Issue column.
6. Add the two new records shown in Figure 3-30 to the end of the BUSINESS ARTICLES table. Notice the format of the Issue field and enter the two new Issue field values in the exact same format.

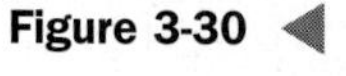

Figure 3-30

	Article Title	Type	Issue	Article Length	Writer ID
Record 1:	The Economy Under Sub-Zero Population Growth	BUS	1995 Dec	1020	E235
Record 2:	New York City Fiscal Crisis	POL	1975 Nov	1477	N425

7. Resize the datasheet columns so that all field names and field values appear on the screen. Sort the records in ascending order by Article Length. What is the title of the shortest article?
8. Save your changes, then print and close the datasheet.
9. Import into the Issue25 database the TYPES table from the Vision database in the Tutorial folder on your Student Disk.
10. Use Access's Spelling feature to correct the spelling of values in the Description column of the TYPES table.
11. Back up the Issue25 database from your Student Disk to your backup disk.
12. Compact the Issue25 database using Issue25 as the filename in the Compact Database Into dialog box.

Case Problems

1. Walkton Daily Press Carriers Robin Witkop has created a database to help Grant Sherman track newspaper carriers and their outstanding balances. Grant starts his maintenance of the CARRIERS table. He imports data to his database and then adds, changes, and deletes data to update the CARRIERS table.

Start Access and do the following:

1. Open the Press database in the Cases folder on your Student Disk and maximize the Database window.
2. Delete the CARRIERS table.
3. Import the CARRIERS-RW table from the Walkton database on your Student Disk.
4. Change the table name CARRIERS-RW to CARRIERS.
5. Open the CARRIERS table, which should contain 19 records.
6. Delete the record that has a value of 10 in the Carrier ID field. This is the record for Joe Carrasco.

7. In the Last Name field of the record having a Carrier ID value of 11, change Thompson to Thomson.
8. Make the following changes to the record that has a Carrier ID value of 17—the record for Bradley Slachter. Change the First Name field value to Sean; change the Birthdate field value 3/4/79 to 3/14/79.
9. Add the two new records shown in Figure 3-31 to the end of the CARRIERS table. Because Access automatically controls fields that are assigned an auto-number data type, press the Tab key instead of typing a field value in the Carrier ID field. Notice that Access assigns a unique number for the Carrier ID field value.

Figure 3-31

	Carrier ID	Last Name	First Name	Carrier Phone	Birthdate
Record 1:	AutoNumber	Rivera	Nelia	281-3787	6/3/80
Record 2:	AutoNumber	Hansen	Gunnar	949-6745	4/30/81

10. Sort the records in descending order by Last Name. Whose name appears last alphabetically? Put the records back in original order by sorting the Carrier ID field in ascending order.
11. Import the BILLINGS table from the Walkton database on your Student Disk. Use the Lookup Wizard to change the data type of the Carrier ID field to look up the Carrier ID in the CARRIERS table. Tell the Lookup Wizard to display the Carrier ID, Carrier Last Name and Carrier First Name fields when the Carrier ID field is selected.
12. Change the font and type style of the Billings table to settings of your choosing.
13. Save your changes, then print and close the datasheet.
14. Back up the Press database from your Student Disk to your backup disk.
15. Compact the Press database using Press as the filename in the Database to Compact Database Into dialog box.

2. Lopez Lexus Dealerships Maria and Hector Lopez have created a database to track their car inventory in the lots they own throughout Texas. They start their maintenance of the CARS table. They import data and then add, change, and delete data to update the CARS table.

Start Access and do the following:

1. Open the Lexus database in the Cases folder on your Student Disk and maximize the Database window.
2. Delete the CARS and LOCATIONS tables.
3. Import the CARS-LL table from the Lopez database on your Student Disk.
4. Change the table name CARS-LL to CARS.
5. Open the CARS table. It should contain 25 records.
6. Delete the record that has the value JT4AA in the Vehicle ID field. The record is for a Lexus GS300.
7. In the record having the Vehicle ID QQRT6, which is a Lexus LS400, change the value of the Cost field from $36,700 to $36,900. Change the value of the Class field from S1 to S5. You might need to scroll the datasheet to see these values.
8. Make the following changes to the record that has the Vehicle ID value AB7J8, which is a Lexus SC300. Change the Model field from SC300 to SC400; change the Cost field value from $41,300 to $42,300.
9. Add the two new records shown in Figure 3-32 to the end of the CARS table.

	Vehicle ID	Manufacturer	Model	Class	Transmission Type	Year	Location Code	Cost	Selling Price
Record 1:	MX8M4	Lexus	ES300	S4	A4	1996	P1	31,700	37,600
Record 2:	BY7BZ	Lexus	LS400	S5	M5	1996	H1	47,900	55,150

Figure 3-32

10. Resize the datasheet columns so that all field names and field values appear on the screen. Sort the records in descending order by Selling Price. What is the most expensive car?
11. Print the datasheet. If any columns are too narrow to print all field names and values, or if more than one page is needed to print the datasheet, resize the datasheet columns and reprint the datasheet.
12. Import the CLASSES, LOCATIONS, and TRANSMISSIONS tables from the Lopez database on your Student Disk. (*Hint*: Press the Control key to highlight and import all three tables together.)
13. Open the TRANSMISSIONS table and use Access's Spelling feature to check the spelling of values in the Transmission Desc field. Correct any misspelled words.
14. Change the font in the TRANSMISSIONS table to Arial, the size to 10, and the style to normal. Close the TRANSMISSIONS table.
15. Open the CARS table. Use the Lookup Wizard to change the data type for the Class, Transmission Type, and Location Code fields to Lookup Wizard. Define the following lookups:
    Class—look up the Class Type field in the CLASSES table. Display Class Type and Class Description.
    Transmission Type—look up the Transmission Type in the TRANSMISSIONS table. Display the Transmission Type and Transmission Desc fields.
    Location Code—look up the Location Code in the LOCATIONS table. Display the Location Code and Location Name fields.
    Close the CARS table, saving changes.
16. Back up the Lexus database from your Student Disk to your backup disk.
17. Compact the Lexus database using Lexus as the filename in the Compact Database Into dialog box.

3. Tophill University Student Employment Lee Chang has created a database to help Olivia Tyler track employers and their advertised part-time jobs for students. Olivia starts her maintenance of the JOBS table. She imports data to her database and then adds, changes, and deletes data to update the JOBS table.

Start Access and do the following:

1. Open the Parttime database in the Cases folder on your Student Disk and maximize the Database window.
2. Delete the JOBS table.
3. Import the JOBS-LC table from the Tophill database on your Student Disk.
4. Change the table name JOBS-LC to JOBS.
5. Open the JOBS table. It should contain 17 records.
6. Delete the record that has a value of 16 in the Job# field. This record describes a position for a night stock clerk.
7. In the Job Title field of the record having a Job# value of 3, change Computer Analyst to Computer Lab Associate.
8. Make the following changes to the record that has a Job# value of 13–the record describing a position for an actuarial aide. Change the Employer ID field to BJ93; change the Wage field value $8.40 to $9.25.

9. Add the two new records shown in Figure 3-33 to the end of the JOBS table. Because Access automatically controls fields that are assigned an autonumber data type, press the Tab key instead of typing a field value in the Job Order field. Notice that Access assigns a unique number for the Job Order field value. This number is not necessarily the next in sequence.

Figure 3-33

	Job Order	Hours/ Week	Employer ID	Job Title	Wages
Record 1:	AutoNumber	21	ME86	Lab Technician	5.30
Record 2:	AutoNumber	18	BJ92	Desktop Publishing Aide	5.80

10. Print the datasheet. If any columns are too narrow to print all field names and values, or if more than one page is needed to print the datasheet, resize the datasheet columns and reprint the datasheet.
11. Delete the EMPLOYERS table. Import the EMPLOYERS table from the Tophill database on your Student Disk. Redefine the data type of the Employer ID field in the JOBS table to Lookup Wizard. Link the Employer ID field in the JOBS table to the Employer ID field in the EMPLOYERS table. Display the Employer ID and Employer Name fields.
12. Sort the records in the JOBS table in descending order by Wages. Which Job Title earns the most? Return the records to their original order by sorting the Job# field in ascending order.
13. Use Access's Spelling feature to check the spelling of values in the Job Title field. Correct any spelling errors.
14. Open the EMPLOYERS table and change the font in the Employers table to one of your choosing. Print the datasheet, then close the datasheet, saving changes.
15. Back up the Parttime database from your Student Disk to your backup disk.
16. Compact the Parttime database using Parttime as the filename in the Compact Database Into dialog box.

4. Rexville Business Licenses Chester Pearce has created a database to help him track the licenses issued to businesses in the town of Rexville. Chester starts his maintenance of the BUSINESSES table. He imports data to his database and then adds, changes, and deletes data to update the BUSINESSES table.

Start Access and do the following:

1. Open the Buslic database in the Cases folder on your Student Disk and maximize the Database window.
2. Delete the BUSINESSES table.
3. Import the BUSINESSES-CP table from the Rexville database on your Student Disk.
4. Change the table name BUSINESSES-CP to BUSINESSES.
5. Open the BUSINESSES table. It should contain 12 records.
6. Switch to Design View. Enter the Caption property value Bus ID for the Business ID field and the Caption property value Phone# for the Phone Number field.
7. Use the best-fit method to resize the datasheet columns.
8. Delete the record that has a value of 3 in the Business ID field. The content of the Business Name field for this record is Take a Chance.
9. In the Street Name field of the record having a Business ID value of 9, change West Emerald Street to East Emerald Street.
10. Make the following changes to the record that has a Business ID value of 8. The Business Name for this field reads Lakeview House. Change the Business Name field to Rexville Billiards; change the Street# field value 2425 to 4252.

11. Add the two new records shown in Figure 3-34 to the end of the BUSINESSES table. Because Access automatically controls fields that are assigned an auto-number data type, press the Tab key instead of typing a field value in the Business ID field.

	Business ID	Business Name	Street Number	Street Name	Phone Number	Proprietor
Record 1:	AutoNumber	Kyle Manufacturing, Inc.	4818	West Paris Road	942-9239	Myron Kyle
Record 2:	AutoNumber	Merlin Auto Body	2922	Riverview Drive	243-5525	Lester Tiahrt

Figure 3-34

12. Sort the records in the BUSINESSES table in ascending order by Business Name. Print the datasheet. If any columns are too narrow to print all field names and values, or if more than one page is needed to print the datasheet, resize the datasheet columns and reprint the datasheet.
13. Restore the BUSINESSES table records to their original order by sorting the Business ID field in ascending order.
14. Import the ISSUED LICENSES table from the Rexville database on your Student Disk. Redefine the Business ID field to Lookup Wizard. Link the Business ID field in the ISSUED LICENSES table to the Business ID field in the BUSINESSES table. Display the Business ID and Business Name fields.
15. Delete the LICENSES table and then import the LICENSES table from the Rexville database in the Cases folder on your Student Disk. Use Access's Spelling feature to check the spelling of the values in the License Description field. Correct any misspelled words.
16. Redefine the data type of the License Type field in the ISSUED LICENSES table to Lookup Wizard. Link the License Type field in the ISSUED LICENSES table to the License Type field in the LICENSES table. Display the License Description and License Type fields.
17. Change the font in the LICENSES table to one of your choosing. Print the datasheet, then close the Datasheet window, saving changes.
18. Back up the Buslic database from your Student Disk to your backup disk.
19. Compact the Buslic database using Buslic as the filename in the Compact Database Into dialog box.

TUTORIAL 4

Querying Database Tables

Querying the Issue25 Database at Vision Publishers

OBJECTIVES

In this tutorial you will:

- Create and modify a query
- Run a query and view the results
- Save and open a query
- Define record selection criteria
- Sort records in a query
- Print selected query results
- Perform query calculations
- Add relationships between tables
- Create a parameter query

CASE

Vision Publishers

At the next progress meeting on the special 25th-anniversary issue of *Business Perspective*, Brian Murphy, Elena Sanchez, Judith Rossi, and Harold Larson discuss the information each needs to obtain from the database. Brian asks for a list of the freelancers, their phone numbers, and the amounts owed to them.

Judith and Elena decide to develop two writer contact lists, one based on specific area codes and the other based on the last dates the writers were contacted. Because Elena is starting the magazine layout process, she also wants to see the article titles and lengths.

Harold plans to highlight the diversity of articles in his marketing campaign, so he needs a list of writers and article titles, arranged by article type. Harold also wants to spotlight one or two writers in the marketing campaign, and the group decides that Valerie Hall and Wilhelm Seeger should be featured. Elena agrees to get Harold the contact information for these two writers.

Elena will use Access' query capability to obtain the answers to the preliminary list of questions shown in Figure 4-1.

Figure 4-1 Elena's questions about the Issue25 database

Answer these questions:

1. What are the names and phone numbers of and amounts owed to the freelancers?
2. What is the contact information for writers with specific area codes?
3. What is the contact information for Valerie Hall and Wilhelm Seeger?
4. What is the contact information for writers, arranged in order by last contact date?
5. What are the article titles, types, and lengths for each writer, arranged by article type?
6. What are the article titles and writer names, in order by article type?

Using a Query

A **query** is a question you ask about the data stored in a database in order to retrieve specific records. It means you don't have to scan through an entire database to find the information you need. Elena's list of questions about the Issue25 database are examples of queries. You create a query based on the specific information you need to extract from the database. A **criterion** is a rule that determines which records are selected. The query will tell Access which fields you need and what criterion (or criteria) Access should use to obtain the necessary information for you.

Access has a powerful query capability that can do the following:

- display selected fields and records from a table
- sort records
- perform calculations
- generate data for forms, reports, and other queries
- access data from two or more tables

The specific type of Access query that Elena will use to answer her questions is called a select query. A **select query** asks a question about the data stored in a database and returns an answer in a datasheet format. When you create a select query, you specify the conditions that the fields must meet in order for the records to be selected. The select query conditions are stored in the Query Design grid and can be stored as a file for later use. A second type of query, called a **filter**, is used with forms and is often created for one-time use. (You will work with filters in the next tutorial.) In the remainder of this tutorial, a select query will simply be called a query.

To create a query, you can use the Query Wizards, the Query Design window, or Structured Query Language (SQL). SQL (pronounced *sequel* or *ess cue ell*) is a powerful computer language used in querying, updating, and managing relational databases. In this tutorial, you will create queries using the Simple Query Wizard and the Query Design window. You will not use SQL here, as it is a more advanced Access capability.

SESSION 4.1

In this session, you will create a query using the Simple Query Wizard, run a query, view the query results, save a query design, and open a saved query design. You will also define selection criteria for a query and exclude a query field from the query results.

Creating a Query with the Simple Query Wizard

Query Wizards can be used for simple queries or for more complex queries. A simple query allows you to select records and fields and perform calculations and summaries. A complex query allows you to find duplicate records in a table, copy table records to a new table, or update groups of records. Because Elena has not created queries before, she decides first to practice by using the Simple Query Wizard. She begins by creating a query that will use all the records in the WRITERS table to answer the question: What are the names and phone numbers of and amounts owed to all writers?

CREATING A QUERY WITH THE SIMPLE QUERY WIZARD

- Click the Queries tab in the Database window to display the Queries list.
- Click the New button.
- In the New Query dialog box, select the Simple Query Wizard, then click the OK button.
- Select the table to be used in the query.
- Select the fields to be used in the query, then click the Next > button.
- Enter a name for the query.
- Click the Finish button.

To create a new query using the Simple Query Wizard:

1. If you have not done so, place your Student Disk in the appropriate drive, start Access, open the Issue25 database in the Tutorial folder on your Student Disk, maximize the Database window, then click the **Queries** tab in the Database window to display the Queries list. The Queries list box is empty because you haven't defined any queries yet.
2. Click the **New** button to open the New Query dialog box.
3. Click **Simple Query Wizard** to select it, then click the **OK** button. Access starts the Simple Query Wizard. See Figure 4-2.

   Clicking the Tables/Queries list arrow allows you to choose the table (or previous query) from which you will select fields. The Available Fields list box displays the fields from the chosen table. You click a field to highlight it, then click [>] to move the field to the Selected Fields list box. Clicking [>>] moves all available fields to the Selected Fields list box. Clicking [<] moves the highlighted field from the Selected Fields list box to the Available Fields list box and clicking [<<] moves all fields in the Selected Fields list box to the Available Fields list box.

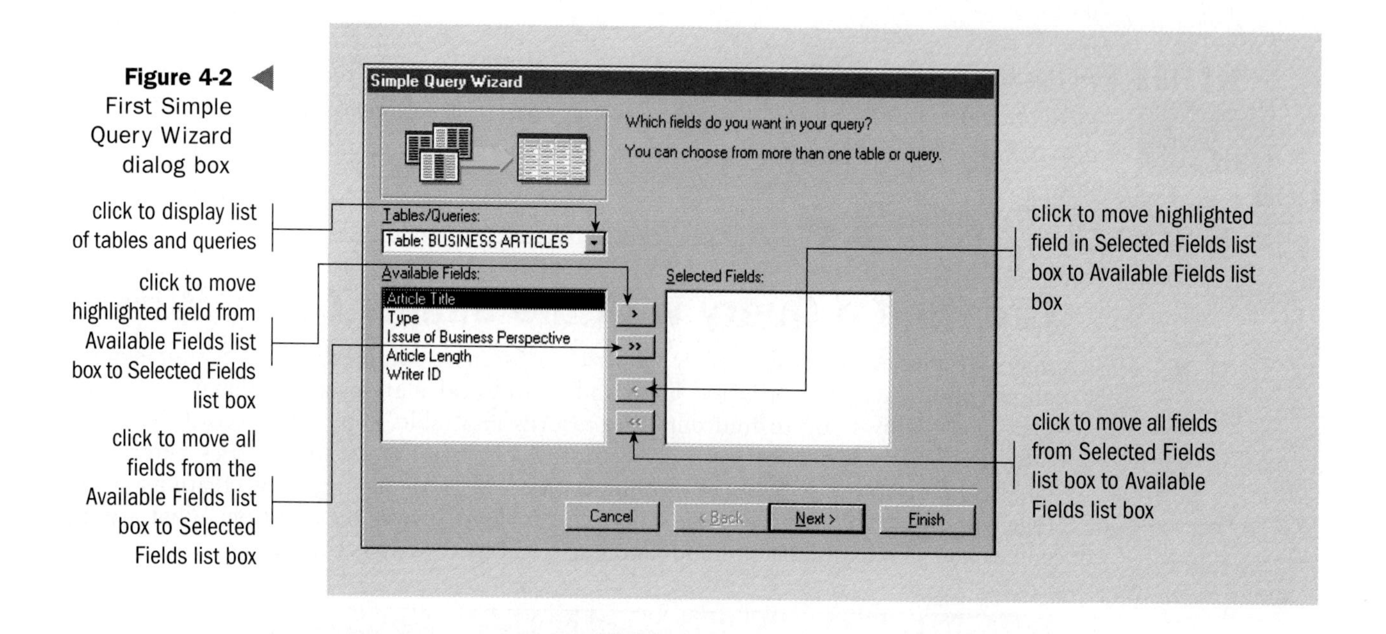

Figure 4-2 First Simple Query Wizard dialog box

Elena needs the Last Name, First Name, Writer Phone, and Freelancer Reprint Payment Amount fields from the WRITERS table.

To select fields for a query:

1. Click the **Tables/Queries** list arrow, then click **Table:WRITERS** to select the WRITERS table.
2. Click **Last Name** in the Available Fields list box, then click [>] to move it to the Selected Fields list box.
3. Using the same procedure, move the First Name, Writer Phone, and Freelancer Reprint Payment Amount fields to the Selected Fields list box, then click the [Next >] button to display the next Simple Query Wizard dialog box.

   This dialog box asks you to choose between a detail or a summary query. A detail query shows every field of every record that answers the query.
4. Make sure the Detail radio button is selected, then click the [Next >] button to display the next Simple Query Wizard dialog box.

   This dialog box asks you to enter the name you will use for this query. The name will appear in the list of queries in the Database window.
5. Type **Practice List Query**. Make sure the radio button is selected next to "Open the query to view information", then click the **Finish** button. See Figure 4-3.

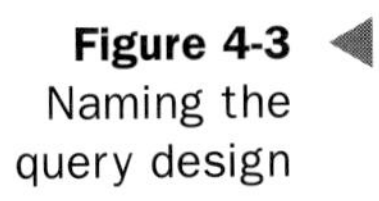
Figure 4-3 Naming the query design

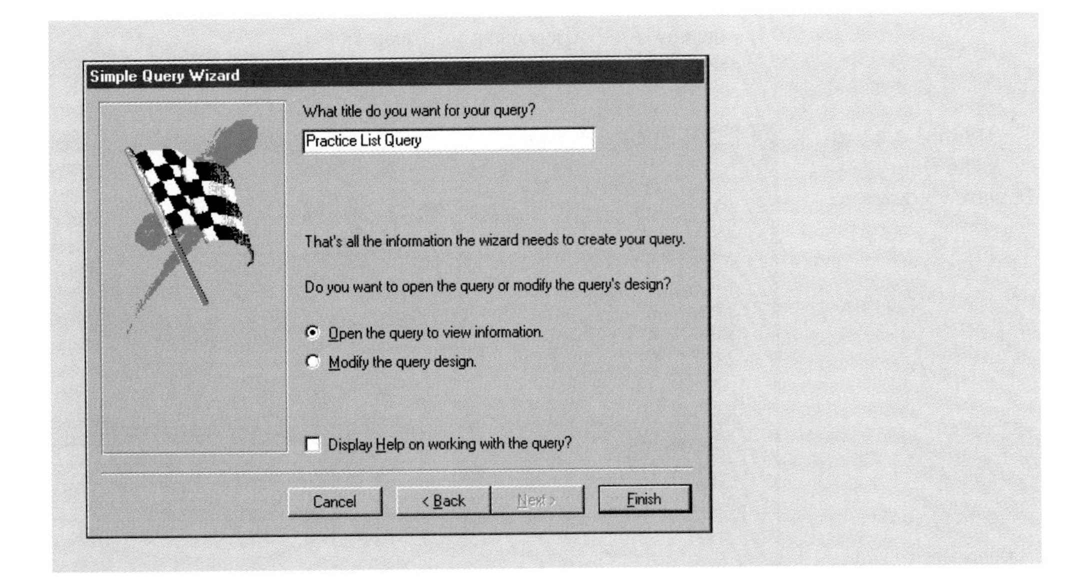

Access saves the query design and then runs the query. The query results are displayed in the Datasheet View window for the query.

Viewing the Query Results

The Datasheet View of the query results contains only the fields that you selected for the Practice List Query. These fields are displayed for each record in the WRITERS table. Although the query results look just like a table's datasheet and appear in the same Datasheet View window, the results are temporary and are not stored as a table on the disk. Instead, the query design is stored on the disk; you can re-create the query results at any time by running the query again.

In the Datasheet View of the query results, if you change a field value in a record, the change will be recorded in the underlying table. Records deleted from the query results will be deleted from the underlying table as well. In this case, however, you cannot add a record to the Practice List Query results, because each new record must have a value for the primary key field (Writer ID), which is not a field selected by the query. In general, to avoid any inconsistencies or errors, any changes to the data should be made directly to the underlying table.

Elena views the results of running the Practice List Query and decides that she would like to make some changes to the query design. She switches to the Query Design window to make the changes.

To switch to the Query Design window:

1. Click the **Query View** button on the toolbar. Access opens the Query Design window.

The Query Design Window

The Query Design window contains a standard title bar, menu bar, toolbar, and status bar. As shown in Figure 4-4, the title bar displays the query type, Select Query, and the query name, Practice List Query. You can use the Query Design window to make changes to existing queries. In addition to the standard window components, the Query Design window contains a field list and the Query Design grid. The field list, which appears in the upper-left part of the window, states the table name and contains all the fields from the table you are querying. The primary key is shown in bold. If your query needs fields from two or more tables, each table's field list appears in this upper portion of the Query Design window.

Figure 4-4
The Query Design window

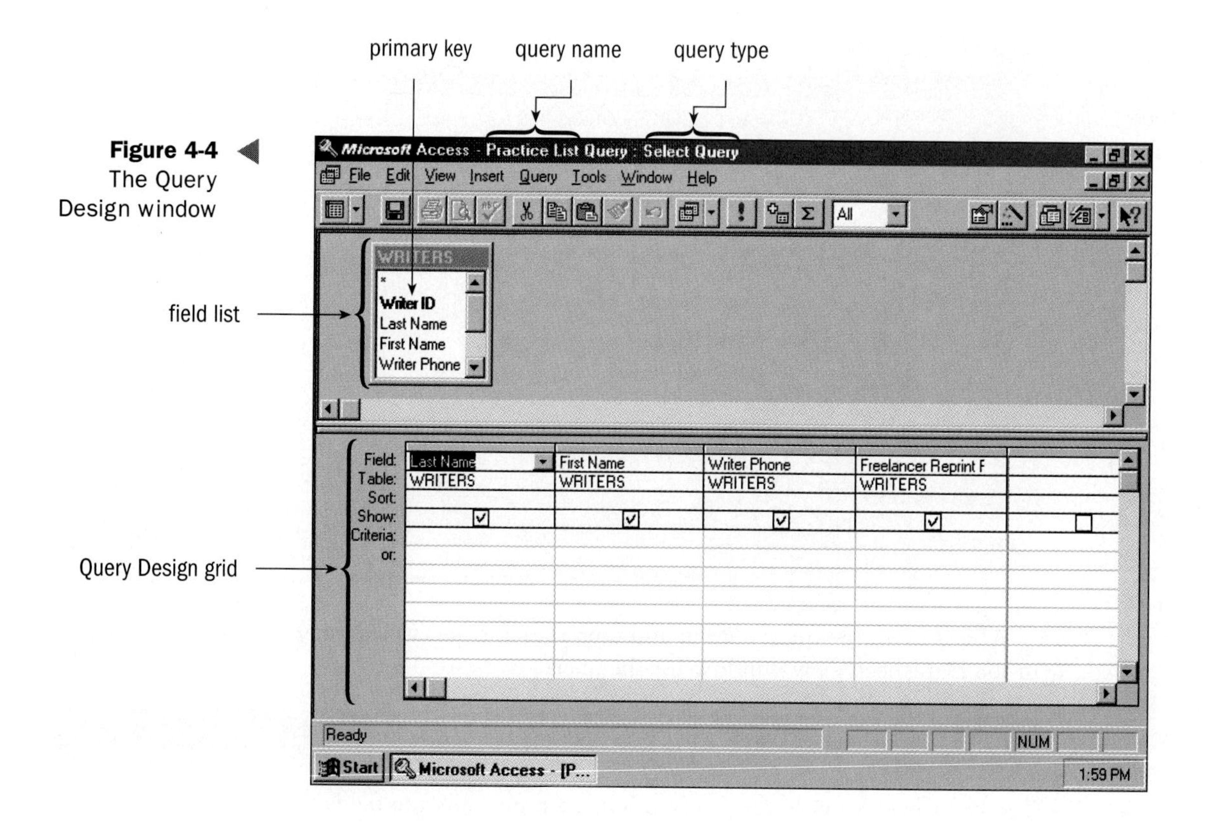

In the Query Design window, you can specify the data you want to see by constructing a query by example. When you create a **query by example (QBE)**, you give Access an example of the information you are requesting. Access then retrieves the information that precisely matches your example. In the Query Design grid, you include the fields and record selection criteria for the information you want to obtain. Each column in the Query Design grid contains specifications about a field you will use in the query. If the Query Design grid contains many fields depending upon your computer system you may need to use the horizontal scroll bar to view all of them.

Elena thinks reading the Practice List Query results will be easier if the First Name field precedes the Last Name field. She uses the Query Design grid in the Query Design window to make this change.

Moving a Field

The Query Design grid displays the fields in the order in which they appear in the query results. Elena moves the First Name field to the left of the Last Name field so that it will appear first in the query results.

To move a field in the Query Design grid:

1. Click the **First Name** field selector to highlight the entire column. (The field selectors are the gray bars above the Field row.) Click the **First Name** field selector again and drag the pointer, which appears as , to the left. When the pointer is anywhere in the Last Name column, release the mouse button. Access moves the First Name field to the left of the Last Name field. See Figure 4-5.

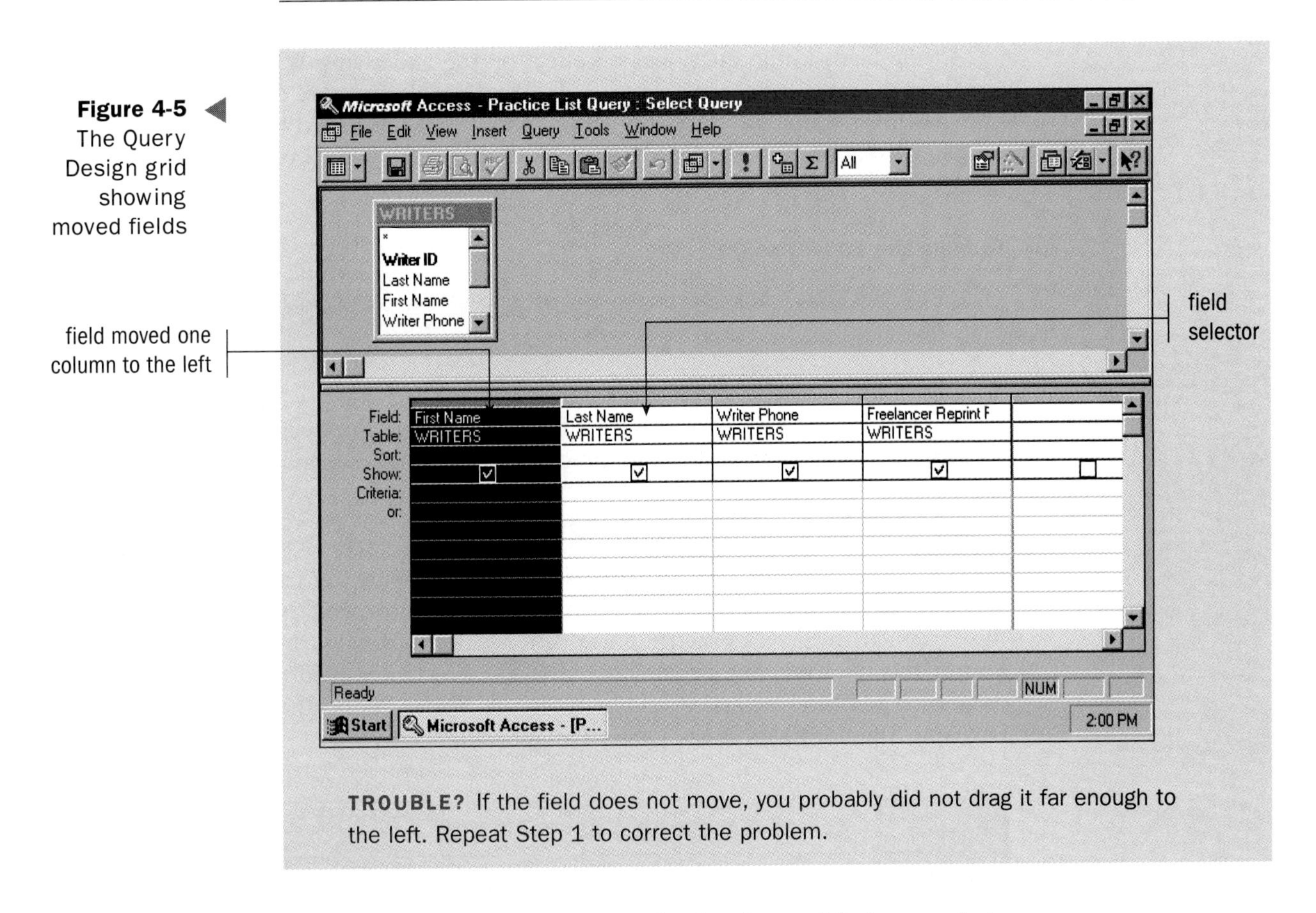

Figure 4-5 The Query Design grid showing moved fields

TROUBLE? If the field does not move, you probably did not drag it far enough to the left. Repeat Step 1 to correct the problem.

Elena now runs the query results for the modified query design.

To run a query:

1. Click the **Run** button on the toolbar. Access displays the query results in Datasheet View. See Figure 4-6. The First Name field now appears to the left of the Last Name field.

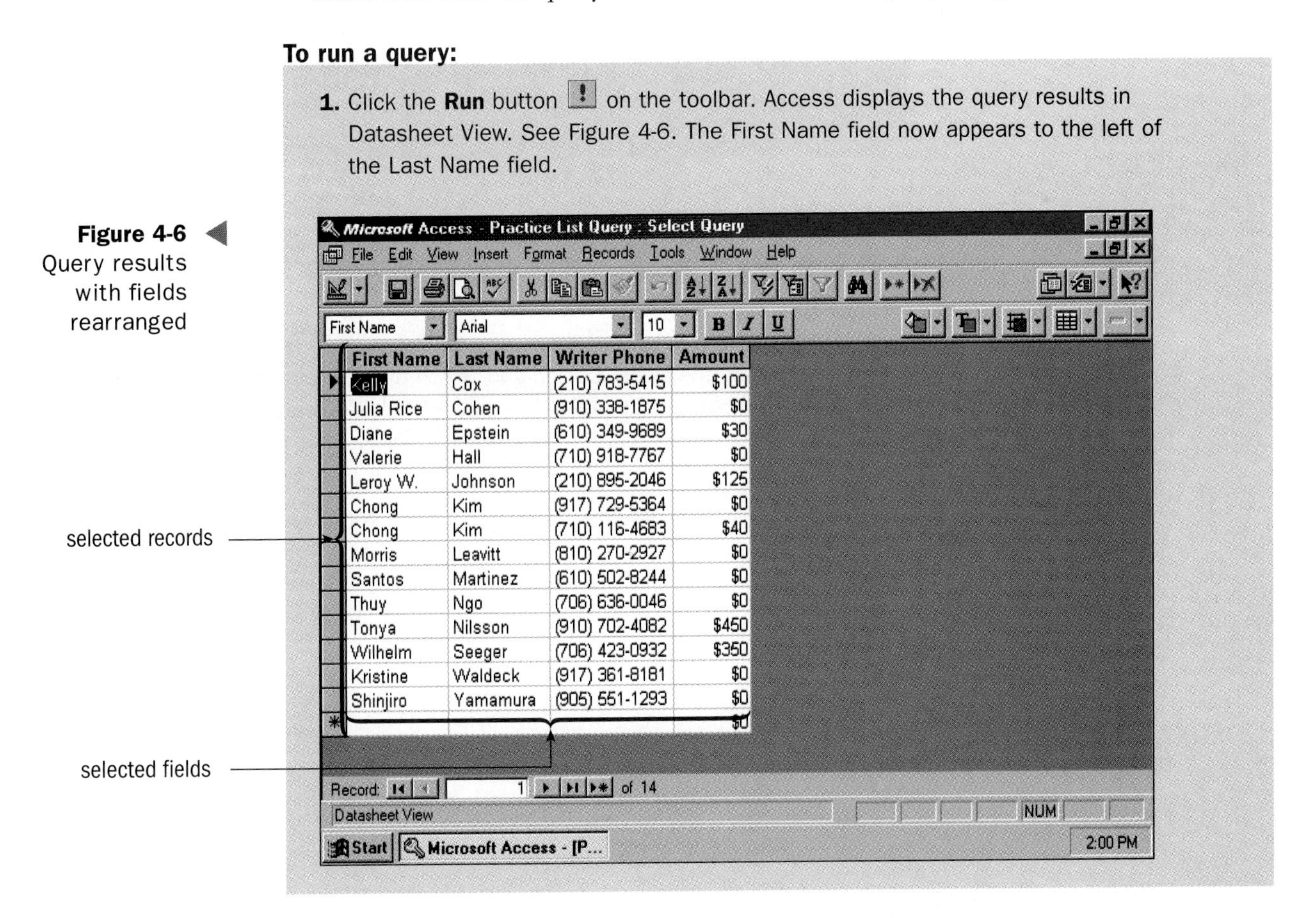

First Name	Last Name	Writer Phone	Amount
Kelly	Cox	(210) 783-5415	$100
Julia Rice	Cohen	(910) 338-1875	$0
Diane	Epstein	(610) 349-9689	$30
Valerie	Hall	(710) 918-7767	$0
Leroy W.	Johnson	(210) 895-2046	$125
Chong	Kim	(917) 729-5364	$0
Chong	Kim	(710) 116-4683	$40
Morris	Leavitt	(810) 270-2927	$0
Santos	Martinez	(610) 502-8244	$0
Thuy	Ngo	(706) 636-0046	$0
Tonya	Nilsson	(910) 702-4082	$450
Wilhelm	Seeger	(706) 423-0932	$350
Kristine	Waldeck	(917) 361-8181	$0
Shinjiro	Yamamura	(905) 551-1293	$0
			$0

Figure 4-6 Query results with fields rearranged

Moving fields in the query has no effect on the underlying WRITERS table. All fields remain in the table in the order you specified in the table structure design. With queries, you can view information any way you want without being restricted by the table structure.

Elena is satisfied with the appearance of the query and saves this modified query design.

To save the query design:

1. Click the **Save** button on the toolbar. Access saves the modified query design.

Remember that when Access saves the query design, the query results are not saved. You can view the query results any time by opening and rerunning the query.

Adding a Field to a Query

Elena is ready to consider the first question she needs to answer from the WRITERS table: What are the names and phone numbers of and amounts owed to all freelancers? Because this is similar to Elena's practice query, she decides to modify the Practice List Query to answer this question. She begins by adding the Freelancer field to the query design. She decides to add the Freelancer field between the Writer Phone and the Freelancer Reprint Payment Amount fields in the Query Design grid.

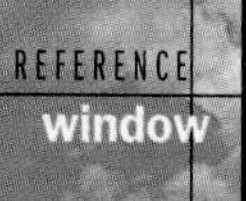

ADDING A FIELD TO A QUERY DESIGN

- Drag the field name from the field list to the Query Design grid or double-click the field name in the field list. Use the first method if you want to position the new field between other fields in the Query Design grid. When you use the second method, the new field becomes the last field in the Query Design grid.

To add a field to the query design:

1. Click the **Query View** button on the toolbar to switch to the Query Design window.
2. Scroll the field list in the upper panel until the Freelancer field is visible. Drag the **Freelancer** field to the Query Design grid. When the pointer moves over the Query Design grid, it changes to . Position the anywhere in the column for the Freelancer Reprint Payment Amount and release the mouse button.

   The Freelancer field is now inserted between the Writer Phone and the Freelancer Reprint Payment Amount fields in the Query Design grid. See Figure 4-7.

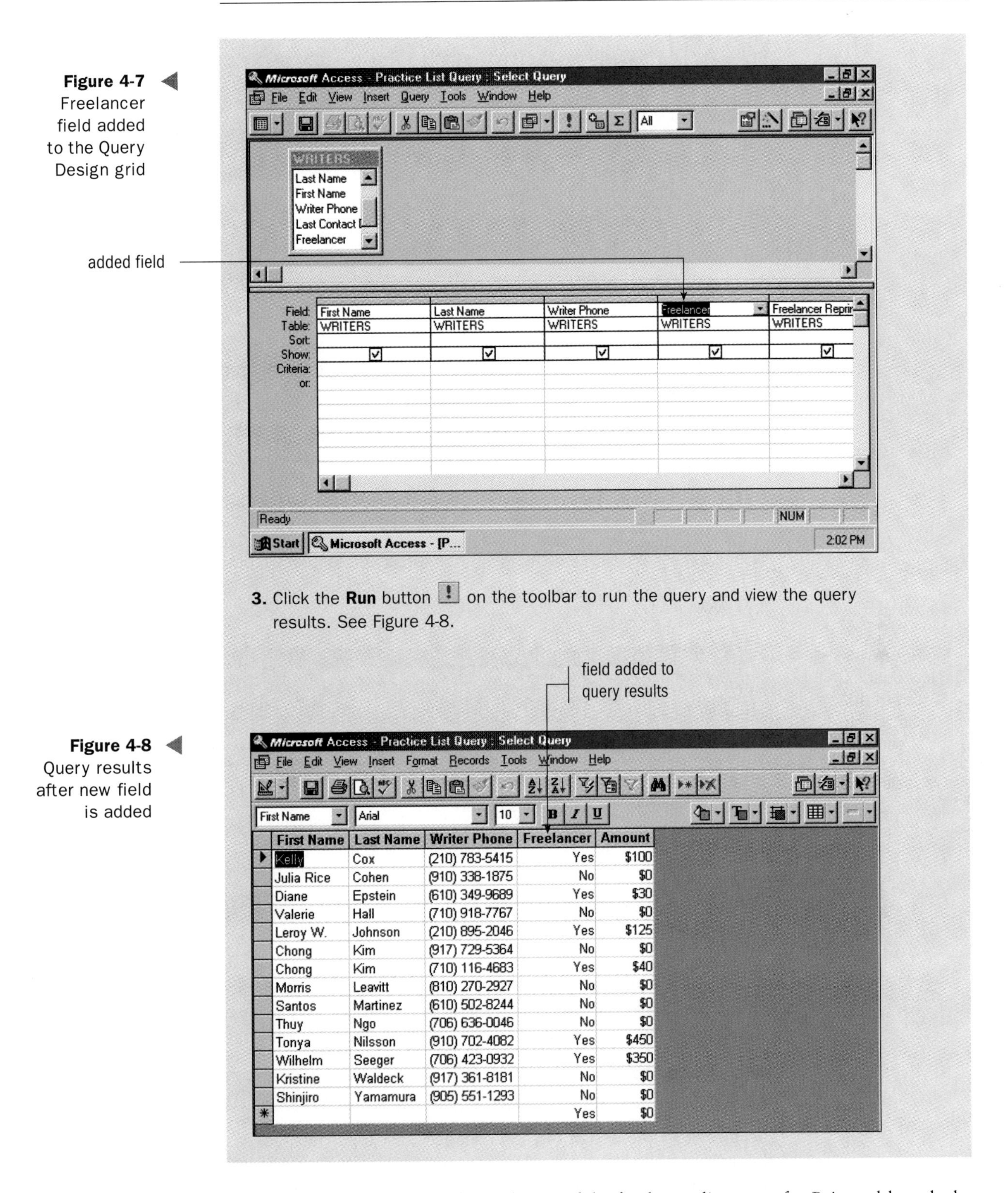

Figure 4-7
Freelancer field added to the Query Design grid

3. Click the **Run** button on the toolbar to run the query and view the query results. See Figure 4-8.

Figure 4-8
Query results after new field is added

First Name	Last Name	Writer Phone	Freelancer	Amount
Kelly	Cox	(210) 783-5415	Yes	$100
Julia Rice	Cohen	(910) 338-1875	No	$0
Diane	Epstein	(610) 349-9689	Yes	$30
Valerie	Hall	(710) 918-7767	No	$0
Leroy W.	Johnson	(210) 895-2046	Yes	$125
Chong	Kim	(917) 729-5364	No	$0
Chong	Kim	(710) 116-4683	Yes	$40
Morris	Leavitt	(810) 270-2927	No	$0
Santos	Martinez	(610) 502-8244	No	$0
Thuy	Ngo	(706) 636-0046	No	$0
Tonya	Nilsson	(910) 702-4082	Yes	$450
Wilhelm	Seeger	(706) 423-0932	Yes	$350
Kristine	Waldeck	(917) 361-8181	No	$0
Shinjiro	Yamamura	(905) 551-1293	No	$0
*			Yes	$0

Elena has completed the basic design of the freelancer list query for Brian, although she still needs to modify it. Before making any further changes, however, Elena decides to save the query design under a different name.

Elena saves the query, so that she and others can open and run it again in the future. Since she has modified the Practice List Query, Access will use that name for this query if Elena uses the Save button to save it now. Instead, Elena wants to save this query under a new name: Freelancer List for Brian Query.

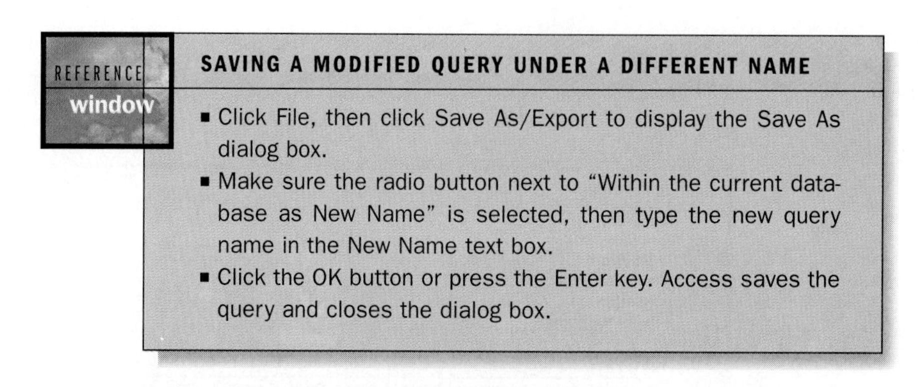

REFERENCE window

SAVING A MODIFIED QUERY UNDER A DIFFERENT NAME

- Click File, then click Save As/Export to display the Save As dialog box.
- Make sure the radio button next to "Within the current database as New Name" is selected, then type the new query name in the New Name text box.
- Click the OK button or press the Enter key. Access saves the query and closes the dialog box.

To save a query with a new name:

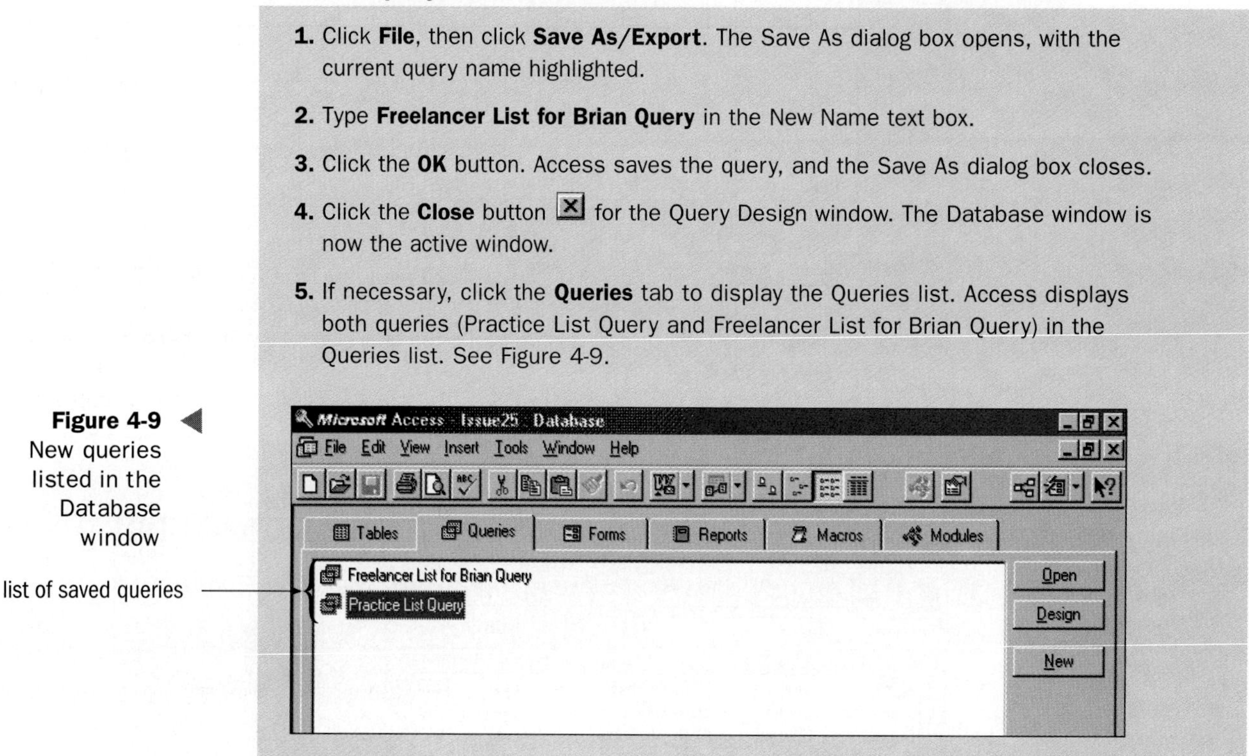

1. Click **File**, then click **Save As/Export**. The Save As dialog box opens, with the current query name highlighted.
2. Type **Freelancer List for Brian Query** in the New Name text box.
3. Click the **OK** button. Access saves the query, and the Save As dialog box closes.
4. Click the **Close** button for the Query Design window. The Database window is now the active window.
5. If necessary, click the **Queries** tab to display the Queries list. Access displays both queries (Practice List Query and Freelancer List for Brian Query) in the Queries list. See Figure 4-9.

Figure 4-9 New queries listed in the Database window

You can use the same procedure to save a query from the Design View window. If you try to close either the Design View window or the Datasheet View window without saving the query, Access displays a dialog box asking if you want to save the query. If you click the Yes button, Access saves the query under its current name.

Opening a Saved Query

Elena reviews the design of the Freelancer List for Brian Query. She already knows that the query results should display only the records for writers who are freelancers. Elena realizes there will then be no need to display the Freelancer column in the query results. She opens the Freelancer List for Brian Query to make these changes.

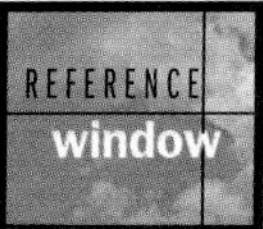

OPENING A SAVED QUERY

- Click the Query tab to display the Queries list in the Database window.
- To view the query results, click the query name and then click the Open button.
- To view the query design, click the query name and then click the Design View button.

To open a saved query to change its design:

1. If necessary, click the **Queries** tab to display the Queries list.
2. If necessary, click **Freelancer List for Brian Query** in the Queries list to select it, then click the **Design** button. The Query Design window appears with the saved query on the screen.

Defining Record Selection Criteria

Elena wants to modify the query design to include information on freelancers only. Some of the other questions in her list include finding contact information on Valerie Hall and Wilhelm Seeger and locating writers who have specific area codes. Unlike her Practice List Query, which selected some fields but all records from the WRITERS table, these questions ask Access to select specific records based on a criterion. Remember that a criterion determines which records are selected, based on conditions set for a field value.

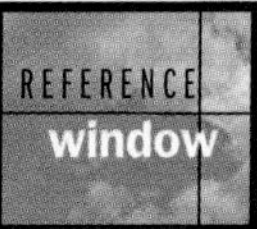

DEFINING RECORD SELECTION CRITERIA

- In the Query Design grid, click the Criteria text box for the field for which you want to define a selection criterion.
- Enter the selection criterion. Use an exact match, pattern match, list-of-values match, range-of-values match, or non-matching value criterion.
- Click the Run button on the toolbar. Access executes the query, selects the records that match the selection criterion, and displays the selected records in the Datasheet View window.

To define a condition for a field, you place the condition in the Query Design grid Criteria text box for the field. When you select records based on one criterion (for a single field), you are using a simple condition. To form a simple condition, you enter a comparison operator and a value. A **comparison operator** asks Access to compare the relationship between the criterion value and the field value and to select the record if the relationship is true. For example, because Elena wants records selected if they meet the condition that a writer is a freelancer, the simple condition =Yes for the Freelancer field selects all records having Freelancer field values equal to Yes. The Access comparison operators are shown in Figure 4-10.

Figure 4-10 Access comparison operators

Operator	Meaning	Example
=	equal to (optional, default operator)	="Hall"
<	less than	<#1/1/94#
<=	less than or equal to	<=100
>	greater than	>"C400"
>=	greater than or equal to	>=18.75
<>	not equal to	<>"Hall"
Between ... And...	between two values (inclusive)	Between 50 And 325
In ()	in a list of values	In ("Hall", "Seeger")
Like	matches a pattern that includes wildcards	Like "706*"

When you specify a comparison value for a Text field, the value should be enclosed in quotation marks. The quotation marks are optional for text that contains no spaces or punctuation, but it is usually a good idea to use them whenever you specify a text value. Similarly, when entering a date or time value in a Date/Time field, enclose the value with the # character.

Simple conditions fit into the following categories, you'll have an opportunity to use them in this tutorial:

- exact match
- pattern match
- list-of-values match
- non-matching value
- range-of-values match

Using an Exact Match

An **exact match** selects records that have a value for the selected field exactly matching the simple condition value. Elena modifies the Freelancer List for Brian Query to select only the records for freelancers. She enters the simple condition =Yes in the Criteria text box for the Freelancer field. When Elena runs the query, Access selects records that have the exact value Yes in the Freelancer field.

To select records that match a specific value:

1. Click the **Criteria** text box in the Query Design grid for the Freelancer field and then type **=Yes**. See Figure 4-11. Access will select a record only if the Freelancer field value is Yes. (You can also omit the equals symbol and just type Yes, because the equals sign is the default comparison operator automatically inserted by Access. However, it is good practice to type the comparison operator.)

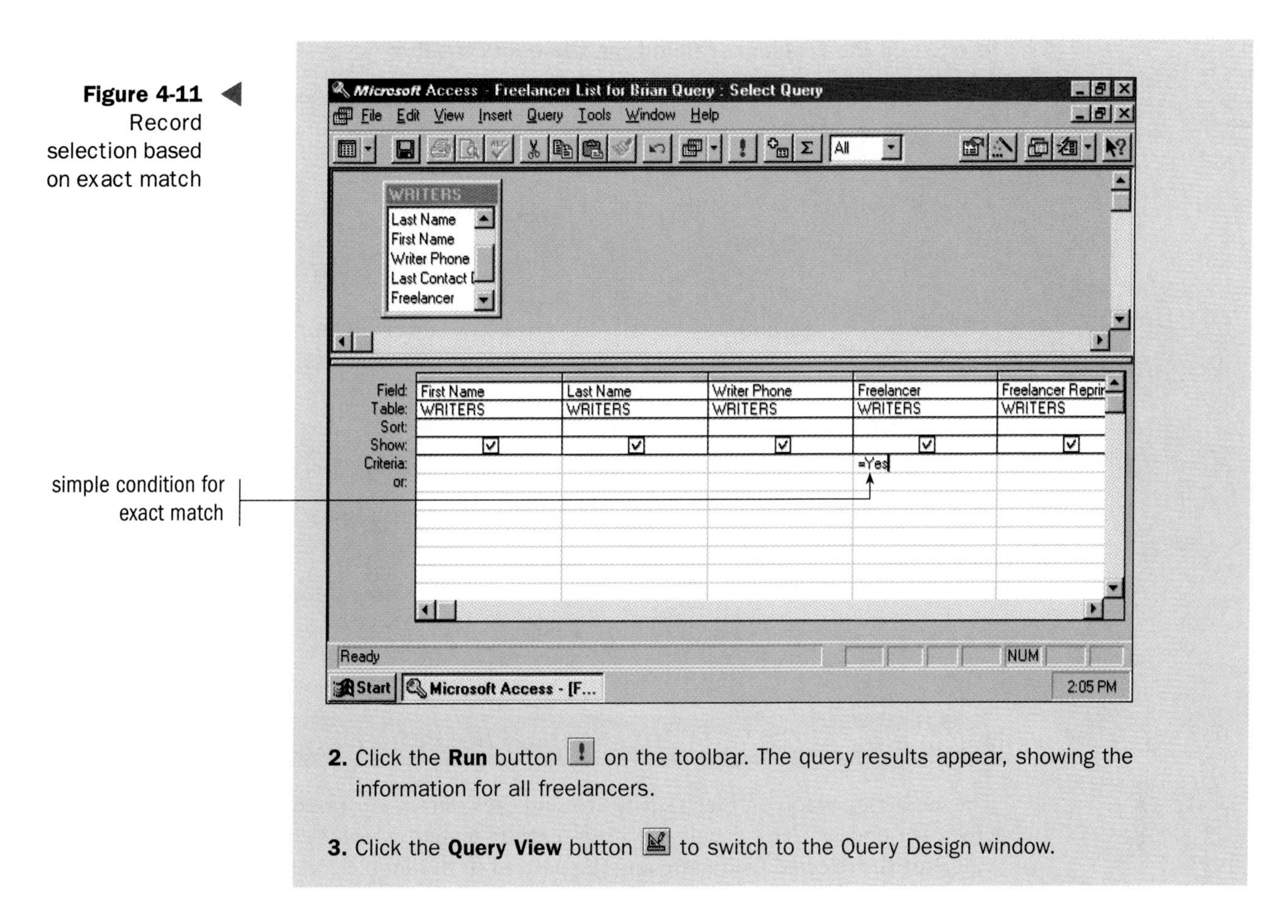

Figure 4-11 Record selection based on exact match

2. Click the **Run** button on the toolbar. The query results appear, showing the information for all freelancers.

3. Click the **Query View** button to switch to the Query Design window.

Now that the query design selects only the freelancer records, it is not necessary to display the Freelancer column in the query results. Elena next excludes the Freelancer column from the display.

Excluding a Field from the Query Results

Elena cannot delete the Freelancer column from the Query Design grid because it is needed to specify the selection criterion. Instead, she can click the Show box in the Query Design grid for the Freelancer column to remove the check mark from the Show box and prevent the field from appearing in the query results. Clicking the Show box again re-inserts the check mark in the Show box and includes the field in the query results.

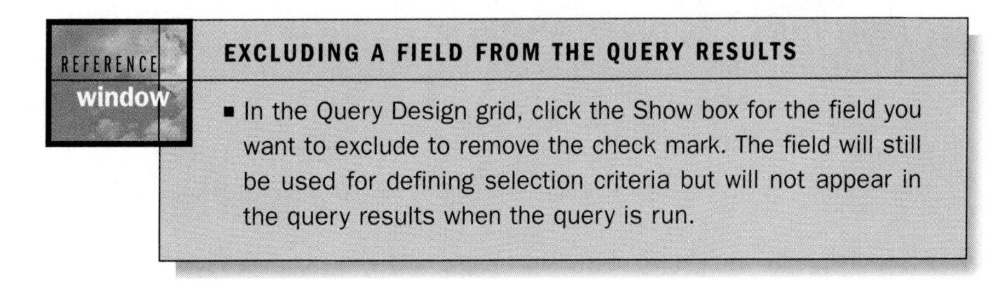
REFERENCE window

EXCLUDING A FIELD FROM THE QUERY RESULTS

- In the Query Design grid, click the Show box for the field you want to exclude to remove the check mark. The field will still be used for defining selection criteria but will not appear in the query results when the query is run.

To exclude the Freelancer field from the query results:

1. Click the **Show** box in the Freelancer column to remove the check mark. Access will no longer show the Freelancer field in the query results.
2. Click the **Run** button on the toolbar to display the query results. Only records for freelancers are selected, and the Freelancer field does not appear in the query results.

Elena is now satisfied with the design of the Freelancer List for Brian Query. She prints the query results, saves the query design, and returns to the Database window.

To print the query results and save the query design:

1. Click the **Print** button on the toolbar. Access prints the query results.
2. Click the **Save** button on the toolbar. Access saves the changes that you have made to the query design.
3. Click the **Close** button in the Datasheet View window. Access closes the window and returns to the Database window.

Using a Pattern Match

The second question on Elena's list is to find the contact information for writers with specific area codes. Elena decides to use a **pattern match**, which selects records that have a value for the selected field matching the pattern of the simple condition value, in this case, to select writers with 706 area codes. Elena does this using the Like comparison operator.

The Like comparison operator selects records by matching field values to a specific pattern that includes one or more wildcard characters—asterisk (*), question mark (?), and number symbol (#). The asterisk represents any string of characters, the question mark represents any single alphabetic character, and the number symbol represents any single digit. Using a pattern match is similar to using an exact match, except that a pattern match includes wildcard characters.

As further practice, Elena also decides to create the query design directly in the Query Design window.

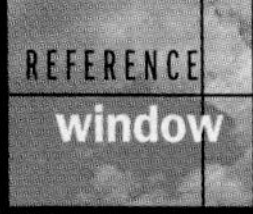

CREATING A QUERY DESIGN IN THE QUERY DESIGN WINDOW

- In the Queries list in the Database window, click the New button.
- Make sure that Design View is selected, then click the OK button.
- In the Show Table dialog box, select the table(s) on which the query is based, then click the OK button.
- In the Query Design window, select the fields to appear in the query results.
- Specify selection criteria and sorting options.
- Click the Save button on the toolbar to save the query design.

To create the query design in the Query Design window:

1. In the Queries list of the Database window, click the **New** button. Access displays the New Query dialog box. Design View is highlighted in the list box.
2. Click the **OK** button. Access displays the Query Design window and the Show Table dialog box.

   The Show Table dialog box allows you to select the tables and queries to be used in the query design. Elena needs only the WRITERS table for this query.
3. Click **WRITERS**, then click the **Add** button. See Figure 4-12.

Figure 4-12 The Show Table dialog box

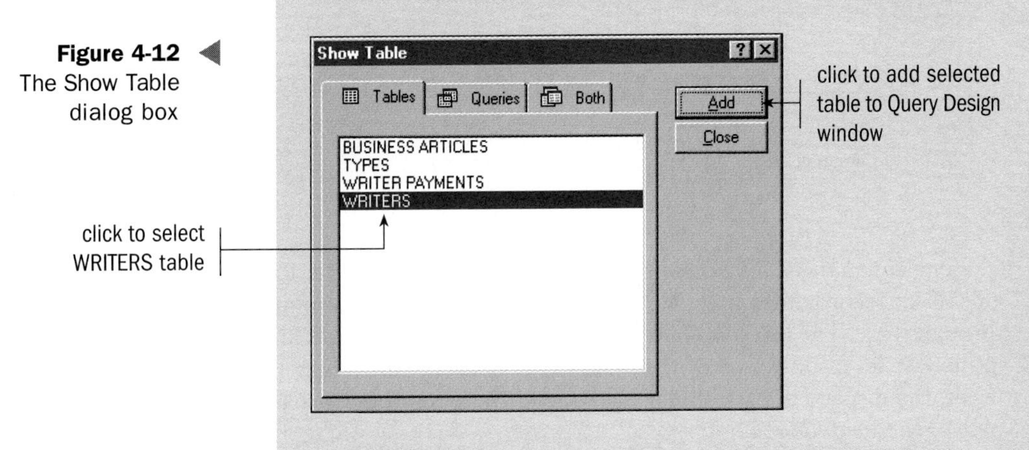

4. Click the **Close** button to close the Show Table dialog box. The WRITERS table now appears in the upper panel of the Query Design window. No fields appear in the Query Design grid because no fields have been selected yet.

Elena wants to use all the fields from the WRITERS table in the query. She could drag each field individually, but Access has two other methods for moving all of the fields at once. One method is to click the asterisk at the top of the field list. Access then places WRITERS.* in the Query Design grid, which represents all fields of the WRITERS table. The advantage of using this method over dragging each field individually is that you do not need to change the query if you add or delete fields from the underlying table structure. All changes to the table's fields will automatically appear in the query. However, this does not allow rearranging the order of the fields, sorting the records, or adding selection criteria. Elena uses a third method instead.

To include all fields in the query:

1. Double-click the **title bar** of the WRITERS field list to highlight, or select, all the fields in the table. Notice that the asterisk in the first row of the field list is not highlighted.
2. Click and hold the mouse button anywhere in the highlighted area of the WRITERS field list, then drag the pointer to the Query Design grid's first column Field box. As you near the destination Field box, the pointer changes to [pointer icon]. Release the mouse button in the Field box. Access adds each field in a separate Field box, from left to right. See Figure 4-13. If necessary, scroll right in the Query Design grid to see the fields that are off the screen.

Figure 4-13 Adding all fields to the query by the dragging method

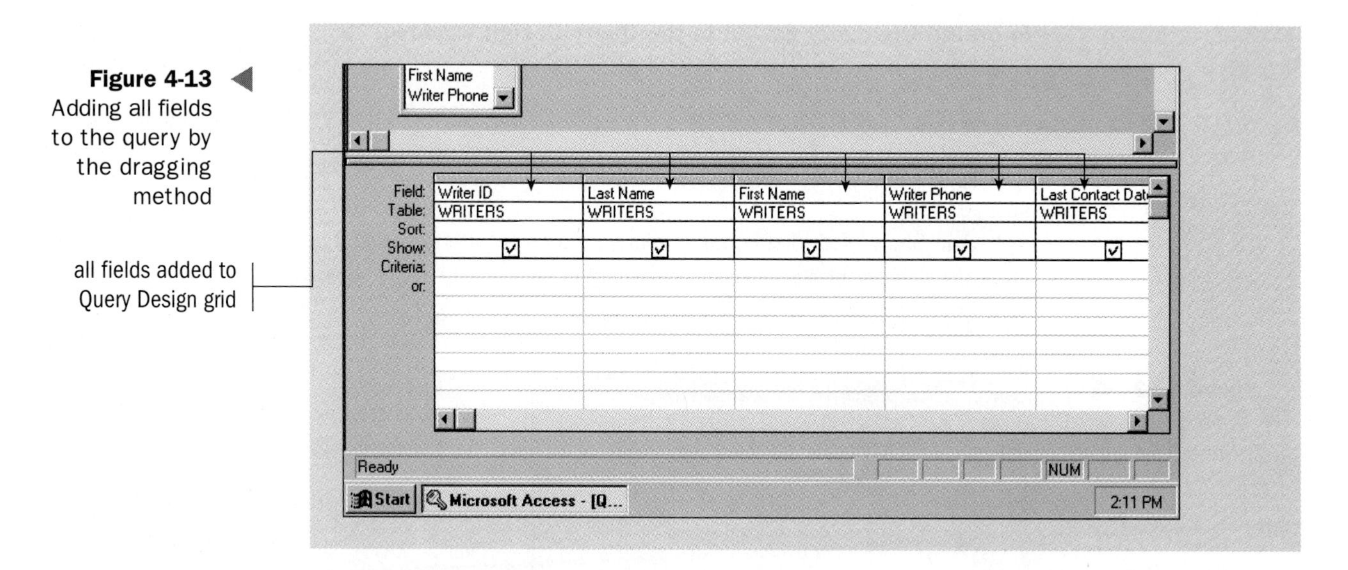

Elena enters the simple condition Like "706*" for the Writer Phone field so that Access will select records that have a Writer Phone field value containing 706 in positions one through three. The asterisk (*) wildcard character specifies that any characters can appear in the last seven positions of the field value. Because the Writer Phone field has an input mask, the displayed placeholder characters (the parentheses, space, and hyphen) are not part of the field value.

To select records that match a specific pattern:

1. Click the **Criteria** text box in the Query Design grid for the Writer Phone field and then type **Like "706*"**. See Figure 4-14. (Note that Access will automatically add Like and the quotation marks to the simple condition if you omit them.)

Figure 4-14 Record selection based on matching a specific pattern

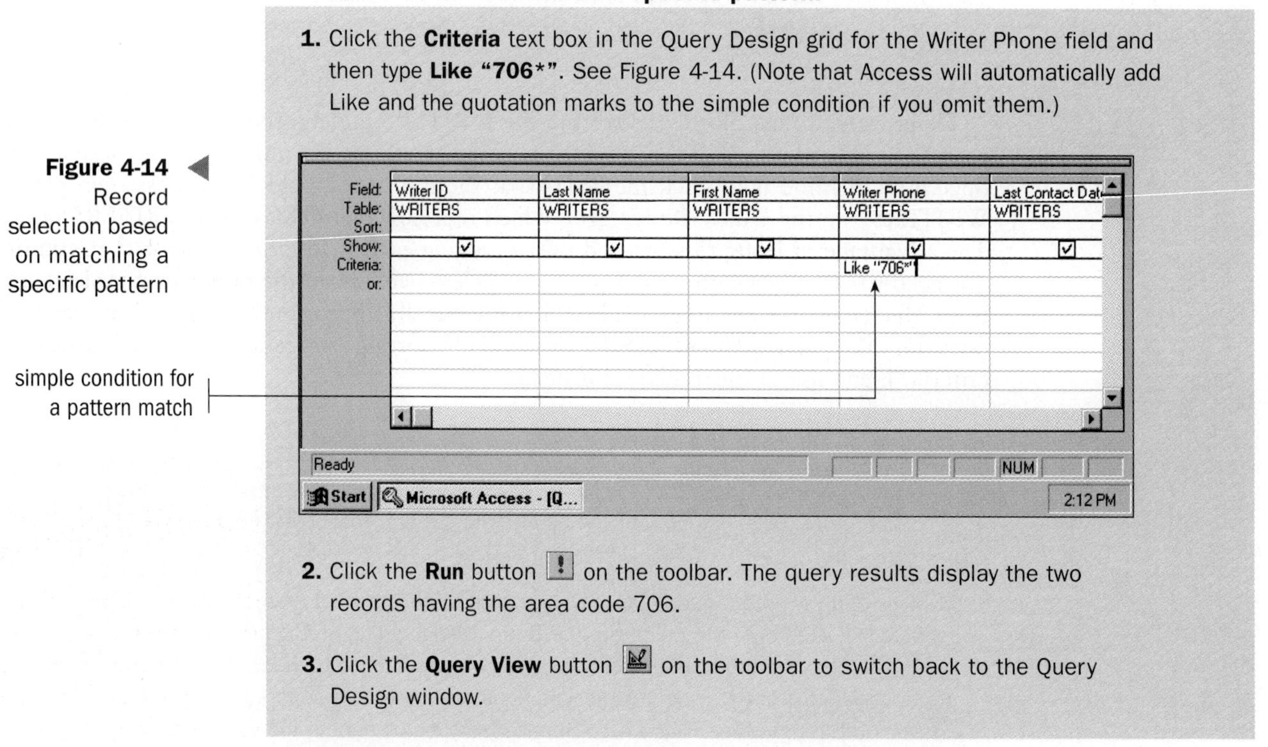

2. Click the **Run** button on the toolbar. The query results display the two records having the area code 706.

3. Click the **Query View** button on the toolbar to switch back to the Query Design window.

Elena prints her results and decides that she will next obtain the contact information for Valerie Hall and Wilhelm Seeger by using a list-of-values match.

Using a List-of-Values Match

A **list-of-values match** selects records that have a value for the selected field matching one of two or more simple condition values. Elena uses the In comparison operator to create the condition to find the contact information needed by Harold for Valerie Hall and Wilhelm Seeger. The In comparison operator allows you to define a condition with two or more values. If a record's field value matches at least one value from the list of values, Access selects that record.

Elena wants records selected if the Last Name field value is equal to Hall or to Seeger. These are the values she will use with the In comparison operator. The simple condition she enters is: In ("Hall","Seeger"). Because matching is not case-sensitive, hall and HALL and other variations will also match Hall. Notice that when you make a list of values, you place them inside parentheses.

To select records having a field value that matches a value in a list of values:

1. Click the **Criteria** text box for the Writer Phone field, press the **F2** key to highlight the entire condition, and then press the **Delete** key to remove the previous condition.

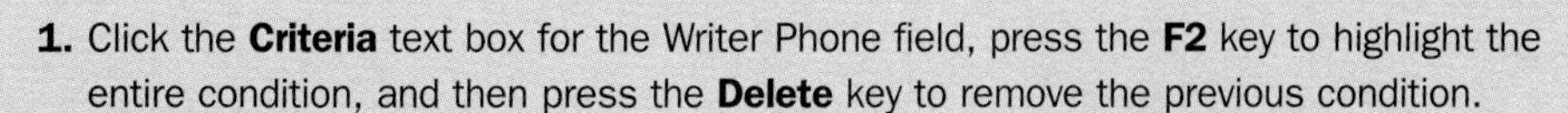

2. Scroll left in the Query Design grid if necessary to display the Last Name column. Click the **Criteria** text box for the Last Name field and then type **In ("Hall", "Seeger")**. See Figure 4-15.

Figure 4-15 Record selection based on matching field values to a list of values

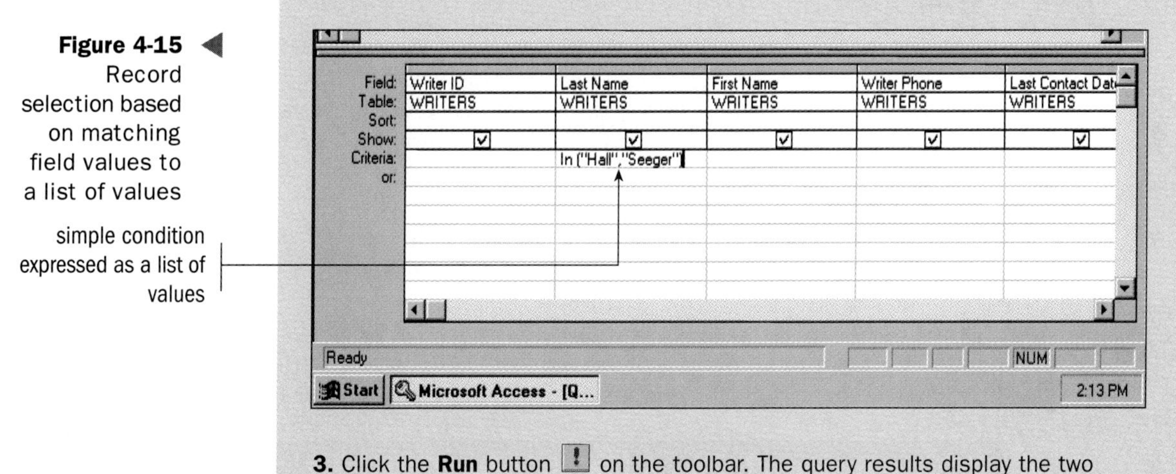

3. Click the **Run** button on the toolbar. The query results display the two records having Hall or Seeger in the Last Name field.

Elena prints the query results for Harold and proceeds to her next query.

Using a Non-Matching Value

Judith offers to help Elena with the task of contacting the writers and will call those writers with 706 area codes; Elena will contact the rest. Elena therefore needs to find all writers who do not have 706 area codes. To obtain this information, Elena uses a **non-matching value**, which selects records that have a value for the selected field that does not match the simple condition value. She will use a combination of the Like comparison operator and the Not logical operator. The Not logical operator allows you to find records that do not match a value. If Elena wants to find all records that do not have Hall in the Last Name field, for example, her condition is Not ="Hall".

Elena enters the simple condition Not Like "706*" in the Writer Phone field to select writers who do not have 706 area codes.

To select records having a field value that does not match a specific pattern:

1. Click the **Query View** button on the toolbar to switch back to the Query Design window.
2. If necessary, click the **Criteria** text box for the Last Name field, press the **F2** key to highlight the entire condition, and then press the **Delete** key to remove the previous condition.
3. Click the **Criteria** text box for the Writer Phone field and then type **Not Like "706*"**. See Figure 4-16. Access will select a record only if the Writer Phone field value does not have a 706 area code.

Figure 4-16 Record selection based on not matching a specific pattern

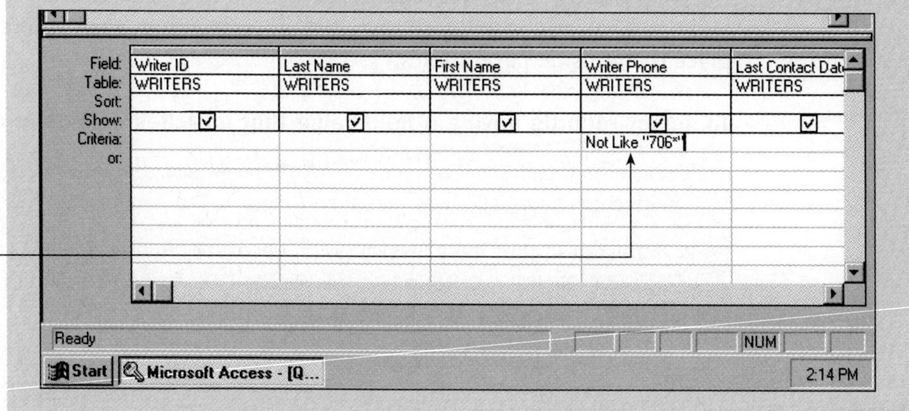

4. Click the **Run** button on the toolbar. The query results display only those records having a Writer Phone field value that does not have a 706 area code. Elena prints the results.
5. Click the **Query View** button to switch back to the Query Design window.

Elena is ready to go on to the next question on her list when Harold drops by with a new request. He needs to know all writers who were last contacted prior to 1994 for a meeting he will attend in an hour. To find this information, Elena will use a range-of-values match.

Using a Range-of-Values Match

A **range-of-values match** selects records that have a value for the selected field within a range specified in the simple condition. For Harold's request, Elena uses the less than (<) comparison operator with a date value of 1/1/94 and enters <#1/1/94# as the simple condition. Access will select records that have, in the Last Contact Date field, a date anywhere in the range of dates prior to January 1, 1994. You place date and time values inside number symbols (#). (If you omit the number symbols, Access will automatically include them, but it is good practice to include them yourself.)

To select records having a field value in a range of values:

1. Click the **Criteria** text box for the Writer Phone field, press the **F2** key to highlight the entire condition, and then press the **Delete** key to remove the previous condition.
2. Click the **Criteria** text box for the Last Contact Date field and then type **<#1/1/94#**. See Figure 4-17. Access will select a record only if the Last Contact Date field value is a date prior to January 1, 1994.

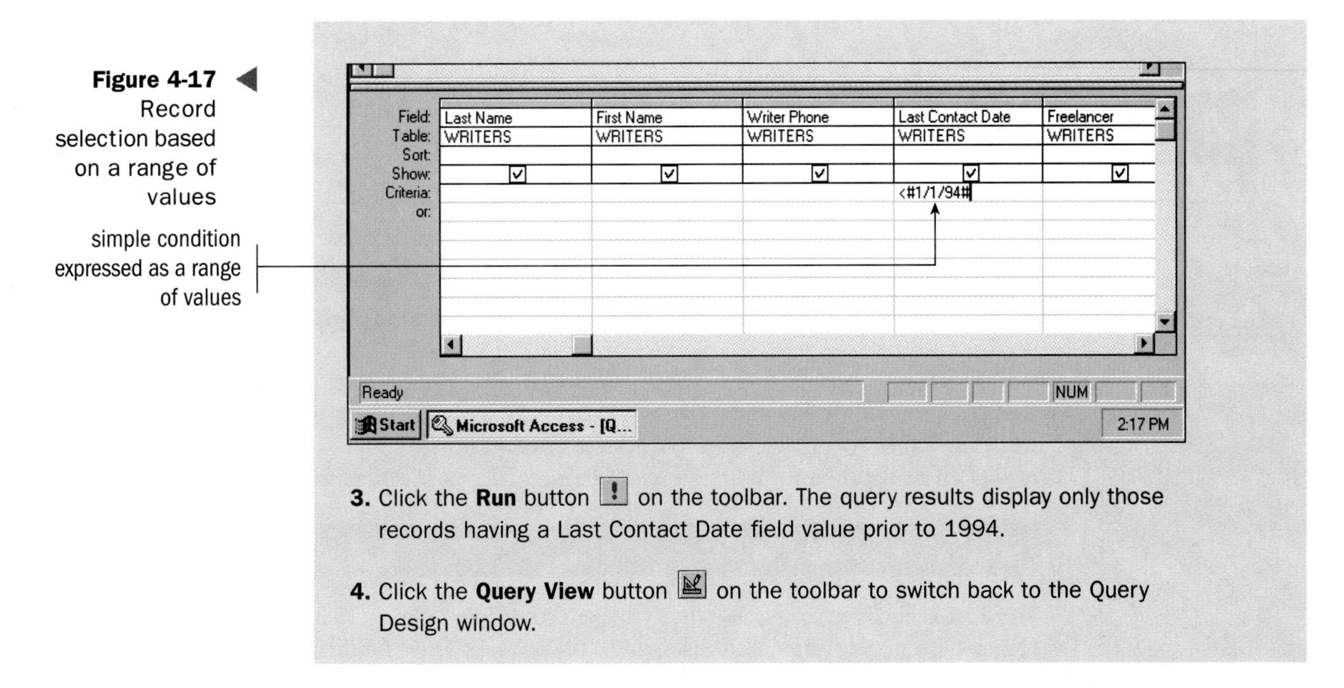

Figure 4-17 Record selection based on a range of values

3. Click the **Run** button on the toolbar. The query results display only those records having a Last Contact Date field value prior to 1994.

4. Click the **Query View** button on the toolbar to switch back to the Query Design window.

As Elena finishes and prints her query, Harold stops by to pick up the information and also reminds her that she also needs to attend the meeting. Because creating this query was easy and she wants to conserve disk space, Elena closes the Query Design window without saving the query.

To close the Query Design window without saving the query:

1. Click the Query Design window **Close** button. A dialog box asks if you want to save changes to the design of the Query1 query.

2. Click the **No** button. Access closes the Query Design window without saving the query.

If you want to take a break and resume the tutorial at a later time, exit Access. When you resume the tutorial, place your Student Disk in the appropriate drive, start Access, open the Issue25 database in the Tutorial folder on your Student Disk, click the Queries tab in the Database window to display the Queries list, and maximize the Database window.

Quick Check

1. What is the Simple Query Wizard?
2. In what format do the query results appear? What are the advantages of this format?
3. What is QBE?
4. What are two methods for adding a field from a table to the Query Design grid?
5. What are the two components of a simple condition?
6. How do you exclude a field that appears in the Query Design grid from the query results?
7. What comparison operator is used to select records based on a specific pattern?
8. When do you use the In comparison operator?

SESSION 4.2

In this session, you will learn to sort data in a query, print query results, define multiple selection criteria, and perform calculations in a query.

Sorting Data

After the meeting, Elena resumes work on the Issue25 database queries. The next item on her list of questions asks for writers arranged in order by last contact date. Because the WRITERS table displays records in Writer ID, or primary key, sequence, records in the query results will appear in Writer ID sequence as well. Elena will need to sort records from the table to produce the requested information. If you sort records in the query results and save the query design, the sorting order is saved as well.

Sorting a Single Field

You sort records in an Access query by selecting one or more fields to be sort keys in the Query Design grid. Elena chooses the Last Contact Date field to be the sort key for her next query. Because her last Access task was to return to the Database window, she first opens the Query Design window. Elena then adds all the fields from the WRITERS table to the Query Design grid.

To start a new query for a single table:

1. Make sure the Database window is open and maximized and that the Queries list is visible. Click the **New** button to open the New Query dialog box.
2. Make sure that Design View is selected, then click the **OK** button. Access opens the Query Design window.
3. Click **WRITERS** in the Show Table dialog box, then click the **Add** button. The WRITERS table appears in the upper panel of the Query Design window.
4. Click the **Close** button ☒ to close the Show Table dialog box.
5. Double-click the title bar of the WRITERS field list to highlight all the fields in the table.
6. Click and hold the mouse button anywhere in the highlighted area of the WRITERS field list, and then drag the pointer to the Query Design grid's first column Field text box and release the mouse button when the pointer changes to [pointer icon]. Access adds all the fields from the WRITERS table to separate boxes in the Query Design grid.

Elena now selects the Last Contact Date field to be the sort key.

REFERENCE window

SELECTING A SORT KEY IN THE QUERY DESIGN WINDOW

- Click the Sort text box in the Query Design grid for the field designated as the sort key.
- Click the Sort list arrow to display the Sort list.
- Click Ascending or Descending from the Sort list. Access displays the selected sort order in the Sort text box.

Elena decides a descending sort order for the Last Contact Date field (with most recent dates shown first) will be the best way to display the query results, and she now selects the sort key and its sort order. She does this by clicking the Sort list arrow for the Last Contact Date column in the Query Design grid.

To select a sort key and view sorted query results:

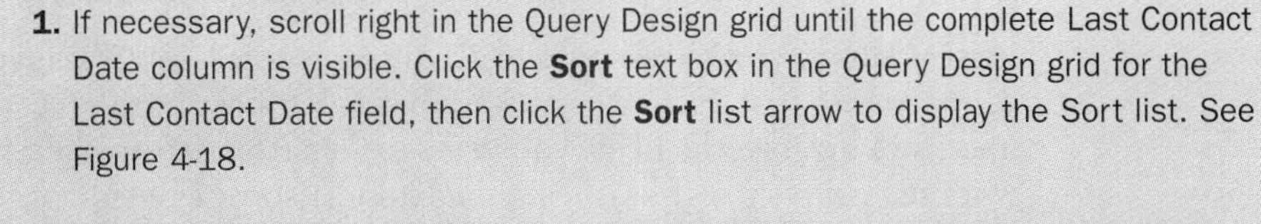

1. If necessary, scroll right in the Query Design grid until the complete Last Contact Date column is visible. Click the **Sort** text box in the Query Design grid for the Last Contact Date field, then click the **Sort** list arrow to display the Sort list. See Figure 4-18.

Figure 4-18 Specifying the sort order for the Last Contact Date field

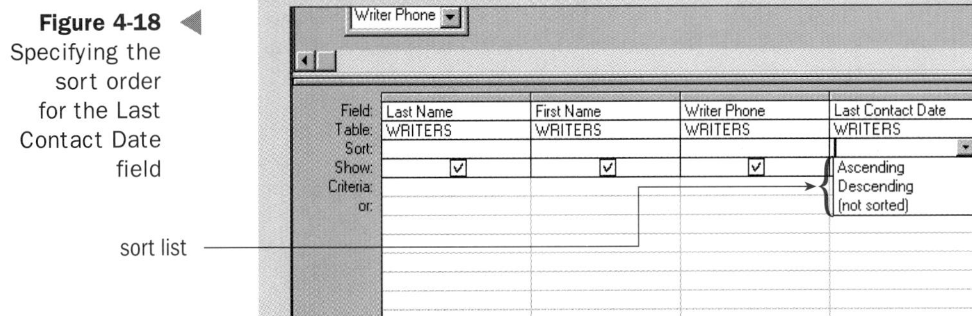

2. Click **Descending** in the Sort list. Descending appears in the Sort text box as the selected sort order.

3. Click the **Run** button on the toolbar. The query results display all the fields of the WRITERS table and all its records in descending order by Last Contact Date. See Figure 4-19.

Figure 4-19 Records sorted in descending order based on Last Contact Date

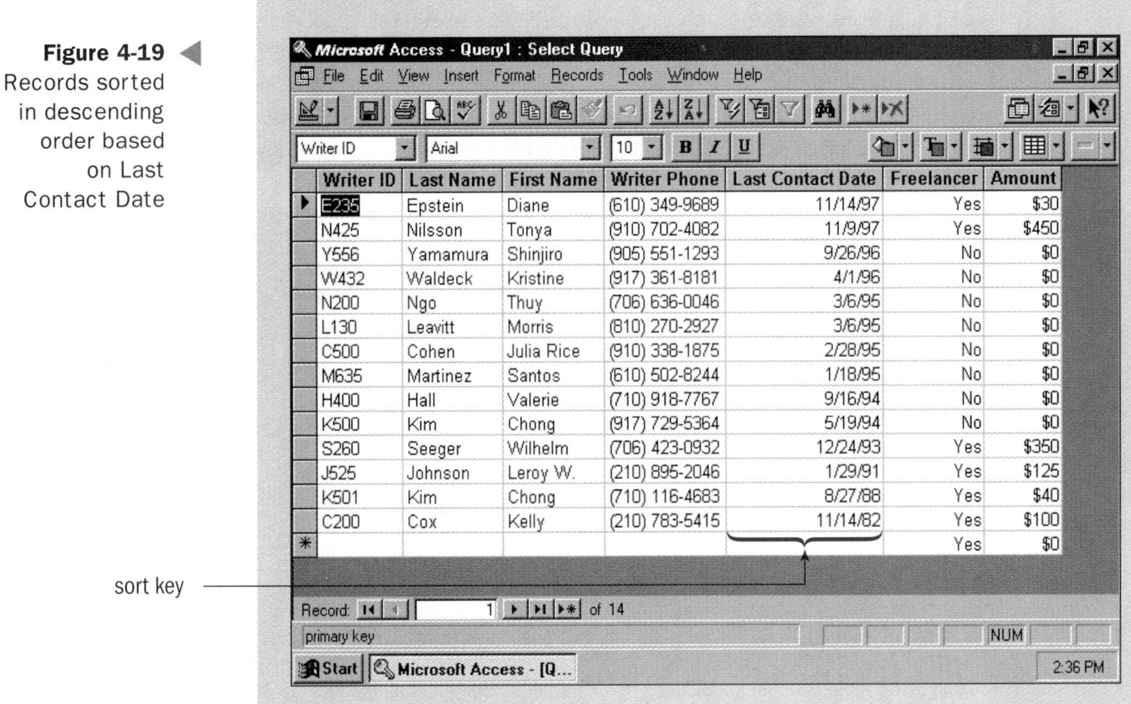

Writer ID	Last Name	First Name	Writer Phone	Last Contact Date	Freelancer	Amount
E235	Epstein	Diane	(610) 349-9689	11/14/97	Yes	$30
N425	Nilsson	Tonya	(910) 702-4082	11/9/97	Yes	$450
Y556	Yamamura	Shinjiro	(905) 551-1293	9/26/96	No	$0
W432	Waldeck	Kristine	(917) 361-8181	4/1/96	No	$0
N200	Ngo	Thuy	(706) 636-0046	3/6/95	No	$0
L130	Leavitt	Morris	(810) 270-2927	3/6/95	No	$0
C500	Cohen	Julia Rice	(910) 338-1875	2/28/95	No	$0
M635	Martinez	Santos	(610) 502-8244	1/18/95	No	$0
H400	Hall	Valerie	(710) 918-7767	9/16/94	No	$0
K500	Kim	Chong	(917) 729-5364	5/19/94	No	$0
S260	Seeger	Wilhelm	(706) 423-0932	12/24/93	Yes	$350
J525	Johnson	Leroy W.	(210) 895-2046	1/29/91	Yes	$125
K501	Kim	Chong	(710) 116-4683	8/27/88	Yes	$40
C200	Cox	Kelly	(210) 783-5415	11/14/82	Yes	$100
					Yes	$0

Elena studies the query results and decides the information would be more helpful if it was also sorted into staff writers and freelancers. This entails using two sort keys. Elena needs to select Freelancer as the primary sort key and Last Contact Date as the secondary sort key.

Sorting Multiple Fields

Access allows you to select up to 10 different sort keys. When you have two or more sort keys, Access first uses the sort key that is leftmost in the Query Design grid. You must therefore arrange the fields you want to sort from left to right in the Query Design grid, with the primary sort key being the leftmost sort key field.

The Freelancer field appears to the right of the Last Contact Date field in the Query Design grid. Because the Freelancer field is the primary sort key, Elena must move it to the left of the Last Contact Date field.

To move a field in the Query Design grid:

1. Click the **Query View** button on the toolbar to switch back to the Query Design window.
2. Click the **right arrow** button of the Query Design grid horizontal scroll bar until the Last Contact Date and Freelancer fields are visible.
3. Click the **Freelancer** field selector to highlight the entire column.
4. Click the **Freelancer** field selector again and drag the pointer, which appears as , to the left. When the pointer is anywhere in the Last Contact Date column, release the mouse button. Access moves the Freelancer field one column to the left.

   TROUBLE? If the Freelancer column does not move to the correct place, click the Freelancer field selector and move it to the correct position.

Elena previously selected the Last Contact Date field to be a sort key, and it is still in effect. She now chooses the appropriate sort order for the Freelancer field. Elena wants staff writers, which are identified in the Freelancer field by a value of No, to appear first in the query. Elena uses a descending sort order for the Freelancer field so that all No values appear first (Yes is considered to be less than No for the purpose of sorting Yes/No values). The Freelancer field will serve as the primary sort key, and the Last Contact Date field will be the secondary sort key.

To select a sort key:

1. Click the **Sort** text box in the Query Design grid for the Freelancer field, then click the **Sort** list arrow to display the Sort list.
2. Click **Descending** in the Sort list. Descending appears in the Sort text box as the selected sort order. See Figure 4-20.

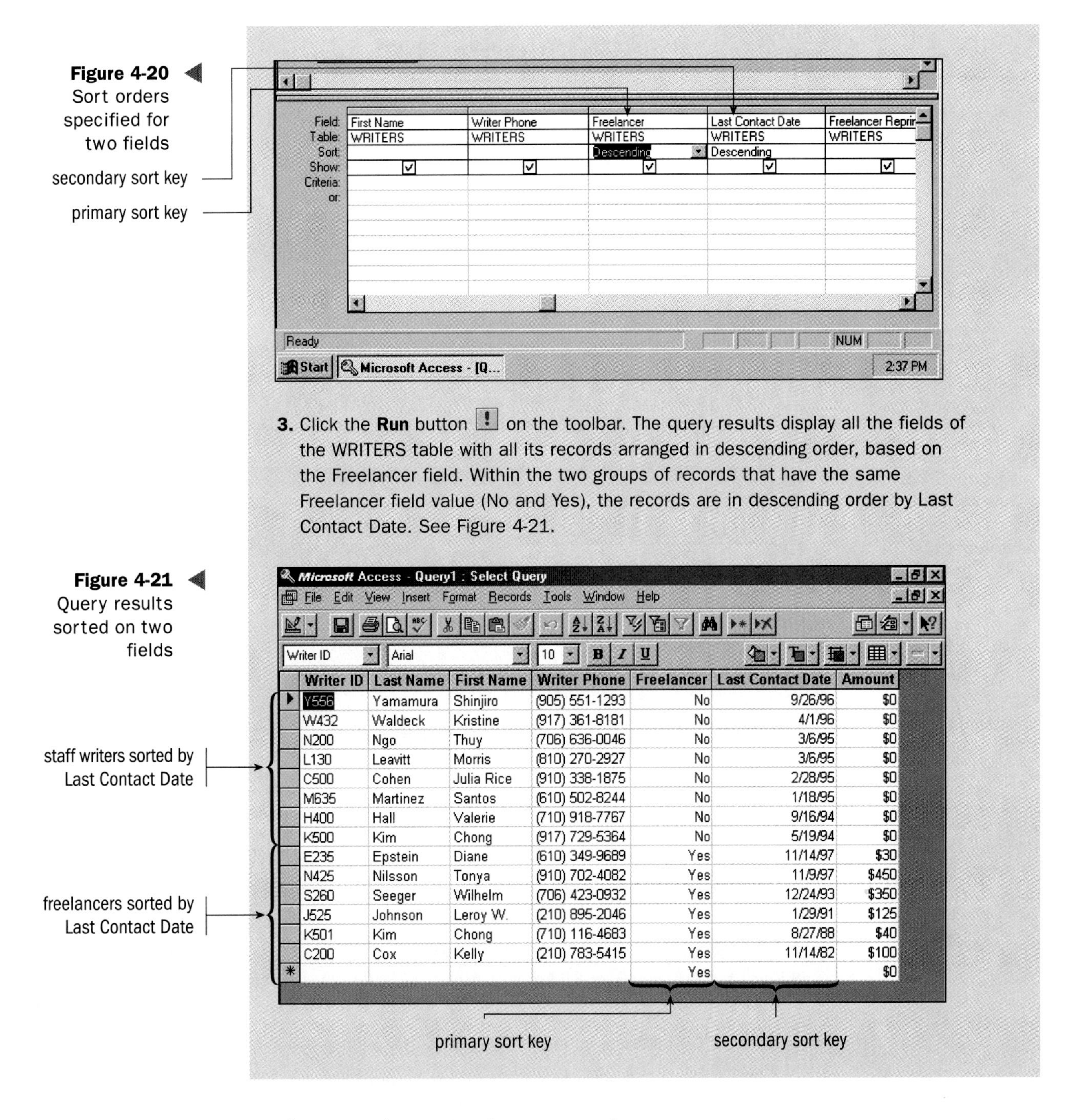

Figure 4-20 ◀ Sort orders specified for two fields

3. Click the **Run** button on the toolbar. The query results display all the fields of the WRITERS table with all its records arranged in descending order, based on the Freelancer field. Within the two groups of records that have the same Freelancer field value (No and Yes), the records are in descending order by Last Contact Date. See Figure 4-21.

Figure 4-21 ◀ Query results sorted on two fields

Writer ID	Last Name	First Name	Writer Phone	Freelancer	Last Contact Date	Amount
Y556	Yamamura	Shinjiro	(905) 551-1293	No	9/26/96	$0
W432	Waldeck	Kristine	(917) 361-8181	No	4/1/96	$0
N200	Ngo	Thuy	(706) 636-0046	No	3/6/95	$0
L130	Leavitt	Morris	(810) 270-2927	No	3/6/95	$0
C500	Cohen	Julia Rice	(910) 338-1875	No	2/28/95	$0
M635	Martinez	Santos	(610) 502-8244	No	1/18/95	$0
H400	Hall	Valerie	(710) 918-7767	No	9/16/94	$0
K500	Kim	Chong	(917) 729-5364	No	5/19/94	$0
E235	Epstein	Diane	(610) 349-9689	Yes	11/14/97	$30
N425	Nilsson	Tonya	(910) 702-4082	Yes	11/9/97	$450
S260	Seeger	Wilhelm	(706) 423-0932	Yes	12/24/93	$350
J525	Johnson	Leroy W.	(210) 895-2046	Yes	1/29/91	$125
K501	Kim	Chong	(710) 116-4683	Yes	8/27/88	$40
C200	Cox	Kelly	(210) 783-5415	Yes	11/14/82	$100
*				Yes		$0

Elena is ready to print the query results.

Printing Selected Query Results

Rather than print the staff writers and freelancers together, Elena wants to print the staff writers and the freelancers as separate lists. Elena could change the query to select one group, run the query, print the query results, and then repeat the process for the other group. Instead, she uses a quicker method by selecting one group in the query results, printing the selected query results, and then doing the same for the other group.

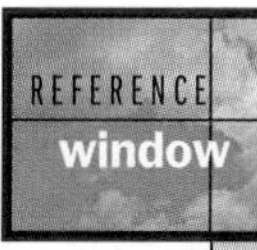

PRINTING SELECTED QUERY RESULTS

- In the query results window, select the records you want to print.
- Click File, then click Print to open the Print dialog box.
- Click the Selected Record(s) radio button to print the selected records.
- Click the OK button to initiate printing.

To print selected query results:

1. Click the **record selector** for the first query results record and, while holding down the mouse button, drag the pointer to the record selector of the last record that has a No value in the Freelancer field. Release the button. The group of records with Freelancer field values of No is highlighted. See Figure 4-22.

Figure 4-22 Query results records selected for printing

Microsoft Access - Query1 : Select Query

Writer ID	Last Name	First Name	Writer Phone	Freelancer	Last Contact Date	Amount
Y556	Yamamura	Shinjiro	(905) 551-1293	No	9/26/96	$0
W432	Waldeck	Kristine	(917) 361-8181	No	4/1/96	$0
N200	Ngo	Thuy	(706) 636-0046	No	3/6/95	$0
L130	Leavitt	Morris	(810) 270-2927	No	3/6/95	$0
C500	Cohen	Julia Rice	(910) 338-1875	No	2/28/95	$0
M635	Martinez	Santos	(610) 502-8244	No	1/18/95	$0
H400	Hall	Valerie	(710) 918-7767	No	9/16/94	$0
K500	Kim	Chong	(917) 729-5364	No	5/19/94	$0
E235	Epstein	Diane	(610) 349-9689	Yes	11/14/97	$30
N425	Nilsson	Tonya	(910) 702-4082	Yes	11/9/97	$450
S260	Seeger	Wilhelm	(706) 423-0932	Yes	12/24/93	$350
J525	Johnson	Leroy W.	(210) 895-2046	Yes	1/29/91	$125
K501	Kim	Chong	(710) 116-4683	Yes	8/27/88	$40
C200	Cox	Kelly	(210) 783-5415	Yes	11/14/82	$100
*				Yes		$0

record selectors

records selected for printing

2. Click **File**, then click **Print** to open the Print dialog box.
3. Click the Selected Record(s) radio button to print just those records that are highlighted in the query results.
4. Click the **OK** button to initiate printing. After the printing dialog box closes, you are returned to the query results.

   TROUBLE? If the selected query results are not printed, make sure your printer is on-line and that your computer's printer is selected in the Printer section of the Print dialog box.

5. Use the same procedure to print the records for the Freelancers.

Defining Multiple Selection Criteria

The previous queries that Elena created involved just one condition—for example, a condition to obtain information for freelancers. What if Elena needs to find all freelancers who were last contacted prior to 1990? This query involves two conditions.

Multiple conditions require you to use logical operators to combine two or more simple conditions. When you want a record selected only if all conditions are met, then you need to use the And logical operator. To use the And logical operator, you place two or more simple conditions in the same Criteria row of the Query Design grid. If a record meets every one of the conditions in the Criteria row, then Access selects the record.

If you place multiple conditions in different Criteria rows, Access selects a record if at least one of the conditions is satisfied. If none of the conditions is satisfied, then Access does not select the record. This is known as the Or logical operator. The difference between the two logical operators is illustrated in Figure 4-23.

Figure 4-23 Logical operators And and Or for multiple selection criteia

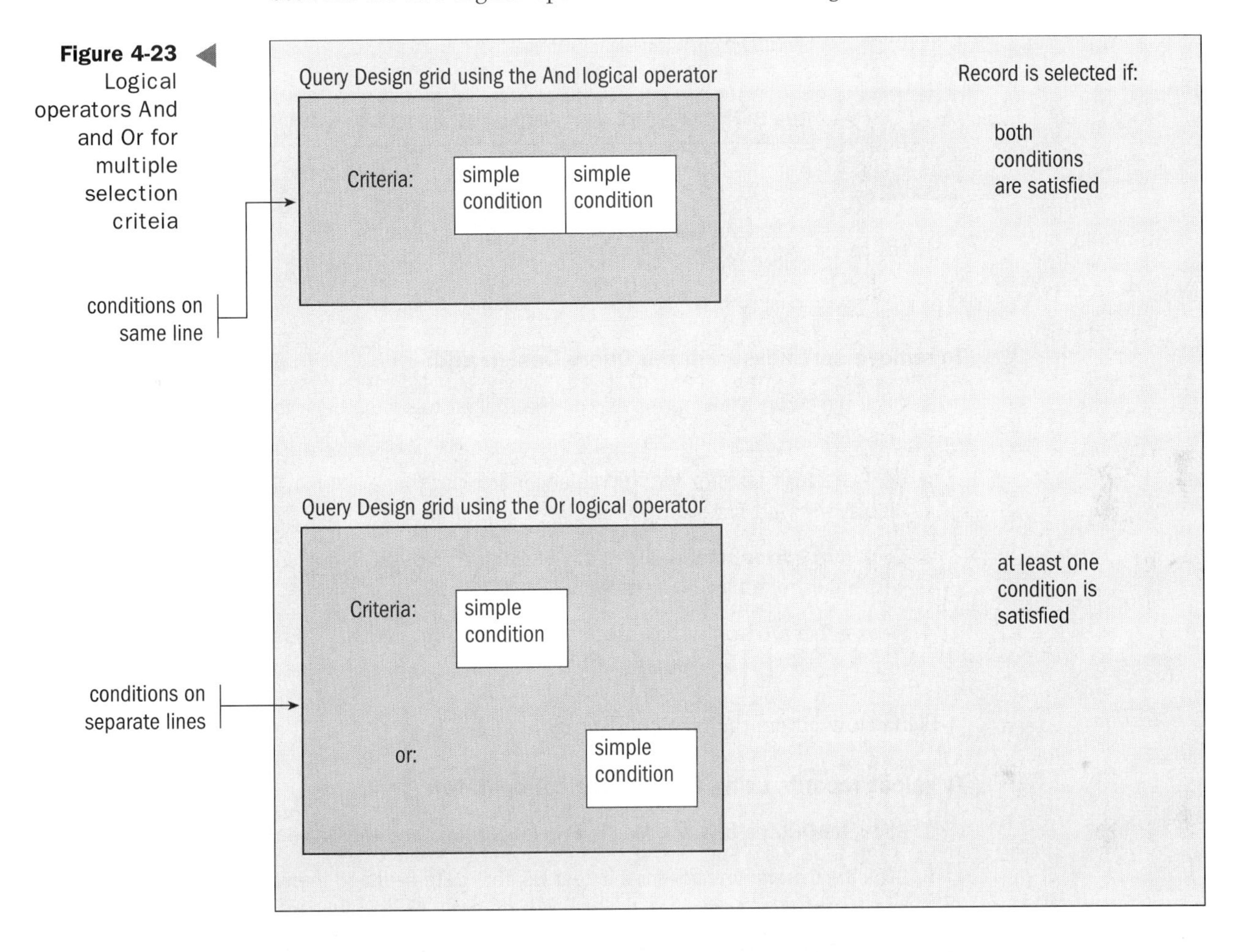

REFERENCE window

DEFINING MULTIPLE SELECTION CRITERIA

- In the Query Design grid, enter the first condition in the Criteria text box for the appropriate field.
- To create an And condition, enter the second condition on the same line as the first condition.
- To create an Or condition, enter the second condition on a different line from the first condition.

The use of the word "and" in a question is usually a clue that you should use the And logical operator. The word "or" usually means that you should use the Or logical operator. To obtain information on all writers who are freelancers *and* who were last contacted prior to 1990, Elena uses the And logical operator.

The And Logical Operator

Elena will use the And logical operator and enter conditions for the Freelancer field and the Last Contact Date field in the same Criteria row. She will enter =Yes as the condition for the Freelancer field and <#1/1/90# as the condition for the Last Contact Date field to obtain information on all writers who are freelancers and who were last contacted prior to 1990. Because the conditions appear in the same Criteria row, Access selects records only if both conditions are met.

Elena's new query does not need sort keys, so Elena first removes the sort keys for the Freelancer and Last Contact Date fields.

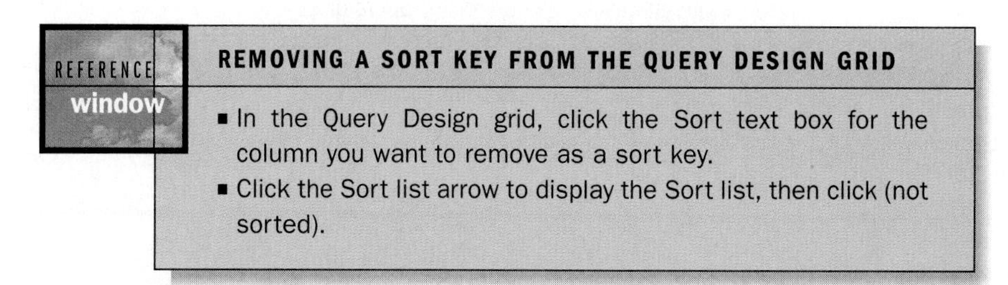

REFERENCE window

REMOVING A SORT KEY FROM THE QUERY DESIGN GRID

- In the Query Design grid, click the Sort text box for the column you want to remove as a sort key.
- Click the Sort list arrow to display the Sort list, then click (not sorted).

To remove sort keys from the Query Design grid:

1. Click the **Query View** button on the toolbar to switch back to the Query Design window.
2. Click the **Sort** text box in the Freelancer column, then click the **Sort** list arrow to display the Sort list.
3. Click **(not sorted)** in the Sort list. The Sort list closes, and Access removes the sort order from the Sort text box.
4. Repeat this procedure to remove the sort key from the Last Contact Date column.

Elena now enters the two conditions.

To select records using the And logical operator:

1. Click the **Criteria** text box for the Freelancer field and then type **=Yes**.
2. Click the **Criteria** text box for the Last Contact Date field and then type **<#1/1/90#**. See Figure 4-24. Access will select a record only if both conditions are met.

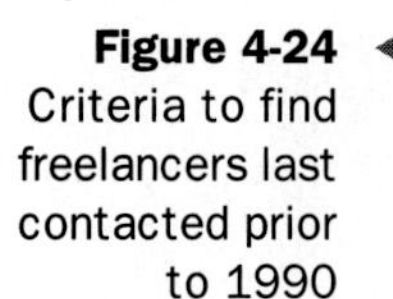

Figure 4-24 Criteria to find freelancers last contacted prior to 1990

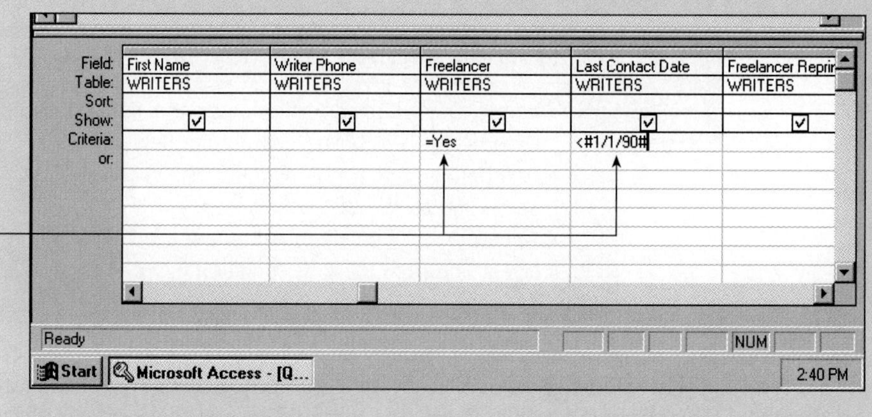

And condition: conditions entered in same row

3. Click the **Run** button on the toolbar. The query results display only those records for freelancers last contacted prior to 1990.
4. Click the **Query View** button on the toolbar to switch back to the Query Design window.

Elena is pleased with how easy it is to use multiple selection criteria. She decides to try the Or logical operator next.

The Or Logical Operator

Elena practices using the Or logical operator by creating a query that asks for those writers who have 210 or 706 area codes. For this query, Elena will enter Like "210*" in one row and Like "706*" in another row. Because the conditions appear in different Criteria rows, Access selects records if either condition is satisfied.

To select records using the Or logical operator:

1. Move the pointer to the left side of the Criteria text box for the first column (Writer ID) and click when the pointer changes to ➡. Access highlights the entire Criteria row.
2. Press the **Delete** key to remove all of the previous conditions from the Query Design grid.
3. Click the **Criteria** text box in the Writer Phone column and then type **Like "210*"**.
4. Click the **or:** text box below the one you just used and type **Like "706*"**. See Figure 4-25. Access will select a record if either condition is met.

Figure 4-25 ◀ Criteria to find writers with 210 or 706 area codes

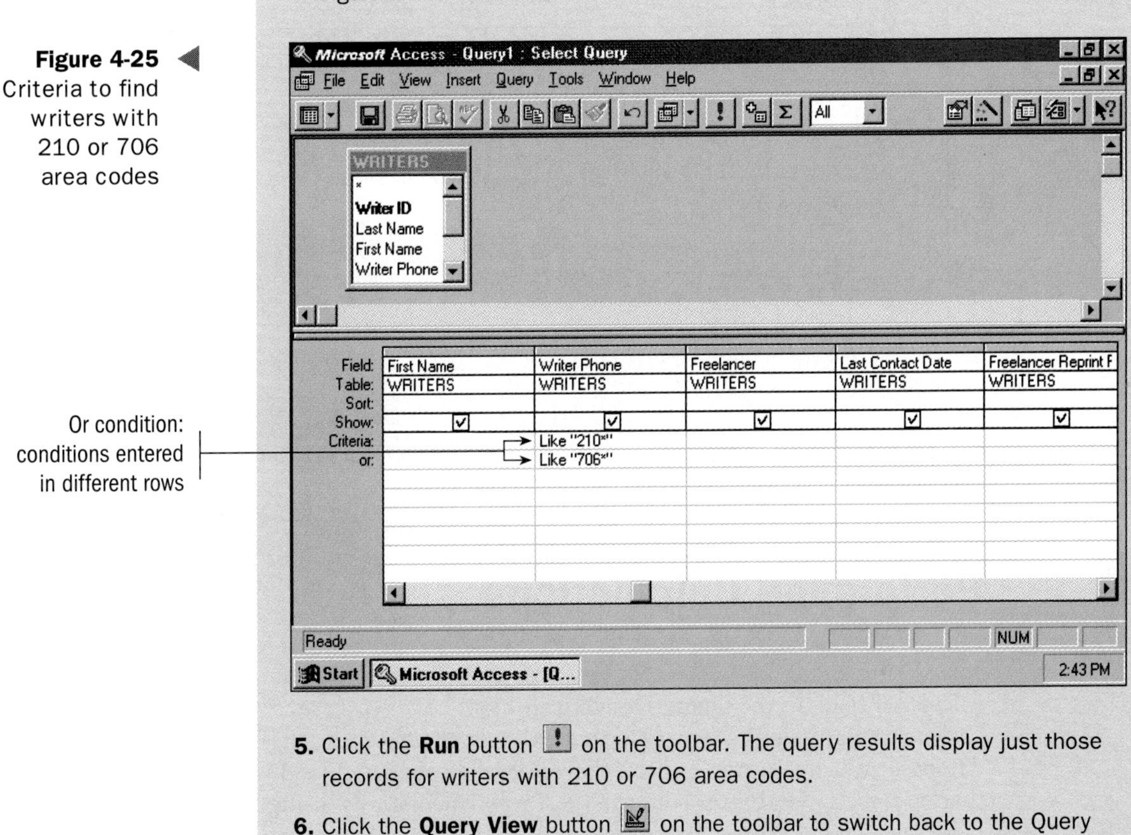

5. Click the **Run** button on the toolbar. The query results display just those records for writers with 210 or 706 area codes.
6. Click the **Query View** button on the toolbar to switch back to the Query Design window.

Using And with Or

Now that Elena has used both the And and Or logical operators, she wants to know if she can combine both operators to obtain information. Can she, for example, create a query that will select only freelancers who have 210 or 706 area codes? In other words, she wants writers who are freelancers *and* have 210 area codes, *or* who are freelancers *and* have 706 area codes. To create this query, she needs to add the =Yes condition for the Freelancer field to both rows that already contain the Writer Phone conditions. Access will select a record if either And condition is met. Only freelancers will be selected, and only if their area codes are 210 or 706.

Elena needs to add the Freelancer conditions to the Query Design grid to complete her new query.

To select records using the And logical operator with the Or logical operator:

1. Click the **Criteria** text box in the Freelancer column and then type **=Yes**.
2. Press the **down arrow** button and then type **=Yes**. Access will select a record if either And condition is met.

   Because she is listing only Freelancer records, Elena removes the Freelancer field from the query results.
3. Click the **Show** box for the Freelancer field to remove the check mark. See Figure 4-26.

Figure 4-26 Criteria to find freelancers who have 210 or 706 area codes

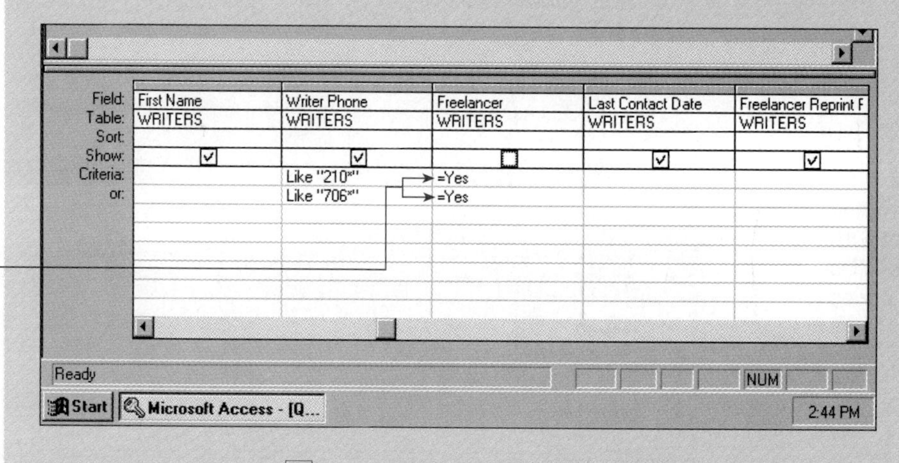

4. Click the **Run** button on the toolbar. The query results display only those records for freelancers with 210 or 706 area codes.
5. Click the **Query View** button on the toolbar to switch back to the Query Design window.

Performing Calculations

Brian thanks Elena for the list of freelancers that she printed out for him earlier. He is now considering giving all freelancers an extra $50. This query requires a new field, called a calculated field, in the Query Design grid.

A **calculated field** is a new field that exists in the query results but does not exist in the database. When you run a query, the value of a calculated field is determined from fields that are in a database. You can perform calculations using Number, Currency, or Date/Time fields from your database. Among the arithmetic operators you can use are those for addition (+), subtraction (−), multiplication (*), and division (/).

Using Calculated Fields

Elena creates a calculated field that adds 50 to the amount stored in the Freelancer Reprint Payment Amount field. Whenever a calculation includes a field name, you place brackets around the name to tell Access that the name is a field name from your database. Elena's calculation, for example, will be expressed as [Freelancer Reprint Payment Amount]+50.

Access supplies the default name Expr1 for the first calculated field, but Elena changes the name to Add50. Because the Field text box is too small to show the entire calculated field, Elena uses the Zoom box while she enters the calculated field. The Zoom box is a large text box for entering text or other values. You can open the Zoom box by using the shortcut menu.

The new query will select all Freelancer records in the WRITERS table, so Elena must remove the unnecessary conditions in the Criteria rows. At the same time, she decides to delete the fields that are not needed for her query: Writer ID, Last Name, First Name, Writer Phone, and Last Contact Date.

To delete fields and remove conditions from the Query Design grid:

1. Scroll to make the Writer ID column visible. Click the **Writer ID** field selector to highlight the entire column. Click the right mouse button in the Writer ID field selector to display the shortcut menu and click **Cut** to delete the column.
2. Use the same procedure to delete the Last Name, First Name, Writer Phone, and Last Contact Date columns in the Query Design grid.
3. Move the pointer to the left side of the or: text box for the first column. When the pointer changes to ➡, click to highlight the entire row. Press the **Delete** key to remove the previous Or condition from the Query Design grid.

The Query Design grid now contains two fields: Freelancer and Freelancer Reprint Payment Amount. Elena next adds the calculated field.

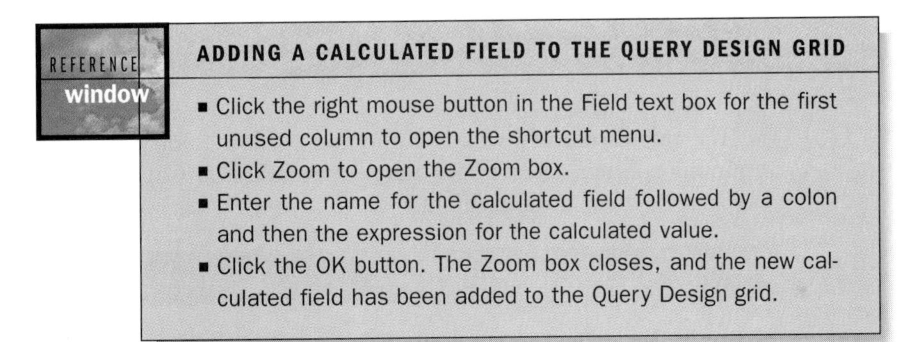

ADDING A CALCULATED FIELD TO THE QUERY DESIGN GRID

- Click the right mouse button in the Field text box for the first unused column to open the shortcut menu.
- Click Zoom to open the Zoom box.
- Enter the name for the calculated field followed by a colon and then the expression for the calculated value.
- Click the OK button. The Zoom box closes, and the new calculated field has been added to the Query Design grid.

To add a calculated field to the Query Design grid and run the query:

1. Click the right mouse button in the Field text box for the first unused column (the third column) to open the shortcut menu.
2. Click **Zoom** to open the Zoom box.
3. Type **Add50:[Freelancer Reprint Payment Amount]+50**. See Figure 4-27.

Figure 4-27 The Zoom box for entering long calculations

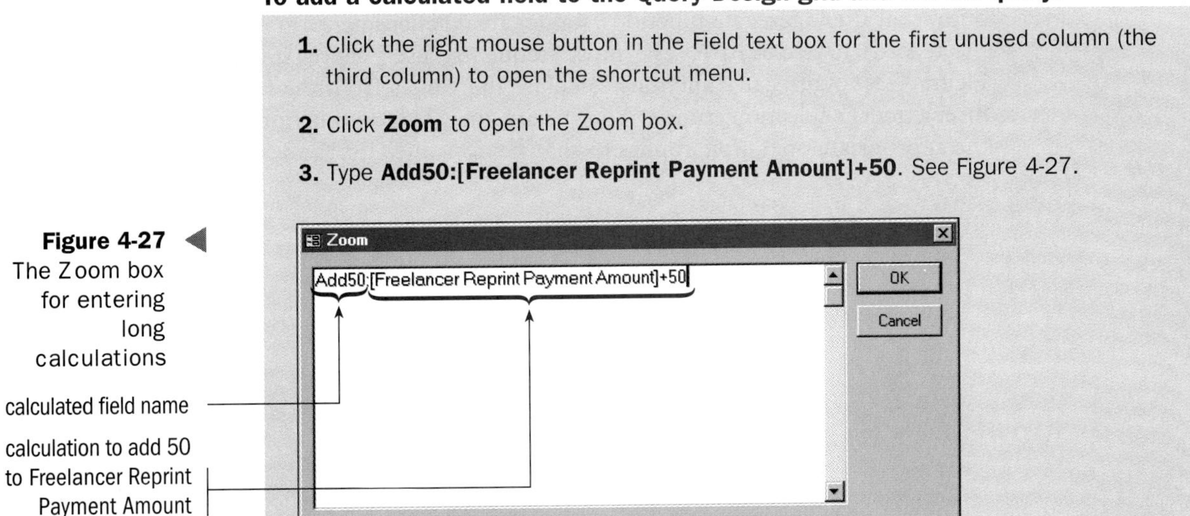

4. Click the **OK** button. The Zoom box closes, and the new calculated field appears as the third column in the Query Design grid.

5. Click the **Run** button on the toolbar. The query results display all records in the WRITERS table and include the new calculated field. See Figure 4-28.

Figure 4-28 Query results with calculated field

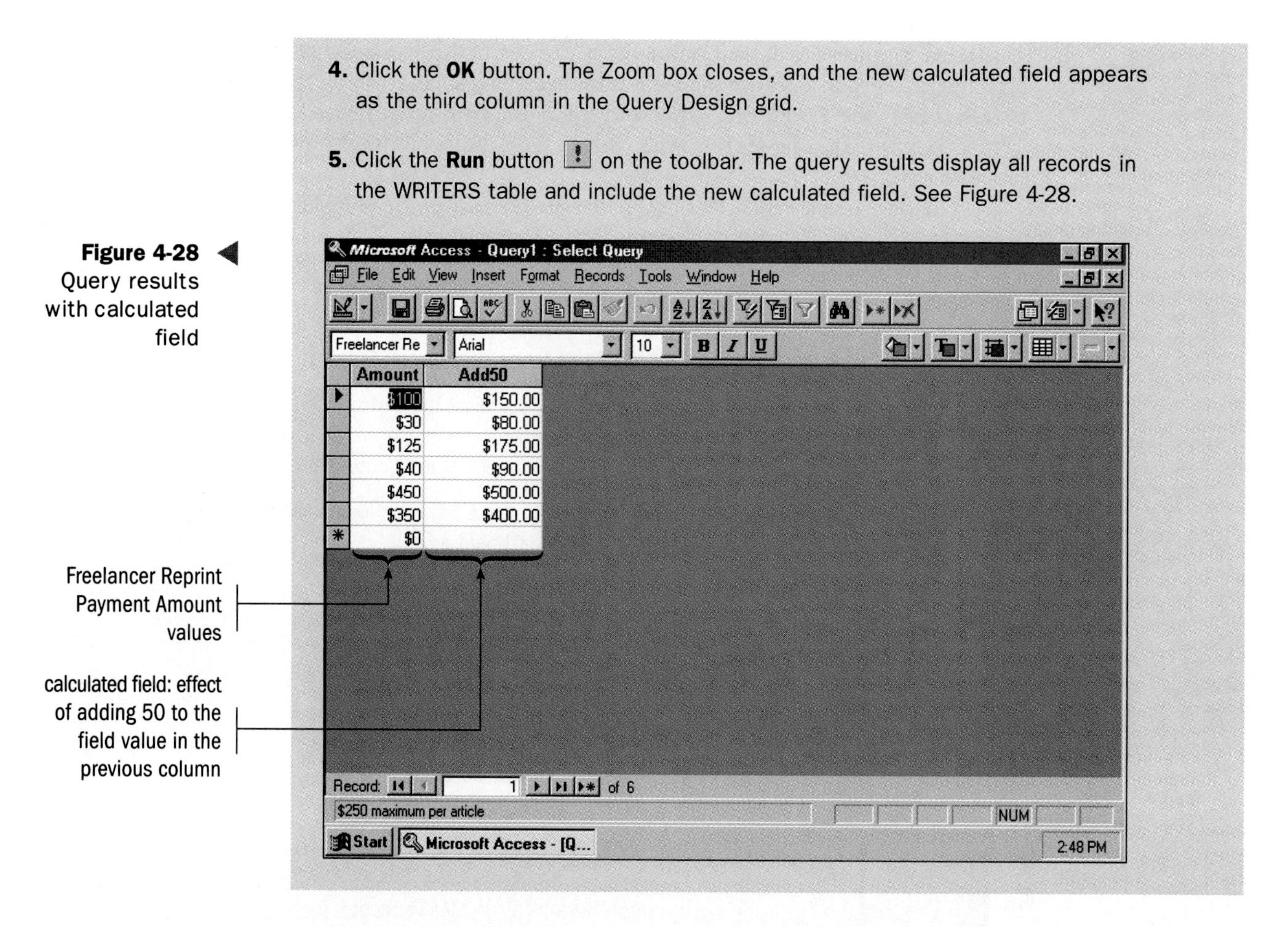

The calculated field values in the new Add50 column are $50 more than those in the Amount column. (Remember that Amount is the Caption property for the Freelancer Reprint Payment Amount field.)

Using Aggregate Functions

Brian looks at the numbers and thinks giving the freelancers an extra $50 is possible. However, before he gives the go-ahead, he wants to know both the total cost and the average cost, with and without the extra $50. To obtain this information, Elena will create a query that uses aggregate functions. **Aggregate functions** perform arithmetic operations on the records in a database. The most frequently used aggregate functions are listed in Figure 4-29. Aggregate functions calculate the values from the fields in the records that meet a query's selection criteria. You specify an aggregate function for a specific field, and the appropriate operation applies to that field's values for the selected records.

Figure 4-29 Frequently used aggregate functions

Function	Meaning
Avg	average of the field values for the selected records
Count	number of records selected
Min	lowest field value for the selected records
Max	highest field value for the selected records
Sum	total of the field values for the selected records

REFERENCE window

USING AGGREGATE FUNCTIONS IN THE QUERY DESIGN GRID

- In the Query Design window, click the Totals button on the toolbar. Access adds a Totals row to the Query Design grid.
- Click in the Total text box for the field you want to aggregate.
- Click the Total list arrow to display the list of available aggregate functions.
- Click the function you want to select it.

Elena uses the Sum and Avg aggregate functions for both the Freelancer Reprint Payment Amount field and for the Add50 calculated field she just created in her previous query. The Sum aggregate function gives the total of the selected field values, and the Avg aggregate function gives the average of the selected field values. Elena's query results will contain one record displaying the four requested aggregate function values.

To use aggregate functions in the Query Design window, you click the toolbar Totals button. Access inserts a Total row between the Table and Sort rows in the Query Design grid. You specify the aggregate functions you want to use in the Total row. When you run the query, one record appears in the query results with your selected aggregate function values. The individual table records themselves do not appear.

Elena has three fields in the Query Design grid: the Freelancer and Freelancer Reprint Payment Amount fields, and the Add50 calculated field. She needs a column for the Sum aggregate function and a column for the Avg aggregate function for each of the Freelancer Reprint Payment Amount and Add50 fields. The columns will allow her to find the total cost and average cost for freelancers with and without the extra $50. She inserts a second copy of the Freelancer Reprint Payment Amount field in the Query Design grid. She then renames the first Freelancer Reprint Payment Amount field AmountSum and the second AmountAvg. She likewise makes a second copy of the Add50 calculated field and renames the first one Add50Sum and the second Add50Avg.

First Elena adds the copy of the Freelancer Reprint Payment Amount field to the Query Design grid and renames the four summary fields.

To add and rename fields in the Query Design grid:

1. Click the **Query View** button on the toolbar. If necessary, scroll to the left to make all fields visible in the Query Design grid. Click **Freelancer Reprint Payment Amount** in the WRITERS field list, drag it to the Add50 calculated field column in the Query Design grid, and then release the mouse button. The four fields in the Query Design grid, from left to right, are Freelancer, Freelancer Reprint Payment Amount, Freelancer Reprint Payment Amount, and Add50.

2. Click the beginning of the Field box for the first Freelancer Reprint Payment Amount field and type **AmountSum:**.

3. Click the beginning of the Field box for the second Freelancer Reprint Payment Amount field and type **AmountAvg:**.

4. Click just before the colon in the Field box for the Add50 calculated field and type **Sum**. The name of the calculated field is now Add50Sum.

Elena next selects aggregate functions for these three fields.

To select aggregate functions:

1. Click the **Totals** button Σ on the toolbar. The Total row appears in the Query Design grid.

2. Click in the **Total** text box for the AmountSum field, then click the **Total** list arrow, then click **Sum** in the Total list box. See Figure 4-30.

Figure 4-30 Aggregate function selection

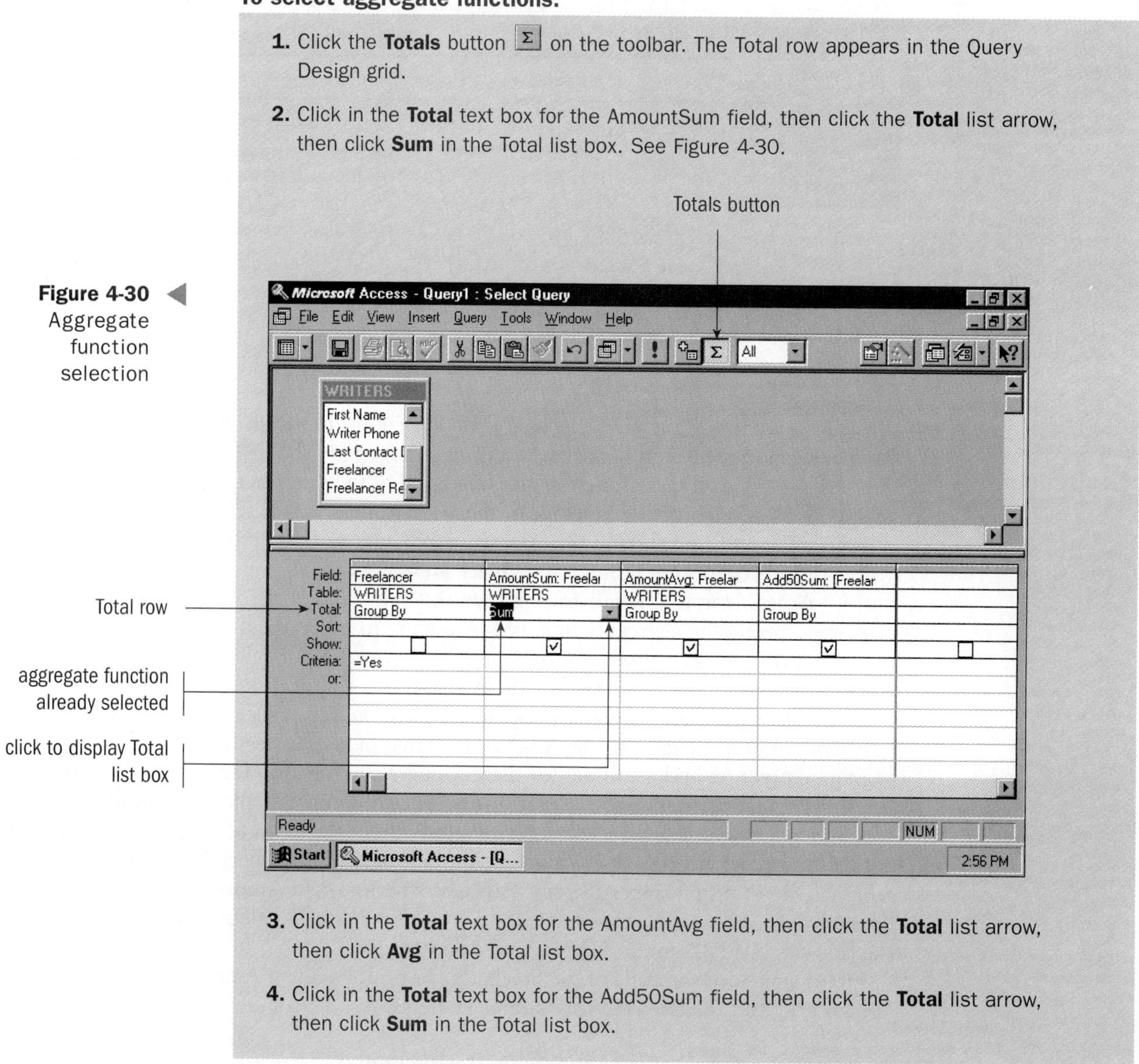

3. Click in the **Total** text box for the AmountAvg field, then click the **Total** list arrow, then click **Avg** in the Total list box.

4. Click in the **Total** text box for the Add50Sum field, then click the **Total** list arrow, then click **Sum** in the Total list box.

Elena's last steps are to copy a calculated field, paste it into the fifth column, rename the new field Add50Avg, and change its Total text box to Avg.

To copy and paste a new calculated field with an aggregate function:

1. Click the **Add50Sum** field selector to highlight the entire column.
2. Click the right mouse button in the Add50Sum field selector to display the shortcut menu and then click **Copy** to copy the column to the Clipboard.
3. Click the field selector for the fifth column to highlight the entire column. Click the right mouse button in the fifth column's field selector to display the shortcut menu and then click **Paste**. A copy of the fourth column appears in the fifth column.
4. Highlight **Sum** in the Field text box for the fifth column and type **Avg**. The renamed field name is now Add50Avg.
5. Click in the **Total** text box for the Add50Avg column, then click the **Total** list arrow, and then click **Avg** in the Total list box. See Figure 4-31.

Figure 4-31 Calculating total cost and average cost of freelancers with and without an extra $50

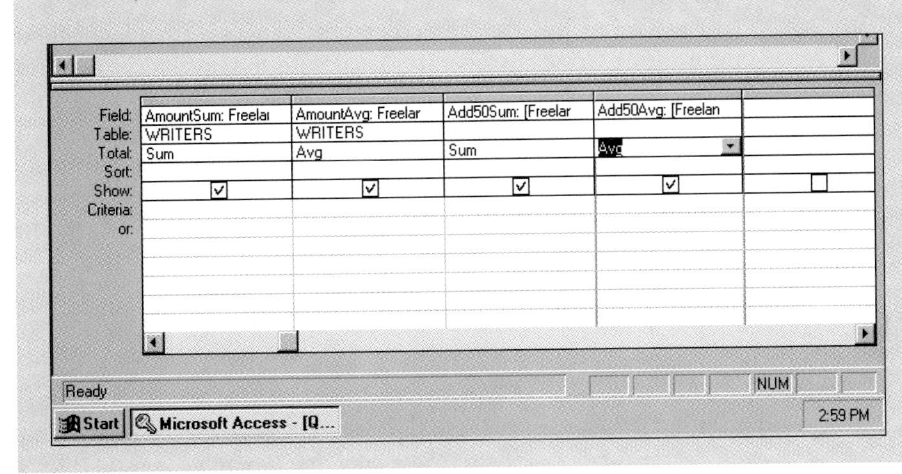

As her final step, Elena runs the query and then views the query results.

To run the query and view the query results:

1. Click the **Run** button on the toolbar. The query results display one record containing the four aggregate function values. See Figure 4-32.

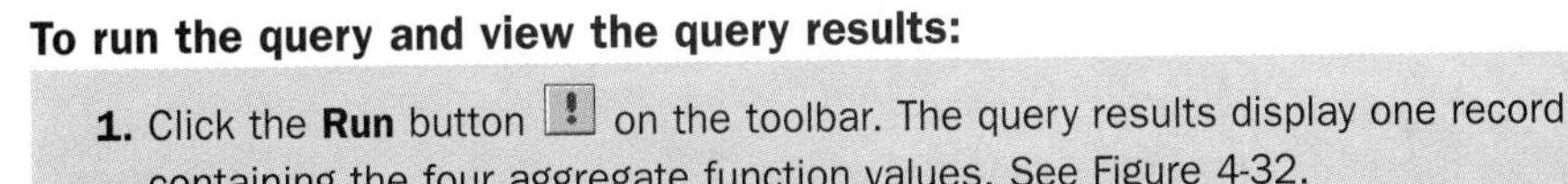

Figure 4-32 Results of a query using aggregate functions

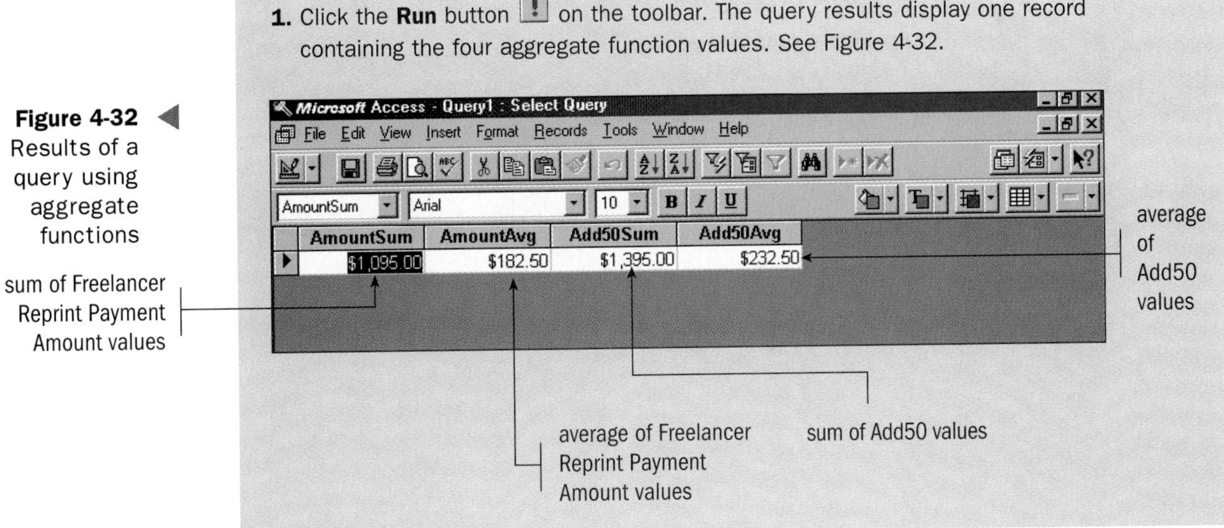

Elena prints the query results to give to Brian. Then she saves the query and closes the Datasheet window.

To save the query and close the Datasheet window:

1. Click the **Save** button on the toolbar. Access displays the Save As dialog box. Type **Freelancer Summary Query**, then click the **OK** button. Access saves the query design.
2. Click the Datasheet View window **Close** button. Access closes the Datasheet window.

Using Record Group Calculations

Elena has one more query to create requiring the use of aggregate functions. Brian wants to know how many staff writers and how many freelancers there are in the WRITERS table. To do this, Elena creates a query that uses the Group By operator and the Count function.

The Group By operator combines records with identical field values into a single record. The Group By operator used with the Freelancer field results in two records: one record for the Yes field values and another for the No field values. If you use aggregate functions, Access will calculate the value of the aggregate function for each group. The Count function counts the number of records that match the criteria. When Elena uses the Group By operator with the Freelancer field, and the Count function with the Writer ID field, Access will count the number of Writer IDs for freelancers and the number of Writer IDs for staff writers.

Elena creates a new query containing the Writer ID and Freelancer fields, and specifies the necessary operator and aggregate function.

To create the new query:

1. In the Queries list of the Database window, click the **New** button to open the New Query dialog box. Make sure that Design View is selected, then click the **OK** button. Access opens the Query Design window.
2. Click **WRITERS** in the Show Table dialog box, then click the **Add** button. The WRITERS table appears in the upper panel of the Query Design window.
3. Click the **Close** button to close the Show Table dialog box.
4. Double-click **Writer ID** in the field list to add the Writer ID field to the Query Design grid.
5. Scroll down the field list, then double-click **Freelancer** in the field list to add the Freelancer field to the Query Design grid.
6. Click the **Totals** button Σ on the toolbar. The Total row appears in the Query Design grid. By default, the Group By operator appears in the Total row for each column.
7. Click in the **Total** text box for the Writer ID field, then click the **Total** list arrow, then click **Count**. See Figure 4-33.

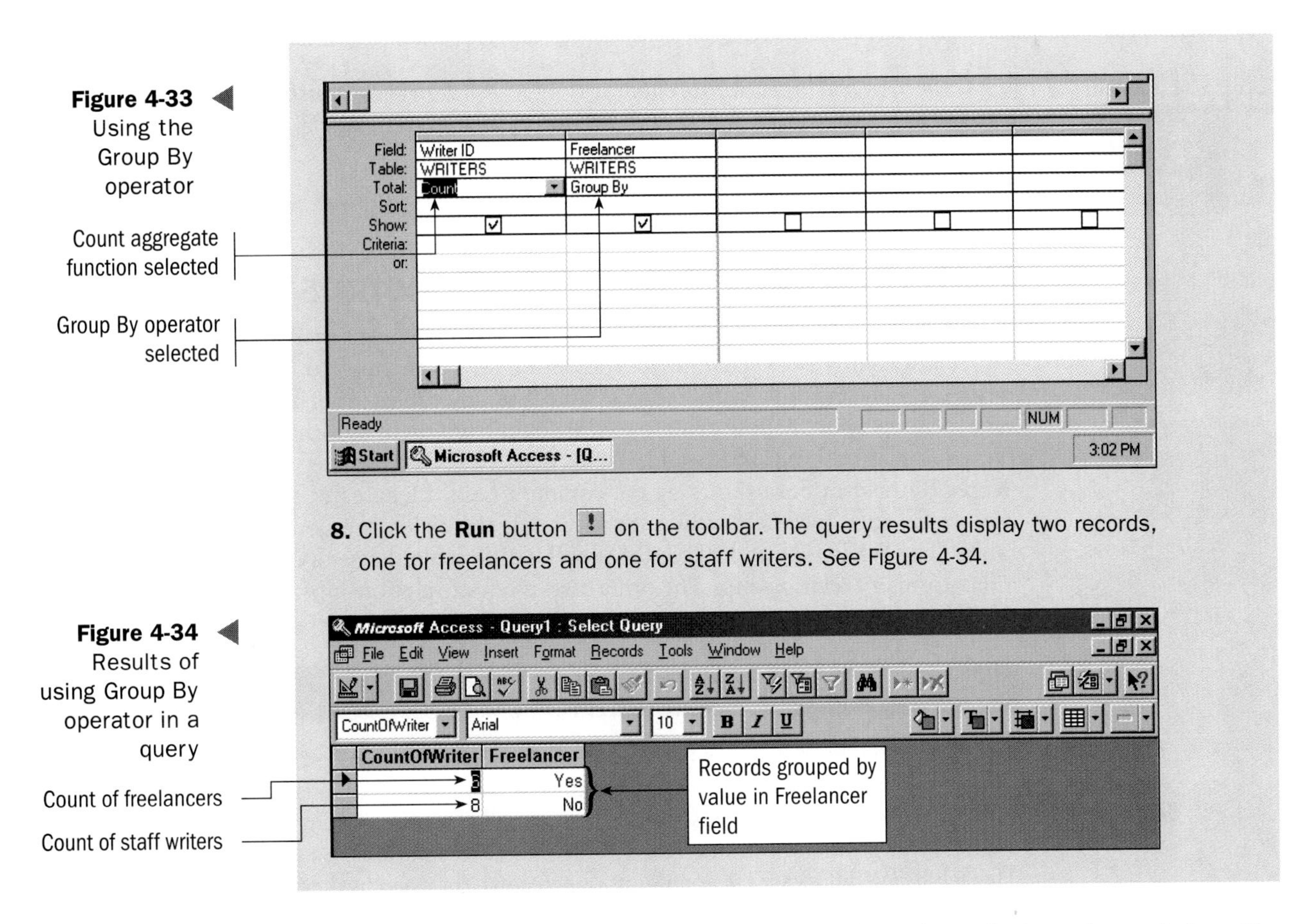

Figure 4-33 Using the Group By operator

8. Click the **Run** button on the toolbar. The query results display two records, one for freelancers and one for staff writers. See Figure 4-34.

Figure 4-34 Results of using Group By operator in a query

After printing the results to submit to Brian, Elena closes the Datasheet window. She decides not to save the latest query because she won't need to obtain this information again.

To close the Datasheet window without saving the query:

1. Click the Datasheet View window **Close** button. A dialog box asks if you want to save changes to the Query1 query.
2. Click the **No** button. Access closes the dialog box and then closes the Datasheet View window without saving the query.

If you want to take a break and resume the tutorial at a later time, exit Access. When you resume the tutorial, place your Student Disk in the appropriate drive, start Access, open the Issue25 database in the Tutorial folder on your Student Disk, and click the Queries tab to display the Queries list.

Quick Check

1. Why might you need to sort a single field?
2. How must you position the fields in the Query Design grid when you have multiple sort keys?
3. Why might you print selected query results?
4. When do you use logical operators?
5. What is a calculated field?
6. When do you use an aggregate function?
7. What does the Group By operator do?

SESSION 4.3

In this session, you will learn more about how to establish relationships between tables, design a query using related tables, and create a parameter query.

Understanding Table Relationships

One of the most powerful features of a database management system is its ability to establish relationships between tables. You've already seen how to use a common field to relate, or link, one table with another table. Linking tables (often called performing a **join**) with a common field allows you to extract data from them as if they were one larger table. For example, the WRITERS and BUSINESS ARTICLES tables are linked by using the Writer ID field in both tables as the common field. Elena can use a query to extract all the article data for each writer, even though the fields are contained in two separate tables. The WRITERS and BUSINESS ARTICLES tables have a type of relationship called a one-to-many relationship. The other two types of relationships are the one-to-one relationship and the many-to-many relationship.

Types of Relationships

A **one-to-one relationship** exists between two tables when each record in one table has exactly one matching record in the other table. Suppose, for example, Elena invites all of the writers to attend a meeting. Since most of the writers will be coming from out of town, she creates a table to keep track of airline reservations, hotel reservations, and other appropriate data. The RESERVATIONS table contains one record for each writer, with Writer ID as the primary key. In this example the WRITERS table and the RESERVATIONS table have a one-to-one relationship, as shown in Figure 4-35. Both tables have Writer ID as the primary key, which is also the common field between the two tables. Each record in the WRITERS table matches one record in the RESERVATIONS table through the common field.

Figure 4-35 One-to-one relationship

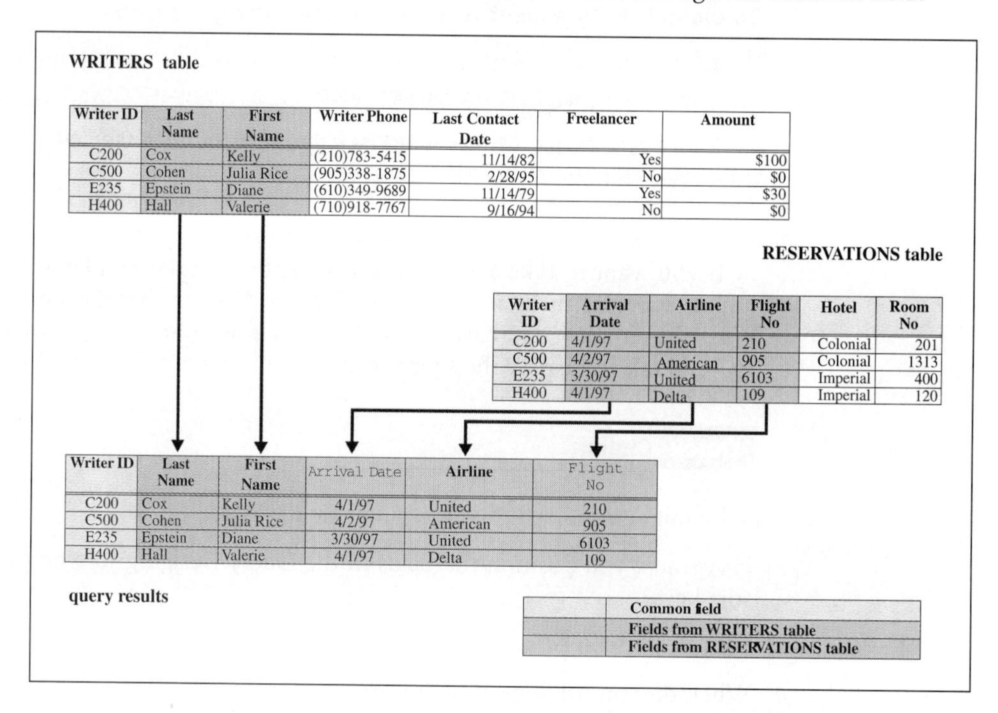

WRITERS table

Writer ID	Last Name	First Name	Writer Phone	Last Contact Date	Freelancer	Amount
C200	Cox	Kelly	(210)783-5415	11/14/82	Yes	$100
C500	Cohen	Julia Rice	(905)338-1875	2/28/95	No	$0
E235	Epstein	Diane	(610)349-9689	11/14/79	Yes	$30
H400	Hall	Valerie	(710)918-7767	9/16/94	No	$0

RESERVATIONS table

Writer ID	Arrival Date	Airline	Flight No	Hotel	Room No
C200	4/1/97	United	210	Colonial	201
C500	4/2/97	American	905	Colonial	1313
E235	3/30/97	United	6103	Imperial	400
H400	4/1/97	Delta	109	Imperial	120

query results

Writer ID	Last Name	First Name	Arrival Date	Airline	Flight No
C200	Cox	Kelly	4/1/97	United	210
C500	Cohen	Julia Rice	4/2/97	American	905
E235	Epstein	Diane	3/30/97	United	6103
H400	Hall	Valerie	4/1/97	Delta	109

A **one-to-many relationship** exists between two tables when one record in the first table matches many records in the second table, but one record in the second table matches only one record in the first table. The relationship between the WRITERS table and the BUSINESS ARTICLES table, as shown in Figure 4-36, is an example of a one-to-many relationship. Each record in the WRITERS table may match many records in the BUSINESS ARTICLES table. Valerie Hall's record in the WRITERS table with a Writer ID of H400, for example, links to three records in the BUSINESS ARTICLES table: 25% Tax Cut Bill Approved, The BCCI Scandal and Computers in the Future. Conversely, each record in the BUSINESS ARTICLES table links only to a single record in the WRITERS table, with Writer ID used as the common field.

Figure 4-36 One-to-many relationship

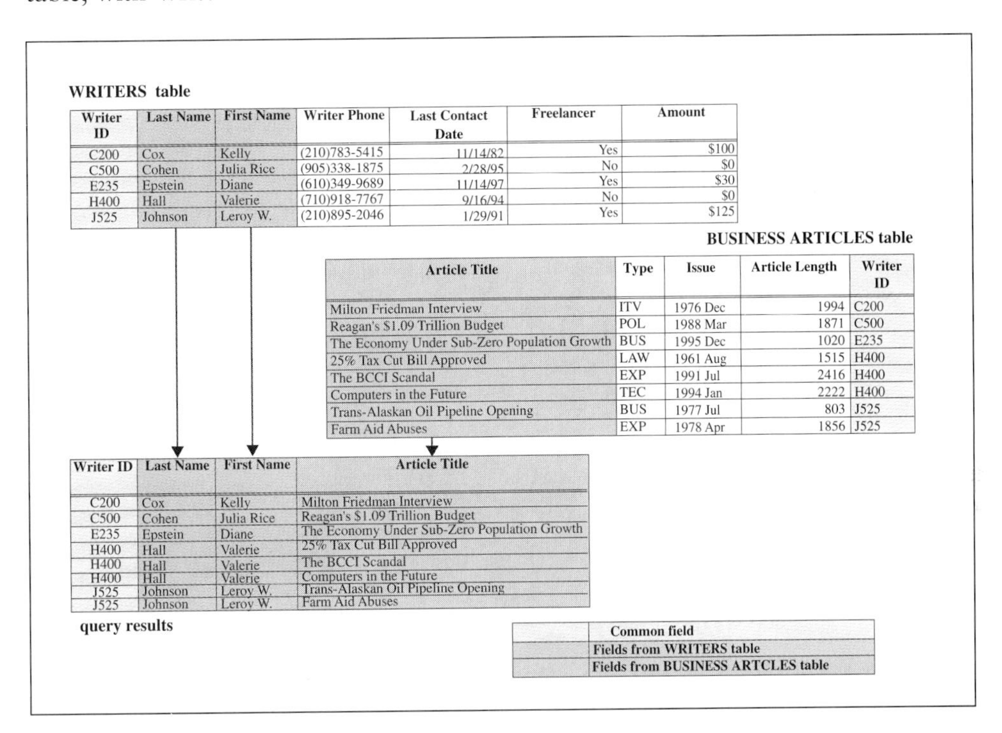

WRITERS table

Writer ID	Last Name	First Name	Writer Phone	Last Contact Date	Freelancer	Amount
C200	Cox	Kelly	(210)783-5415	11/14/82	Yes	$100
C500	Cohen	Julia Rice	(905)338-1875	2/28/95	No	$0
E235	Epstein	Diane	(610)349-9689	11/14/97	Yes	$30
H400	Hall	Valerie	(710)918-7767	9/16/94	No	$0
J525	Johnson	Leroy W.	(210)895-2046	1/29/91	Yes	$125

BUSINESS ARTICLES table

Article Title	Type	Issue	Article Length	Writer ID
Milton Friedman Interview	ITV	1976 Dec	1994	C200
Reagan's $1.09 Trillion Budget	POL	1988 Mar	1871	C500
The Economy Under Sub-Zero Population Growth	BUS	1995 Dec	1020	E235
25% Tax Cut Bill Approved	LAW	1961 Aug	1515	H400
The BCCI Scandal	EXP	1991 Jul	2416	H400
Computers in the Future	TEC	1994 Jan	2222	H400
Trans-Alaskan Oil Pipeline Opening	BUS	1977 Jul	803	J525
Farm Aid Abuses	EXP	1978 Apr	1856	J525

Writer ID	Last Name	First Name	Article Title
C200	Cox	Kelly	Milton Friedman Interview
C500	Cohen	Julia Rice	Reagan's $1.09 Trillion Budget
E235	Epstein	Diane	The Economy Under Sub-Zero Population Growth
H400	Hall	Valerie	25% Tax Cut Bill Approved
H400	Hall	Valerie	The BCCI Scandal
H400	Hall	Valerie	Computers in the Future
J525	Johnson	Leroy W.	Trans-Alaskan Oil Pipeline Opening
J525	Johnson	Leroy W.	Farm Aid Abuses

query results

A **many-to-many relationship** exists between two tables when one record in the first table may match many records in the second table, and one record in the second table may match many records in the first table. Suppose, for example, that an article has two authors. The relationship between the WRITERS and BUSINESS ARTICLES tables is then a many-to-many relationship, as shown in Figure 4-37. Access does not allow you to define a many-to-many relationship between two tables. To handle this type of relationship, you would need to create a primary key for the BUSINESS ARTICLES table. An AutoNumber-field named Article ID could be added as a primary key. Then you would create a new table with a primary key that combines the primary keys of the other two tables. The WRITERS AND BUSINESS ARTICLES table would have the combination of Article ID and Writer ID as its primary key. Each record in this new table represents one article and one of the article's writers. Even though an Article ID and Writer ID value can appear more than once, each combination of Article ID and Writer ID is unique.

Figure 4-37 Many-to-many relationship

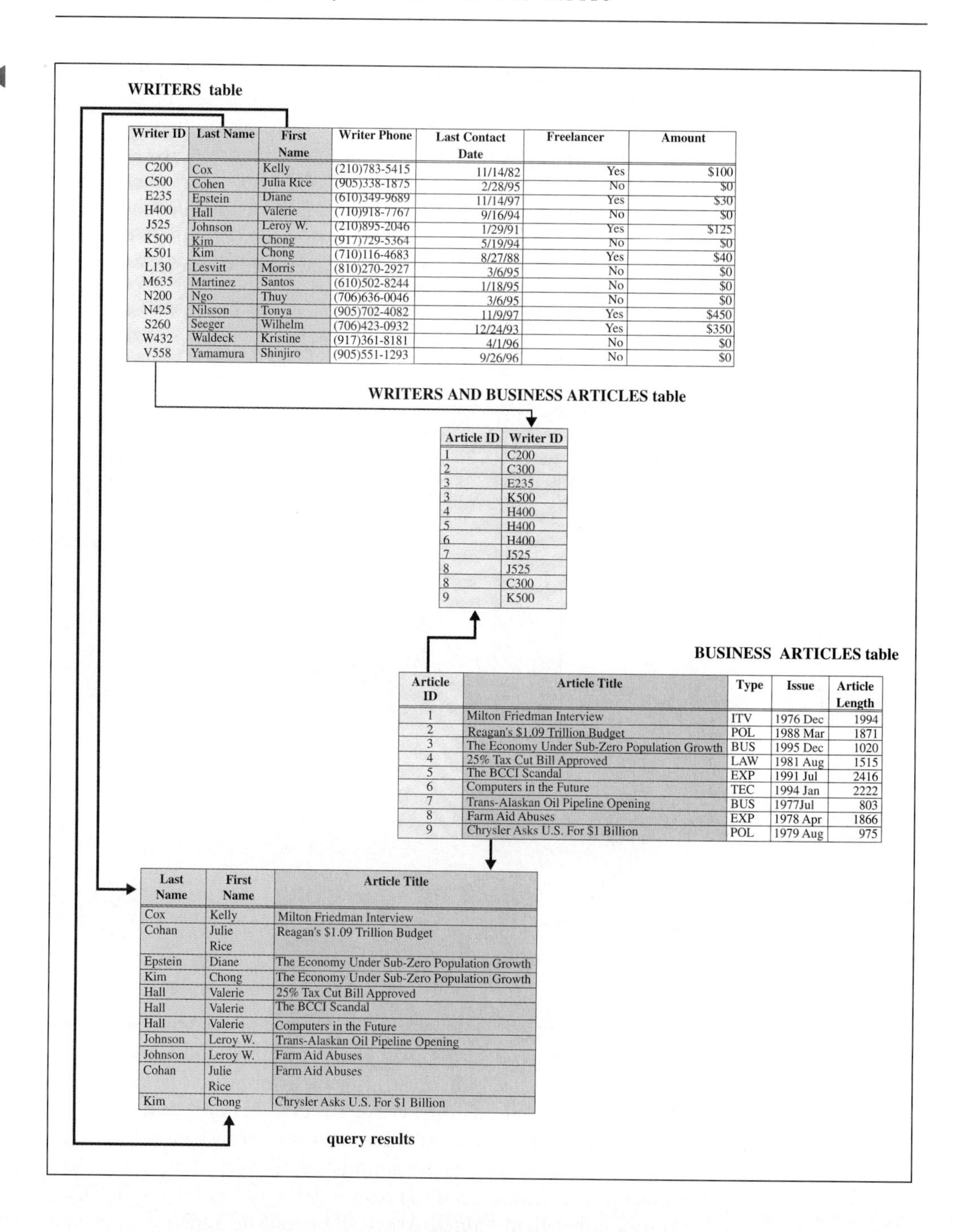

WRITERS table

Writer ID	Last Name	First Name	Writer Phone	Last Contact Date	Freelancer	Amount
C200	Cox	Kelly	(210)783-5415	11/14/82	Yes	$100
C500	Cohen	Julia Rice	(905)338-1875	2/28/95	No	$0
E235	Epstein	Diane	(610)349-9689	11/14/97	Yes	$30
H400	Hall	Valerie	(710)918-7767	9/16/94	No	$0
J525	Johnson	Leroy W.	(210)895-2046	1/29/91	Yes	$125
K500	Kim	Chong	(917)729-5364	5/19/94	No	$0
K501	Kim	Chong	(710)116-4683	8/27/88	Yes	$40
L130	Lesvitt	Morris	(810)270-2927	3/6/95	No	$0
M635	Martinez	Santos	(610)502-8244	1/18/95	No	$0
N200	Ngo	Thuy	(706)636-0046	3/6/95	No	$0
N425	Nilsson	Tonya	(905)702-4082	11/9/97	Yes	$450
S260	Seeger	Wilhelm	(706)423-0932	12/24/93	Yes	$350
W432	Waldeck	Kristine	(917)361-8181	4/1/96	No	$0
V558	Yamamura	Shinjiro	(905)551-1293	9/26/96	No	$0

WRITERS AND BUSINESS ARTICLES table

Article ID	Writer ID
1	C200
2	C300
3	E235
3	K500
4	H400
5	H400
6	H400
7	J525
8	J525
8	C300
9	K500

BUSINESS ARTICLES table

Article ID	Article Title	Type	Issue	Article Length
1	Milton Friedman Interview	ITV	1976 Dec	1994
2	Reagan's $1.09 Trillion Budget	POL	1988 Mar	1871
3	The Economy Under Sub-Zero Population Growth	BUS	1995 Dec	1020
4	25% Tax Cut Bill Approved	LAW	1981 Aug	1515
5	The BCCI Scandal	EXP	1991 Jul	2416
6	Computers in the Future	TEC	1994 Jan	2222
7	Trans-Alaskan Oil Pipeline Opening	BUS	1977Jul	803
8	Farm Aid Abuses	EXP	1978 Apr	1866
9	Chrysler Asks U.S. For $1 Billion	POL	1979 Aug	975

Last Name	First Name	Article Title
Cox	Kelly	Milton Friedman Interview
Cohan	Julie Rice	Reagan's $1.09 Trillion Budget
Epstein	Diane	The Economy Under Sub-Zero Population Growth
Kim	Chong	The Economy Under Sub-Zero Population Growth
Hall	Valerie	25% Tax Cut Bill Approved
Hall	Valerie	The BCCI Scandal
Hall	Valerie	Computers in the Future
Johnson	Leroy W.	Trans-Alaskan Oil Pipeline Opening
Johnson	Leroy W.	Farm Aid Abuses
Cohan	Julie Rice	Farm Aid Abuses
Kim	Chong	Chrysler Asks U.S. For $1 Billion

query results

By creating the WRITERS AND BUSINESS ARTICLES table, you change the many-to-many relationship between the WRITERS and BUSINESS ARTICLES tables into two one-to-many relationships. The WRITERS table has a one-to-many relationship with the WRITERS AND BUSINESS ARTICLES table, and the BUSINESS ARTICLES table has a one-to-many relationship with the WRITERS AND BUSINESS ARTICLES table.

Access refers to the two tables that form a relationship as the primary table and the related table. The **primary table** is the "one" table in a one-to-many relationship, and the **related table** is the "many" table. In a one-to-one relationship, you can choose either table as the primary table and the other table as the related table.

Elena's next step is to define relationships for the WRITERS and BUSINESS ARTICLES tables. She will then use these relationships to obtain additional information from the Issue25 database.

Adding a Relationship Between Two Tables

When two tables have a common field, you can define the relationship between them in the Relationships window. The **Relationships window** illustrates the one-to-one and one-to-many relationships among a database's tables. In this window you can view or change existing relationships, define new relationships between tables, rearrange the layout of the tables, and change the structures of the related tables.

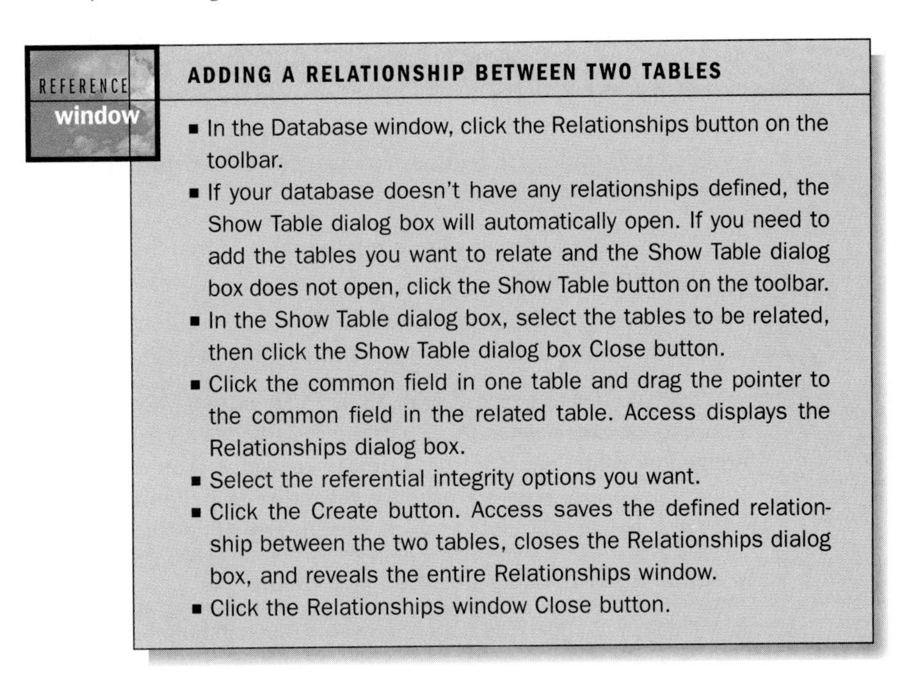

REFERENCE window

ADDING A RELATIONSHIP BETWEEN TWO TABLES

- In the Database window, click the Relationships button on the toolbar.
- If your database doesn't have any relationships defined, the Show Table dialog box will automatically open. If you need to add the tables you want to relate and the Show Table dialog box does not open, click the Show Table button on the toolbar.
- In the Show Table dialog box, select the tables to be related, then click the Show Table dialog box Close button.
- Click the common field in one table and drag the pointer to the common field in the related table. Access displays the Relationships dialog box.
- Select the referential integrity options you want.
- Click the Create button. Access saves the defined relationship between the two tables, closes the Relationships dialog box, and reveals the entire Relationships window.
- Click the Relationships window Close button.

Elena defines the one-to-many relationship between the WRITERS and BUSINESS ARTICLES tables. First, she opens the Relationships window.

To open the Relationships window:

1. Make sure the Issue25 database is open and the Queries list is displayed. Click the **Relationships** button on the toolbar. Access displays the Relationships window. See Figure 4-38.

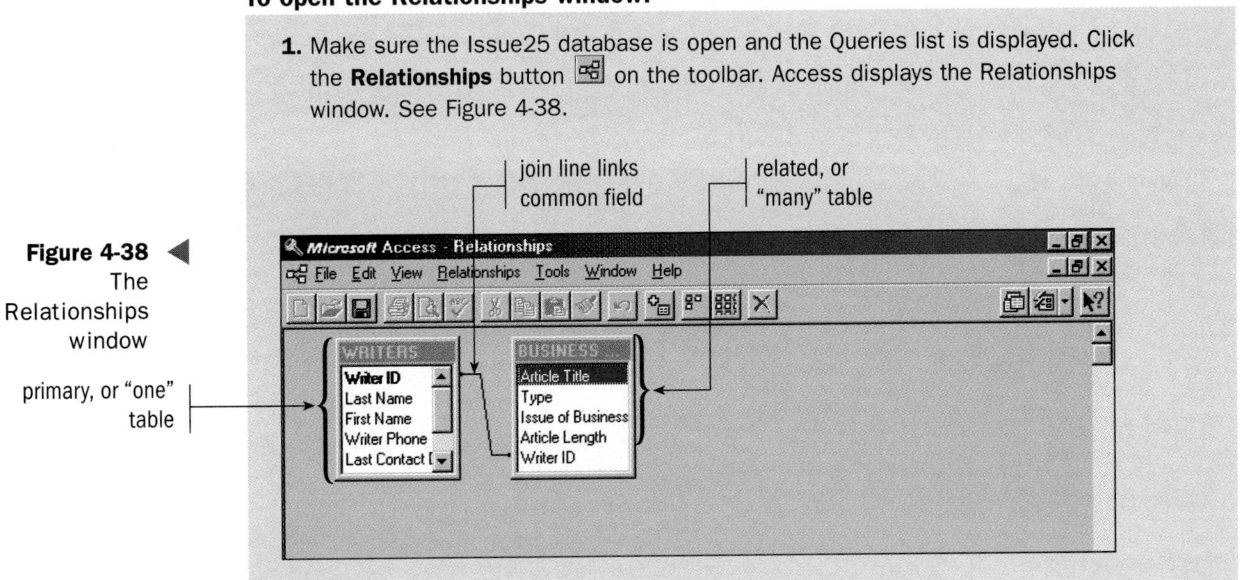

Figure 4-38 The Relationships window

The Relationships window shows the WRITERS table and the BUSINESS ARTICLES table and a line connecting them. This line is called the **join line** and identifies the common field in the two tables in the relationship. Recall that in Tutorial 3, you defined the Writer ID field in the BUSINESS ARTICLES table as a Lookup Wizard field and linked it to the Writer ID field in the WRITERS table. When you did this, Access automatically created a relationship between the WRITERS table and the BUSINESS ARTICLES table with the Writer ID field as the common field.

If you had not already defined the relationship, you could do so by adding the tables to the Relationships window using the Show Table dialog box. Then, you would drag the common field from one table to the other table to create the join line. Specifically, you would click the primary key field in the primary table and drag it to the foreign key field in the related table.

When two tables are related, you can choose to enforce referential integrity rules. The **referential integrity rules** are:

- When you add a record to a related table, a matching record must already exist in the primary table.
- You cannot delete a record from a primary table if matching records exist in the related table, unless you choose to cascade deletes.

When you delete a record with a particular primary key value from the primary table and choose to **cascade deletes**, Access automatically deletes from related tables all records having foreign key values equal to that primary key value. You can also choose to cascade updates. When you change a table's primary key value and choose to **cascade updates**, Access automatically changes all related tables' foreign-key values that equal that primary key value.

To define a relationship between two tables:

1. Click on the **join line** between the WRITERS and the BUSINESS ARTICLES table to highlight it. Click **Relationships**, then click **Edit Relationship**. Access displays the Relationships dialog box. Access analyzes the relationship and determines that it is one-to-many.
2. Click the **Enforce Referential Integrity** check box to turn on this option.
3. Click the **Cascade Update Related Fields** check box to turn on this option. See Figure 4-39. Do not turn on the Cascade Delete Related Records option.

Figure 4-39 The Relationships dialog box

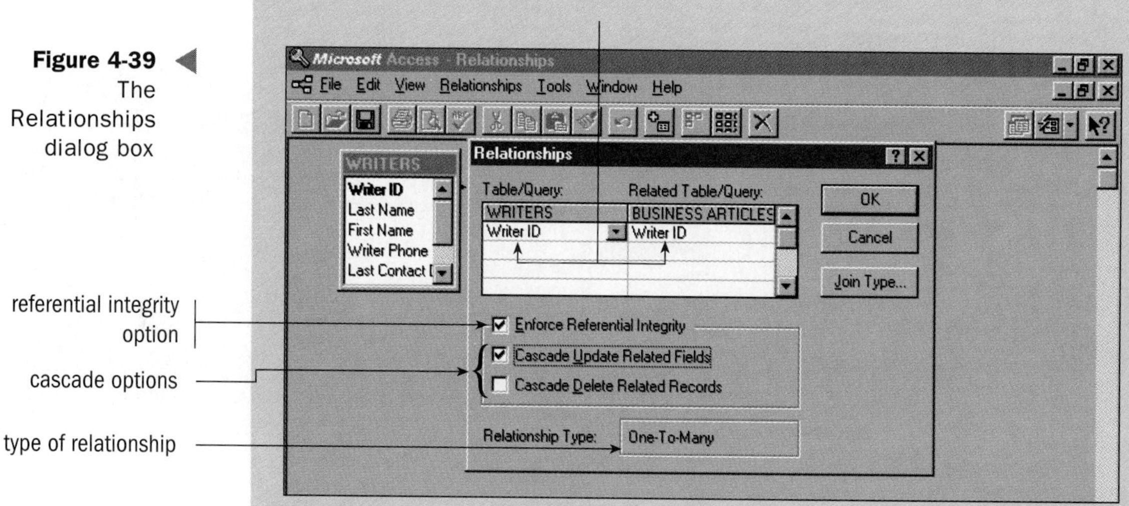

4. Click the **Create** button. Access saves the relationship defined between the two tables, closes the Relationships dialog box, and displays the entire Relationships window. See Figure 4-40.

Figure 4-40 Two tables related with a join line

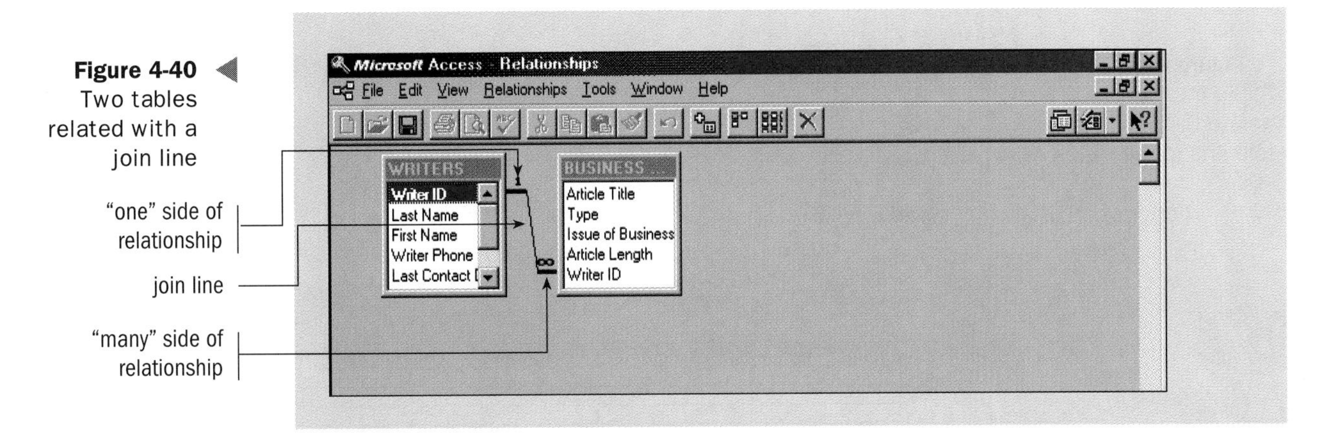

Notice the join line that connects the Writer ID fields common to the two tables. The common fields link (or join) the two tables, which have either a one-to-one or one-to-many relationship. The join line is bold at both ends; this signifies that you have chosen the option to enforce referential integrity. If you do not select this option, the join line is thin at both ends. The "one" side of the relationship has the digit 1 at its end (to indicate the primary table), and the "many" side of the relationship has the infinity symbol (∞) at its end (to indicate the related table). Although the two tables are still separate tables, you have now defined the one-to-many relationship between them.

Now that she has defined the relationship between the WRITERS and BUSINESS ARTICLES tables, Elena closes the Relationships window.

To close the Relationships window:

1. Click the Relationships window **Close** button. Access closes the dialog box and the Relationships window, and returns you to the Database window.

Elena can now build her next query, which requires data from both the WRITERS and BUSINESS ARTICLES tables.

Querying More Than One Table

Elena's present task is to obtain information about the article titles, types, and lengths for each writer, arranged by article type. This query involves fields from both the WRITERS and BUSINESS ARTICLES tables and requires a sort.

Elena first opens the Query Design window and selects the two needed tables.

To start a query using two tables:

1. Make sure that the Queries tab is selected in the Database window and then click the **New** button. The New Query dialog box opens.
2. Make sure that Design View is selected, then click the **OK** button. The Show Table dialog box appears on top of the Query Design window.
3. Double-click **WRITERS** and then double-click **BUSINESS ARTICLES** in the Tables list box. In the upper panel of the Query Design window, Access displays the WRITERS and BUSINESS ARTICLES field lists and indicates their relationship.
4. Click the **Close** button. The Show Table dialog box closes. See Figure 4-41.

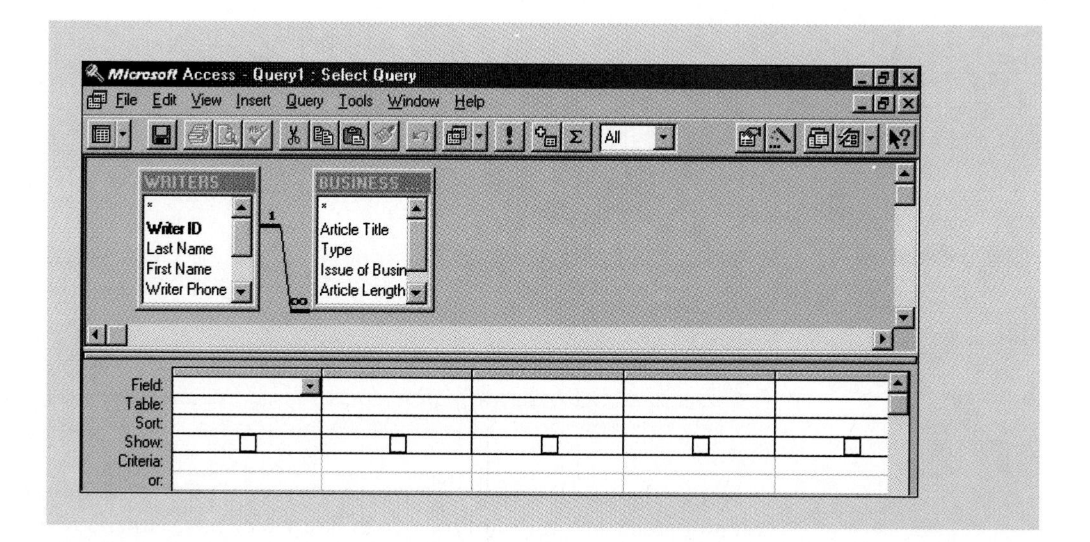

Figure 4-41 Two tables related with a join line in the Query Design window

Elena now defines the query. In the Query Design grid, she inserts the Article Title, Type, and Article Length fields from the BUSINESS ARTICLES table. She inserts the Last Name and First Name fields from the WRITERS table. She then saves the query.

To define and save a query using two tables:

1. Double-click **Article Title** in the BUSINESS ARTICLES field list. Access places this field in the first column's Field text box.
2. Using the same procedure, select Type and Article Length from the BUSINESS ARTICLES field list as the second and third columns, and Last Name and First Name from the WRITERS field list as the fourth and fifth columns. See Figure 4-42.

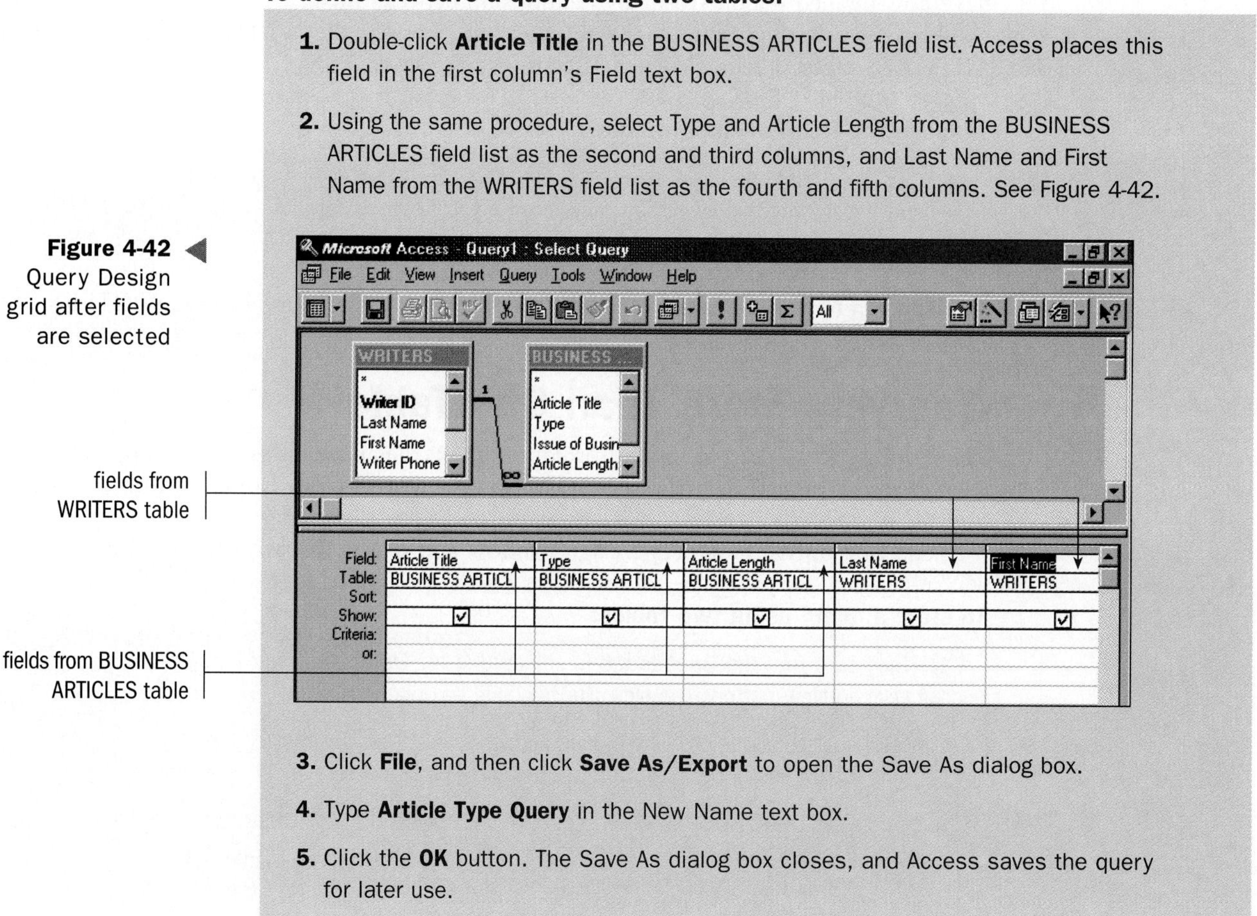

Figure 4-42 Query Design grid after fields are selected

3. Click **File**, and then click **Save As/Export** to open the Save As dialog box.
4. Type **Article Type Query** in the New Name text box.
5. Click the **OK** button. The Save As dialog box closes, and Access saves the query for later use.

Elena runs the query to view the query results.

To view the query results:

1. Click the **Run** button on the toolbar. The query results display the fields from the two tables.
2. If necessary, click the Datasheet View window's **Maximize** button to see all the fields and records. See Figure 4-43.

Figure 4-43 Results of a query using fields from two tables

fields from BUSINESS ARTICLES table

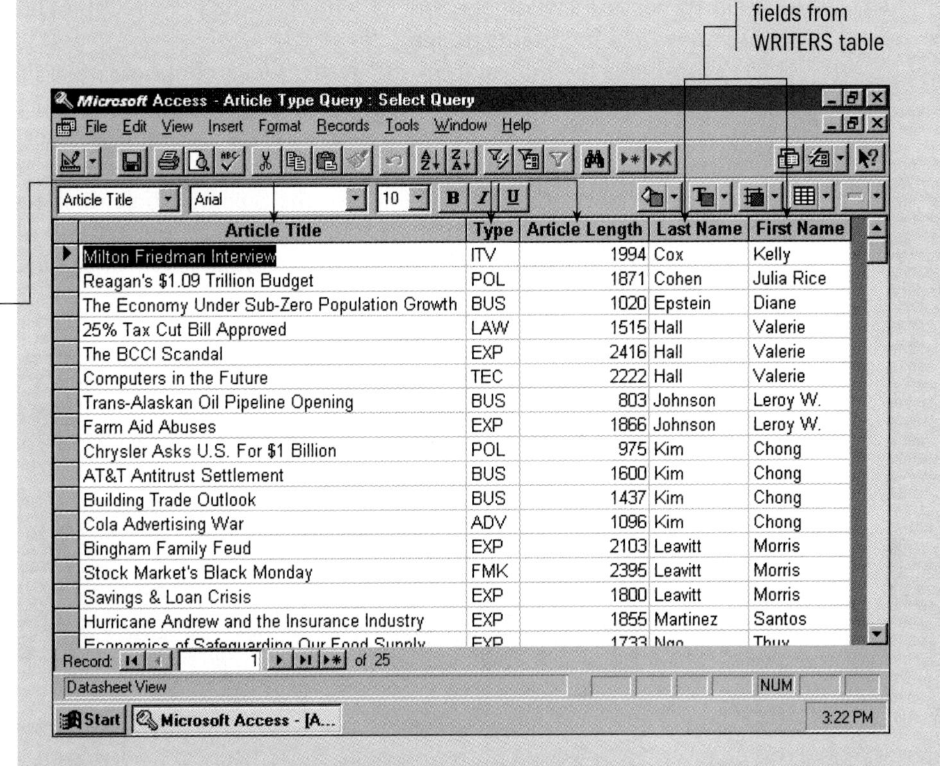

Article Title	Type	Article Length	Last Name	First Name
Milton Friedman Interview	ITV	1994	Cox	Kelly
Reagan's $1.09 Trillion Budget	POL	1871	Cohen	Julia Rice
The Economy Under Sub-Zero Population Growth	BUS	1020	Epstein	Diane
25% Tax Cut Bill Approved	LAW	1515	Hall	Valerie
The BCCI Scandal	EXP	2416	Hall	Valerie
Computers in the Future	TEC	2222	Hall	Valerie
Trans-Alaskan Oil Pipeline Opening	BUS	803	Johnson	Leroy W.
Farm Aid Abuses	EXP	1866	Johnson	Leroy W.
Chrysler Asks U.S. For $1 Billion	POL	975	Kim	Chong
AT&T Antitrust Settlement	BUS	1600	Kim	Chong
Building Trade Outlook	BUS	1437	Kim	Chong
Cola Advertising War	ADV	1096	Kim	Chong
Bingham Family Feud	EXP	2103	Leavitt	Morris
Stock Market's Black Monday	FMK	2395	Leavitt	Morris
Savings & Loan Crisis	EXP	1800	Leavitt	Morris
Hurricane Andrew and the Insurance Industry	EXP	1855	Martinez	Santos
Economics of Safeguarding Our Food Supply	EXP	1733	Ngo	Thuy

TROUBLE? You should see 25 records in the query results. If you don't see any, then you probably did not import the BUSINESS ARTICLES table correctly with the Data and Structure option. Save the query with the name Article Type Query. Delete the table and import it again. Then try running the query. If you see more than 25 records, then you created the relationship between the two tables incorrectly. Save the query with the name Article Type Query, repeat the steps for adding the relationship between the two tables, and then try running the query again.

Elena notices that she neglected to sort the query results by Type. She can do that now in the Datasheet View window.

3. Click the field selector for the Type field to select the column.
4. Click the **Sort Ascending** button to sort the query results in ascending order by Type.

After printing the query results, Elena saves the changes to the query and then closes the Datasheet View window.

To save changes to a query and close the Datasheet View window:

1. Click the Datasheet View window **Close** button. Access displays the Save changes? dialog box.
2. Click the **Yes** button to save the changes you made to the sort order for this query. The Save changes? dialog box closes and the Database window becomes the active window.

Creating a Parameter Query

Elena's final query task is to obtain the article titles and writer names for specific article types—examples of article types are advertising (ADV), business (BUS), exposé (EXP), and political (POL). She will use the BUSINESS ARTICLES table for the Article Title and Type fields, and the WRITERS table for the Last Name and First Name fields. Article Title will be the sort key and will have an ascending sort order. Because this query is similar to her last saved query, Elena will open the Article Type Query in the Query Design window and modify its design.

To obtain the information she needs, Elena could create a simple condition using an exact match for the Type field that she would change in the Query Design window every time she runs the query. Instead, Elena creates a parameter query. A **parameter query** is a query that prompts you for information when the query runs. In this case, Elena wants to create a query that prompts her for the type of article to select from the table.

When Access runs the query, it will display a dialog box and prompt Elena to enter the article type. Access then creates the query results just as if she had changed the criteria in the Query Design window.

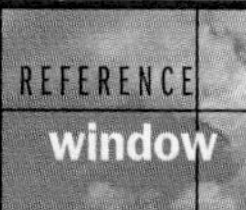

CREATING A PARAMETER QUERY

- Create a select query that includes all the fields that will appear in the query results. Also choose the sort keys and set the criteria that do not change when you run the query.
- Decide on the fields that will have prompts when you run the query. For each of them, type the prompt you want in the field's Criteria box and enclose the prompt in brackets.
- Highlight the prompt, but do not highlight the brackets. Click Edit and then click Copy to copy the prompt to the Clipboard.
- Click Query and then click Parameters to open the Query Parameters dialog box.
- Press Ctrl + V to paste the contents of the Clipboard into the Parameter text box. Press the Tab key and select the field's data type.
- Click the OK button to close the Query Parameters dialog box.

Elena opens the Article Type Query in the Query Design window and changes its design.

To open a saved query and modify its design:

1. Make sure that the Database window is active and the Queries tab is selected. Click **Article Type Query** in the Queries list and then click the **Design** button to open the Query Design window.
2. To add a sort key for the Article Title field, click the **Sort** text box, then click the **Sort** list arrow, and then click **Ascending**.

Elena has completed the changes to the select query. She now changes the query to a parameter query.

To create a parameter query:

1. Click the **Criteria** text box for the Type field and type **[Enter an Article Type:]**. See Figure 4-44.

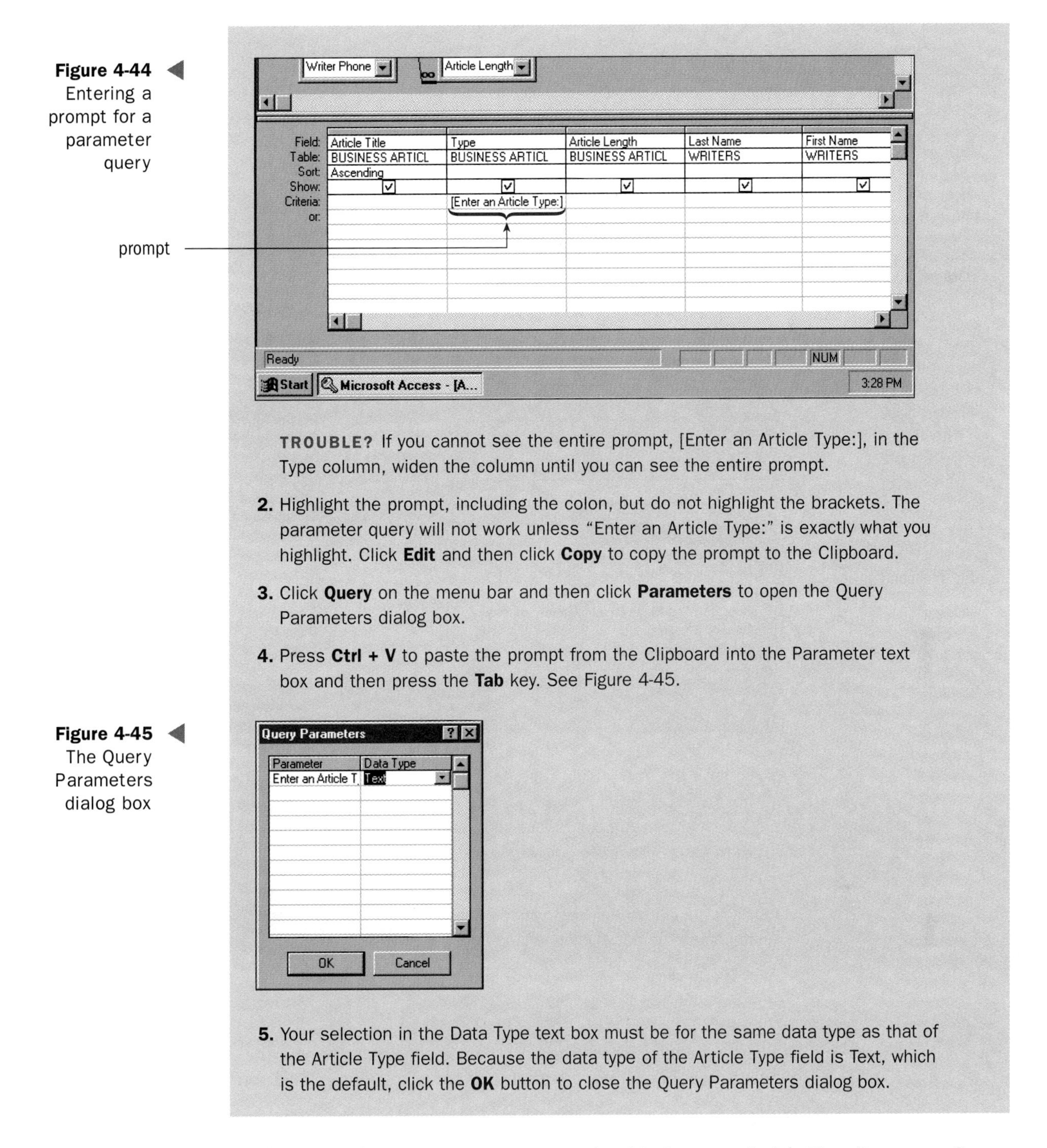

Figure 4-44 Entering a prompt for a parameter query

TROUBLE? If you cannot see the entire prompt, [Enter an Article Type:], in the Type column, widen the column until you can see the entire prompt.

2. Highlight the prompt, including the colon, but do not highlight the brackets. The parameter query will not work unless "Enter an Article Type:" is exactly what you highlight. Click **Edit** and then click **Copy** to copy the prompt to the Clipboard.

3. Click **Query** on the menu bar and then click **Parameters** to open the Query Parameters dialog box.

4. Press **Ctrl + V** to paste the prompt from the Clipboard into the Parameter text box and then press the **Tab** key. See Figure 4-45.

Figure 4-45 The Query Parameters dialog box

5. Your selection in the Data Type text box must be for the same data type as that of the Article Type field. Because the data type of the Article Type field is Text, which is the default, click the **OK** button to close the Query Parameters dialog box.

Elena runs the parameter query, saves it with the name Article Type Parameter Query, and closes the query results. She then exits Access.

To run and save a parameter query and exit Access:

1. Click the **Run** button on the toolbar. The Enter Parameter Value dialog box appears with your prompt above the text box.

2. To see all the articles that are exposés, type **EXP** in the text box. See Figure 4-46.

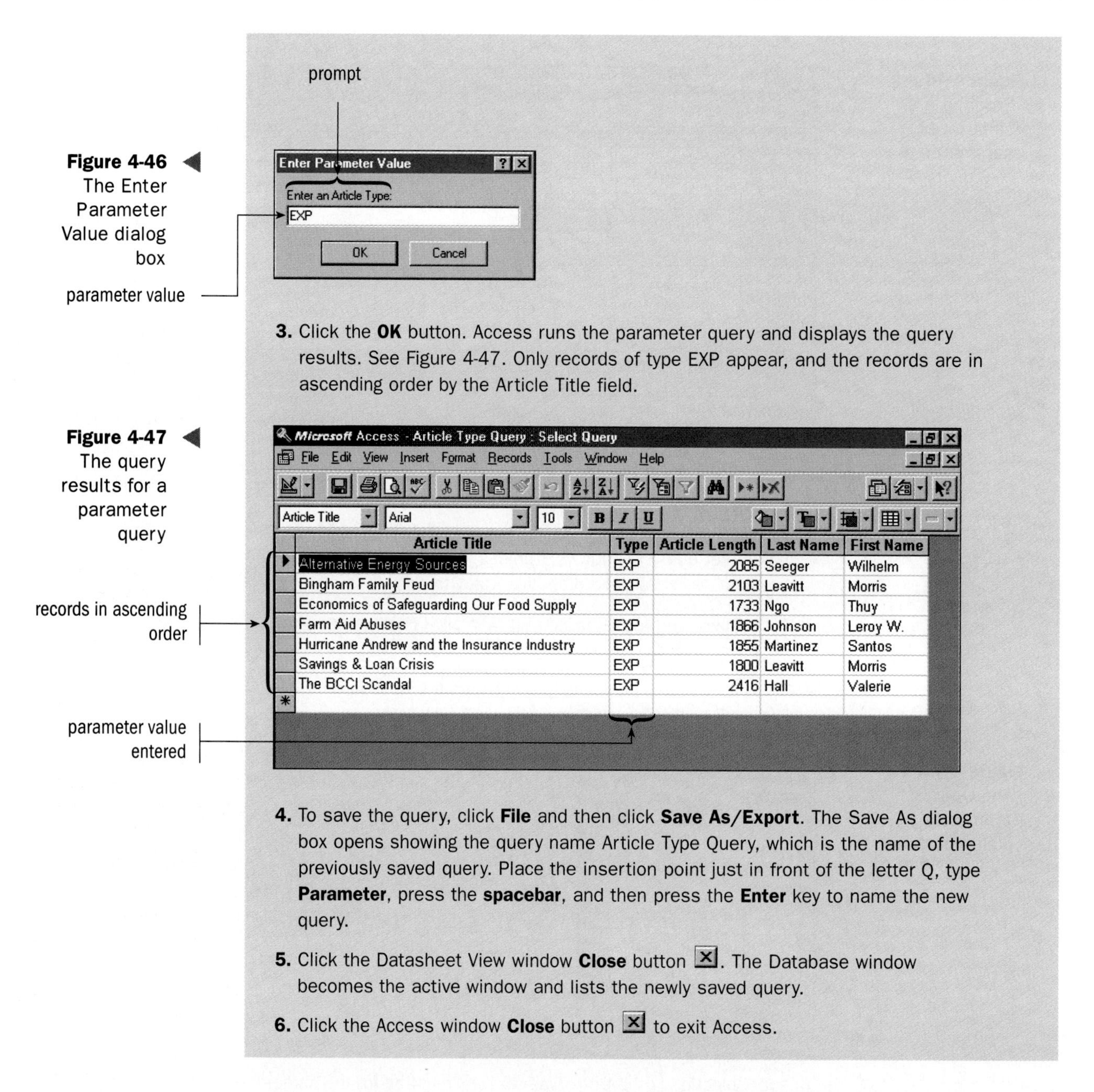

Article Title	Type	Article Length	Last Name	First Name
Alternative Energy Sources	EXP	2085	Seeger	Wilhelm
Bingham Family Feud	EXP	2103	Leavitt	Morris
Economics of Safeguarding Our Food Supply	EXP	1733	Ngo	Thuy
Farm Aid Abuses	EXP	1866	Johnson	Leroy W.
Hurricane Andrew and the Insurance Industry	EXP	1855	Martinez	Santos
Savings & Loan Crisis	EXP	1800	Leavitt	Morris
The BCCI Scandal	EXP	2416	Hall	Valerie

Figure 4-46 The Enter Parameter Value dialog box

3. Click the **OK** button. Access runs the parameter query and displays the query results. See Figure 4-47. Only records of type EXP appear, and the records are in ascending order by the Article Title field.

Figure 4-47 The query results for a parameter query

4. To save the query, click **File** and then click **Save As/Export**. The Save As dialog box opens showing the query name Article Type Query, which is the name of the previously saved query. Place the insertion point just in front of the letter Q, type **Parameter**, press the **spacebar**, and then press the **Enter** key to name the new query.

5. Click the Datasheet View window **Close** button. The Database window becomes the active window and lists the newly saved query.

6. Click the Access window **Close** button to exit Access.

Elena schedules a meeting with her colleagues to review the results of her queries. In the next tutorial, she will create forms for displaying records on the screen.

Quick Check

1. What is a join?
2. Describe the difference between a one-to-many relationship and a one-to-one relationship.
3. What functions can you perform in the Relationships window?
4. What are the two referential integrity rules?
5. What does a join line signify?
6. How do you query more than one table?
7. When do you use a parameter query?

Tutorial Assignments

Elena creates several queries using the BUSINESS ARTICLES table that she imported into the Issue25 database. Start Access, open the Issue25 database in the Tutorial folder on your Student Disk, and maximize the Database window.

For each of the following questions, prepare an appropriate query in the Query Design window and print the query results.

If fields are listed in any of the questions, display the fields in the order listed. Unless the question explicitly says to save, do not save the queries.

1. Which articles are of type BUS? Print all fields for this query.
2. What are the article titles and article lengths for all articles that have a length greater than 2103?
3. What are the article titles, article lengths, and writer IDs for all articles written by writers with Writer IDs H400 or W432?
4. What are the article titles, article lengths, writer IDs, and issues for all articles published in *Business Perspective* in the 1980s?
5. What are the article lengths, article titles, writer IDs, and issues for all articles of type EXP that have a length less than 2100?
6. What are the article titles, writer IDs, and issues for all articles of type ITV or that were written by writer L130?
7. What are the article lengths, writer IDs, issues, types, and article titles for all articles that have a length less than 2000 and are of type BUS or LAW? Print in ascending order by the Article Length field.
8. What are the article lengths, writer IDs, issues, types, and article titles for all articles in descending order by the Article Length field?
9. What are the writer IDs, article titles, issues, types, and article lengths for all articles? Display the query results in ascending order, with Writer ID as the primary sort key and Article Length as the secondary sort key.
10. What are the article titles, writer IDs, issues, types, article lengths, and costs per article for all articles, based on a cost per article of three cents per word? Use the name CostPerArticle for the calculated field, assume that the Article Length field gives the number of words in the article, and use ascending sort order for the Article Length field.
11. What is the total cost, average cost, lowest cost, and highest cost for all articles? Assume that the Article Length field gives the number of words in an article and that the cost per article is three cents per word.
12. What is the total cost, average cost, lowest cost, and highest cost for all articles by type? Assume that the Article Length field gives the number of words in an article and that the cost per article is three cents per word.

13. Using the BUSINESS ARTICLES and WRITERS tables, list the article titles, article types, issues, writer last names, and writer first names in ascending order by the Article Length field for all articles of type BUS, LAW, or POL. Do not print the Article Length field in the query results. Be sure that there is no Total row in the Query Design grid. Remember to change the name of the Issue of Business Perspective field to Issue in the query results.
14. Using the BUSINESS ARTICLES and WRITERS tables, list the article titles, issues, writer last names, and writer first names in ascending order by the Article Length field for a selected article type. This query should be a parameter query. Save the query as Business Articles and Writers Parameter Query.

Case Problems

1. Walkton Daily Press Carriers Grant Sherman has created and updated his Press database and is now ready to query it. Start Access and do the following:

1. Open the Press database in the Cases folder on your Student Disk and maximize the Database window.
   Grant creates several queries using the CARRIERS table. For each of the following questions, prepare an appropriate query in the Query Design window and print its entire query results. Whenever you use one of the carrier name fields, rename it omitting the word Carrier. Whenever fields are listed in the question, display the fields in the order listed.
2. What is all the carrier information on Ashley Shaub?
3. What is all the information on those carriers whose last names begin with the letter S?
4. What are the birthdates, phone numbers, first names, and last names of carriers born in 1981 or later?
5. What are the birthdates, phone numbers, last names, and first names of carriers whose phone numbers end with the digits 4 or 7?
6. What are the birthdates, carrier IDs, first names, and last names of those carriers born prior to 1980 who have a carrier ID either less than 5 or greater than 10?
7. What are the birthdates, carrier IDs, first names, last names, and phone numbers of all carriers in descending order by birthdate?

Close the query results to return to the Database window without saving your queries. Complete the following queries using the BILLINGS table.

8. What is the total, average, lowest, and highest balance amount for all carriers? Your four calculated fields should use the Balance Amount field as is. Note that Balance Amount is the table field name and Balance is the Caption property name.

9. What is the total, average, lowest, and highest balance amount, grouped by carrier?
10. Create a parameter query to display all the fields in the BILLINGS table based on a selected Carrier ID.
11. Open the BILLINGS table. For the records with Route ID J311 and J314, change the Carrier ID to 11. Then add a one-to-many relation between the CARRIERS and BILLINGS tables using Carrier ID as the common field. Create a query to find the Route ID, Carrier ID, Carrier Last Name and Carrier First Name sorted by Carrier Last Name.

2. Lopez Lexus Dealerships Maria and Hector Lopez have created and updated their Lexus database and are now ready to query it. Start Access and do the following:

1. Open the Lexus database in the Cases folder on your Student Disk and maximize the Database window.
   Maria and Hector create several queries using the CARS table. For each of the following questions, prepare an appropriate query in the Query Design window and print its entire query results. Whenever fields are listed in the question, display the fields in the order listed. If a field has a Caption property, rename the field to match the caption in the Query Design window.
2. What are the models, years, and selling prices for all cars?
3. What are the years, costs, and selling prices for ES300 models?
4. What are the models, classes, years, costs, and selling prices for cars manufactured in 1995 and having either an S4 or an S5 class?
5. What are the models, classes, years, costs, and selling prices for all cars in descending sequence by selling price?
6. Create a field that calculates the difference (profit) between the Selling Price and the Cost and name it Diff. What are the models, classes, years, costs, selling prices, and profits for all cars?

7. What is the total cost, total selling price, total profit, and average profit for all the cars?
8. What is the total cost, total selling price, total profit, and average profit for all the cars, grouped by model?
9. What is the total cost, total selling price, total profit, and average profit grouped by year?
10. Create a parameter query to display all the fields from the CARS table based on a selected model.

Close the query results Datasheet View window to return to the Database window without saving your query, and then complete the following problem.

11. Using a one-to-many relationship between the LOCATIONS and CARS tables using Location Code as the common field. Create a query to find the models, selling prices, location names, and manager names for all cars in descending sequence by manager name.

3.Tophill University Student Employment Olivia Tyler has created and updated her Parttime database and is now ready to query it. Start Access and do the following:

1. Open the Parttime database in the Cases folder on your Student Disk and maximize the Database window.

Olivia creates several queries using the JOBS table. For each of the following questions, prepare an appropriate query in the Query Design window and print its entire query results. Whenever fields are listed in the question, display the fields in the listed order. If a field has a Caption property, rename the field to match the caption in the Query Design window.

2. What is all the job information on job order 7?
3. What is all the information on jobs having job titles that begin with the word "Computer?"
4. What are the job titles, hours per week, and wages of jobs paying wages greater than or equal to $7.05?
5. What are the job titles, hours per week, employer IDs, and wages of jobs requiring between 20 and 24 hours per week, inclusive?
6. What are the job titles, hours per week, employer IDs, and wages of jobs requiring between 20 and 24 hours per week, inclusive, and paying wages less than or equal to $6.75?
7. What are the job titles, hours per week, employer IDs, and wages of all jobs in ascending order by hours per week (the primary sort key) and in descending order by job title (the secondary sort key)?
8. Create a calculated field that is the product of hours per week and wage, and name it Weekly. What are the hours per week, wages, weekly wages, and job titles for all jobs?

9. What is the total, average, lowest, and highest weekly wage for all the jobs listed in the jobs table?
10. What is the total, average, lowest, and highest weekly wage for all jobs grouped by employer ID?
11. Create a parameter query to display all the fields in the JOBS table based on a selected employer ID.
12. Add a one-to-many relationship between the EMPLOYERS and JOBS tables using the Employer ID as the common field. Create a query to find the Employer ID, Employer Name, Job Order and Job Title, sorted by Employer Name.

4. Rexville Business Licenses Chester Pearce has created and updated his Buslic database and is now ready to query it. Start Access and do the following:

1. Open the Buslic database in the Cases folder on your Student Disk and maximize the Database window.

Chester creates several queries using the BUSINESSES table. For each of the following questions, prepare an appropriate query in the Query Design window and print its entire query results. Whenever fields are listed in the question, display the fields in the listed order. If a field has a Caption property, rename the field to match the caption in the Query Design window.

2. What is all the information for business ID 11?
3. What is all the information on those businesses that have the word "avenue" in the Street Name field?
4. What are the business names, street numbers, street names, and proprietors for businesses having street numbers greater than 5100?
5. What are the business names, street numbers, street names, proprietors, and phone numbers for businesses having phone numbers starting 243 or 942?
6. What are the proprietors, business names, street numbers, street names, and phone numbers of all businesses in ascending sequence by business name?

Close the query results to return to the Database window without saving your queries. Complete the following queries using the ISSUED LICENSES table.

7. What is the total amount, total count, and average amount for all issued licenses?

8. What is the total amount, total count, and average amount for all issued licenses grouped by license type?
9. Create a parameter query to display all the fields based on a selected business ID.
10. Add a one-to-many relationship between the BUSINESSES and the ISSUES LICENSES tables using the Business ID as the common field. Add a one-to-many relationship between the LICENSES and the ISSUES LICENSES tables using the License Type as the common field. Create a query to find the Business ID, Business Name, License Type and License Description sorted by Business Name.

TUTORIAL 5

Designing Forms

Creating Forms at Vision Publishers

OBJECTIVES

In this tutorial you will:

- Create forms using AutoForm and the Form Wizard
- Save and open a form
- View and maintain data using forms
- Use a filter to select and sort records in a form
- Design and create a custom form
- Select, move, and delete controls
- Use Control Wizards
- Add form headers and footers

Vision Publishers

At the next progress meeting on the special 25th-anniversary issue of *Business Perspective*, Brian Murphy, Judith Rossi, and Harold Larson are pleased when Elena Sanchez presents her query results from the Issue25 database. They agree that Elena should place the Issue25 database on the company network so that everyone can access and query the data. To make the selected data easier to read and understand, Elena decides to create several forms to display the information. She begins by creating a form to display information about one writer at a time on the screen. This will be easier to read than a datasheet, and Elena can also use the form to make changes to a writer's data or to add new writers to the database.

Using a Form

A **form** is an object you use to maintain, view, and print records from a database. A form is used to display records on the screen in a more attractive and readable format. In Access, you can design your own form using several different methods:

- **AutoForm** uses all of the fields in the underlying table or query, and is a quick way to create a basic form that you can use as is or customize. AutoForm creates a form in one of three standard formats: Columnar, Tabular, or Datasheet. A **columnar form** displays the fields, one on a line, vertically on the form. Field values appear in boxes. Labels, which are the table field names, appear to the left of the field values. A **tabular form** displays multiple records and field values in a row-and-column format. Field values appear in boxes with the table field names as column headings. A **datasheet form** displays records in the same format as in the Datasheet View window. Figure 5-1 shows forms created from the BUSINESS ARTICLES table in each of these three formats.

Figure 5-1 Forms created by AutoForm from the BUSINESS ARTICLES table

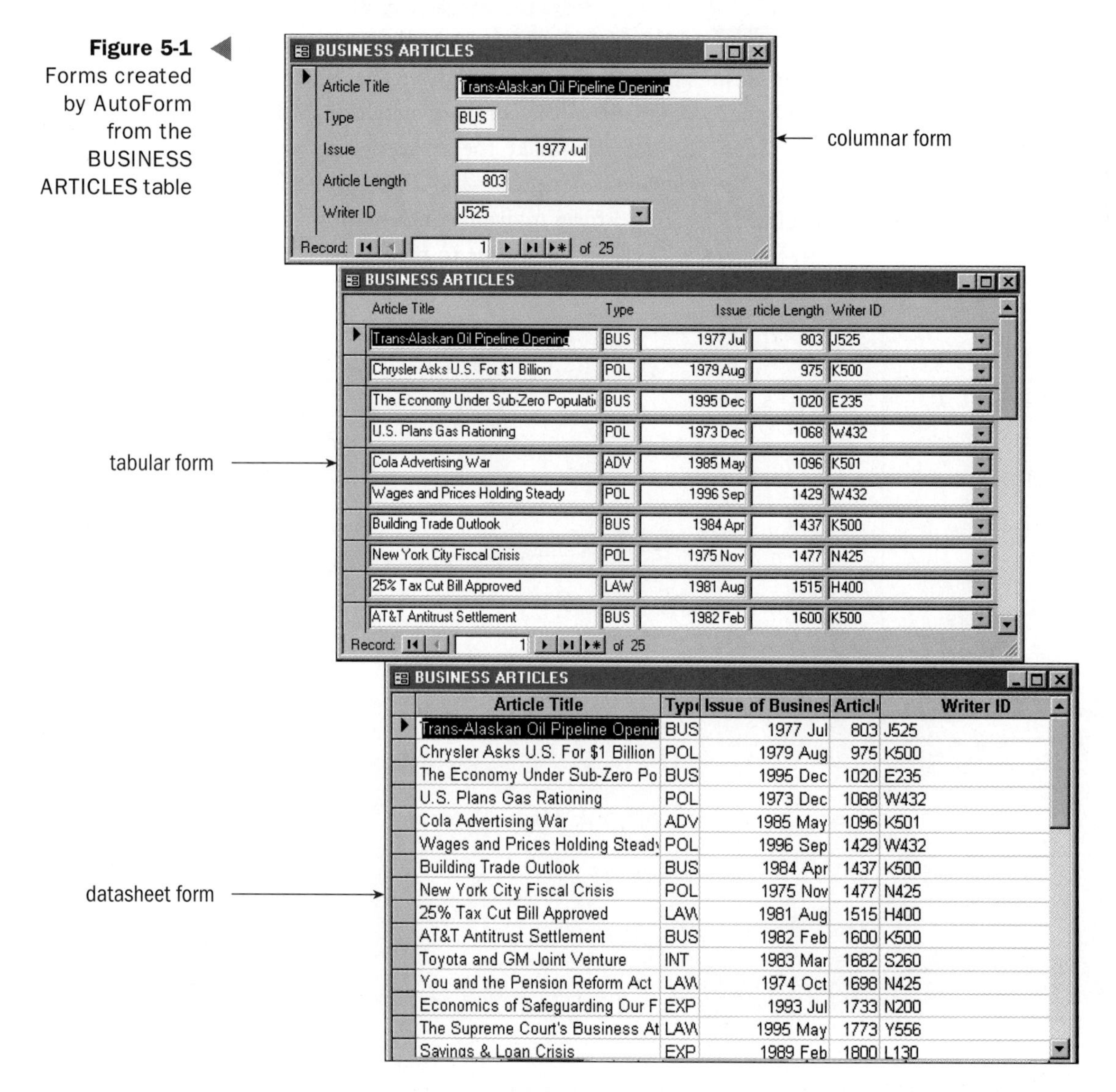

- The **Form Wizard** asks you a series of questions and then creates a form based on your answers. Using the Form Wizard, you can select the fields that you want to appear in the form.
- The **Form Design** window allows you to create your own customized form that you design directly on the screen.

- The **Chart Wizard** displays a graph created from your data.
- The **Pivot Table** form displays a Pivot Table created in Microsoft Excel. A Pivot Table summarizes the data in a table or query and can be based on the data in your Access table or query.

SESSION 5.1

In this session, you will create a form using AutoForm, create a main/subform form with the Form Wizard, save a form, and use a form for navigating in and updating records in a database table. You will also learn to use filter by selection and filter by form to select records in the table, and to save a filter as a query so that you can use it again at a later time.

Creating a Columnar Form with AutoForm

The quickest way to create a form is to use AutoForm. Once you select the type of form and the table or query upon which the form is based, AutoForm selects all the fields from the table or query, creates a form for these fields, and displays the form on the screen.

REFERENCE window

CREATING A FORM WITH AUTOFORM

- In the Database window, click the Forms tab to display the Forms list.
- Click the New button to display the New Form dialog box.
- In the list box, select an AutoForm design (Columnar, Tabular, or Datasheet).
- Click the "Choose the table or query where the object's data comes from" list arrow to display the list of available tables and queries.
- Click the table or query you want as the basis for the form.
- Click the OK button. AutoForm creates the form and displays the first record.

Because Elena wants to create a form to display information about one writer at a time on the screen, she chooses the AutoForm columnar design for her form and bases it on the WRITERS table.

To create a columnar form using AutoForm:

1. If you have not done so, place your Student Disk in the appropriate drive, start Access, open the Issue25 database in the Tutorial folder on your Student Disk, and maximize the Database window. Click the **Forms** tab to display the Forms list. No forms appear in the list yet.
2. Click the **New** button. Access displays the New Form dialog box.
3. Click **AutoForm: Columnar** in the list box to highlight it.
4. Click the **Choose the table or query where the object's data comes from** list arrow to display a list of available tables.
5. Click **WRITERS** to select the WRITERS table. See Figure 5-2.

Figure 5-2 ◀
Completed New Form dialog box

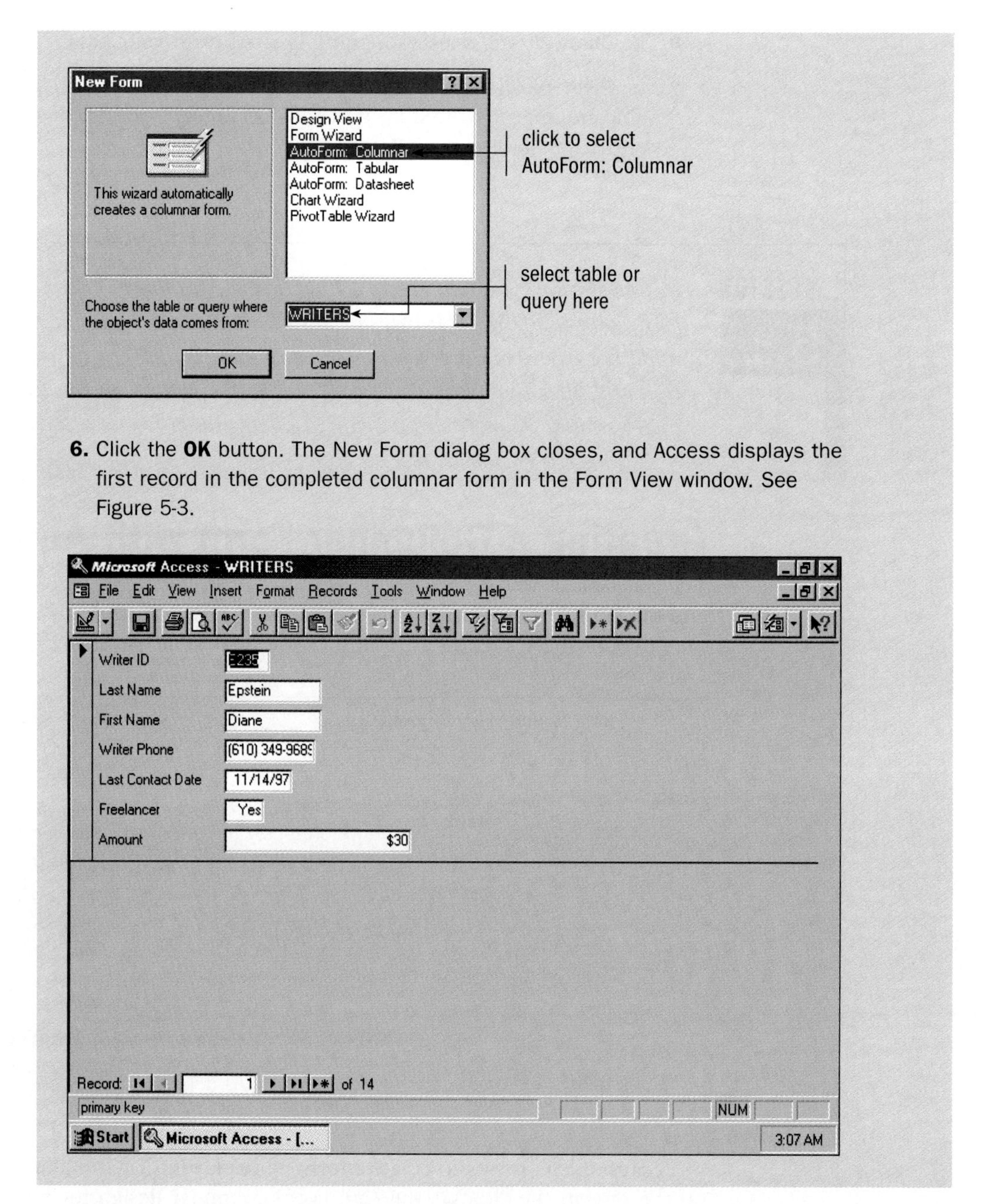

6. Click the **OK** button. The New Form dialog box closes, and Access displays the first record in the completed columnar form in the Form View window. See Figure 5-3.

Figure 5-3 ◀
First record in the completed columnar form for the WRITERS table

Access displays the first record from the WRITERS table in the new form. If you want to view other records from the WRITERS table, click the form navigation buttons. Or, if you know the specific record, type its number in the record number text box that is displayed between the form navigation buttons.

Saving a Form

Elena saves the form so that she and others can use it for future work with data from the WRITERS table. Elena saves the form with the name Writers Column Form and then closes the Form View window.

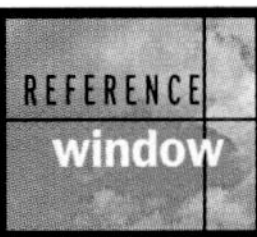

SAVING A NEW FORM

- Click the Save button on the toolbar. Access opens the Save As dialog box.
- Type the new form name in the Form Name text box.
- Click the OK button. Access saves the form and closes the dialog box.

To save and close a new form:

1. Click the **Save** button on the toolbar. Because you have not provided a name for this form yet, the Save As dialog box opens.
2. Type **Writers Column Form** in the Form Name text box.
3. Click the **OK** button. The Save As dialog box closes, and Access saves the form. The new form name will appear in the Forms list.
4. Click the Form View window **Close** button. The Form View window closes, and the Database window becomes the active window.

Next, Elena creates a form to show a specific writer, using data from the WRITERS table, and his or her articles, using data from the BUSINESS ARTICLES table. Elena will use this form to update the records in the WRITERS and BUSINESS ARTICLES tables.

Creating a Form with the Form Wizard

Because AutoForm creates forms based only on a single table or query, Elena must use a different method to create her next form. She decides to use the Form Wizard to create this new form. To base the form on two tables, Elena needs a main form and a subform. Elena will choose the WRITERS table data for the main form and the BUSINESS ARTICLES table data for the subform, so that the form will display the information for a single writer with a subform displaying all the articles by that writer. If Elena had decided to select the BUSINESS ARTICLES table data to be the main form and the WRITERS table data to be the subform instead, the form would display a single article with the information for the article's writer.

The main/subform form type uses data from two (or more) tables; therefore, the tables must be related. Elena has already defined a one-to-many relationship between the WRITERS and the BUSINESS ARTICLES tables, so she can create the form now.

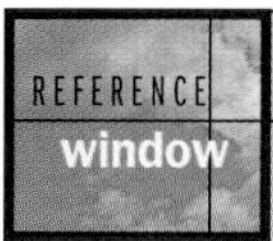

CREATING A MAIN/SUBFORM FORM WITH THE FORM WIZARD

- In the Forms list of the Database window, click the New button to display the New Form dialog box.
- Click Form Wizard, then click the OK button.
- Select the fields from tables and queries upon which the form will be based, then click the Next > button.
- Select the way in which you will view the records in the form, then click the Next > button.
- Select tabular or datasheet style for the subform, then click the Next > button.
- Select the predefined form style you want, then click the Next > button.
- Enter a name for the main form and for the subform, then click the Finish button. Access creates the form and saves the main form and the subform on the disk. Access opens the form and displays the first record in Form View.

Elena creates the form using the Form Wizard.

To create a main/subform form:

1. Click the **New** button. The New Form dialog box opens. Click **Form Wizard** to highlight it, then click the **OK** button. Access starts the Form Wizard, and the first Form Wizard dialog box is displayed. See Figure 5-4.

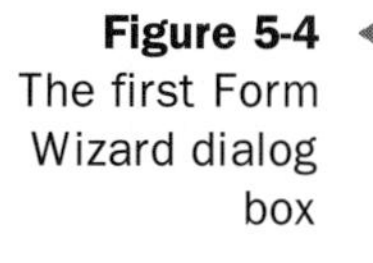

Figure 5-4 The first Form Wizard dialog box

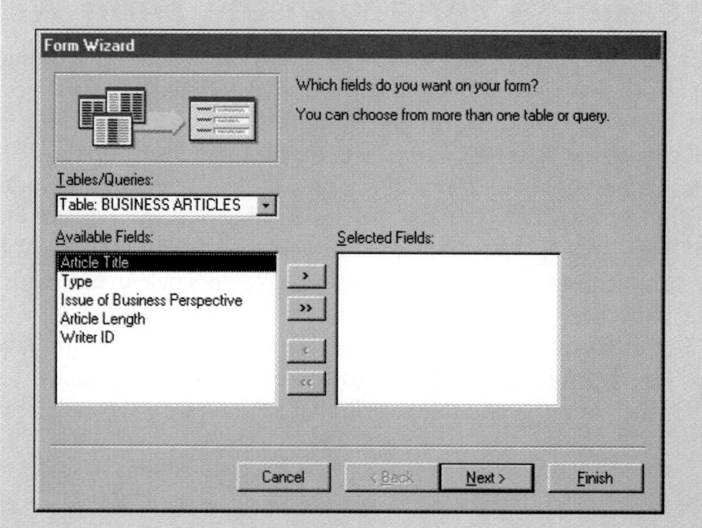

In this dialog box, you select the fields to be used in the form. The Tables/Queries list box displays Table: BUSINESS ARTICLES, the currently selected table or query, and the Available Fields list box displays the fields that are available in the selected table or query. Elena selects the WRITERS table fields first to create the main form.

2. Click the **Tables/Queries** list arrow to display the list of available tables and queries and then click **Table: WRITERS**.

3. Click the >> button to move all fields from the WRITERS table from the Available Fields list box to the Selected Fields list box.

Elena is now ready to select all the fields from the BUSINESS ARTICLES table except for the Writer ID field (which was already included with the WRITERS table).

4. Click the **Tables/Queries** list arrow to display the list of available tables and queries, then click **Table: BUSINESS ARTICLES**. Use the > button to move the Article Title, Type, Issue of Business Perspective, and Article Length fields to the Selected Fields list.

5. Click the Next > button to display the next Form Wizard dialog box.

   This dialog box allows you to choose how to view the records in this form. Elena wants to view the records by writer.

6. If necessary, click **by WRITERS** in the list box. Make sure the radio button next to "Form with subform(s)" is selected. See Figure 5-5. Click the Next > button to display the next Form Wizard dialog box.

Figure 5-5 The next Form Wizard dialog box

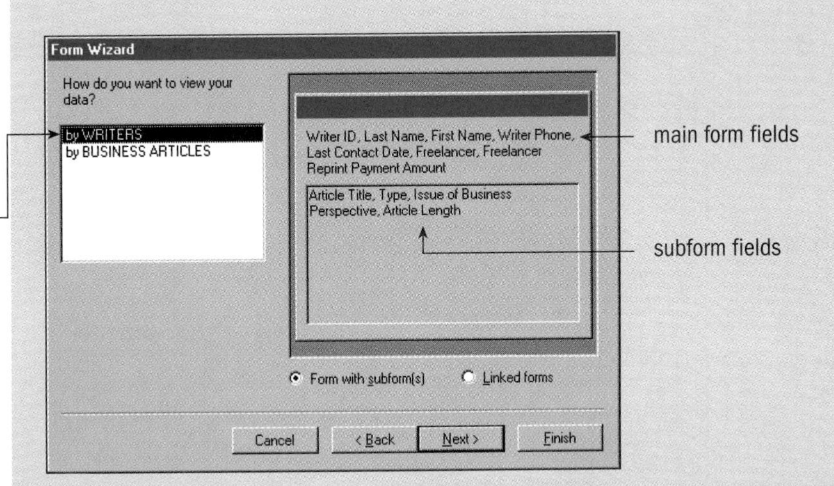

   This dialog box allows you to choose between two layouts for the subform: tabular or datasheet. The main form will use a columnar layout, but you can choose tabular or datasheet layout for the subform. Elena chooses Tabular.

7. Click the **Tabular** radio button. Click the Next > button to display the next Form Wizard dialog box.

   This dialog box allows you to choose a style for the form. Access has several predefined styles that use various background patterns and styles for the labels and data text boxes. Elena uses the standard style.

8. If necessary, click **Standard** to select it, then click the Next > button to display the next Form Wizard box. See Figure 5-6.

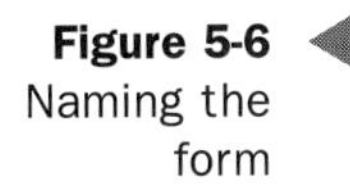

Figure 5-6 Naming the form

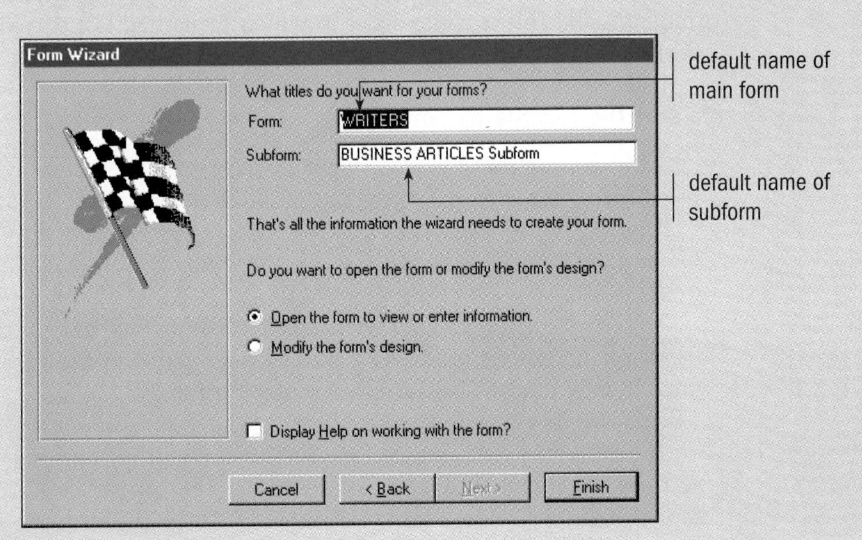

This dialog box lets you name the form. Access displays the default name WRITERS for the main form and BUSINESS ARTICLES Subform for the subform. Elena decides a more descriptive name for the main form will be helpful and that using a mix of uppercase and lowercase letters for the subform name will make it more consistent with the other form names.

9. Type **Writers and Business Articles Form** in the Form text box, press the **Tab** key, then type **Business Articles Subform** in the Subform text box. Make sure the radio button next to "Open the form to view or enter information" is selected, then click the **Finish** button. Access saves the main form and the subform and displays the first WRITERS record with the related BUSINESS ARTICLES records. See Figure 5-7.

Figure 5-7 The completed Writers and Business Articles Form

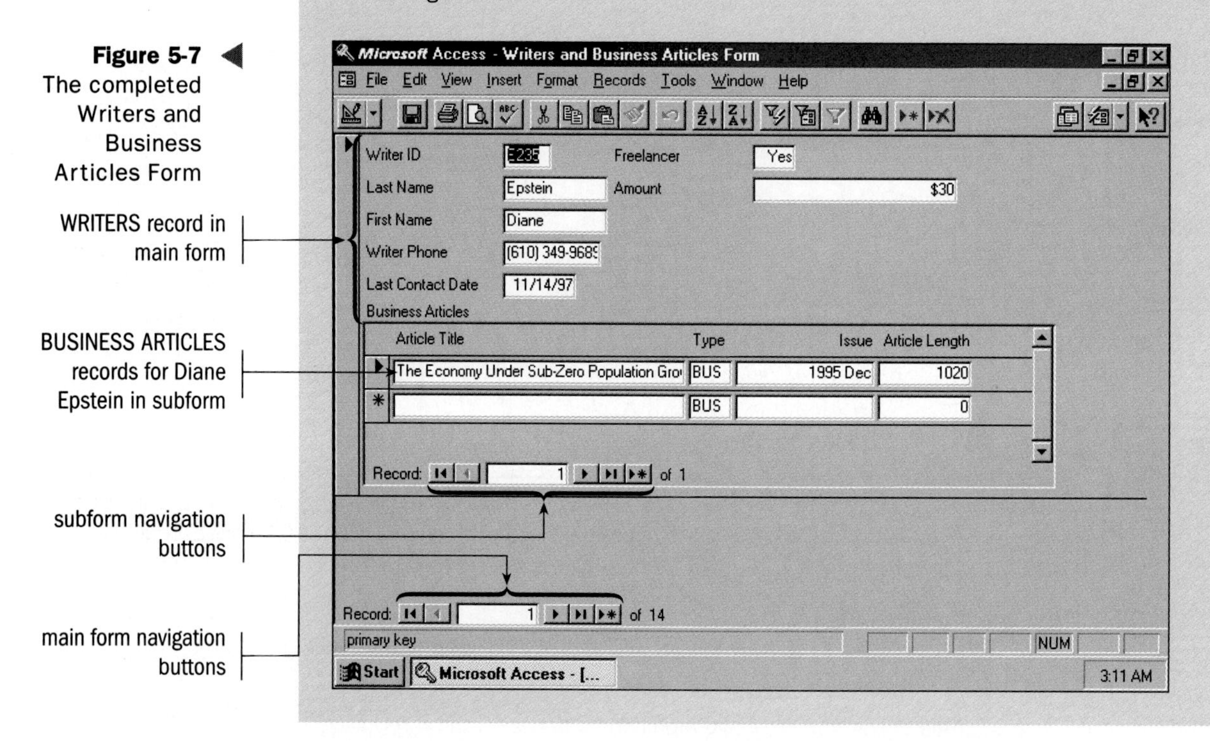

Because the Form View window is maximized, the form title is displayed in the Access title bar. Access displays the fields from the first record in the WRITERS table in the main form in a columnar format. The records in this main form appear sorted in ascending order by the Freelancer field and subsorted in ascending order by the Freelancer Reprint Payment Amount field. This was the order in which Elena had last sorted the table. She decides to sort the records in primary key sequence (by Writer ID) to view the records in the form.

To sort the records by Writer ID:

1. If necessary, click in the **Writer ID** text box to select it, then click the **Sort Ascending** button on the toolbar. Access sorts the records in ascending order by Writer ID.

The record for Kelly Cox (Writer ID C200) now appears in the form, since her Writer ID is alphabetically first. Kelly Cox has one record in the BUSINESS ARTICLES table, which is shown in the subform in tabular format.

Elena wants to view the data for a writer who has more than one record in the BUSINESS ARTICLES table. Two sets of navigation buttons appear at the bottom of the form, as shown in Figure 5-7. You use the top set of navigation buttons to select records from the related table (BUSINESS ARTICLES) in the subform and the bottom set to select records from the primary table (WRITERS) in the main form.

To navigate to different main and subform records:

1. To find a writer who has more than one record in the BUSINESS ARTICLES table, click the main form **Next Record** button ▶ three times. Access displays the record for Valerie Hall in the main form and her three articles in the subform.
2. Click the subform **Next Record** button ▶ once. Access changes the current record to the second article in the subform.
3. Click the main form **First Record** button ◀|. The main form displays the record for Kelly Cox and the subform displays the BUSINESS ARTICLES record for Kelly Cox.

   If you know which record you want to view, you can enter the record number in the text box between the navigation buttons. Elena wants to view the record for Leroy W. Johnson, the fifth record in the WRITERS table.
4. Click the record number that is displayed between the main form navigation buttons and then press the **F2** key to highlight the number. Type **5** and then press the **Enter** key. The form now displays the record for Leroy W. Johnson, record number 5 in the WRITERS table.

Now that Elena has created the Writers and Business Articles Form, she is ready to use it to update the records in the WRITERS and the BUSINESS ARTICLES tables.

Maintaining Table Data Using a Form

Elena needs to add a new article to the Issue25 database for a writer already listed in the WRITERS table, and a new writer to the WRITERS table and an article by that writer to the BUSINESS ARTICLES table. She also wants to make two changes to the record for one of Valerie Hall's articles. These database modifications involve both tables, as shown in Figure 5-8.

Figure 5-8 Changes to records in the Issue25 database

Table	Action
WRITERS	Add new writer Writer ID: L350 Last Name: Lawton First Name: Pat Writer Phone: (705) 677-1991 Last Contact Date: 9/4/94 Freelancer: No Amount: 0
BUSINESS ARTICLES	Add: Article Title: Law Over the Past 25 Years (by Pat Lawton) Type: LAW Issue: 1994 Dec Article Length: 2834 Add: Article Title: Advertising Over the Past 25 Years (by Thuy Ngo) Type: ADV Issue: 1994 Dec Article Length: 3285 Change: Article Title: The BCCI Scandal (by Valerie Hall) New Issue Date: 1991 Aug New Article Length: 2779

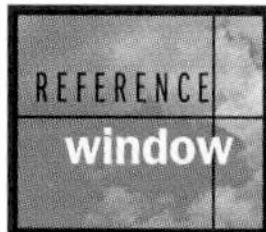

MAINTAINING TABLE DATA USING A FORM

- To add a new record in the main form, click the main form New Record button, then enter the data for the new record.
- To add a new record in the subform, locate the correct main form record, click the subform New Record button, then enter the data for the new record.
- To modify a record in the main form or the subform, locate the correct main form record and the correct subform record, click in the field you want to modify and enter the changes.

Elena begins by adding the new article for Thuy Ngo. Elena knows from her previous work with the Issue25 database that there is already a record for Thuy Ngo in the WRITERS table, record number 10.

To add a record in a subform:

1. Click the record number text box that is displayed between the main form navigation buttons and then press the **F2** key to highlight the number. Type **10** and then press the **Enter** key. Thuy Ngo's record appears, and the Writer ID field is selected in the main form.

2. Click the **New Record** button in the subform. Access displays a blank record in the Business Articles Subform.

   TROUBLE? If the entire form appears blank, you may have clicked the New Record button for the main form. Repeat Steps 1 and 2.

3. Type **Advertising Over the Past 25 Years**, press the **Tab** key, type **ADV**, press the **Tab** key, type **1994 Dec**, press the **Tab** key, type **3285**, and then press the **Tab** key. See Figure 5-9. Access has added this record not just to the Writers and Business Articles Form but also to the BUSINESS ARTICLES table.

Figure 5-9 Adding a record in a subform

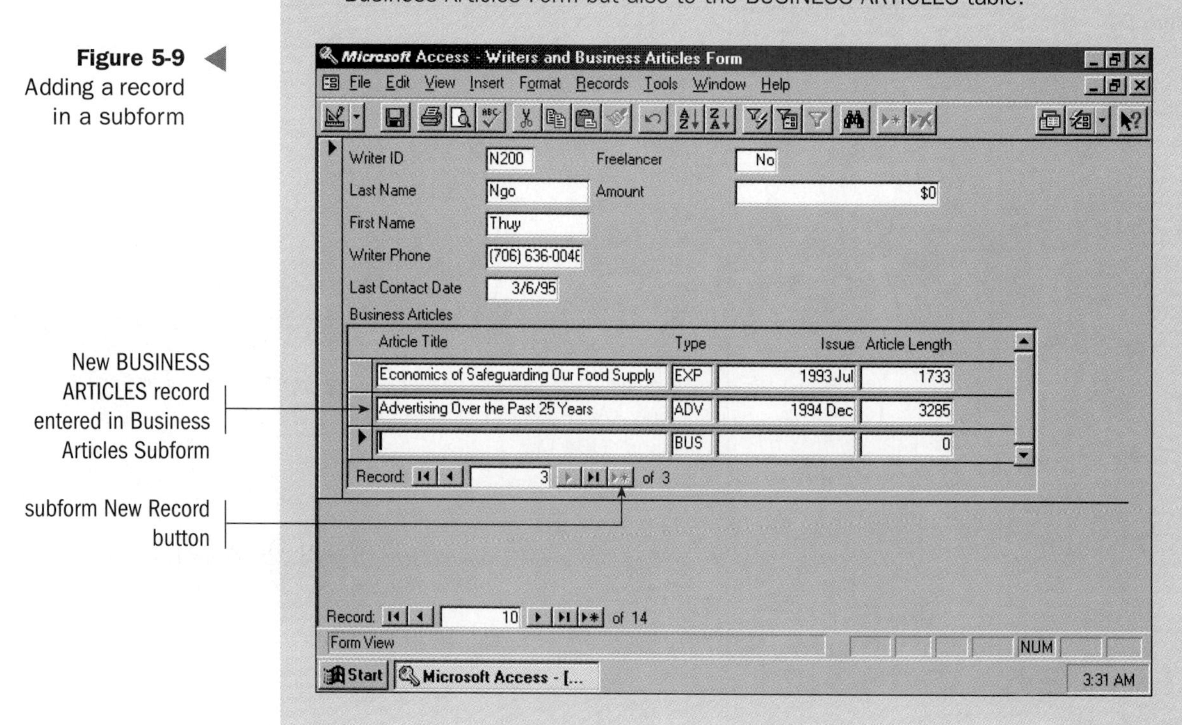

When you created the Writers and Business Articles Form, you selected all fields from the WRITERS table for the main form. However, you did not select the Writer ID field for the Business Articles Subform. Because the Writer ID field is the common field between the two tables, Access uses the Writer ID field value from the main form when it saves the subform new record in the BUSINESS ARTICLES table. Therefore, Thuy's article will be saved with his current Writer ID value.

Next, Elena adds the new writer, Pat Lawton, to the WRITERS table and then adds her article to the BUSINESS ARTICLES table.

To add a new writer and a new article using a form:

1. Click the main form's **New Record** button ▶*. Access moves to record 15 in the main form and to record 1 in the subform. These new records contain no data. Click in the main form's Writer ID field to position the pointer there.
2. To enter the first five field values, type **L350**, press the **Tab** key, type **Lawton**, press the **Tab** key, type **Pat**, press the **Tab** key, type **7056771991**, press the **Tab** key, type **9/4/94,** and then press the **Tab** key.
3. Type **No** to change the Freelancer field value to No, and then press the **Tab** key to move to the Amount field.
4. Press the **Tab** key. Access automatically enters the field value of $0, saves the new record in the WRITERS table, and then positions the insertion point in the Article Title field in the subform.
5. Type **Law Over the Past 25 Years**, press the **Tab** key, type **LAW**, press the **Tab** key, type **1994 Dec**, press the **Tab** key, and then type **2834**.
6. Press the **Tab** key. Access saves the new record in the BUSINESS ARTICLES table and positions the insertion point in the Article Title field for the next available record in the Business Articles Subform. See Figure 5-10.

Figure 5-10 Adding records in a main form and a subform

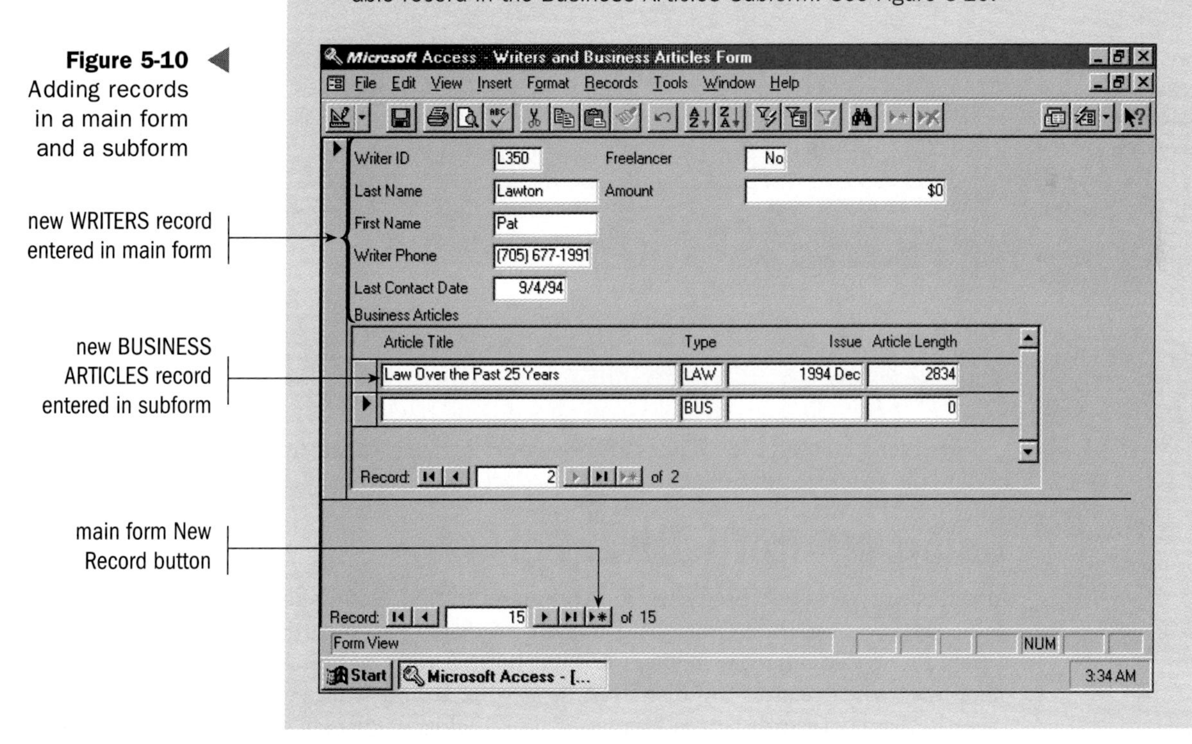

Finally, Elena finds the record for Valerie Hall and makes the two changes to one of her articles.

To find a record and change table field values using a form:

1. Click the **First Record** button in the main form. Access displays the record for Kelly Cox. Click in the Last Name text box for the record.
2. Click **Edit**, then click **Find** to display the Find in Field dialog box. Be sure that the Search Only Current field box is not selected.
3. Type **Hall** in the Find What text box, then click the **Find First** button. Access displays the record for Valerie Hall.
4. Click the Find in Field **Close** button to close the dialog box.
5. Double-click **Jul** in the Issue field for the article title The BCCI Scandal and then type **Aug** as the correct month value for the Issue field.
6. Press the **Tab** key to move to and highlight the Article Length field.
7. Type **2779** as the correct field value for the Article Length field.

Elena has completed her maintenance tasks, which have been automatically saved to the underlying tables. She closes the Form View window and returns to the Database window.

To close the Form View window:

1. Click the Form View window **Close** button. The Form View window closes and the Database window becomes the active window. Notice that both Business Articles Subform and Writers and Business Articles Form appear in the Forms list. See Figure 5-11.

Figure 5-11 The Forms list in the Database window

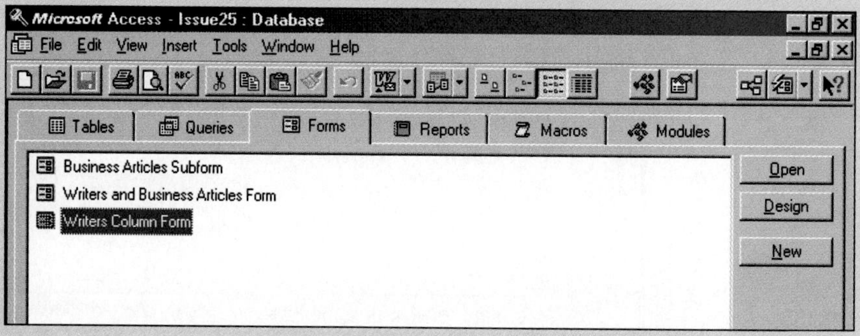

First Elena created the Writers and Business Articles Form, then she used the form to update the records, now she can use it to select records from the table.

Using a Filter with a Form

In Datasheet View, you used the Find command to find records that match a specific field value, and you used the Quick Sort buttons to display all records in a specified order by a field or by two adjacent fields. The Find button and the Quick Sort buttons work the same way when records are displayed in a form. If you want Access to display selected records, display records sorted by two or more fields, or display selected records and sort them, you use a filter.

A **filter** is a set of criteria that describes the records you want to see in a form and specifies their sequence. A filter is similar to a query, but it applies only to the form that is currently in use. If you want to use a filter at another time, you can save the filter as a query.

Access has three filter tools that allow you to specify and apply filters: filter by selection, filter by form, and advanced filter/sort. With filter by selection and filter by form, you specify the record selection criteria directly in the form. Filter by selection finds records that match a particular field value. Filter by form finds records that match multiple selection criteria using the same Access logical And and Or comparison operators discussed in Tutorial 4. After applying a filter by selection or filter by form, you can rearrange the records using the Quick Sort buttons.

Advanced filter/sort allows you to specify multiple selection criteria and to specify a sort order for the selected records in the Advanced Filter/Sort window, in the same way you specify record selection criteria and sort order for a query in the Query Design window. Since you are already familiar with using the Query Design window to specify selection criteria and sort order, you will only use filter by selection and filter by form in this tutorial.

Using Filter by Selection

Harold asks Elena to select all the records for freelancers, as he needs their names and phone numbers. Elena uses a filter by selection to specify the criterion that only records for freelancers be selected. In filter by selection, you first display a record that contains the field value you want and then apply the filter. Access selects all records that have a matching value in the same field.

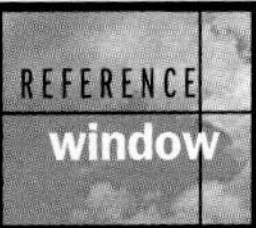

SELECTING RECORDS WITH FILTER BY SELECTION

- Open the form you want to use for selecting and viewing records.
- In the Form View window, display a record that contains a field that meets the selection criterion.
- Click in that field's text box to indicate that this is the value you want to match.
- Click the Filter By Selection button on the toolbar. Access selects all records that meet the selection criterion.

Because Elena needs information from the WRITERS table, she uses the Writers Column Form created earlier to view the records.

To find records for freelancers using filter by selection:

1. Double-click **Writers Column Form** to select and open the form. Access opens the form and displays the first record.
2. The first record displayed is for Diane Epstein, a freelancer, which matches the selection criterion. The record for Diane Epstein is the first record because the last time this table was sorted (by Freelancer field and then by Freelancer Reprint Payment Amount), her record appeared first in the sorted table. Click in the **Freelancer** text box to indicate that this is the value you want to match.
3. Click the **Filter By Selection** button on the toolbar. Access searches the WRITERS table and finds all records that have Yes as the Freelancer field value. See Figure 5-12.

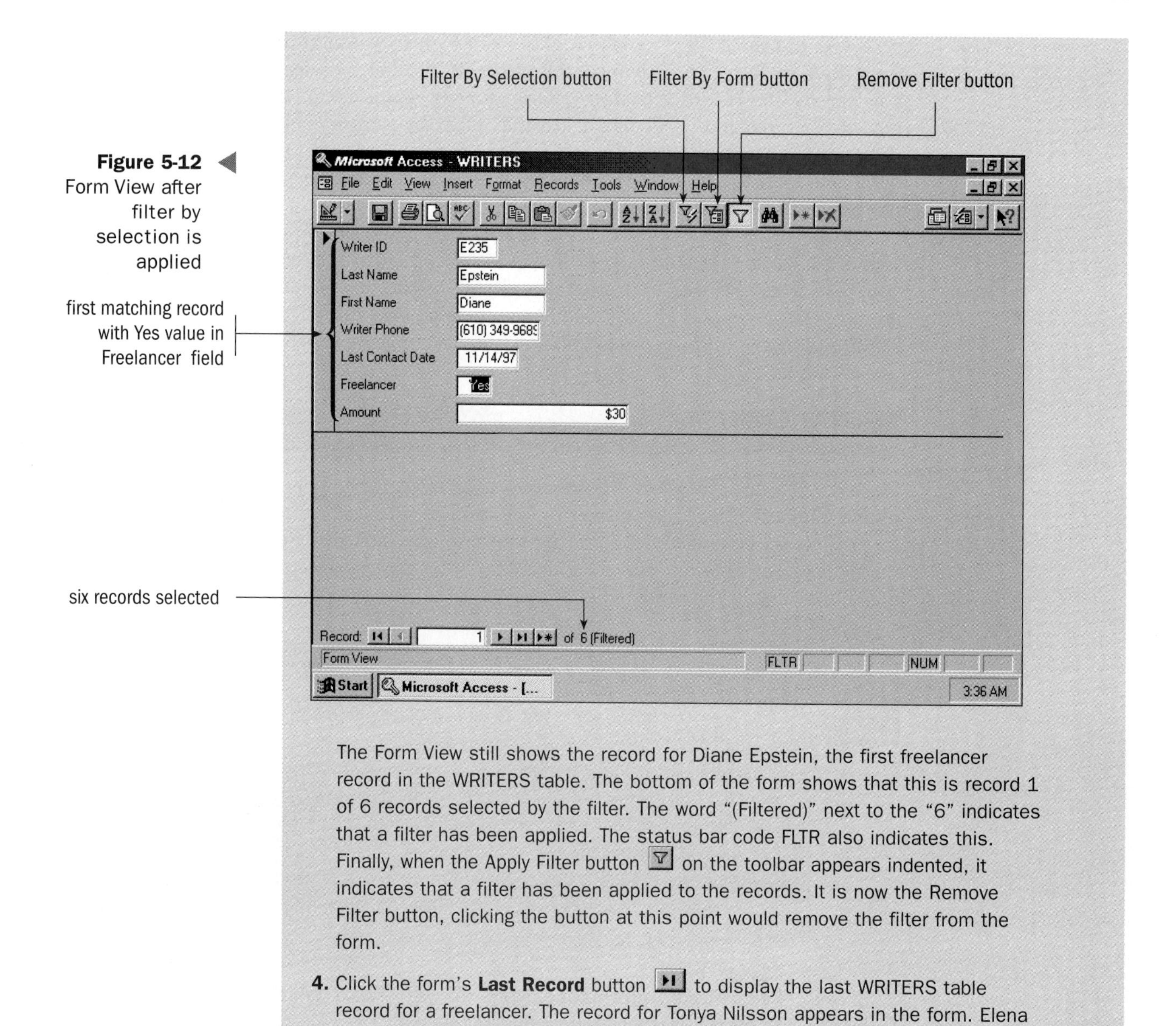

Figure 5-12 Form View after filter by selection is applied

The Form View still shows the record for Diane Epstein, the first freelancer record in the WRITERS table. The bottom of the form shows that this is record 1 of 6 records selected by the filter. The word "(Filtered)" next to the "6" indicates that a filter has been applied. The status bar code FLTR also indicates this. Finally, when the Apply Filter button on the toolbar appears indented, it indicates that a filter has been applied to the records. It is now the Remove Filter button, clicking the button at this point would remove the filter from the form.

4. Click the form's **Last Record** button to display the last WRITERS table record for a freelancer. The record for Tonya Nilsson appears in the form. Elena then prints the records for Harold.

5. Click the **Print** button on the toolbar. Access prints the six selected records, fitting as many records as possible on each page.

Elena is finished finding the freelancers' names and phone numbers for Harold so she removes the filter and closes the Form View window.

To remove the filter and close the Form View window:

1. Click the **Remove Filter** button on the toolbar. The Apply Filter button appears raised, Access removes the filter, and the bottom of the screen again shows there are 15 records. The FLTR code in the status bar disappears.

2. Click the **Close** button on the Form View window. Access closes the Form View window, and the Database window becomes active.

Using Filter by Form

After she gives the list of freelancers and their phone numbers to Harold, Elena is given another task by Brian. He asks Elena to create a form that displays all recent (that is, printed after 1990) business articles of type EXP (exposé) or BUS (business). He would like the list sorted in ascending order, from earliest to the most recent publication date. Because this requires data from the BUSINESS ARTICLES table only, Elena first creates a columnar form based on the BUSINESS ARTICLES table, then uses filter by form to find the requested records, and then uses the Quick Sort buttons to sort the information.

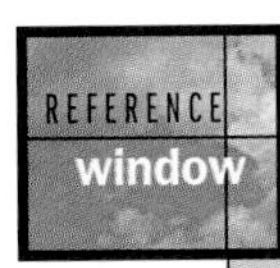

SELECTING RECORDS WITH FILTER BY FORM

- Open the form you want to use for selecting and viewing records.
- In the Form View window, click the Filter By Form button on the toolbar.
- Enter a simple selection criterion or an And condition in the first form by entering the selection criteria in the text boxes for the appropriate fields.
- If there is an Or condition, click the Or tab and enter the second part of the Or condition in the second form. Continue to enter Or conditions on separate forms by using the Or tab.
- Click the Apply Filter button on the toolbar. Access applies the filter and displays the first record matching the selection criteria.

To create the columnar form based on the BUSINESS ARTICLES table:

1 If necessary, click the **Forms** tab to display the Forms list. Click the **New** button. Access displays the New Form dialog box.

2. Click **AutoForm: Columnar** in the list box to highlight it.

3. Click the **Choose the table or query where the object's data comes from** list arrow to display a list of available tables.

4. Click **BUSINESS ARTICLES** to select the BUSINESS ARTICLES table.

5. Click the **OK** button. The New Form dialog box closes, and Access displays the completed form.

Elena saves this form for later use.

To save a form:

1. Click the **Save** button on the toolbar. Access displays the Save As dialog box.

2. Type **Business Articles Column Form** in the Form Name text box, then click the **OK** button to save the form.

Elena is now ready to use a filter by form to select the records from the Business Articles Column Form. The multiple selection criteria Elena wants to specify are: BUS article *and* after 12/31/90 *or* EXP article *and* after 12/31/90.

To select records using filter by form:

1. Click the **Filter By Form** button on the toolbar. Access displays a blank form. See Figure 5-13.

Figure 5-13 Blank form for filter by form

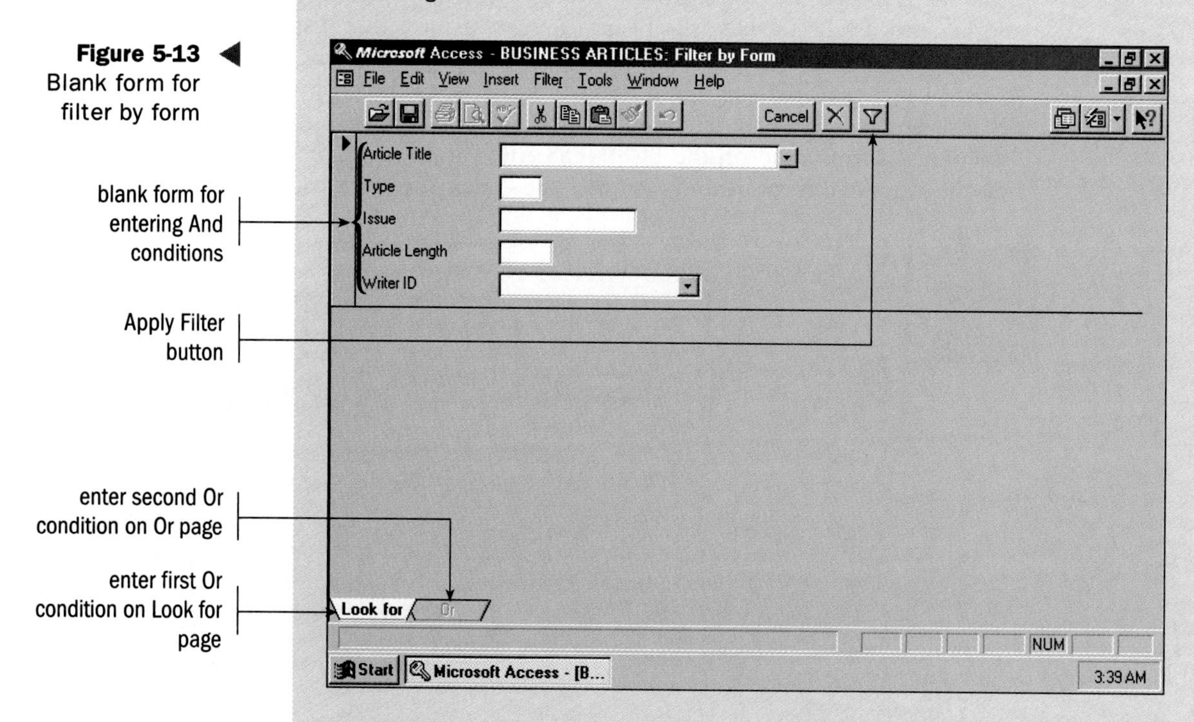

In this blank form, you specify multiple selection criteria by entering conditions in the text boxes for the fields in a record. If you enter criteria in more than one field, you create the equivalent of an And condition: Access will select any record that matches all of the criteria. To create an Or condition, you enter the criteria for the first part of the Or in the field on the first (Look for) blank form, then click the Or tab. The Or tab displays a new blank form. You enter the criteria for the second part of the Or in the same field on this new blank form. Access selects any record that matches either all criteria on the first form *or* all criteria on the second form. Elena uses the blank form to enter the criteria for the first part of the Or condition.

2. Click the **Type** text box, then click the **Type** list arrow, then click **BUS** to select the BUS type.
3. Click the **Issue** text box and type **>#12/31/90#**. You have now specified the logical operator (And) and the comparison operator (>) for the condition BUS type article *and* after 12/31/90. To add the second part of the Or condition, Elena displays the second blank form.
4. Click the **Or** tab to display a second blank form. The cursor is in the text box for the Issue field.
5. Click the **Type** text box, then click the **Type** list arrow, then click **EXP**.
6. Click the **Issue** text box and type **>#12/31/90#**. The form now contains the equivalent of the second And condition: EXP type article *and* after 12/31/90. See Figure 5-14.

Figure 5-14 Completed filter by form

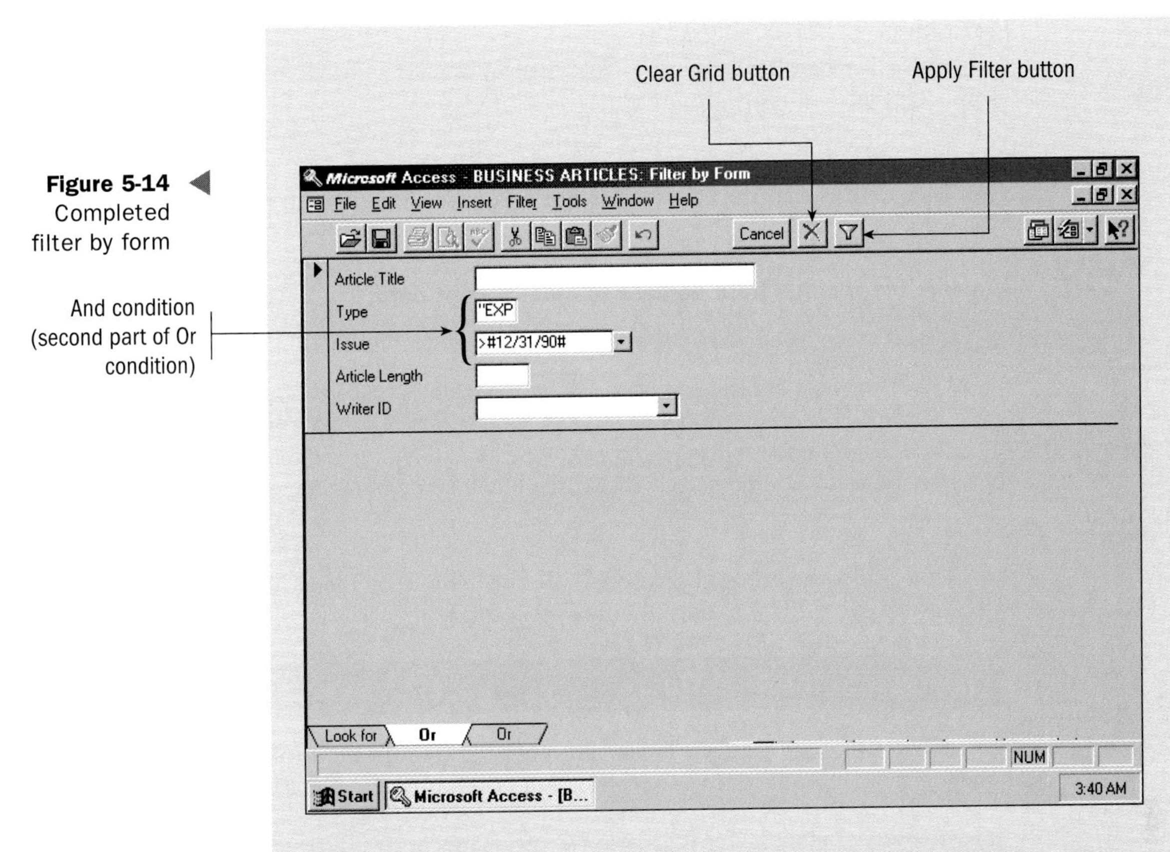

Combined with the first form, you now have the Or condition, and the filter by form conditions are complete.

7. Click the **Apply Filter** button on the toolbar to apply the filter to the records in the BUSINESS ARTICLES table. Access applies the filter and displays the first record (The Economy Under Sub-Zero Population Growth, a BUS article in the 1995 Dec issue) that matches the selection criteria. The bottom of the screen shows that four records were selected. See Figure 5-15.

Figure 5-15 First record that matches the selection criteria

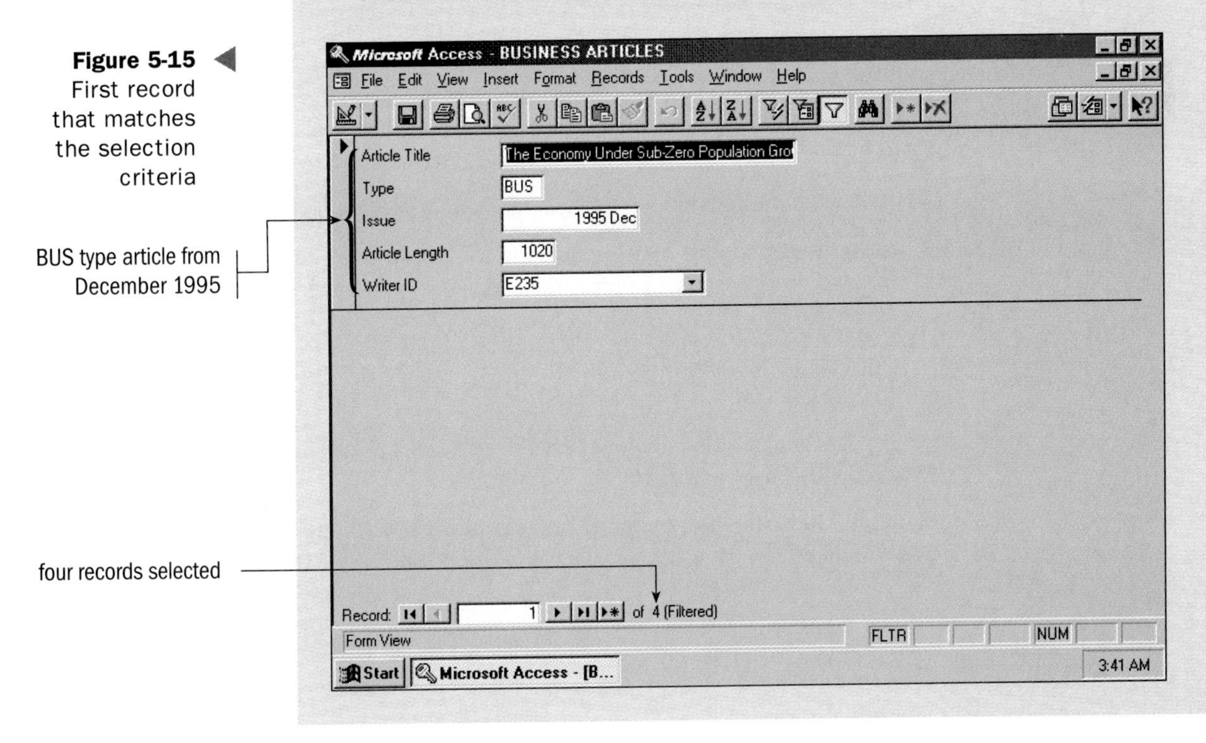

8. Click the **Last Record** button to display the last selected record (The BCCI Scandal).

Elena notices that the records are not sorted from earliest to most recent date, so she does that now.

To sort the records from earliest to most recent date:

1. Click in the **Issue** text box on the form to select that field.
2. Click the **Sort Ascending** button on the toolbar. Access sorts the selected records in ascending order by issue. The record for "The BCCI Scandal" article, the earliest of the selected records, appears in the form and the record number at the bottom of the screen shows that it is the first of the four selected records.

Elena prints the selected records for Brian. Now that Elena has defined the filter, she decides she would like to save the filter as a query.

Saving a Filter As a Query

By saving a filter as a query, Elena can reuse the filter in the future by opening the saved query. The saved query stores the selection criteria used in the filter.

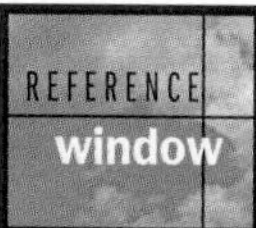

SAVING A FILTER AS A QUERY

- Create a filter by form.
- Click the Save button on the toolbar to display the Save As Query dialog box.
- Type the name for the query, then click the OK button. Access saves the query.

To save a filter as a query:

1. Click the **Filter By Form** button on the toolbar. Access displays the form with the selection criteria.
2. Click the **Save** button on the toolbar. The Save As Query dialog box opens.
3. Type **Recent BUS and EXP Articles Query** in the Query Name text box and then click the **OK** button. Access saves the filter as a query, and the Save As Query dialog box closes.

   Next, Elena clears the selection criteria, closes the filter window, and returns to the Form View window.

4. Click the Filter window Close button . The filter window closes and the Form View window becomes active.
5. Click the the **Remove Filter** button on the toolbar. The bottom of the screen shows that there are 27 records available in the BUSINESS ARTICLES table.

Elena wants to check that the filter was saved as a query, so she closes the Form View window.

To close the Form View window and view the query list:

1. Click the Form View window **Close** button ☒. Access closes the Form View window and opens the Database window.
2. Click the **Queries** tab to display the Queries list. See Figure 5-16. Recent BUS and EXP Articles Query is now listed.

Figure 5-16 Queries list in the Database window

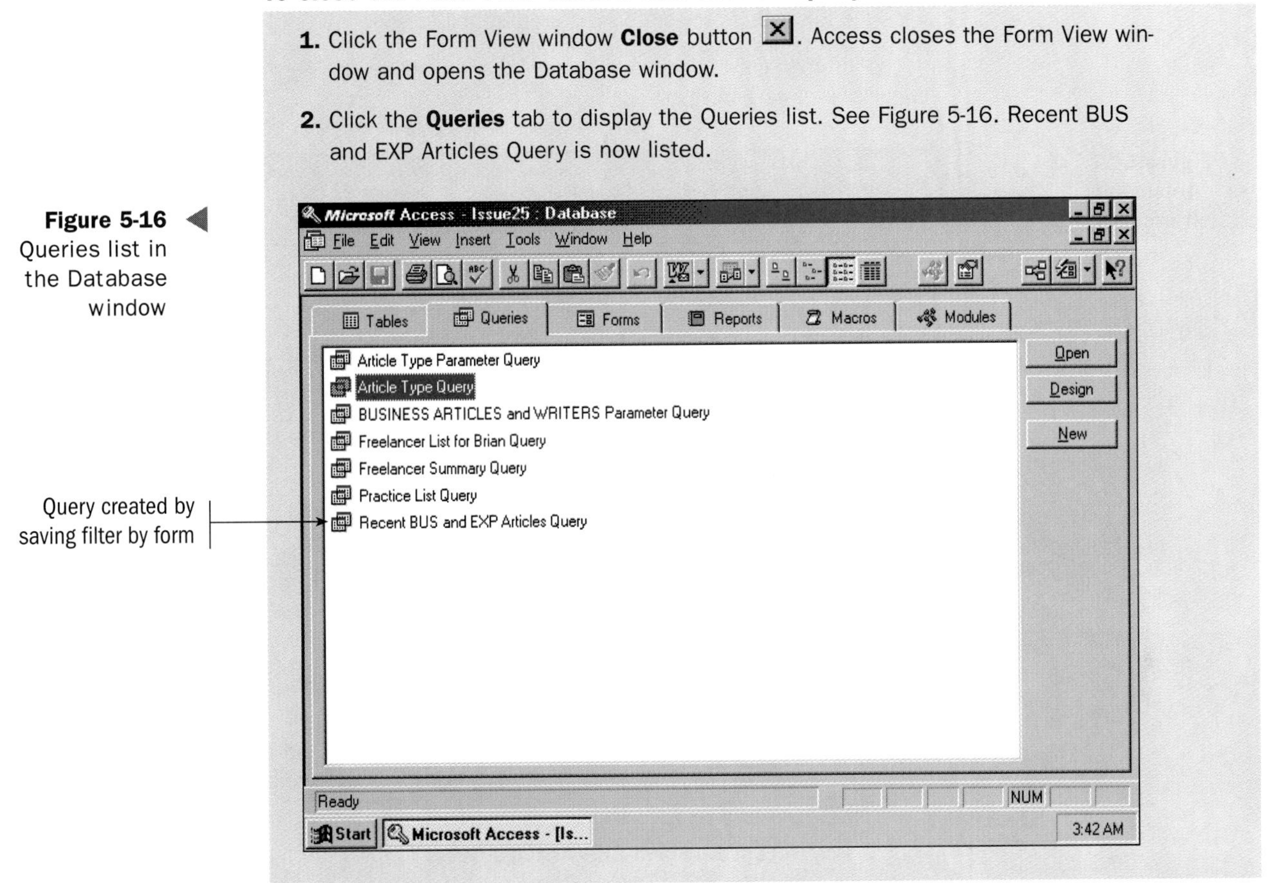

Next, Elena wants to practice applying a filter that was saved as a query.

Applying a Filter That Was Saved As a Query

Elena opens the Business Articles Column Form and applies the Recent BUS and EXP Articles Query as a filter.

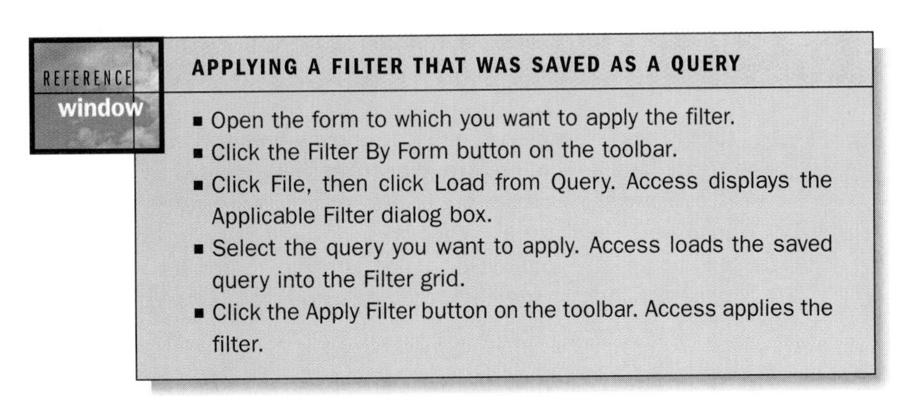
REFERENCE window

APPLYING A FILTER THAT WAS SAVED AS A QUERY

- Open the form to which you want to apply the filter.
- Click the Filter By Form button on the toolbar.
- Click File, then click Load from Query. Access displays the Applicable Filter dialog box.
- Select the query you want to apply. Access loads the saved query into the Filter grid.
- Click the Apply Filter button on the toolbar. Access applies the filter.

To apply a filter that was saved as a query:

1. Click the **Forms** tab in the Database window and double-click **Business Articles Column Form** in the Forms list. The Form View window opens.
2. Click the **Filter By Form** button on the toolbar.
3. Click **File**, then click **Load from Query**. Access displays the Applicable Filter dialog box. See Figure 5-17.

Figure 5-17 Applicable Filter dialog box

query selected to apply

Apply Filter button

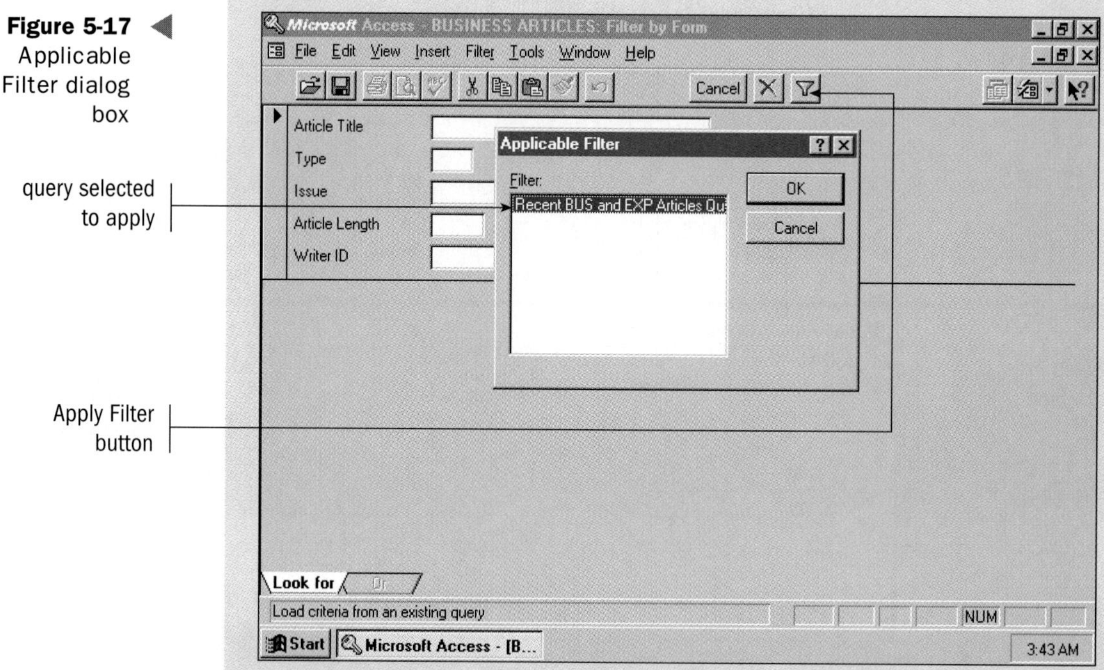

4. Double-click **Recent BUS and EXP Articles Query** in the Filter list box. The Applicable Filter dialog box closes, and Access loads the saved query into the Filter grid.
5. Click the **Apply Filter** button on the toolbar. Access applies the filter and displays the first record in the form. Notice that the first record is for the article "The Economy Under Sub-Zero Population Growth." This is not the article that appeared first when you sorted the articles by date. The saved query did not save the sort order.
6. Click the Form View window **Close** button. The Form View window closes, and the Database window becomes the active window.

In the next session, you will learn how to create a custom form. Custom forms allow you to create layouts that are different from those created by the Form Wizard and AutoForm.

If you want to take a break and resume the tutorial at later time, exit Access. When you resume the tutorial, place your Student Disk in the appropriate drive, start Access, open the Issue25 database in the Tutorial folder on your Student Disk, maximize the Database window, and click the Forms tab to display the Forms list.

Quick Check

1. What is a form?
2. What are three form designs that you can create with AutoForm?
3. What formats does the Form Wizard use to display records in a main/subform form?
4. How many sets of navigation buttons appear in a main/subform form, and what does each set control?
5. What is a filter?
6. What is the purpose of filter by selection? Filter by form?
7. How can you tell if a Form View window is displaying records to which a filter has been applied?
8. How do you reuse a filter in the future?

SESSION 5.2

In this session, you will learn to create a custom form using the Form Design window; add, delete, and modify controls on a form; add a form header; and add a graphic image to a form. You will also learn to change object colors and add special effects to form controls.

Creating a Custom Form

Elena places the Issue25 database on the company network, so others can use it to answer their questions. The most popular query proves to be the Article Type Query (created in Tutorial 4), which lists the article title, type, and length, and the writer's first and last names. Harold suggests that Elena present the same information in a more attractive layout. Elena designs a custom form based on the query to display this information.

To create a custom form, Elena can modify a form created by the Form Wizard or AutoForm, or design and create a form directly in the Form Design window. A custom form can be designed to match a paper form. It can display some fields side by side and others top to bottom; it can include color highlighting and special buttons and list boxes.

Designing a Custom Form

Elena plans to create a relatively simple custom form. Whether she creates a simple or complex custom form, she knows it is always best to plan the form's content and appearance first. Elena's sketch for her finished design is shown in Figure 5-18. The designed form displays all fields from the Article Type Query in single-column format, except for the writer's First Name and Last Name fields, which are side by side. Each field value will appear in a text box and will be preceded by a label (Access's default label name is the field name or the Caption property if there is one). Elena indicates the locations and lengths of each field value by a series of X's. The three X's that follow the Type field label indicate that the field value will be three characters wide. Elena also wants a graphic image for the 25th-anniversary issue to appear at the top of the form.

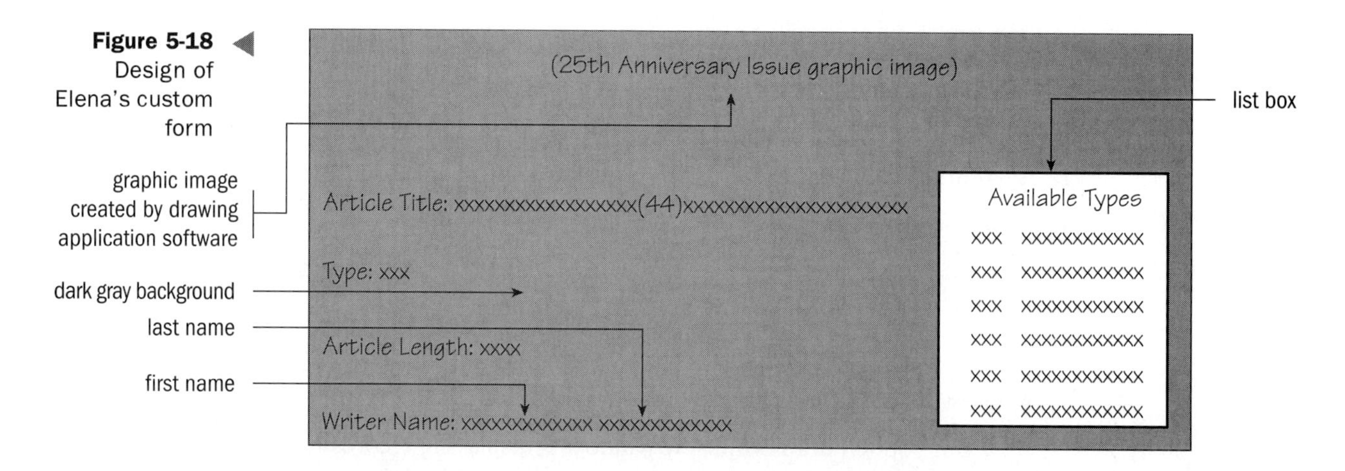

Figure 5-18 Design of Elena's custom form

Because many of her co-workers are unfamiliar with the article type codes, a list box containing the article type codes and their meaning will appear on the right. Elena also plans to add a dark gray background to improve the contrast of the form and make it easier to read.

Unlike her previous forms, which were based on tables, Elena's custom form will be based on the Article Type Query, which obtains data from both the BUSINESS ARTICLES and WRITERS tables and displays records in ascending order by the Type field. The form, which Elena plans to name Article Type Form, will likewise display records in ascending order by the Type field.

Now that she has planned her custom form, Elena is ready to create it. Elena could use AutoForm or the Form Wizard to create a basic form and then customize it in the Form Design window. Because her custom form differs from a basic form in many details, however, she decides to design the entire form directly in the Form Design window.

The Form Design Window

You use the Form Design window to create and modify forms. To create the custom form, Elena creates a blank form based on the Article Type Query in the Form Design window.

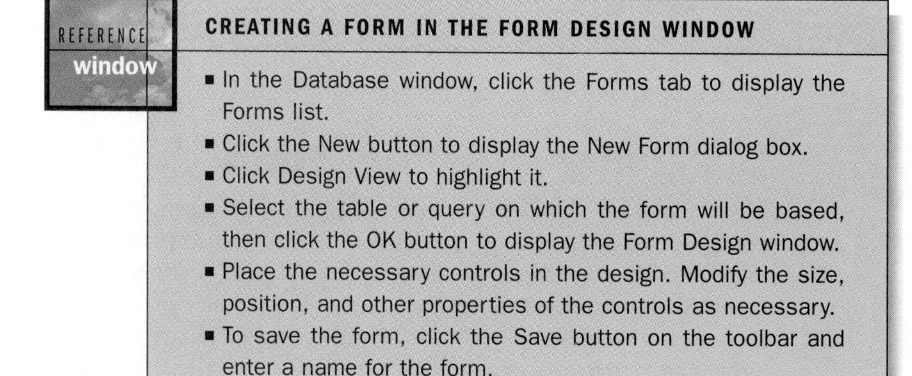

REFERENCE window

CREATING A FORM IN THE FORM DESIGN WINDOW

- In the Database window, click the Forms tab to display the Forms list.
- Click the New button to display the New Form dialog box.
- Click Design View to highlight it.
- Select the table or query on which the form will be based, then click the OK button to display the Form Design window.
- Place the necessary controls in the design. Modify the size, position, and other properties of the controls as necessary.
- To save the form, click the Save button on the toolbar and enter a name for the form.

To create a blank form in the Form Design window:

1. Make sure the Issue25 database from the Tutorial folder on your Student Disk is open, the Database window is maximized, and the Forms list is displayed in the Database window, then click the **New** button. The New Form dialog box opens.

2. If necessary, click Design View to select it, then click the **text box** list arrow. Scroll, if necessary, then click **Article Type Query**, and then click the **OK** button. The Form Design window opens. See Figure 5-19.

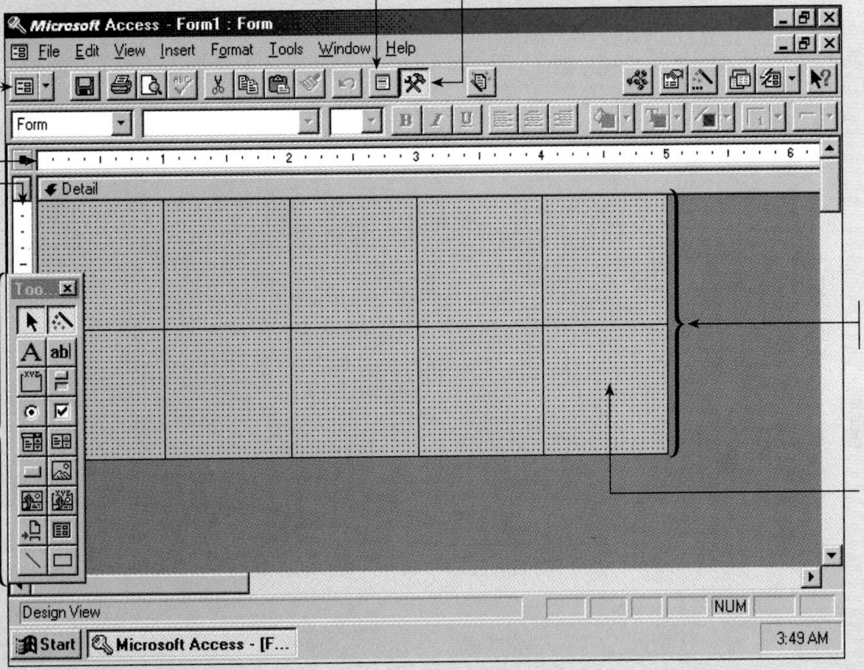

Field List button
Toolbox button
Form View button
rulers
toolbox
Detail section
grid

Figure 5-19 The Form Design window

TROUBLE? If the rulers, grid, or toolbox do not appear, click View on the menu bar and then click Ruler, Grid, or Toolbox to display any missing components in the Form Design window. If the grid is still invisible, see your technical support person or instructor for assistance. If the toolbox is not visible, click the Toolbox button to open it. If the toolbox is not positioned as in Figure 5-19, click the toolbox title bar and drag it to the position shown.

The Form Design window contains the tools necessary to create a custom form. You create the form by placing objects in the blank form in the window. Each object, such as a text box, list box, rectangle, or command button, that you place in a form is called a **control**; there are three kinds of controls that you can place on the form:

- A **bound control** is linked, or bound, to a field in the underlying table or query. You use a bound control to display table field values.
- An **unbound control** is not linked to a field in the underlying table or query. You use an unbound control to display text, such as a form title or instructions, or to display graphics and pictures from other software programs. An unbound control that displays text is called a **label**.
- A **calculated control** displays a value calculated from data from one or more fields.

To create a bound control, you click the toolbar Field List button to display a list of fields available from the underlying table or query. You drag fields from the field list box to the Form Design window and place the bound controls where you want them to appear on the form. Clicking the Field List button a second time closes the field list box.

To place other controls on a form, you use the tool buttons on the toolbox. The **toolbox** is a specialized toolbar containing buttons that represent the tools you use to place controls on a form or a report. ToolTips are available for each tool. If you want to show or hide the toolbox, click the toolbar Toolbox button. The tools available in the toolbox are described in Figure 5-20.

Figure 5-20 Summary of tools available in the toolbox for a form or a report

Button	Tool Name	Control Purpose on a Form or a Report	Control Wizard
	Select Objects	Selects, moves, sizes, and edits controls	
	Control Wizards	When selected, activates Control Wizards for certain other toolbox tools	
	Label	Displays text, such as title or instructions; an unbound control	
	Text Box	Displays a label attached to a text box that contains a bound control or a calculated control	
	Option Group	Displays a group frame containing toggle buttons, option buttons, or check boxes	Yes
	Toggle Button	Displays a toggle button control bound to a Yes/No field	Yes
	Option Button	Displays a radio button control bound to a Yes/No field	Yes
	Check Box	Displays a check box control bound to a Yes/No field	Yes
	Combo Box	Displays a control that combines the features of a list box and a text box. You can type in the text box or select an entry in the list box to add a value to an underlying field	Yes
	List Box	Displays a control that contains a scrollable list of values	Yes
	Command Button	Displays a control button you can use to link to an action—for example, finding a record, printing a record, or applying a form filter	Yes
	Image	Displays a graphic image in the form or report	Yes
	Unbound Object Frame	Displays a frame for enclosing an unbound OLE object, such as a Microsoft Excel spreadsheet, on a form or report	Yes
	Bound Object Frame	Displays a frame for enclosing a bound OLE object stored in an Access database table	Yes
	Page Break	Begins a new screen on a form or a new page on a report	
	Subform/Subreport	Displays data from more than one table on a form or report	Yes
	Line	Displays a line on a form or report	
	Rectangle	Displays a rectangle on a form or report	

The Form Design window also contains a Detail section, which appears as a light gray rectangle. You place the fields, labels, and values for your form in the Detail section. You can change the size of the Detail section by dragging the edges. The grid consists of dots that appear in the Detail section to help you to position controls precisely on a form. The rulers at the top and at the left edge of the Detail section define the horizontal and vertical dimensions of the form and serve as a guide to the placement of controls on the form.

Elena's first task in the Form Design window is to add bound controls to the form Detail section for all the fields from the Article Type Query.

Adding Fields to a Form

When you add a bound control to a form, Access adds a field-value text box and, to its left, a label. To create a bound control, you display the field list by clicking the Field List button. Then you select one or more fields from the field list box and drag them to the form. You select a single field by clicking the field. You select two or more fields by holding down the Ctrl key and clicking each field, and you select all fields by double-clicking the field list title bar.

Elena adds bound controls to the form Detail section for all the fields in the field list. To make more of the Form Design window visible, she closes the toolbox for now.

To close the toolbox and add bound controls for all the fields in the field list:

1. Click the **Close** button on the toolbox to close it.
2. Click the **Field List** button on the toolbar. The field list box opens.
3. Double-click the **field list** title bar to select all the fields in the field list. Access highlights the field list box.
4. Click anywhere in the highlighted area of the field list box and drag to the form's Detail section. Release the mouse button when the is positioned at the 1.5" mark on the horizontal ruler and the .25" mark on the vertical ruler. Access adds bound controls for the five selected fields. Each bound control consists of a text box and, to its left, an attached label. See Figure 5-21.

Figure 5-21 Text boxes and attached labels added to a form as bound controls

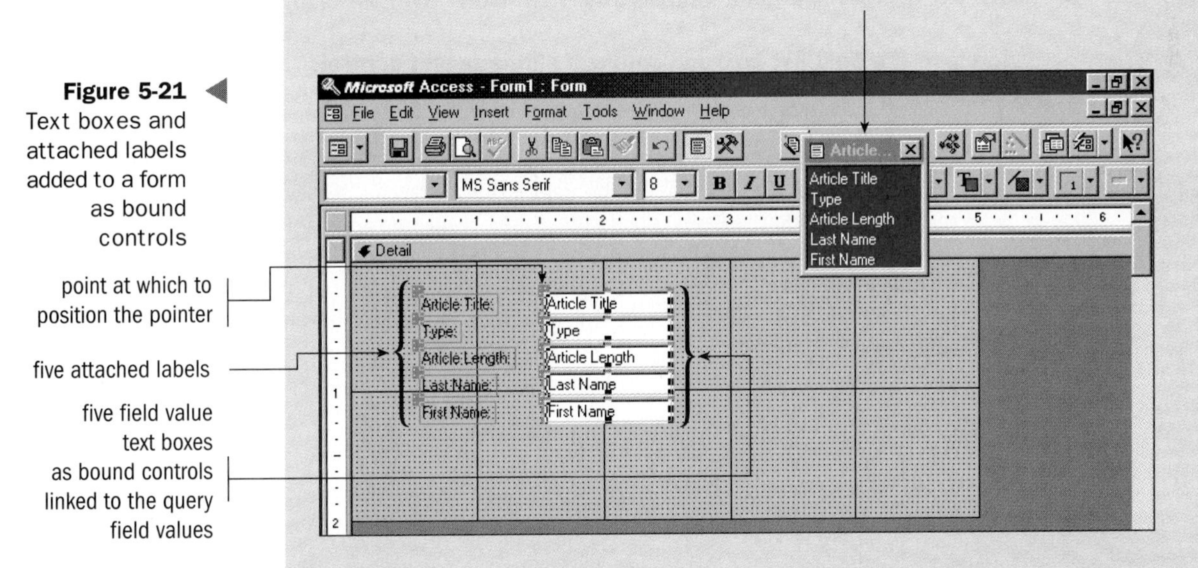

TROUBLE? If you did not position the bound controls properly in the Detail section, click the Undo button to delete the text boxes and labels from the Detail section. Repeat Step 4 to position the bound controls.

Performing operations in the Form Design window might seem awkward at first. With practice you will become comfortable with creating a custom form. Remember that you can always click the Undo button immediately after you make an undesired form adjustment.

Five text boxes now appear in a column in the form Detail section. Each text box is a bound control linked to a field in the underlying query and has an attached label box to its left. This means that if you move the text box, the label will move with it. Each text box and each label is an object on the form, and each appears with square boxes on the corners and edges. These boxes are called **handles**. Handles appear around an object when it is selected and they allow you to move or resize the control.

Selecting, Moving, and Deleting Controls

Elena is done with the field list box and closes it by clicking the Field List button. Elena next compares the form Detail section with her design. She needs to arrange the Last Name and First Name text boxes side by side to agree with her form design.

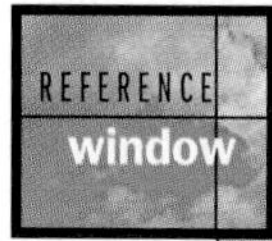

SELECTING, MOVING, AND DELETING CONTROLS

- Click on any control to select it. To select several controls at once, press the Shift key while clicking on each control. Handles appear around selected controls.
- To move a single selected control, click the control's move handle and drag it to its new position.
- To move a group of selected controls, click anywhere in a selected control (but not on its move handle) and drag the group of selected controls to its new position.
- To delete selected controls, point to any selected control, then click the right mouse button to display the shortcut menu. Click Cut to delete the selected controls.

To move a single bound control, Elena needs to select just that control. All controls are currently selected and will all move together if Elena moves any one of them. Elena first deselects all of the bound controls and then selects the Last Name control to move it.

To close the field list box and select a single bound control:

1. Click the **Field List** button on the toolbar to close the field list box.
2. Two boxes in the Detail section have Last Name inside them. The box on the left is the label box, and the box on the right is the field-value text box. Click in the gray area outside the Detail section to deselect any previous selection and then click the **Last Name** field-value text box to select it. Move handles, the larger handles, appear in the upper-left corner of the field-value text box and its attached label box. Sizing handles also appear, but only on the field-value text box. See Figure 5-22.

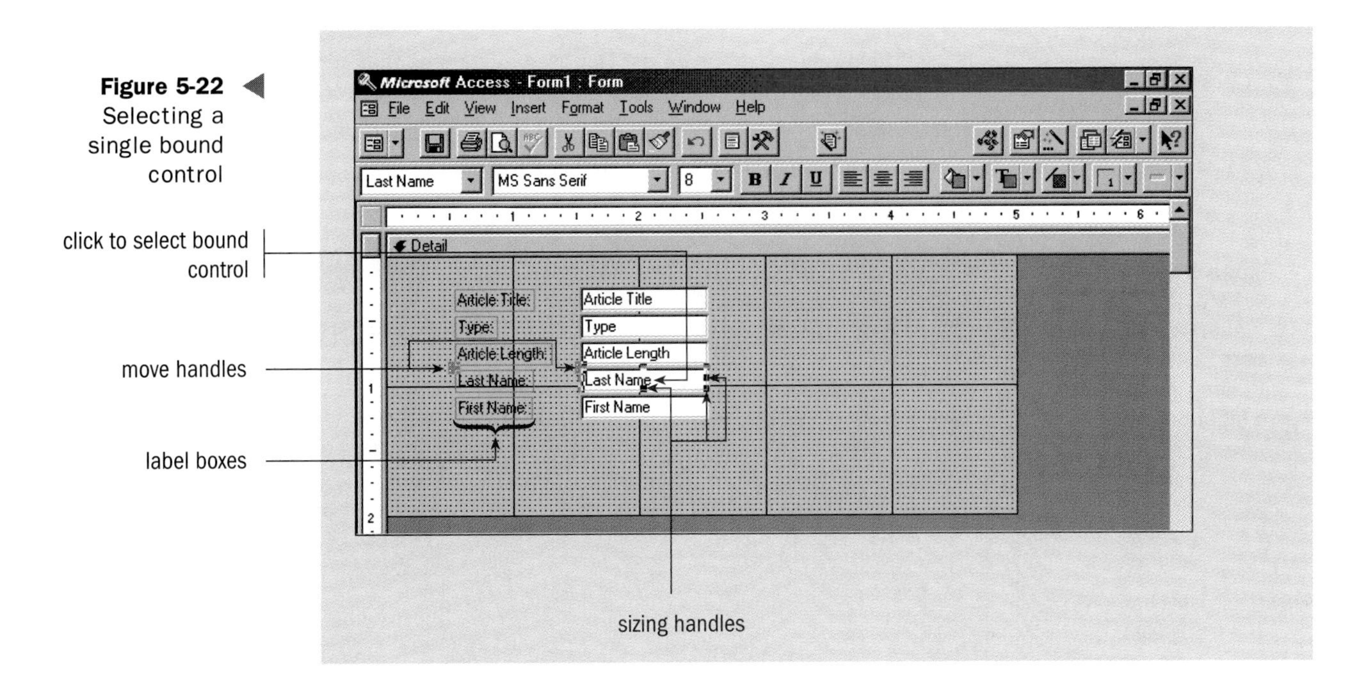

Figure 5-22 Selecting a single bound control

You can move a field-value text box and its attached label box together. To move them, place the pointer anywhere on the border of the field-value text box, but not on a move handle or a sizing handle. When the pointer changes to, you can drag the field-value text box and its attached label box to the new location. As you move the boxes, their outline moves to show you the changing position.

You can also move either the field-value text box or its label box individually. If you want to move the field-value text box but not its label box, for example, place the pointer on the text box's move handle. When the pointer changes to, drag the field-value text box to the new location. You use the label box's move handle to move just the label box.

You can delete a field-value text box and its attached label box or delete just the label box. To delete both boxes together, click inside the field-value text box to select both boxes, click the right mouse button inside the text box to open its shortcut menu, and then click Cut. To delete just the label box, use the same procedure but click inside the label box instead of the field-value text box.

To arrange the Last Name and First Name text boxes to agree with her design, Elena must move the Last Name field-value text box to the right without moving its label box, move the First Name field-value text box (without its label box) up beside the Last Name label box, delete the First Name label box, and then change the Last Name label box to read Writer Name. Elena first moves the field-values text boxes and deletes the First Name label box.

To move field-value text boxes and delete labels:

1. Move the pointer to the Last Name field-value text box move handle. When the mouse pointer changes to, drag the text box horizontally to the right, leaving enough room for the First Name field-value text box to fit in its place. An outline of the box appears as you change its position to guide you in the move operation. Use the grid dots in the Detail section to help you position the box outline.

   TROUBLE? If you move the field-value text box incorrectly, click the Undo button and then repeat Step 1.

2. Click the **field-value** text box for the First Name field and then move the pointer to its move handle. When the mouse pointer changes to [pointer], drag the box up to the position previously occupied by the Last Name field-value text box.

3. Click the **First Name** label box with the right mouse button to open the shortcut menu and then click **Cut**. The First Name label box is deleted. See Figure 5-23.

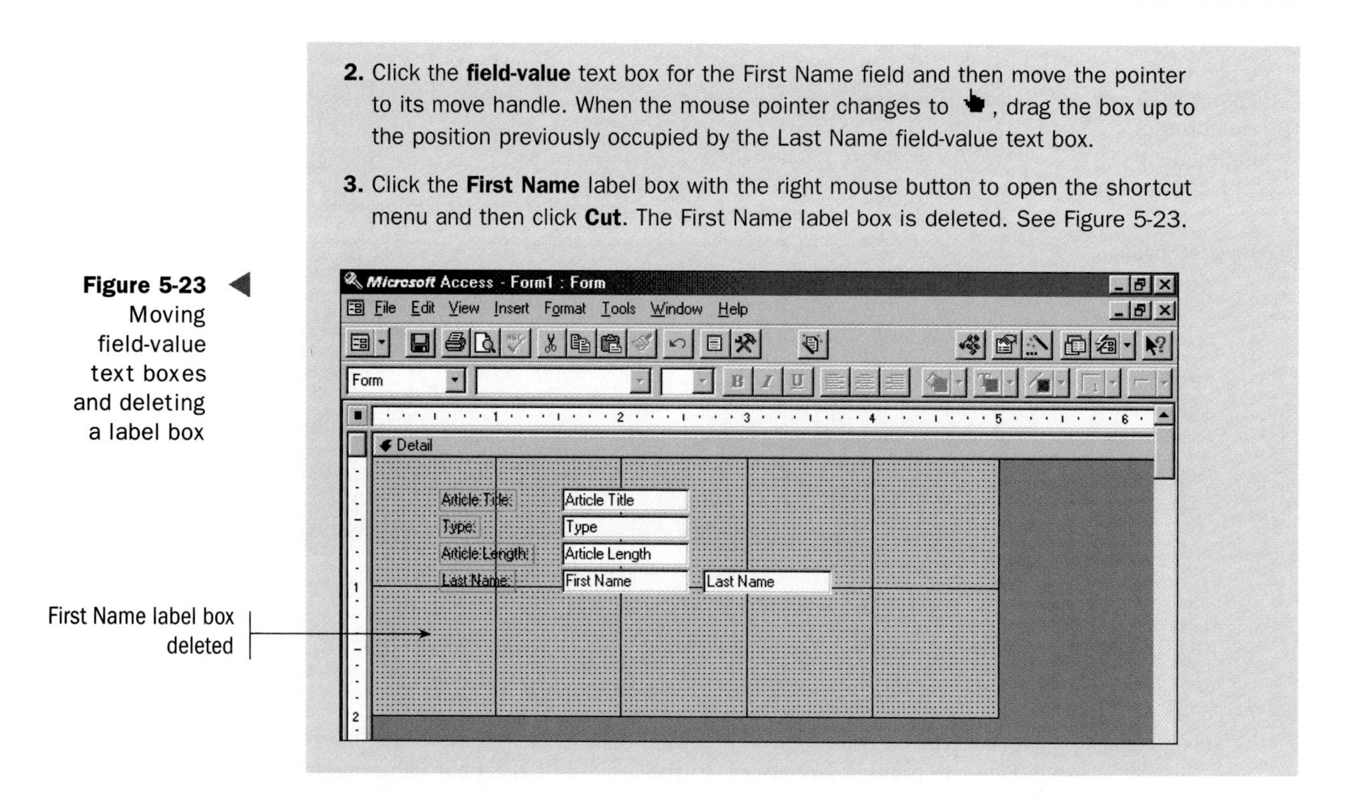

Figure 5-23 Moving field-value text boxes and deleting a label box

Next, Elena changes the text in the Last Name label box to Writer Name.

Changing a Label's Caption

The text in a label is defined by the field name or Caption property.

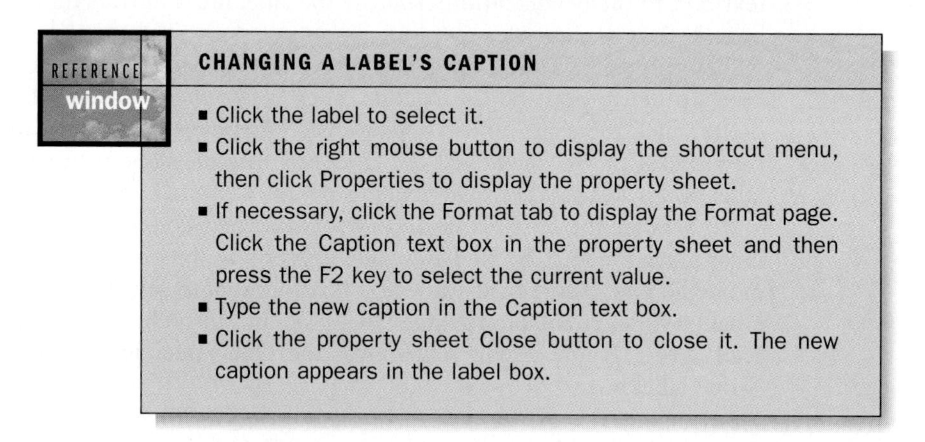

REFERENCE window

CHANGING A LABEL'S CAPTION

- Click the label to select it.
- Click the right mouse button to display the shortcut menu, then click Properties to display the property sheet.
- If necessary, click the Format tab to display the Format page. Click the Caption text box in the property sheet and then press the F2 key to select the current value.
- Type the new caption in the Caption text box.
- Click the property sheet Close button to close it. The new caption appears in the label box.

Elena uses the label's property sheet to change the Caption property value.

To change the Caption property value for a label:

1. Click the **Last Name** label box to select it.

2. Click the right mouse button to display the shortcut menu, then click **Properties**. The property sheet for the Last Name label opens.

3. If necessary, click the **Format** tab to display the Format page. Click the **Caption** text box in the property sheet and then press the **F2** key to select the entire value.

4. Type **Writer Name:**. Be sure to type a colon at the end of the caption. See Figure 5-24.

Figure 5-24 Changing a property for a label

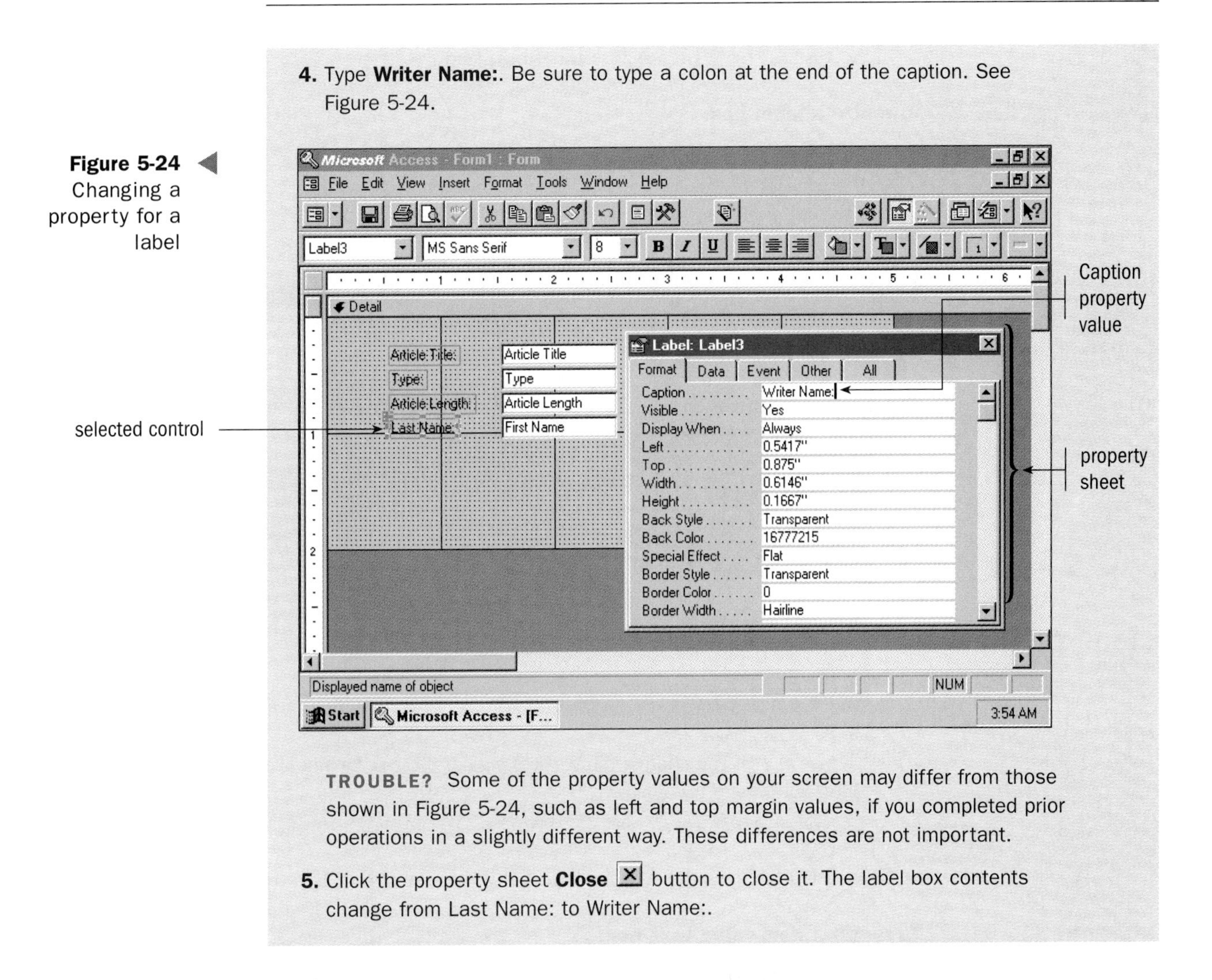

TROUBLE? Some of the property values on your screen may differ from those shown in Figure 5-24, such as left and top margin values, if you completed prior operations in a slightly different way. These differences are not important.

5. Click the property sheet **Close** [X] button to close it. The label box contents change from Last Name: to Writer Name:.

Resizing a Control

Looking at her new Writer Name caption, Elena notices that only part of the new caption is visible in the label box. Elena must resize the label box. Elena also notices that the Article Title field-value text box is too small to contain long titles, so she must resize it as well.

A selected object displays seven sizing handles: one on each side of the object and one at each corner, except the upper-left corner. The upper-left corner displays the move handle. Moving the pointer over a sizing handle changes the pointer to a two-headed arrow; the pointer's direction indicates the direction in which you can move the sizing handle. When you drag the sizing handle, you resize the control. Thin lines appear, which guide you as you drag the control.

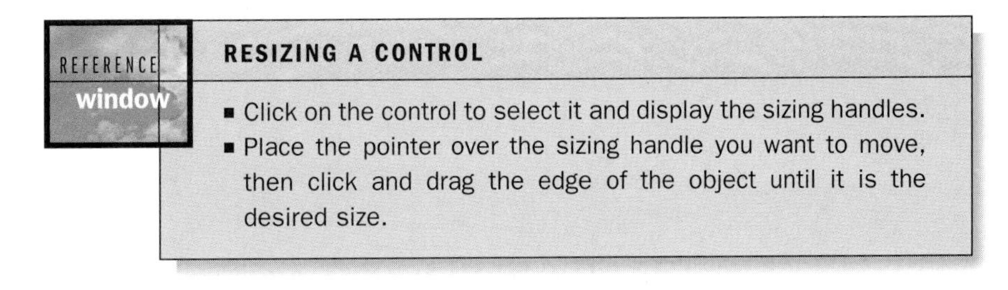

REFERENCE window

RESIZING A CONTROL

- Click on the control to select it and display the sizing handles.
- Place the pointer over the sizing handle you want to move, then click and drag the edge of the object until it is the desired size.

Elena resizes the Writer Name label box first.

To resize a label box:

1. The Writer Name label box is still the selected control, so move the pointer to the left side of the control over the middle handle. When the pointer changes to ↔ , drag the left border horizontally to the left two entire sets of grid dots. See Figure 5-25.

Figure 5-25 Resizing the Writer Name label box

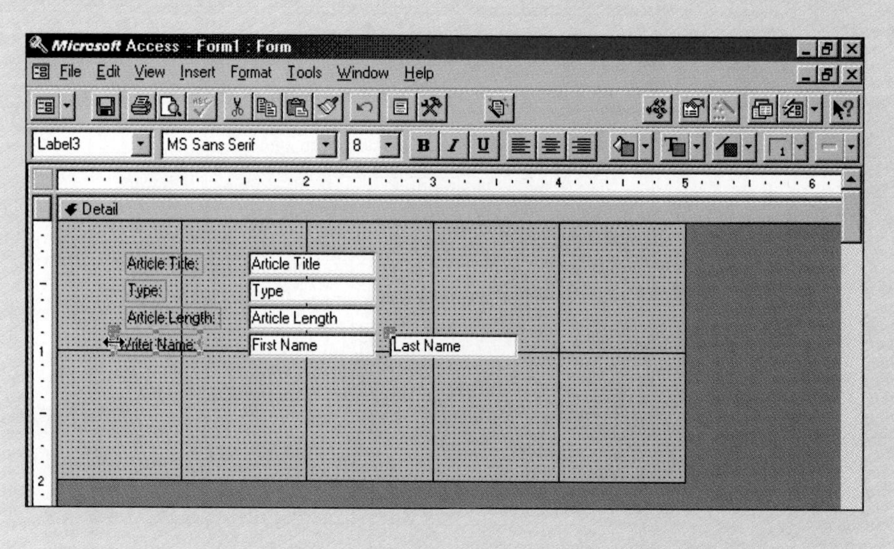

TROUBLE? If you change the vertical size of the box by mistake, just click the Undo button and try again.

Next, Elena resizes the Article Title field-value text box by stretching it to the right.

To resize a field-value text box:

1. Click the **Article Title** field-value text box to select it. Move handles and sizing handles appear.
2. Move the pointer to the right side of the box over the middle handle. The pointer changes to ↔ .
3. Drag the right border horizontally to the right until the right edge is at the 4" mark on the horizontal ruler. The text box will now accommodate longer Article Title field values.

Aligning Controls

Elena next notices that the top three label boxes are left-justified; that is, they are aligned on the left edges. She feels that the form will look better if all the labels are right-justified, or aligned on their right edges.

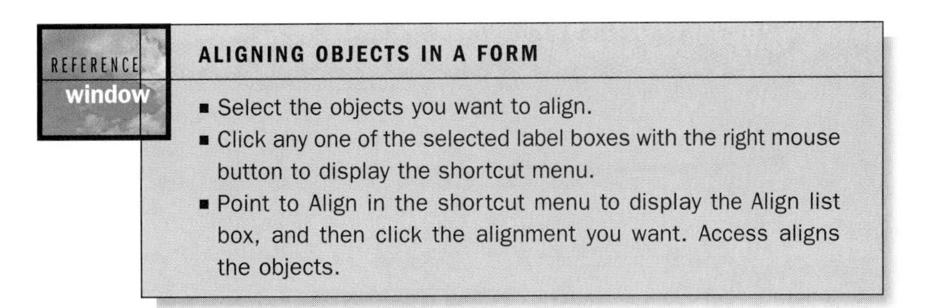

REFERENCE window

ALIGNING OBJECTS IN A FORM

- Select the objects you want to align.
- Click any one of the selected label boxes with the right mouse button to display the shortcut menu.
- Point to Align in the shortcut menu to display the Align list box, and then click the alignment you want. Access aligns the objects.

Elena selects all of the labels and uses the shortcut menu to align them.

To select and align all label boxes on the right:

1. Click in the **Article Title** label box to select it.
2. Press the **Shift** key and hold it as you click each of the remaining label boxes so that all four are selected, and then release the Shift key.
3. Click any one of the selected label boxes with the right mouse button to display the shortcut menu.
4. Point to **Align** in the shortcut menu to display the Align list box, and then click **Right**. Access aligns the label boxes on their right edges. See Figure 5-26.

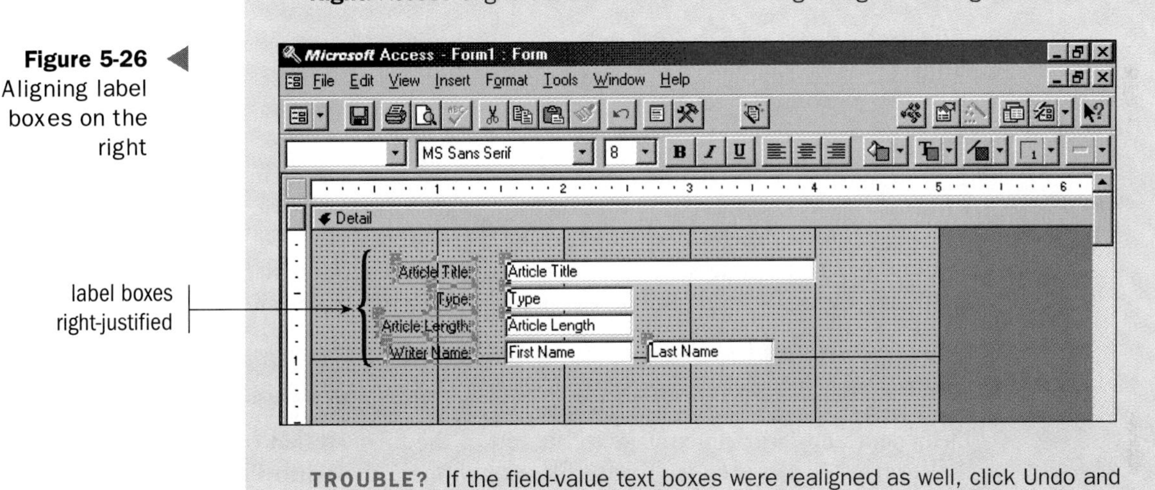

Figure 5-26 Aligning label boxes on the right

TROUBLE? If the field-value text boxes were realigned as well, click Undo and repeat Steps 1 through 4, making sure to select only the label boxes.

Before Elena makes further changes in the Form Design window, she saves her work and then switches to the Form View window to study her form.

To save the form:

1. Click the **Save** button on the toolbar. The Save As dialog box opens.
2. Type **Article Type Form** and then click the **OK** button. Access saves the custom form.

Viewing a Form in the Form View Window

When you create a form, you should periodically check your progress in the Form View window. You might see adjustments you want to make on your form in the Form Design window.

To switch to the Form View window:

1. Click the **Form View** button on the toolbar. Access closes the Form Design window and opens the Form View window. See Figure 5-27.

Figure 5-27 The Form View window

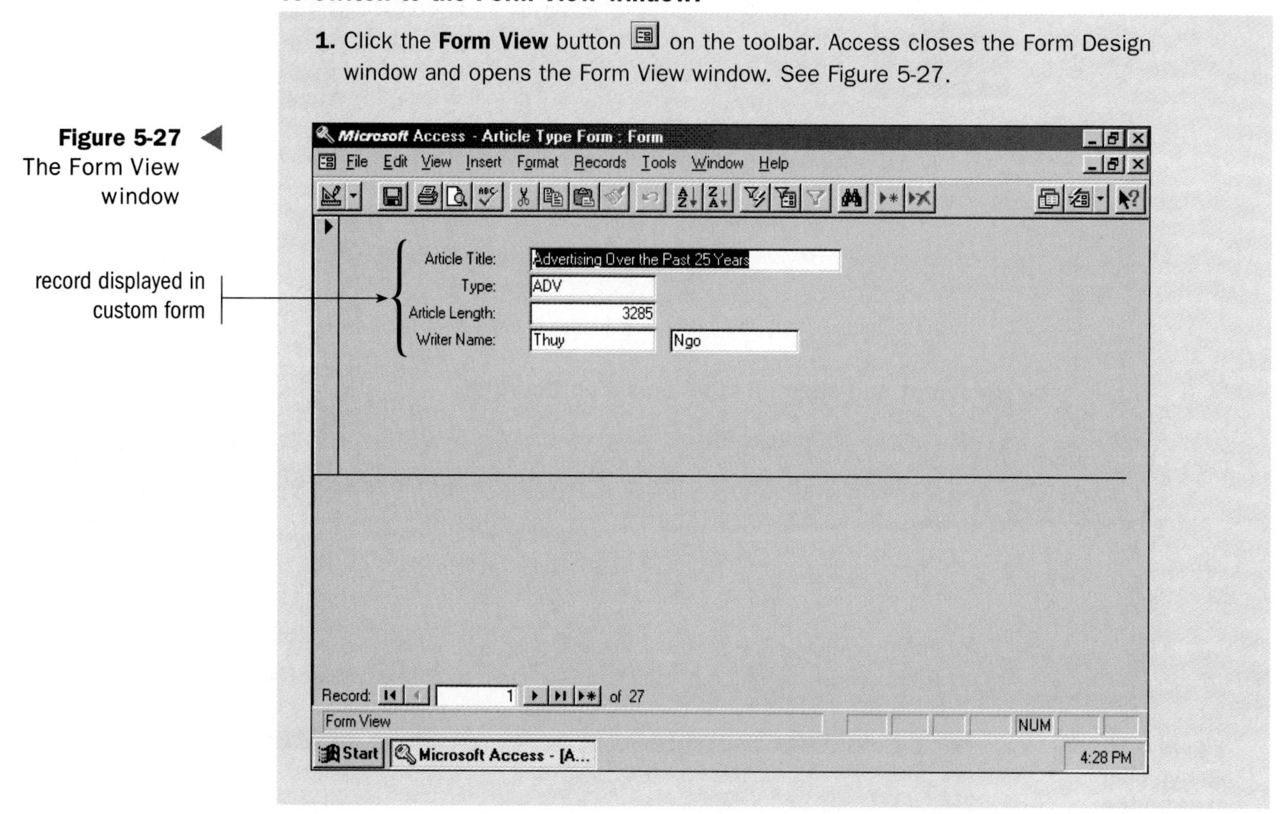

Your form uses the Article Type Query to sort the records in ascending order by the Type field. Access displays the first record in this sort order. You can use navigation buttons to view other records from the query on the form.

Elena sees some adjustments she wants to make to her design. She wants to add a form title, with a graphic, and add the list box for the article types and descriptions.

Using Form Headers and Footers

Elena next adds a graphic image to the top of the form so that others can easily identify the form when they see it. To do this, she chooses the Form Header/Footer command from the View menu to add header and footer sections to the form. She then places the graphic image in the Form Header section and deletes the Form Footer section by decreasing its height to zero.

In the Form Header and Form Footer sections you can add titles, instructions, command buttons, and other information to the top and bottom of your form. You add the Form Header and Form Footer as a pair. If your form needs one of them but not the other, you can remove the one you don't want by setting its height to zero, which is the method you would use to remove any section on a form.

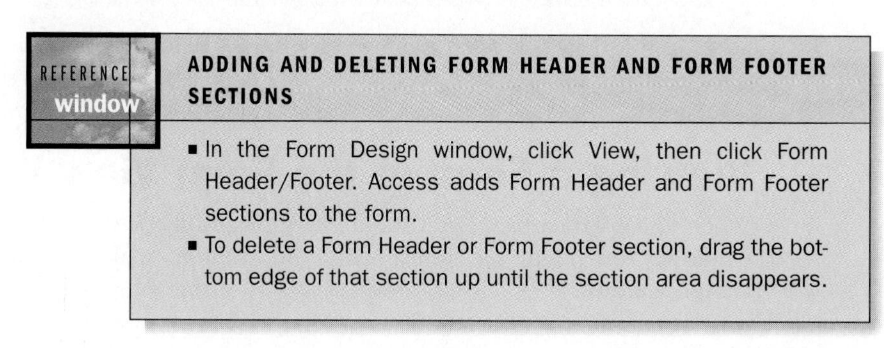

REFERENCE window

ADDING AND DELETING FORM HEADER AND FORM FOOTER SECTIONS

- In the Form Design window, click View, then click Form Header/Footer. Access adds Form Header and Form Footer sections to the form.
- To delete a Form Header or Form Footer section, drag the bottom edge of that section up until the section area disappears.

Elena adds the Form Header and Form Footer sections to the form.

To add Form Header and Form Footer sections to a form:

1. Click the **Form View** button on the toolbar. Access closes the Form View window and opens the Form Design window.
2. Click **View**, and then click **Form Header/Footer**. Access inserts a Form Header section above the Detail section and a Form Footer section below the Detail section. See Figure 5-28.

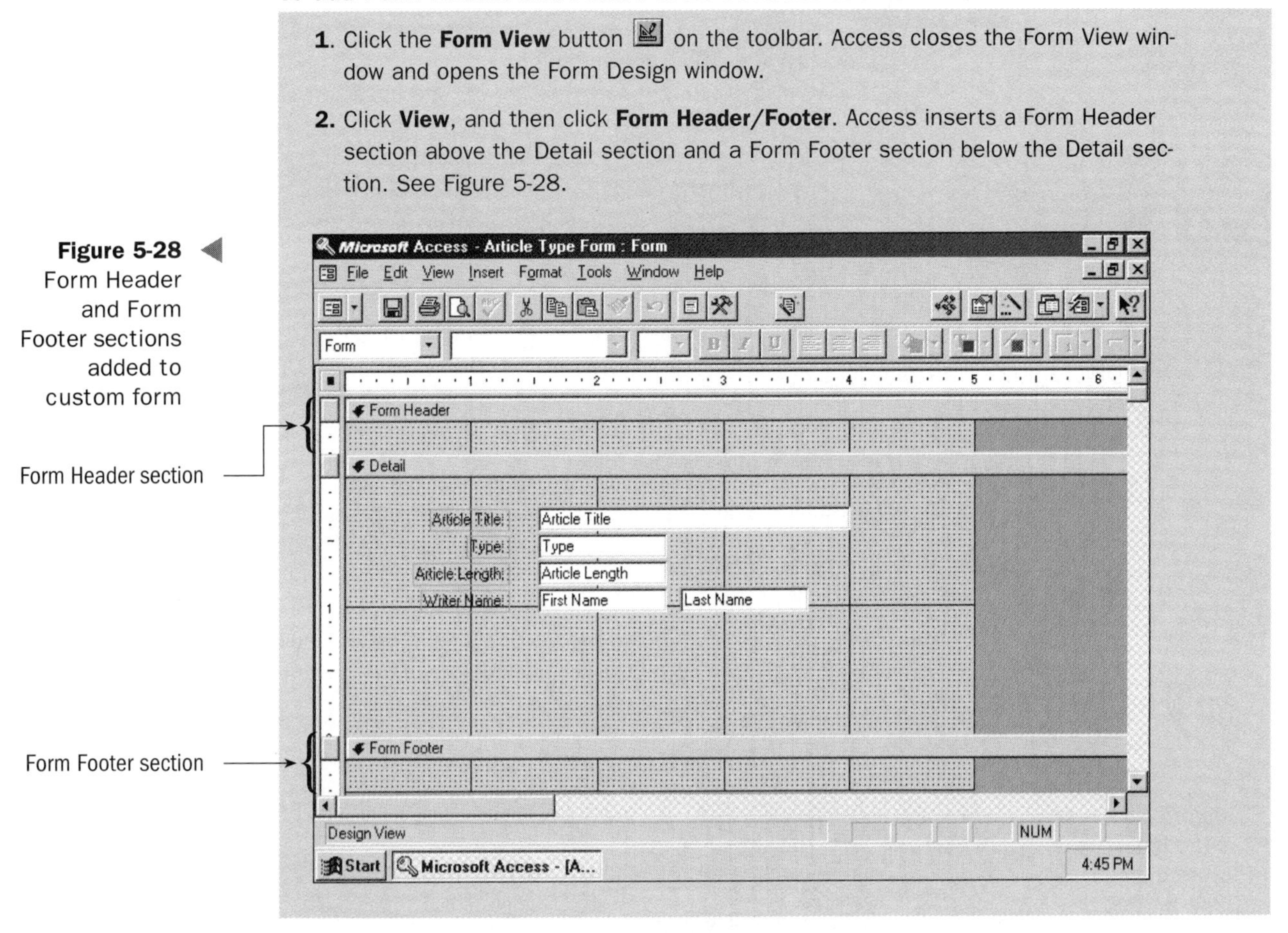

Figure 5-28 Form Header and Form Footer sections added to custom form

Elena does not want to use a Form Footer section in this form, so she removes it by making its height zero.

To remove the Form Footer section:

1. Move the pointer to the bottom edge of the Form Footer section. When the pointer changes to ✛, drag the bottom edge upward until it disappears. Even though the words "Form Footer" remain, the area defining the section is set to zero, and the section will not appear in the form.

Elena now adds the graphic image to the Form Header section with the toolbox Image tool.

Adding a Graphic Image to a Form

Elena has designed a small graphic image that she wants displayed in the header. Access has the ability to use files and data created by other software programs. In this case, Elena has used a drawing program and saved her image in a file named 25th. To place the image in the form header, she uses the toolbox Image tool.

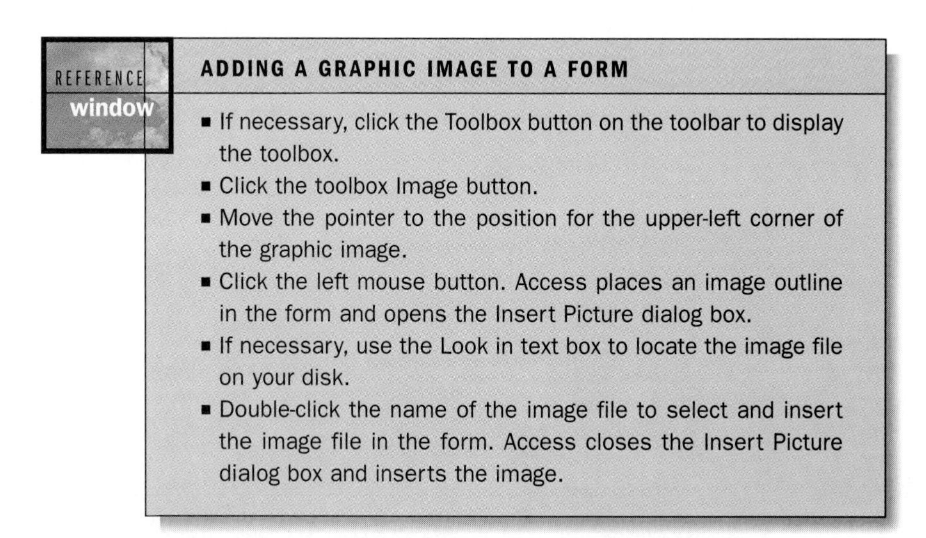

REFERENCE window

ADDING A GRAPHIC IMAGE TO A FORM

- If necessary, click the Toolbox button on the toolbar to display the toolbox.
- Click the toolbox Image button.
- Move the pointer to the position for the upper-left corner of the graphic image.
- Click the left mouse button. Access places an image outline in the form and opens the Insert Picture dialog box.
- If necessary, use the Look in text box to locate the image file on your disk.
- Double-click the name of the image file to select and insert the image file in the form. Access closes the Insert Picture dialog box and inserts the image.

To place a graphic image on the form:

1. Click the **Toolbox** button on the toolbar to display the toolbox.
2. Click the toolbox **Image** button.
3. Move the pointer to the Form Header. The pointer changes to . Use the ruler bar to place the pointer slightly below the top of the Form Header, approximately 1" from the left edge. This will be the upper-left corner of the image.
4. Click the left mouse button. Access places an image outline in the Form Header and opens the Insert Picture dialog box. See Figure 5-29.

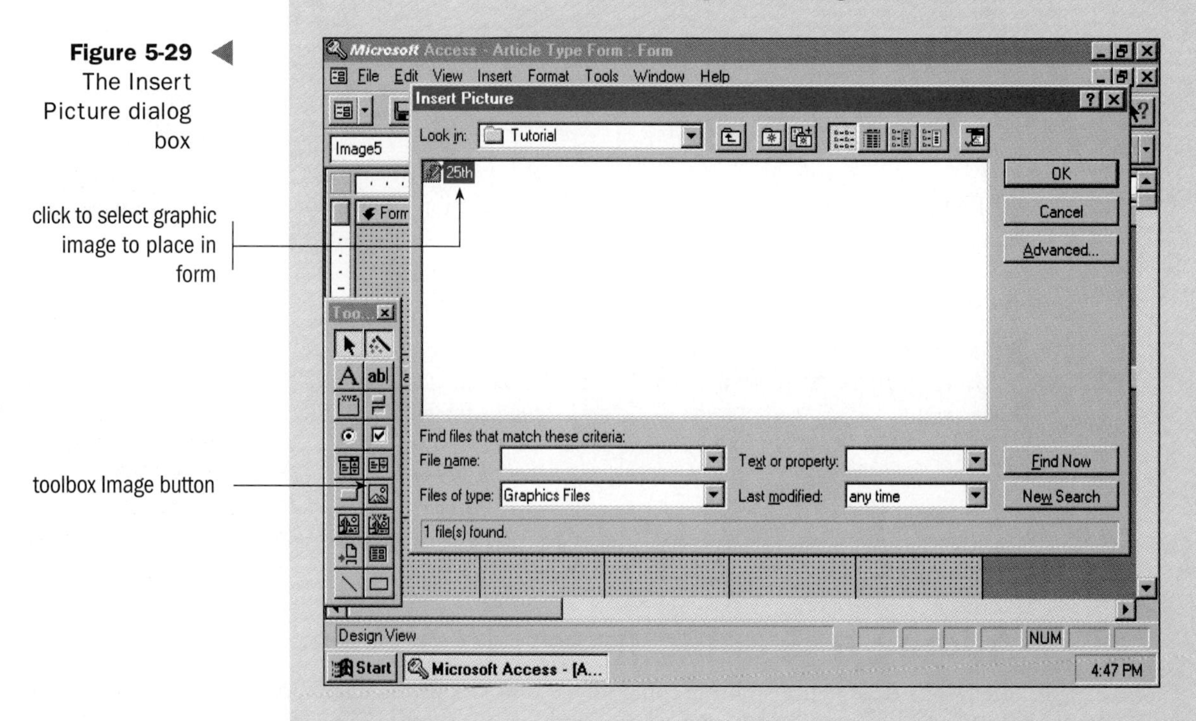

Figure 5-29 The Insert Picture dialog box

Elena is ready to insert her image. The image is saved under the name "25th" in your Tutorial folder.

5. If necessary, click the **Look in** list arrow to display the contents of the Tutorial folder on your Student Disk.
6. Double-click **25th** to select and insert the image file in the Form Header.

Access closes the Insert Picture dialog box and inserts the image. The Form Header section automatically becomes larger to accommodate the size of the image.

Elena views the form with the new header.

7. Click the **Form View** button on the toolbar to view the form. See Figure 5-30.

Figure 5-30 New header in Form View

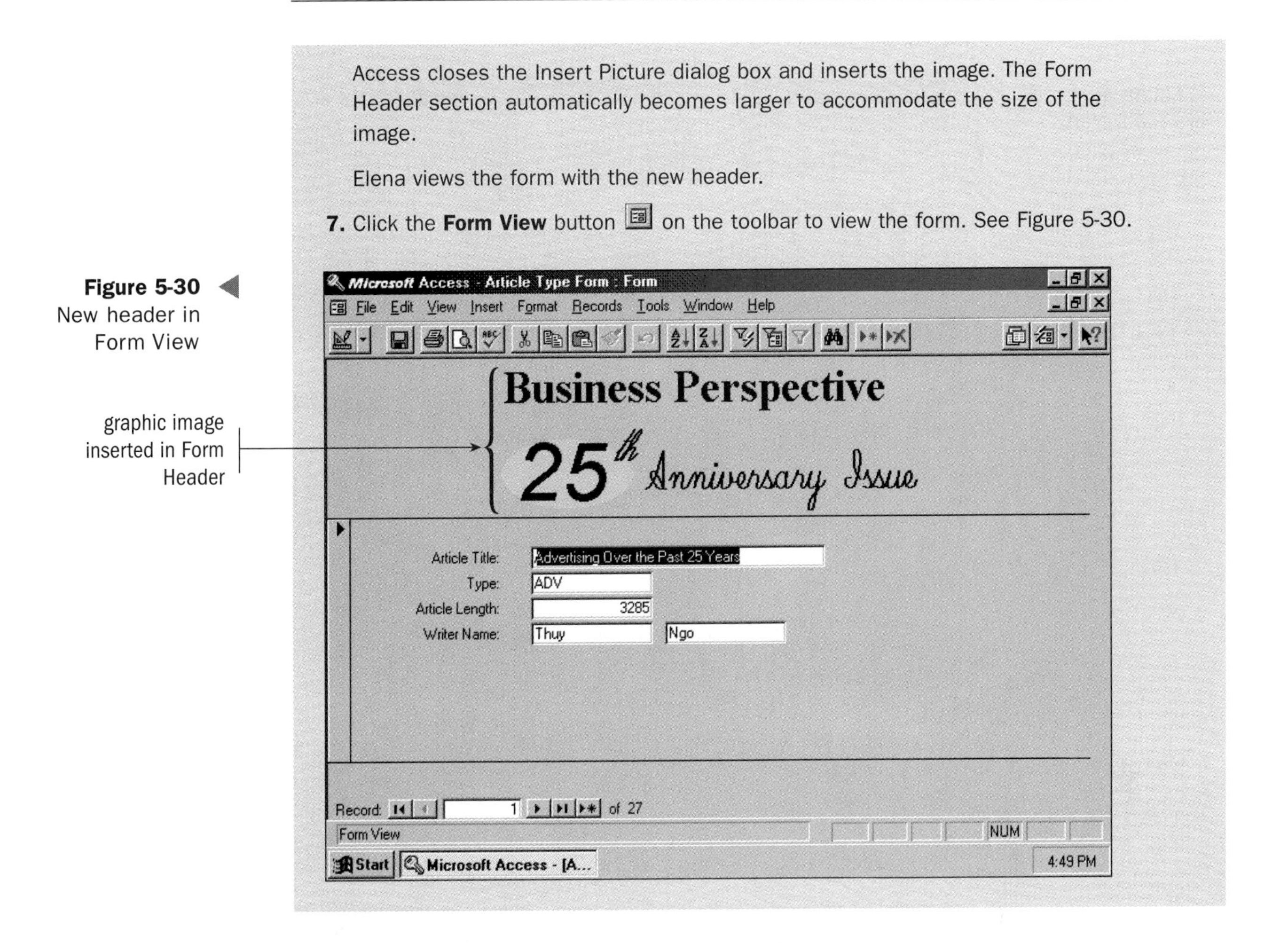

Adding a List Box with Control Wizards

Because many of her co-workers are unfamiliar with the various article type codes, Elena adds a list box to the form's Detail section. A **list box** is a control that displays a list of values. The list box in this form will display all the article types and their full descriptions from the TYPES table so that anyone using this form will not need to remember all the Type field values. Clicking one of the list box values will replace the form's Type field value with the clicked value. Thus, you can eliminate the need to enter a Type field value from the keyboard. When you add a list box to a form, by default Access adds a label box to its left.

You use the toolbox List Box tool to add a list box to a form. If you want help in defining the list box, you can first select one of Access's Control Wizards. A **Control Wizard** asks you a series of questions and then creates a control on a form or report based on your answers. Access offers Control Wizards for the toolbox Combo Box tool, List Box tool, Option Group tool, Command Button tool, and the Subform/Subreport tool, among others.

Elena will use the List Box Wizard to add the list box for the article types and descriptions. Before she adds the list box, Elena increases the width of the Detail section (and the Form Header section) to make room for the list box.

To resize the Detail section:

1. Click the **Form View** button on the toolbar to switch to the Form Design window.

2. Drag the right edge of the Detail section to the horizontal ruler's 6" mark. The Form Header section is also widened. See Figure 5-31.

Figure 5-31
Resized Detail section

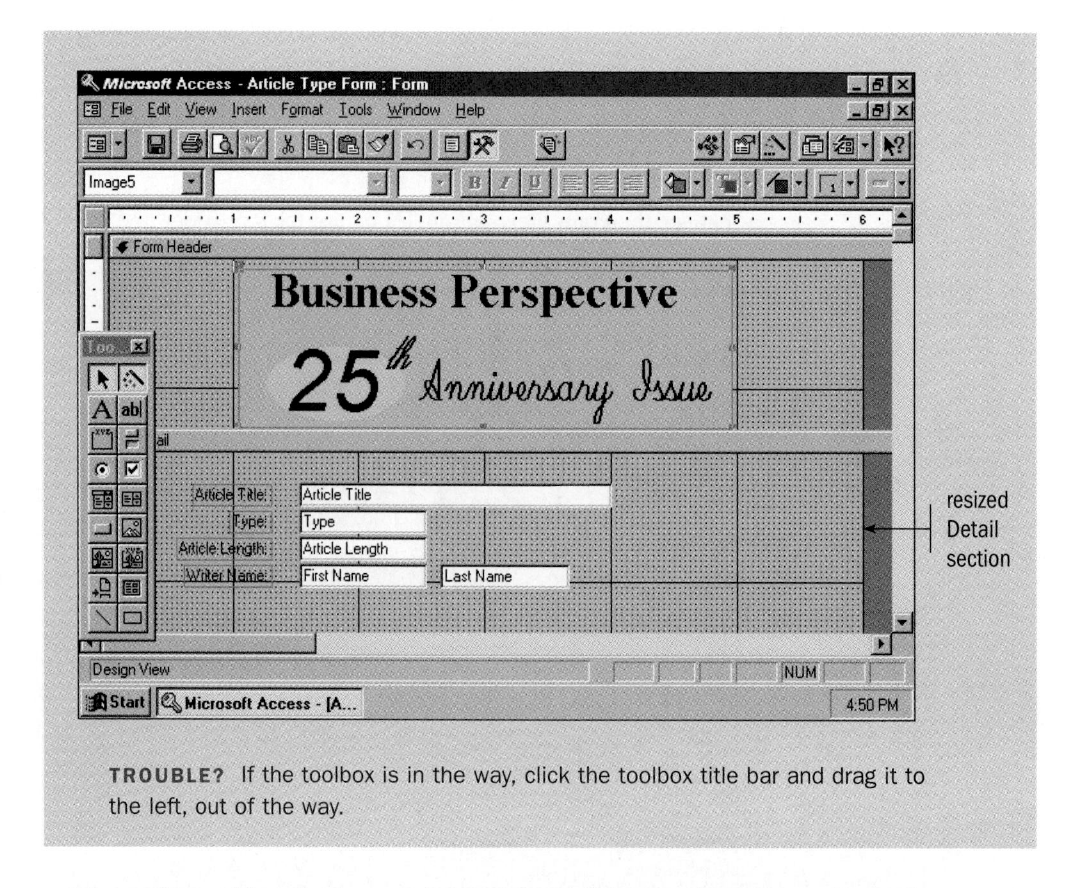

TROUBLE? If the toolbox is in the way, click the toolbox title bar and drag it to the left, out of the way.

Next, Elena adds a list box to the Detail section using the List Box Wizard.

Using the List Box Wizard

Elena will use the List Box Wizard to add the list box for the article types and descriptions.

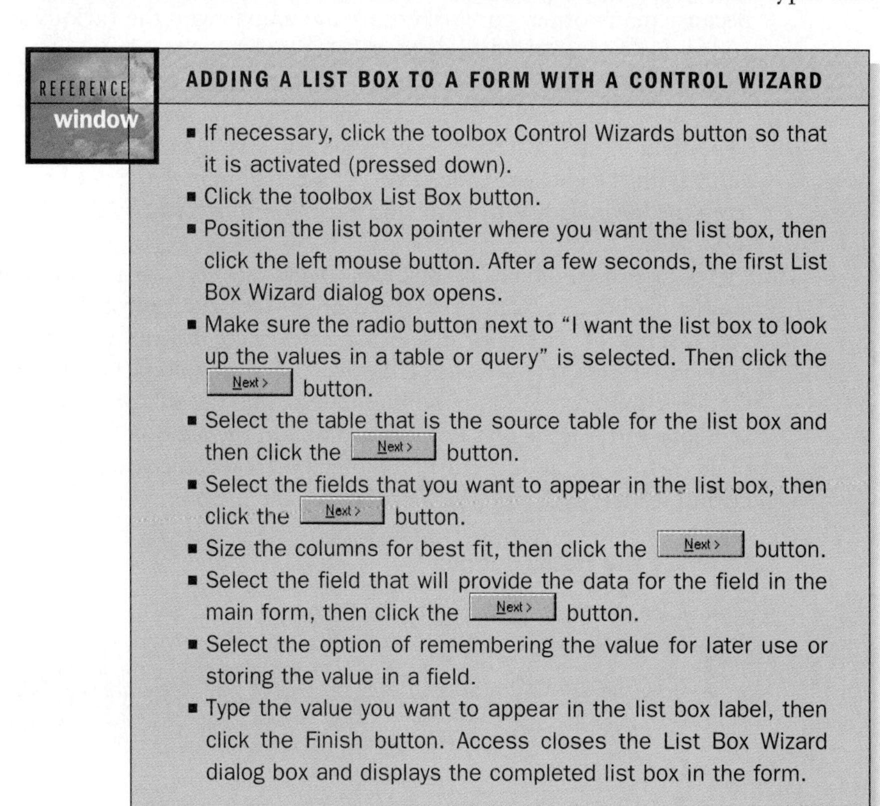

REFERENCE window

ADDING A LIST BOX TO A FORM WITH A CONTROL WIZARD

- If necessary, click the toolbox Control Wizards button so that it is activated (pressed down).
- Click the toolbox List Box button.
- Position the list box pointer where you want the list box, then click the left mouse button. After a few seconds, the first List Box Wizard dialog box opens.
- Make sure the radio button next to "I want the list box to look up the values in a table or query" is selected. Then click the Next > button.
- Select the table that is the source table for the list box and then click the Next > button.
- Select the fields that you want to appear in the list box, then click the Next > button.
- Size the columns for best fit, then click the Next > button.
- Select the field that will provide the data for the field in the main form, then click the Next > button.
- Select the option of remembering the value for later use or storing the value in a field.
- Type the value you want to appear in the list box label, then click the Finish button. Access closes the List Box Wizard dialog box and displays the completed list box in the form.

To start the List Box Wizard:

1. If necessary, click the toolbox **Control Wizards** button so that it is activated (pressed down).
2. Click the toolbox **List Box** button. As you move the pointer away from the toolbox, the pointer changes to . See Figure 5-32.

Figure 5-32 Positioning a list box

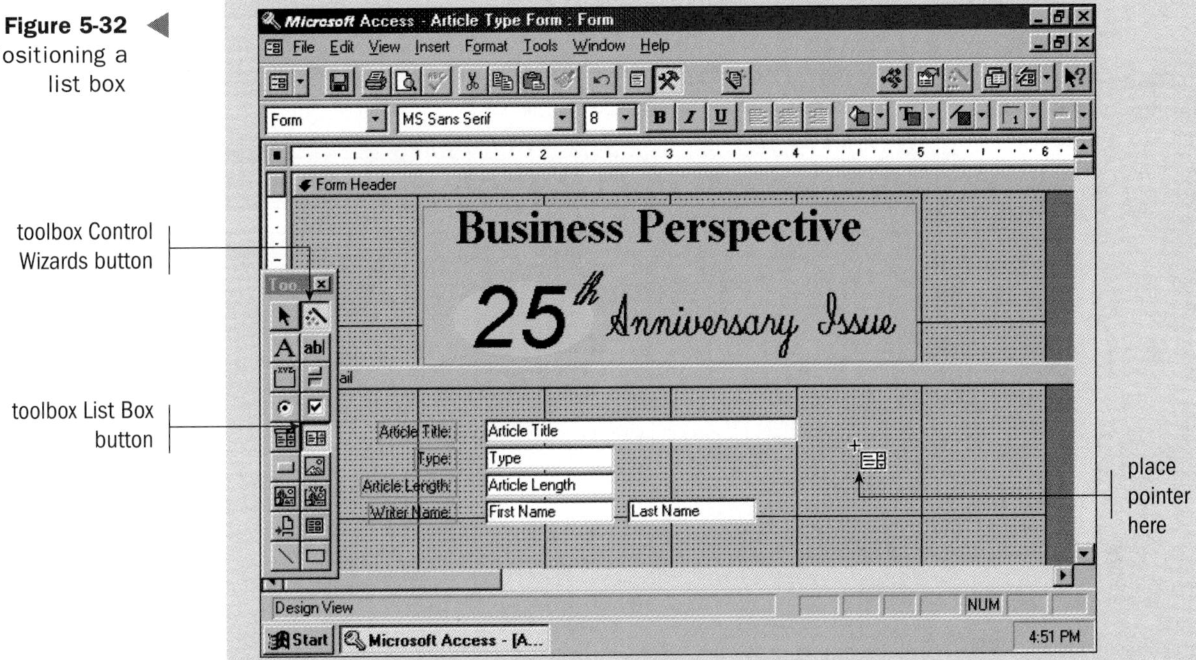

toolbox Control Wizards button

toolbox List Box button

place pointer here

3. Click when the list box pointer is positioned as shown in Figure 5-32. After a few seconds, the first List Box Wizard dialog box opens.

Elena uses the List Box Wizard to display the two fields from the TYPES table: the Type field and the Description field. She also uses the List Box Wizard dialog box to size the two fields' column widths and to add the label Article Types.

To add a list box using the List Box Wizard:

1. The TYPES table will supply the values for the list box, so make sure the radio button next to "I want the list box to look up the values in a table or query" is selected. Then click the Next > button. The next List Box Wizard dialog box opens.
2. Click **TYPES** as the source table for the list box and then click the Next > button. The next List Box Wizard dialog box opens.
3. Because you want both the Type and Description fields to appear in the list box, click the >> button to select both fields and then click the Next > button. The next List Box Wizard dialog box opens.
4. For both columns, double-click the right edge of each column selector to get the best column fit and then click the Next > button. The next List Box Wizard dialog box opens.
5. If Type is not selected in the Available Fields list box, click it to select it. Then click the Next > button.

6. Click the radio button beside "Store that value in this field," click the **text box** list arrow, and click **Type**. Then click the Next > button. Access will store the Type value selected from the TYPES table in the Type field of the BUSINESS ARTICLES record.

7. For a label, type **Article Types:** in the text box and then click the **Finish** button. Access closes the List Box Wizard dialog box and displays the completed list box in the Detail section of the form. See Figure 5-33.

Figure 5-33 List box added to a form

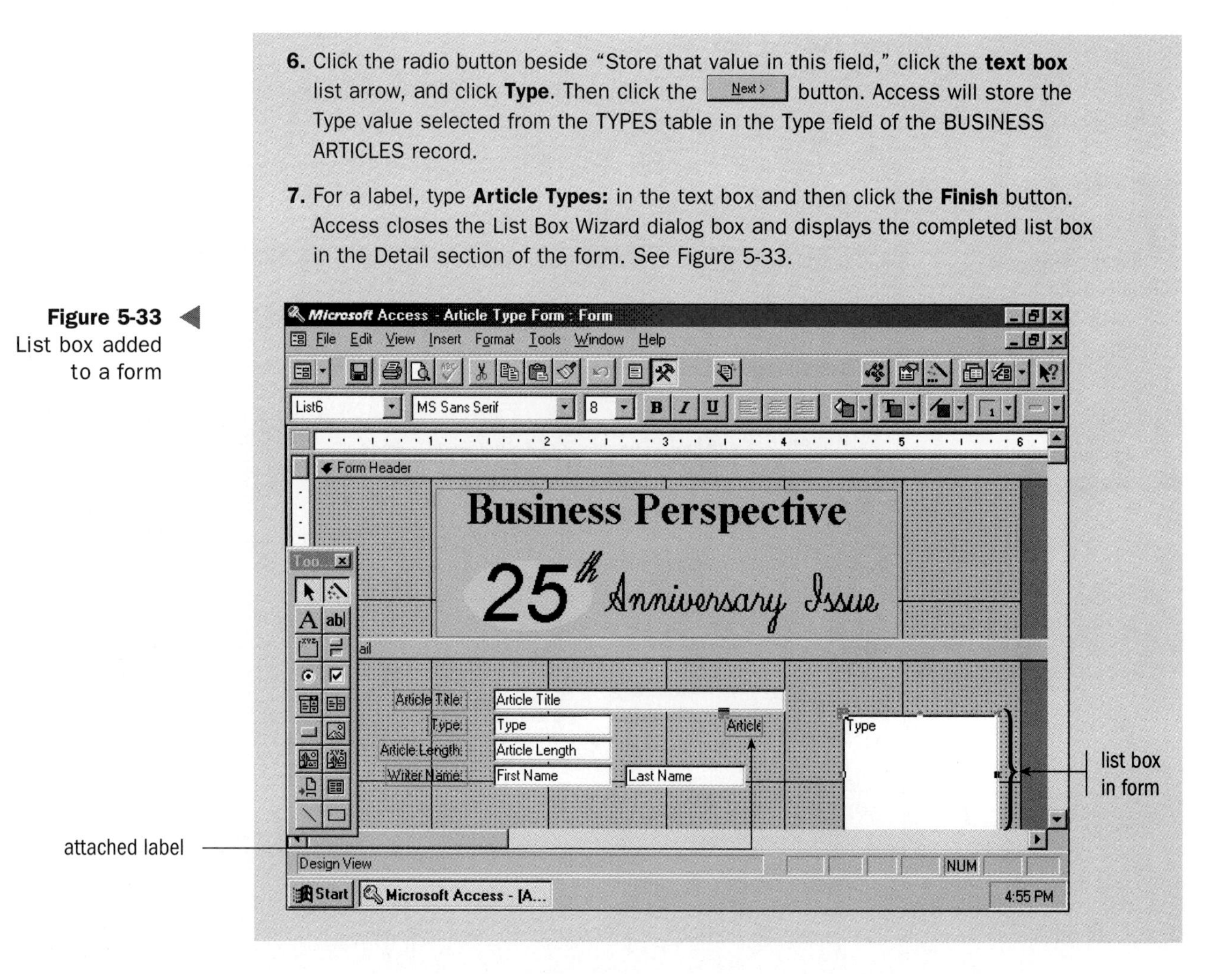

Elena notices that the attached label does not fit in the label box and also that it appears too far to the left of the list box. She resizes the label and then moves it above the list box.

To resize and move a label:

1. Click the **label box** attached to the list box to select it.

2. Click **Format**, click **Size**, and then click **to Fit**. The label's entire caption is now visible.

3. Click and drag the label box's **move handle** to position the label box above the list box. See Figure 5-34.

Figure 5-34
Resizing and moving a label

Elena's final tasks are to add background colors to the Form Header and Detail sections and to change the style of the graphic image.

Adding Background Colors and Special Effects to a Form

Elena changes the background of the Detail and Form Header sections to a darker gray and applies a special effect to the graphic image to make it stand out.

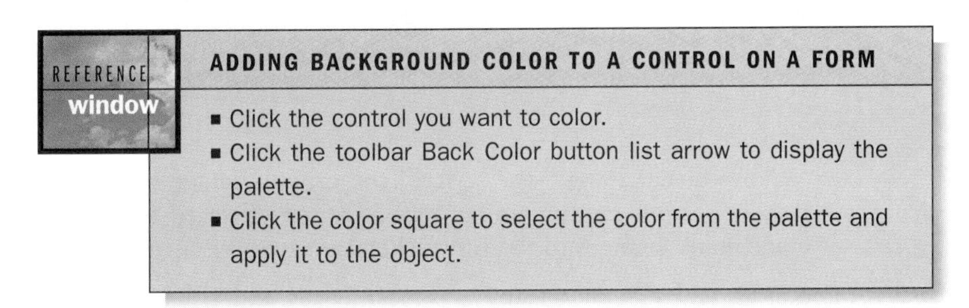

REFERENCE window

ADDING BACKGROUND COLOR TO A CONTROL ON A FORM

- Click the control you want to color.
- Click the toolbar Back Color button list arrow to display the palette.
- Click the color square to select the color from the palette and apply it to the object.

Elena changes the background colors of the two form sections.

To change the background colors of the form sections:

1. Click the **Detail** section, but do not click any of the controls in that section. This makes the Detail section the selected control.
2. Click the **Back Color** button list arrow on the toolbar. Access displays the color palette. See Figure 5-35.

Figure 5-35 Back color palette

Click the **dark gray color box** in the color palette (at the right end of the second row). The Detail section displays the dark gray background.

TROUBLE? If your screen shows a different color palette, select any dark gray color of your choice.

3. Click the Form Header section, but do not click the graphic image. This makes the Form Header section the selected control.

4. Click the **Back Color** button (not the list arrow) on the toolbar. The Form Header section appears with the dark gray background.

Now Elena changes the style of the graphic image so that it stands out in the Form Header section by applying a special raised effect to the graphic image. Since she has made many changes to the form, she also saves the form again

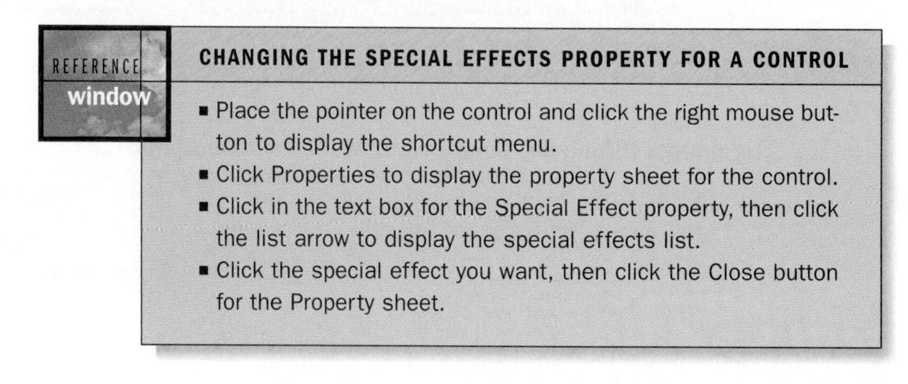

REFERENCE window

CHANGING THE SPECIAL EFFECTS PROPERTY FOR A CONTROL

- Place the pointer on the control and click the right mouse button to display the shortcut menu.
- Click Properties to display the property sheet for the control.
- Click in the text box for the Special Effect property, then click the list arrow to display the special effects list.
- Click the special effect you want, then click the Close button for the Property sheet.

To apply the special effect to the graphic image and save the form:

1. Position the pointer in the graphic image, then click the right mouse button to display the shortcut menu.
2. Click **Properties** to display the property sheet for the graphic image.
3. If necessary, click the **Format** tab to display the Format page. Then use the elevator bar in the property sheet to scroll down until the Special Effect property is visible. Click in the text box for the Special Effect property, then click the **list arrow** to display the special effects list. See Figure 5-36.

Figure 5-36 Adding a special effect to the graphic image

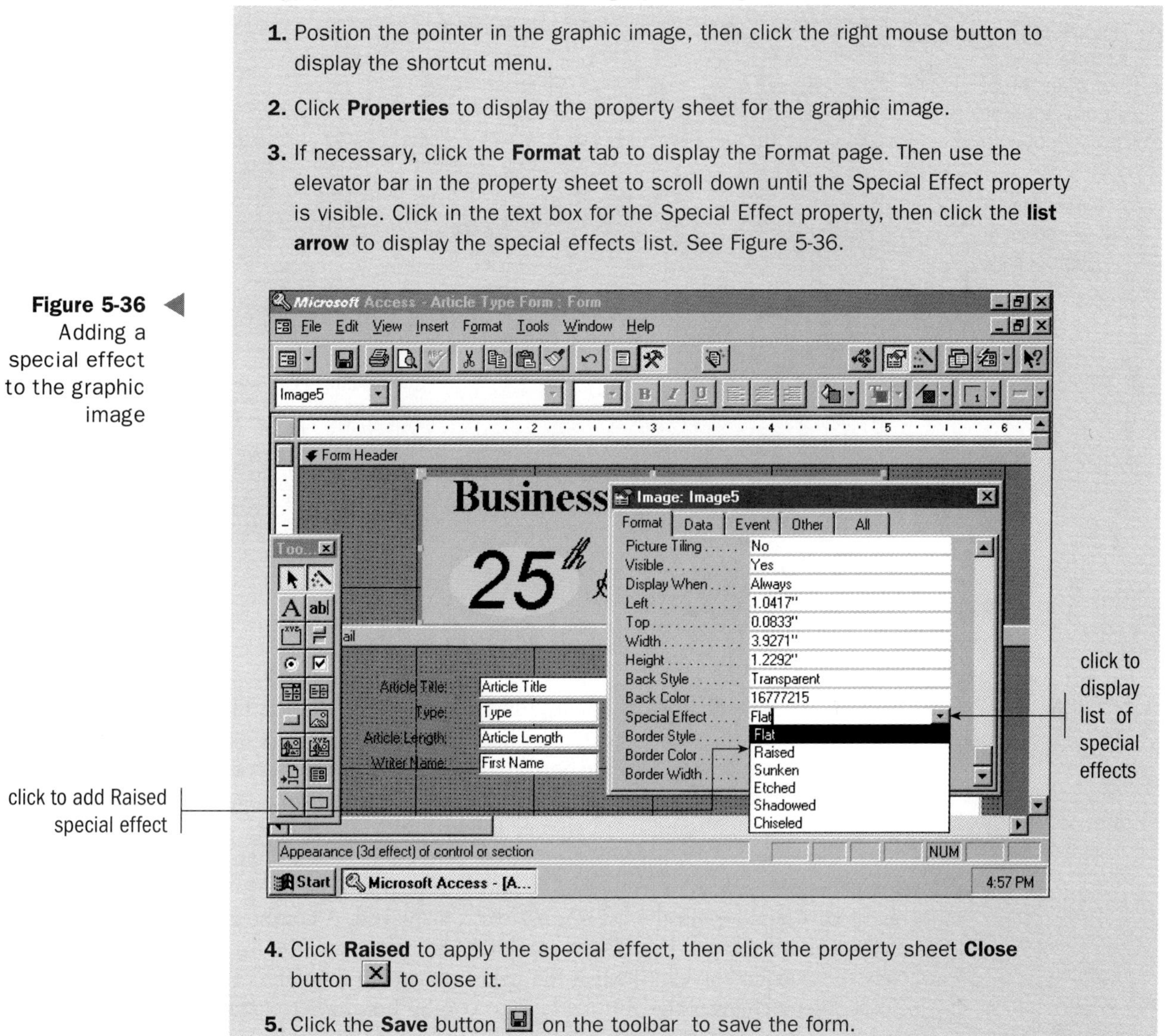

4. Click **Raised** to apply the special effect, then click the property sheet **Close** button to close it.
5. Click the **Save** button on the toolbar to save the form.

Making Final Revisions to a Custom Form

Elena switches to the Form View window to review the custom form. She wants to see if there are any further changes she needs to make to the form.

To switch to the Form View window to review a custom form:

1. Click the **Form View** button on the toolbar. Access closes the Form Design window and opens the Form View window. See Figure 5-37.

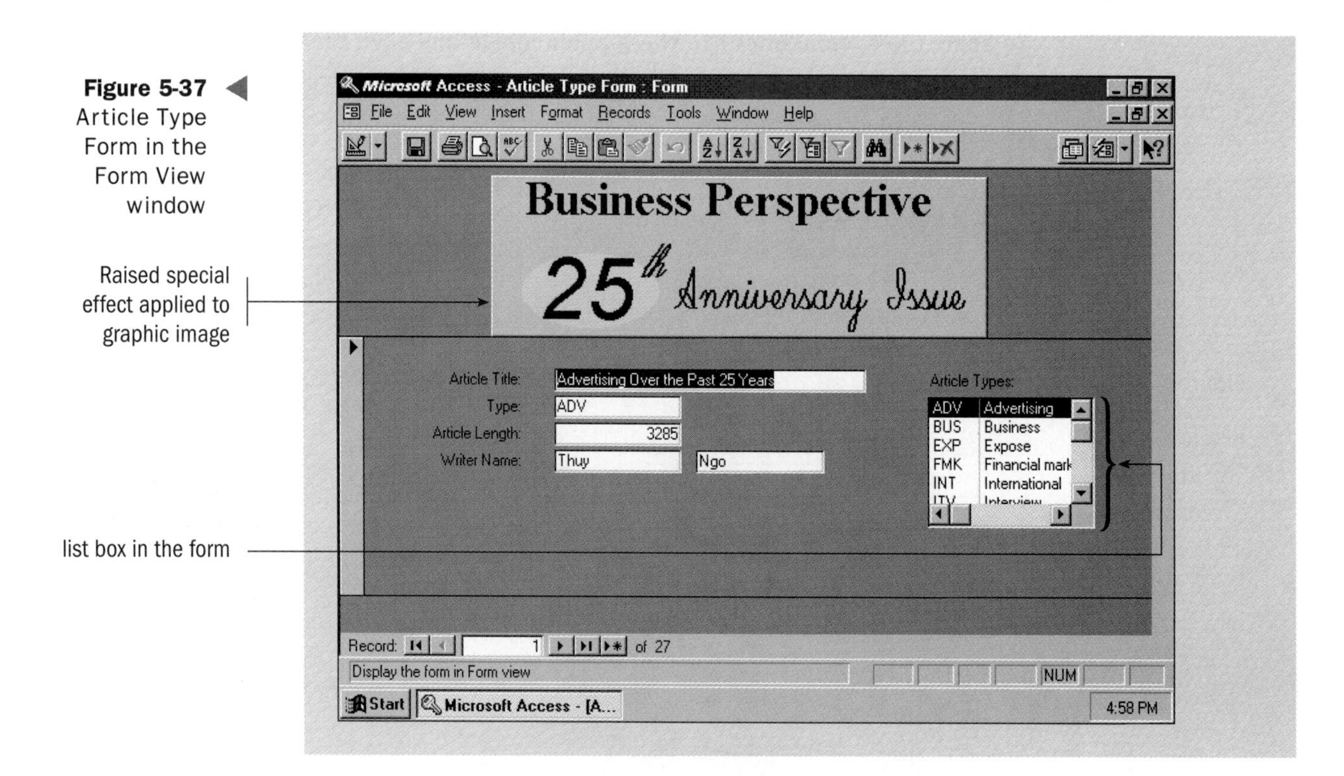

Figure 5-37 Article Type Form in the Form View window

Elena sees two changes she would like to make. She doesn't like the appearance of the Article Types list box and decides to change it to a combo box control. She also sees that the graphic image extends to the bottom of the Form Header section and rests on the dividing line. She decides to increase the height of the Form Header section. She switches back to the Form Design window to change the list box control first.

As you have seen, a list box contains a field-value text box and a list displayed below. You can select any item from the list and it appears in the field-value text box. A combo box is very similar, but the list is not always displayed. A combo box contains a list arrow instead of a displayed list. When you click the list arrow, the list is displayed. When you click to select an entry in the list, the value appears in the field-value text box, and the list closes. Elena changes the control type to combo box in her custom form.

Changing the Control Type with Control Morphing

To change the control type, Elena could delete the list box control on the form and replace it with a combo box control. However, Access also allows you to change a control's type directly on the form. This is known as **control morphing**. Elena will use control morphing to change the list box control to a combo box control.

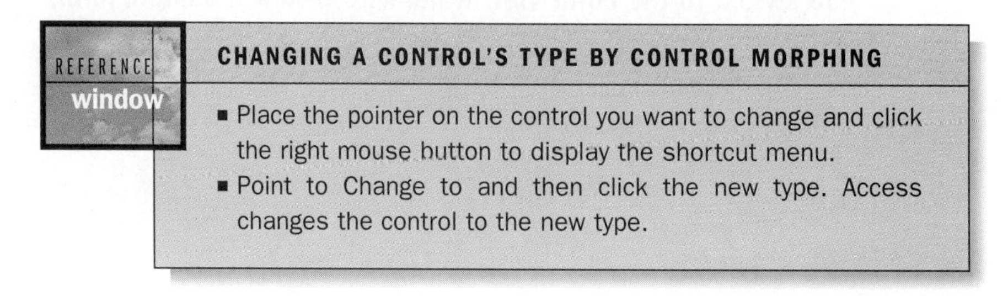
REFERENCE window

CHANGING A CONTROL'S TYPE BY CONTROL MORPHING

- Place the pointer on the control you want to change and click the right mouse button to display the shortcut menu.
- Point to Change to and then click the new type. Access changes the control to the new type.

To change the list box control to a combo box control:

1. Click the **Form View** button on the toolbar. Access closes the Form View window and opens the Form Design window.
2. Place the pointer on the list box control and click the right mouse button to display the shortcut menu.
3. Point to **Change to** and then click **Combo Box**. Access changes the control to a combo box.

As her final task to complete her custom form, Elena resizes the Form Header section.

To resize the Form Header section:

1. Position the pointer at the top edge of the bar that divides the Form Header section from the Detail section. When the pointer changes to ✛, drag the divider down approximately .25", then release the mouse button.

   TROUBLE? If you move the divider too far, drag the divider again until it is correctly positioned.

2. Switch back and forth between the Form View window and the Form Design window until the Form Header section is the correct size. See Figure 5-38.

Figure 5-38 The final version of a custom form in the Form View window

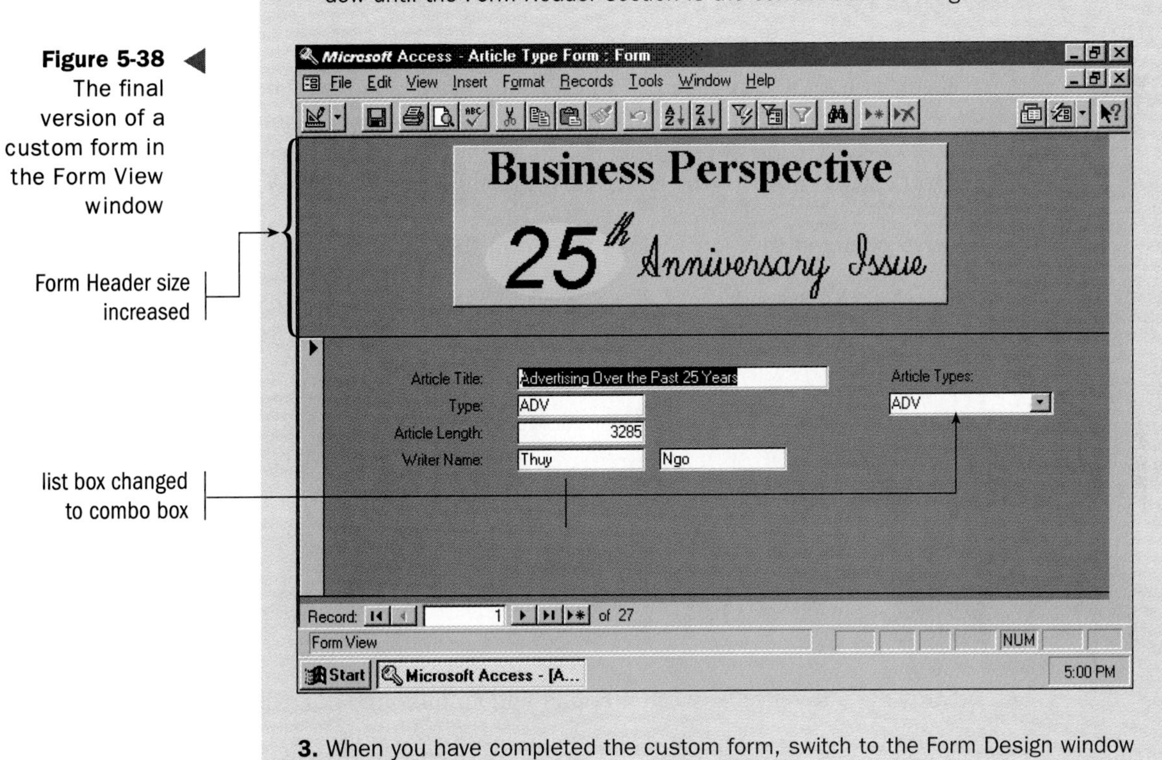

3. When you have completed the custom form, switch to the Form Design window to view the form's final design. See Figure 5-39.

Figure 5-39 The final version of a custom form in the Form Design window

Elena prints the completed form and shows it to Harold, who tells her this format is much easier to read and use than the Article Type Query results. Elena then saves her changes to the Article Type Form, and closes the Form Design window. Having completed her work with forms for the Issue25 database, Elena also exits Access at this time.

To save changes to a form, close the Form Design window, and exit Access:

1. Click the **Save** button on the toolbar. Access saves the form.
2. Click the Form Design window **Close** button. Access closes the Form Design window and switches to the Database window.
3. Click the Access window **Close** button to exit Access.

In the next tutorial, Elena will create reports that will allow her to print table records and query results in a useful hardcopy format.

Quick Check

1. What is the difference between a bound and an unbound control?
2. How do you move a control and its label together, and how do you move each separately?
3. How do you change a label name?
4. How would you resize a control?
5. What is the Form Header section?
6. Describe how you would use a Control Wizard to add a list box to a form.
7. How do you insert into a form a graphic created with another software program?
8. What is control morphing?

Tutorial Assignments

Elena creates two new forms for the Issue25 database. Start Access, open the Issue25 database in the Tutorial Folder on your Student Disk, and do the following:

1. Use the Form Wizard to create a columnar form based on the BUSINESS ARTICLES table. Select all the fields from the table in the order in which they are stored in the table, and use the form title Business Articles Columnar Form.
2. Open the Form View window and then print the first page.
3. Change the form's design so that the Article Length text box and its attached label box are to the right of, and on the same line as, the Issue field.
4. Move the Writer ID text box and its attached label box up to the position previously occupied by the Article Length bound control.
5. Change the Caption property for the Article Length label box to Length followed by a colon.
6. Resize the Article Title text box so that the field value for each record is completely displayed.
7. Verify your design changes in the Form View window by navigating through all records.
8. Print the first page and close the Form View window.

Elena next creates a custom form and names it Business Articles by Issue and Length Form. Use the Issue25 database in the Tutorial folder on your Student Disk to do the following:

9. Create a query by selecting the BUSINESS ARTICLES and WRITERS tables and selecting the following fields in the order given here: Article Title, Type, Issue of Business Perspective, Article Length, Last Name, and First Name. Rename the Issue of Business Perspective field as Issue. Then sort the records based on Issue as the primary sort key in descending order and Article Length as the secondary sort key in ascending order. Print the entire query results for this query. Finally, save the query, naming it Articles Sorted by Issue and Length Query, and switch to the Database window.
10. Create a custom form by selecting the query Articles Sorted by Issue and Length Query, clicking the New button, and selecting Design View.
11. Add all the fields from the query Articles Sorted by Issue and Length Query to the Detail section and print the first page of the form.
12. Change the Caption property for the Article Length label box to Length, right-align all the label boxes, resize the Article Title text box so that the field-value for each record is completely displayed, and print the first page of the form.
13. Move the First Name text box to the right of, and on the same line as, the Last Name text box; delete the First Name label; change the Caption property for the Last Name label to Writer Name; resize the Writer Name label; and print the first page of the form.
14. Use the Format menu's to Fit option under the Size command for the five labels and then right-align all the labels. Print the first page of the form.
15. Change the form width to 4.5" and then move the Issue text box and its attached label to the right of, and on the same line as, the Type field. Move all the lines that follow the Type and Issue fields up to eliminate blank lines. If necessary, right-align all the labels that appear on the left of the form and then left align the field-value text boxes to their immediate right. Print the first page of the form.
16. Add Form Header and Form Footer sections; delete the Form Footer section; add to the Form Header section the form title Business Articles by Issue and Length Form. Add the graphic image 25th to the Form Header, change the height of the Detail section to accommodate the title and graphic image, and print the first page of the form.

17. Use the List Box Wizard to create a list box to display all the article types and their descriptions. Position the list box under all the fields. Use the TYPES table for the list box, and display both table fields. Use Types as the label and position it just to the left of the list box. Resize the list box to display all types and descriptions.

18. In Design View, use AutoFormat to change the style of the form (click Format, then AutoFormat). Select Colorful 2 as the style. Print the first and last pages of the form.
19. Save the form as Business Articles by Issue and Length Form.

20. Import the WRITER PAYMENTS-JR table from the Vision database in the Tutorial folder on your Student Disk. Delete the WRITER PAYMENTS table you created in Tutorial 2 and rename WRITER PAYMENTS-JR as WRITER PAYMENTS. Create a custom form using the WRITER PAYMENTS table. Since this table contains records of checks, make your form resemble a check
21. Save the form with the name WRITERS PAYMENT form.

Case Problems

1. Walkton Daily Press Carriers Grant Sherman uses the Form Wizard to create a form for his Press database. Start Access, open the Press database in the Cases folder on your Student Disk, and do the following:

1. Use AutoForm to create a columnar form based on the CARRIERS table.
2. Open the Form View window and then print the second page.
3. Save the form with the name Carriers Form and close the Form View window on your screen.

Grant creates a custom form named Carriers by Name and Route ID Form. Use the Press database in the Cases folder on your Student Disk to do the following:

4. Create a query by selecting the BILLINGS and CARRIERS tables. If necessary, create a join line for the Carrier ID fields and select fields in the order given here: Carrier Last Name, Carrier First Name, Carrier Phone, Route ID, and Balance Amount. Rename the Balance Amount field simply Balance, and then sort the records based on Carrier Last Name as the primary sort key in ascending order and on Route ID as the secondary sort key in ascending order. Print the entire query results for this query. Finally, save the query, naming it Carriers Sorted by Name and Route ID Query. Switch to the Database window.
5. Create a custom form based on the Carriers Sorted by Name and Route ID Query.
6. To the Detail section of the form, add all the fields from the Carriers Sorted by Name and Route ID Query. Print the first page of the form.
7. Move the Carrier Last Name text box without its attached label to the right on the same line, leaving room to move the Carrier First Name text box from the line below up in front of it. Then move the Carrier First Name text box without its attached label up between the Carrier Last Name label box and the Carrier Last Name text box. Delete the Carrier First Name label box, change the Caption property for the Last Name label box to Carrier Name: (include the colon), resize the Carrier Name label box to accommodate the caption, and print the first page of the form.
8. Move the Carrier Phone text box and its attached label up one line, and move the Route ID text box and its attached label up one line. Move the Balance text box and its attached label to the right of, and on the same line as, the Route ID bound control. Print the first page of the form.
9. Move the Balance label to the right, so that it is closer to its attached text box.
10. Right-align all the labels on the left side of the form.
11. Change the Detail section background color to blue-green (third color from the right in the second row of the palette).

12. Add Form Header and Form Footer sections. Add to the Form Header section the form title Carriers by Name and Route ID. (*Hint:* use the toolbox Label tool.) Add to the Form Footer section the label Press Database, and print the first page of the form.
13. Save the form as Carriers by Name and Route ID Form.

2. Lopez Lexus Dealerships Hector Lopez uses the Form Wizard to create a form for his Lexus database. Start Access, open the Lexus database in the Cases folder on your Student Disk, and do the following:

1. Use the Form Wizard to create a columnar form type with the Colorful 1 style based on the CARS table. Select all the fields from the table in the order in which they are stored in the table. Use the form title Cars Data.
2. Open the Form View window, print the first two pages, then close the Form View window.

Maria Lopez creates a custom form, naming it Cars by Model and Year Form. Use the Lexus database on your Student Disk to do the following:

3. Create a query by selecting the CLASSES, LOCATIONS, CARS, and TRANSMISSIONS tables. You need join lines between the two Transmission Type fields, between the two Location Code fields, and between Class Type and Class. If any of these join lines are not shown, then create them. Select fields in the order given here: Manufacturer, Model, Class Description, Transmission Desc, Year, Location Name, Manager Name, Cost, and Selling Price. Sort the records based on Model as the primary sort key in ascending order and on Year as the secondary sort key in ascending order. Print the entire query results for this query. Finally, save the query, naming it Cars by Model and Year Query.
4. Create a custom form based on the Cars by Model and Year Query.
5. Add to the Detail section all the fields from the Cars by Model and Year Query. Place the fields at the left edge of the Design View. Print the fourth page of the form.
6. Resize the field-value text boxes, as necessary, so that, in the Form View window, all the field values for each record are completely displayed without unnecessary extra space. Navigate through the records in the Form View window to be sure the box sizes are correct. The Class Description and Transmission Desc text boxes should be widened, for example, and the Year, Cost, and Selling Price text boxes should be narrowed.
7. Change the width of the Detail section to 5.75" and its height to 2.75".
8. Move the Model text box and its attached label to the right of, and on the same line as, the Manufacturer bound control. Then move the Model text box to the left to be one grid dot away from its related label.
9. Move the Year text box and its attached label to the right of, and on the same line as, the Model bound control. Then move the Year label to the right to be one grid dot away from its related text box.
10. Move the Manager Name text box and its attached label to the right of, and on the same line as, the Location Name bound control. Move the Selling Price text box and its attached label to the right of, and on the same line as, the Cost bound control.
11. Eliminate blank lines by moving text boxes and their attached labels up, and then print the fourth page of the form.
12. Change the Caption properties for these labels: Class Description to Class, Transmission Desc to Trans, and Location Name to Location.
13. Apply the Format menu's to Fit option under the Size command for the labels on the left side of the form, right-align these labels, and then print the fourth page of the form.

14. Use the List Box Wizard to add two list boxes to the form—one for class types and descriptions and one for location codes and names. Position the list boxes side by side below all the control boxes in the Detail section, placing the one containing class types and descriptions on the left. For the class list box, use the CLASSES table, display both table fields, and enter Classes for the label. For the location list box, use the LOCATIONS table, display the Location Code and Location Name fields, and enter Locations as the label. Resize and move the labels and list boxes to display as much of each record as possible.
15. Use control morphing to change the location list box to a combo box.
16. Print the fourth page of the form.
17. Save the form as Cars by Model and Year Form.

3. Tophill University Student Employment Olivia Tyler uses the Form Wizard to create a form for her Parttime database. Start Access, open the Parttime database in the Cases folder on your Student Disk, and do the following:

1. If you have not already defined a one-to-many relation from the EMPLOYERS table to the JOBS table, use the Relationships window to do so now.
2. Use the Form Wizard to create a tabular main/subform form type based on the EMPLOYERS table as the primary table for the main form and the JOBS table as the related table for the subform. Choose your own style for the form. Select all the fields from the EMPLOYERS table in the order in which they are stored in the table. Select all the fields from the JOBS table, except for the Employer ID field, in the order in which they are stored in the table. Save the form with the name Employers and Jobs Form, save the subform with the name Jobs Subform.
3. Open the Form View window and print the first page, then close the Form View window.

Olivia creates a custom form named Jobs by Employer and Job Title Form. Use the Parttime database on your Student Disk to do the following:

4. Create a query by selecting the EMPLOYERS and JOBS tables and, if necessary, create a join line for the Employer ID fields. Select all the fields from the EMPLOYERS table in the order in which they are stored in the table, and then select fields from the JOBS table in the order given here: Hours/Week, Job Title, and Wage. Sort the records based on Employer Name as the primary sort key in ascending order and on Job Title as the secondary sort key in ascending order. Print the query results for this query. Finally, save the query, naming it Jobs Sorted by Employer and Job Title Query.
5. Create a custom form based on the query Jobs Sorted by Employer and Job Title Query.
6. Add all the fields from Jobs Sorted by Employer and Job Title Query to the Detail section and then print the first page of the form.
7. Resize the Employer Name and Job Title text boxes and print the first page of the form.
8. Right-align all the labels.
9. Add Form Header and Form Footer sections, add to the Form Header section the form title Jobs by Employer and Job Title, add to the Form Footer section the Tophill University logo graphic image TU from the Cases folder on your student disk, and print the first page of the form.
10. Save the form as Jobs by Employer and Job Title Form.

4. Rexville Business Licenses Chester Pearce uses AutoForm to create a form for his Buslic database. Start Access, open the Buslic database in the Cases folder on your Student Disk, and do the following:

1. Use AutoForm to create a columnar form based on the BUSINESSES table.
2. Open the Form View window and then print the first two pages.
3. Save the form as Businesses Form and close the Form View window.

Chester creates a custom form, naming it Businesses by License Type and Business Name Form. Use the Buslic database on your Student Disk to do the following:

4. Create a query by selecting the BUSINESSES, ISSUED LICENSES, and LICENSES tables and, if necessary, create join lines for the Business ID fields and the License Type fields. Select all the fields, except the Business ID field, from the BUSINESSES table in the order in which they are stored in the table; select the License Number, License Type, Amount, and Date Issued fields (in the order given here) from the ISSUED LICENSES table; and then select the License Description and Basic Cost fields from the LICENSES table. Rename the License Description field simply License. Sort the records based on License Type as the primary sort key in ascending order and on Business Name as the secondary sort key in ascending order, but do not show the License Type field in the query results. Print the entire query results for this query. Finally, save the query, naming it Businesses Sorted by License Type and Business Name Query.
5. Create a custom form by selecting the Businesses Sorted by License Type and Business Name Query.
6. Add all the fields from Businesses Sorted by License Type and Business Name Query to the Detail section and then print the first page of the form.
7. Resize the Business Name and License text boxes, and print the first page of the form.
8. Right-align all the labels.
9. Change the Detail section background color to blue-green (third color from the right in the second row on the palette), and then print the first page of the form.
10. Add Form Header and Form Footer sections, add to the Form Header section the form title Businesses by License Type and Business Name, add to the Form Footer section the label Buslic Database, and print the first page of the form.
11. Save the form as Businesses by License Type and Business Name Form.

TUTORIAL 6

Creating Reports

Creating a Marketing Report at Vision Publishers

OBJECTIVES

In this tutorial you will:

- Create a report using AutoReport and the Report Wizard
- Save and print a report
- Design and create a custom report
- Modify report controls and properties
- Sort and group data
- Calculate group and overall totals
- Hide duplicate values
- Embed and link objects in a report

CASE

Vision Publishers

At the next progress meeting on the special 25th-anniversary issue of *Business Perspective*, Harold Larson mentions to Elena Sanchez that the forms she created from the Issue25 database certainly provided information in a more attractive, readable format than query results. Now he needs information from the Issue25 database presented even more professionally, for an upcoming meeting with several advertisers in New York for the special 25th-anniversary issue of *Business Perspective*. He asks Elena to produce a report that includes information about the articles and authors to help him discuss the special issue with potential advertisers.

Using a Report

A **report** is a formatted hardcopy of the contents of one or more tables from a database. Although you can format and print data using datasheets, queries, and forms, reports allow you greater flexibility and provide a more professional, custom appearance. Reports can be used, for example, to print billing statements and mailing labels.

An Access report is divided into sections. Each report can have seven different sections, which are described in Figure 6-1. You do not need to use all seven report sections in a report. When you design your report, you determine which sections to use and what information to place in each section. Figure 6-2 shows a sample report produced from the Issue25 database.

Figure 6-1 Access report sections

Report Section	Description
Report Header	Appears once at the beginning of a report. Use it for report titles, company logos, report introductions, and cover pages.
Page Header	Appears at the top of each page of a report. Use it for column headings, report titles, page numbers, and report dates. If your report has a Report Header section, it precedes the first Page Header section.
Group Header	Appears once at the beginning of a new group of records. Use it to print the group name and the field value that all records in the group have in common. A report can have up to 10 grouping levels.
Detail	Appears once for each record in the underlying table or query. Use it to print selected fields from the table or query and to print calculated values.
Group Footer	Appears once at the end of a group of records. Use it to print totals for the group.
Report Footer	Appears once at the end of the report. Use it for report totals and other summary information.
Page Footer	Appears at the bottom of each page of a report. Use it for page numbers and brief explanations of symbols or abbreviations. If your report has a Report Footer section, it precedes the Page Footer section on the last page of the report.

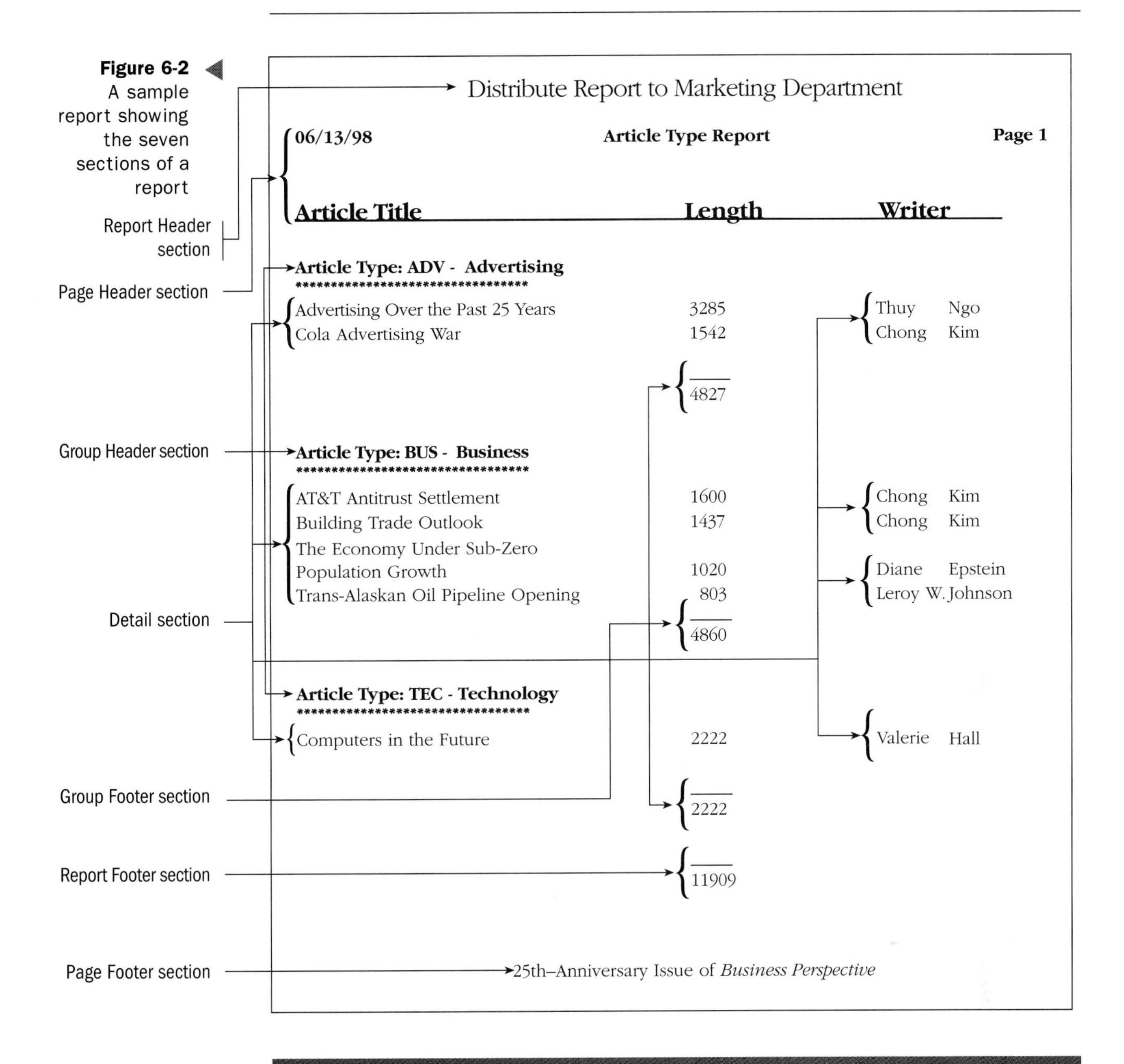

Figure 6-2 A sample report showing the seven sections of a report

Creating a Report

In Access, there is more than one way to create your own report:

- **AutoReport** creates a report in one of two standard formats, columnar or tabular; it uses all of the fields in the underlying table or query. This is a quick way to create a basic report that you can use without modification or that you can customize later. Figure 6-3 shows columnar and tabular reports created from the WRITERS table with AutoReport. In Figure 6-3, notice that the report created by AutoReport would have to be modified to include the entire Writer Phone field values.

Figure 6-3A ◀ The AutoReport Columnar

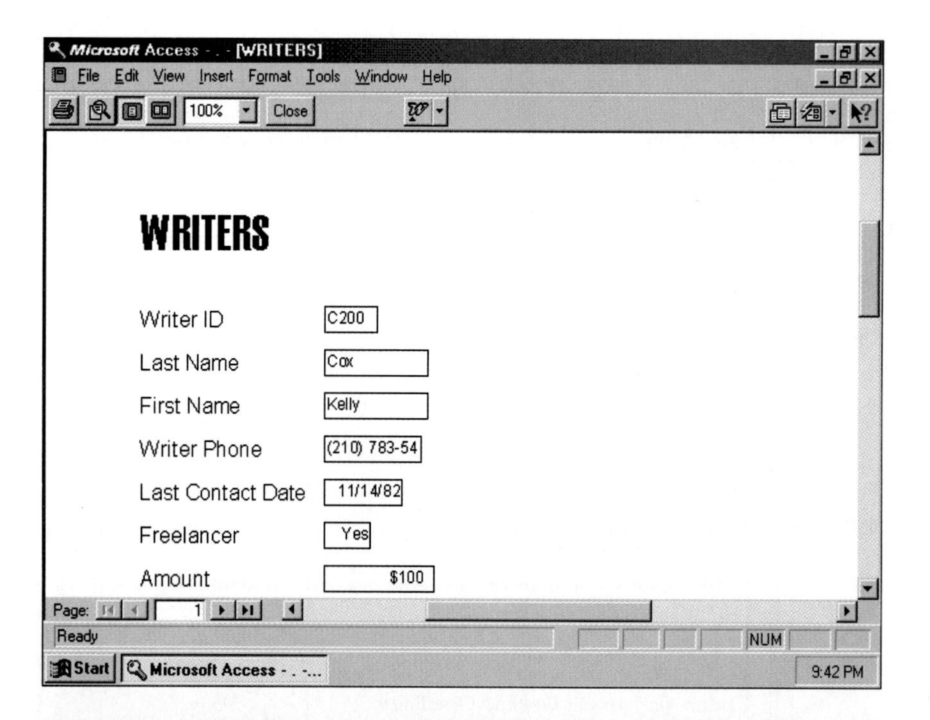

Figure 6-3B ◀ The AutoReport Tabular

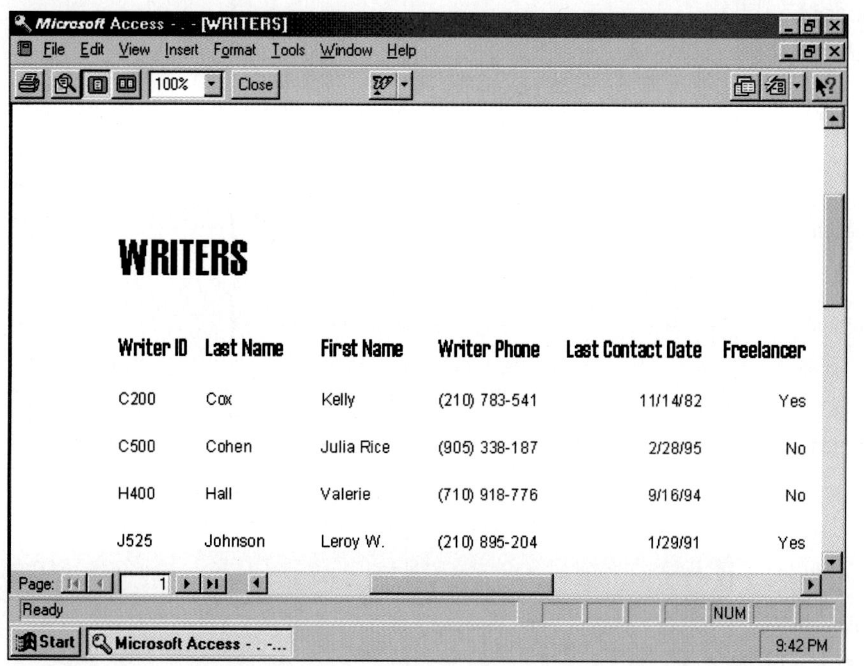

- The **Report Wizard** asks you a series of questions and then creates a report based on your answers. Using the Report Wizard, you can select fields that you want to appear in the report.
- The **Report Design** window allows you to create your own customized report that you design directly on the screen.
- The **Chart Wizard** designs a graph based on your data.
- The **Label Wizard** designs labels (such as mailing labels) based on your data.

Elena has never created an Access report, so she first familiarizes herself with AutoReport.

SESSION 6.1

In this session, you will create reports using AutoReport and the Report Wizard, save a report, and print a report. You will also create a blank report and then begin to customize it by adding and modifying fields.

Creating a Report with AutoReport

The quickest way to create a report is to use AutoReport. AutoReport uses all the fields from the selected table or query, creates a columnar or tabular report for these fields, and displays the report on the screen in the Print Preview window.

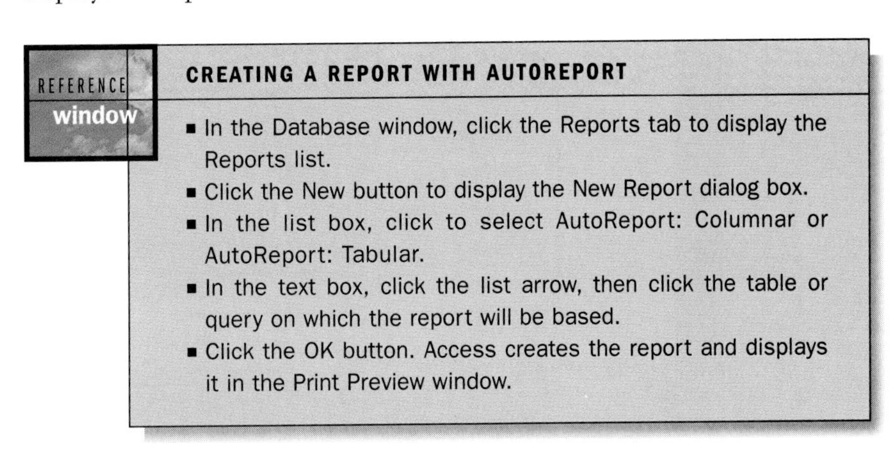

REFERENCE window

CREATING A REPORT WITH AUTOREPORT

- In the Database window, click the Reports tab to display the Reports list.
- Click the New button to display the New Report dialog box.
- In the list box, click to select AutoReport: Columnar or AutoReport: Tabular.
- In the text box, click the list arrow, then click the table or query on which the report will be based.
- Click the OK button. Access creates the report and displays it in the Print Preview window.

In order to become familiar with AutoReport, Elena uses AutoReport: Columnar to create a report containing all the fields from the WRITERS table.

To create a columnar report using AutoReport:

1. If you have not done so, place your Student Disk in the appropriate drive, start Access, and open the Issue25 database in the Tutorial folder on your Student Disk. Click the **Reports** tab to display the Reports list. No reports appear in the list yet.
2. Click the **New** button. Access displays the New Report dialog box.
3. Click **AutoReport: Columnar** in the list box to highlight it.
4. Click the **list arrow** in the text box to display a list of available tables and queries.
5. If necessary, scroll the list until WRITERS is visible. Click **WRITERS** to select the WRITERS table. See Figure 6-4.

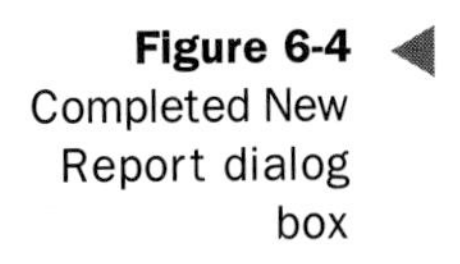

Figure 6-4 Completed New Report dialog box

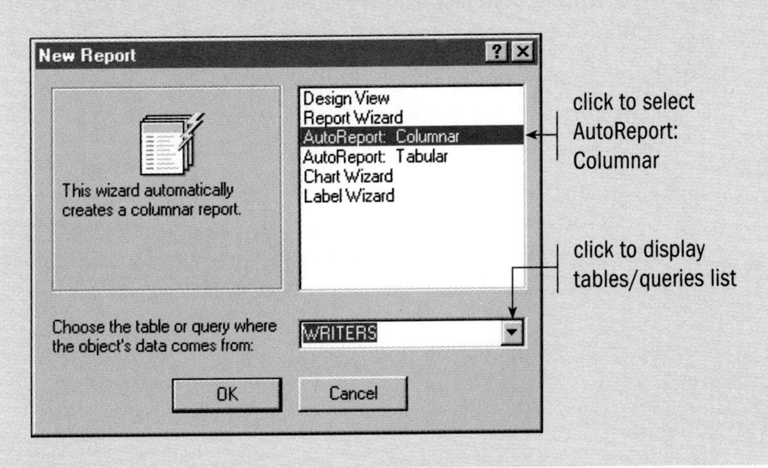

6. Click the **OK** button. The New Report dialog box closes, and Access displays the completed columnar report in the Print Preview window. Click the Print Preview window **Maximize** button. See Figure 6-5. You can use the elevator bar to scroll down and display all the fields of the report.

Figure 6-5 The completed columnar report in the Print Preview window

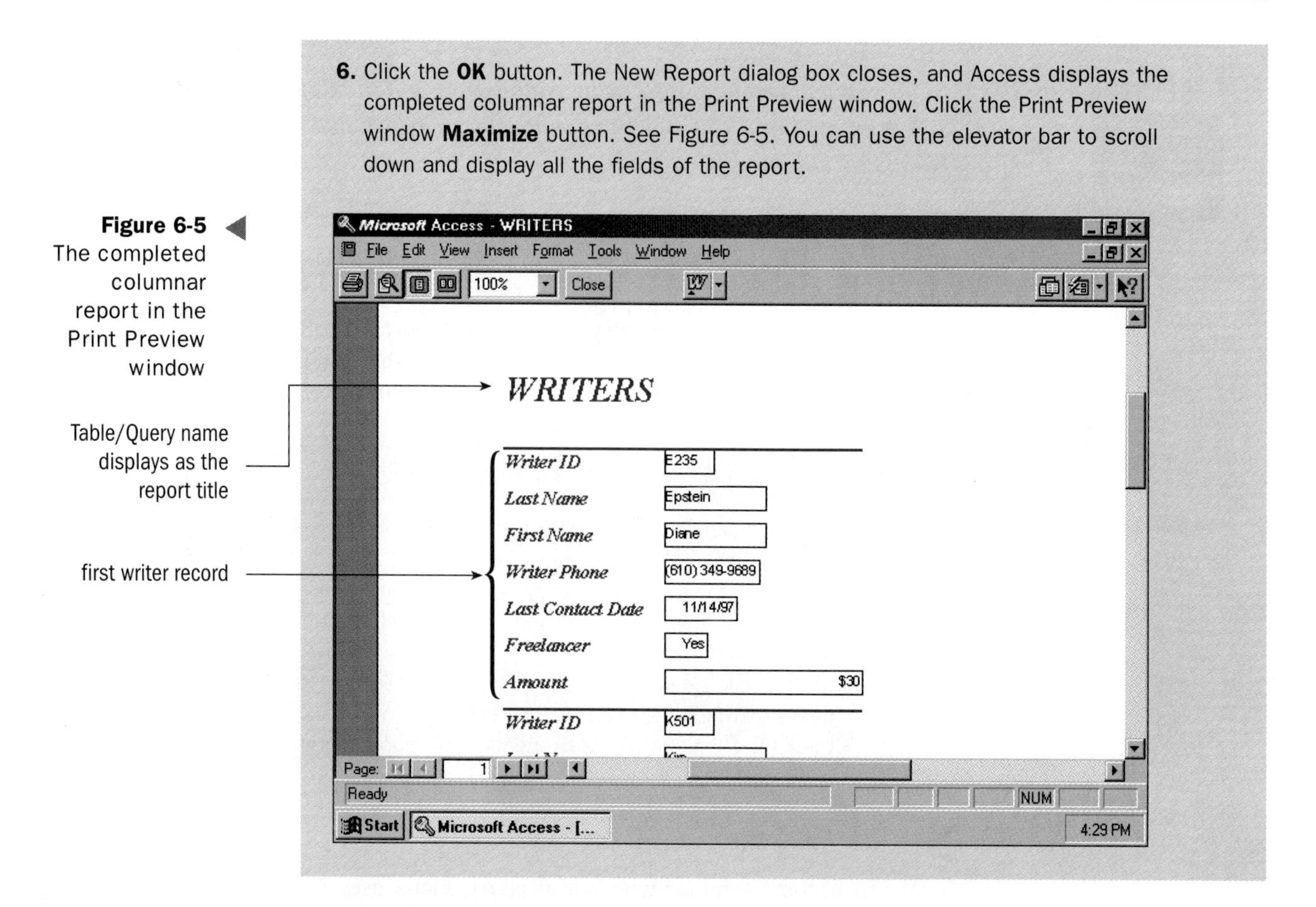

After viewing the report, Elena saves it.

Saving a Report

Elena saves her report so that she and others can print it whenever they need an updated copy. When you save a report, you actually save the report design. When you preview or print the report later, Access uses the current data from the underlying table or query to create the report.

Elena saves the report using the name Writers Columnar Report and then closes the Print Preview window.

To save and close a new report:

1 Click **File** and then click **Save As/Export** to display the Save As dialog box.

2 Type **Writers Columnar Report** in the New Name text box and then click the **OK** button. The Save As dialog box closes, and Access saves the report.

3 Click the Print Preview window **Close** button ☒ (in the upper-right corner) to close the report and return to the Database window. Notice that Writers Columnar Report appears in the Reports list.

TROUBLE? If Access switches to the Report Design window instead of the Database window, you clicked the Close button on the Print Preview toolbar. Click the Report Design window Close button to return to the Database window.

Creating a Report with the Report Wizard

After viewing the columnar report created by AutoReport, Elena decides that she would like to create a report listing selected fields from the WRITERS table in a tabular format. She wants to use a different title and style for the report and to print the staff writers and freelancers in separate groups. Since AutoReport uses all of the fields in the selected table and creates a standard title and layout, Elena would have to make many modifications to a report created by AutoReport. Instead, Elena uses the Report Wizard to create her report.

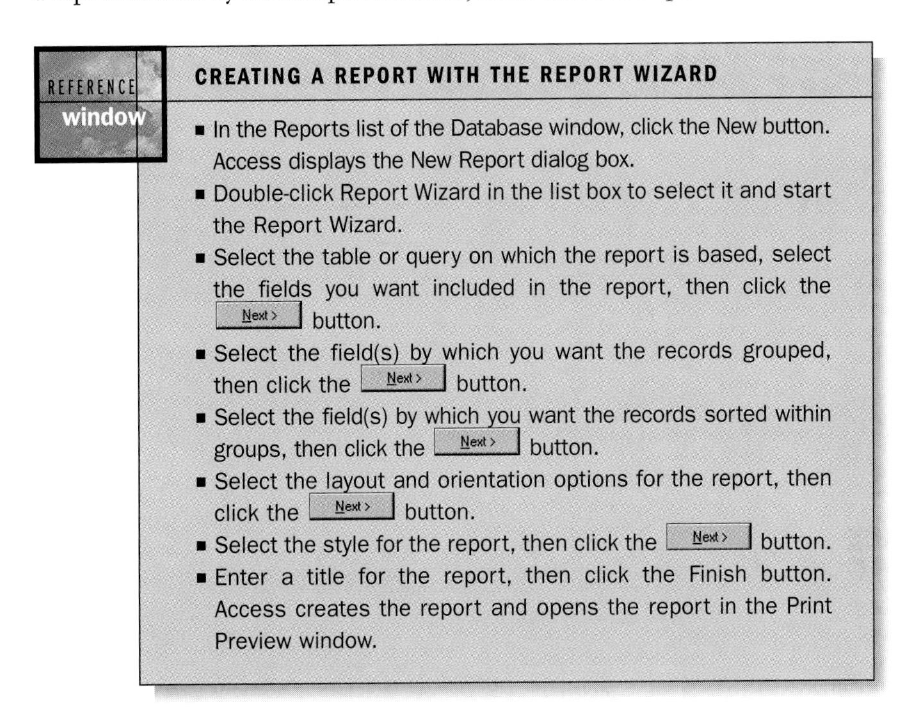

REFERENCE window

CREATING A REPORT WITH THE REPORT WIZARD

- In the Reports list of the Database window, click the New button. Access displays the New Report dialog box.
- Double-click Report Wizard in the list box to select it and start the Report Wizard.
- Select the table or query on which the report is based, select the fields you want included in the report, then click the Next > button.
- Select the field(s) by which you want the records grouped, then click the Next > button.
- Select the field(s) by which you want the records sorted within groups, then click the Next > button.
- Select the layout and orientation options for the report, then click the Next > button.
- Select the style for the report, then click the Next > button.
- Enter a title for the report, then click the Finish button. Access creates the report and opens the report in the Print Preview window.

Elena creates a report with the Report Wizard.

To start the Report Wizard and select a report type:

1. In the Reports list of the Database window, click the **New** button. Access displays the New Report dialog box. Double-click **Report Wizard** in the list box to select it and start the Report Wizard. The first Report Wizard dialog box appears.

2. If necessary, click the **Tables/Queries** list arrow and then click **Table: WRITERS** to select the WRITERS table.

   Elena wants to include the Last Name, First Name, Writer ID, Last Contact Date, and Freelancer fields from the WRITERS table.

3. Click **Last Name** to select it, then click the > button to move the Last Name field from the Available Fields list box to the Selected Fields list box. Use the same procedure to move the First Name, Writer ID, Last Contact Date, and Freelancer fields from the Available Fields list box to the Selected Fields list box.

4. Click the Next > button to display the next Report Wizard dialog box. This dialog box allows you to select the grouping for the records in the report. To print the staff writers and freelancers in separate groups, click **Freelancer**, then click the > button to select grouping by the value in the Freelancer field. The sample panel on the right changes to show grouping by the Freelancer field. See Figure 6-6.

Figure 6-6 Selecting the grouping field

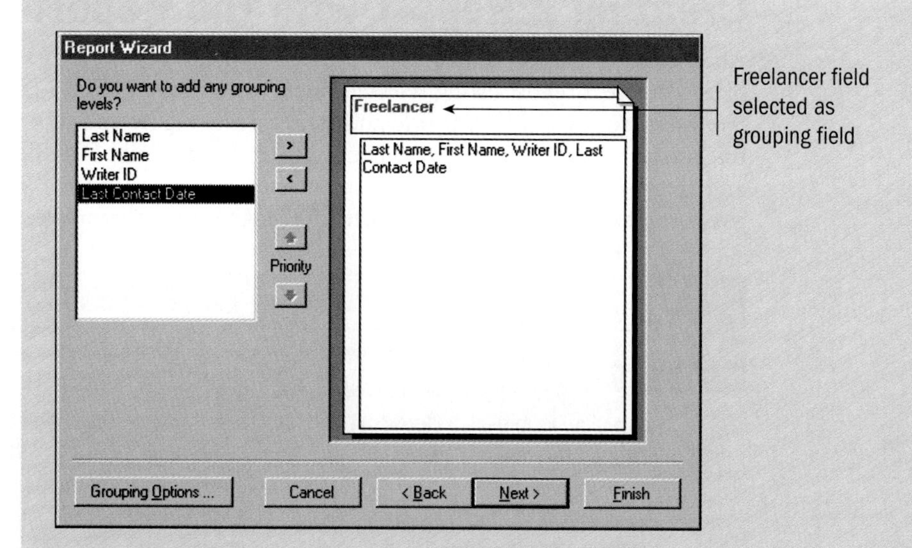

Click the Next > button to display the next Report Wizard dialog box.

This dialog box allows you to select the sort order for records within groups. Elena decides to sort the records by the Last Name field.

5. Click the first **sort order** list arrow to display the field list, then click **Last Name** to select sorting by the Last Name field. See Figure 6-7.

Figure 6-7 Selecting the sort order

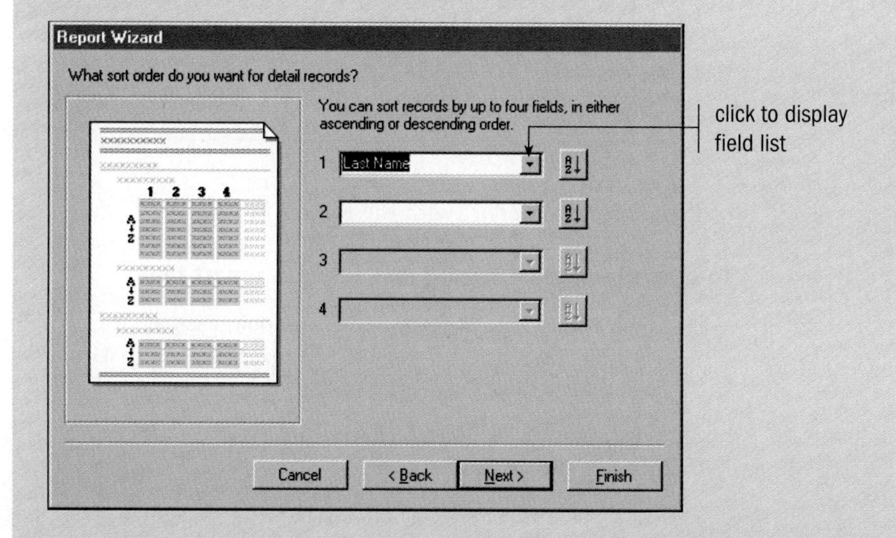

6. Click the Next > button to display the next Report Wizard dialog box. This dialog box allows you to select from several predefined layouts for the report. "Layout" refers to the physical placement of fields, titles, page numbers, and other objects on the report page. The sample box on the left displays the selected layout. Elena clicks different layout radio buttons to view the samples and decides on the layout called Outline 1.

7. If necessary, click the **Outline 1** radio button to select this layout. Make sure that the Portrait orientation radio button is selected and that the check box next to "Adjust field width so all fields fit on a page" is checked, then click the Next > button to display the next Report Wizard dialog box.

This dialog box allows you to select a predefined style for the report. "Style" refers to the use of color, fonts, and other formatting options applied to objects on the report page.

8. If necessary, click **Corporate** to select the Corporate style, then click the Next > button to display the next Report Wizard dialog box.

   This dialog box allows you to specify a title for the report. This title will appear at the top of the printed report and will also appear as the name of the report in the Reports list in the Database window.

9. Type **Freelancer/Staff Writer Report** in the text box. Make sure the radio button next to "Preview the report" is selected, then click the **Finish** button. The Report Wizard closes and the report is displayed in the Print Preview window. See Figure 6-8.

Figure 6-8 The completed report in the Print Preview window

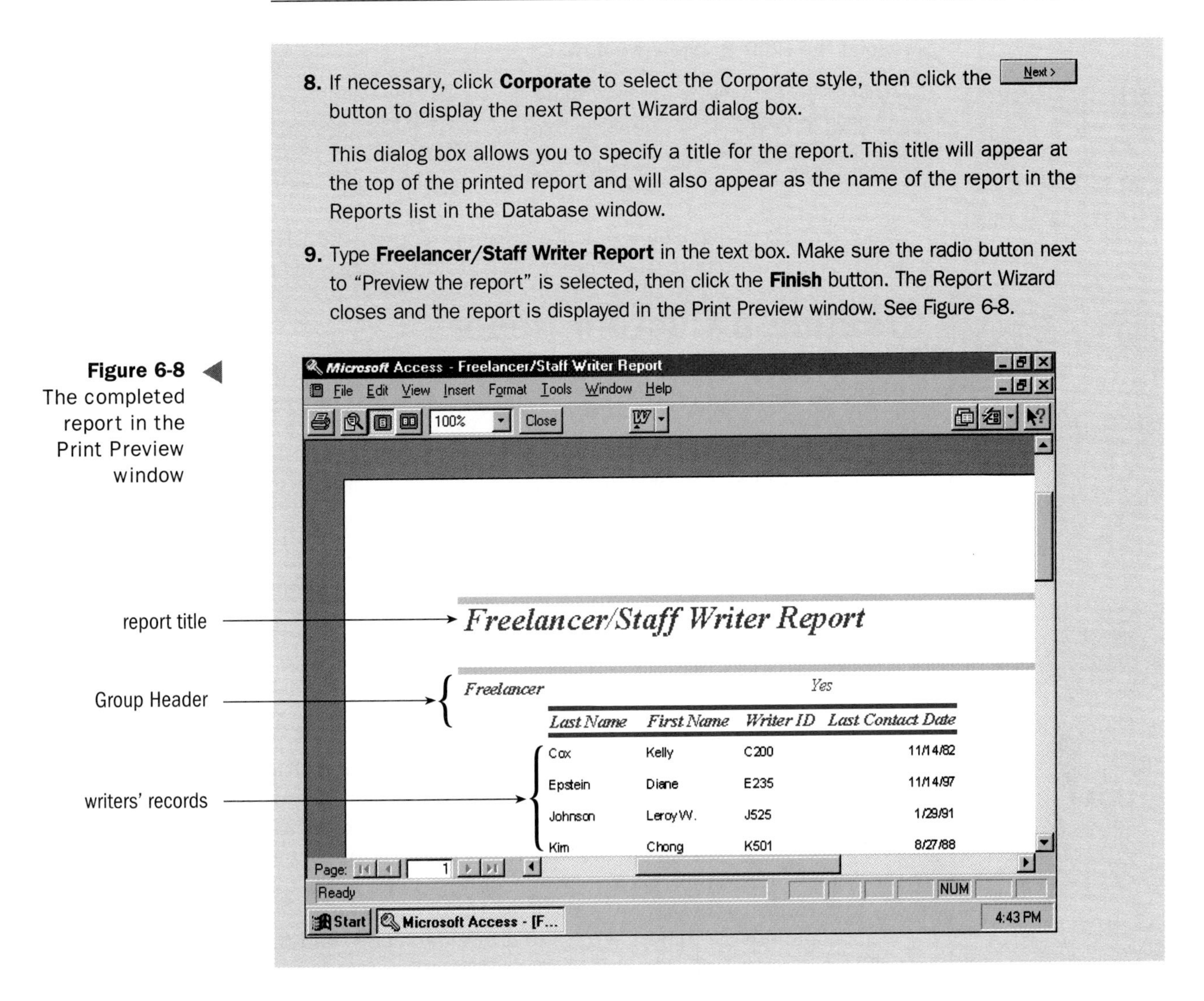

Access displays the report title at the top of the report page. Lines are used to separate the title from the rest of the report page. Since the records are grouped by the value in the Freelancer field, there is a Group Header for each group. The header consists of the label Freelancer and the value of the Freelancer field (Yes or No) for the group. The Group Header also includes labels for the columns in the Detail section. Remember that the default label is the field name or Caption property for that field.

Below each Group Header are column headings and the detail records for that group, in ascending order by the Last Name field. You can use the elevator bar and horizontal scroll bar to view the other records in the report. At the bottom of the page is the Page Footer, which contains the date of the report and page number for each page. Since all of the WRITERS records fit on one page, there is only one page for this report.

Printing a Report

Next, Elena prints the report from the Print Preview window.

To print the report from the Print Preview window:

1. Make sure your printer is on-line and ready to print. Click the **Print** button on the toolbar. Access prints the report.

Elena closes the Print Preview window. Since this report was created by the Report Wizard, Access has already saved the report, using the report title as the report name.

To close the Print Preview window:

1. Click the Print Preview window **Close** button ☒. The Print Preview window closes and the Database window becomes the active window. The new report appears in the Reports list.

Now that Elena has some practice creating reports, she is ready to begin work on Harold's requested report. She meets with Harold to discuss his requirements.

Creating a Custom Report

Elena and Harold discuss his report requirements and decide that the report for his meeting with the advertisers should contain the following four different report sections:

- A Page Header section that shows the current date, report title, page number, and column headings for each field.
- A Detail section that lists the title, type, and length of each article, and the name of the writer. Records should be grouped by the Type field value and the groups printed in ascending order. Within each group, records should appear in descending order based on the Article Length field.
- A Group Footer section that prints subtotals of the Article Length field for each Type group.
- A Report Footer section that prints the overall total of the Article Length field.

The report will not include Report Header, Group Header, or Page Footer sections.

From her work with AutoReport and the Report Wizard, Elena knows that, by default, Access places the report title in the Report Header section and the date and page number in the Page Footer section. Harold prefers all three items at the top of each page, so Elena needs to place that information in the Page Header section.

Elena could use the Report Wizard to create the report, and then modify the report to match her report design. The Report Wizard would construct the majority of the report, so Elena would save time and reduce the possibility for errors. However, Elena decides to create a custom report using the Report Design window so that she can control the precise placement of fields and labels and become more skilled at constructing reports.

If you modify a report created by AutoReport or the Report Wizard, or if you design and create your own report, you produce a **custom report**. You should create a custom report whenever AutoReport or the Report Wizard cannot automatically create the specific report you need.

Designing a Custom Report

Before she creates the custom report, Elena first plans the report's contents and appearance. Elena's completed design is shown in Figure 6-9. The Page Header section contains the report title, Article Type Report, and below that, descriptive column heads. The Page Header section also contains the current date and page number on the same line as the report title.

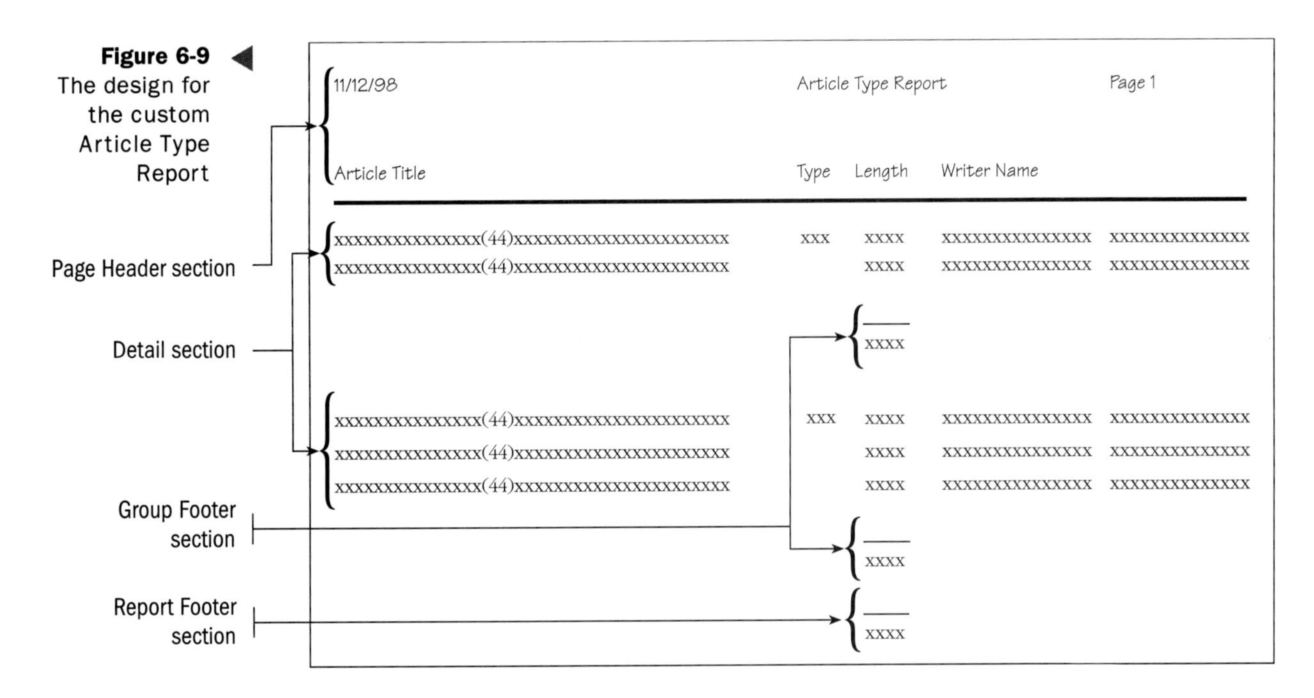

Figure 6-9 The design for the custom Article Type Report

In the Detail section, Elena indicates the locations and lengths of the field values by a series of X's. The three X's under the Type field label indicate that the field value will be three characters wide. The Type field value will appear only with the first record of a group.

The subtotals for each group will appear in the Group Footer section, and an overall total will appear in the Report Footer section. Article Length is the only field for which totals will appear.

The data for a report can come either from a single table or from a query based on one or more tables. Elena's report will contain data from the WRITERS and BUSINESS ARTICLES tables; therefore, she must use a query for this report. She will use the Article Type Query she created earlier because it contains the fields she needs from the two tables.

The Report Design Window

Elena's first step is to create a blank report in the Report Design window. You use the Report Design window to create and modify reports.

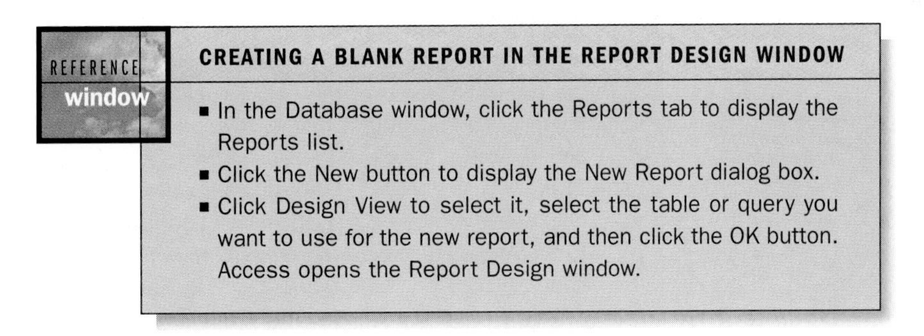
REFERENCE window

CREATING A BLANK REPORT IN THE REPORT DESIGN WINDOW

- In the Database window, click the Reports tab to display the Reports list.
- Click the New button to display the New Report dialog box.
- Click Design View to select it, select the table or query you want to use for the new report, and then click the OK button. Access opens the Report Design window.

Elena creates a blank report.

To create a blank report in the Report Design window:

1. If necessary, click the **Reports** tab to display the Reports list then click the **New** button to open the New Report dialog box.
2. If necessary, click **Design View** to select it, then click the **text box** list arrow to display the list of Issue25 database tables and queries.
3. Click **Article Type Query** to select it, then click the **OK** button. The Report Design window opens.

The Report Design window has several components in common with the Form Design window. The toolbar for both windows has a Properties button, a Field List button, and a Toolbox button. Both windows also have horizontal and vertical rulers, a grid, and a format toolbar.

The Report Design window displays one new toolbar button, the Sorting and Grouping button. Recall that to display records in a specific order for a form, you use a filter. In reports, you use the **Sorting and Grouping button** to establish sort keys and grouping fields. A maximum of 10 fields can serve as sort keys, and any number of these can be grouping fields.

Unlike the Form Design window, which initially displays only the Detail section on a blank form, the Report Design window also displays a Page Header section and a Page Footer section. Reports often contain these sections, so Access automatically includes them in a blank report.

Adding Fields to a Report

Elena's first task is to add bound controls to the report Detail section for all the fields from the Article Type Query. You use bound controls to print field values from a table or query on a report, and add them to a report the same way you added them to a form. In fact, every task that you accomplished in the Form Design window is done in a similar way in the Report Design window.

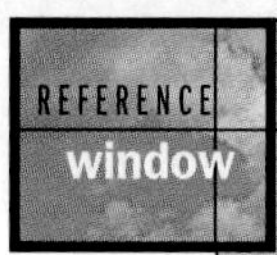

ADDING FIELDS TO A REPORT

- In the Report Design window, click the Field List button on the toolbar to display the field list.
- To place all fields in the report, double-click the field list title bar to highlight all the fields in the field list. Then click anywhere in the highlighted area of the field list and drag to the report. Release the mouse button when the pointer is correctly positioned. Access places all the field in the report.
- To place a single field in the report, place the pointer on the field name in the field list, then click and drag the field name to the report. Release the mouse button when the pointer is correctly positioned. Access places the field in the report.

Elena begins her custom report.

To open the field list box and add bound controls for all the fields in the field list:

1. Click the **Field List** button on the toolbar. The field list box opens. See Figure 6-10.

Figure 6-10 The blank Report Design window

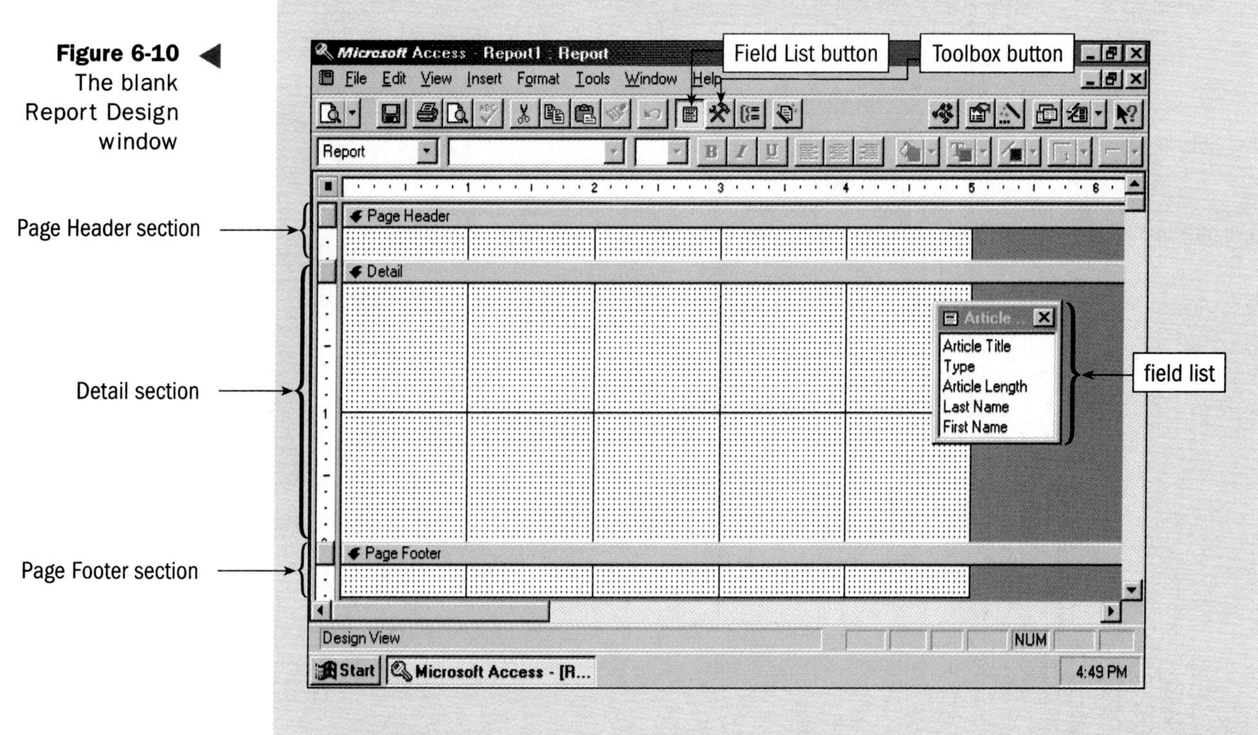

TROUBLE? If the rulers or grid do not appear, click View on the menu bar and then click Ruler or Grid to display the missing component in the Report Design window. A check mark appears in front of these components when they are displayed in the Report Design window. If the grid is still invisible, see your technical support person or instructor for assistance.

If the toolbox is visible, click the Close button for the toolbox to hide it.

2. Double-click the **field list** title bar to highlight all the fields in the Article Type Query field list.

3. Click anywhere in the highlighted area of the field list and drag to the report Detail section. Release the mouse button when the is positioned at the top of the Detail section and at the 1.25" mark on the horizontal ruler. Access resizes the Detail Section and adds bound controls for the five selected fields. Each bound control consists of a text box and, to its left, an attached label. See Figure 6-11. Notice that the text boxes align at the 1.25" mark.

Figure 6-11 Bound controls added to a report

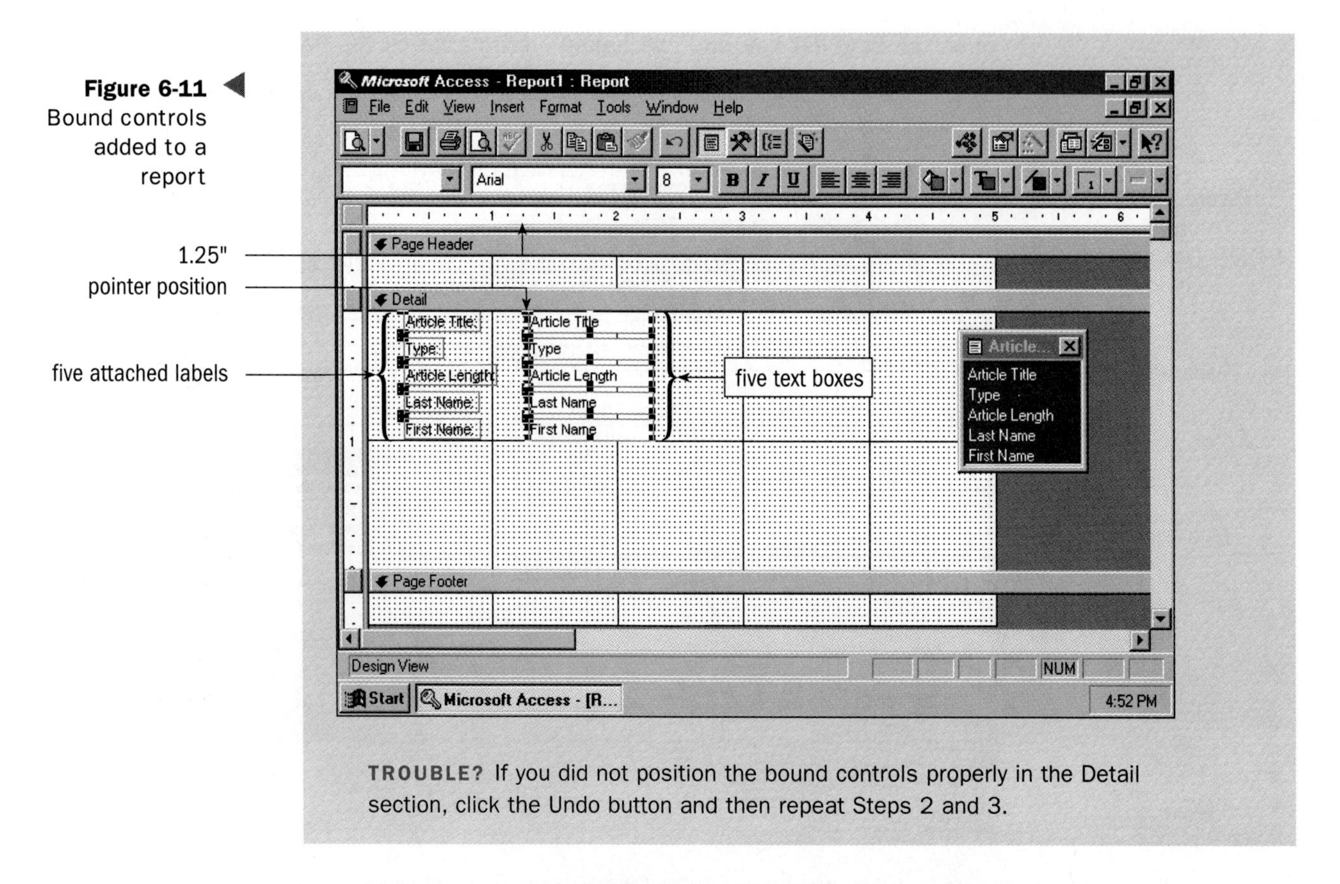

TROUBLE? If you did not position the bound controls properly in the Detail section, click the Undo button and then repeat Steps 2 and 3.

Performing operations in the Report Design window will become easier with practice. Remember, you can always click the Undo button immediately after you make a report design change that has undesired results. You can also click the toolbar Print Preview button at any time to view your progress on the report. Recall that you return to the Report Design window by clicking the Print Preview window Close button on the toolbar.

Using Controls

Five text boxes now appear in a column in the Detail section. Each text box is a bound control linked to a field in the underlying query and has, to its left, an attached label box. Because she is done with the field list box, Elena closes it by clicking the Close button on the field list box. Elena next compares the report Detail section with her design. She needs to move all the label boxes to the Page Header section, and then reposition the label boxes and text boxes so that they agree with her report design.

To close the field list and move all label boxes to the Page Header section:

1. Click the **Close** button on the field list box to close the field list.
2. Click anywhere in the Page Footer section to deselect the five text boxes and their attached label boxes. While pressing and holding the **Shift** key, click each of the five label boxes in the Detail section, then release the Shift key. This action selects all the label boxes in preparation for cutting them from the Detail section and pasting them in the Page Header section.
3. Position the pointer in any one of the selected label boxes. The pointer turns to . Click the right mouse button to display the shortcut menu.
4. Click **Cut** in the shortcut menu to delete the label boxes from the Detail section and place them in the Windows Clipboard. See Figure 6-12.

Figure 6-12
Label boxes cut from the Detail section

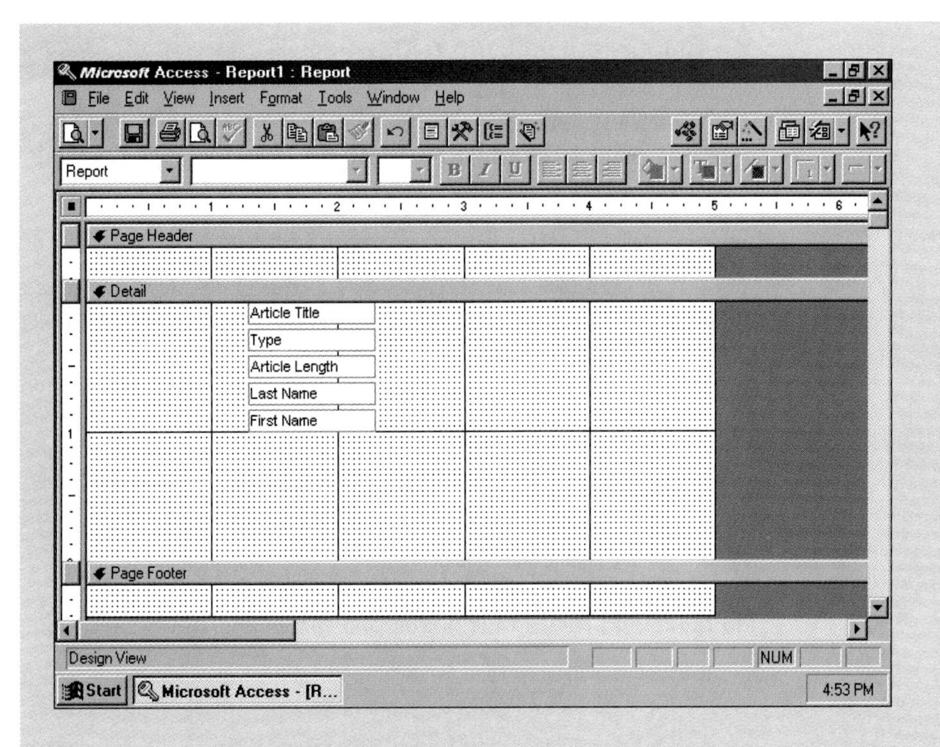

TROUBLE? If you selected both the label boxes and the text boxes, click Undo and repeat Steps 2 through 4, selecting only the label boxes.

5. Click anywhere in the Page Header section, click the right mouse button in the Page Header section to open the shortcut menu, and then click **Paste**. Access pastes all the label boxes from the Windows Clipboard into the Page Header section and automatically resizes that section to display the label boxes. See Figure 6-13.

Figure 6-13
Label boxes pasted in the Page Header section

pasted labels

Page Header section automatically resized

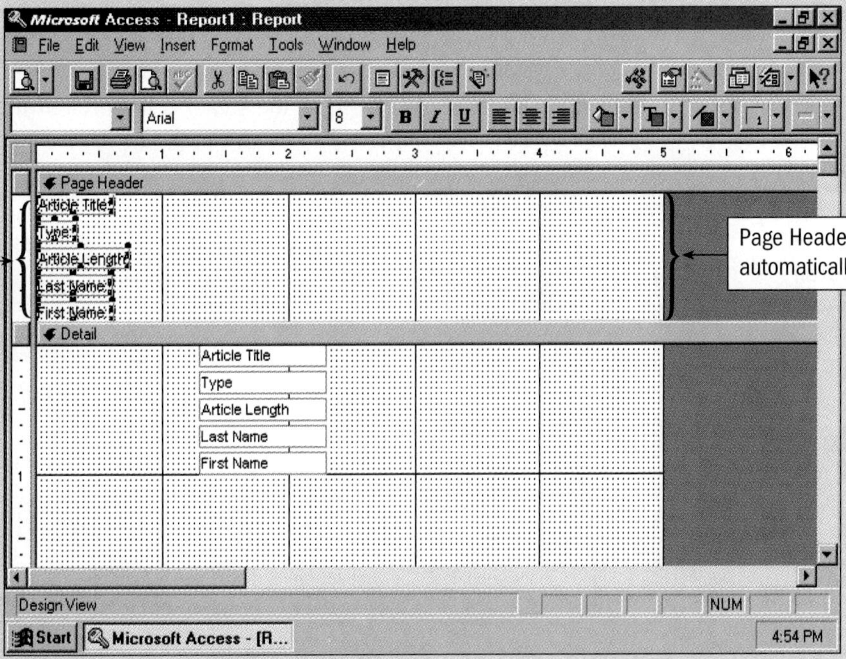

Moving the label boxes has unlinked them from their attached text boxes. You can now select and move either a label box or a text box, but not both at once.

Moving and Resizing Controls

Elena needs to reposition the text boxes and label boxes. She first drags the Article Title text box to the left into the corner of the Detail section and resizes it. She then moves and resizes the other four text boxes and resizes the Detail section.

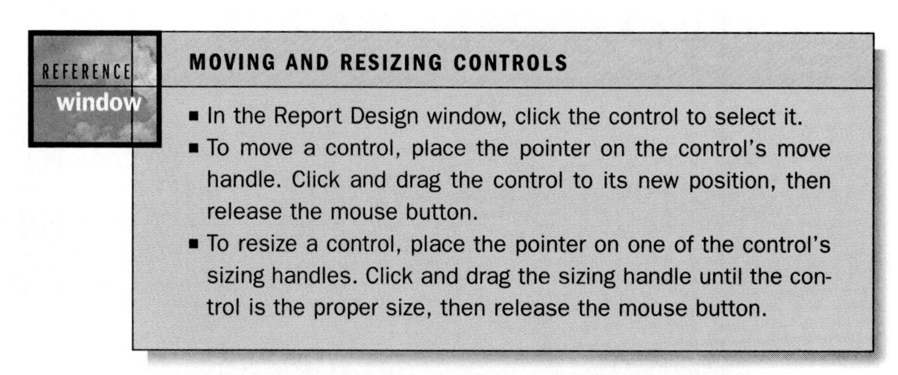

REFERENCE window

MOVING AND RESIZING CONTROLS

- In the Report Design window, click the control to select it.
- To move a control, place the pointer on the control's move handle. Click and drag the control to its new position, then release the mouse button.
- To resize a control, place the pointer on one of the control's sizing handles. Click and drag the sizing handle until the control is the proper size, then release the mouse button.

To move and resize text boxes and resize the Detail section:

1. Click the **Article Title** field-value text box in the Detail section, move the pointer to the move handle in the upper-left corner of the field-value text box, and drag to the upper-left corner of the Detail section.
2. Next, move the pointer to the middle sizing handle on the right side of the Article Title field-value text box. When the pointer changes to ↔, drag the right border horizontally to the right, to the 2.5" mark on the horizontal ruler.
3. Use the same procedure to move and resize each of the other four field-value text boxes in the Detail section, using the sketch of the report design (See Figure 6-9) as a guide.
4. If necessary, scroll down to display the bottom edge of the Detail section. Move the pointer to the bottom edge of the Detail section. When the pointer changes to ✛, drag the bottom edge upward to align with the bottom of the field-value text boxes. If necessary, scroll up to display the top of the report. See Figure 6-14. When the Detail section height is the same as the text-box height, the lines in the Detail section of the report will be single spaced.

Figure 6-14 ◀ Field-value text boxes moved and Detail section resized

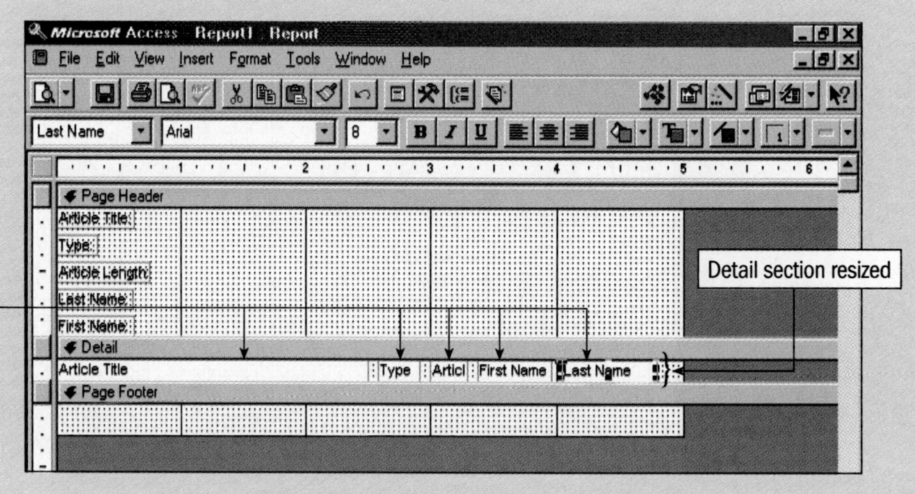

TROUBLE? If Access widens the report too much while you are moving and resizing the text boxes, wait until you are finished with these operations and then reduce the width of the report. To reduce the report's width, start by moving the pointer to the right edge of the Detail section. When the pointer changes to ✛, drag the right edge to the left to narrow the report's width to 5".

Next, Elena deletes the First Name label and changes the Caption property for all other labels in the Page Header section.

Deleting Controls

To match her report design, Elena must change the Last Name Caption property to Writer Name and the Article Length Caption property to Length. She also deletes the colons in the Caption properties for the Article Title label and the Type label.

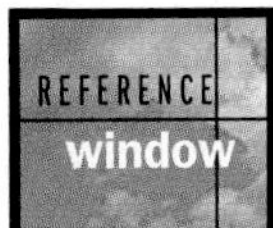

DELETING CONTROLS

- In the Report Design window, click the control to select it.
- With the pointer on the control, click the right mouse button to display the shortcut menu.
- Click Cut to delete the control.

Elena makes these changes now.

To delete a label and change label Caption properties:

1. Move the pointer to the First Name label box, then click the right mouse button to open the shortcut menu, and then click **Cut** to delete the First Name label box.
2. Move the pointer to the Last Name label box, then click the right mouse button to display the shortcut menu, and then click **Properties** to display the property sheet for the Last Name label. If necessary, click the **Format** tab to display the Format page of the property sheet. The Caption property value is selected.
3. Type **Writer Name** to replace the Caption property value.
4. Click the **Article Length** label box to select it. The property sheet changes to show the properties for the Article Length field. Click the **Caption** text box in the property sheet, press the **F2** key to select the caption property value, and then type **Length**.
5. Click the **Type** label box to select it. Click near the end of the Caption text box in the property sheet and press the **Backspace** key to remove the colon from the caption.
6. Use the same procedure to remove the colon from the caption in the Article Title label box.
7. Click the property sheet **Close** button ☒ to close the property sheet.

After checking her report design, Elena realizes she needs to resize the Length and Writer Name label boxes and rearrange the label boxes in the Page Header section.

To resize and move labels:

1. Click in an unoccupied area of the grid to deselect the Article Title label box. While holding down the **Shift** key, click the **Length** label box and then click the **Writer Name** label box to select both of them.
2. Click **Format**, point to **Size**, and then click **to Fit**. Access resizes the two label boxes to fit around the captions.
3. Individually select and move each of the label boxes in the Page Header section, following the sketched report design. See Figure 6-15.

Figure 6-15 Label boxes resized and positioned above their field-value text boxes

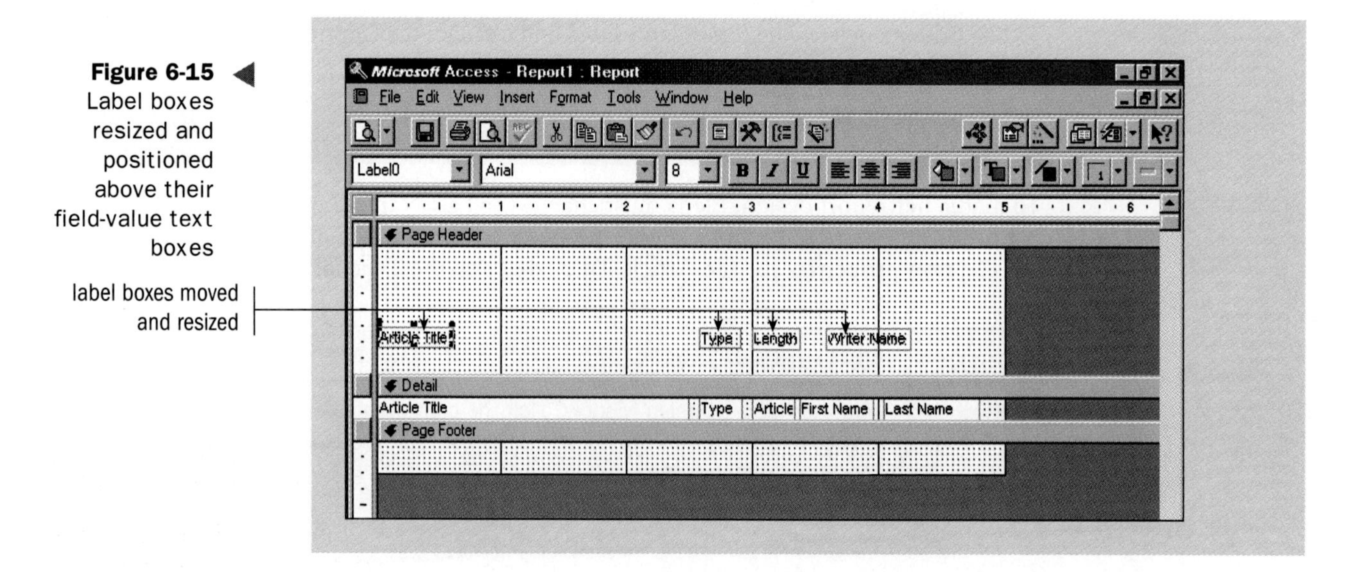

Elena has made many modifications to the report design, so she saves the report before proceeding.

To save the report design:

1. Click the **Save** button on the toolbar. Access displays the Save As dialog box.
2. Type **Article Type Report** in the Report Name text box, then click the **OK** button. The dialog box closes and Access saves the report.

If you want to take a break and resume the tutorial at a later time, exit Access by clicking the Access window Close button. When you resume the tutorial, open the Issue25 database, and select Article Type Report in the Reports list. Click the Design button to open the Report Design window and maximize the window.

Quick Check

1. What are the seven Access report sections?
2. What types of reports can AutoReport create and what is the difference between them?
3. What is a group?
4. Why is it not necessary to save manually a report created by the Report Wizard?
5. What is a custom report?
6. What does the Report Design window have in common with the Form Design window? What is different?
7. In the Report Design window, how is adding, moving, resizing, and deleting controls different from accomplishing these tasks in the Form Design window?

SESSION 6.2

In this session, you will add a title, a page number and date, and a Report Footer. You will also sort and group records, add a Group Footer, calculate group and overall totals, and hide duplicate values in a report.

Adding a Title, Date, and Page Number to a Report

To match her design, Elena must also include a report title, date, and page number in the Page Header section. She does these tasks next.

Adding a Title to a Report

Elena's report design includes the title Article Type Report. She places this report title in the Page Header section using the toolbox Label tool. To make the report title stand out, Elena will increase the report title font size from 8, the default, to 10 (the default typeface is Arial).

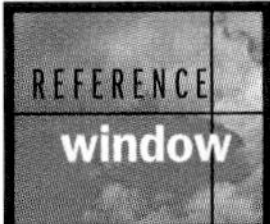

ADDING A LABEL TO THE REPORT

- In the Report Design window, click the toolbox Label tool.
- Move the pointer to the position in the report where you want to place the label, then click to place the label.
- Type the label text, then press the Enter key.

To add a report title to the Page Header section and change the font size:

1. Click the **Toolbox** button on the toolbar to display the toolbox.
2. Click the **toolbox Label** button.
3. Move the pointer into the Page Header section. As you move the pointer into the report, the pointer changes to +A. Click the left mouse button when the pointer's plus symbol (+) is positioned at the top of the Page Header section at the 2" mark on the horizontal ruler. Access places a narrow text box in the Page Header section.
4. Type **Article Type Report** and then press the **Enter** key. See Figure 6-16.

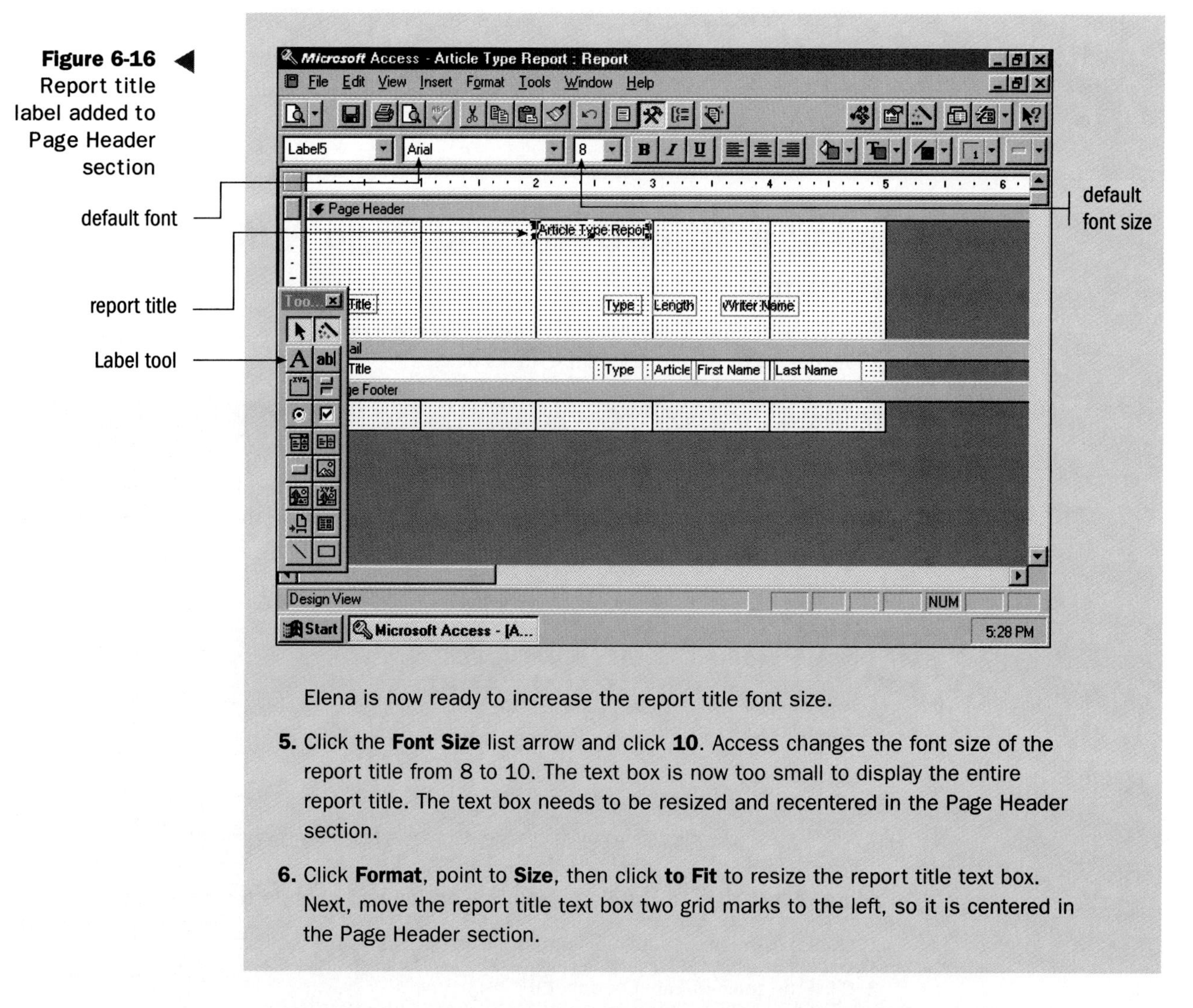

Figure 6-16 Report title label added to Page Header section

Elena is now ready to increase the report title font size.

5. Click the **Font Size** list arrow and click **10**. Access changes the font size of the report title from 8 to 10. The text box is now too small to display the entire report title. The text box needs to be resized and recentered in the Page Header section.

6. Click **Format**, point to **Size**, then click **to Fit** to resize the report title text box. Next, move the report title text box two grid marks to the left, so it is centered in the Page Header section.

Next, Elena adds a text box to the Page Header section in which she will insert the Date function.

Adding a Date to a Report

You use the toolbox Text Box tool to add a text box with an attached label to a report or form. Text boxes are most often used to contain bound controls or calculated controls. In this case, the text box will contain the Date function, which is a type of calculated control. It will print the current date each time the report is generated.

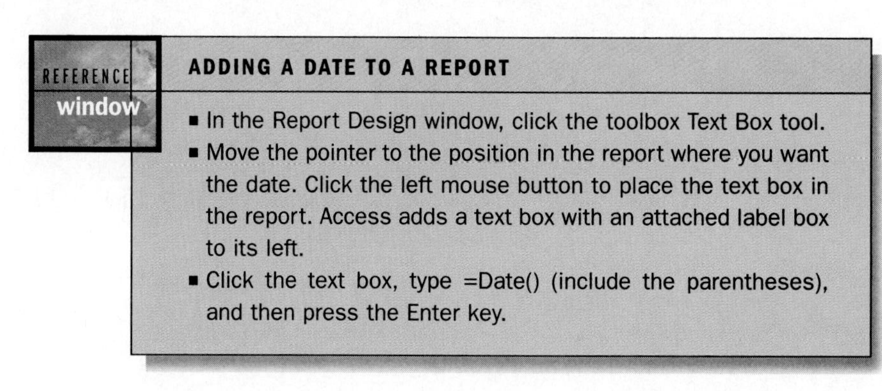

REFERENCE window

ADDING A DATE TO A REPORT

- In the Report Design window, click the toolbox Text Box tool.
- Move the pointer to the position in the report where you want the date. Click the left mouse button to place the text box in the report. Access adds a text box with an attached label box to its left.
- Click the text box, type =Date() (include the parentheses), and then press the Enter key.

Elena adds the date to the Page Header section.

To use the Text Box tool to add the Date function:

1. Click the **toolbox Text Box** button. Move the pointer into the Page Header section. As you move the pointer into the report, the pointer changes to. Click the left mouse button when the pointer's plus (+) symbol is positioned at the top of the Page Header section just to the right of the .75" mark on the horizontal ruler. Access adds a text box with an attached label box to its left. Inside the text box is the description Unbound.
2. Click the **Unbound** text box, type **=Date()** (type the left and right parentheses), and then press the **Enter** key. See Figure 6-17.

Figure 6-17 Current date added to a report

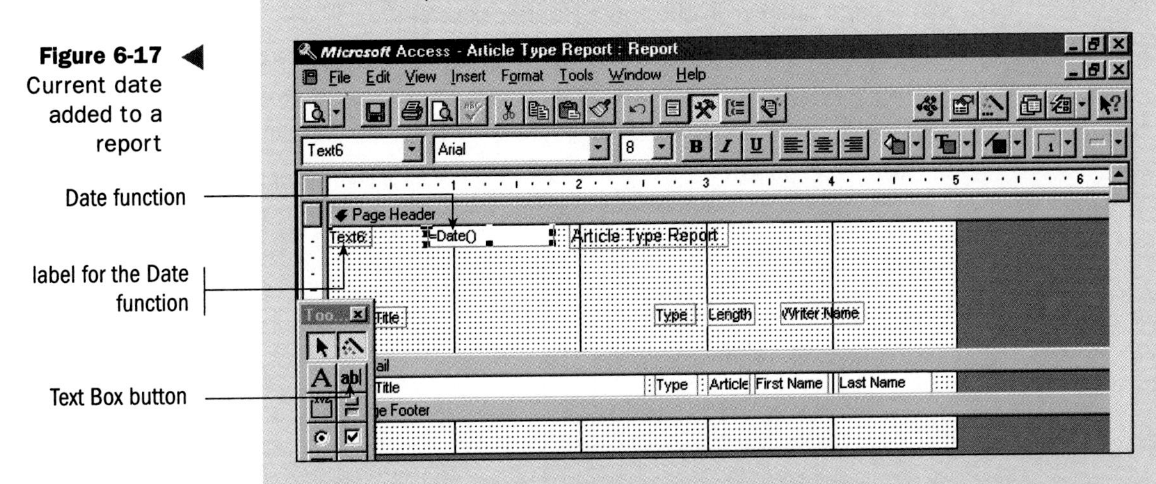

TROUBLE? If your text box and attached label box are too close together, resize and reposition the text box using Figure 6-17 as a guide. The attached label box on your screen might have a Caption other than the one shown (such as "Text7"), depending on the exact way you completed previous steps. This causes no problem.

When Access prints your report, the current date replaces the Date function you entered in the Unbound text box. Because a current date in a Page Header section does not usually need a label, Elena deletes the label box. She then changes the Date text box to font size 10 and moves it to the upper-left corner of the Page Header section.

3. Position the pointer on the Date label box, which is located in the upper-left corner of the Page Header section. Click the right mouse button to open the shortcut menu and then click **Cut** to delete the label.
4. Click the **Date** text box and then drag its move handle to the upper-left corner of the Page Header section.
5. Click the **Font Size** list arrow and click **10** to change the font size of the Date text box.

Elena is now ready to complete her report's Page Header section by adding page numbers.

Adding Page Numbers to a Report

Elena adds the page number to the upper-right corner of the Page Header section. The page number function automatically prints the correct page number on each page of a report.

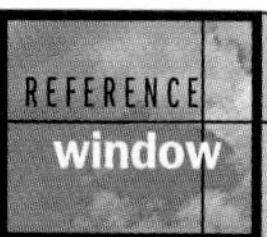

ADDING PAGE NUMBERS TO A REPORT

- In the Report Design window, click in the section where you want to place the page numbers.
- Click Insert, then click Page Number to display the Page Numbers dialog box.
- Select the formatting, position, and alignment options you want.
- Click the OK button to place the page number in the report.

To add a page number in the Page Header section:

1. Click **Insert**, then click **Page Number** to display the Page Numbers dialog box. Make sure that the Page N radio button is selected in the Format panel and that the Top of Page [Header] radio button is selected in the Position panel.

2. Click the **Alignment** list arrow to display the list of alignment options, then click **Right**. Make sure that the Show Number on First Page check box is checked. See Figure 6-18.

Figure 6-18 Completed Page Numbers dialog box

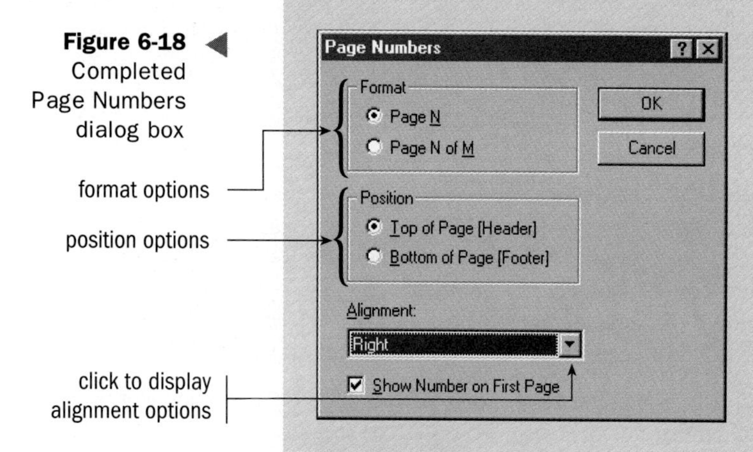

3. Click the **OK** button to place the page number in the report. Access adds a text box to the upper-right corner of the Page Header section. See Figure 6-19. The value ="Page" & [Page] means that, when it is printed, the report will show the word "Page" followed by the page number.

Figure 6-19 Page property added to the Report Design window

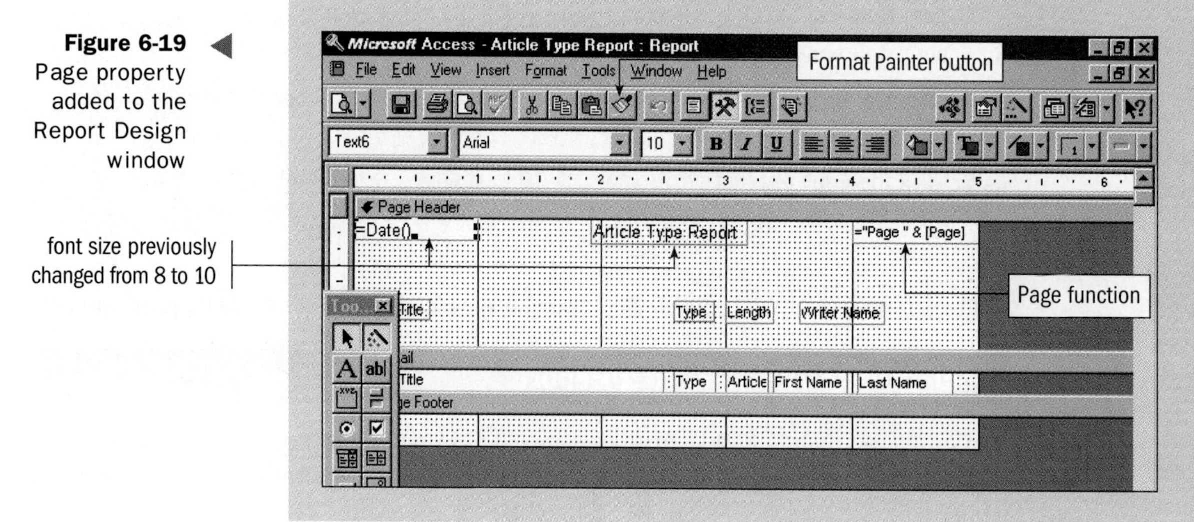

Elena wants to change the Page Number text box to font size 10 to match the date and report title. To duplicate the formatting of the Date text box, she can use the Format Painter. The Format Painter allows you to copy the format of an object to other objects in the report. This makes it easy to create several objects having the same font style and size, the same color, and the same special effect.

To use the Format Painter to format the Page Number text box:

1. If necessary, click the **Date** text box to select it.
2. Click the **Format Painter** button on the toolbar. The Format Painter button appears indented.
3. Click the **Page Number** text box. The Format Painter automatically formats the Page Number text box like the Date text box (with a font size of 10) and resizes the text box to fit. The label ="Page" & [Page] is now larger than the text box, but the actual page number will fit when the report is printed. Notice that after you use the Format Painter, the Format Painter button is no longer indented, meaning it is inactive.

Now that Elena has completed the Page Header section of her report, she switches to the Print Preview window to check the appearance of the report against her design.

To view a report in the Print Preview window:

1. Click the **Print Preview** button on the toolbar to open the Print Preview window. See Figure 6-20.

Figure 6-20 A custom report in the Print Preview window

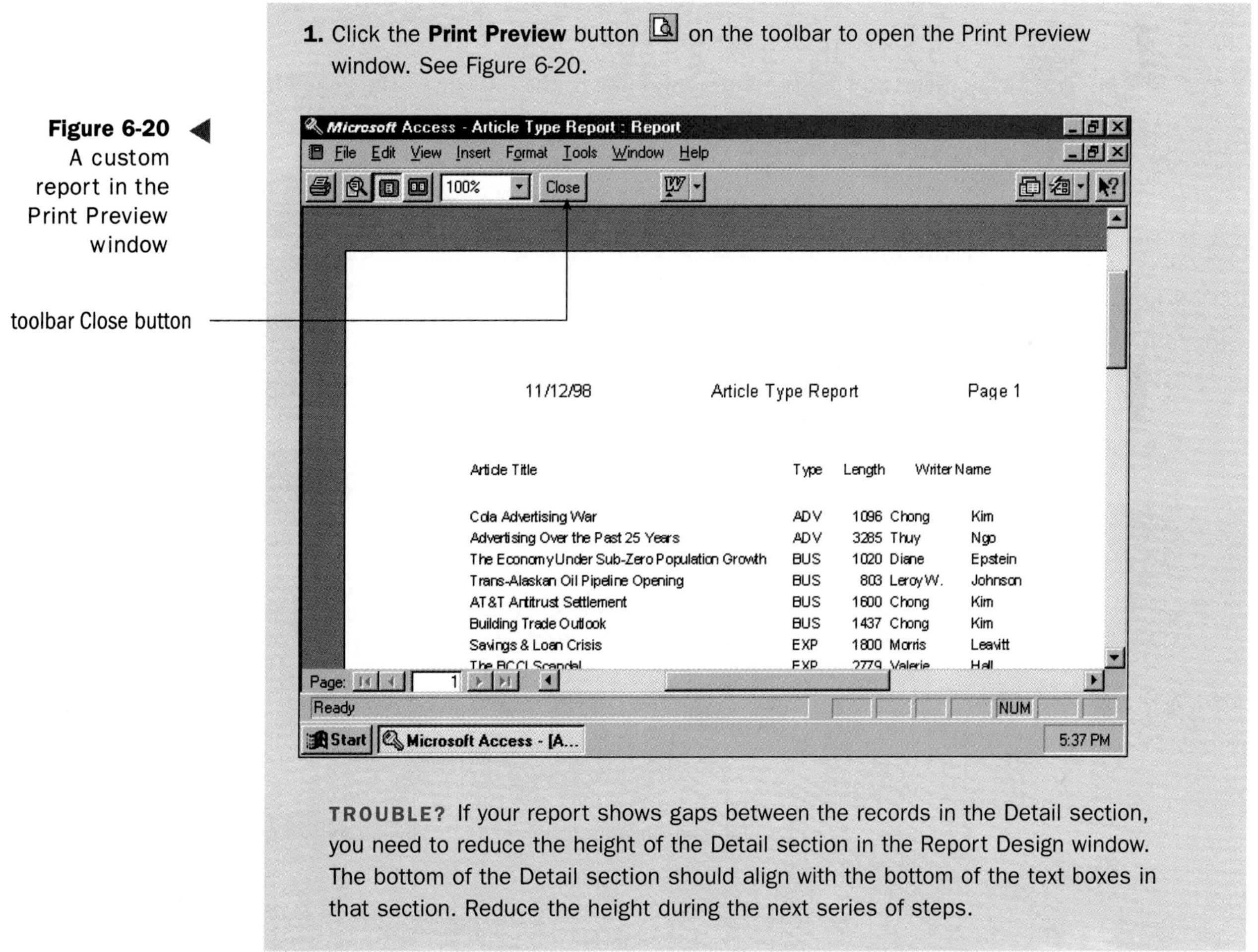

TROUBLE? If your report shows gaps between the records in the Detail section, you need to reduce the height of the Detail section in the Report Design window. The bottom of the Detail section should align with the bottom of the text boxes in that section. Reduce the height during the next series of steps.

Adding Lines to a Report

Looking at her report, Elena decides to reposition the column heading labels just below the report title line and decrease the height of the Page Header section. She also decides to add a horizontal line to the Page Header section below the column heads.

To move labels and decrease the Page Header section height:

1. Click the toolbar **Close** button to close the Print Preview window and return to the Report Design window.
2. Click in the Page Header section, but not on any object, to deselect the Date text box. While pressing and holding down the **Shift** key, click each of the four label boxes in the Page Header section to select them. When the pointer changes to ✋, drag the label boxes up so they are positioned just below the report title. Position the labels so that the top of each label box is at the .25" mark on the vertical ruler.

   TROUBLE? If the label boxes do not move, the Page Number text box is probably selected along with the label boxes. Click in any unoccupied portion of the Page Header section to deselect all boxes, then repeat Step 2.
3. Move the pointer to the bottom edge of the Page Header section. When the pointer changes to ✛, drag the bottom edge upward to reduce the height of the Page Header section. Align the bottom edge with the grid marks that are just below the .5" mark on the vertical ruler.

Elena now adds a horizontal line to the bottom of the Page Header section to separate it visually from the Detail section when the report is printed. You use the toolbox Line tool to add a line to a report or form.

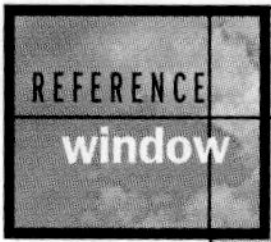

ADDING A LINE TO A REPORT

- In the Report Design window, click the toolbox Line button on the toolbox.
- Move the pointer to position one end of the line.
- Click and hold the left mouse button, drag the pointer to the position of the other end of the line, and then release the mouse button.

To add a line to a report:

1. Click the **toolbox Line** button ⧅. Move the pointer into the Page Header section; the pointer changes to +╲. Position the pointer's plus (+) symbol at the left edge of the Page Header section just below the column headings.
2. Click and hold the left mouse button, drag a horizontal line from left to right, ending just after the 4.25" mark on the horizontal ruler, and then release the mouse button.

   Elena views the line and decides to increase its thickness to make it stand out more.
3. To increase the thickness of the line, position the pointer on the line, click the right mouse button to display the shortcut menu, then click **Properties** to display the property sheet. The Border Width property controls width, or thickness, of lines.

4. Click the **Border Width** text box in the property sheet, then click the **Border Width** list arrow that appears, and then click **3 pt**. The line's width increases to 3 points. See Figure 6-21.

Figure 6-21 Changing the width of a line

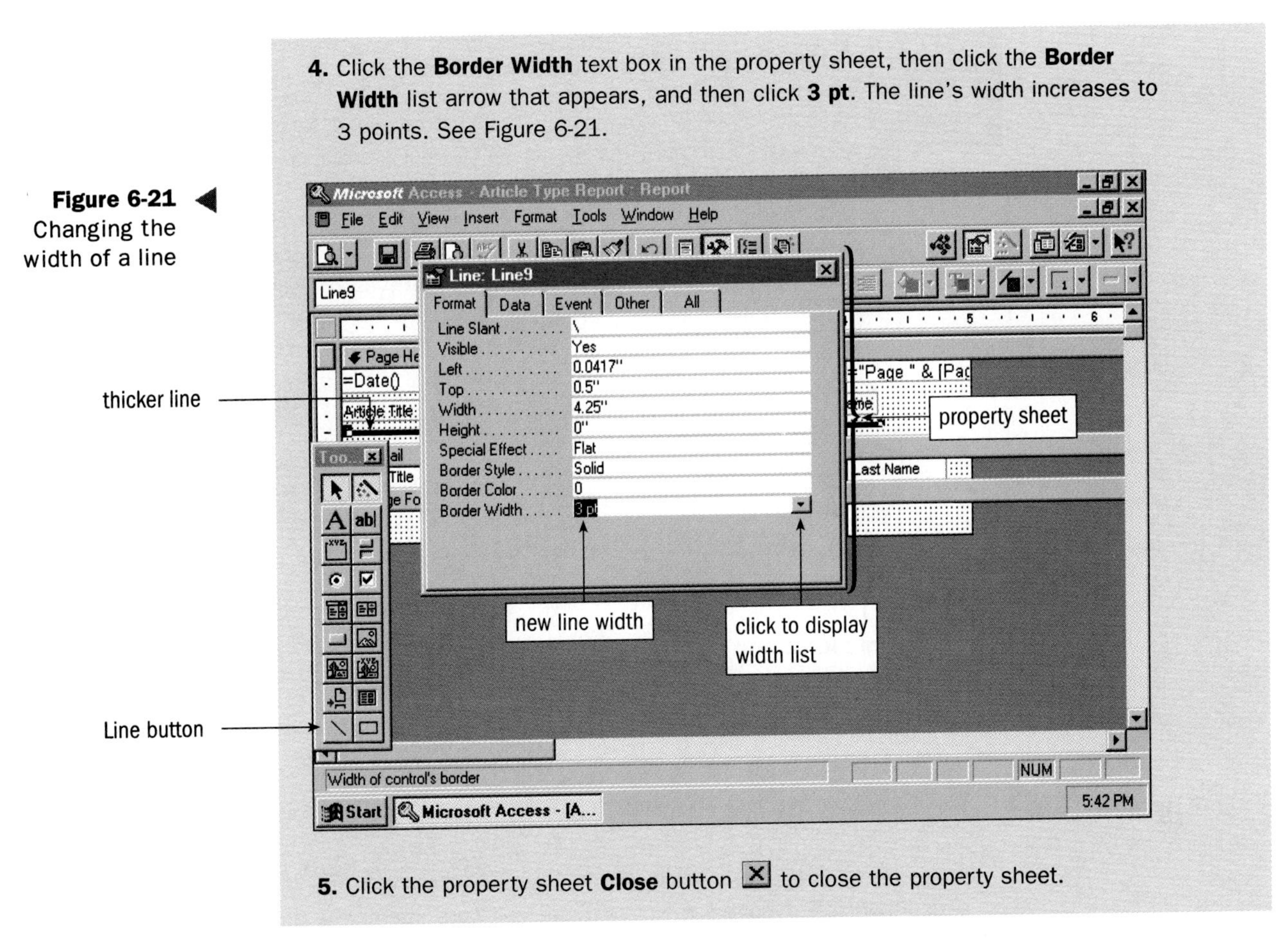

5. Click the property sheet **Close** button to close the property sheet.

Elena has finished formatting the Page Header section. She decides to save her report before she chooses the sort fields and the grouping field for the report.

To save the report:

1. Click the **Save** button on the toolbar. Access saves the report design.

Sorting and Grouping Data in a Report

Elena wants Access to print records in ascending order based on the Type field and to print subtotals for each set of Type field values. The Type field is both the primary sort key and the grouping field. Elena wants the records within a Type to be printed in descending order based on the Article Length field. This makes Article Length the secondary sort key.

You use the Sorting and Grouping button on the toolbar to select sort keys and grouping fields. Each report can have up to 10 sort fields, and any of the sort fields can also be grouping fields.

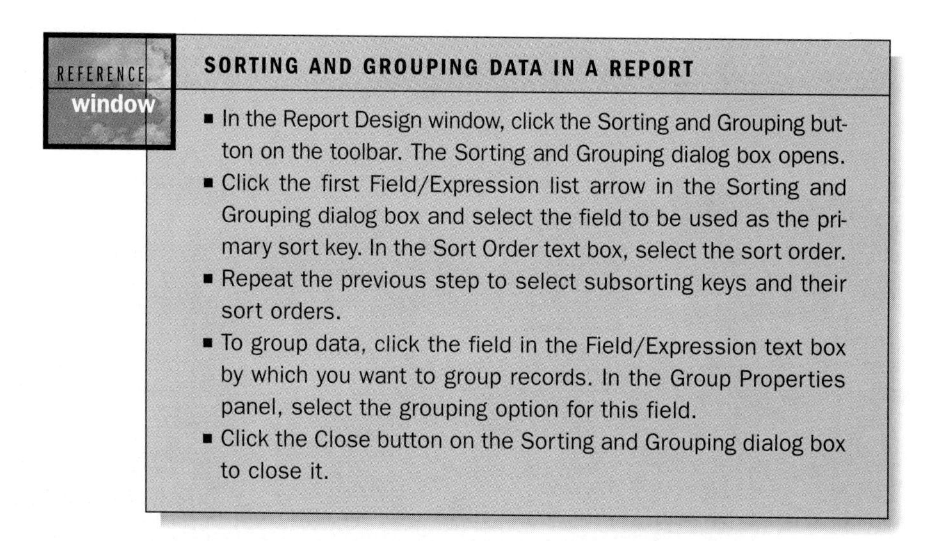

REFERENCE window

SORTING AND GROUPING DATA IN A REPORT

- In the Report Design window, click the Sorting and Grouping button on the toolbar. The Sorting and Grouping dialog box opens.
- Click the first Field/Expression list arrow in the Sorting and Grouping dialog box and select the field to be used as the primary sort key. In the Sort Order text box, select the sort order.
- Repeat the previous step to select subsorting keys and their sort orders.
- To group data, click the field in the Field/Expression text box by which you want to group records. In the Group Properties panel, select the grouping option for this field.
- Click the Close button on the Sorting and Grouping dialog box to close it.

Elena selects the sort keys and grouping fields now.

To select sort keys and grouping fields:

1. If you haven't done so already, click the **toolbox title bar** and drag the toolbox to the right side of the Report Design window. This will make it easier to see the report sections.
2. Click the **Sorting and Grouping** button on the toolbar. The Sorting and Grouping dialog box opens.
3. Click the first **Field/Expression** list arrow in the Sorting and Grouping dialog box and then click **Type**. Ascending is the default sort order in the Sort Order text box.
4. Click anywhere in the second Field/Expression text box in the Sorting and Grouping dialog box, click the **list arrow** that appears, and then click **Article Length**. Ascending, the default sort order, needs to be changed to Descending in the Sort Order text box.
5. Click anywhere in the second Sort Order text box, click the **list arrow** that appears, and then click **Descending**. See Figure 6-22.

Figure 6-22
The Sorting and Grouping dialog box

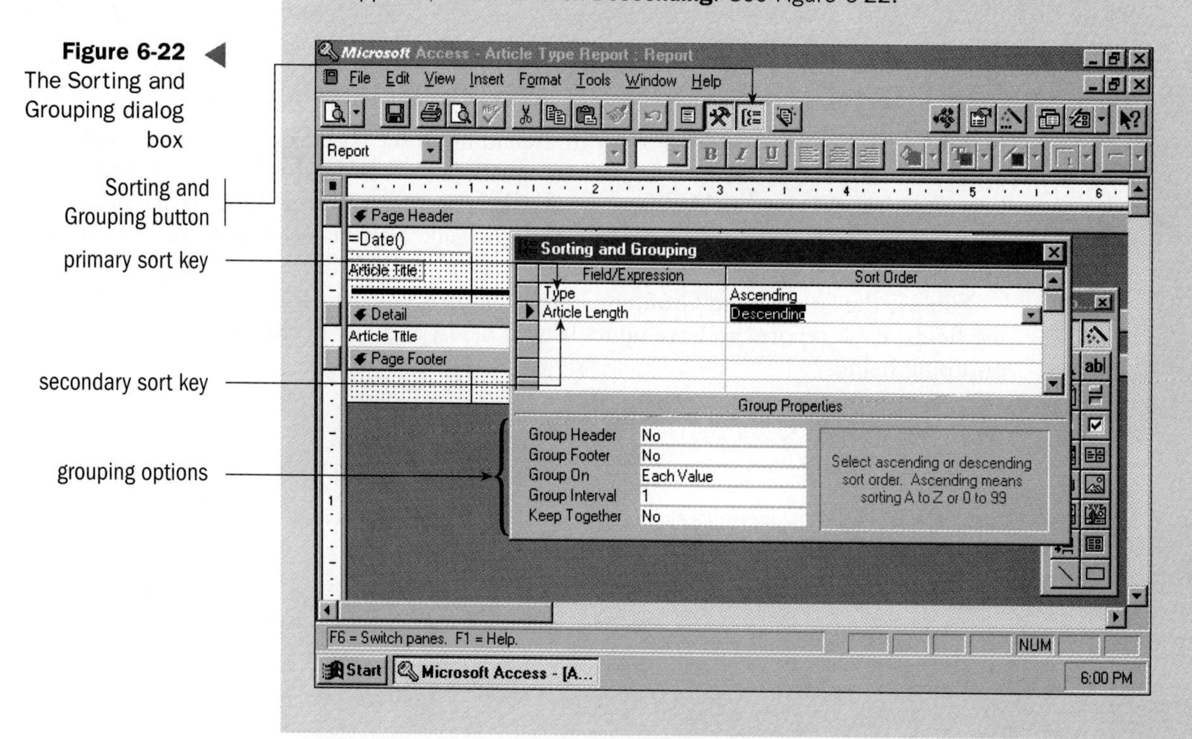

Elena uses the Group Properties panel to add a Group Footer to the report. To add a Group Footer, she must choose the Group Footer option for the Type field in the Sorting and Grouping dialog box.

To add a Group Footer to a report:

1. Click the **Field/Expression** text box for the Type field in the Sorting and Grouping dialog box, click the **Group Footer** text box, click the **list arrow** that appears, and then click **Yes**. Access adds a Group Footer section called Type Footer to the Report Design window. See Figure 6-23.

Figure 6-23 Adding a Group Footer section

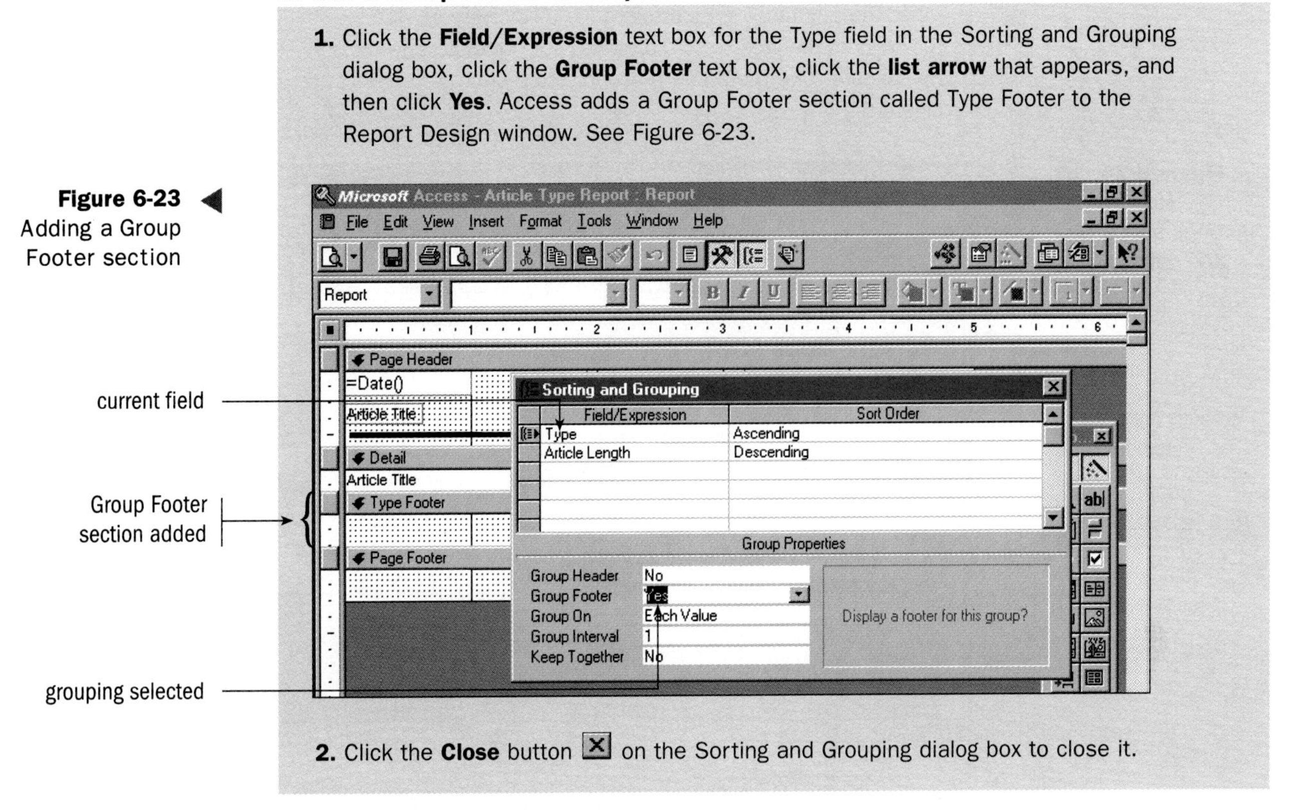

2. Click the **Close** button on the Sorting and Grouping dialog box to close it.

Adding and Deleting a Report Header and Footer

Elena compares her progress against her report design again and sees that she is almost done. Next she adds a Report Footer section to her report. To add this new section, Elena must add both the Report Header and Report Footer sections to the report together. She does not need the Report Header section, so she then deletes it. She also deletes the Page Footer section that was automatically included when the Report Design window was opened.

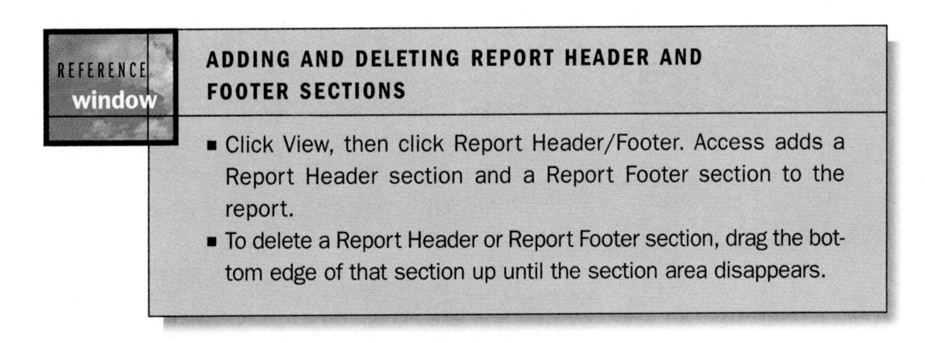

ADDING AND DELETING REPORT HEADER AND FOOTER SECTIONS

- Click View, then click Report Header/Footer. Access adds a Report Header section and a Report Footer section to the report.
- To delete a Report Header or Report Footer section, drag the bottom edge of that section up until the section area disappears.

To add and delete sections from a report:

1. Click **View** and then click **Report Header/Footer**. Access creates a Report Header section at the top of the report and a Report Footer section at the bottom of the report.

2. Move the pointer to the bottom edge of the Report Header section. When the pointer changes to ┼, drag the bottom edge upward until the section disappears. Use the same procedure to delete the Page Footer section. See Figure 6-24.

Figure 6-24 Report sections added and deleted

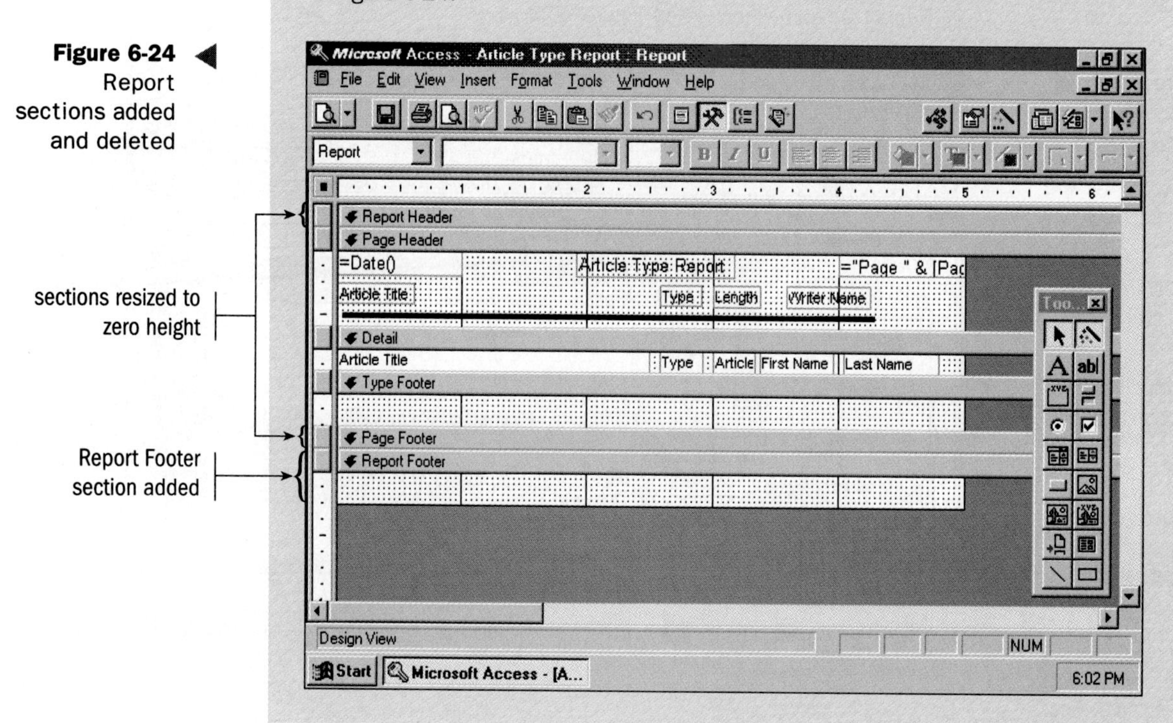

Calculating Group Totals and Overall Totals

Elena wants the report to print subtotals for each Type group, as well as an overall total, based on the Article Length field. To calculate these totals for the Article Length field, Elena uses the **Sum function**. She places the Sum function in a Group Footer section to print each group total and in the Report Footer section to print the overall total. The format for the Sum function is =Sum([*field name*]). You use the toolbar Text Box tool to create appropriate text boxes in the footer sections.

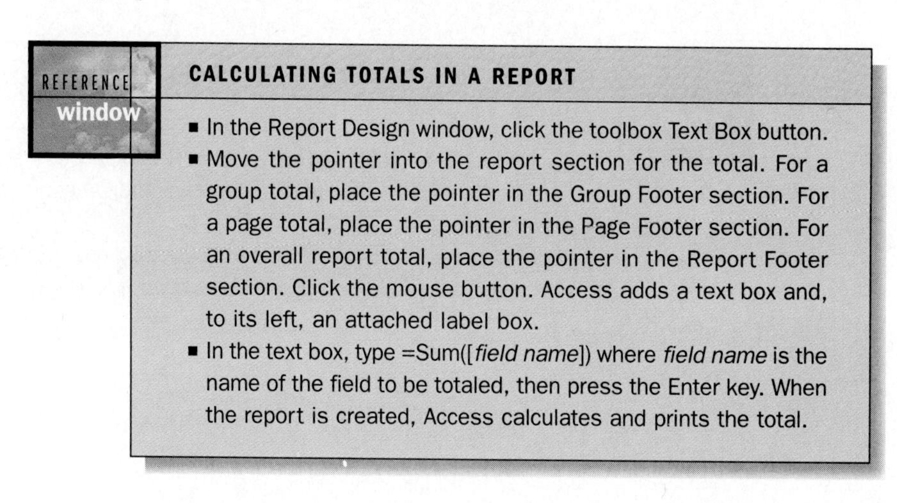

REFERENCE window

CALCULATING TOTALS IN A REPORT

- In the Report Design window, click the toolbox Text Box button.
- Move the pointer into the report section for the total. For a group total, place the pointer in the Group Footer section. For a page total, place the pointer in the Page Footer section. For an overall report total, place the pointer in the Report Footer section. Click the mouse button. Access adds a text box and, to its left, an attached label box.
- In the text box, type =Sum([*field name*]) where *field name* is the name of the field to be totaled, then press the Enter key. When the report is created, Access calculates and prints the total.

In the Type Footer (the Group Footer for Type) and Report Footer sections, Elena adds text boxes, deletes the attached labels for both, and adds the Sum function to each text box. She also draws lines above each Sum function so that the totals will be separated visually from the Detail section field values.

To add text boxes to footer sections and to delete labels:

1. Increase the height of the Type Footer section to .5" and increase the height of the Report Footer section to .5". These heights will allow sufficient room for the totals in these sections.
2. Click the **toolbox Text Box** button abl. Move the pointer into the Type Footer section. Click the mouse button when the pointer's plus (+) symbol is positioned in the second row of grid lines and vertically aligned with the right edge of the Type field-value text box. Access adds a text box and, to its left, an attached label box.
3. Click the **toolbox Text Box** button abl. Move the pointer into the Report Footer section. Click the mouse button when the pointer's plus (+) symbol is positioned in the fourth row of grid lines and vertically aligned with the right edge of the Type field-value text box. Access adds a text box, and, to its left, an attached label box. See Figure 6-25.

Figure 6-25 Text boxes added to footer sections

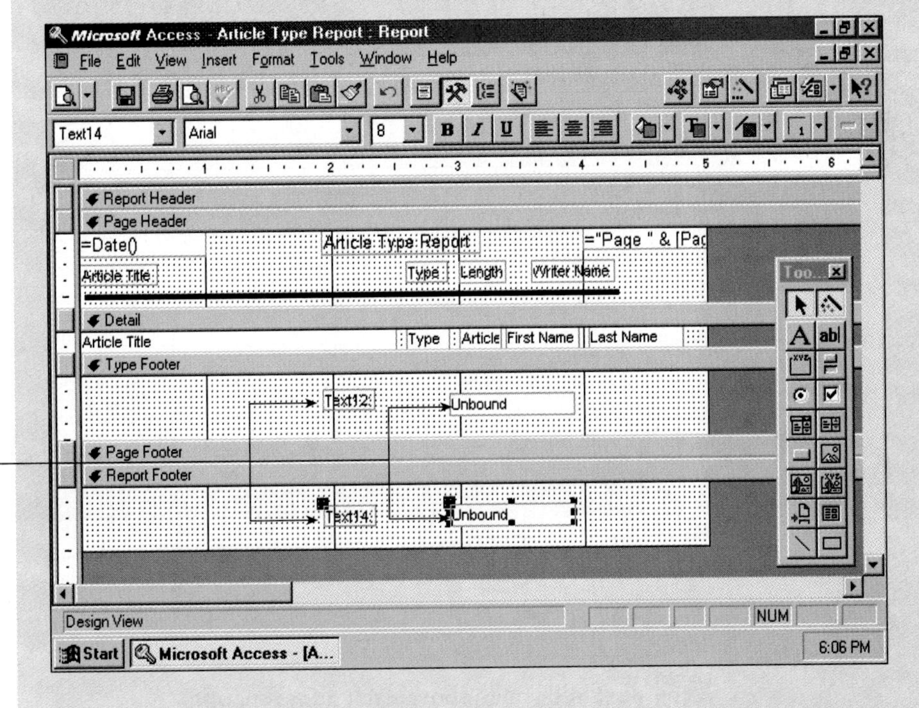

4. Click anywhere in the Type Footer section, outside both boxes, to deselect all boxes.
5. While you press and hold the **Shift** key, click the **label box** in the Type Footer section, and then click the **label box** in the Report Footer section. You have selected both boxes.
6. Click either label box with the right mouse button to open the shortcut menu and then click **Cut** to delete both label boxes.

Elena now adds the Sum function to the two footer section text boxes.

To add the Sum function to calculate group and overall totals:

1. Click the **text box** in the Type Footer section, type **=Sum([Article Length])**, and then press the **Enter** key. The text box in the Type Footer section needs to be narrower to align with the Article Length field in the Detail section.

   TROUBLE? Be sure that you enter the field name Article Length correctly. If you misspell Article Length, you will receive an error message later, when you preview or print the report.

2. Click the **middle sizing handle** on the right side of the text box and drag it to the left until the right edge of the box lines up with the right edge of the Article Length field-value text box in the Detail section. Although the formula doesn't fit in the text box, the calculated value will fit.
3. Click the **text box** in the Report Footer section, type **=Sum([Article Length])**, and then press the **Enter** key.
4. Resize the text box in the Report Footer section so that its right edge lines up with the right edge of the Article Length field-value text box in the Detail section. See Figure 6-26.

Figure 6-26 Group total and overall total formulas added to text boxes

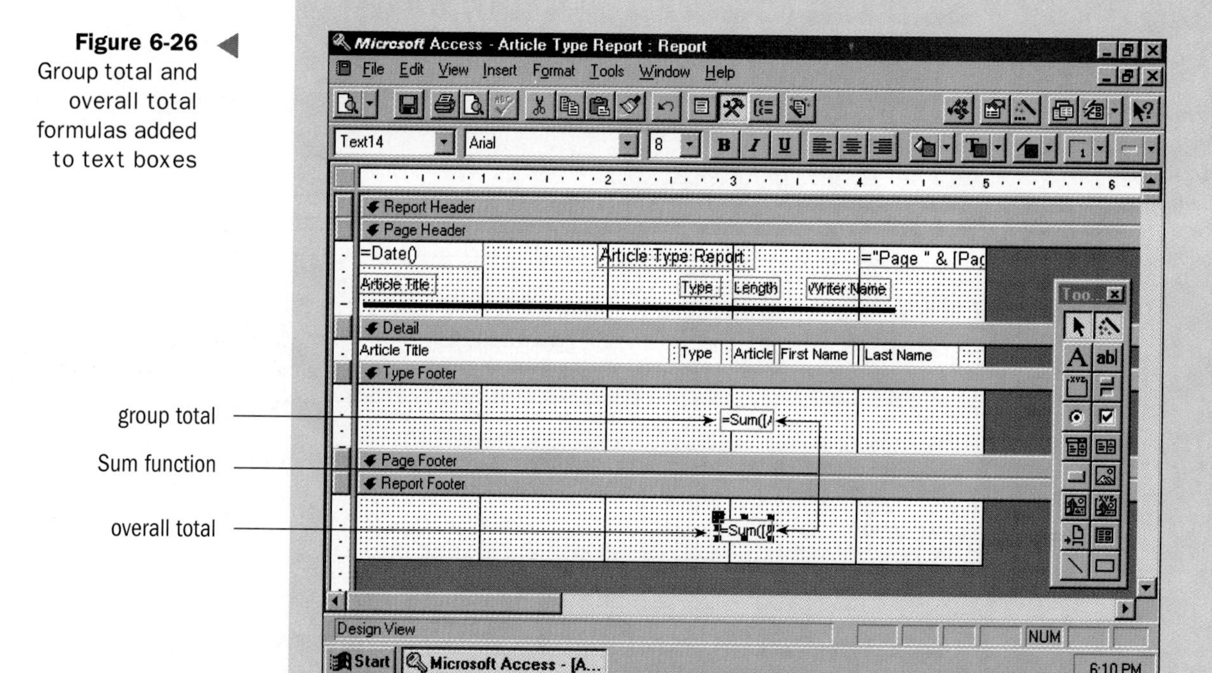

Elena next adds lines above each Sum function.

To add lines above totals:

1. Click the **toolbox Line** button. Move the pointer into the Type Footer section; the pointer changes to a line pointer. Position the pointer's plus (+) symbol in the second row of grid lines and align it vertically with the right edge of the Type field-value text box in the Detail section above it.
2. Click and hold the left mouse button to drag a horizontal line to the right until the right end of the line is below the right edge of the Article Length field-value text box.
3. Repeat Steps 1 and 2 for the Report Footer section. See Figure 6-27.

Figure 6-27 Horizontal lines added above group and overall totals

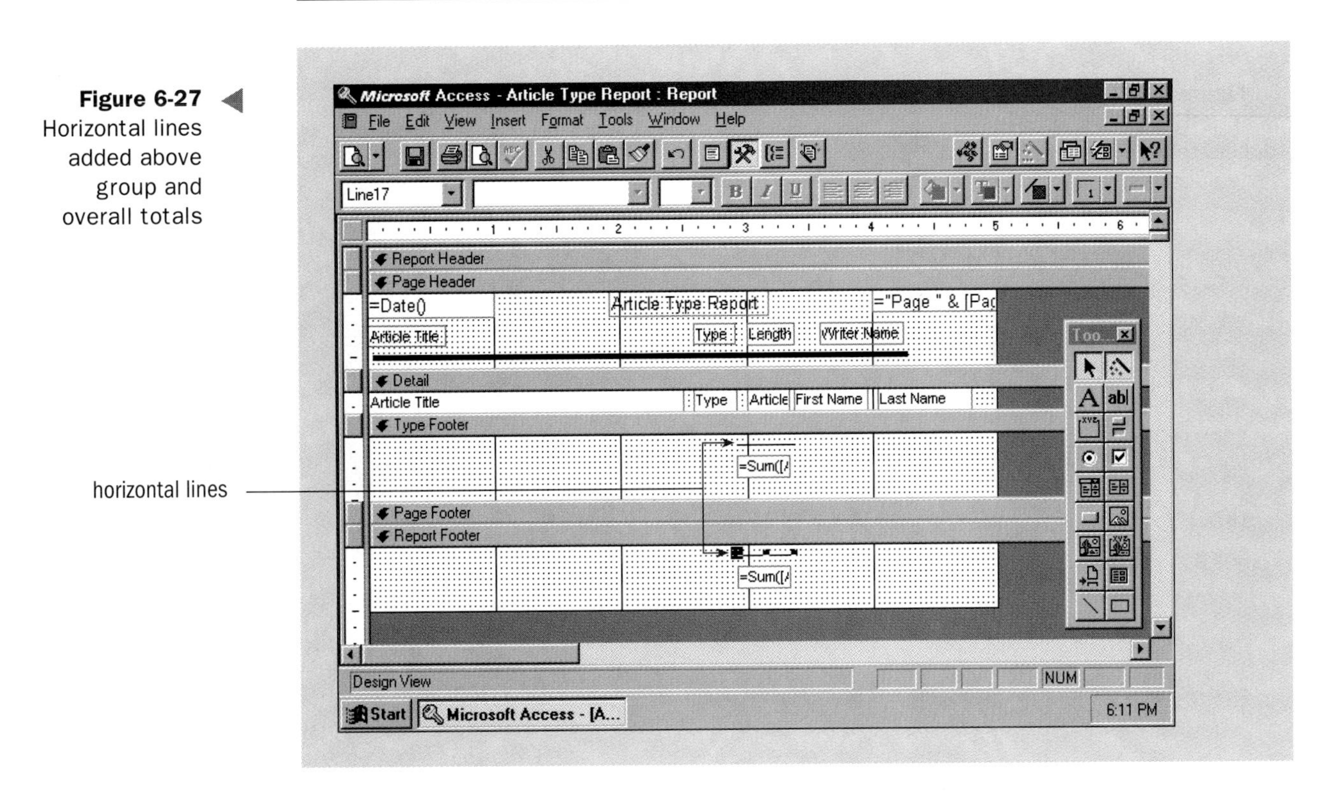

Elena's report is almost finished. There remain, however, some changes she can make to improve its appearance.

Hiding Duplicate Values in a Report

Elena's next change is to display the Type value only in the first record in a group. Within a group, all Type field values are the same, so if you display only the first one, you simplify the report and make it easier to read.

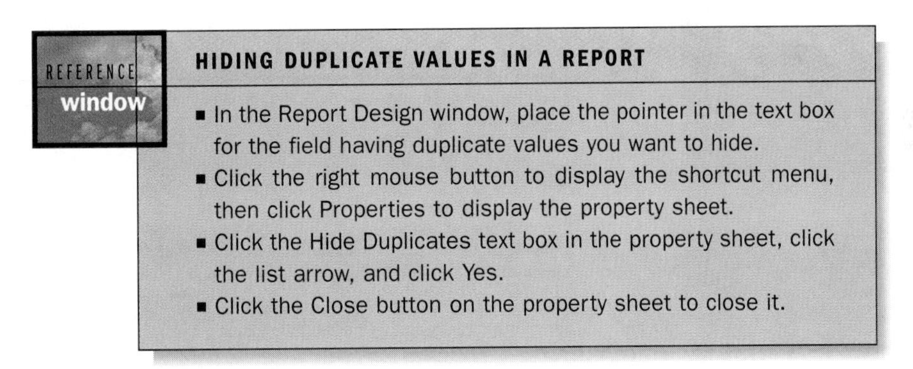
REFERENCE window

HIDING DUPLICATE VALUES IN A REPORT

- In the Report Design window, place the pointer in the text box for the field having duplicate values you want to hide.
- Click the right mouse button to display the shortcut menu, then click Properties to display the property sheet.
- Click the Hide Duplicates text box in the property sheet, click the list arrow, and click Yes.
- Click the Close button on the property sheet to close it.

Elena hides the duplicate Type values now.

To hide duplicate values:

1. Place the pointer in the Type text box in the Detail section and then click the right mouse button to display the shortcut menu, then click **Properties** to display the property sheet.
2. Click the **Hide Duplicates** text box in the property sheet, click the **list arrow**, then click **Yes**. See Figure 6-28.

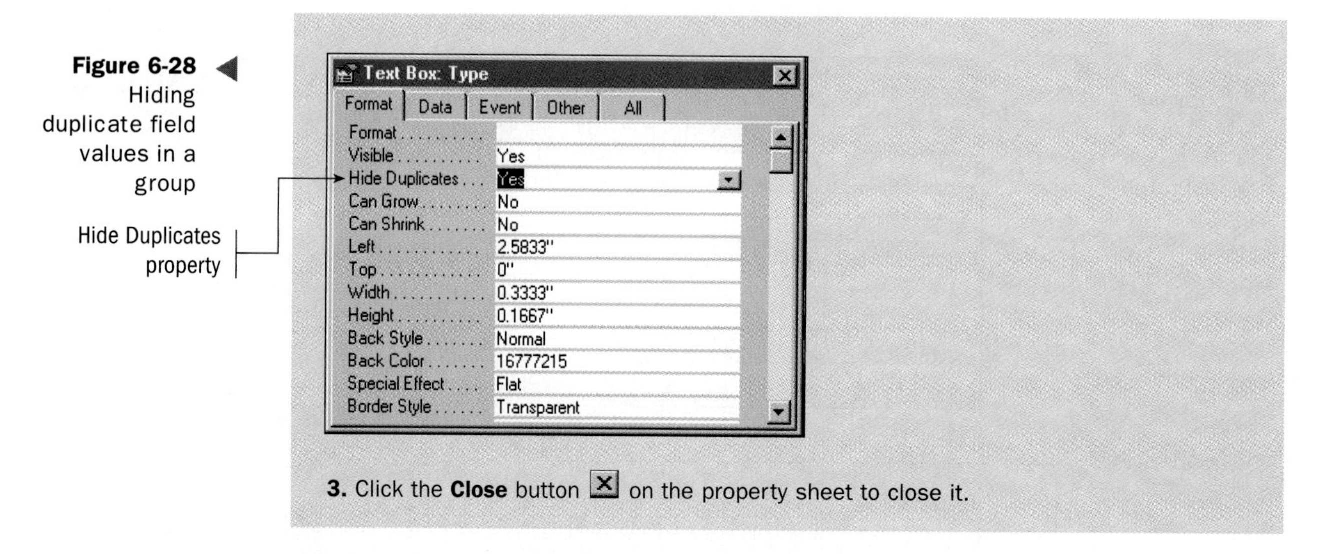

Figure 6-28 Hiding duplicate field values in a group

3. Click the **Close** button on the property sheet to close it.

Elena views the report in the Print Preview window, then prints and saves the report.

To view, print, and save a report:

1. Click the **Print Preview** button on the toolbar. Access displays the first page of the report. See Figure 6-29.

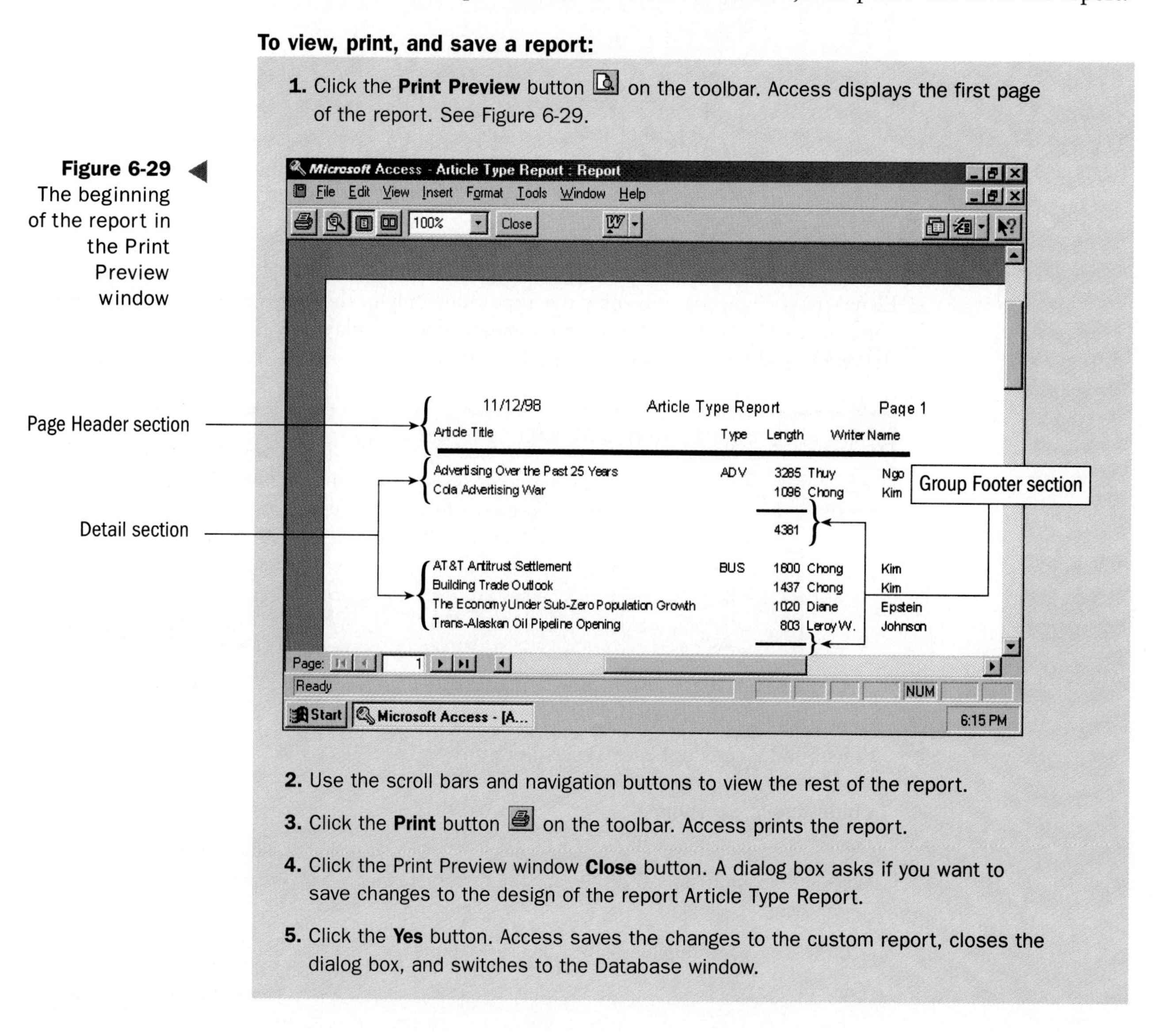

Figure 6-29 The beginning of the report in the Print Preview window

2. Use the scroll bars and navigation buttons to view the rest of the report.
3. Click the **Print** button on the toolbar. Access prints the report.
4. Click the Print Preview window **Close** button. A dialog box asks if you want to save changes to the design of the report Article Type Report.
5. Click the **Yes** button. Access saves the changes to the custom report, closes the dialog box, and switches to the Database window.

Elena brings her printed report to Harold. He is very pleased, and feels that the report will help ensure a successful meeting with the advertisers.

If you want to take a break and resume the tutorial at a later time, exit Access. When you resume the tutorial, place your Student Disk in the appropriate drive, start Access, open the Issue25 database in the Tutorial folder on your Student Disk, maximize the Database window, and click the Reports tab to display the Reports list.

Quick Check

1. When do you use the toolbox Text Box tool?
2. What do you type in a text box to tell Access to print the current date?
3. How do you insert a page number in a Page Header section?
4. What is the function of the Sorting and Grouping button?
5. How do you add a Report Footer section to a report without adding a Report Header section?
6. How do you calculate group totals and overall totals?
7. Why might you want to hide duplicate values in a group report?

SESSION 6.3

In this session, you will learn to integrate Access with other Windows 95 applications. You will create an embedded chart in a report and place a linked graphic image in a Page Header, and then edit the chart and the graphic image.

Integrating Access with Other Windows 95 Applications

Harold is so pleased with the report that Elena created for him that he immediately thinks of another report that would be helpful to include for his meeting with the advertisers. He asks Elena if she can create a report with a graph showing the number of articles of each type that are included in the 25th-anniversary issue. Elena says she will investigate creating such a report for him.

Integrating Applications

When you create a report or form in Access, you might want to include more than just the formatted listing of records. You may want to include objects such as a long text passage, a graphic image, or a graph summarizing the data. Creating long text passages is difficult with Access, and Access is also not able to create graphic images or graphs. Instead, you can create these objects with other applications and then place them in a report or form.

Access offers three ways for you to include objects created by other applications in a form or report, as shown in Figure 6-30:

- **Importing:** When you import an object, you include the contents of a file in the form or report. In Tutorial 5, for example, you imported a graphic image created by the drawing application called Microsoft Paint. Once the object is imported, it has no relation to the application that created it. It is simply an object in the form or report.

- **Embedding**: When you embed an object, you preserve its connection to the application that created it. You can edit the object by double-clicking on it. This starts the application that created it. Any changes you make in the object are reflected in the form or report in which it has been embedded. These changes affect only the copy of the object in the form or report; they do not affect the original copy of the object in the file from which it was embedded.
- **Linking:** When you link an object to a form or report, you preserve its connection to the original file from which it came. You can edit the object by double-clicking on it. This starts the application that created it, and any changes you make in the object are reflected in the form or report and in the original file from which it came. You can also start the application outside of Access and edit the object's original file. Any changes are reflected in the original file and in the linked object in the Access form or report.

Figure 6-30 Integration techniques

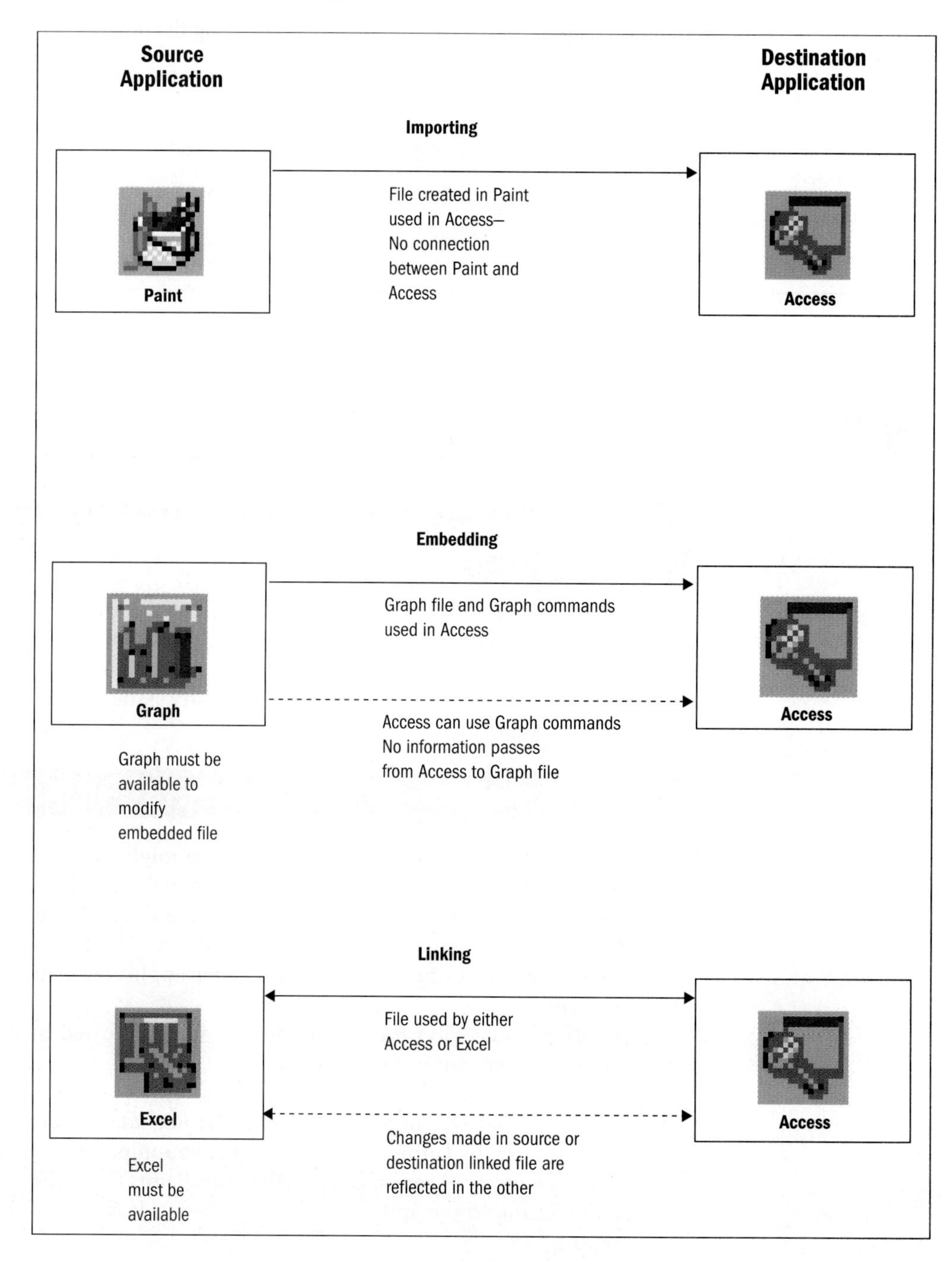

Not all applications support **Object Linking and Embedding (OLE)**, although most application software does. If you have difficulty linking or embedding objects from an application, it is possible that the application you are using does not support OLE.

Elena's design for the report requested by Harold, shown in Figure 6-31, will include an embedded chart showing the distribution of articles in the BUSINESS ARTICLES table by Type, and a linked graphic image in the Page Header.

Figure 6-31 Elena's design for Harold's chart report

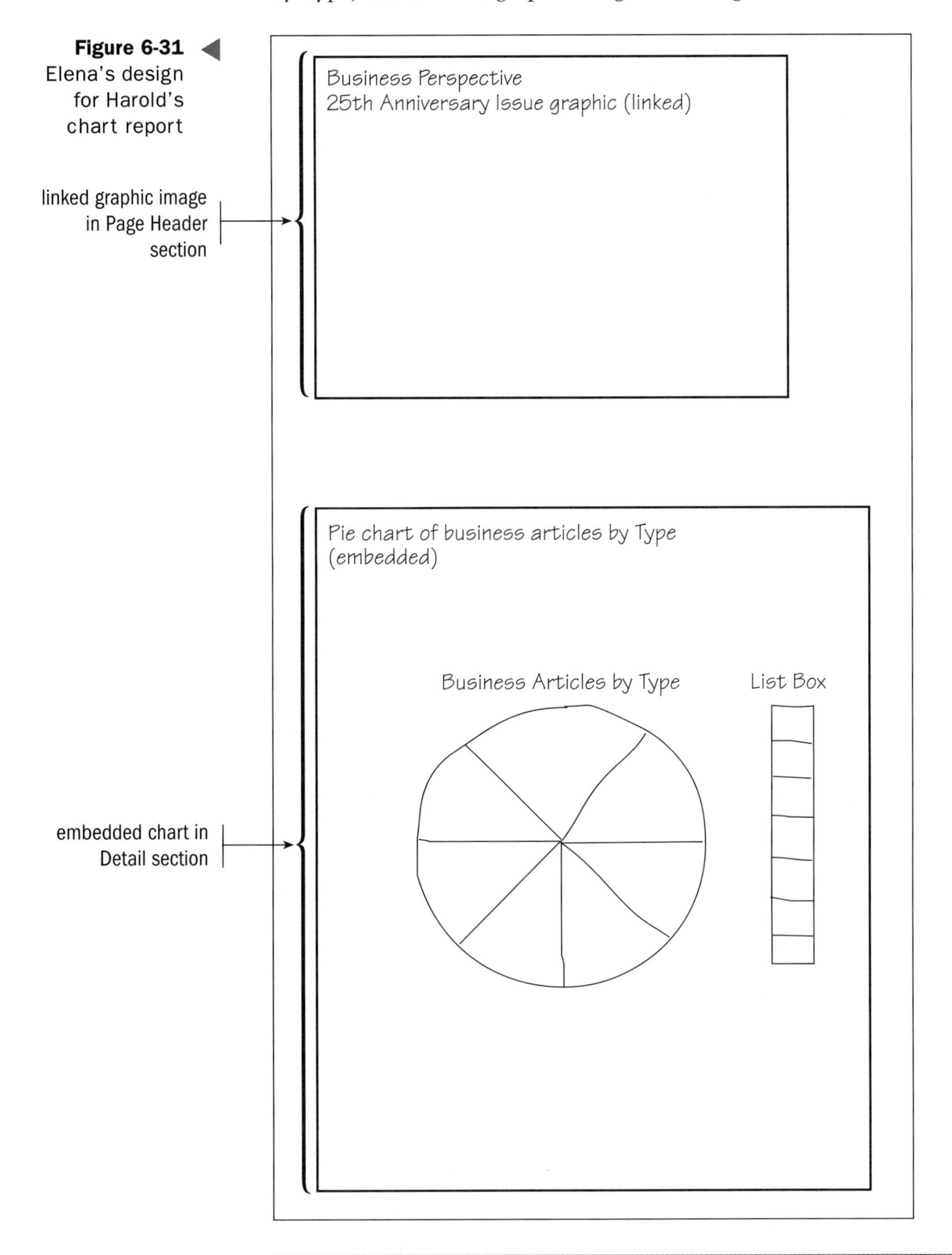

Embedding a Chart in a Report

Elena begins by creating a report with an embedded chart. Access provides the Chart Wizard to assist you in embedding the chart. The chart itself is actually created by another application, Microsoft Graph. After embedding the chart in the report, you can edit it by using the Graph program.

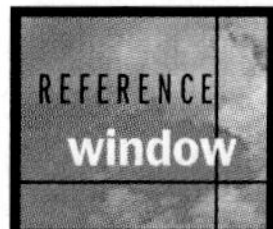

USING THE CHART WIZARD TO CREATE A REPORT WITH AN EMBEDDED CHART

- In the Database window, click the Reports tab to display the Reports list.
- Click the New button to open the New Report dialog box.
- Click Chart Wizard, select the table or query on which the report is based, then click the OK button. Access starts the Chart Wizard.
- Select the field(s) that contain the data for the chart, then click the Next > button.
- Select the type of chart you want, then click the Next > button.
- Make any modifications you want in the layout of the chart, then click the Next > button.
- Enter a title for the chart, then click the Finish button. Access places (embeds) the chart in the report. You can modify the chart by double-clicking on it and using Graph to make the modifications.

Elena creates a new report that will contain an embedded chart.

To create a report with an embedded chart:

1. In the Reports list box of the Database window, click the **New** button to display the New Report dialog box.
2. Click **Chart Wizard** to select it, click the **list arrow** in the text box, click **BUSINESS ARTICLES** to select the table, then click the **OK** button. Access starts the Chart Wizard and displays the first Chart Wizard dialog box.

   This dialog box allows you to select the fields that contain the data for the chart. Elena wants to graph the distribution of BUSINESS ARTICLES by Type, so she selects the Type field.
3. Click **Type** in the Available Fields list box to select it, then click the > button to move the Type field to the Fields for graph list. Click the Next > button. Access displays the next Chart Wizard dialog box, which allows you to select the type of graph you want.

   A pie chart is a good type of graph for showing the relative sizes of different categories (the number of articles of each type) to the whole (the total number of articles). Elena chooses it.
4. Click the **pie chart** button (first button in the third row) to select the pie chart type, then click the Next > button. See Figure 6-32.

Figure 6-32 Selecting the type of graph

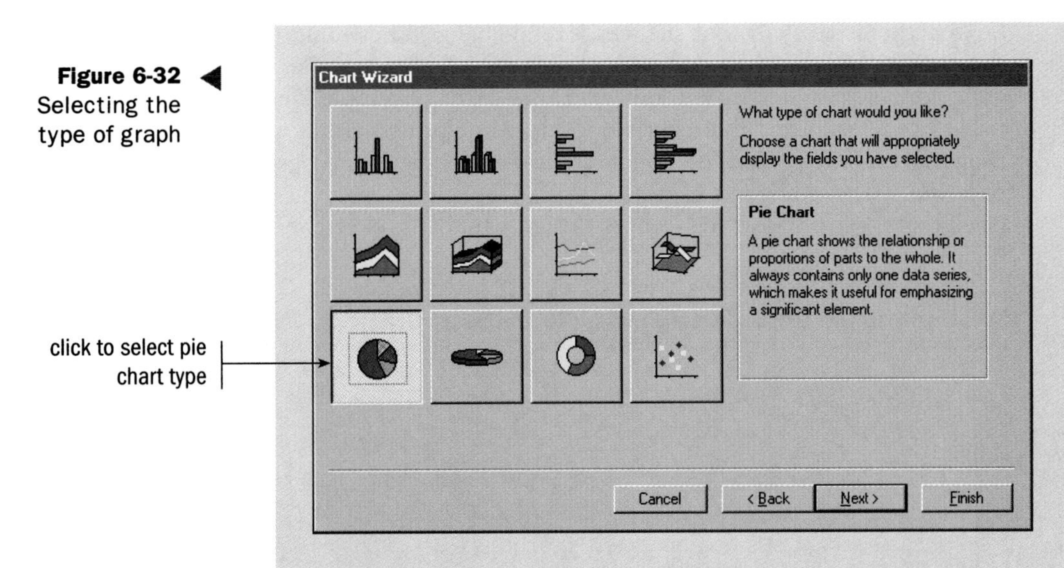

Access displays the next Chart Wizard dialog box. This dialog box allows you to modify the layout of the chart. Elena decides to use the default layout and to modify it later, if necessary, once she has seen the chart in the report.

5. Click the Next > button. This dialog box allows you to enter the title that will appear at the top of the graph.
6. Type **Business Articles by Type** in the text box. Make sure the radio buttons next to the following options are selected: Yes, display a legend and Open the report with the graph displayed on it. Make sure the option, Display help showing me how to work with my chart, is not checked, then click the **Finish** button. Access creates the report and displays it, with the embedded chart, in the Print Preview window.
7. Click the Print Preview window **Maximize** button, then use the elevator bar to scroll until the entire chart is visible. See Figure 6-33.

Figure 6-33 The embedded chart in the Print Preview window

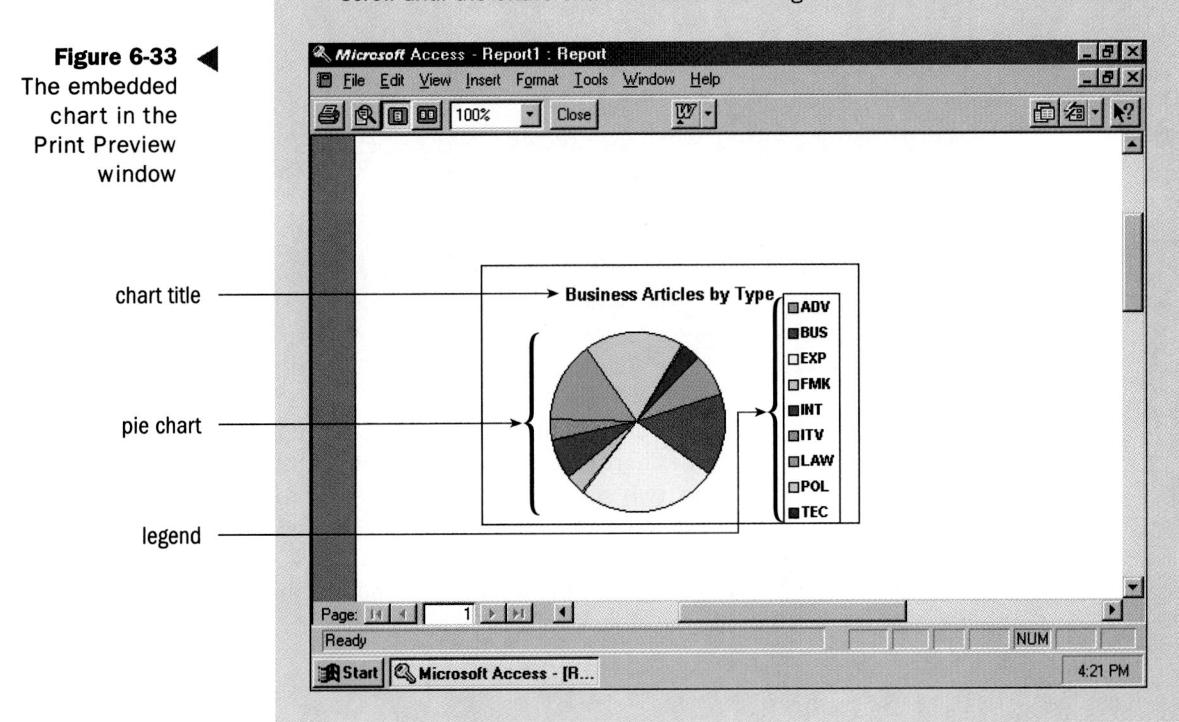

Elena likes the chart, but she sees several changes she would like to make. She wants the chart to be larger and centered on the page. She notices that the wedges in the chart are color-coded and a legend appears to the right of the pie. She thinks that the colors might not reproduce well on her black-and-white printer and it will therefore be difficult to match the wedges with the article types that appear in the legend. She would prefer to have the wedges themselves marked with the article type. She prepares to make these changes by switching to the Report Design window and starting Graph so she can edit the chart.

To switch to the Report Design window and start Graph:

1. Click the **Close** button on the toolbar to close the Print Preview window and switch to the Report Design window. The chart appears in the Detail section of the report.
2. Double-click the **chart object**. Graph starts and the chart appears in the Graph window. Click the Graph window **Maximize** button. See Figure 6-34. Because Elena has not yet saved her report, it bears the default name Report1.

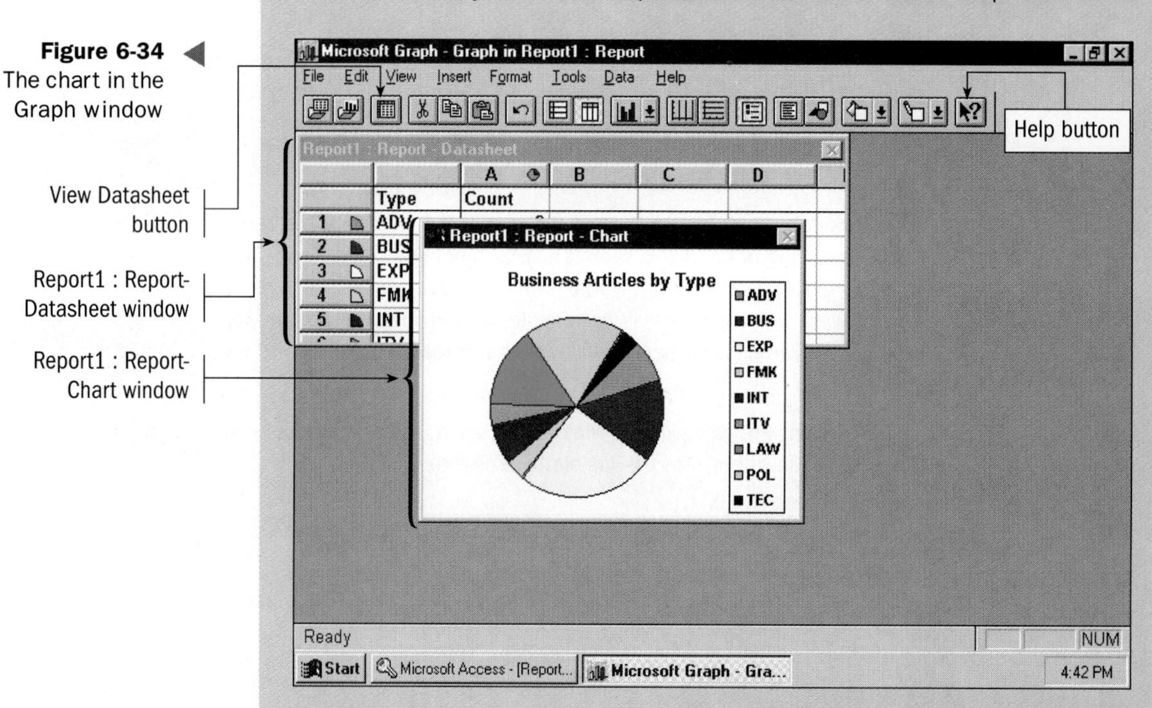

Figure 6-34 The chart in the Graph window

TROUBLE? If the chart appears with the incorrect legend and appears to have the incorrect wedges, this is a minor Access display error. It will not affect the chart or the report. Continue with the tutorial.

Graph is the application that created the original chart. Since the chart is embedded in the report, double-clicking the chart object starts Graph and allows you to edit the chart. The Graph window contains two smaller windows: Report1 : Report - Datasheet and Report1 : Report - Chart. The Report1 : Report - Datasheet window displays the data on which the chart is based. The Report1 : Report - Chart window displays the chart itself. All of Elena's changes will be made in the Report1 : Report - Chart window.

Elena starts by enlarging the chart.

To enlarge the chart:

1. Click in the title bar of the Report1 : Report - Chart window and drag the window up and to the left until it is directly under the toolbar and the left edge is lined up with the left edge of the View Datasheet button. Release the mouse button.
2. Position the pointer on the lower right corner of the Report1 : Report - Chart window. When the pointer turns to ↘, drag the lower right corner down and to the right until the bottom of the window is just above the status bar and the right edge is aligned with the right edge of the Help button. Release the mouse button. See Figure 6-35.

Figure 6-35 The resized chart

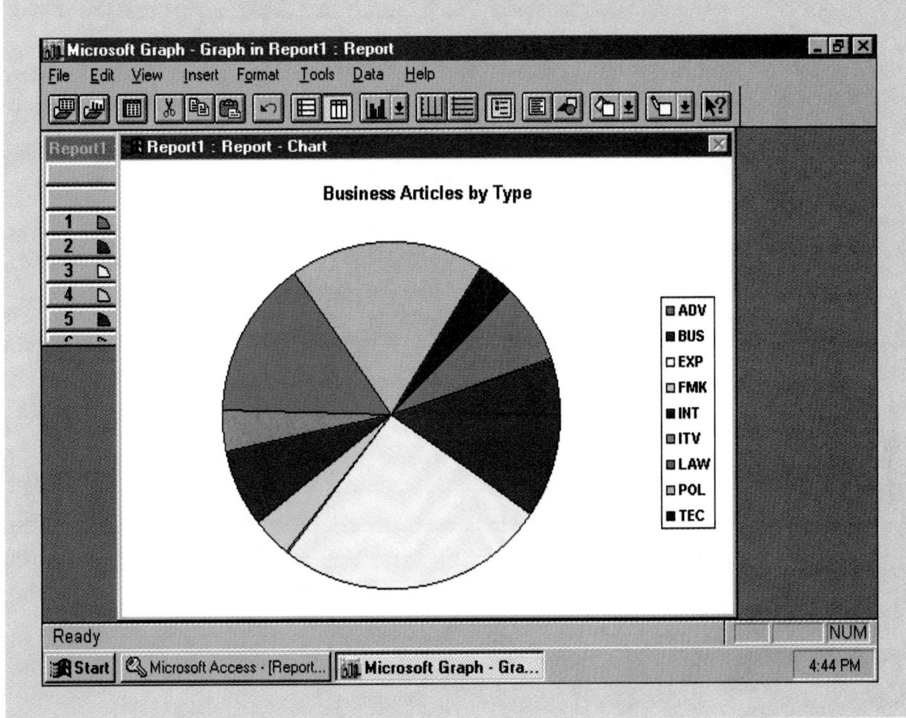

Elena now deletes the legend from the chart and creates labels for the wedges.

To delete the legend and create labels:

1. Click anywhere in the legend in the Report1 : Report - Chart window to select it. Handles appear around the edges of the legend object.
2. With the pointer inside the legend object, click the right mouse button to display the shortcut menu, then click **Clear** to remove the legend from the graph.
3. Click anywhere in the pie chart. Handles appear around the edges of the pie chart object.
4. With the pointer inside the pie chart object, click the right mouse button to display the shortcut menu, then click **Insert Data Labels** to display the Data Labels dialog box. See Figure 6-36.

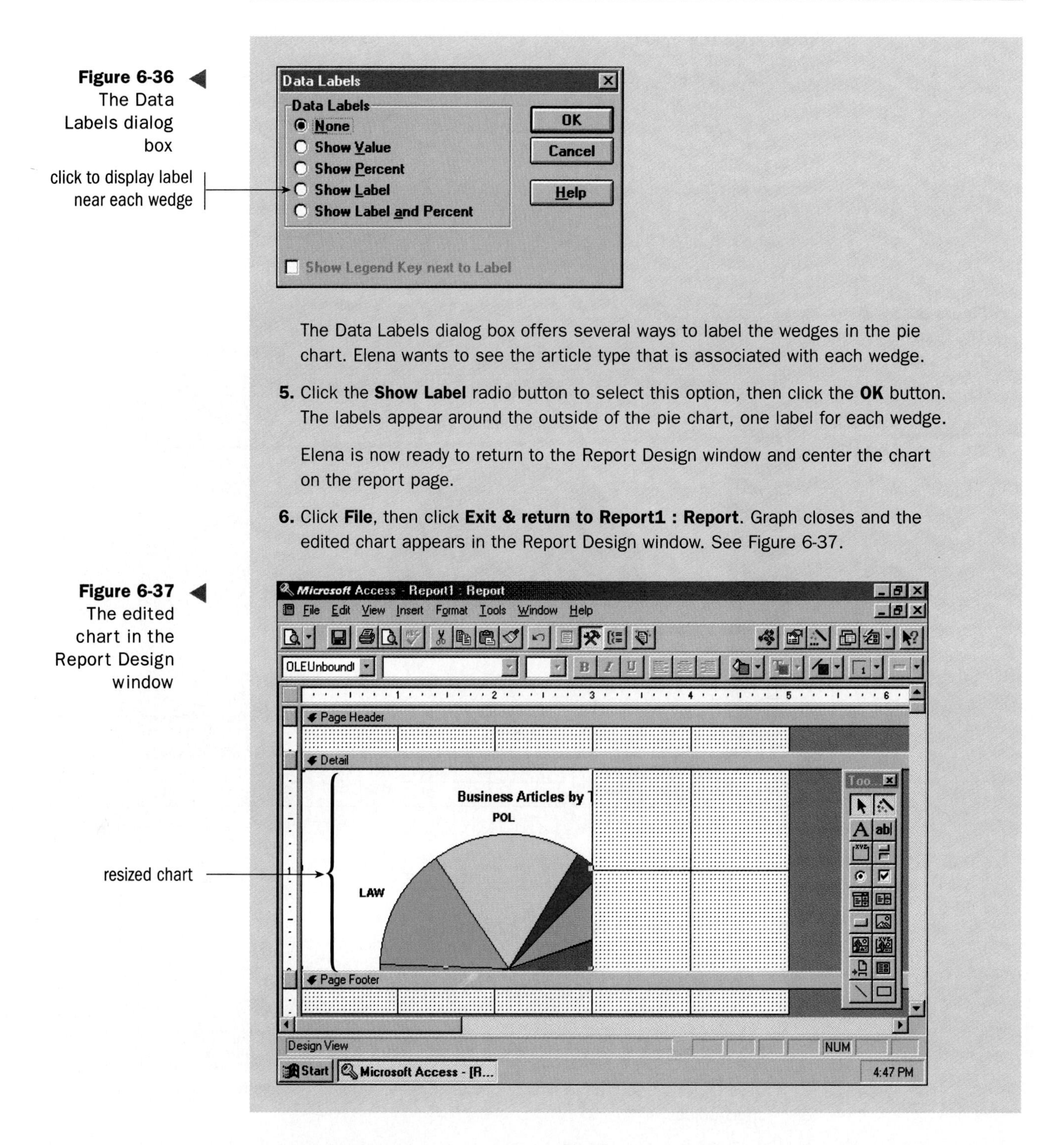

Figure 6-36 The Data Labels dialog box

The Data Labels dialog box offers several ways to label the wedges in the pie chart. Elena wants to see the article type that is associated with each wedge.

5. Click the **Show Label** radio button to select this option, then click the **OK** button. The labels appear around the outside of the pie chart, one label for each wedge.

   Elena is now ready to return to the Report Design window and center the chart on the report page.

6. Click **File**, then click **Exit & return to Report1 : Report**. Graph closes and the edited chart appears in the Report Design window. See Figure 6-37.

Figure 6-37 The edited chart in the Report Design window

Although the chart is now larger, the box in which it appears in the Detail section of the report is still its original size. The box needs to be enlarged and centered in the report page.

To enlarge and center the box:

1. Click the toolbox **Close** button to hide the toolbox.

2. Position the pointer on the right edge of the report page in the Detail section. When the pointer turns to ✛, click and drag the right edge to the 6" mark on the horizontal ruler. Release the mouse button.

3. Position the pointer in the chart object. When the pointer turns to ✋, click and drag the chart object to the right until the left edge of the chart object is at the 1" mark on the horizontal ruler.

4. Position the pointer on the sizing handle in the middle of the right edge of the chart object. When the pointer turns to ↔, click and drag the right edge of the chart object to the 5.5" mark on the horizontal ruler. Release the mouse button.

5. Move the pointer to the bottom of the Detail section. When the pointer changes to ✛, click and drag the bottom of the Detail section to the 4" mark on the vertical ruler. Notice that the report automatically scrolls when the pointer reaches the bottom of the screen.

   TROUBLE? If you did not get the bottom of the Detail section positioned correctly, simply click and drag the bottom of the Detail section up or down as necessary. Then proceed with the following steps.

6. If necessary, scroll until the bottom of the chart object is visible, then position the pointer on the sizing handle in the middle of the bottom of the chart object. When the pointer changes to ↕, click and drag the bottom of the chart object to the bottom of the Detail section.

7. Use the elevator bar to scroll to the top of the report. See Figure 6-38.

Figure 6-38 The resized chart object

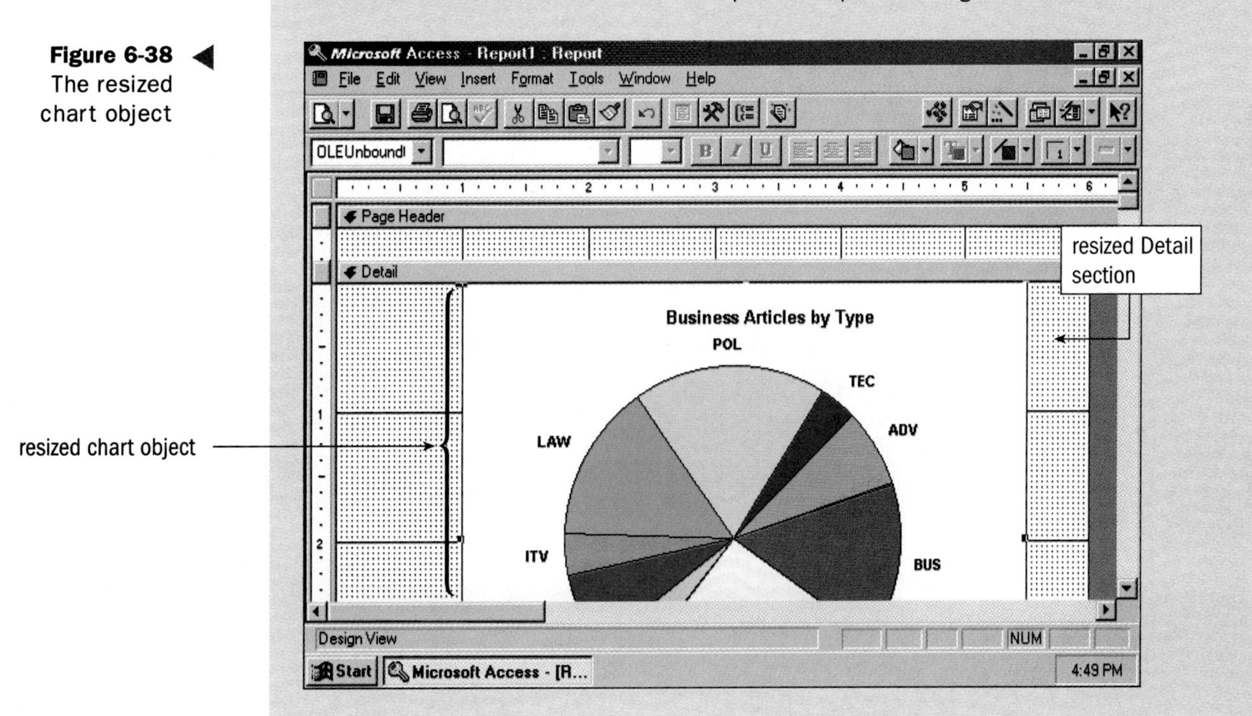

Now that the chart is properly positioned on the report page, Elena is ready to place the graphic object in the Page Header section. Since she has made many changes to the report design, she saves it before proceeding.

To save the report:

1. Click the **Save** button on the toolbar. Access displays the Save As dialog box.

2. Type **Type Pie Chart Report**, then click the **OK** button. Access saves the report.

Linking an Object in a Report

Elena decides to use the same 25th anniversary issue graphic image that she used in the Article Type Form (created in Tutorial 5). She inserts it in the Page Header, but this time, she uses linking to insert the image. That way, if she changes the graphic image later using the Microsoft Paint program, the change will also be updated in the Page Header section of the Type Pie Chart Report.

REFERENCE window

INSERTING A LINKED OBJECT IN A REPORT

- In the Report Design window, click in the report section where you want to place the linked object.
- Click Insert, then click Object to display the Insert Object dialog box.
- Click the Create from File radio button. The dialog box now displays a File Name text box.
- Enter the name of the file containing the object, or use the Browse button to display the Browse dialog box. Use the Browse dialog box to locate and select the file.
- Click the Link check box to place a check mark in it.
- Click the OK button. Access inserts the object in the report and creates a link to the original file from which the object came.

Elena first resizes the Page Header and then inserts the linked graphic image.

To resize the Page Header and insert the linked graphic image:

1. Position the pointer at the bottom of the Page Header section. When the pointer turns to ✛, click and drag the bottom of the Page Header section down until the bottom is at the 2" mark on the vertical ruler. Release the mouse button.
2. Click anywhere in the Page Header section, then click **Insert,** then click **Object** to display the Insert Object dialog box.
3. Click the **Create from File** radio button to select this option. The dialog box changes to display the File text box, the Browse button, and the Link check box. See Figure 6-39.

Figure 6-39 The Insert Object dialog box

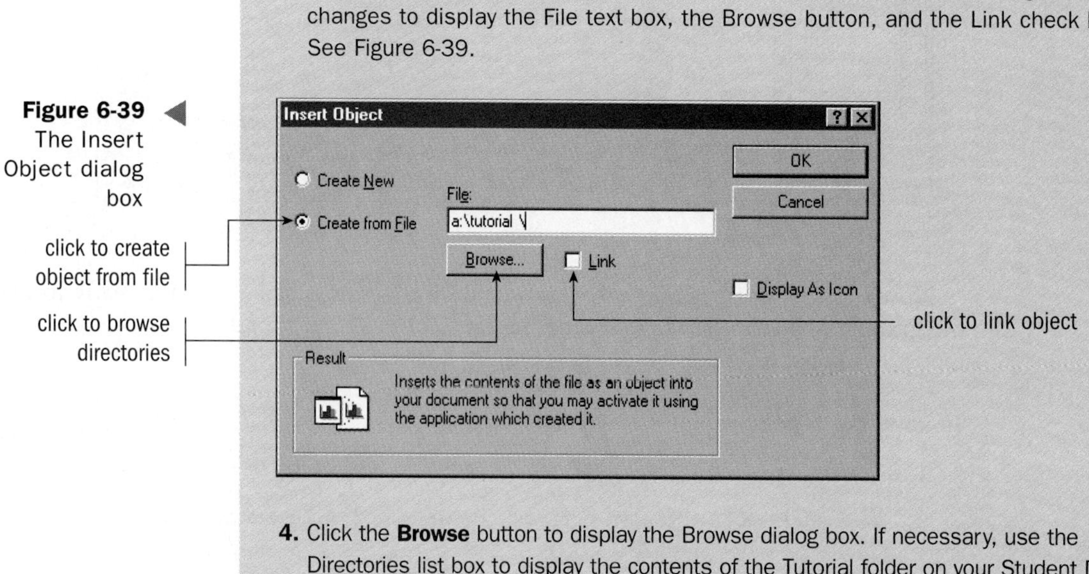

4. Click the **Browse** button to display the Browse dialog box. If necessary, use the Directories list box to display the contents of the Tutorial folder on your Student Disk.
5. In the files list box, click **25th** to select the graphic image file, then click the **OK** button. The Browse dialog box closes.

6. Click the **Link** check box to place a check mark in the box, then click the **OK** button. The Insert Object dialog box closes, and the graphic image is placed in the Page Header section.

7. Position the pointer in the graphic image object. When the pointer turns to ✋, click and drag the graphic image down and to the right until the top of the image is aligned with the fourth row of grid dots and the left edge is at the 1.25" mark on the horizontal ruler. See Figure 6-40.

Figure 6-40 The linked graphic image in the Page Header section

linked graphic image

resized Page Header section

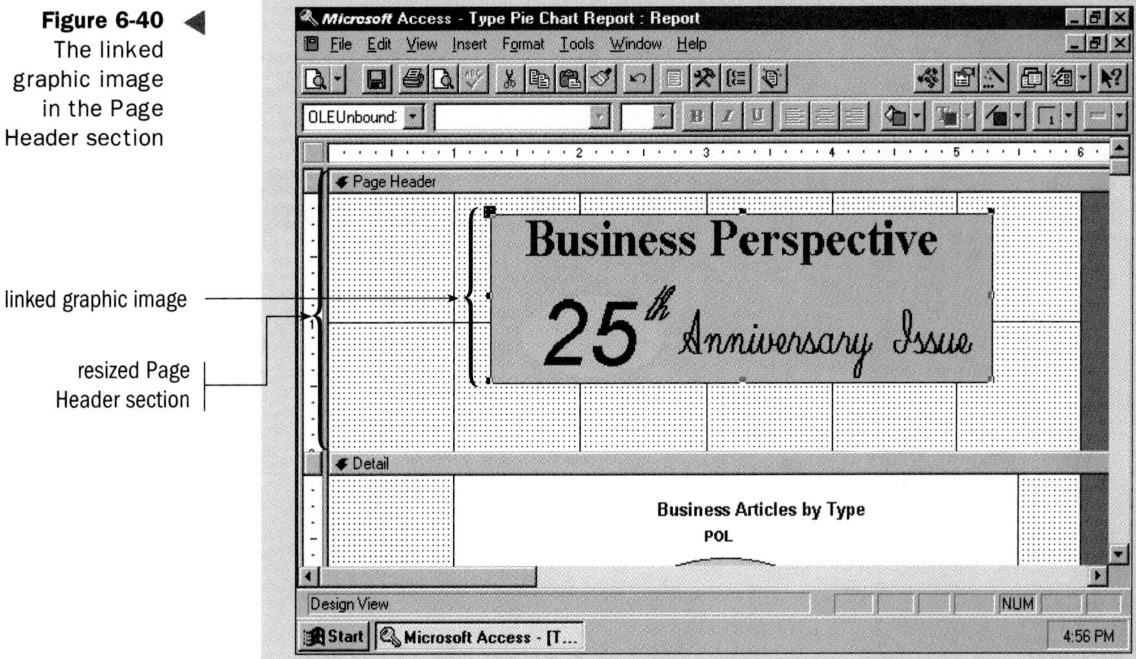

8. Click the **Print Preview** button to view the completed report. See Figure 6-41.

Figure 6-41 Completed Type Pie Chart Report

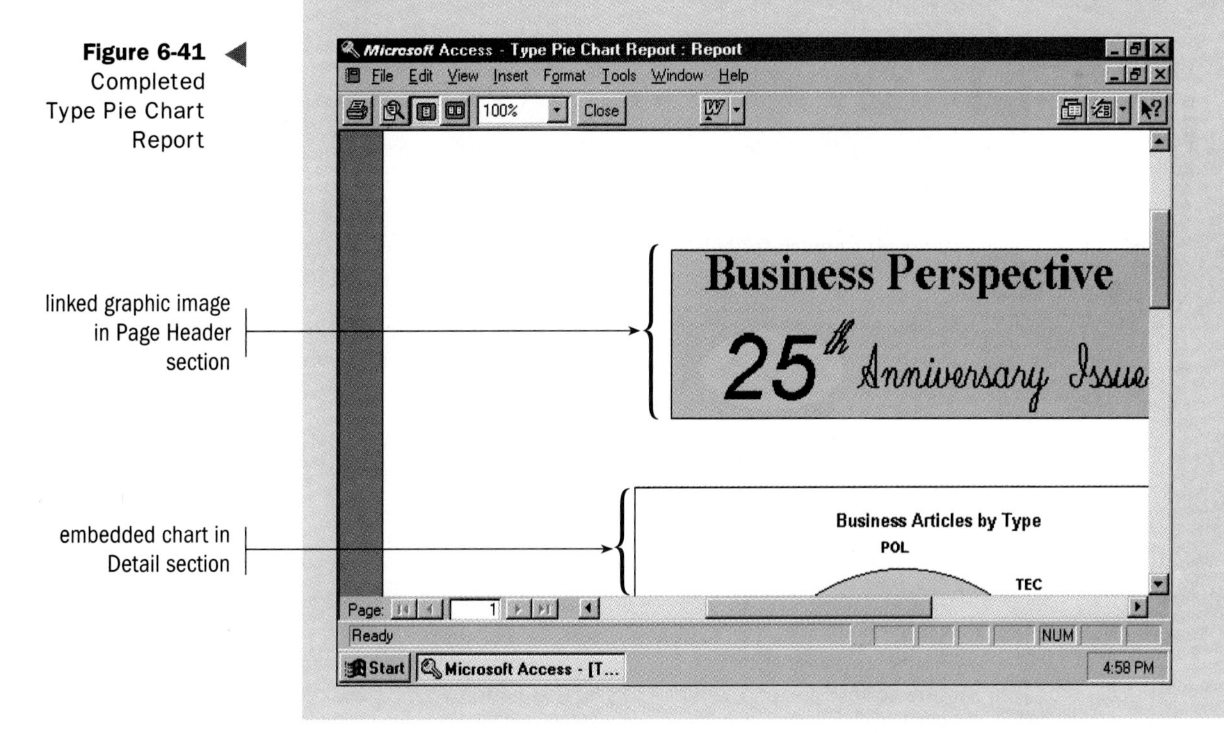

Because you checked the Link check box, the graphic image in the Page Header is *linked* to the 25th file in the Paint program that contains the original image. Any changes made to the original will automatically be included in the image that appears in the Page Header of the report. If you had not checked the Link check box, the graphic image would be *embedded.*

To see how linking works, Elena makes a change to the original graphic image using the Paint application and views the results in the Report Design window.

To make a change to the original graphic image:

1. Click the **Close** button on the toolbar to return to the Report Design window, then click the **Start** button at the bottom of the screen, point to **Programs**, point to **Accessories**, then click **Paint**. The Paint program starts and the Paint window opens. Click the Paint window **Maximize** button. See Figure 6-42.

Figure 6-42 The Paint window

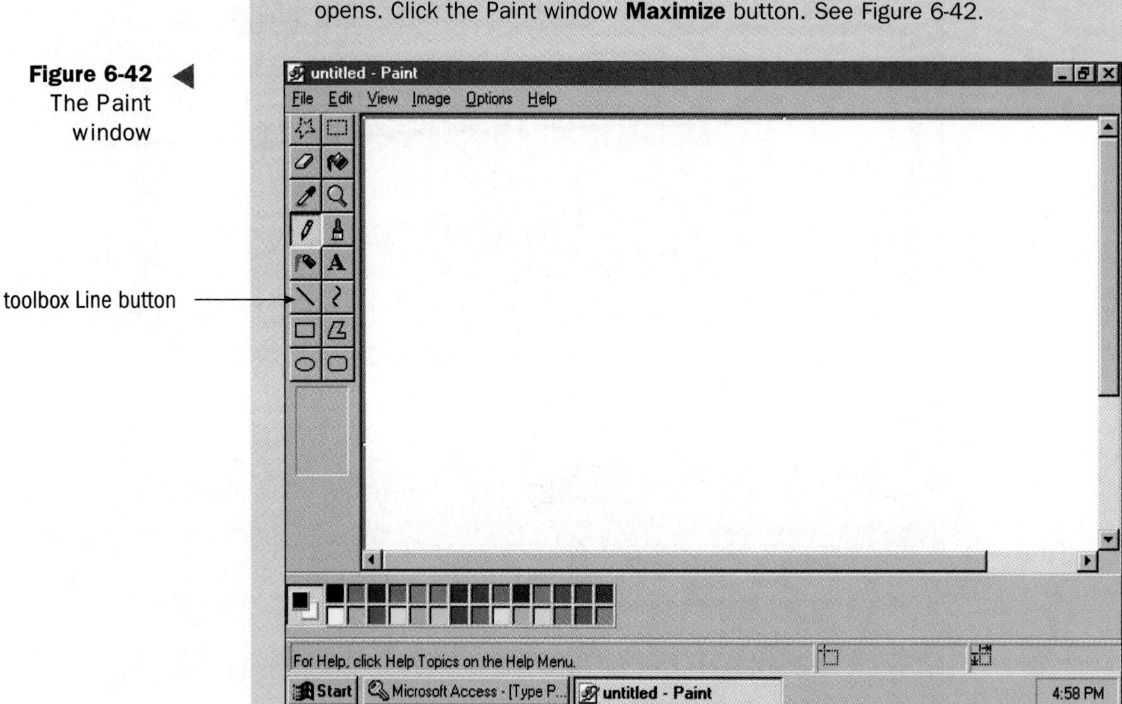

TROUBLE? If you cannot locate the Paint program in the Accessories group, it may be located in another program group on your computer. Try looking through other program groups to find it. If you cannot find it, ask your instructor or technical support person for help. If the Paint program is not installed on your computer, click in the Access window to close the Program list and skip Steps 2 through 8.

2. Click **File**, then click **Open** to display the Open dialog box. Use the Look in text box to open the Tutorial folder on your Student Disk, then double-click **25th** in the file list to open the graphic image file.

   Elena decides to place a line under the Business Perspective title in the graphic image.

3. Click the **toolbox Line** button. Move the pointer onto the image. The pointer changes shape to +.

4. Position the pointer approximately .25" under the "B" in "Business." Click and drag the pointer to the right until it is under the right edge of the final "e" in "Perspective." Paint displays a line as you move the pointer. When the pointer is in the correct position, release the mouse button. Paint places the line in the image. See Figure 6-43.

Figure 6-43 The modified graphic image

TROUBLE? If the line is not straight or is misplaced, click Edit, click Undo, and then repeat Steps 3 and 4.

5. Click **File**, then click **Save** to save the modified image, then click the Paint window **Close** button to exit Paint. The Paint window closes, and the Access Report Design window becomes active.

   The graphic image in the Page Header section does not yet reflect the change Elena made in the original file. If you close the Report Design window and then reopen the report, Access updates the link. Access automatically updates the links to linked objects whenever a form or report is opened. To see the reflected change now, you can also update the link manually.

6. Click **Edit**, then click **OLE/DDE Links** to display the Links dialog box. This dialog box allows you to select the linked objects to be updated.
7. Click **25th** in the Links list box to select it. See Figure 6-44.

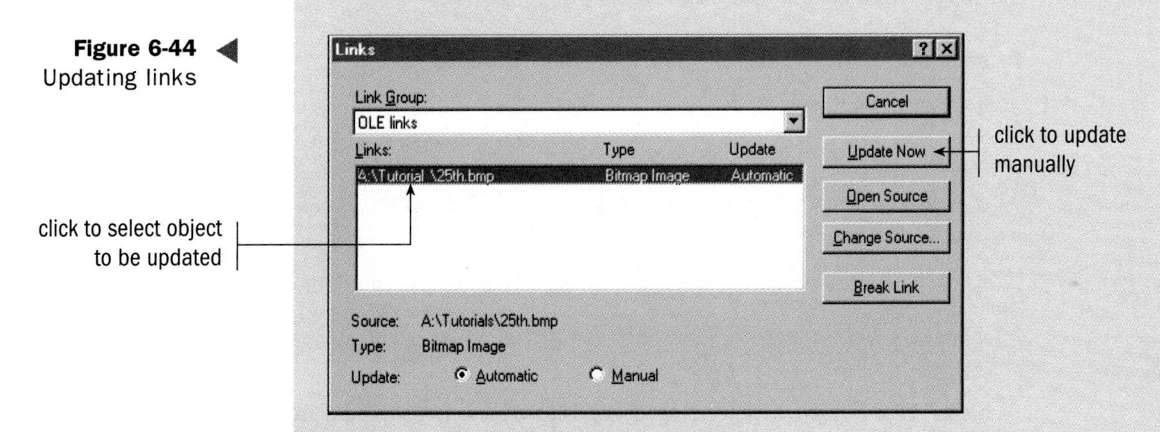

Figure 6-44 Updating links

8. Click the **Update Now** button. Access opens the 25th file on your Student Disk and updates the image in the Page Header. Click the **Close** button to close the Links dialog box and view the updated graphic image. The modified graphic image appears in the Page Header. See Figure 6-45.

Figure 6-45 The report with modified graphic image in the Page Header

Elena is satisfied with the appearance of the report. She saves the report design, prints the report for Harold, and exits Access.

To save and print the report and then exit Access:

1. Click the **Save** button on the toolbar. Access saves the report.
2. Click the **Print** button on the toolbar to print the report.
3. Click the Report Design window **Close** button to close the Report Design window and return to the Database window.
4. Click the Access window **Close** button to exit Access and return to the Windows 95 desktop.

Elena gives Harold the printed report, which he can use in his meetings with the advertisers.

Brian, Judith, and Harold are all pleased with the Issue25 database that Elena has created. They know that Access will make it easier to keep track of the information for the 25th-anniversary issue of *Business Perspective.*

Quick Check

1. Why might you want to embed or link an object in an Access report?
2. What is the difference between embedding and linking?
3. What is OLE?
4. When you insert an object in a report or form using the Insert Object dialog box, how do you specify that the object is to be linked rather than embedded?
5. If you modify a linked object, in what application do you make the changes?
6. What are two ways to update links to linked objects in a report?

Tutorial Assignments

Elena uses the Report Wizard to create a report, named Business Articles Report, for the Issue25 database. Start Access, open the Issue25 database in the Tutorial folder on your Student Disk, and do the following:

1. Use the Report Wizard to create a report based on the BUSINESS ARTICLES table. Use the Align Left 1 layout and the Corporate style for the report. Select all the fields from the table in the order in which they are stored in the table, group the records by Writer ID, select no sort key fields, and enter Business Articles Report as the report title.
2. Display the report in the Print Preview window and then print the entire report.
3. Return to the Database window.

Elena next creates a custom report. Use the Issue25 database on your Student Disk to do the following. Use the report shown in Figure 6-2 as a model for your report design.

4. Create a blank report based on the WRITERS table.
5. Include in your report these sections: Page Header, Freelancer Header, Detail, Freelancer Footer, Page Footer, and Report Footer.
6. In the Page Header section at the beginning of the first line, enter Freelancer Group Totals as the report title. Enter the current date at the beginning of the second line. Position the labels under these lines. Add a single line below the column heads line. Do not place any lines above the column heads or above the report title.
7. Use Freelancer for the grouping field. There are no sorting fields in this report. In the Freelancer Header section, include the Freelancer field value.
8. In the Detail section, include field values for WriterID, Last Name, First Name, Writer Phone, Last Contact Date, and Freelancer Reprint Payment Amount.
9. In the Freelancer Footer section, include the group total for the Freelancer Reprint Payment Amount field.
10. In the Page Footer section, include a page number aligned with the right edge of the Freelancer Reprint Payment Amount field.
11. In the Report Footer section, include the overall total for the Freelancer Reprint Payment Amount field.
12. Embed the 25th Anniversary Issue graphic image (the file named 25th) in the Page Header.
13. When you finish creating the report, print the entire report.
14. Save the report, naming it Freelancer Group Totals Report, and then exit Access.

Case Problems

1. Walkton Daily Press Carriers Grant Sherman uses the Report Wizard to create a report for his Press database. Start Access, open the Press database in the Cases folder on your Student Disk, and do the following:

1. Use the Report Wizard to create a report based on the CARRIERS table. Select all the fields from the table in the order in which they are stored in the table. Do not select a grouping field, use the tabular format, use the compact style, and enter Carriers Report as the report title.
2. Save the report and return to the Database window.

Grant next modifies the design of this report. Open the newly created Carriers Report in the Report Design window and do the following:

3. Move the day/date (Now()) and page number text fields to the Page Header section. Change the sort order of the records to ascending order by Carrier Last Name.
4. Click the Print Preview button to display the report and then print the entire report.

5. Use Save As to save the report, naming it Carriers Report #2, and return to the Database window.

Grant next creates a custom report. Use the Press database on your Student Disk to do the following:

6. Create a blank report using the query Carriers Sorted by Name and Route ID Query.

7. Sketch a design for the report based on the requirements described in Steps 8 through 12, and then create the report following these same steps.
8. Include in your report these sections: Report Header, Page Header, Detail, Group Footer, and Report Footer.
9. In the Page Header section at the beginning of the first line, enter Carriers Sorted by Name and Route ID Report as the report title. Enter the current date at the beginning of the second line and the page number at the end of the second line. Position under these elements a row of column heads with these labels: Last Name, First Name, Carrier Phone, Route ID, and Balance. Add a single horizontal line under the column heads.
10. In the Detail section, include field values for Last Name, First Name, Carrier Phone, Route ID, and Balance. Hide duplicates for the Last Name, First Name, and Carrier Phone fields.
11. In the Group Footer section, print the group total for the Balance field. Select Last Name as the primary sort key, and use this field as a grouping field. Select Route ID as the secondary sort key, but do not use it as a grouping field. Choose ascending sort order for each sort key.
12. In the Report Footer section, print the overall total for the Balance field.

13. Insert an embedded WordPad document in the Report Header. In the document, write a short paragraph describing the contents of the report. Include your name as the creator of the report.
14. When you finish creating the report, print the entire report.
15. Save the report, and then exit Access.

2. Lopez Lexus Dealerships Maria Lopez uses the Report Wizard to create a report for her Lexus database. Start Access, open the Lexus database in the Cases folder on your Student Disk, and do the following:

1. Use the Report Wizard to create a report in the Corporate style based on the CARS table. Select all the fields from the table in the order in which they are stored in the table. Do not select a grouping field, use the tabular layout, and enter Cars by Year Report as the report title.
2. Save the report and return to the Database window.

Maria next modifies the design of this report. Open the newly created report Cars by Year Report in the Report Design window and do the following:

3. Move the day/date (Now()) and page number text fields to the Report Header section. Adjust the font size and widths in the column headings so the entire labels are visible.
4. Click the Print Preview button to display the report and then print the entire report.
5. Use Save As to save the report, naming it Cars Report #2, and return to the Database window.

Maria next creates a custom report. Use the Lexus database in the Cases folder on your Student Disk and do the following:

6. Create a blank report using the CARS table.

7. Sketch a design for the report based on the requirements described in Steps 8 through 12, and then create the report following these same steps.
8. Include in your report these sections: Page Header, Detail, Group Footer, and Report Footer.
9. In the Page Header section at the beginning of the first line, enter the report title Cars Sorted by Model and Year. Enter the current date at the beginning of the second line and the page number at the end of the second line.

Position under these elements a row of column heads with these labels: Manufacturer, Model, Year, Cost, and Selling Price. Add a single horizontal line under the column heads.

10. In the Detail section, include the field values for Manufacturer, Model, Year, Cost, and Selling Price. Hide duplicates for the Manufacturer field.
11. In the Group Footer section, print the group total for the Cost and Selling Price fields. Select Model as the primary sort key and as the grouping field. Select Year as the secondary sort key but do not use it as a grouping field. Choose ascending sort order for the sort keys.
12. In the Report Footer section, print the overall totals for the Cost and Selling Price fields.
13. When you finish creating the report, print the entire report.
14. Save the report, naming it Cars by Model and Year Report.
15. Use the Chart Wizard to create a pie chart report based on Model. Each wedge in the pie should represent the count of cars of each model. Insert percents as labels for each wedge. Save the report as Model Pie Chart Report. Print the report and exit Access.

3. Tophill University Student Employment Olivia Tyler uses the Report Wizard to create a report for her Parttime database. Start Access, open the Parttime database in the Cases folder on your Student Disk, and do the following:

1. Use the Report Wizard to create a tabular layout report based on the JOBS table. Select all the fields from the table in the order in which they are stored in the table. Do not select a grouping field and enter Jobs Report as the report title. Use the corporate style.
2. Save the report, naming it Jobs Report, and return to the Database window.

Olivia next modifies the design of this report. Open the newly created report Jobs Report in the Report Design window and do the following:

3. Adjust the size of the Detail section so that there are no blank lines between the printed records. Add double lines in the Page Footer, separating the Day/Date and Page Number text boxes from the Detail section.
4. Click the Print Preview button to display the report and then print the entire report.
5. Use Save As to save the report, naming it Jobs Report #2, and return to the Database window.

Olivia next creates a custom report. Use the Parttime database on your Student Disk to do the following:

6. Create a blank report using Jobs Sorted by Employer and Job Title Query.
7. Sketch a design for the report based on the requirements described in Steps 8 through 11, and then create the report following these same steps.
8. Include in your report a Page Header section and a Detail section.
9. In the Page Header section at the beginning of the first line, enter Jobs Sorted by Employer and Job Title as the report title. Enter the current date at the beginning of the second line and the page number at the end of the second line. Position under these elements a row of column heads with these labels: Employer Name, Hours/Week, Job Title, and Wages. Add a single horizontal line under the column heads.
10. In the Detail section, include the field values for Employer Name, Hours/Week, Job Title, and Wages. Hide duplicates for the Employer Name field.
11. Select Employer Name as the primary sort key and Job Title as the secondary sort key. Do not select a grouping field. Choose ascending sort order for each sort key.

12. Insert the graphic image file TU as a linked object in the Page Header. Edit the graphic image file in the Paint program and change the background of the TU logo to bright yellow. Save the changes to the image and view the report in the Print Preview window.
13. When you finish creating the report, print the entire report.
14. Save the report, naming it Jobs Sorted by Employer and Job Title Report and then exit Access.

4. Rexville Business Licenses Chester Pearce uses the Report Wizard to create a report for his Buslic database. Start Access, open the Buslic database in the Cases folder on your Student Disk, and do the following:

1. Use the Report Wizard to create a report in the Bold style based on the BUSINESSES table. Select all the fields from the table in the order in which they are stored in the table. Do not select a grouping field, select tabular layout, and enter Businesses Report as the report title.
2. Return to the Database window.

Chester next modifies the design of this report. Open the newly created report Businesses Report in the Report Design window and do the following:

3. In the Report Header section, center the title label.
4. Click the Print Preview button to display the report and then print the entire report.
5. Use Save As to save the report, naming it Businesses Report #2, and then return to the Database window.

Chester next creates a custom report. Use the Buslic database on your Student Disk to do the following:

6. Create a blank report using Businesses Sorted by License Type and Business Name Query.
7. Sketch a design for the report based on the requirements described in Steps 8 through 12, and then create the report following these same steps.

8. Include in your report these sections: Page Header, Detail, Group Footer, and Report Footer.
9. In the Page Header section at the beginning of the first line, enter Businesses Sorted by License Type and Business Name as the report title. Enter the current date at the beginning of the second line and the page number at the end of the second line. Position under these elements a row of column heads with these labels: License, Basic Cost, Business Name, and Amount. Add a single horizontal line under the column heads.
10. In the Detail section, include the field values for License (do not use License Number), Basic Cost, Business Name, and Amount. Hide duplicates for the License and Basic Cost fields.
11. In the Group Footer section, print the group total for the Amount field. Select License as the primary sort key and as the grouping field. Select Business Name as the secondary sort key, but do not use it as a grouping field. Choose ascending sort order for each sort key.
12. In the Report Footer section, print the overall totals for the Amount field.
13. When you finish creating the report, print the entire report.
14. Save the report, naming it Businesses Sorted by License Type and Business Name Report.

15. Use the Chart Wizard to create a 3-D column chart based on the License Type and Amount fields of the Issued Licenses table. Accept the default layout. Add a label to the X (horizontal) axis of the graph. The label should be License Types. Delete the legend. Insert an embedded WordPad document in the Detail section that explains that these numbers are license types. In the document, write a short description of the graph.
16. Print the report and save it with the name License Fee Graph Report, and then exit Access.

Answers to Quick Check Questions

SESSION 1.1

1 What three steps should you generally follow to create and store a new type of data?
When you create and store new types of data either manually or on a computer, you follow a general three-step procedure:
- Identify the individual fields.
- Group fields for each entity in a table.
- Store the field values for each record.

2 What are fields and entities, and how are they related?
An entity is a person, place, object, event, or idea that you are recording in a table. Each record in a table corresponds to an individual entity. Each entity has certain characteristics or attributes. Each attribute is represented by a field. For example, the records in a mailing list table correspond to the individual persons on the mailing list. Each person has characteristics such as Last Name, First Name, Street Address, etc. Each of these characteristics is a field in the table.

3 What are the differences between a primary key and a foreign key?
A primary key is a field, or a collection of fields, whose values uniquely identify each record in a table. When we include a primary key from one table in a second table to form a relationship between the two tables, we call it a foreign key in the second table.

4 Describe what a DBMS is designed to do.
A database management system (DBMS) is a software package that lets us create databases and then manipulate data in the databases.

5 Describe the six different objects you can create for an Access database.
A table is a structure that contains all fields for a specific entity. Records are stored in a table. A query is a question you can ask about the data from your tables. A form allows you do display records from a table for viewing or editing. A report describes a customized format for printing the data from tables. A macro is a saved list of operations to be performed on data, which Access carries out when you run the macro. Finally, Access has a built-in programming language called Visual Basic. A module is a set of one or more Visual Basic programmed procedures.

6 What do the columns and rows of a datasheet represent?
Each row is a separate record in the table, and each column, headed by a field name, contains the field values for one field from the table.

7 Name the fields in the CHECKS table. How many records are in the CHECKS table? What is the primary key of the CHECKING ACCOUNTS table?
Field names: Account Number, Check Number, Date, Amount. There are 5 records in the CHECKS table. The primary key is Account Number.

SESSION 1.2

1 What does the Form View window show?
The Form View window displays records from a table in a custom form. A custom form can be used to display records in a more readable or usable format than that used by the Datasheet View window.

2 Name the five ways you can use Access's Help system to get on-line information.
You can use Access's Help system to get on-line information through:
- Help Contents — displays a list of the major Help topics.
- Help Index — allows you to find topics related to a key word or phrase.
- Help Find — allows you to search the entire Help system for specific words.

- Answer Wizard — analyzes your typed question and suggests related Help topics.
- Context-Sensitive Help — displays short help information about objects on the current screen.

3 How does the Help Index differ from the Answer Wizard?
The Help Index searches for topics related to a specific word or phrase that you enter. The Help Index, like an index in a book, is a list of topics available in Help. When you enter a word or phrase, the Help Index searches for the word or phrase in the index and displays the relevant section of the Index. You can then ask for help on the topic displayed. The Answer Wizard analyzes a question that you enter and displays a list of topics related to your question. It is not necessary for you to enter words that exactly match the words in Help's list of topics. The Answer Wizard can use synonyms and analyze questions in various forms.

4 How would you find out the meaning of the button?
Use context-sensitive help to learn that is the Spelling button. It is used to check the spelling of text entries in Datasheet View of tables, queries, and forms. It also can be used to check the spelling of selected text in a text box in Form View.

5 What is the purpose of a shortcut menu, and why would you use it?
A shortcut menu contains a list of commands that relate to the object you click. Using a shortcut menu is often faster than using a menu or toolbar button.

6 How do you open and close a shortcut menu?
To display a shortcut menu window, you position the mouse pointer on a specific object or area and click the right mouse button. To close a shortcut menu window, you click the left mouse button outside the window.

SESSION 2.1

1 What two types of keys represent a common field when you form a relationship between tables?
A primary key and a foreign key.

2 What is data redundancy?
Data redundancy occurs when you store the same data in more than one place. With the exception of common fields to relate tables, you should avoid redundancy.

3 Name and describe three Access data types.
There are nine Access data types:

- Text allows field values containing letters, digits, spaces, and special characters. Text fields can be up to 255 characters long.
- Memo, like the Text data type, allows field values containing letters, digits, spaces, and special characters. Memo fields, however, can be up to 64,000 characters long and are used for long comments or explanations.
- Number limits field values to digits, an optional leading sign (+ or –), and an optional decimal point.
- Date/Time allows field values containing valid dates and times only.
- Currency allows field values similar to those for the Number data type. Unlike calculations with Number data type decimal values, calculations performed using the Currency data type will not be subject to round-off error.
- AutoNumber consists of integers with values automatically controlled by Access. Access automatically inserts a value in the field as each new record is created.
- Yes/No limits field values to yes and no entries.
- OLE Object allows field values that are created in other software packages as objects, such as photographs, video images, graphics, drawings, sound recordings, voice-mail messages, spreadsheets, and word processing documents.
- Lookup Wizard creates a field that lets you to select a value from another table or from a predefined list of values.

4 Why might including a field description in a table be helpful?
The field description helps the table designer identify the purpose of a field. It is an annotation to help document the table.

5 What is one advantage of designating a primary key?
Access prevents the user from entering a new record that has a primary key value identical to that of an existing record. This guarantees uniqueness of primary key values.

6 Which data types need to have field sizes determined?
You must define field sizes for Text and Number fields. Other fields have predefined sizes.

7 Describe two different ways to select a field's data type.
- Click the Data Type text box, then click the Data Type list arrow that appears, then click the data type you want.
- In the Data Type text box, type the first letter of the name of the data type. Access fills in the name of the data type in the Data Type text box.

8 How do you switch from one view window to another?
Click the Table View button to switch to a different view of the table.

SESSION 2.2

1 What is a caption?
A caption is a shorter version of a longer, more descriptive table field name.

2 Describe three different ways to resize a datasheet column.
- You can use the Format menu to display the Column Width dialog box. Specify the desired width.
- You can use the mouse pointer to drag the right edge of a selected column.
- You can use the best-fit column width method to resize a selected column Access automatically resizes the column to accommodate its largest value, including the field name at the top of the column. To use this method, you position the mouse pointer at the right edge of the column selector for the field and, when the mouse pointer changes to ↔, double-click the left mouse button. Access then automatically resizes the column.

3 Why would you assign a default value to a field?
When you assign a default value to a field, Access automatically supplies that value for each new record. This makes data entry easier and minimizes the chance of error.

4 What are the steps for changing decimal places?
In the Design View window, select the field for which you want to change decimal places. Click the text box for the Decimal places property, then click the list arrow that appears, then select the correct number of decimal places.

5 What is an input mask?
An input mask is a description of the format for data entered in a particular field. When you enter data in the field, Access requires that you enter the data according to the format specified by the input mask

6 Describe two recommended ways to create an Access table.
Create an Access Table using the Table Wizard or by designing the table directly in the Design View window.

7 What is an index and why is it useful?
An index is a list of primary key values and their corresponding record numbers. An index makes searching for and sorting records more efficient. An index also allows you to define relations between tables.

SESSION 3.1

1 What operations are performed when you update a database?
Adding records, deleting records, and modifying records are the basic operations when you update a database.

2 What does a pencil symbol signify in a record selector? An asterisk symbol?
The pencil symbol indicates a record that has been modified but not saved. The asterisk is the new record symbol.

3 Which button do you use to move to the last record in the table?
Use the Last Record button ▶|.

4 If you change field values in a table, what do you have to do to save your changes?
Once you have entered or modified data in a field, Access automatically saves the changes.

5 If you delete a record from a table, do all field values disappear? Which field values, if any, remain?
Access deletes the record from the table. The Datasheet View window will still show the default values for any blank record visible in the window.

6 What are some advantages of importing data?
Importing data saves time since you don't have to reenter the data. Importing also minimizes the chance of error in data entry.

7 When would you use the Table Analyzer Wizard?
Use the Table Analyzer Wizard to check the design of a table. The Table Analyzer Wizard makes suggestions for changes to the table design that may make the design more efficient.

8 How do you change a datasheet's font?
Use the Format toolbar to change a datasheet's font. You can change the font type, size, and style.

SESSION 3.2

1 How can you find a specific field value in a table?
Click in the field column you want to search. Click the Find button, then type the search value in the Find What text box. Select the search options, then click the Find First button to find the first occurrence of the field value.

2 Why do you need to be cautious about using the Replace All option when replacing table field values?
When you use the Replace All option, Access cannot undo the replacements after they are made.

3 What are the advantages of sorting a datasheet's records?
By sorting a datasheet's records, you can view the records in a more convenient order. You can sort the records on different fields, allowing different users to view the records in the order they need and making it easy to find and view groups of records.

4 When might you consider using a secondary sort key?
A secondary key is useful to subsort records that have matching values for the primary sort key. For example, if you wish to sort employee records by name, the Last Name would be an appropriate primary sort key and First Name would be an appropriate secondary sort key.

5 What are some advantages of using Access's Spelling feature?
Access's Spelling feature allows you to check the spelling of values entered in a Text field. This reduces the chance of error in the data and allows you to check many records quickly.

6 What is the purpose of the Lookup Wizard?
The Lookup Wizard assists you in defining a Table Lookup field. It prompts you for the necessary information to describe the source of the data and which value should be stored.

7 How many different files do you copy when you back up one Access database that includes three tables?
You only need to copy one file.

8 What is the purpose of compacting a database?
When records or objects are deleted from a database, the space does not become immediately available. Compacting a database removes deleted records and objects, creates a smaller version of the database, and releases the space for future use.

SESSION 4.1

1 What is the Simple Query Wizard?
The Simple Query Wizard assists you in creating a query design by prompting you for the tables and fields to be used in the query and by automatically saving the query design.

2 In what format do the query results appear? What are the advantages of this format?
The query results appear in the Datasheet View window. These results are temporary and are not saved as a table. Any changes you make to the data in the query results will be made in the underlying table(s).

3 What is QBE?
QBE means Query By Example. You can define a query using the Query Design grid by describing an example of the information you want. Access then retrieves the records that match you example.

4 What are two methods for adding a field from a table to the Query Design grid?
You can add a field from a table by clicking and dragging the field from the field list to the Query Design grid or by double-clicking on the field name in the field list.

5 What are the two components of a simple condition?
A simple condition is composed of a comparison operator (such as = or <) and a value.

6 How do you exclude a field that appears in the Query Design grid from the query results?
You exclude a field from the query results by removing the check mark in the Show box for that field in the Query Design grid.

7 What comparison operator is used to select records based on a specific pattern?
The Like comparison operator is used to select records based on a pattern.

8 When do you use the In comparison operator?
Use the In comparison operator to specify a list of values. A record is selected if its field value matches any value in the list.

SESSION 4.2

1 Why might you need to sort a single field?
You would sort query results for a single field in order to view the records ordered by the values in that field.

2 How must you position the fields in the Query Design grid when you have multiple sort keys?
The sort key that appears leftmost in the Query Design grid is the primary sort key. If two records match in the primary sort key field, Access uses the next leftmost sort key to subsort.

3 Why might you print selected query results?
You would print a query results selection if you want to print only some of the records in the query results.

4 When do you use logical operators?
Logical operators And and Or are used to create multiple selection criteria. For the And logical operator, Access selects all records that meet all selection criteria. For the Or logical operator, Access selects all records that meet any of the selection criteria.

5 What is a calculated field?
A calculated field is a field in the Query Design grid that is calculated from values in other fields.

6 When do you use an aggregate function?
Aggregate functions summarize data. For example, to calculate the sum of values in a field, use the SUM aggregate function.

7 What does the Group By operator do?
The Group By operator combines records with identical field values into a single record.

SESSION 4.3

1 What is a join?
A join is a relationship between two tables.

2 Describe the difference between a one-to-many relationship and a one-to-one relationship.
In a one-to-many relationship, a single record in the primary table is related to one or more records in the related table. In a one-to-one relationship, a single record in the primary table is related to only one record in the related table.

3 What functions can you perform in the Relationships window?
In the Relationships window, you can view or change existing relationships, define new relationships between tables, rearrange the layout of tables, and change the structures of related tables.

4 What are the two referential integrity rules?
The two referential integrity rules are:
- When you add a record to a related table, there must be a matching record in the primary table.
- You cannot delete a record in the primary table if matching records exist in the related table.

5 What does a join line signify?
A join line in a relationship diagram indicates the common field in the two tables, the nature of the relationship (one-to-one, one-to-many, etc.), and the enforcement of integrity rules.

6 How do you query more than one table?
You query more than one table by defining a relationship between the tables and then selecting fields from those tables in the Query Design grid.

7 When do you use a parameter query?
Use a parameter query when you want Access to prompt you for the selection criteria when you run the query.

SESSION 5.1

1 What is a form?
A form displays records from an Access database in a more attractive and readable format. You can use a form to maintain, view, and print records of data.

2 What are three form designs that you can create with AutoForm?
AutoForm creates a form in one of three standard designs: Columnar, Tabular, or Datasheet.

3 What formats does the Form Wizard use to display records in a main/subform form?
The main form is displayed in columnar format. The subform can be displayed in either tabular or datasheet format, depending on your choice when you create the subform.

4 How many sets of navigation buttons appear in a main/subform form, and what does each set control?
There are two sets of navigation buttons in a main/subform form. The bottom set controls navigation through the records displayed in the main form. The upper set controls navigation through the records displayed in the subform.

5 What is a filter?
A filter is a set of criteria that describes the records you want to see in a form and their sequence. Unlike a query, a filter applies only to the form that is currently in use. You can save the filter as a query.

6 What is the purpose of filter by selection? Filter by form?
Filter by selection allows you to specify an exact match simple selection condition by using an actual record as a model. Filter by form allows you to specify multiple selection criteria directly in a blank form. A filter by form can be saved as a query.

7 How can you tell that the Form View window is displaying records to which a filter has been applied?
The Form View window displays three indicators that a filter has been applied:
- The Apply Filter button appears pressed down.
- The word "(Filtered)" appears near the navigation buttons.
- The indicator "FLTR" appears in the status line.

8 How do you reuse a filter in the future?
After specifying a filter by form or designing a filter in the Filter Design window, you can save the filter as a query for future use. Open the form and click the Filter By Form button on the toolbar. Click File, then click Load from Query, and select the saved query. Click the Apply Filter button on the toolbar to run the query.

SESSION 5.2

1 What is the difference between a bound and an unbound control?
A bound control, such as a field-value text box, is associated with a field from a table record. The field value appears in the bound control. An unbound control, such as a label, is not associated with any field in a table.

2 How do you move a control and its label together, and how do you move each separately?
Click in the control or label to select both, then place the pointer inside either object. Click the left mouse button to change the pointer to 🖐 and drag the two controls

together to their new location. To move a single selected control, click the control's move handle and drag it to its new position.

3 How do you change a label name?
Click in the label to select it, click the right mouse button to display the property sheet window. Change the Caption property value, then close the property sheet window.

4 How would you resize a control?
Click the control to select it, place the pointer on a sizing handle, and click and drag the edge of the control.

5 What is the Form Header section?
The Form Header section defines the controls that will appear at the top of each form.

6 Describe how you would use a Control Wizard to add a list box to a form.
In the toolbox, click the Control Wizards button, then click the toolbox List Box button. Place the pointer on the form and click to position the list box. Complete the Control Wizard dialog boxes to create the list box.

7 How do you insert into a form a graphic created with another software program?
In the toolbox, click the toolbox Image button. Position the pointer in the form at the position for the upper-left corner of the graphic image. Select the image from the Insert Picture dialog box.

8 What is control morphing?
Control morphing allows you to change the control type for a control without having to delete it and redefine it.

SESSION 6.1

1 What are the seven Access report sections?
- Report Header — Appears once at the beginning of a report.
- Page Header — Appears at the top of each page of a report.
- Group Header — Appears once at the beginning of a new group of records.
- Detail — Appears once for each record in the underlying table or query.
- Group Footer — Appears once at the end of a group of records.
- Report Footer — Appears once at the end of the report.
- Page Footer — Appears at the bottom of each page of a report.

2 What types of reports can AutoReport create and what is the difference between them?
AutoReport creates a report in one of two standard formats: columnar or tabular. A Columnar report lists records one field per line, vertically on the report page. A Tabular report lists one record per line, horizontally on the report page.

3 What is a group?
A group is a set of records that share a common value for one or more fields.

4 Why is it not necessary to save manually a report created by the Report Wizard?
The Report Wizard automatically saves the report before displaying it in the Print Preview window.

5 What is a custom report?
A custom report is any report you create in the Report Design window or any modified report created by AutoReport or the Report Wizard.

6 What does the Report Design window have in common with the Form Design window? What is different?
The Report Design window and the Form Design window are similar in most respects, except that the Report Design window displays a new toolbar button, the Sorting and Grouping button. By default, the Form Design window displays only a Detail section. The Report Design window displays a Page Header and Page Footer section as well as the Detail section.

7 In the Report Design window, how is adding, moving, resizing, and deleting controls different from accomplishing these tasks in the Form Design window?
Each object in the Form Design window or the Report Design window is a control. The process of adding, moving, resizing, and deleting controls is essentially the same in both windows.

SESSION 6.2

1 When do you use the toolbox Text Box tool?
The Text Box tool is used to place a bound control in the Report Design window.

2 What do you type in a text box to tell Access to print the current date?
The function =Date() will print the current date.

3 How do you insert a page number in a Page Header section?
In the Report Design window, click Insert, then click Page Number.

4 What is the function of the Sorting and Grouping button?
The Sorting and Grouping button allows you to specify how the records will be sorted when they are printed in a report. Each sort key can also be used as a grouping field for the records.

5 How do you add a Report Footer section to a report without adding a Report Header section?
Click View, then click Report Header/Footer in the Report Design window. Then reduce the height of the Report Header section to zero.

6 How do you calculate group totals and overall totals?
Place a text box in the Group Footer or Report Footer section. In the text box, enter the expression =Sum([*field name*]), where *field name* is the name of the field you want to total.

7 Why might you want to hide duplicate values in a group report?
Duplicate values clutter up the report. Hiding them makes the report easier to read.

SESSION 6.3

1 Why might you want to embed or link an object in an Access report?
You embed or link objects in an Access report to include objects created by other applications. These can be objects of a type Access cannot create (e.g., graphs).

2 What is the difference between embedding and linking?
An embedded object preserves its connection to the application that created it. You can edit the object by double-clicking on it and using the parent application. Any changes you make in the object are reflected in the Access embedded file, not in the original file. A linked object also preserves its connection to the original file from which it came. You can edit the object by double-clicking on it and using the parent application, or you can edit it outside of Access using the parent application. Any changes you make in the object are reflected in both the Access file and in the original file from which it came.

3 What is OLE?
OLE stands for Object Linking and Embedding. An application that supports OLE can create objects that can be embedded or linked in another application. Not all applications allow object linking or embedding.

4 When you insert an object in a report or form using the Insert Object dialog box, how do you specify that the object is to be linked rather than embedded?
Insert the object from a file and check the Link check box.

5 If you modify a linked object, in what application do you make the changes?
When you modify a linked object, you use the application that was originally used to create the object.

6 What are two ways to update links to linked objects in a report?
Each linked object is updated automatically when the report is opened. You can also update the links manually by clicking Edit, then clicking Update OLE/DDE links in the Report Design window.

Index

Task Reference

TASK	PAGE #	RECOMMENDED METHOD	NOTES
Access, exiting	AC 10	Click the Access window Close button ☒	
Access, starting	AC 9	Click Start, point to Programs, then click Microsoft Access	
Aggregate function, adding to a query	AC 141	See Reference Window: Using Aggregate Function in the Query Design Grid	
Answer Wizard, accessing	AC 24	Click Help, then click Answer Wizard	
AutoForm form, creating	AC 163	See Reference Window: Creating a Form with AutoForm	
AutoReport report, creating	AC 217	See Reference Window: Creating a Report with AutoReport	
Blank report, creating	AC 223	See Reference Window: Creating a Blank Report in the Report Design Window	
Calculated field, adding to a query	AC 139	See Reference Window: Adding a Calculated Field to the Query Design Grid	
Caption, entering for a field	AC 49	Type caption in the Caption property text box in the Design View window	
Caption, changing a label's	AC 188	See Reference Window: Changing a Label's Caption	
Change, undoing		Click	
Chart, embedding in a report	AC 248	See Reference Window: Using the Chart Wizard to Create a Report with an Embedded Chart	
Colors, changing in a form	AC 199	See Reference Window: Adding Background Color to a Control on a Form	
Column, resizing	AC 50	See Reference Window: Resizing Columns in a Datasheet	
Control, deleting	AC 229	See Reference Window: Deleting Controls	
Control, morphing	AC 202	Right click the control, point to Change to, then click the new type	
Control, resizing	AC 189	Click the control to display sizing handles, then drag a sizing handle	
Controls, aligning on a form	AC 191	See Reference Window: Aligning Objects in a Form	
Controls, arranging on a form	AC 186	See Reference Window: Selecting, Moving and Deleting Controls	
Controls, arranging on a report	AC 228	See Reference Window: Moving and Resizing Controls	
Custom form, creating	AC 182	See Reference Window: Creating a Form in the Form Design Window	

Task Reference

TASK	PAGE #	RECOMMENDED METHOD	NOTES
Data, finding in a datasheet	AC 88	See Reference Window: Finding Data in a Table	
Data, maintaining using a form	AC 170	See Reference Window: Maintaining Table Data Using a Form	
Data, replacing in a datasheet	AC 91	See Reference Window: Replacing Data in a Table	
Database, backing up	AC 103	See Reference Window: Backing Up an Access Database	
Database, closing	AC 22	Click the Database window Close button	
Database, compacting	AC 105	See Reference Window: Compacting a Database	
Database, creating	AC 37	See Reference Window: Creating a Database	
Database, opening	AC 11	Click , then select the file from the Open dialog box	
Datasheet View, switching to	AC 47	Click	
Datasheet, printing	AC 47	Click	
Data type, assigning to field	AC 40	Select data type from the data type list in the Design View window	
Date, adding to a report	AC 233	See Reference Window: Adding a Date to a Report	
Decimal places, changing the number of in a field	AC 53	Select decimal places in Decimal Places property text box in the Design View window	
Default value, defining for a field	AC 52	Type default value in Default Value property text box in the Design View window	
Design View, switching to	AC 47	Click	
Duplicate values, hiding in a report	AC 243	See Reference Window: Hiding Duplicate Values in a Report	
Embedded object, editing	AC 246	Double-click the object to start the application that created it	
Field, adding to a form or report	AC 185	Click field name in the field list box, then drag the field to the form	
Field, adding to a table structure	AC 59	See Reference Window: Adding a Field to a Table Structure	
Field, deleting from a table structure	AC 58	See Reference Window: Deleting a Field from a Table Structure	
Field, deleting from the Query Design grid	AC 139	Right click the field selector, then click Cut	
Field, excluding from the query results	AC 123	Click the field's Show box in the Query Design grid to remove the check mark	

Task Reference

TASK	PAGE #	RECOMMENDED METHOD	NOTES
Field, inserting in Query Design grid	AC 118	Drag the field name from the field list to the Query Design grid	
Field description, assigning	AC 42	Type description in Description text box in Design View window	
Field size, assigning	AC 43	Select or enter field size in Field Size text box in the Design View window	
Field values, changing	AC 79	See Reference Window: Changing Field Values in a Record	
Fields, adding all to a Query Design grid	AC 118	Double-click field list box title bar, then drag the field list to the Query Design grid	
Fields, naming	AC 40	Type name in the Field Name text box in the Design View window	
Filter, applying	AC 179	Click	
Filter by form, creating	AC 175	See Reference Window: Selecting Records with Filter by Form	
Filter by selection, creating	AC 173	See Reference Window: Selecting Records with Filter by Selection	
Filter saved as a query, applying	AC 179	See Reference Window: Applying a Filter that Was Saved as a Query	
Filter, removing	AC 174	Click	
Filter, saving as a query	AC 178	See Reference Window: Saving a Filter as a Query	
First record, moving to	AC 17	Click	
Font, changing a datasheet's	AC 86	See Reference Window: Changing a Datasheet's Font Properties	
Form Header and Footer, adding to a form	AC 185	Click View, then click Form Header/Footer	
Form View, switching to	AC 192	Click	
Form, creating using AutoForm	AC 163	See Reference Window: Creating a Form with AutoForm	
Form, creating in the Form Design Window	AC 182	See Reference Window: Creating a Form in the Form Design Window	
Form, creating using the Form Wizard	AC 166	See Reference Window: Creating a Main/Subform Form using the Form Wizard	
Form, opening	AC 21	Select the form in the Database window, then click the Open button	
Form, printing	AC 174	Click	

Task Reference

TASK	PAGE #	RECOMMENDED METHOD	NOTES
Form, saving	AC 165	Click	
Graphic image, adding to a form	AC 194	See Reference Window: Adding a Graphic Image to a Form	
Graphic image, linking in a report	AC 254	See Reference Window: Inserting a Linked Object in a Report	
Grouping fields, adding to a report	AC 224	Click , then either double-click the field list title bar to highlight all the fields and drag to the report, or place pointer on field names and drag to the report	
Help, accessing	AC 23	Click Help on the menu bar	
Index, creating	AC 67	Type Yes in the Indexed property text box in the Design View window	
Indexes, displaying a table's	AC 67	Click	
Input mask, defining for a field	AC 54	See Reference Window: Creating an Input Mask with the Input Mask Wizard	
Label, adding to a form or report	AC 231	See Reference Window: Adding a Label to a Report	
Last record, moving to	AC 17	Click	
Lines, adding to a form or report	AC 236	See Reference Window: Adding a Line to a Report	
Linked object, editing	AC 250	Start the application that created the object, open the object and edit it	
Links, updating	AC 257	Click Edit, then click OLE/DDE Links, select the object, then click the Update Now button	
List box, adding to a form or report	AC 196	See Reference Window: Adding a List Box to a Form with the Control Wizard	
Lookup Wizard field, defining	AC 98	See Reference Window: Defining a Lookup Wizard Field	
Multiple selection criteria, defining in Query Design grid	AC 135	See Reference Window: Defining Multiple Selection Criteria	
Next record, moving to	AC 17	Click	
Page numbers, adding to a report	AC 234	See Reference Window: Adding Page Numbers to a Report	
Parameter query, creating	AC 154	See Reference Window: Creating a Parameter Query	
Previous record, moving to	AC 17	Click	

Task Reference

TASK	PAGE #	RECOMMENDED METHOD	NOTES
Primary key, defining	AC 42	Click	
Record, creating a new blank	AC 77	Click	
Relationship, establishing	AC 151	See Reference Window: Adding a Relationship Between Two Tables	
Query results, printing	AC 133	Click	
Query results, sorting a single field	AC 130	See Reference Window: Selecting a Sort Key in the Query Design Window	
Query results, viewing	AC 115	Click	
Query, creating with the Simple Query Wizard	AC 113	See Reference Window: Creating a Query with the Simple Query Wizard	
Query, opening	AC 120	Click the query name, then click the Open button	
Query, running	AC 117	Click	
Query, saving	AC 120	Click	
Query, saving under a new name	AC 120	Click File, click Save As/Export, type new name in the New Name text box, then click the OK button	
Record group calculations, adding to a query	AC 144	See Reference Window: Using Record Group Calculations	
Record, adding to a table	AC 77	See Reference Window: Adding a Record to a Table	
Record, deleting from a table	AC 80	Right click record selector, then click Cut	
Records, printing selected	AC 132	Select records in Datasheet View, then click	
Records, quick sorting on a single field	AC 95	See Reference Window: Sorting Records on a Single Field in Datasheet View with Quick-Sort	
Records, grouping in a report	AC 238	See Reference Window: Sorting and Grouping Data in a Report	
Records, sorting in a report	AC 238	See Reference Window: Sorting and Grouping Data in a Report	
Records, quick sorting on multiple fields	AC 95	See Reference Window: Sorting Records on Multiple Fields in Datasheet View with Quick-Sort	
Records, sorting in a query	AC 130	See Reference Window: Selecting a Sort Key in the Query Design Window	

Task Reference

TASK	PAGE #	RECOMMENDED METHOD	NOTES
Relationship, defining between tables	AC 152	See Reference Window: Adding a Relationship Between Two Tables	
Report Header and Footer, adding to a report	AC 239	Click View, then click Report Header and Footer	
Report, creating using AutoReport	AC 217	See Reference Window: Creating a Report with AutoReport	
Report, creating using the Report Wizard	AC 219	See Reference Window: Creating a Report with the Report Wizard	
Report, printing	AC 221	Click	
Report, saving	AC 218	Click	
Selection criteria, defining in Query Design grid	AC 121	See Reference Window: Defining Record Selection Criteria	
Selection criteria, deleting in Query Design grid	AC 127	Click in criterion text box, press the [F2] key, then press the [Delete] key	
Shortcut menu, displaying an object's	AC 29	Right click on object	
Sort keys, adding to a report	AC 238	See Reference Window: Sorting and Grouping Data in the Report	
Special effects, adding to an object	AC 200	See Reference Window: Changing the Special Effects Property for a Control	
Spelling, checking in records	AC 97	See Reference Window: Using Access's Spelling Feature to Check Spelling of Field Values	
Table structure, saving	AC 46	Click	
Table, creating in Design View	AC 39	See Reference Window: Creating a Table in Design View	
Table, creating using Table Wizard	AC 63	See Reference Window: Creating a Table with the Table Wizard	
Table, deleting	AC 85	See Reference Window: Deleting a Table	
Table, importing	AC 82	See Reference Window: Importing an Access Table	
Table, opening	AC 15	Click the table name, then click the Open button	
Table, renaming	AC 85	Right click table name, then click Rename	
Table Analyzer Wizard, using	AC 83	See Reference Window: Using the Table Analyzer Wizard	

Task Reference

TASK	PAGE #	RECOMMENDED METHOD	NOTES
Text box, adding to a form or report	AC 231	Click the Text Box button in the toolbox, move the pointer to the form or report, then click the mouse button to place the text box	
Totals, calculating in a report	AC 240	See Reference Window: Calculating Totals in a Report